American Experiences

Readings in American History

Second Edition

American Experiences

Readings in American History

Second Edition

■

Randy Roberts
Purdue University

■

James S. Olson
Sam Houston State University

SCOTT, FORESMAN/LITTLE, BROWN HIGHER EDUCATION
A Division of Scott, Foresman and Company
Glenview, Illinois   London, England

Cover: "Baltimore Street Looking West from Calvert," Baltimore, Maryland, c. 1851, The Maryland Historical Society.

LIBRARY OF CONGRESS CATALOGING-IN-PUBLICATION DATA
American experiences/[edited by] Randy Roberts, James S. Olson.—
  2nd ed.
     p. cm.
   Includes bibliographies.
   Contents: v. 1. 1607-1877—v. 2. 1877 to the present.
   ISBN 0-673-38862-X (v. 1): $12.00.—ISBN 0-673-38863-8 (v. 2):
$12.00
   1. United States—History.   I. Roberts, Randy
II. Olson, James Stuart
E178.6.A395   1990
973—dc20   89-10428
                                                      CIP

Preface

American History instructors enjoy talking about the grand sweep of the American past. Many note the development of unique traditions such as the American political tradition and the American diplomatic tradition. They employ the article "the" so often that they depict history as a seamless garment and Americans as all cut from the same fabric. Nothing could be further from the truth. America is a diverse country, and its population is the most ethnically varied in the world—white and black, Indian and Chicano, rich and poor, male and female. No single tradition can encompass this variety. *American Experiences* shows the complexity and richness of the nation's past by focusing on the people themselves—how they coped with, adjusted to, or rebelled against America. The readings examine them as they worked and played, fought and made love, lived and died.

We designed *American Experiences* as a supplement to the standard textbooks used in college survey classes in American history. Unlike other readers, it covers ground not usually found in textbooks. For example, instead of an essay on the effect of the New Deal, it includes a selection on life in the Hill Country of Texas before rural electrification. Instead of a discussion of the political impact of the Populist Movement, it explores the *Wizard of Oz* as a Populist parable. In short, it presents different slants on standard and not-so-standard topics.

We have tested each essay in classrooms so that *American Experiences* reflects not only our interest in social history but student interests in American history in general. We have selected essays that are readable, interesting, and help illuminate important aspects of America's past. For example, to show the nature of the class system in the South and to introduce the topic of southern values, we selected one essay on gambling and horse racing in the Old South and another on gouging matches in the southern backcountry. As an introduction to the conventional and medical view of women in the late nineteenth century, we selected an essay about Lizzie Borden. Each essay, then, serves at least two purposes: to tell a particular story well, and to help illuminate the social or political landscape of America.

This reader presents a balanced picture of the experiences of Americans. The characters in these volumes are not exclusively white males from the Northeast, whose eyes are continually focused on Boston, New York and Washington. Although their stories are certainly important, so, too, are the stories of blacks adjusting with dignity to a barbarous labor system, Chicanos coming to terms with Anglo society, and women striving for increased opportunities in a sexually restrictive society. We have looked at all of these stories and, in doing so, we have assumed that Americans express themselves in a variety of ways, through work, sex, and games, as well as politics and diplomacy.

During the last three years, we have solicited a variety of opinions, from colleagues and students, about the selections for *American Experiences*. Based on that feedback we have made a number of changes in the second edition, always with the intention of selecting articles that undergraduate students will find interesting and informative. The new articles for this first volume of *American Experiences*, Second Edition, include James S. Olson and Raymond Wilson's "The World of Native Americans," Estelle Kleiger's "Vanity in the 19th Century," Martin Kaufman's '' 'Step Right Up, Ladies and Gentlemen': Patent Medicines in 19th-Century America," a selection from Harriet Beecher Stowe's *Uncle Tom's Cabin*, Henry Tragle's "The Southampton Slave Revolt," Bell Wiley's "Johnny Reb and Billy Yank," and Dee Brown's "Day of the Longhorns."

Each volume of *American Experiences* is divided into standard chronological and topical parts. Each part is introduced by a brief discussion of the major themes of the period or topic. In turn, each individual selection is preceded by a short discussion of how it fits into the part's general theme. We employ this method to give students some guidance through the complexity of the experiences of Americans. At the conclusion of each selection is a series of study questions and a brief bibliographic essay. These are intended to further the usefulness of *American Experiences* for students as well as teachers.

Randy Roberts
James S. Olson

Contents

Part Seven

CIVIL WAR AND RECONSTRUCTION
page 310

JOHNNY REB AND BILLY YANK
Bell I. Wiley
page 312

MASTERS WITHOUT SLAVES
James L. Roark
page 320

THE KNIGHTS OF THE RISING SUN
Allen W. Trelease
page 330

DAY OF THE LONGHORNS
Dee Brown
page 340

American Experiences

Readings in American History

Second Edition

Part One

PURITAN LIFE

John Winthrop, the first governor of the Puritan settlement of Massachusetts Bay, was charged with a sense of mission. He and his Puritan followers had braved the North Atlantic to establish a society which would totally observe the will of God. On his way to the new world aboard the flagship *Arbella* in April 1630, Winthrop explained their "errand into the wilderness." The Puritans felt that they were a unique people who had been given "a special commission" to create a kingdom of God on earth. By working together, defeating selfishness, and keeping the Lord foremost in their thoughts, they strove to blaze a trail for the future of mankind. As Winthrop said, "we shall be as a Citty upon a hill, the eyes of all people are uppon us."

The Puritans' Lord was a stern master, and their religion was as uncompromising as the cold rocky shores of New England. At the heart of their religion was the doctrine of predestination. Since humanity was too sinful to deserve salvation, God simply saved the souls of a select few, while condemning the rest to eternal damnation. There was nothing an individual could do to alter this decision. Nor could an individual ever know if he or she was saved or damned.

The ultimate mystery of predestination created an underlying tension in Puritan society. The Puritans searched constantly for some sign that they had received God's gift of salvation. In their diaries they scrutinized their actions and thoughts, examining their lives for demonstrations of the sin that was inherent in all people. Often they were disappointed with themselves, for they believed sin could be as passive as an envious thought or as active as a violent deed.

The Puritans believed that God constantly intervened in their daily affairs to punish those who disobeyed his laws. A bolt of lightning or a debilitating disease might very well be a sign of God's disfavor. The devil, who similarly was a part of their everyday lives, lurked in the New England forests and among the Indian tribes, ready to claim those with weak hearts and bodies.

Nevertheless, the Puritans were not one-dimensional people; their sins, excesses, and great accomplishments were only human. The following essays present the Puritans at their best and worst. Each essay shows how the Puritans used their religion to interpret and determine the course of their lives. In the end, you'll see how the history of American Puritanism is the history of a religious idea.

PEQUOTS AND PURITANS: THE CAUSES OF THE WAR OF 1637

Alden T. Vaughan

In 1637 the New England colonists and the Pequot Indians fought a bloody and decisive war that destroyed the Pequot tribe and opened most of southern New England for settlement. Alden T. Vaughan, however, does not believe that the Puritan's land-hunger and aggression caused the war. Instead he believes that the fighting was the result of a complex series of events in which Pequots as well as Puritans were guilty of excessive violence and narrow-minded attitudes.

At the heart of the conflict were unstated and therefore misunderstood assumptions. The Puritans assumed that they had the right to act as a police force for New England. They believed that they were God's chosen people, ordained by a special covenant to do God's work on earth. The Pequots, who had recently acquired hegemony over New England, did not share the Puritans' self-righteous beliefs. More practical, the Pequots based their right to control the area on their military, not their moral, strength. The consequence of these two attitudes was war. It would not be the last time that Americans confused the power to influence others with the right to do so.

The war of 1637 between the Puritans and the Pequot Indians was one of the most dramatic episodes in early New England history, possessing an intensity and a significance deserving of far more attention than it has usually been accorded. While more limited in scope than King Philip's War, and less tied to controversial issues than the Antinomian crisis or the banishment of Roger Williams, the Pequot War had unique elements which made it memorable in its own right. It resulted in the extermination of the most powerful tribe in New England, it witnessed one of the most sanguinary battles of all Indian wars—when some five hundred Pequot men, women, and children were burned to death in the Puritans' attack on Mystic Fort—and it opened southern New England to rapid English colonization. The war was not soon forgotten by the other tribes in the northeast, nor by the English who memorialized the victory in prose and poetry. It even found its way into *Moby Dick* when Herman Melville chose the name of the vanquished tribe for Captain Ahab's ill-fated whaling vessel.

As in the case of most wars, the conflict between the Pequot Indians and the Puritans of New England raises for its historian the twin problems of cause and responsibility. Involved is the whole question of Indian-white relations during the first century of English settlement in New England, the basic nature of the Puritan experiment, and the justice and humanity of the participants. Writers in eighteenth-century New England tended to side with their ancestors and view the conflict as a defensive maneuver on the part of the righteous forces of Puritanism prodded into action by the Pequot hordes, or, as Puritan rhetoric would have it, by Satan himself. Later historians sharing a popular antipathy toward Puritansim and all its works concluded that the war was a simple case of Puritan aggression and

"Pequots and Puritans: The Causes of the War of 1637" by Alden T. Vaughan in *The William and Mary Quarterly*, 3rd Series, XXI, April 1964, pp. 256–269. Reprinted by permission.

Pequot retaliation. Others would have us believe that it was fundamentally a manifestation of English land-hunger with the Pequots fighting for their lands as well as their lives. The well-established facts seem to indicate that the proper explanation lies in none of these interpretations alone, but in a blend of the first two, modified by a radical restatement of the third.

Although the early history of the Pequot tribe is shrouded in obscurity, it is generally accepted that prior to the tribe's arrival in southern New England, it had inhabited lands in northern New Netherland close to the Mohawk Indians. For reasons that will probably always remain uncertain, the Pequot tribe, then called Mohegan, migrated into west central New England in the early seventeenth century and then turned southward until it reached the shores of the Atlantic Ocean. Unlike the Pilgrims who were exploring and settling Plymouth harbor at about the same time, the Mohegans gained their territory by force of arms. Along the route of their journey they made innumerable enemies and incurred such a reputation for brutality that they became known as "Pequots," the Algonquin word for "destroyers of men." Animosity toward the Pequots was particularly strong among the small tribes of the Connecticut Valley who were forced to acknowledge the suzerainty of the intruders and to pay them annual tribute. Equally unfriendly were the Narragansetts, the Pequots' nearest neighbors to the east, who resented the presence of a militarily superior tribe and refused to be cowed by it. The result was almost constant warfare between the Narragansetts and the Pequots, the final campaign of which was one phase of the Pequot War of 1637.

Not only were the Pequots unable to live peacefully with their Indian neighbors, they alienated the adjacent European settlers as well. In 1634 the Pequots were at war with both Dutch New Netherland and the Narragansetts. In the same year they made their first hostile move against the English with the assassination of Captain John Stone of Virginia and eight other

Englishmen. Friendly Indians informed the Massachusetts authorities that the Pequots had assassinated the ship captain while he was sleeping in his bunk, had murdered the rest of his crew, and plundered his vessel. The Puritans could hardly let the murder of nine colonists go unchallenged if they intended to maintain their precarious foothold in a land where the natives vastly outnumbered them.

With the English demanding revenge for the murder of John Stone, the Pequots decided that this was one enemy too many, and late in October 1634 they sent ambassadors to Massachusetts to treat for peace and commerce, reinforcing their appeal with gifts of wampum. The Puritan authorities, after consulting with some of the clergy, demanded Stone's assassins as a prelude to negotiations. The Pequots replied with an account of Stone's death that differed markedly from the colonists' version. Stone, the Indians contended, had seized and bound two braves who had boarded his ship to trade. It was after this, they said, that several of the braves' friends ambushed the captain when he came ashore. They also insisted that the sachem responsible for the ambush had since been killed by the Dutch and all but two of his henchmen had fallen victim to the pox.

The Pequots told their story "with such confidence and gravity" that the English were inclined to accept it, and after several days of negotiations the Pequots and the Bay Colony signed a treaty on November I, 1634. By its terms the Indians agreed to hand over the two remaining assassins when sent for and "to yield up Connecticut," by which they probably meant as much of the valley as the English desired for settlement. In addition, the Pequots promised to pay an indemnity of four hundred fathoms of wampum, forty beaver and thirty otter skins. Commercial relations were projected by an agreement that Massachusetts would send a trading vessel to the Pequots in the near future. Peace was thus maintained in New England. Commerce between the Bay Colony and the Pequots did not materialize, however. When

John Oldham took his trading ship into Pequot territory the next spring, he found them "a very false people" and disinclined to amicable trade.

Peace between the Bay Colony and the Pequots lasted until the fall of 1636, but those two years witnessed a rapid deterioration of the relations between the two. The Pequots failed to surrender the remaining assassins of Stone, the indemnity was paid only in part, and reports of further Pequot disingenuousness began to drift into Boston. By midsummer of 1636, Massachusetts had lost patience and commissioned John Winthrop, Jr., then in Connecticut, to demand that Chief Sassacus of the Pequots surrender at once the assassins of Captain Stone and reply to several other charges of bad faith. Should the Pequots fail to meet these demands, the Bay Colony threatened to terminate the league of amity and to "revenge the blood of our Countrimen as occasion shall serve." But before Winthrop could fulfill his mission, an event occurred that put an end to all peaceful dealings with the Pequot tribe.

Late in July, John Gallop, en route by sea to Long Island, spied near Block Island John Oldham's pinnace, its deck crowded with Indians and no sign of a white man. When no one answered his hail, Gallop tried to board to investigate; a frenzied battle followed in which Gallop routed the Indians. On board he found the naked and mutilated body of Oldham.

At first it appeared that the Narragansetts were responsible for Oldham's murder. The Block Island tribe was subservient to them, and according to one report, all the Narragansett sachems except Canonicus and Miantonomo (the two leading chiefs) had conspired with the Block Islanders against Oldham because of his attempts to trade with the Pequots the previous year. The Massachusetts leaders contemplated war with the Narragansetts and warned Roger Williams "to look to himself." But Canonicus and Miantonomo speedily regained the confidence of the English by returning Oldham's two boys and his remaining goods from Block Island,

and by assuring the Bay Colony, through Roger Williams, that most of the culprits had been killed by Gallop. Meanwhile the few surviving assassins sought refuge with the Pequots.

The upshot of all this was a punitive expedition of ninety Massachusetts volunteers under magistrate John Endicott against Block Island. The troops were also ordered to visit Pequot territory to secure the remaining murderers of Stone and Oldham and assurances of future good behavior on the part of the Pequots. But when in early September the expedition made contact with the tribe, the Pequot spokesmen obstinately refused to comply with Puritan demands, first offering a new version of the killing of Stone that absolved them of any blame, then claiming that their leading chiefs were on Long Island, and finally insisting that they were still trying to discover who the culprits were. After a few hours of futile negotiations, the English became convinced that the delay was a camouflage for ambush, particularly when they observed the Pequots "convey away their wives and children, and bury their chiefest goods." A brief clash ensued in which a few Pequots were slain, several wounded, and much Pequot property seized or destroyed by the Massachusetts troops.

The Pequots retaliated by torturing and slaying every Englishman they could find. Fort Saybrook at the mouth of the Connecticut River was put under virtual siege, and several of its garrison were ambushed during the next few months. English traders entering the Connecticut River fell victim to Pequot raiding parties. When reinforcements arrived from Massachusetts in the spring of 1637, the Pequots shifted their attacks to the unprotected plantations farther up the river. Early on the morning of April 23, 1637, two hundred howling Pequot braves descended on a small group of colonists at work in a meadow near Wethersfield, Connecticut. Nine of the English were slain, including a woman and child; and the Pequots carried to their stronghold two young women whom the sachems hoped could make gunpowder for the tribe's few fire-

arms. With some thirty Englishmen dead at Pequot hands, the New England colonies had no alternative but to wage war. Massachusetts Bay had in fact already declared war two weeks before the Wethersfield raid but had done nothing to stop the pattern of massacres. Connecticut could wait no longer, and on May 1, 1637, its General Court declared "that there shalbe an offensive warr against the Pequoitt." Settlers as well as Pequots had engaged in the series of attacks, retaliations, and counter-retaliations preceding the formal declaration, but the wantonness, scope, and cruelty of the Indian raids cast upon them a very heavy burden of responsibility for the war that followed.

The reaction of the other Indian tribes to the outbreak of war reveals much about the nature of the conflict. The Narragansetts, thanks to some last-minute diplomacy by Roger Williams, had already made an offensive alliance with Massachusetts. The Mohegans, a secessionist faction of the Pequot tribe that had revived the old tribal name and separated from Chief Sassacus the year before, also fought on the English side, against their blood brothers. The small valley tribes along the Connecticut River enthusiastically backed the Puritans, whom they had encouraged to settle in the valley as early as 1631 in hope of gaining protection against the Pequots. Connecticut's declaration of war was, in fact, partly due to the urging of these tribes. "The Indians here our frends," wrote Thomas Hooker from Hartford, "were so importunate with us to make warr presently that unlesse we had attempted some thing we had delivered our persons unto contempt of base feare and cowardise, and caused them to turne enemyes agaynst us." Of the hundreds of casualties the Pequots suffered, scores were inflicted by the Indians of southern New England and Long Island. As Captain John Mason, leader of the Connecticut forces observed, "Happy were they that could bring in their Heads to the English: Of which there came almost daily to Winsor, or Hartford." And the greatest prize of all, the head of Chief Sassacus, was delivered by the

■ ■ *In this 1638 drawing we see the Puritans, led by Captain John Mason and Captain John Underhill, defeat the Pequots by razing the Indian settlement on Block Island.*

Mohawks. Sassacus had sought asylum with his former neighbors, but afraid of the Englishmen's "hot-mouthed weapons," the Mohawks seized him and forty of his warriors, cut off their heads and hands, and confiscated their wampum. The Pequots, for their part, were unable to find any important allies among the Indians. Clearly, this was no racial conflict between white man and red. Rather, the Pequot War saw the English colonies, eagerly assisted by several Indian tribes, take punitive action against the one New England tribe that was hated and feared by Indian and white alike.

The short career of the Pequots in history, then, was of a people apparently incapable of maintaining the trust and forbearance of any of their neighbors, red or white, English or Dutch. A prima facie case exists for the claims of Puritan apologists, and its partial validity is undeniable. Unfortunately, it is not the whole story.

The weightiest criticism of Puritan policy, and the one stressed most often by scholars hostile to the New Englanders, is that the conduct of the settlers was incessantly heavy-handed and provocative. It can even be argued that long before the Endicott expedition the English had treated the Pequots with something less than equity. For example, the character of Captain John Stone was such as to lend an air of plausibility to the Pequot version of his death.

Captain Stone, it seems, had piloted a shipload of cattle from Virginia to Boston in 1634. At each stop along the way he managed so to embroil himself with the local authorities that he was soon *persona non grata* in every community north of the Hudson. His first escapade was in New Amsterdam, where he attempted to steal a Plymouth bark and was thwarted only at the last minute by some Dutch seamen. Later, in Plymouth, he almost stabbed Governor Thomas Prence. He acted little better in Massachusetts Bay where he "spake contemptuously of [the] magistrates, and carried it lewdly in his conversation," in particular calling Judge Roger Ludlow "a just as." On top of this he was charged with excessive drinking and adultery. He was tried and acquitted for lack of evidence on the major charge, but his lesser indiscretions earned him a suspended fine of one hundred pounds and banishment from the colony under penalty of death. Stone was on his way back to Virginia, accompanied by Captain Walter Norton and crew, when he stopped off to explore the trading prospects of the Connecticut River and there met his death. As might be expected, news of his fate did not elicit universal mourning: some of the

English, secure in their piety, concluded with Roger Clap that "thus did God destroy him that so proudly threatened to ruin us."

These circumstances perhaps explain why no military action was taken against the Pequots in 1634. It should be noted, however, that the treaty the Puritans extracted from the Pequots later that year was hardly a lenient one. Still, hostilities did not break out until the Bay Colony dispatched the Endicott expedition in 1636 to avenge the death of John Oldham. And here again, the Puritans' conception of just retribution was stern indeed. Endicott's instructions were to kill all Indian men on Block Island, seize the women and children, and take possession of the island. He was then to proceed to the Pequot territory and demand the murderers of Stone and Oldham, one thousand fathoms of wampum, and some Pequot children as hostages. Should the Pequots refuse to comply with the terms of this ultimatum, the expedition was to impose them by force. And Endicott vigorously complied with these instructions. He secured a beachhead on Block Island in the face of brief resistance, routed the defenders, and devastated the island. While the Indians of Block Island sought refuge in the swamps, the Massachusetts troops burned wigwams, destroyed cornfields, and smashed canoes. Dissatisfied by the small number of Indian casualties, the English soldiers heartlessly "destroyed some of their dogs instead of men." After two busy days of destruction, the expedition set sail for Pequot territory.

Four days later Endicott's fleet entered Pequot Harbor. The Indians greeted the fleet's appearance with "doleful and woful cries," for it was obvious to the Pequots that this was no friendly mission. And whatever chance there may have been for peaceful negotiations rapidly vanished. When the Pequots refused to meet his demands and began their annoying delays, Endicott landed his troops and took station on a commanding hilltop. Some of the Indians' excuses for delay may have been legitimate, but the English rejected them, and Endicott interpreted a final Pequot suggestion that both sides lay down their arms as a dastardly ruse. "We rather chose to beat up the drum and bid them battle," recorded Captain John Underhill. A volley from the musketeers sent the Pequot warriors scurrying for shelter, and the pattern established on Block Island was repeated. The colonists spent the next two days in rampant destruction and looting. In deference to English firepower, the Indians kept a respectful distance.

By the fourteenth of September, less than three weeks after their departure from Boston, the Massachusetts troops were back in the Bay Colony with but two casualties, neither fatal. The Pequots were mourning far greater losses: several killed and a score of more wounded in addition to the destruction of their property. Ironically, the first Pequot life may well have been taken by Chief Cutshamekin of the Massachusetts Indians, who had joined Endicott as an interpreter and guide. In any event, harsh Puritan "justice" had been imposed; harsh Pequot retaliation soon followed.

The Endicott attack spurred the Pequots to seek retribution. Although the Pequots had suffered few casualties, it was inconceivable that this proud tribe would not insist on revenge. Its land had been invaded, its chief subjected to arrogant demands, and its tribesmen assaulted. The other Puritan colonies were quick to blame the Bay Colony for the massacres that ensued. Spokesmen for Plymouth, Connecticut, and Fort Saybrook (then under separate government) all condemned the Endicott expedition, and even Governor Winthrop later tacitly admitted that Massachusetts had provoked hostilities. Lion Gardiner, commander of the Saybrook garrison, expressed the prevalent opinion even before the Endicott expedition reached Pequot soil. "You come hither," he protested, "to raise these wasps about my ears, and then you will take wing and flee away." His prophecy was accurate; Endicott upset the nest, but the stings were first felt by the few hundred settlers of Connecticut and Fort Saybrook.

There remains the question of why the Bay Colony had resorted to coercive action after having tolerated the crimes attributed to the Pequots prior to their harboring of Oldham's assassins. The explanation may be threefold. In the first place, the Bay Colony, now considering herself the dominant authority in New England, was determined strictly to enforce the peace, a policy more easily undertaken since she was the least likely to feel the brunt of any retaliation. Secondly, shortly before the Endicott expedition was formed Roger Williams had reported a heady boast of the Pequots that they could by witchcraft defeat any English expedition, a challenge hardly designed to soothe Puritan tempers. Finally, Massachusetts was then in the throes of civil and religious controversy. Roger Williams had been ousted but a few months earlier for "divers dangerous opinion," the Crown had recently instituted quo warranto proceedings against the colony's charter, and the first rumblings of the Antinomian movement were faintly audible. If frustration is a prime cause of aggression, the Bay Colony had been overripe for Endicott's blow at Satan's horde.

Added to Pequot perfidy, then, was the harshness of Massachusett's remedial action. Both contributed to the outbreak of the war.

That the war was a product of English land hunger and Pequot defense of its tribal territory, finds little documentation. It seems doubtful that in 1636 English settlers wanted land with which the Indians were unwilling to part. The Connecticut Valley tribes were welcoming the English and encouraging their settlement there. Neither the Narragansetts nor the Mohegans seem to have been disturbed by colonial expansion; the former had made sizable grants to Roger Williams, and the latter were to make the most vigorous Indian contribution to the downfall of the Pequots. Nor is there any evidence that the Pequots themselves feared immediate English encroachment on their tribal lands. It is true that the Pequots did try to gain Narragansett aid against Massachusetts Bay by raising the specter of future Indian extermination at the hands of the English, but they did not argue that the present danger of dispossession was great. By the treaty of November 1634, the Pequots themselves had granted the Bay Colony the right to settle in Connecticut, though of course the local valley tribes would have denied the right of the Pequots to make such a grant. The English settlement nearest to Pequot territory was at Saybrook, which had a garrison of only twenty men. It was situated, in fact, in the Mohegans' territory after their secession in 1636.

A few historians have attempted to find evidence of a ravenous Puritan land hunger in the rhetoric of Puritan theology, but the evidence presented in support of such a view appears to consist for the most part of theological generalizations—in many cases uttered by Puritan leaders before embarking for the New World—concerning the holiness of their venture and the certainty that God had laid aside for them the lands necessary for its fulfillment. It is far more germane to establish how the Puritans, once settled in New England and confronted with its realities, went about the mundane business of evolving and administering a practicable land policy. The records clearly demonstrate that the bulk of the settlers proceeded upon the assumption that the Indian—heathen or not—had legal title to the lands upon which he lived, a title that could be changed only through the civilized conventions of sale and formal transfer. Only two instances exist in which the New Englanders acquired any substantial amounts of land from the Indians by means other than treaties. One was the Pequot War of 1637, the other King Philip's War of 1675–76; neither can reasonably be explained as campaigns for territorial expansion.

In seeking to identify the causes of the war and apportion responsibility for its outbreak, one must begin with the fact established by the testimony of all the whites and most Indians that the Pequots were blatantly and persistently provocative and aggressive. Perhaps brilliant diplomacy could have prevented the intransigence of the Pequots from leading to open warfare; but even Roger Williams, the most likely man for the role of arbiter, had no influence upon the Pequots. On the other hand, it is undeniable that Puritan

severity in the Endicott campaign provided the spark that set off the ultimate conflagration. Although the harshness of the Bay Colony's policy in the summer of 1636 is understandable, it cannot be excused.

While land as such was plainly not at issue, the Endicott expedition may well have represented something even more fundamental at stake here—the struggle between Puritans and Pequots for ultimate jurisdiction over the region both inhabited. The Puritans, determined to prevent Indian actions that might in any way threaten the New World Zion, had assumed through their governments responsibility for maintaining law and order among all inhabitants, Indian and white. The Plymouth magistrates had accepted this responsibility to the full limit of their resources, and had labored to curb both Indian and English when either threatened the peace. Massachusetts Bay, at first too weak to exert its authority beyond its immediate area of settlement, was by 1636 ready to enforce its fiat on all Indians in southern New England. Prior to the formation of the Confederation of New England in 1643, each colony endeavored to exercise full authority over natives as well as its own people within its own borders; yet Massachusetts, in its dealings with the Narragansetts and Pequots, was obviously assuming jurisdiction over areas outside its charter limits. It did so for the simple reason that otherwise Indians could molest white men, and vice versa, with impunity.

At bottom it was the English assumption of the right to discipline neighboring Indians that led to war in 1637. The Endicott expedition of 1636 was sent primarily to act as a police force, with orders to inflict punishment upon Block island and obtain sureties of good behavior from the Pequots. The Pequots naturally resented the interference of Massachusetts in an area over which they had but recently acquired hegemony, and rejected the Bay Colony's assumption of the right to impose authority. The result was war. It may be the Puritans of Massachusetts were begging for trouble by extending their authority beyond their chartered territory; but the other tribes of New England not only submitted to the exertion of authority by Massachusetts Bay to keep the peace but even appeared at times to invite it. As the alternative was anarchy outside the settled areas, it is difficult to condemn the policy of Massachusetts, except in its application by Endicott. In short, the Pequot War, like most wars, cannot be attributed to the unmitigated bellicosity of one side and the righteous response of the other. Persistent aggression by the Pequot tribe, the desire for autonomy from or revenge against the Pequots by various other tribes, the harshness of the Endicott campaign, and divergent concepts as to the Englishman's jurisdiction all contributed to the outbreak of New England's first Indian war.

The war itself was brief, brutal, and its outcome thoroughly satisfying to the English and their Indian allies. The toll in human life was extremely high and makes the Pequot War one of the most regrettable episodes in early New England history. Still, it is small, though real, consolation that the blame lies somewhat more heavily upon the Pequots than the Puritans. It may also be hoped that the troubled conscience with which the modern American historian often views our past relations with the Indians can find some balm in contemplating an episode in which the white man groped for workable formulas of friendship and justice, and in which he was not solely responsible for their ultimate failure.

■■■

STUDY QUESTIONS

1. How were the Pequots viewed by their Indian neighbors?

2. What were the origins of the bad relations between the Pequots and the Puritans?

3. How did the Puritans regard the Indians of New England?

4. What problems in Puritan society in the mid-1630s affected the Puritan's reaction to the Pequot threat?

5. Ultimately, who or what caused the Pequot War of 1637?

BIBLIOGRAPHY

The relations between the colonists and the Indians has long been a central concern for historians. Wilcomb E. Washburn's *The Indian in America* (1975) is the best general survey. For an excellent survey of early Indian culture see Francisco Guerra, *The Pre-Columbian Mind* (1971). Gerald B. Nash surveys early Indian-colonist relations in *Red, White, and Black* (1982). On the long-term consequences of the conquest of America, see Alfred W. Crosby, Jr., *The Columbian Exchange: Biological and Cultural Consequences of 1492* (1972). For specific descriptions of Indian-European relations in New England, see Alden T. Vaughan, *New England Frontier: Puritans and Indians* (1965); Neal Salisbury, *Manitou and Providence: Indians, Europeans and the Making of New England* (1982); and Francis Jennings, *The Invasion of America: Indians, Colonialism, and the Cant of Conquest* (1975).

THE PURITANS AND SEX

Edmund S. Morgan

During the 1920s, as many Americans challenged nineteenth century social norms and moved toward greater sexual freedom, historians often blamed their Puritan forefathers for the restrictive elements they saw in their own society. For them, the Puritans were narrow-minded bigots who were intent on banning all that was natural, joyful, and refreshing in society. H. L. Mencken best captured this attitude by defining Puritanism as "the haunting fear that someone, somewhere, may be happy."

   This stereotype of Puritans as humorless and sexually repressed has maintained a firm hold on the popular historical imagination. Reay Tannahill, in her recent book *Sex in History,* refers to the "dour moral standards" of Puritans. However, the Puritans were not as inhibited as popularly believed. As Edmund S. Morgan demonstrates, the Puritans were intensely religious people who nevertheless understood that humans were often morally weak. Indeed, they "showed none of the blind zeal or narrow-minded bigotry which is too often supposed to have been characteristic of them. The more one learns about these people, the less do they appear to have resembled the sad and sour portraits which their . . . critics have drawn of them."

Henry Adams once observed that Americans have "ostentatiously ignored" sex. He could think of only two American writers who touched upon the subject with any degree of boldness—Walt Whitman and Bret Harte. Since the time when Adams made this penetrating observation, American writers have been making up for lost time in a way that would make Bret Harte, if not Whitman, blush. And yet there is still more truth than falsehood in Adams's statement. Americans, by comparison with Europeans or Asiatics, are squeamish when confronted with the facts of life. My purpose is not to account for this squeamishness, but simply to point out that the Puritans, those bogeymen of the modern intellectual, are not responsible for it.

At the outset, consider the Puritans' attitude toward marriage and the role of sex in marriage. The popular assumption might be that the Puritans frowned on marriage and tried to hush up the physical aspect of it as much as possible, but listen to what they themselves had to say. Samuel Willard, minister of the Old South Church in the latter part of the seventeenth century and author of the most complete textbook of Puritan divinity, more than once expressed his horror at "that Popish conceit of the Excellency of Virginity." Another minister, John Cotton, wrote that

Women are Creatures without which there is no comfortable Living for man: it is true of them what is wont to be said of Governments, That bad ones are better than none: *They are a sort of Blasphemers then who dispise and decry them, and call them* a necessary Evil, for they are a necessary Good.

These sentiments did not arise from an interpretation of marriage as a spiritual partnership, in which sexual intercourse was a minor or inci-

dental matter. Cotton gave his opinion of "Platonic love" when he recalled the case of

one who immediately upon marriage, without ever approaching the Nuptial Bed, *indented with the* Bride, *that by mutual consent they might both live such a life, and according did sequestring themselves according to the custom of those times, from the rest of mankind, and afterwards from one another too, in their retired Cells, giving themselves up to a Contemplative life; and this is recorded as an instance of no little or ordinary Vertue; but I must be pardoned in it, if I can account it no other than an effort of blind zeal, for they are the dictates of a blind mind they follow therein, and not of that Holy Spirit, which saith* It is not good that man should be alone.

Here is as healthy an attitude as one could hope to find anywhere. Cotton certainly cannot be accused of ignoring human nature. Nor was he an isolated example among the Puritans. Another minister stated plainly that "the Use of the Marriage Bed" is "founded in mans Nature," and that consequently any withdrawal from sexual intercourse upon the part of husband or wife "Denies all reliefe in Wedlock vnto Human necessity: and sends it for supply vnto Beastiality when God gives not the gift of Continency." In other words, sexual intercourse was a human necessity and marriage the only proper supply for it. These were the views of the New England clergy, the acknowledged leaders of the community, the most Puritanical of the Puritans. As proof that their congregations concurred with them, one may cite the case in which the members of the First Church of Boston expelled James Mattock because, among other offenses, "he denyed Coniugall fellowship vnto his wife for the space of 2 years together vpon pretense of taking Revenge upon himself for his abusing of her before marryage." So strongly did the Puritans insist upon the sexual character of marriage that one New Englander considered himself slandered when it was reported, "that he Brock his deceased wife's hart with Greife, that he wold be absent from her 3 weeks together when he

"The Puritans and Sex" by Edmund S. Morgan in *New England Quarterly,* XV, December 1942, pp. 591–607. Reprinted by permission.

was at home, and wold never come nere her, and such Like.''

There was just one limitation which the Puritans placed upon sexual relations in marriage: sex must not interfere with religion. Man's chief end was to glorify God, and all earthly delights must promote that end, not hinder it. Love for a wife was carried too far when it led a man to neglect his God:

. . . sometimes a man hath a good affection to Religion, but the love of his wife carries him away, a man may bee so transported to his wife, that hee dare not bee forward in Religion, lest hee displease his wife, and so the wife, lest shee displease her husband, and this is an inordinate love, when it exceeds measure.

Sexual pleasures, in this respect, were treated like other kinds of pleasure. On a day of fast, when all comforts were supposed to be foregone in behalf of religious contemplation, not only were tasty food and drink to be abandoned but sexual intercourse, too. On other occasions, when food, drink, and recreation were allowable, sexual intercourse was allowable too, though of course only between persons who were married to each other. The Puritans were not ascetics; they never wished to prevent the enjoyment of earthly delights. They merely demanded that the pleasures of the flesh be subordinated to the greater glory of God: husband and wife must not become ''so transported with affection, that they look at no higher end than marriage it self.'' ''Let such as have wives,'' said the ministers, ''look at them not for their own ends, but to be fitted for Gods service, and bring them nearer to God.''

Toward sexual intercourse outside marriage the Puritans were as frankly hostile as they were favorable to it in marriage. They passed laws to punish adultery with death, and fornication with whipping. Yet they had no misconceptions as to the capacity of human beings to obey such laws. Although the laws were commands of God, it was only natural—since the fall of Adam—for human beings to break them. Breaches must be

punished lest the community suffer the wrath of God, but no offense, sexual or otherwise, could be occasion for surprise or for hushed tones of voice. How calmly the inhabitants of seventeenth-century New England could contemplate rape or attempted rape is evident in the following testimony offered before the Middlesex County Court of Massachusetts:

The examination of Edward Wire taken the 7th of October and alsoe Zachery Johnson. who sayeth that Edward Wires mayd being sent into the towne about busenes meeting with a man that dogd hir from about Joseph Kettles house to goody marches. She came into William Johnsones and desired Zachery Johnson to goe home with her for that the man dogd hir. accordingly he went with her and being then as far as Samuell Phips his house the man over tooke them. which man caled himselfe by the name of peter grant would have led the mayd but she oposed itt three times: and coming to Edward Wires house the said grant would have kist hir but she refused itt: wire being at prayer grant dragd the mayd between the said wiers and Nathanill frothinghams house. hee then flung the mayd downe in the street and got atop hir; Johnson seeing it hee caled vppon the fellow to be sivill and not abuse the mayd then Edward wire came forth and ran to the said grant and took hold of him asking him what he did to his mayd, the said grant asked whether she was his wife for he did nothing to his wife: the said grant swearing he would be the death of the said wire. when he came of the mayd; he swore he would bring ten men to pul down his house and soe ran away and they followed him as far as good[y] phipses house where they mett with John Terry and George Chin with clubs in there hands and soe they went away together. Zachy Johnson going to Constable Heamans, and wire going home. there came John Terry to his house to ask for beer and grant was in the streete but afterward departed into the town, both Johnson and Wire both aferme that when grant was vppon the mayd she cryed out severall times.

Deborah hadlocke being examined sayth that

*she mett with the man that cals himselfe peeter
grant about good prichards that he dogd hir and
followed hir to hir masters and there threw hir
downe and lay vppon hir but had not the use of
hir body but swore several othes that he would ly
with hir and gett hir with child before she got
home.*

*Grant being present denys all saying he was
drunk and did not know what de did.*

The Puritans became inured to sexual
offenses, because there were so many. The
impression which one gets from reading the
records of seventeenth-century New England
courts is that illicit sexual intercourse was fairly
common. The testimony given in cases of fornication and adultery—by far the most numerous
class of criminal cases in the records—suggests
that many of the early New Englanders possessed a high degree of virility and very few inhibitions. Besides the case of Peter Grant, take the
testimony of Elizabeth Knight about the manner
of Richard Nevars's advances toward her:

*The last publique day of Thanksgiving (in the year
1674) in the evening as I was milking Richard
Nevars came to me, and offered me abuse in
putting his hand, under my coates, but I turning
aside with much adoe, saved my self, and when I
was settled to milking he agen took me by the
shoulder and pulled me backward almost, but I
clapped one hand on the Ground and held fast the
Cows teatt with the other hand, and cryed out,
and then came to mee Jonathan Abbot one of my
Masters Servants, whome the said Never asked
wherefore he came, the said Abbot said to look
after you, what you doe unto the Maid, but the
said Never bid Abbot goe about his businesse but I
bade the lad to stay.*

One reason for the abundance of sexual
offenses was the number of men in the colonies
who were unable to gratify their sexual desires in
marriage. Many of the first settlers had wives in
England. They had come to the new world to
make a fortune, expecting either to bring their
families after them or to return to England with

some of the riches of America. Although these
men left their wives behind, they brought their
sexual appetites with them; and in spite of laws
which required them to return to their families,
they continued to stay, and more continued to
arrive, as indictments against them throughout
the seventeenth century clearly indicate.

Servants formed another group of men, and
of women too, who could not ordinarily find
supply for human necessity within the bounds of
marriage. Most servants lived in the homes of
their masters and could not marry without their
consent, a consent which was not likely to be
given unless the prospecitve husband or wife
also belonged to the master's household. This
situation will be better understood if it is recalled
that most servants at this time were engaged by
contract for a stated period. They were, in the
language of the time, "covenant servants," who
had agreed to stay with their masters for a number of years in return for a specified recompense,
such as transportation to New England or education in some trade (the latter, of course, were
known more specifically as apprentices). Even
hired servants who worked for wages were usually single, for as soon as a man had enough
money to buy or build a house of his own and to
get married, he would set up in farming or trade
for himself. It must be emphasized, however,
that anyone who was not in business for himself
was necessarily a servant. The economic organization of seventeenth-century New England had
no place for the independent proletarian work-
man with a family of his own. All production
was carried on in the household by the master of
the family and his servants, so that most men
were either servants or masters of servants; and
the former, of course, were more numerous than
the latter. Probably most of the inhabitants of
Puritan New England could remember a time
when they had been servants.

Theoretically no servant had a right to a private life. His time, day or night, belonged to his
master, and both religion and law required that
he obey his master scrupulously. But neither
religion nor law could restrain the sexual

impulses of youth, and if those impulses could not be expressed in marriage, they had to be given vent outside marriage. Servants had little difficulty in finding the occasions. Though they might be kept at work all day, it was easy enough to slip away at night. Once out of the house, there were several ways of meeting with a maid. The simplest way was to go to her bedchamber, if she was so fortunate as to have a private one of her own. Thus Jock, Mr. Solomon Phipps's Negro man, confessed in court

that on the sixteenth day of May 1682, in the morning, betweene 12 and one of the clock, he did force open the back doores of the House of Laurence Hammond in Charlestowne, and came in to the House, and went up into the garret to Marie the Negro.

He doth likewise acknowledge that one night the last week he forced into the House the same way, and went up to the Negro Woman Marie and that the like he hath done at severall other times before.

Joshua Fletcher took a more romantic way of visiting his lady:

Joshua Fletcher . . . doth confesse and acknowledge that three severall nights, after bedtime, he went into Mr Fiskes Dwelling house at Chelmsford, at an open window by a ladder that he brought with him. the said windo opening into a chamber, whose was the lodging place of Gresill Juell servant to mr. Fiske. and there he kept company with the said mayd. she sometimes having her cloathes on, and one time he found her in her bed.

Sometimes a maidservant might entertain callers in the parlor while the family were sleeping upstairs. John Knight described what was perhaps a common experience for masters. The crying of his child awakened him in the middle of the night, and he called to his maid, one Sarah Crouch, who was supposed to be sleeping with the child. Receiving no answer, he arose and

went downe the stayres, and at the stair foot, the latch of doore was pulled in. I called severall times

and at the last said if shee would not open the dore, I would breake it open, and when she opened the doore shee was all undressed and Sarah Largin with her undressed, also the said Sarah went out of doores and Dropped some of her clothes as shee went out. I enquired of Sarah Crouch what men they were, which was with them. Shee made mee no answer for some space of time, but at last shee told me Peeter Brigs was with them, I asked her whether Thomas Jones was not there, but shee would give mee no answer.

In the temperate climate of New England it was not always necessary to seek out a maid at her home. Rachel Smith was seduced in an open field "about nine of the clock at night, being darke, neither moone nor starrs shineing." She was walking through the field when she met a man who

asked her where shee lived, and what her name was and shee told him. and then shee asked his name, and he told her Saijing that he was old Good-man Shepards man. Also shee saith he gave her strong liquors, and told her that it was not the first time he had been with maydes after his master was in bed.

Sometimes, of course, it was not necessary for a servant to go outside his master's house in order to satisfy his sexual urges. Many cases of fornication are on record betweeen servants living in the same house. Even where servants had no private bedroom, even where the whole family slept in a single room, it was not impossible to make love. In fact many love affairs must have had their consummation upon a bed in which other people were sleeping. Take for example the case of Sarah Lepingwell. When Sarah was brought into court for having an illegitimate child, she related that one night when her master's brother, Thomas Hawes, was visiting the family, she went to bed early. Later, after Hawes had gone to bed, he called to her to get him a pipe of tobacco. After refusing for some time,

at the last I arose and did lite his pipe and cam and lay doune one my one bead and smoaked

■ ■ *Punishments were often designed not to reform, but to deter others from committing the same offense. This woodcut shows one of the humiliating punishments used in both the Old and New Worlds.*

about half the pip and siting vp in my bead to giue him his pip my bead being a trundell bead at the sid of his bead he reached beyond the pip and Cauth me by the wrist and pulled me on the side of his bead but I biding him let me goe he bid me hold my peas the folks wold here me and if it be replyed come why did you not call out I Ansar I was posed with fear of my mastar least my master shold think I did it only to bring a scandall on his brothar and thinking thay wold all beare witnes agaynst me but the thing is true that he did then begete me with child at that tim and the Child is Thomas Hauses and noe mans but his.

In his defense Hawes offered the testimony of another man who was sleeping "on the same side of the bed," but the jury nevertheless accepted Sarah's story.

The fact that Sarah was intimidated by her master's brother suggests that maidservants may have been subject to sexual abuse by their masters. The records show that sometimes masters did take advantage of their position to force unwanted attentions upon their female servants. The case of Elizabeth Dickerman is a good example. She complained to the Middle-sex County Court,

against her master John Harris senior for profiring abus to her by way of forsing her to be naught with him: . . . he has tould her that if she tould her dame: what cariag he did show to her shee

had as good be hanged and shee replyed then shee
would run away and he sayd run the way is befor
you: . . . she says if she should liwe ther shee shall
be in fear of her lif.

The court accepted Elizabeth's complaint and
ordered her master to be whipped twenty
stripes.

So numerous did cases of fornication and
adultery become in seventeenth-century New
England that the problem of caring for the children of extra-marital unions was a serious one.
The Puritans solved it, but in such a way as to
increase rather than decrease the temptation to
sin. In 1668 the General Court of Massachusetts
ordered:

that where any man is legally convicted to be the
Father of a Bastard childe, he shall be at the care
and charge to maintain and bring up the same, by
such assistance of the Mother as nature requireth,
and as the Court from time to time (according to
circumstances) shall see meet to Order: and in case
the Father of a Bastard, by confession or other
manifest proof, upon trial of the case, do not
appear to the Courts satisfaction, then the Man
charged by the Woman to be the Father, shee
holding constant in it, (especially being put upon
the real discovery of the truth of it in the time of
her Travail) shall be the reputed Father, and
accordingly be liable to the charge of maintenance
as aforesaid (though not to other punishment)
notwithstanding his denial, unless the
circumstances of the case and pleas be such, on the
behalf of the man charged, as that the Court that
have the cognizance thereon shall see reason to
acquit him, and otherwise dispose of the Childe
and education thereof.

As a result of this law a girl could give way to
temptation without the fear of having to care for
an illegitimate child by herself. Furthermore, she
could, by a little simple lying, spare her lover the
expense of supporting the child. When Elizabeth
Wells bore a child, less than a year after this stat-
ute was passed, she laid it to James Tufts, her
master's son. Goodman Tufts affirmed that

Andrew Robinson, servant to Goodman Dexter,
was the real father, and he brought the following
testimony as evidence:

Wee Elizabeth Jefts aged 15 ears and Mary tufts
aged 14 ears doe testyfie that their being one at our
hous sumtime the last winter who sayed that thear
was a new law made concerning bastards that If
aney man wear aqused with a bastard and the
woman which had aqused him did stand vnto it in
her labor that he should bee the reputed father of
it and should mayntaine it. Elizabeth Wells
hearing of the sayd law she sayed vnto vs that If
shee should bee with Child shee would bee sure to
lay it vn to won who was rich enough abell to
mayntayne it wheather it wear his or no and shee
farder sayed Elizabeth Jefts would not you doe so
likewise If it weare your case and I sayed no by no
means for right must tacke place: and the sayd
Elizabeth wells sayed If it wear my Caus I think I
should doe so.

A tragic unsigned letter that somehow found
its way into the files of the Middlesex County
Court gives more direct evidence of the practice
which Elizabeth Wells professed:

der loue i remember my loue to you hoping your
welfar and i hop to imbras the but now i rit to you
to let you nowe that i am a child by you and i wil
ether kil it or lay it to an other and you shal have
no blame at al for i haue had many children and
none have none of them. . . . [i.e., none of their
fathers is supporting any of them.]

In face of the wholesale violation of the sexual
codes to which all these cases give testimony, the
Puritans could not maintain the severe penalties
which their laws provided. Although cases of
adultery occurred every year, the death penalty
is not known to have been applied more than
three times. The usual punishment was a whipping or a fine, or both, and perhaps a branding,
combined with a symbolical execution in the
form of standing on the gallows for an hour with
a rope about the neck. Fornication met with a
lighter whipping or a lighter fine, while rape was
treated in the same way as adultery. Though the

Puritans established a code of laws which demanded perfection—which demanded, in other words, strict obedience to the will of God, they nevertheless knew that frail human beings could never live up to the code. When fornication, adultery, rape, or even buggery and sodomy appeared, they were not surprised, nor were they so severe with the offenders as their codes of law would lead one to believe. Sodomy, to be sure, they usually punished with death; but rape, adultery, and fornication they regarded as pardonable human weaknesses, all the more likely to appear in a religious community, where the normal course of sin was stopped by wholesome laws. Governor Bradford, in recounting the details of an epidemic of sexual misdemeanors in Plymouth, wrote resignedly:

it may be in this case as it is with waters when their streames are stopped or damned up, when they gett passage they flow with more violence, and make more noys and disturbance, then when they are suffered to rune quietly in their owne chanels. So wickednes being here more stopped by strict laws, and the same more nerly looked unto, so as it cannot rune in a comone road of liberty as it would, and is inclined, it searches every wher, and at last breaks out wher it getts vente.

The estimate of human capacities here expressed led the Puritans not only to deal leniently with sexual offenses but also to take every precaution to prevent such offenses, rather than wait for the necessity of punishment. One precaution was to see that children got married as soon as possible. The wrong way to promote virtue, the Puritans thought, was to "ensnare" children in vows of virginity, as the Catholics did. As a result of such vows, children, "not being able to contain," would be guilty of "unnatural pollutions, and other filthy practices in secret: and too oft of horrid Murthers of the fruit of their bodies," said Thomas Cobbett. The way to avoid fornication and perversion was for parents to provide suitable husbands and wives for their children:

Lot was to blame that looked not out seasonally for some fit matches for his two daughters, which had formerly minded marriage (witness the contract between them and two men in Sodom, *called therfore for his Sons in Law, which had married his daughters, Gen. 19. 14.) for they seeing no man like to come into them in a conjugall way . . . then they plotted that incestuous course, whereby their Father was so highly dishonoured.*

As marriage was the way to prevent fornication, successful marriage was the way to prevent adultery. The Puritans did not wait for adultery to appear; instead, they took every means possible to make husbands and wives live together and respect each other. If a husband deserted his wife and remained within the jurisdiction of a Puritan government, he was promptly sent back to her. Where the wife had been left in England, the offense did not always come to light until the wayward husband had committed fornication or bigamy, and of course there must have been many offenses which never came to light. But where both husband and wife lived in New England, neither had much chance of leaving the other without being returned by order of the county court at its next sitting. When John Smith of Medfield left his wife and went to live with Patience Rawlins, he was sent home poorer by ten pounds and richer by thirty stripes. Similarly Mary Drury, who deserted her husband on the pretense that he was impotent, failed to convince the court that he actually was so, and had to return to him as well as to pay a fine of five pounds. The wife of Phillip Pointing received lighter treatment: when the court thought that she had overstayed her leave in Boston, they simply ordered her "to depart the Towne and goe to Tanton to her husband." The courts, moreover, were not satisfied with mere cohabitation; they insisted that it be peaceful cohabitation. Husbands and wives were forbidden by law to strike one another, and the law was enforced on numerous occasions. But the courts did not stop there. Henry Flood was required to give bond for good behavior because he had abused his wife simply by "ill words calling her whore and cursing of her." The wife of Christopher Collins was presented for railing at her husband and calling him "Gurley gutted divill." Apparently in this case the court thought that Mistress Collins was right, for although the fact was proved by two witnesses, she was discharged. On another occasion the court favored the husband: Jacob Pudeator, fined for striking and kicking his wife, had the sentence moderated when the court was informed that she was a woman "of great provocation."

Wherever there was strong suspicion that an illicit relation might arise between two persons, the authorities removed the temptation by forbidding the two to come together. As early as November, 1630, the Court of Assistants of Massachusetts prohibited a Mr. Clark from "cohabitacion and frequent keepeing company with Mrs. Freeman, vnder paine of such punishment as the Court shall thinke meete to inflict." Mr. Clark and Mr. Freeman were both bound "in XX£ apeece that Mr. Clearke shall make his personall appearance att the nexte Court to be holden in March nexte, and in the meane tyme to carry himselfe in good behaviour towards all people and espetially towards Mrs. Freeman, concerneing whome there is stronge suspicion of incontinency." Forty-five years later the Suffolk County Court took the same kind of measure to protect the husbands of Dorchester from the temptations offered by the daughter of Robert Spurr. Spurr was presented by the grand jury

for entertaining persons at his house at unseasonable times both by day and night to the greife of theire wives and Relations & The Court having heard what was alleaged and testified against him do Sentence him to bee admonish't and to pay Fees of Court and charge him upon his perill not to entertain any married men to keepe company with his daughter especially James Minott and Joseph Belcher.

In like manner Walter Hickson was forbidden to keep company with Mary Bedwell, "And if at any time hereafter hee bee taken in company of the saide Mary Bedwell without other company to bee forthwith apprehended by the Constable and to be whip't with ten stripes." Elizabeth Wheeler and Joanna Peirce were admonished "for theire disorderly carriage in the house of Thomas Watts being married women and founde sitting in other mens Laps with theire Armes about theire Necks." How little confidence the Puritans had in human nature is even more clearly displayed by another case, in which Edmond Maddock and his wife were brought to court "to answere to all such matters as shalbe objected against them concerning Haarkwoody and Ezekiell Euerells being at their house at unseasonable tyme of the night and her being up with them after her husband was gone to bed." Haarkwoody and Everell had been found "by the Constable Henry Bridghame about tenn of the Clock at night sitting by the fyre at the house of Edmond Maddocks with his wyfe a suspicious weoman her husband being on sleepe [*sic*] on the bedd." A similar distrust of human ability to resist temptation is evident in the following order of the Connecticut Particular Court:

James Hallett is to returne from the Correction house to his master Barclyt, who is to keepe him to hard labor, and course dyet during the pleasure of the Court provided that Barclet is first to remove his daughter from his family, before the sayd James enter therein.

These precautions, as we have already seen, did not eliminate fornication, adultery, or other sexual offenses, but they doubtless reduced the number from what it would otherwise have been.

In sum, the Puritan attitude toward sex, though directed by a belief in absolute, God-given moral values, never neglected human nature. The rules of conduct which the Puritans regarded as divinely ordained had been formulated for men, not for angels and not for beasts. God had created mankind in two sexes; He had ordained marriage as desirable for all, and sexual intercourse as essential to marriage. On the other hand, He had forbidden sexual intercourse outside of marriage. These were the moral principles which the Puritans sought to enforce in New England. But in their enforcement they took cognizance of human nature. They knew well enough that human beings since the fall of Adam were incapable of obeying perfectly the laws of God. Consequently, in the endeavor to enforce those laws they treated offenders with patience and understanding, and concentrated their efforts on prevention more than on punishment. The result was not a society in which most of us would care to live, for the methods of prevention often caused serious interference with personal liberty. It must nevertheless be admitted that in matters of sex the Puritans showed none of the blind zeal or narrow-minded bigotry which is too often supposed to have been characteristic of them. The more one learns about these people, the less do they appear to have resembled the sad and sour portraits which their modern critics have drawn of them.

■■■

STUDY QUESTIONS

1. What limitations did Puritans place on sexual relations within marriage?

2. What was the Puritans' attitude toward sexual relations outside marriage?

3. What special sexual problems did servants in Puritan society face?

4. How did the Puritan view of human nature govern their attitudes toward illicit sexual relations?

5. How did Puritans try to prevent fornication and adultery?

BIBLIOGRAPHY

Historians have only recently begun to explore the significance of attitudes toward sex. On a popular level, Reay Tannahill, *Sex in History* (1980) and Gay Talese, *Thy Neighbor's Wife* (1980) examine changing attitudes toward the subject. More scholarly examinations of early American sexual attitudes include Laurel Ulrich, *Good Wives: Image and Reality in the Lives of Women in Northern New England, 1650–1750* (1982); Ellen K. Rothman, "Sex and Self-Control: Middle-Class Courtship in America, 1770–1870," *Journal of Social History* (1982); Linda Hyman, "The Greek Slave by Hiram Powers: High Art as Popular Culture," *Art Journal* (1976); and Lyle Koehler, *A Search for Power: "The Weaker Sex" in Seventeenth-Century New England* (1974).

Puritan theology, on the other hand, has been richly studied. The books by Perry Miller and Edmund Morgan are the best starting point. Miller's ideas are presented clearly in *Errand into the Wilderness* (1956). Equally valuable is Morgan's *Puritan Dilemma: The Story of John Winthrop* (1958).

THE WITCHES OF SALEM VILLAGE

Kai T. Erikson

Most of the "facts" of the Salem witchcraft trials and executions are known. The trouble started during the cold winter of 1691–92. By the end of the summer, nineteen people were adjudged to be witches and hanged. One other person, Giles Cory, refused to plead innocent or guilty. Because of his refusal, he was to be placed between two boards. Heavy stones were to be piled on the top board until a plea was given. Giles was slowly crushed to death; his last words were "more weight." His death brought the total executions to twenty.

What is difficult to determine is the reason why the trials ever took place. Certainly the belief in witchcraft was nearly universal in seventeenth-century New England, and perhaps a few of the people executed had even practiced witchcraft. But the vast majority had been as innocent as Sarah Good, whose last words to her minister were, "I am no more a witch than you are a wizard, and if you take away my life, God will give you blood to drink."

For almost a century, historians have debated the cause of the outbreak of the witchcraft hysteria. Many have blamed the girls who set the dreadful events into motion. Others have stressed the community conflicts within Salem and the general social and religious tensions created by an expanding society and declining religiosity. One historian has even claimed the real problem was the actual existence of witches.

Kai T. Erikson sides with the historians who stress the social conflict in Puritan society. In his thought-provoking examination of the events, he describes a society that had lost its bearing and that looked toward the future with fear and anxiety.

The witchcraft hysteria that began in Salem Village (a town some miles away from Salem itself) is probably the best known episode of Massachusetts history and has been described in a number of careful works. In the pages which follow, then, the story will be sketched in rather briefly: readers interested in a fuller account of those unusual events are urged to consult *The Devil in Massachusetts* by Marion L. Starkey, a book that captures all the grim drama of the period without losing any of its merit as a scholarly work.

Between the end of the Quaker persecutions in 1665 and the beginning of the Salem witchcraft outbreak in 1692, the colony had experienced some very trying days. To begin with, the political outlines of the commonwealth had been subject to sudden, often violent, shifts, and the people of the colony were quite uncertain about their own future. The King's decrees during the Quaker troubles had provoked only minor changes in the actual structure of the Puritan state, but they had introduced a note of apprehension and alarm which did not disappear for thirty years; and no sooner had Charles warned the Massachusetts authorities of his new interest in their affairs then he dispatched four commissioners to the Bay to look after his remote dominions and make sure that his occasional orders were being enforced. From that moment, New England feared the worst. The sermons of the period were full of dreadful prophecies about the future of the Bay, and as New England moved through the 1670's and 1680's the catalogue of political calamities grew steadily longer and more serious. In 1670, for example, a series of harsh arguments occurred between groups of magistrates and clergymen, threatening the alliance which had been the very cornerstone of the New England Way. In 1675 a

brutal and costly war broke out with a confederacy of Indian tribes led by a wily chief called King Philip. In 1676 Charles II began to review the claims of other persons to lands within the jurisdiction of Massachusetts, and it became increasingly clear that the old charter might be revoked altogether. In 1679 Charles specifically ordered Massachusetts to permit the establishment of an Anglican church in Boston, and in 1684 the people of the Bay had become so pessimistic about the fate of the colony that several towns simply neglected to send Deputies to the General Court. The sense of impending doom reached its peak in 1686. To begin with, the charter which had given the colony its only legal protection for over half a century was vacated by a stroke of the royal pen, and in addition the King sent a Royal Governor to represent his interests in the Bay who was both an Anglican and a man actively hostile to the larger goals of New England. For the moment, it looked as if the holy experiment was over: not only had the settlers lost title to the very land they were standing on, but they ran the very real risk of witnessing the final collapse of the congregational churches they had built at so great a cost.

The settlers were eventually rescued from the catastrophes of 1686, but their margin of escape had been extremely narrow and highly tentative. In 1689 news began to filter into the Bay that William of Orange had landed in England to challenge the House of Stuart, and hopes ran high throughout the colony; but before the people of the Bay knew the outcome of this contest in England, a Boston mob suddenly rose in protest and placed the Royal Governor in chains. Luckily for Massachusetts, William's forces were successful in England and the Boston insurrection was seen as little more than a premature celebration in honor of the new King. Yet for all the furor, little had changed. At the time of the witchcraft hysteria, agents of Massachusetts were at work in London trying to convince William to restore the old charter, or at least to issue a new one giving Massachusetts all the advantages it had enjoyed in the past, but everyone

Reprinted with permission of Macmillan Publishing Company from *Wayward Puritans: A Study in the Sociology of Deviance* by Kai T. Erikson. Copyright © 1966.

knew that the colony would never again operate under the same autonomy. As the people of the Bay waited to hear about the future of their settlement, then, their anxiety was understandably high.

Throughout this period of political crisis, an even darker cloud was threatening the colony, and this had to do with the fact that a good deal of angry dissension was spreading among the saints themselves. In a colony that depended on a high degree of harmony and group feeling, the courts were picking their way through a maze of land disputes and personal feuds, a complicated tangle of litigations and suits. Moreover, the earnest attempts at unanimity that had characterized the politics of Winthrop's era were now replaced by something closely resembling open party bickering. When John Josselyn visited Boston in 1668, for instance, he observed that the people were "savagely factious" in their relations with one another and acted more out of jealousy and greed than any sense of religious purpose. And the sermons of the day chose even stronger language to describe the decline in morality which seemed to darken the prospects of New England. The spirit of brotherhood which the original settlers had counted on so heavily had lately diffused into an atmosphere of commercial competition, political contention, and personal bad feeling.

Thus the political architecture which had been fashioned so carefully by the first generation and the spiritual consensus which had been defended so energetically by the second were both disappearing. At the time of the Salem witchcraft mania, most of the familiar landmarks of the New England Way had become blurred by changes in the historical climate, like signposts obscured in a storm, and the people of the Bay no longer knew how to assess what the past had amounted to or what the future promised. Massachusetts had become, in Alan Heimert's words, "a society no longer able to judge itself with any certainty."

In 1670, the House of Deputies took note of the confusion and fear which was beginning to spread over the country and prepared a brief inventory of the troubles facing the Bay:

Declension from the primitive foundation work, innovation in doctrine and worship, opinion and practice, an invasion of the rights, liberties and privileges of churches, an usurpation of a lordly and prelatical power over God's heritage, a subversion of the gospel order, and all this with a dangerous tendency to the utter devastation of these churches, turning the pleasant gardens of Christ into a wilderness, and the inevitable and total extirpation of the principles and pillars of the congregational way; these are the leaven, the corrupting gangrene, the infecting spreading plague, the provoking image of jealousy set up before the Lord, the accursed thing which hath provoked divine wrath, and doth further threaten destruction.

The tone of this resolution gives us an excellent index to the mood of the time. For the next twenty years, New England turned more and more to the notion that the settlers must expect God to turn upon them in wrath because the colony had lost its original fervor and sense of mission. The motif introduced in this resolution runs like a recurrent theme through the thinking of the period: the settlers who had carved a commonwealth out of the wilderness and had planted "the pleasant gardens of Christ" in its place were about to return to the wilderness. But there is an important shift of imagery here, for the wilderness they had once mastered was one of thick underbrush and wild animals, dangerous seasons and marauding Indians, while the wilderness which awaited them contained an entirely different sort of peril. "The Wilderness thro' which are passing to the Promised Land," Cotton Mather wrote in a volume describing the state of New England at the time of the witchcraft difficulties, "is all over fill'd with Fiery flying serpents. . . . All our way to Heaven, lies by the Dens of Lions, and the Mounts of Leopards; there are incredible Droves of Devils in our way." We will return to discussion of this wilderness theme at the conclusion of the chapter, but for the moment it is important to note that Massachusetts had lost much of its concern for institutions and policies and had begun to seek some vision of its future by looking into a ghostly, invisible world.

It was while the people of the colony were preoccupied with these matters that the witches decided to strike.

I

No one really knows how the witchcraft hysteria began, but it originated in the home of the Reverend Samuel Parris, minister of the local church. In early 1692, several girls from the neighborhood began to spend their afternoons in the Parris' kitchen with a slave named Tituba, and it was not long before a mysterious sorority of girls, aged between nine and twenty, became regular visitors to the parsonage. We can only speculate what was going on behind the kitchen door, but we know that Tituba had been brought to Massachusetts from Barbados and enjoyed a reputation in the neighborhood for her skills in the magic arts. As the girls grew closer together, a remarkable change seemed to come over them: perhaps it is not true, as someone later reported, that they went out into the forest to celebrate their own version of a black mass, but it is apparent that they began to live in a state of high tension and shared secrets with one another which were hardly becoming to quiet Puritan maidens.

Before the end of winter, the two youngest girls in the group succumbed to the shrill pitch of their amusements and began to exhibit a most unusual malady. They would scream unaccountably, fall into grotesque convulsions, and sometimes scamper along on their hands and knees making noises like the barking of a dog. No sooner had word gone around about this extraordinary affliction than it began to spread like a contagious disease. All over the community young girls were groveling on the ground in a panic of fear and excitement, and while some of the less credulous townspeople were tempted to reach for their belts in the hopes of strapping a little modesty into them, the rest could only stand by in helpless horror as the girls suffered their torments.

The town's one physician did what he could to stem the epidemic, but he soon exhausted his meagre store of remedies and was forced to conclude that the problem lay outside the province of medicine. The Devil had come to Salem Village, he announced; the girls were bewitched. At this disturbing news, ministers from many of the neighboring parishes came to consult with their colleague and offer what advice they might. Among the first to arrive was a thoughtful clergyman named Deodat Lawson, and he had been in town no more than a few hours when he happened upon a frightening exhibition of the devil's handiwork. "In the beginning of the evening," he later recounted of his first day in the village,

I went to give Mr. Parris a visit. When I was there, his kinswoman, Abigail Williams, (about 12 years of age,) had a grievous fit; she was at first hurried with violence to and fro in the room, (though Mrs. Ingersoll endeavored to hold her,) sometimes making as if she would fly, stretching up her arms as high as she could, and crying ''whish, whish, whish!'' several times. . . . After that, she run to the fire, and began to throw fire brands about the house; and run against the back, as if she would run up the chimney, and, as they said, she had attempted to go into the fire in other fits.

Faced by such clear-cut evidence, the ministers quickly agreed that Satan's new challenge would have to be met with vigorous action, and this meant that the afflicted girls would have to identify the witches who were harassing them.

It is hard to guess what the girls were experiencing during those early days of the commotion. They attracted attention everywhere they went and exercised a degree of power over the adult community which would have been exhilarating under the sanest of circumstances. But whatever else was going on in those young minds, the thought seems to have gradually occurred to the girls that they were indeed bewitched, and after they had been coaxed over and over again to name their tormentors, they finally singled out three women in the village and accused them of witchcraft.

Three better candidates could not have been found if all the gossips in New England had met to make the nominations. The first, understandably, was Tituba herself, a woman who had grown up among the rich colors and imaginative legends of Barbados and who was probably acquainted with some form of voodoo. The second, Sarah Good, was a proper hag of a witch if Salem Village had ever seen one. With a pipe clenched in her leathery face she wandered around the countryside neglecting her children and begging from others, and on more than one occasion the old crone had been overheard muttering threats against her neighbors when she was in an unusually sour humor. Sarah Osburne, the third suspect, had a higher social standing than either of her alleged accomplices, but she had been involved in a local scandal a year or two earlier when a man moved into her house some months before becoming her husband.

A preliminary hearing was set at once to decide whether the three accused women should be held for trial. The girls were ushered to the front row of the meeting house, where they took full advantage of the space afforded them by rolling around in apparent agony whenever some personal fancy (or the invisible agents of the devil) provoked them to it. It was a remarkable show. Strange creatures flew about the room pecking at the girls or taunting them from the rafters, and it was immediately obvious to everyone that the women on trial were responsible for all the disorder and suffering. When Sarah Good and Sarah Osburne was called to the stand and asked why they sent these spectres to torment the girls, they were too appalled to say much in their defense. But when Tituba took the stand she had a ready answer. A lifetime spent in bondage is poor training for standing up before a bench of magistrates, and anyway Tituba was an excitable woman who had breathed the warmer winds of the Caribbean and knew things about magic her crusty old judges would never learn. Whatever the reason, Tituba gave her audience one of the most exuberant confessions ever recorded in a New England courtroom. She spoke of the creatures who inhabit the invisible world, the dark rituals which bind them together in the service of Satan; and before she had ended her astonishing recital she had convinced everyone in Salem Village that the problem was far worse then they had dared imagine. For Tituba not only implicated Sarah Good and Sarah Osburne in her own confession but announced that many other people in the colony were engaged in the devil's conspiracy against the Bay.

So the hearing that was supposed to bring a speedy end to the affair only stirred up a hidden hornet's nest, and now the girls were urged to identify other suspects and locate new sources of trouble. Already the girls had become more than unfortunate victims: in the eyes of the community they were diviners, prophets, oracles, mediums, for only they could see the terrible spectres swarming over the countryside and tell what persons had sent them on their evil errands. As they became caught up in the enthusiasm of their new work, then, the girls began to reach into every corner of the community in a search for likely suspects. Martha Corey was an upstanding woman in the village whose main mistake was to snort incredulously at the girls' behavior. Dorcas Good, five years old, was a daughter of the accused Sarah. Rebecca Nurse was a saintly old woman who had been bedridden at the time of the earlier hearings. Mary Esty and Sarah Cloyce were Rebecca's younger sisters, themselves accused when they rose in energetic defense of the older woman. And so it went—John Proctor, Giles Corey, Abigail Hobbs, Bridgit Bishop, Sarah Wild, Susanna Martin, Dorcas Hoar, the Reverend George Burroughs: as winter turned into spring the list of suspects grew to enormous length and the Salem

■■
The English witchcraft executions first started in the sixteenth century and peaked by the mid-seventeenth century. It wasn't until the late seventeenth century that Massachusetts Bay began its witchcraft executions.

jail was choked with people awaiting trial. We know nothing about conditions of life in prison, but it is easy to imagine the tensions which must have echoed within those grey walls. Some of the prisoners had cried out against their relatives and friends in a desperate effort to divert attention from themselves, others were witless persons with scarcely a clue as to what had happened to them, and a few (very few, as it turned out) were accepting their lot with quiet dignity. If we imagine Sarah Good sitting next to Rebecca Nurse and lighting her rancid pipe or Tituba sharing views on supernatural phenomena with the Reverend George Burroughs, we may have a rough picture of life in those crowded quarters.

By this time the hysteria had spread well beyond the confines of Salem Village, and as it grew in scope so did the appetites of the young girls. They now began to accuse persons they had never seen from places they had never visited (in the course of which some absurd mistakes were made), yet their word was so little questioned that it was ordinarily warrant enough to put respected people in chains.

From as far away as Charlestown, Nathaniel Cary heard that his wife had been accused of witchcraft and immediately traveled with her to

Salem "to see if the afflicted did know her." The two of them sat through an entire day of hearings, after which Cary reported:

I observed that the afflicted were two girls of about ten years old, and about two or three others, of about eighteen. . . . The prisoners were called in one by one, and as they came in were cried out of. . . . The prisoner was placed about seven or eight feet from the Justices, and the accusers between the Justices and them; the prisoner was ordered to stand right before the Justices, with an officer appointed to hold each hand, lest they should therewith afflict them, and the prisoner's eyes must be constantly on the Justices; for if they looked on the afflicted, they would either fall into their fits, or cry out of being hurt by them. . . . Then the Justices said to the accusers, "which of you will go and touch the prisoner at the bar?" Then the most courageous would adventure, but before they had made three steps would ordinarily fall down as in a fit. The Justices ordered that they should be taken up and carried to the prisoner, that she might touch them; and as soon as they were touched by the accused, the Justices would say "they are well," before I could discern any alteration. . . . Thus far I was only as a spectator, my wife also was there part of the time, but no notice taken of her by the afflicted, except once or twice they came to her and asked her name.

After this sorry performance the Carys retired to the local inn for dinner, but no sooner had they taken seats than a group of afflicted girls burst into the room and "began to tumble about like swine" at Mrs. Cary's feet, accusing her of being the cause of their miseries. Remarkably, the magistrates happened to be sitting in the adjoining room—"waiting for this," Cary later decided—and an impromptu hearing took place on the spot.

Being brought before the Justices, her chief accusers were two girls. My wife declared to the Justices that she never had any knowledge of them before that day; she was forced to stand with her arms stretched out. I did request that I might hold one of her hands, but it was denied me; then she desired me to wipe the tears from her eyes, and the sweat from her face, which I did; then she desired she might lean herself on me, saying she should faint. Justice Hathorne replied, she had strength enough to torment those persons, and she should have strength enough to stand. I speaking something against their cruel proceedings, they commanded me to be silent, or else I should be turned out of the room. An Indian . . . was also brought in to be one of her accusers: being come in, he now (when before the Justices) fell down and tumbled about like a hog, but said nothing. The Justices asked the girls, "who afflicted the Indian?", they answered "she" (meaning my wife). . . . The Justices ordered her to touch him, in order of his cure . . . but the Indian took hold of her in a barbarous manner; then his hand was taken off, and her hand put on his, and the cure was quickly wrought. . . . Then her mittimus was writ.

For another example of how the hearings were going, we might listen for a moment to the examination of Mrs. John Proctor. This record was taken down by the Reverend Samuel Parris

himself, and the notes in parentheses are his. Ann Putnam and Abigail Williams were two of the most energetic of the young accusers.

JUSTICE: Ann Putnam, doth this woman hurt you?

PUTNAM: Yes, sir, a good many times. (Then the accused looked upon them and they fell into fits.)

JUSTICE: She does not bring the book to you, does she?

PUTNAM: Yes, sir, often, and saith she hath made her maid set her hand to it.

JUSTICE: Abigail Williams, does this woman hurt you?

WILLIAMS: Yes, sir, often.

JUSTICE: Does she bring the book to you?

WILLIAMS: Yes.

JUSTICE: What would she have you do with it?

WILLIAMS: To write in it and I shall be well.

PUTNAM TO MRS. PROCTOR: Did you not tell me that your maid had written?

MRS. PROCTOR: Dear child, it is not so. There is another judgment, dear child. (Then Abigail and Ann had fits. By and by they cried out, "look you, there is Goody Proctor upon the beam." By and by both of them cried out of Goodman Proctor himself, and said he was a wizard. Immediately, many, if not all of the bewitched, had grievous fits.)

JUSTICE: Ann Putnam, who hurt you?

PUTNAM: Goodman Proctor and his wife too. (Some of the afflicted cried, "there is Proctor going to take up Mrs. Pope's feet—and her feet were immediately taken up.)

JUSTICE: What do you say Goodman Proctor to these things?

PROCTOR: I know not. I am innocent.

WILLIAMS: There is Goodman Proctor going to Mrs. Pope (and immediately said Pope fell into a fit).

JUSTICE: You see, the Devil will deceive you. The children could see what you was going to do before the woman was hurt. I would advise you to repentance, for the devil is bringing you out.

This was the kind of evidence the magistrates were collecting in readiness for the trials; and it was none too soon, for the prisons were crowded with suspects. In June the newly arrived Governor of the Bay, Sir William Phips, appointed a special court of Oyer and Terminer to hear the growing number of witchcraft cases pending, and the new bench went immediately to work. Before the month was over, six women had been hanged from the gallows in Salem. And still the accused poured in.

As the court settled down to business, however, a note of uncertainty began to flicker across the minds of several thoughtful persons in the colony. To begin with, the net of accusation was beginning to spread out in wider arcs, reaching not only across the surface of the country but up the social ladder as well, so that a number of influential people were now among those in the overflowing prisons. Nathaniel Cary was an important citizen of Charlestown, and other men of equal rank (including the almost legendary Captain John Alden) were being caught up in the widening circle of panic and fear. Slowly but surely, a faint glimmer of skepticism was introduced into the situation; and while it was not to assert a modifying influence on the behavior of the court for some time to come, this new voice had become a part of the turbulent New England climate of 1692.

Meantime, the girls continued to exercise their extraordinary powers. Between sessions of the court, they were invited to visit the town of Andover and help the local inhabitants flush out whatever witches might still remain at large among them. Handicapped as they were by not knowing anyone in town, the girls nonetheless managed to identify more than fifty witches in the space of a few hours. Forty warrants were signed on the spot, and the arrest total only stopped at that number because the local Justice of the Peace simply laid down his pen and refused to go on with the frightening charade any longer—at which point, predictably, he became a suspect himself.

Yet the judges worked hard to keep pace with their young representatives in the field. In early August five persons went to the gallows in Salem. A month later fifteen more were tried and condemned, of which eight were hung promptly and the others spared because they were presumably ready to confess their sins and turn state's evidence. Nineteen people had been executed, seven more condemned, and one pressed to death under a pile of rocks for standing mute at his trial. At least two more persons had died in prison, bringing the number of deaths to twenty-two. And in all that time, not one suspect brought before the court had been acquitted.

At the end of this strenuous period of justice, the whole witchcraft mania began to fade. For one thing, the people of the Bay had been shocked into a mood of sober reflection by the deaths of so many persons. For another, the afflicted girls had obviously not learned very much from their experience in Andover and were beginning to display an ambition which far exceeded their credit. It was bad enough that they should accuse the likes of John Alden and Nathaniel Cary, but when they brought up the name of Samuel Willard, who doubled as pastor of Boston's First Church and President of Harvard College, the magistrates flatly told them they were mistaken. Not long afterwards, a brazen finger was pointed directly at the executive mansion in Boston, where Lady Phips awaited her husband's return from an expedition to Canada, and one tradition even has it that Cotton Mather's mother was eventually accused.

This was enough to stretch even a Puritan's boundless credulity. One by one the leading men of the Bay began to reconsider the whole question and ask aloud whether the evidence accepted in witchcraft hearings was really suited to the emergency at hand. It was obvious that people were being condemned on the testimony of a few excited girls, and responsible minds in the community were troubled by the thought that the girls' excitement may have been poorly diagnosed in the first place. Suppose the girls were directly possessed by the devil and not touched by intermediate witches? Suppose they were simply out of their wits altogether? Suppose, in fact, they were lying? In any of these events the rules of evidence used in court would have to be reviewed—and quickly.

Deciding what kinds of evidence were admissible in witchcraft cases was a thorny business at best. When the court of Oyer and Terminer had first met, a few ground rules had been established to govern the unusual situation which did not entirely conform to ordinary Puritan standards of trial procedure. In the first place, the scriptural rule that two eye-witnesses were necessary for conviction in capital cases was modified to read that any two witnesses were sufficient even if they were testifying about different events—on the interesting ground that witchcraft was a "habitual" crime. That is, if one witness testified that he had seen Susanna Martin bewitch a horse in 1660 and another testified that she had broken uninvited into his dreams twenty years later, then both were witnesses to the same general offense. More important, however, the court accepted as an operating principle the old idea that Satan could not assume the shape of an innocent person, which meant in effect that any spectres floating into view which resembled one of the defendants must be acting under his direct instruction. If an afflicted young girl "saw" John Proctor's image crouched on the window sill with a wicked expression on his face, for example, there could be no question that Proctor himself had placed it there, for the devil could not borrow that disguise without the permission of its owner. During an early hearing, one of the defendants had been asked: "How comes your appearance to hurt these [girls]?" "How do I know," she had answered testily, "He that appeared in the shape of Samuel, a glorified saint, may appear in anyone's shape." Now this was no idle retort, for every man who read his Bible knew that the Witch of Endor had once caused the image of Samuel to appear before Saul, and this scriptural evidence that the devil might indeed be able to impersonate an innocent person proved a difficult matter for the court to handle. Had the defendant been able to win her

point, the whole machinery of the court might have fallen in pieces at the magistrates' feet; for if the dreadful spectres haunting the girls were no more than free-lance apparitions sent out by the devil, then the court would have no prosecution case at all.

All in all, five separate kinds of evidence had been admitted by the court during its first round of hearings. First were trials by test, of which repeating the Lord's Prayer, a feat presumed impossible for witches to perform, and curing fits by touch were the most often used. Second was the testimony of persons who attributed their own misfortunes to the sorcery of a neighbor on trial. Third were physical marks like warts, moles, scars, or any other imperfection through which the devil might have sucked his gruesome quota of blood. Fourth was spectral evidence, of the sort just noted; and fifth were the confessions of the accused themselves.

Now it was completely obvious to the men who began to review the court's proceedings that the first three types of evidence were quite inconclusive. After all, anyone might make a mistake reciting the Lord's Prayer, particularly if the floor was covered with screaming, convulsive girls, and it did not make much sense to execute a person because he had spiteful neighbors or a mark upon his body. By those standards, half the people in Massachusetts might qualify for the gallows. This left spectral evidence and confessions. As for the latter, the court could hardly maintain that any real attention had been given to that form of evidence, since none of the executed witches had confessed and none of the many confessors had been executed. Far from establishing guilt, a well-phrased and tearfully delivered confession was clearly the best guarantee against hanging. So the case lay with spectral evidence, and legal opinion in the Bay was slowly leaning toward the theory that this form of evidence, too, was worthless.

In October, Governor Phips took note of the growing doubts by dismissing the special court of Oyer and Terminer and releasing several suspects from prison. The tide had begun to turn, but still there were 150 persons in custody and some 200 others who had been accused.

In December, finally, Phips appointed a new session of the Superior Court of Judicature to try the remaining suspects, and this time the magistrates were agreed that spectral evidence would be admitted only in marginal cases. Fifty-two persons were brought to trial during the next month, and of these, forty-nine were immediately acquitted. Three others were condemned ("two of which," a contemporary observer noted, "were the most senseless and ignorant creatures that could be found"), and in addition death warrants were signed for five persons who had been condemned earlier. Governor Phips responded to these carefully reasoned judgments by signing reprieves for all eight of the defendants anyway, and at this, the court began to empty the jails as fast as it could hear cases. Finally Phips ended the costly procedure by discharging every prisoner in the colony and issuing a general pardon to all persons still under suspicion.

The witchcraft hysteria had been completely checked within a year of the day it first appeared in Salem Village.

II

Historically, there is nothing unique in the fact that Massachusetts Bay should have put people on trial for witchcraft. As the historian Kittredge has pointed out, the whole story should be seen "not as an abnormal outbreak of fanaticism, not as an isolated tragedy, but as a mere incident, a brief and transitory episode in the biography of a terrible, but perfectly natural, superstition."

The idea of witchcraft, of course, is as old as history; but the concept of a malevolent witch who makes a compact with Satan and rejects God did not appear in Europe until the middle of the fourteenth century and does not seem to have made a serious impression on England until well into the sixteenth. The most comprehensive study of English witchcraft, for example,

opens with the year 1558, the first year of Elizabeth's reign, and gives only passing attention to events occurring before that date.

In many ways, witchcraft was brought into England on the same current of change that introduced the Protestant Reformation, and it continued to draw nourishment from the intermittent religious quarrels which broke out during the next century and a half. Perhaps no other form of crime in history has been a better index to social disruption and change, for outbreaks of witchcraft mania have generally taken place in societies which are experiencing a shift of religious focus—societies, we would say, confronting a relocation of boundaries. Throughout the Elizabethan and early Stuart periods, at any rate, while England was trying to establish a national church and to anchor it in the middle of the violent tides which were sweeping over the rest of Europe, increasing attention was devoted to the subject. Elizabeth herself introduced legislation to clarify the laws of dealing with witchcraft, and James I, before becoming King of England, wrote a textbook on demonology which became a standard reference for years to come.

But it was during the Civil Wars in England that the witchcraft hysteria struck with full force. Many hundreds, probably thousands of witches were burned or hung between the time the Civil Wars began and Oliver Cromwell emerged as the strong man of the Commonwealth, and no sooner had the mania subsided in England than it broke out all over again in Scotland during the first days of the Restoration. Every important crisis during those years seemed to be punctuated by a rash of witchcraft cases. England did not record its last execution for witchcraft until 1712, but the urgent witch hunts of the Civil War period were never repeated.

With this background in mind, we should not be surprised that New England, too, should experience a moment of panic; but it is rather curious that this moment should have arrived so late in the century.

During the troubled years in England when

countless witches were burned at the stake or hung from the gallows, Massachusetts Bay showed but mild concern over the whole matter. In 1647 a witch was executed in Connecticut, and one year later another woman met the same fate in Massachusetts. In 1651 the General Court took note of the witchcraft crisis in England and published an almost laconic order that "a day of humiliation" be observed throughout the Bay, but beyond this, the waves of excitement which were sweeping over the mother country seemed not to reach across the Atlantic at all. There was no shortage of accusations, to be sure, no shortage of the kind of gossip which in other days would send good men and women to their lonely grave, but the magistrates of the colony did not act as if a state of emergency was at hand and thus did not declare a crime wave to be in motion. In 1672, for example, a curious man named John Broadstreet was presented to the Essex County Court for "having familiarity with the devil," yet when he admitted the charge the court was so little impressed that he was fined for telling a lie. And in 1674, when Christopher Brown came before the same court to testify that he had been dealing with Satan, the magistrates flatly dismissed him on the grounds that his confession seemed "inconsistent with truth."

So New England remained relatively calm during the worst of the troubles in England, yet suddenly erupted into a terrible violence long after England lay exhausted from its earlier exertions.

In many important respects, 1692 marked the end of the Puritan experiment in Massachusetts, not only because the original charter had been revoked or because a Royal Governor had been chosen by the King or even because the old political order had collapsed in a tired heap. The Puritan experiment ended in 1692, rather, because the sense of mission which had sustained it from the beginning no longer existed in any recognizable form, and thus the people of the Bay were left with few stable points of reference to help them remember who they were. When they looked back on their own history, the settlers had to conclude that the trajectory of the past pointed in quite a differnt direction than the one they now found themselves taking: they were no longer participants in a great adventure, no longer residents of a "city upon a hill," no longer members of that special revolutionary elite who were destined to bend the course of history according to God's own word. They were only themselves, living alone in a remote corner of the world, and this seemed a modest end for a crusade which had begun with such high expectations.

In the first place, as we have seen, the people of the colony had always pictured themselves as actors in an international movement, yet by the end of the century they had lost many of their most meaningful contacts with the rest of the world. The Puritan movement in England had scattered into a number of separate sects, each of which had been gradually absorbed into the freer climate of a new regime, and elsewhere in Europe the Protestant Reformation had lost much of its momentum without achieving half the goals set for it. And as a result, the colonists had lost touch with the background against which they had learned to assess their own stature and to survey their own place in the world.

In the second place, the original settlers had measured their achievements on a yardstick which no longer seemed to have the same sharp relevance. New England had been built by people who believed that God personally supervised every flicker of life on earth according to a plan beyond human comprehension, and in undertaking the expedition to America they were placing themselves entirely in God's hands. These were men whose doctrine prepared them to accept defeat gracefully, whose sense of piety depended upon an occasional moment of failure, hardship, even tragedy. Yet by the end of the century, the Puritan planters could look around them and count an impressive number of accomplishments. Here was no record of erratic providence; here was a record of solid human enterprise, and with this realization, as Daniel Boorstin suggests, the settlers moved from a "sense of mystery" to a "consciousness of mastery," from a helpless reliance on fate to a firm confidence in their own abilities. This shift helped clear the way for the appearance of the shrewd, practical, self-reliant Yankee as a figure in American history, but in the meantime it left the third generation of settlers with no clear definition of the status they held as the chosen children of God.

In the third place, Massachusetts had been founded as a lonely pocket of civilization in the midst of a howling wilderness, and as we have seen, this idea remained one of the most important themes of Puritan imagery long after the underbrush had been cut away and the wild animals killed. The settlers had lost sight of their local frontiers, not only in the sense that colonization had spread beyond the Berkshires into what is now upper state New York, but also in the sense that the wilderness which had held the community together by pressing in on it from all sides was disappearing. The original settlers had landed in a wilderness full of "wild beasts and wilder men"; yet sixty years later, sitting many miles from the nearest frontier in the prosperous seaboard town of Boston, Cotton Mather and other survivors of the old order still imagined that they were living in a wilderness—a territory they had explored as thoroughly as any frontiersmen. But the character of this wilderness was unlike anything the first settlers had ever seen, for its dense forests had become a jungle of mythical beasts and its skies were thick with flying spirits. In a sense, the Puritan community had helped mark its location in space by keeping close watch on the wilderness surrounding it on all sides; and now that the visible traces of that wilderness had receded out of sight, the settlers invented a new one by finding the shapes of the forest in the middle of the community itself.

And as the wilderness took on this new character, it seemed that even the Devil had given up his more familiar disguises. He no longer lurked in the underbrush, for most of it had been cut away; he no longer assumed the shape of hostile Indians, for most of them had retreated inland for the moment; he no longer sent waves of heretics to trouble the Bay, for most of them lived quietly under the protection of toleration; he no longer appeared in the armies of the Counter-Reformation, for the old battlefields were still and too far away to excite the imagination. But his presence was felt everywhere, and when the colonists began to look for his new hiding places they found him crouched in the very heart of the Puritan colony. Quite literally, the people of the Bay began to see ghosts, and soon the boundaries of the New Engalnd Way closed in on a space full of demons and incubi, spectres and evil spirits, as the settlers tried to find a new sense of their own identity among the landmarks of a strange, invisible world. Cotton Mather, who knew every disguise in the Devil's wardrobe, offered a frightening catalogue of the Devil's attempts to destroy New England.

I believe, there never was a poor Plantation, more pursued by the wrath of the Devil, than our poor New-England. . . . It was a rousing alarm to the Devil, when a great Company of English Protestants and Puritans, came to erect Evangelical Churches, in a corner of the world, where he had reign'd without control for many ages; and it is a vexing Eye-sore to the Devil, that our Lord Christ should be known, and own'd and preached in this howling wilderness. Wherefore he has left no Stone unturned, that so he might undermine his Plantation, and force us out of our Country. First, the Indian Powawes, used all their Sorceries to molest the first Planters here; but God said unto them, Touch them not! Then, Seducing spirits came to root in this Vineyard, but God so rated them off, that they have not prevail'd much farther than the edges of our Land. After this, we have had a continual blast upon some of our principal Grain, annually diminishing a vast part of our ordinary Food. Herewithal, wasting Sicknesses, especially Burning and Mortal Agues, have Shot the Arrows of Death in at our Windows. Next, we have had many Adversaries of our own Language, who have been perpetually assaying to deprive us of those English Liberties, in the encouragement whereof these Territories have been settled. As if this had not been enough; the Tawnies among whom we came have watered our Soil with the Blood of many Hundreds of Inhabitants. . . . Besides all which, now at last the Devils are (if I may so speak) in Person come down upon us with such a Wrath, as is justly much, and will quickly be more, the Astonishment of the World.

And this last adventure of the Devil has a quality all its own.

Wherefore the Devil is now making one Attempt more upon us; an Attempt more Difficult, more Surprising, more snarl'd with unintelligible Circumstances than any that we have hitherto Encountered. . . . An Army of Devils is horribly broke in upon the place which is the center, and after a sort, the First-born of our English Settlements: and the Houses of the Good People there are fill'd with the doleful shrieks of their Children and Servants, Tormented by Invisible Hands, with Tortures altogether preternatural.

The witchcraft hysteria occupied but a brief moment in the history of the Bay. The first actors to take part in it were a group of excited girls and a few of the less savory figures who drifted around the edges of the community, but the speed with which the other people of the Bay gathered to witness the encounter and accept an active role in it, not to mention the quality of the other persons who were eventually drawn into this vortex of activity, serves as an index to the gravity of the issues involved. For a few years, at least, the settlers of Massachusetts were alone in the world, bewildered by the loss of their old destiny but not yet aware of their new one, and during this fateful interval they tried to discover some image of themselves by listening to a chorus of voices which whispered to them from the depths of an invisible wilderness.

■■■

STUDY QUESTIONS

1. What were the social, political, and religious problems that confronted New England in the late seventeenth century? How were these problems related to the outbreak of the witchcraft hysteria in Salem?

2. What were the major types of evidence used in a witchcraft trial? What were the unique problems involved in the use of special evidence?

3. What role did the Puritan ministers play in the witchcraft episode?

4. What did the Puritan concept of wilderness entail? How have attitudes toward the wilderness changed over the years?

5. What did the transition from "Puritan" to "Yankee' involve?" How did the character of the New Englander change during the seventeenth and eighteenth centuries?

BIBLIOGRAPHY

The Salem witchcraft episode is the single most studied event in colonial history. Certainly the drama of the event accounts for much of the scholarly interest. However, of equal importance is the fact that the documentation produced by the trials provides the historian with a comprehensive view of Salem society. For students interested in these sources, Paul Boyer and Stephen Nissenbaum, eds., *The Salem Witchcraft Papers: Verbatim Transcripts of the Legal Documents of the Salem Witchcraft Outbreak of 1692,* three volumes (1977), is the best starting place. The same two authors collected an anthology of primary documents in *Witchcraft at Salem Village* (1972). The collections include relevant maps, church records, deeds, wills, and petitions.

The first important history of the events is Charles W. Upham, *Salem Witchcraft,* two volumes (1867), which emphasizes the strains in Salem society. Marion Starkey, *The Devil in Massachusetts* (1949) is a highly readable account of the episode. More scholarly are Chadwick Hansen, *Witchcraft at Salem* (1969) and Paul Boyer and Stephen Nissenbaum, *Salem Possessed: The Social Origins of Witchcraft* (1974). The most recent study, John P. Demos, *Entertaining Satan: Witchcraft and the Culture of Early New England* (1982) combines scholarship with narrative grace.

A number of important books have been published on European witchcraft. The best are Keith Thomas, *Religion and the Decline of Magic* (1971); Alan Macfarlane, *Witchcraft in Tutor and Stuart England: A Regional and Comparative Study* (1970); H. C. Erik Midelfort, *Witch Hunting in Southwestern Germany, 1562–1684: The Social and Intellectual Foundation* (1972); E. William Monter, *Witchcraft in France and Switzerland: The Borderlands during the Reformation* (1976); and Julio Caro Baroja, *The World of the Witches* (1964).

DEATH AND THE PURITAN CHILD

David E. Stannard

The cold statistics of life and death in Puritan New England would have been envied in most parts of the seventeenth-century world. Males who survived the perils of infancy could reasonably expect to celebrate their seventieth birthday, and twenty percent of the men of the first generation reached the age of eighty. Although the figures for women were slightly lower, they were still better than in Europe or any other section of America. This longer life expectancy encouraged family stability. Parents watched their children grow to adulthood and often lived long enough to converse with their grandchildren. So unique was this circumstance, that historian John Murrin claimed that New England "invented" grandparents.

From the vantage of the late twentieth century, however, New England life was still riddled with the dangers of an early death. If pure drinking water, a cool climate, and a dispersed population conspired to prolong life, smallpox plagues, crude medical techniques, and Indian wars shortened life. In the seventeenth century, childhood diseases that we take for granted today—such as chicken pox and measles—were often deadly.

In "Death and the Puritan Child," David E. Stannard interprets the Puritan attitude toward death. As with every aspect of Puritan life, religion was paramount. Although Christian tradition counseled peace and comfort in one's dying hour, Puritanism was a religion that offered very little comfort. Its emphasis on the essentially mysterious nature of predestination and man's depraved and morally polluted soul ensured that the moment of death would be plagued by self-doubt and fear. This was true for children as well as for adults.

Probably at no time in modern history have parents in the West agreed on the matter of the correct and proper approach to child-rearing. Certainly this is true of our own time, but it was equally so in the age of the Puritan.

"A child is a man in a small letter," wrote John Earle in 1628,

yet the best copy of Adam *before hee tasted of* Eve *or the Apple. . . . Hee is natures fresh picture newly drawne in Oyle, which time and much handling dimmes and defaces. His soule is yet a white paper unscribled with observations of the world, wherewith at length it becomes a blurr'd Notebooke. He is purely happy, because he knowes no evill, nor hath made meanes by sinne, to be acquainted with misery. . . . Nature and his Parents alike dandle him, and tice him on with a bait of Sugar, to a draught of Worme-wood. . . . His father hath writ him as his owne little story, wherein hee reads those dayes of his life that hee cannot remember; and sighes to see what innocence he ha's outliv'd.*

In view of this attitude among certain Englishmen of the 17th century—an attitude that, it appears, became prevalent in colonial Maryland and Virginia—it should come as no surprise to read in the report of a visiting Frenchman at the end of the century that "In England they show an extraordinary complacency toward young children, always flattering, always caressing, always applauding whatever they do. At least that is how it seems to us French, who correct our children as soon as they are capable of reason." This judgment was echoed a few years later by an Englishman reflecting on the customs of his people: "In the *Education* of *Children*," wrote Guy Miege in 1707, "the indulgence of Mothers is excessive among the *English*;

"Death and the Puritan Child" by David E. Stannard from *American Quarterly*, XXVI, December 1974, pp. 456–476. Published by the American Studies Association. Copyright © 1974. Reprinted by permission of American Quarterly and the author.

which proves often fatal to their children, and contributes much to the Corruption of the Age. If these be Heirs to great Honours and Estates, they swell with the Thoughts of it, and at last grow unmanageable." Had Miege been writing a bit later in the century he might have sought evidence for his assertion in the life of Charles James Fox who, at age five, had been accidentally deprived of the privilege of watching the blowing up of a garden wall; at his insistence his father had the wall rebuilt and blown up again so that the boy might witness it. On another occasion, when the young Charles announced his intention of destroying a watch, his father's reply was: "Well, if you must, I suppose you must."

But neither John Earle in 1628, nor Charles Fox in 1754 were Puritans; and neither Henri Misson in 1698, nor Guy Miege in 1707 were commenting on Puritan attitudes toward children. Had they been, their reports would have read very differently.

In 1628, the same year that John Earle was rhapsodizing on the innocence and purity of children, and on parental accommodation to them, Puritan John Robinson wrote:

And surely there is in all children, though not alike, a stubbornness, and stoutness of mind arising from natural pride, which must, in the first place, be broken and beaten down. . . . This fruit of natural corruption and root of actual rebellion both against God and man must be destroyed, and no manner of way nourished, except we will plant a nursery of contempt of all good persons and things, and of obstinacy therein. . . . For the beating, and keeping down of this stubbornness parents must provide carefully for two things: first that children's wills and willfulness be restrained and repressed. . . . The second help is an inuring of them from the first, to such a meanness in all things, as may rather pluck them down, than lift them up.

In place of Earle's child, seen as "yet the best copy of Adam before hee tasted of Eve or the Apple," the Puritan child was riddled with sin and corruption, a depraved being polluted with the stain of Adam's sin. If there was any chance of an individual child's salvation, it was not a very good chance—and in any case, the knowledge of who was to be chosen for salvation and who was not to be chosen was not a matter for earthly minds. "Because a small and contemptible number are hidden in a huge multitude," Calvin had written, "and a few grains of wheat are covered by a pile of chaff, we must leave to God alone the knowledge of his church, whose foundation is his secret election." The quest for salvation was at the core of everything the devout Puritan thought and did; it was the primary source of the intense drive that carried him across thousands of miles of treacherous ocean in order to found a Holy Commonwealth in the midst of a wilderness; it was his reason for being. And yet, despite his conviction of God's purposeful presence in everything he did or encountered, from Indian wars to ailing livestock, full confidence in his own or anyone else's salvation was rendered impossible by the inscrutability of his God. He was driven to strive for salvation at the same time that he was told his fate was both predetermined and undetectable.

To be sure, Puritans believed there were signs or "marks," indications of God's will, that laymen and ministers alike could struggle to detect in their persons and in those of members of the congregation. But these signs were subject to interpretation and even feigning, and could never be regarded as more than *suggestions* of sainthood. Further, only very rarely was an apparent childhood conversion accepted as real by a congregation. Thus, Jonathan Edwards devoted a great deal of attention to youthful conversions during the stormy emotionalism of the Great Awakening, but only after first noting: "It has heretofore been looked on as a strange thing, when any have seemed to be savingly wrought upon, and remarkably changed in their childhood." And even James Janeway, whose *A Token For Children: Being an Exact Assessment of the Conversion, Holy and Exemplary Lives, and Joyful Deaths of Several Young Children*, was one of the best-read books of 17th and 18th century Puritans, admitted in a later edition that one of his examples of early spiritual development—that of a child who supposedly began showing signs of salvation between the ages of two and three—seemed to many "scarce credible, and they did fear [it] might somewhat prejudice the authority of the rest."

But if conversion was unlikely at an early age, it was at least possible. Given the alternative, then, of apathetic acceptance of their children as depraved and damnable creatures, it is hardly surprising that Puritan parents urged on their offspring a religious precocity that some historians have interpreted as tantamount to premature adulthood. "You can't begin with them *Too soon*," Cotton Mather wrote in 1689,

They are no sooner wean'd *but they are to be* taught. . . . *Are they* Young? *Yet the* Devil *has been with them already. . . . They go astray as soon as they are born. They no sooner* step *than they* stray, *they no sooner* lisp *than they* ly. *Satan gets them to be proud, profane, reviling and revengeful, as* young *as they are. And I pray, why should you not be afore-hand with* him?

Puritan children, even "the very best" of whom had a "Corrupt Nature in them, and . . . an Evil Figment in their Heart," were thus driven at the earliest age possible both to recognize their depravity and to pray for their salvation. In the event that children proved intractable in this regard the first parental response was to be "what saies the Wise man, *A Rod for the fools back*"; but generally more effective—and more insidious—was the advice "to watch when some *Affliction* or some *Amazement* is come upon them: then God opens their ear to Discipline." If Puritan parents carried out these designs with fervor it was of course out of love and concern for their children. But at least some of the motivation may well have had guilt at its source; as Mather and others were frequently careful to point out: "Your Children are Born Children of Wrath. Tis *through you*, that there is derived unto them the sin which Exposes them to infinite Wrath."

We should not, however, pass too quickly over the matter of the Puritan parent's genuine love for his children. Even a casual reading of the most noted Puritan journals and autobiographies—those of Thomas Shepard, Samuel Sewall, Cotton Mather—reveals a deep-seated parental affection for children as the most common, normal and expected attitude. The relationship between parents and children was often compared with that between God and the Children of God. "That God is often angry with [his children]," Samuel Willard wrote in 1684, "afflicts them, and withdraws the light of his countenance from them, and puts them to grief, is not because he loves them not, but because it is that which their present condition requires; they are but Children, and childish, and foolish, and if they were not sometimes chastened, they would grow wanton, and careless of duty." Indeed, in the same work in which Cotton Mather referred to children as "proud, profane, reviling and revengeful," he warned parents that *"They must give an account of the souls that belong unto their Families. . . .* Behold, thou hast *Lambs* in the *Fold,* Little ones in thy House; God will strain for it,— if wild beasts, and Lusts carry any of them away from the *Service* of God through any neglect of thine thou shalt smart for it in the fiery prison of God's terrible Indignation."

Children, then, were on the one hand deeply loved, "Lambs in the Fold"; as Willard noted: "If others in a Family suffer want, and be pincht with difficulties, yet the Children shall certainly be taken care for, as long as there is anything to be had: they are hard times indeed when Children are denied that which is needful for them. On the other hand they were depraved and polluted; as Benjamin Wadsworth wrote: "Their Hearts naturally, are a meer nest, root, fountain of Sin, and wickedness." Even most innocent infants, dying before they had barely a chance to breathe, could at best be expected to be given, in Michael Wigglesworth's phrase, "the easiest room in Hell."

If the state of a child's spiritual health was an extremely worrisome and uncomfortable matter for the Puritan parent, the state of his physical health was not less so. In recent years historians of colonial New England have convincingly shown that the colonists of certain New England towns in the 17th and early 18th centuries lived longer and healthier lives than did many of their countrymen in England. This finding and the many others by these new demographic historians are important to our understanding of life in early New England; but in acknowledging the relative advantages of life in some New England communities compared with parts of England and Europe in the 17th century, we should be careful to avoid blinding ourselves to the fact that death was to the colonist, as it was to the Englishman and Frenchman, an ever-present menace—and a menace that struck with a particular vengeance at the children of the community.

Philip J. Greven's study of colonial Andover, Massachusetts is noteworthy for both the skill of the author's analysis and the stability and healthiness of the families whose lives he studied. As Greven explicitly points out, compared with Boston and other New England communities, Andover's mortality rate was exceptionally low, though it did climb steadily in the 18th century. It is worth dwelling briefly on the differences between Boston and Andover, because the power and sophistication of Greven's work can tend to suggest an implicit, and erroneous, picture of Andover as a representative New England town. It may or may not be representative of a certain type of Puritan community—a sufficient number of collateral studies have not yet been done to determine this—but demographically it was vastly different from Boston, the hub of the Holy Commonwealth. Mortality rates in Andover during the early 18th century, when those rates were on the increase, fluctuated within a normal annual range of about half those in Boston during the same period—somewhere between fifteen and twenty per thousand in Andover, somewhere between thirty-five and forty per thousand in Boston. Epidemic years are excluded from these calculations in both cases, but it should be noted that Andover's worst epidemic lifted the death rate to seventy-one per

The First, Second, and Last Scene of Mortality.   Prudence Punderson.

■ ■ ■ *Because of the high mortality rates in New England, Puritan children were very early made aware of death. The above needlework, done by seventeen-year-old Prudence Punderson, is her depiction of the three stages of life.*

thousand, while Boston's worst epidemic during the same period pushed the death rate well over one hundred per thousand—or more than 10 per cent of the resident population. In the 17th century, the smallpox epidemic of 1677–78, joined by the normal death rate, probably killed off more than one-fifth of Boston's entire population. "Boston burying-places never filled so fast," wrote a young Cotton Mather:

It is easy to tell the time when we did not use to have the bells tolling for burials on a Sabbath morning by sunrise; to have 7 buried on a Sabbath day night, after Meeting. To have coffins

crossing each other as they have been carried in the street. . . . To attempt a Bill of Mortality, and number the very spires of grass in a Burying Place seem to have a parity of difficulty and in accomplishment.

Indeed, if Andover fares well in comparison with mortality figures for English and European towns, Boston does not: it was not at all uncommon for the death rate in Boston to hover near or even exceed that for English towns like Clayworth that have been cited for their exceptionally high mortality rates.

One of the problems with all these figures,

ever, is the almost inevitable underestimation of infant mortality; as Greven and other demographic analysts freely acknowledge, most infant deaths were unrecorded and their number can now only be guessed at. One such guess, a highly informed one, has been made by Kenneth A. Lockridge. In a study of Dedham, Massachusetts in the 17th and early 18th centuries, Lockridge found that an upward adjustment of ⅑ on the town's birth rate would most likely take account of unrecorded infant deaths. If the same adjustment is made on the birth rate of colonial Andover a fairly accurate comparison of childhood birth and mortality rates can be made.

Although Greven traces a trend throughout the generations examined showing a steady drop in fertility and life expectancy rates as Andover became more urbanized, if we view the period as a whole the town remains a good example of one of the healthier communities in New England. Using the Lockridge adjustment to include unrecorded infant deaths, the average number of children born per family in Andover throughout the century under discussion was 8.8. Of those, an average of 5.9 survived to adulthood. In other words, approximately three of the close to nine children born to the average family would die before reaching their twenty-first birthday. But, as Greven notes, the most vulnerable period in life was that "beyond infancy but prior to adolescence—the age group which appears to have been most susceptible, among other things, to the throat distemper prevalent in the mid-1730s." Again applying the infant mortality adjustment to Greven's figures, the rate of survival to age ten for all children born between 1640 and 1759 was approximately 74 per cent—with a generational high of 83 per cent and a low of 63 per cent, this latter figure of course indicating that at one point fewer than two out of three infants lived to see their tenth birthday. During the period as a whole, more than one child in four failed to survive the first decade of life in a community with an average birth rate per family of 8.8.

Thus a young couple embarking on a marriage did so with the knowledge and expectation that in all probability *two or three* of the children they might have would die before the age of ten. In certain cases, of course, the number was more than two; Greven discusses instances when parents lost six of eleven children in rapid succession, including four in a single month, and four of eight children in less than a year—and this in a town remarkable for the relative health and longevity of its residents. In Boston the rate was much higher and even the most prominent and well cared for residents of that city were constantly reminded of the fragility of life in childhood. Thomas Shepard, for instance, had seven sons, three of whom died in infancy; the other four outlived their father, but he died at 43—having in that short time outlived two wives. As Joseph E. Illick has recently pointed out, Samuel Sewall and Cotton Mather each fathered fourteen children: "One of Sewall's was stillborn, several died as infants, several more as young adults. Seven Mather babies died shortly after delivery, one died at two years and six survived to adulthood, five of whom died in their twenties. Only two Sewall children outlived their father, while Samuel Mather was the only child to survive Cotton."

It is important for us to recognize that conditions for living in colonial New England were sometimes superior to those in 17th century England and Europe. But it is equally important for us not to lose sight of the fact that the Puritan settlements were places where "winter was to be feared," as Kenneth Lockridge has written, where "harvests were a gamble that kept men's minds aware of Providence, plague arose and subsided out of all human control and infants died in numbers that would shock us today."

It has often been noted by writers on the Puritan family that the prescribed and common personal relationship between parents and children was one of restraint and even aloofness, mixed with, as we have seen, an intense parental effort to impose discipline and encourage spiritual precocity. Parents were reminded to avoid becoming "too fond of your children and too familiar with them" and to be on their guard against "not keeping constantly your due distance." Edmund

S. Morgan has shown how this "due distance" worked in both directions, as when Benjamin Colman's daughter Jane wrote to her father requesting forgiveness for the "flow of affections" evident in some of her recent letters. Colman responded by urging her to be "careful against this Error, even when you say your Thoughts of Reverence and Esteem to your Father, or to a Spouse, if ever you should live to have one," and commended her for having "done well to correct yourself for some of your Excursions of this kind toward me." Morgan has also seen the common practice of "putting children out," both to early apprenticeship and simply extended stays with other families, often against the child's will, as linked to the maintenance of the necessary distance between parent and child; "these economically unnecessary removals of children from home," he writes, probably resulted from the fact that "Puritan parents did not trust themselves with their own children, that they were afraid of spoiling them by too great affection."

Morgan's suggested explanation for this practice seems logical and convincing, but there may have been an additional, deeper source for both this practice and the entire Puritan attitude toward severely restrained displays of fondness between parents and children. For children, despite the natural hold they had on their parents' affection, were a source of great emotional discomfort for them as well. In the first place, there was a very real possibility, if not a probability, that parental affection would be rewarded by the death of a child before it even reached puberty; the "due distance" kept by Puritan parents from their children might, at least in part, have been an instinctive response to this possibility, a means of insulating themselves to some extent against the shock that the death of a child might bring. This, of course, would be potentially true of any society with a relatively high rate of childhood mortality. But to the Puritan the child was more than a loved one extremely vulnerable to the ravages of the environment; he was also a loved one polluted with sin and natural depravity. In this, of course, he was no dif-

ferent from any other members of the family or community, including those Visible Saints viewed as the most likely candidates for salvation: Original Sin touched everyone, and all were considered polluted and not worthy of excessive affection. What is important here, however, is not that this dictum touched everyone, but that in the process it touched those most emotionally susceptible to its pernicious effects—the children of the zealous and devoted Puritan.

The Puritans of New England held as doctrine the belief that they were involved in a binding contract or "covenant" with God. This belief was complex and multifaceted, but one aspect of it viewed the entire community as having contracted a "social convenant" with God by which they promised strict obedience to his laws. Failure to obey on the part of any individual within the community could result in God's wrath being vented on the entire community. Thus, whenever signs of God's anger appeared, might they be comets or earthquakes or the deaths of eminent men, Puritans searched for the source of the divine displeasure and fearfully awaited future expressions of it. When the younger Thomas Shepard died in 1677, the Reverend Urian Oakes wrote in lamentation:

What! must we with our God, and Glory part?
Lord is thy Treaty with New England come
Thus to an end? And is War in thy Heart?
That this Ambassadour is called home.
   So Earthly Gods (Kings) when they War intend
   Call home their Ministers, and the Treaties end.

The depraved and ungodly child was, it is true, naturally repellent in his sinfulness; but more than that, the activity that might easily grow out of that sinfulness posed a very real danger to the well-being of the community. In response, understandably enough, the Puritan parent strove mightily to effect conversion or at the least to maintain a strict behavior code, but at the same time—when these effects were combined with the love he felt for his child, the tenuous hold the child had on life, the natural repulsiveness of sin—he may well have been driven to find ways of creating emotional distance between his offspring and himself.

But if separation was emotionally beneficial to the Puritan parent, it may have had precisely the opposite effect on the Puritan child. John Demos has recently speculated on the "profound loss" experienced by many Puritan children in the second and third years of life because of the fact that they were probably weaned at the start of the second year and very often witnessed the arrival of a younger brother or sister at the start of the third year. This in itself, it might be argued, does not make Puritan children unique: the spacing of children at two-year intervals is common among many of the world's cultures, and weaning at twelve months is hardly an exceptional custom. But added to these practices was the conscious effort of Puritan parents to separate themselves from an excessively intimate relationship with their children. If this normal practice of separation was not enough, Cotton Mather was probably echoing a fairly common sentiment in viewing as "the sorest Punishment in the Family" the banishment of the child from the parents' presence. Separation, however, can be both real and imagined, can be both present and anticipated. And, of course, the ultimate separation is death. This was a fact of which the Puritan parent was well aware and which the Puritan child, from the earliest age possible, was never allowed to forget.

May of 1678 was a month of great apprehension in Boston. The smallpox plague referred to earlier had entered the city some months before and had begun its relentless slaying of the population. By May hundreds had died and the governments of the colony and the town were hurriedly passing legislation aimed at holding down the spread of the deadly infection—people were directed not to hang out bedding or clothes in their yards or near roadways, and those who had been touched by the disease and survived were forbidden contact with others for specified periods of time. The worst was yet to come: by the time it was over it was as though, proportionate to the population, an epidemic were to kill over a million and a half people in New York City

during the next eighteen months. The city girded for it.

Only two years earlier New England had endured the devastation of King Philip's War, in which—not counting the enormous numbers of Indian dead—greater casualties were inflicted in proportion to the population than in any other war in subsequent American history. Death was everywhere in 1678 when, on May 5, Increase Mather addressed his Boston congregation and prayed "for a Spirit of Converting Grace to be poured out upon the Children and *Rising Generation* in *New England*." A decade later Increase's son Cotton would write, as I have noted earlier, that a particularly effective means of disciplining children was "to watch when some *Affliction* or *Amazement* is come upon them: then God opens their ear to Discipline." On May 5, 1678, the then teen-aged young man probably witnessed a particularly effective demonstration of this principle as it was directed toward an entire congregation.

Some years earlier—at first against Increase Mather's will, then later with his support—the churches of New England had succumbed to the need for what its detractors later called the "Half-Way Covenant," in which as yet unconverted adult children of church members were acknowledged as church members (with the right to have their own children baptized) but not as full communicants. Bound up with this change in the notion of Puritan exclusivity was the growing belief that, in his covenant with his holy children, God had promised to "be thy God, and the God of thy seed after thee." In his sermon of May 1678, Mather alluded to this belief very early: "Now God hath seen good to cast the line of Election so, as that it doth (though not wholly, and only, yet) for the most part, run through the loins of godly Parents." It is well to remember here that before any comforts could be gained from this doctrine the Puritan parent had also to face the impossibility of ever being truly assured of his own election. But that is not the reason Mather cluttered his sentence with such awkward qualifications—"though not wholly, and only, yet . . . for the most part." God remained inscrutable, and it was heresy to think otherwise; but also: "Men should not think with themselves (as some do) if their children do belong to God, then he will convert them, whether they pray for him or no, but should therefore be stirred up to the more fervency in cries to Heaven, for the blessing promised. *I* (saith the Lord) *will give a new heart to you, and to your Children,* yet you must pray for it."

When he turned to address the youth of the congregation Mather mentioned explicitly the "affliction and amazement" that was at hand:

Young men and young Women, O be in earnest for Converting Grace, before it be too late. It is high time for you to look about you, deceive not yourselves with false Conversions (as many young men do to their eternal ruine) or with gifts instead of Grace. . . . Death waits for you. There is now a Mortal and Contagious Disease in many Houses; the Sword of the Lord is drawn, and young men fall down apace slain under it; do you not see the Arrows of Death come flying over your heads? Why then, Awake, Awake, and turn to God in Jesus Christ whilst it is called today, and know for certain that if you dy in your sins, you will be the most miserable of any poor Creatures in the bottom of Hell.

But Mather's most determined and terrifying words were reserved for the youngest and most vulnerable members of the congregation, those of less "discretion and understanding" than the other youths addressed. It was with them that the specter of parental and ministerial separation and betrayal was merged with the promise of death and damnation. "Beg as for your lives that the God of your Fathers would pour his Spirit upon you," he exhorted these littlest of children,

Go into secret corners and plead it with God. . . . If you dy and be not first new Creatures, better you had never been born: you will be left without excuse before the Lord, terrible witnesses shall rise up against you at the last day. Your godly Parents will testifie against you before the Son of God at that day: And the Ministers of Christ will also be called in as witnesses against you for your condemnation, if you dy in your sins. As for many of you, I have treated with you privately and personally, I have told you, and I do tell you, and make solemn Protestation before the Lord, that if you dy in a Christless, graceless estate, I will most certainly profess unto Jesus Christ at the day of Judgement, Lord, these are the Children, whom I spake often unto thy Name, publickly and privately, and I told them, that if they did not make themselves a new heart, and make sure of an interest in Christ, they should become damned creatures for evermore; and yet they would not repent and believe the Gospel.*

If there is one thing on which modern psychologists have agreed concerning the fear of death in young children it is that such fear is generally rooted in the anticipation of separation from their parents. Time and again experimental studies have shown that, as one writer puts it, "the most persistent of fears associated with death is that of separation—and the one which is most likely to be basic, independent of cultural, religious, or social background." "In children," this writer adds, "dread of separation seems to be basic."

There are, certainly, ways that children seem to have of defending against separation anxiety resulting from anticipation of death. One of these—one that has inspired poets down through the ages—is the expectation of reunion in death, a defense that makes separation a temporary matter. But this was a defense denied the Puritan child. As if addressing this question directly, Increase Mather in 1711 remarked on

What a dismal thing it will be when a Child shall see his Father at the right Hand of Christ in the day of Judgment, but himself at His left Hand: And when his Father shall joyn with Christ in passing a Sentence of Eternal Death upon him, saying, Amen O Lord, thou art Righteous in thus Judging: *And when after the Judgment, children shall see their Father going with Christ to Heaven, but themselves going away into Everlasting Punishment!*

As Edmund S. Morgan has pointed out, this verbal "picture of parent and child at the Day of Judgment . . . was a favorite with many Puritan ministers, for it made the utmost of filial affection." It was probably not of much comfort to the Puritan child to hear that, if he was to be separated from his parents, he would at least still have the companionship of certain playmates—given the circumstances. For, as Jonathan Edwards put it in one of his sermons specifically addressed to young children: "How dreadful it will be to be all together in misery. Then you won't play together any more but will be damned together, will cry out with weeping and wailing and gnashing of teeth together."

Another common defense against childhood fear of separation and death that is mentioned in the psychological literature is supplied by parental interjection that only old people die, not children. Puritan children met precisely the opposite advice. The young "may bear and behave themselves as if imagining their hot blood, lusty bodies, activity, beauty, would last alwayes, and their youthful pleasures never be at an end," acknowledged Samuel Wakeman at a young man's funeral in 1673; "but," he warned, *Childhood and Youth are vanity:* Death may not wait till they be grayheaded; or however, the earliest Morning hastens apace to Noon, and then to Night." From the moment they were old enough to pay attention children were repeatedly instructed regarding the precariousness of their existence. The sermons they listened to, the parents who corrected them, the teachers who instructed them, and eventually the books they read, all focused with a particular intensity on the possibility and even the likelihood of their imminent death. Further, those who died young, it was often noted, died suddenly—"Death is oftentimes as near the young man's back as it is to the old man's face," wrote Wakeman—and matter-of-fact repetitions of this ever-present threat joined with burning pictures of Judgment Day to hammer the theme home. "I know you will die in a little time," the esteemed Jonathan Edwards calmly told a group of children "some sooner than others. 'Tis not likely you will all

live to grow up." The fact that Edwards was only speaking the very obvious truth did not help matters any.

Nor did the literalness with which Puritan children must have taken the descriptions of depravity, sin, imminent death, judgment and hell offer anything in the way of relief. At least since the early writings of Piaget psychologists have been familiar with the various stages of the child's sense of causal reality, one central and persistent component of which is termed "realism." Realism, as one writer puts it, "refers to the fact that initially all things are equally real and real in the same sense and on the same plane: pictures, words, people, things, energies, dreams, feelings—all are equally solid or insubstantial and all mingle in a common sphere of experience. . . . Realism does not imply fatalism or passive resignation, but simply a failure [on the part of the young child] to doubt the reality of whatever comes into awareness." The children observed in the psychological experiments that gave rise to the identification of these stages of reality awareness were the children of 20th century parents, children living in, if not a secular universe, at least one in which a fundamentalist view of divine creation and judgment is largely absent. Puritan children, however, lived in a world in which their parents—indeed, the greatest scientific minds of the time: Bacon, Boyle, Newton—were certain of the reality of witches and subterranean demons. In 1674, surprised at Spinoza's skepticism regarding spiritual entities, a correspondent of the freethinking philosopher doubtless spoke for most men of his time, the famed "Age of Reason," when he replied: "No one of moderns denies specters."

It has long been known that one component of death in the Middle Ages was concern over the fate of the body of the deceased, and worry that a fully disintegrated corpse or one that had been destroyed in war might be unable to be present at the Judgment. It is less well known, or less often acknowledged, that a similar literalism retained a hold on the Puritan mind into the 18th century. Thus in 1692 a highly respected New England minister could effectively deal with questions concerning the Last Judgment in the following manner:

Where will there be room for such a Vast Multitude as Adam, with all his Children? The whole surface of the earth could not hold them all? Ridiculous exception! Allow that this World should Last no less than Ten-Thousand *Years, which it will not; Allow that there are at once alive a* Thousand Millions *of men, which there* are not; *Allow all these to march off every* Fifty years, *with a New Generation rising up in their stead; and allow each of these Individuals a place* Five Foot Square *to stand upon. I think these are Fair Allowances. I would now pray the Objector, if he have any skill at* Arithmetick, *to Compute, Whether a Spot of Ground, much less than* England, *which contains perhaps about Thirty Millions of Acres, but about a* Thousandth Part *of the Terraqueous Glob, and about the* Three Hundred thirty third *part of the Habitable Earth, would not hold them all.*

In a world in which the presence of early death was everywhere, and in which the most sophisticated and well regarded adults expressed such a literal sense of spiritual reality, it is hardly surprising that children would respond with a deadly serious mien to reminders of "how filthy, guilty, odious, abominable they are both by nature and practice," to descriptions of parental desertion at the day of Judgment and subsequent condemnation to the terrors of hell where "the Worm dyeth not . . . [and] the Fire is not quenched," and to the exhortations of respected teachers to "Remember Death; think much of death; think how it will be on a death bed." In such a world it is far from surprising that a girl of seven should react "with many tears"—and her father with tears of sympathy—to a reading of Isaiah 24, in which she would have encountered:

Therefore hath the curse devoured the earth, and they that dwell therein are desolate: therefore the inhabitants of the earth are burned, and few men left. . . . Fear, and the pit, and the snare, are upon thee, O inhabitant of the earth. And it shall come to pass, that he who fleeth from the noise of the fear shall fall into the pit; and he that cometh up out of the midst of the pit shall be taken in the snare: for the windows from on high are open, and the foundations of the earth do shake.

Nor, in such a world, should we consider it unusual that later in her youth this same girl would again and again "burst out into an amazing cry . . . [because] she was afraid she should goe to Hell," would "read out of Mr. Cotton Mather—why hath Satan filled thy heart, which increas'd her Fear," and would eventually be unable to read the Bible without weeping, fearing as she did "that she was a Reprobat, Loved not God's people as she should."

The case of young Elizabeth Sewall is by no means unique. Puritan diaries and sermons are filled with references to similar childhood responses to the terrors of separation, mortality and damnation. As with so many other things Puritan, these fears seem to have reached a crescendo with the emotional outpourings of the Great Awakening in the 1740s. But the fears were always present, following children into adulthood and combining there with the disquieting complexities of Puritan theology and Christian tradition to produce a culture permeated by fear and confusion in the face of death.

The Christian tradition that the Puritans had inherited counseled peace and comfort in one's dying hour. Elaborate procedures for coping with the fear of death had been devised throughout long centuries of experience. Extreme unction, the viaticum, indulgences, requiem masses, the prayers of family and friends—all these served the Catholic as a cushion against an excessively fearful reaction in the face of death. The relative optimism that grew out of this tradition was passed on, in different form, to much of Protestantism during the Renaissance and Reformation. Thus, Renaissance poetry on the theme of death, Edelgard Dubruck observes,

. . . stressed immortality and the afterlife. The word "death" was often avoided and replaced by euphemisms . . . [and] depiction of the realistic

aspects of death was carefully suppressed. . . . In the early sixteenth century, poets dwelt upon fame and immortality rather than death, and in the Reformation writings death had at least lost its sting, and both Lutherans and Calvinists insisted that death was at long last vanquished with the help of Christ.

Although the Puritans inherited, and tried to live with, the *prescription* that a peaceful death was a good death, the deterministic pessimism of the faith was contradictory to Christian tradition and caused exceptional discomfort as the devout Puritan awaited the end of his life. To the adult Puritan the contemplation of death frequently "would make the flesh tremble." To the Puritan child it could do no less.

Puritan New England, in this respect at least, seems a far cry from England in the same period, at least if Peter Laslett is correct when he writes that people there were "inured to bereavement and the shortness of life." But in recognizing this, we should also be wary of finding in Puritan attitudes and behavior too much grist for our psychological mills. The fear of death, to many Freudians, is "closely interwoven with castration fear," a fear which "is so closely united with death fear that it has often been described as its origin." It is, writes psychoanalyst J. D. Howard, "purely . . . a secondary substitutive phenomenon of the castration fear which grew out of an inadequately resolved Oedipal conflict." Turning to Freud himself, a more sophisticated interpreter with some knowledge of Puritanism might seize on the similarity between the Puritan requirement for uncertainty and his preoccupations with death, and Freud's treatment of uncertainty and obsessional neurosis. But interpretations of this type are hopelessly bogged down by the arrogance and myopia of the historical present.

The world of the Puritan—child and adult—was a rational world, in many ways, perhaps, more rational than our own. It is true that it was a world of witches and demons, and of a just and terrible God who made his presence known in the slightest act of nature. But this was the given

reality about which most of the decisions and actions of the age, throughout the entire Western world, revolved. When the Puritan parent urged on his children what we would consider a painfully early awareness of sin and death, it was because the well-being of the child and the community *required* such an early recognition of these matters. It merits little to note that the Puritans (and Bacon and Boyle and Newton) were mistaken in their beliefs in hobgoblins; the fact is they were real to men of the 17th century, as real as Ra and his heavenly vessels were to the ancient Egyptians, and at least as real as the unconscious is to devout followers of Freud; and the responses to that reality were as honest and as rational, in the context of the times, as are the responses to reality of any parent today.

If children were frightened, even terrified, by the prospects of life and death conjured up by their parents and ministers, that too was a natural and rational response. As more than one Puritan writer suggested, to fail to be frightened was a sure sign that one was either spiritually lost, or stupid, or both. Death brought with it, to all but a very few, the prospect of the most hideous and excruciating fate imaginable. One necessary, though by itself, insufficient sign of membership in that select company of saints was the taking to heart of the warning to "beware of indulging yourselves in a stupid secure frame." Thus, wrote Samuel Willard with remarkably cool detachment and insight,

Here we see the reason why the People of God are so often doubtful, disquiet, discontent, and afraid to dy (I put things together). The ground of all this is because they do not as yet see clearly what they shall be: It would be a matter of just wonderment to see the Children of God so easily and often shaken, so disturbed and perplexed in hours of Temptation, were it not from the consideration that at present they know so little of themselves or their happiness: Sometimes their sonship itself doth not appear to them, but they are in the dark, at a loss about the evidencing of it to the satisfaction of their own minds, and from hence it is that many doubtings arise, and their souls are disquieted.

Willard knew first hand of what he spoke. He was often the one chosen to try to calm the fears of those who found the prospect of death too much to bear; Judge Sewall in fact called him in to help with young Elizabeth's disconsolate weeping. It may be, despite their experience, that ministers and parents like Willard were unaware of all the components that went into the making of the Puritan child's fear of death. It was, as we have seen, a complex problem touching on a variety of matters which Puritan children and adults alike had to face every day of their lives. But they did at least know that when a young Betty or Sam Sewall broke down in tears over the prospects of death and damnation, the children—and they were children, not miniature adults—were most often acting normally, out of their own experience in the world, and in response to their parents' solemn, reasoned warnings.

■ ■ ■

STUDY QUESTIONS

1. How did "putting out children" affect Puritan parents and children?

2. How did Puritan parents come to terms with their love for their children and the belief that their offspring were riddled with sin?

3. How were Puritan children prepared for death? How did they view death? What special fears of death did they entertain?

4. How did the Puritans' religion separate them from traditional European thought?

BIBLIOGRAPHY

The classic study of death and dying in western culture is Philippe Aries, *The Hour of Our Death* (1977). Magisterial in his sweep, Aries made use of a wide variety of written and artistic works in his attempt to interpret the changing meaning of death. No such grand overview of the subject has been written about death in America. David E. Stannard, however, has advanced the subject with two works. *The Puritan Way of Death: A Study of Religion, Culture, and Social Change* (1977) explores the unique way the Puritans approached death, and *Death in America* (1975) provides a collection of essays on the attitudes toward death in different cultures.

The quality of New England life has been extensively researched by American historians. John Demos, *A Little Commonwealth: Family Life in Plymouth Colony* (1970) examines the physical setting, family relations, and individual development of the residents of Plymouth. Edmund S. Morgan, *The Puritan Family: Religion and Domestic Relations in Seventeenth-Century New England* (1966) remains a classic exploration of the subject. Several more recent books that make use of demographic evidence are Philip J. Creven, Jr., *Four Generations: Population, Land, and Family in Colonial Andover, Massachusetts* (1970) and Kenneth A. Lockridge, *A New England Town: The First Hundred Years (Dedham, Massachusetts, 1636–1736)* (1970). For comparison, Peter Laslett, *The World We Have Lost* (1965) presents a detailed look at English life during the seventeenth century.

Part Two

SOUTHERN
LIFE

The Southern colonies differed markedly from the New England colonies. Colonial Virginia, for example, never enjoyed the remarkable demographic stability of colonial Massachusetts Bay. Most of the people who traveled to Virginia during the seventeenth century were young, unmarried male servants—indeed, before 1640 males outnumbered females by a ratio of 6 to 1. In addition, the humid lowlands of the Chesapeake fostered high mortality rates. During the seventeenth century, the average life expectancy for Chesapeake males was about forty-three, and for females it was even lower. Only 50 percent of the children born in the region lived past the age of twenty, and many of the survivors suffered illnesses that left them too weak for strenuous labor.

The most obvious result of this demographic nightmare was a severe labor shortage. English immigration to the South simply did not satisfy the labor needs. As a result, colonial planters began to import black Africans as early as 1619. The question of whether these unwilling emigrants were chattel slaves or free servants fulfilling an indentureship remained in doubt for some years, but certainly by 1700 white planters had developed the institution of slavery. This peculiar institution was far more than an economic arrangement; it had a psychological effect on everyone who lived close to its dominion.

More than demographics and slavery separated the Southern colonies from the New England colonies. The first settlers who landed in Jamestown were not concerned with the impurities in the Anglican Church. Instead, they worried about

A TOBACCO PLANTATION

their own economic futures. Most longed to become wealthy—and the faster the better. They were worldly men in search of worldly success. The majority readily accepted not only the Anglican Church but also the English class structure. Their goal was to move up the pyramid, not to level it.

With very few exceptions, their dreams of easy prosperity vanished before the hardships of Southern existence. Indians, swamps, diseases, and backbreaking labor were formidable foes. Men who possessed stronger bodies, quicker minds, or larger bank accounts advanced by buying land and growing tobacco. Their society was brutally competitive and early success was no guarantee of lasting success. But by the 1650s a real colonial aristocracy had begun to emerge. The great Chesapeake families—the Byrds, Carters, Masons, and Burwells—commenced their domination of society and politics.

Without losing their competitive urges, the leaders of the major families began to cooperate to preserve and perpetuate their wealth and status. They intermarried, awarded themselves military titles, and dominated the colonial assemblies throughout the South. By the eighteenth century such bodies as Virginia's House of Burgesses began to resemble a gathering of cousins. Not surprisingly, as the gentry consolidated its control over all aspects of colonial society, it became increasingly more difficult for the ordinary man to rise into the ruling class. This development, however, created few problems. Not many people in the colonial South questioned deferential attitudes.

ENGLISHMEN AND AFRICANS

Winthrop Jordan

The institution of chattel slavery developed gradually in the British seaboard colonies. The first Africans landed in Virginia in 1619, but over the next forty years relatively few others followed. By 1660 only about fifteen hundred blacks lived in Virginia, and their status was unclear. White planters regarded some as slaves, others as indentured servants. But as the black population grew after 1660 and the demand for a steady labor force became critical, white planters adopted the institution of chattel slavery.

Planters masked the economic foundations of slavery with a rhetoric that emphasized humanitarianism and Christianity. As Winthrop D. Jordan emphasizes in his National Book Award winning study, *White Over Black: American Attitudes Toward the Negro, 1550–1812,* from their first meeting, Englishmen viewed Africans as a strange and disturbing people. The Africans' color, religion, and social behavior upset Englishmen. This early form of prejudice laid the intellectual groundwork for later justifications of slavery.

The institution of slavery influenced the development of the entire South and left deep psychological scars both on whites and blacks. In the following essay Jordan discusses the initial English attitude toward Africans.

When the Atlantic nations of Europe began expanding overseas in the sixteenth century, Portugal led the way to Africa and to the east while Spain founded a great empire in America. It was not until the reign of Queen Elizabeth that Englishmen came to realize that overseas exploration and plantations could bring home wealth, power, glory, and fascinating information. By the early years of the seventeenth century Englishmen had developed a taste for empire and for tales of adventure and discovery. More than is usual in human affairs, one man, the great chronicler Richard Hakluyt, had roused enthusiasm for western planting and had stirred the nation with his monumental compilation, *The Principal Navigations, Voyages, Traffiques and Discoveries of the English Nation.* Here was a work to widen a people's horizons. Its exhilarating accounts of voyages to all quarters of the globe constituted a national hymn, a scientific treatise, a sermon, and an adventure story.

English voyagers did not touch upon the shores of West Africa until after 1550, nearly a century after Prince Henry the Navigator had mounted the sustained Portuguese thrust southward for a water passage to the Orient. Usually Englishmen came to Africa to trade goods *with* the natives. The earliest English descriptions of West Africa were written by adventurous traders, men who had no special interest in converting the natives or, except for the famous Hawkins voyages in the 1560's, in otherwise laying hands on them. Extensive English participation in the slave trade did not develop until well into the seventeenth century. Initially English contact with Africans did not take place primarily in a context which prejudged the Negro as a slave, at least not as a slave of Englishmen. Rather, Englishmen met Africans merely as another sort of men.

Englishmen found the peoples of Africa very different from themselves. "Negroes" looked different to Englishmen; their religion was un-Christian; their manner of living was anything but English; they seemed to be a particularly libidinous sort of people. All these clusters of perceptions were related to each other, though they may be spread apart for inspection, and they were related also to the circumstances of contact in Africa, to previously accumulated traditions concerning that strange and distant continent, and to certain special qualities of English society on the eve of its expansion into the New World.

The Blackness Without

For Englishmen, the most arresting characteristic of the newly discovered African was his color. Travelers rarely failed to comment upon it; indeed when describing Africans they frequently began with complexion and then moved on to dress (or, as they saw, lack of it) and manners. At Cape Verde, "These people are all blacke, and are called Negroes, without any apparell, saving before their privities." Robert Baker's narrative poem recounting his two voyages to the West African coast in 1562 and 1563 introduced the people he saw with these engaging lines:

And entering in [a river], we see
  a number of blacke soules,
Whose likelinesse seem'd men to be,
  but all as blacke as coles.
Their Captain comes to me
  as naked as my naile,
Not having witte or honestie
  to cover once his taile.

Englishmen actually described Negroes as *black*—an exaggerated term which in itself suggests that the Negro's complexion had powerful impact upon their perceptions. Even the peoples of northern Africa seemed so dark that Englishmen tended to call them "black" and let further refinements go by the board. In Shakespeare's day, the Moors, including Othello, were commonly portrayed as pitchy black and the terms *Moor* and *Negro* were used almost interchangeably. With curious inconsistency, however, Englishmen recognized that Africans south of the Sahara were not at all the same people as the much more familiar Moors. Sometimes they referred to West Africans as "black Moors" to distinguish them from the peoples of North Africa.

The powerful impact which the Negro's color made upon Englishmen must have been partly owing to suddenness of contact. Though the Bible as well as the arts and literature of antiquity and the Middle Ages offered some slight introduction to the "Ethiope," England's immediate acquaintance with "black" skinned peoples came with relative rapidity. People much darker than Englishmen were not entirely unfamiliar, but really "black" men were virtually unknown except as vaguely referred to in the hazy literature about the sub-Sahara which had filtered down from antiquity. Native West Africans probably first appeared in London in 1554; in that year five "Negroes," as one trader reported, were taken to England, "kept till they could speake the language," and then brought back again "to be a helpe to Englishmen" who were engaged in trade with Africans on the coast. Hakluyt's later discussion of these Africans suggests that these "black Moores" were a novelty to Englishmen. In this respect the English experience was markedly different from that of the Spanish and Portuguese who for centuries had been in close contact with North Africa and had actually been invaded and subjected by people both darker and more "highly civilzed" than themselves. The impact of the Negro's color was the more powerful upon Englishmen, moreover, because England's principal contact with Africans came in West Africa and the Congo, which meant that one of the lightest-skinned of the earth's peoples suddenly came face to face with one of the darkest.

In England perhaps more than in southern Europe, the concept of blackness was loaded with intense meaning. Long before they found that some men were black, Englishmen found in the idea of blackness a way of expressing some of their most ingrained values. No other color except white conveyed so much emotional impact. As described by the *Oxford English Dictionary*, the meaning of *black* before the sixteenth century included, "Deeply stained with dirt; soiled, dirty, foul. . . . Having dark or deadly purposes, malignant; pertaining to or involving death, deadly; baneful, disastrous, sinister. . . . Foul, iniquitous, atrocious, horrible, wicked. . . . Indicating disgrace, censure, liability to punishment, etc." Black was an emotionally partisan color, the handmaid and symbol of baseness and evil, a sign of danger and repulsion.

Embedded in the concept of blackness was its direct opposite—whiteness. No other colors so clearly implied opposition, "beinge coloures utterlye contrary":

Everye white will have its blacke,
And everye sweete its sowre.

White and black connoted purity and filthiness, virginity and sin, virtue and baseness, beauty and ugliness, beneficence and evil, God and the devil. Whiteness, moreover, carried a special significance for Elizabethan Englishmen: it was, particularly when complemented by red, the color of perfect human beauty, especially *female* beauty. This ideal was already centuries old in Elizabeth's time, and their fair Queen was its very embodiment: her cheeks were "roses in a bed of lillies." (Elizabeth was naturally pale but like many ladies then and since she freshened her "lillies" at the cosmetic table.) An adoring nation knew precisely what a beautiful Queen looked like.

Her cheeke, her chinne, her neck, her nose,
This was a lillye, that was a rose;
Her bosome, sleeke as Paris plaster,
Held upp twoo bowles of Alabaster.

By contrast, the Negro was ugly, by reason of his color and also his "horrid Curles" and "disfigured" lips and nose. A century later blackness still required apology: one of the earliest attempts to delineate the West African as a heroic character, the popular story *Oroonoko* (1688), presented Negroes as capable of blushing and turning pale. It was important, if incalculably so, that English discovery of black Africans came at a time when the accepted English standard of ideal beauty was a fair complexion of rose and white. Negroes seemed the very picture of perverse negation.

From the first, however, many English observers displayed a certain sophistication about the Negro's color. Despite an ethnocentric tendency to find blackness repulsive, many writers were fully aware that Africans themselves might have different tastes. As early as 1621 one writer told of the "Jetty coloured" Negroes, "Who in their native beauty most delight,/And in contempt doe paint the Divell white"; this assertion became almost a commonplace. Many accounts of Africa reported explicitly that the Negro's preference in colors was inverse to the European's. Even the Negro's features were conceded to be appealing to Negroes.

The Causes of Complexion

Black human beings were not only startling but extremely puzzling. The complexion of Africans posed problems about its nature, especially its permanence and utility, its cause and origin, and its significance. Although these were rather separate questions, there was a pronounced tendency among Englishmen and other Europeans to formulate the problem in terms of causation alone. If the cause of human blackness could be explained, then its nature and significance would follow.

Not that the problem was completely novel. The ancient Greeks had touched upon it. The story of Phaëton's driving the chariot sun wildly through the heavens apparently served as an explanation for the Ethiopian's blackness even before written records, and traces of this ancient fable were still drifting about during the seventeenth century. Ptolemy had made the important suggestion that the Negro's blackness and woolly hair were caused by exposure to the hot sun and had pointed out that people in northern climates were white and those in temperate areas an intermediate color. Before the sixteenth century, though, the question of the Negro's color can hardly be said to have drawn the attention of Englishmen or indeed of Europeans generally.

The discovery of West Africa and the development of Negro slavery made the question far more urgent. The range of possible answers was rigidly restricted, however, by the virtually universal assumption, dictated by church and Scripture, that all mankind stemmed from a single source. Indeed it is impossible fully to understand the various efforts at explaining the Negro's complexion without bearing in mind the strength of the tradition which in 1614 made the chronicler, the Reverend Samuel Purchas, proclaim vehemently: "the tawney Moore, blacke Negro, duskie Libyan, ash-coloured Indian, olive-coloured American, should with the whiter European become one *sheep-fold*, under *one great Sheepheard* . . . without any more distinction of Colour, Nation, Language, Sexe, Condition, all may bee *One* in him that is One. . . ."

In general, the most satisfactory answer to the problem was some sort of reference to the action of the sun, whether the sun was assumed to have scorched the skin, drawn the bile, or blackened the blood. People living on the Line had obviously been getting too much of it; after all, even Englishmen were darkened by a little exposure. How much more, then, with the Negroes who were "so scorched and vexed with the heat of the sunne, that in many places they curse it when it riseth." This association of the Negro's color with the sun became a commonplace in Elizabethan literature; as Shakespeare's Prince of Morocco apologized, "Mislike me not for my complexion,/ The shadow'd livery of the burnish'd sun,/ To whom I am a neighbour and near bred."

Unfortunately this theory ran headlong into a stubborn fact of nature which simply could not be overridden: if the equatorial inhabitants of Africa were blackened by the sun, why not the people living on the same Line in America? Logic required them to be the same color. Yet by the middle of the sixteenth century it was becoming perfectly apparent that the Indians living in the hottest regions of the New World could by no stretch of the imagination be describe as black. They were "olive" or "tawny," and moreover they had long hair rather than the curious "wool" of Negroes. Clearly the method of accounting for human complexion by latitude just did not work. The worst of it was that the formula did not seem altogether wrong, since it was apparent that in general men in hot climates tended to be darker than in cold ones.

Another difficulty with the climatic explanation of skin color arose as lengthening experience provided more knowledge about Negroes. If the heat of the sun caused the Negro's blackness, then his removal to cold northerly countries ought to result in his losing it; even if he did not himself surrender his peculiar color, surely his descendants must. By mid-seventeenth century it was becoming increasingly apparent that this expectation was ill founded: Negroes in Europe and northern America were simply not whitening up very noticeably.

From the beginning, in fact, some Englishmen were certain that the Negro's blackness was permanent and innate and that no amount of cold was going to alter it. There was good authority in Jeremiah 13:23; "Can the Ethiopian change his skin/ or the leopard his spots?" Elizabethan dramatists used the stock expression "to wash in Ethiop white" as indicating sheer impossibility. In 1578 a voyager and speculative geographer, George Best, announced that the blackness of Negroes "proceedeth of some naturall infection of the first inhabitants of that country, and so all the whole progenie of them descended, are still polluted with the same blot of infection." An essayist in 1695 declared firmly, "A negroe will always be a negroe, carry him to Greenland, give him chalk, feed and manage him never so many ways."

There was an alternative to the naturalistic explanations of the Negro's blackness. Some writers felt that God's curse on Ham (Cham), or upon his son Canaan, and all their descendants was entirely sufficient to account for the color of Negroes. This could be an appealing explanation, especially for men like George Best who wished to stress the "natural infection" of blackness and for those who hoped to incorporate the Negro's complexion securely within the accepted history of mankind. The original story in Genesis 9 and 10 was that after the Flood, Ham had looked upon his father's "nakedness" as Noah lay drunk in his tent, but the other two sons, Shem and Japheth, had covered their father without looking upon him; when Noah awoke he cursed Canaan, son of Ham, saying that he would be a "servant of servants" unto his brothers. Given this text, the question becomes why a tale which logically implied slavery but absolutely nothing about skin color should have become a popular explanation of the Negro's blackness. The matter is puzzling, but probably, over the very long run, the story was supported by the ancient association of heat with sensuality and by the fact that some sub-Saharan Africans had been enslaved by Europeans since ancient times. In addition, the extraordinary persistence of the tale in the face of centuries of constant refutation was probably sustained by a feeling that blackness could scarcely be anything *but* a curse and by the common need to confirm the facts of nature by specific reference to Scripture. In contrast to the climatic theory, God's curse provided a satisfying purposiveness which the sun's scorching heat could not match until the eighteenth century.

In the long run, of course, the Negro's color attained greatest significance not as a scientific problem but as a social fact. Englishmen found blackness in human beings a peculiar and important point of difference. The African's color set him radically *apart* from Englishmen. But then, distant Africa had been known to Christians for ages as a land of men radically different in religion.

Defective Religion

While distinctive appearance set Africans apart in a novel way, their religious condition distinguished them in a more familiar manner. Englishmen and Christians everywhere were sufficiently acquainted with the concept of heathenism that they confronted its living representatives without puzzlement. Certainly the rather sudden discovery that the world was teeming with heathen people made for heightened vividness and urgency in a long-standing problem; but it was the fact that this problem was already well formulated long before contact with Africa which proved important in shaping English reaction to the Negro's defective religious condition.

In one sense heathenism was less a "problem" for Christians than an exercise in self-definition: the heathen condition defined by negation the proper Christian life. In another sense, the presence of heathenism in the world constituted an imperative to intensification of religious commitment. From its origin Christianity was a universalist, proselytizing religion, and the sacred and secular histories of Christianity made manifest the necessity of bringing non-Christians into the fold. For Englishmen, then, the heathenism of Negroes was at once a counterimage of their own religion and a summons to eradicate an important distinction between the two peoples. Yet the interaction of these two facets of the concept of heathenism made for a peculiar difficulty: On the one hand, to act upon the felt necessity of converting Africans would have been to eradicate the point of distinction which Englishmen found most familiar and most readily comprehensible. Yet if they did not act upon this necessity, continued heathenism among Negroes would remain an unwelcome reminder to Englishmen that they were not meeting their obligations to their own faith— nor to the benighted Negroes. Englishmen resolved this implicit dilemma by doing nothing.

Considering the strength of the Christian tradition, it is almost startling that Englishmen failed to respond to the discovery of heathenism in Africa with at least the rudiments of a campaign for conversion. Although the impulse to spread Christianity seems to have been weaker in Englishmen than, say, in the Catholic Portuguese, it cannot be said that Englishmen were indifferent to the obligation imposed upon them by the overseas discoveries of the sixteenth century. While they were badly out of practice at the business of conversion (again in contrast to the Portuguese) and while they had never before been faced with the practical difficulties involved in Christianizing entire continents, they nonetheless were able to contemplate with equanimity and even eagerness the prospect of converting the heathen. Indeed they went so far as to conclude that converting the natives in America was sufficiently important to demand English settlement there. As it turned out, the well-publicized English program for converting Indians produced very meager results, but the avowed intentions certainly were genuine. It was in marked contrast, therefore, that Englishmen did not avow similar intentions concerning Africans until the late eighteenth century. Fully as much as with skin color, though less consciously, Englishmen distinguished between the heathenisms of Indians and of Negroes.

It is not easy to account for the distinction which Englishmen made. On the basis of the travelers' reports there was no reason for Englishmen to suppose Indians inherently superior to Negroes as candidates for conversion. But America was not Africa. Englishmen contemplated settling in America, where voyagers had established the King's claim and where supposedly the climate was temperate; in contrast, Englishmen did not envision settlement in Africa, which had quickly gained notoriety as a graveyard for Europeans and where the Portuguese had been first on the scene. Certainly these very different circumstances meant that Englishmen confronted Negroes and Indians in radically

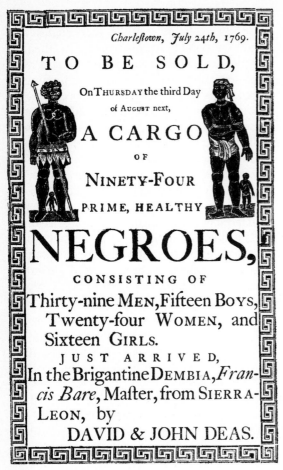

Charleſtown, *July 24th*, 1769.

TO BE SOLD,

On THURSDAY the third Day of AUGUST next,

A CARGO

OF

NINETY-FOUR

PRIME, HEALTHY

NEGROES,

CONSISTING OF

Thirty-nine MEN, Fifteen BOYS, Twenty-four WOMEN, and Sixteen GIRLS.

JUST ARRIVED,

In the Brigantine DEMBIA, *Francis Bare*, Maſter, from SIERRA-LEON, by

DAVID & JOHN DEAS.

■ ■ *A notice announcing the arrival of slaves to be sold at an auction in Charleston, South Carolina.*

the distinction which Englishmen made as to conversion was at least in some small measure modeled after the difference they saw in skin color.

The most important aspect of English reaction to African heathenism was that Englishmen evidently did not regard it as separable from the Negro's other attributes. Heathenism was treated not so much as a specifically religious defect but as one manifestation of a general refusal to measure up to proper standards, as a failure to be English or even civilized. There was every reason for Englishmen to fuse the various attributes they found in Africans. During the first century of English contact with Africa, Protestant Christianity was an important element in English patriotism; especially during the struggle against Spain the Elizabethan's special Christianity was interwoven into his conception of his own nationality, and he was therefore inclined to regard the Negroes' lack of true religion as part of theirs. Being a Christian was not merely a matter of subscribing to certain doctrines; it was a quality inherent in oneself and in one's society. It was interconnected with all the other attributes of normal and proper men: as one of the earliest English travelers described Africans, they were "a people of beastly living, without a God, lawe, religion, or common wealth"—which was to say that Negroes were not Englishmen. Far from isolating African heathenism as a separate characteristic, English travelers sometimes linked it explicitly with blackness and savagery.

Savage Behavior

The condition of savagery—the failure to be civilized—set Negroes apart from Englishmen in an ill-defined but crucial fashion. Africans were *different* from Englishmen in so many ways: in their clothing, housing, farming, warfare, language, government, morals, and (not least important) in their table manners. To judge from the comments of voyagers, Englishmen had an unquenchable thirst for the details of savage life. Englishmen were, indeed, enormously curious about their rapidly expanding world, and it is

different social contexts and that Englishmen would find it far easier to contemplate converting Indians than Negroes. Yet it remains difficult to see why Negroes were not included, at least as a secondary target. The fact that English contact with Africans so frequently occurred in a context of slave dealing does not entirely explain the omission of Negroes, since in that same context the Portuguese and Spanish did sometimes attempt to minister to the souls of Africans and since Englishmen in America enslaved Indians when good occasion arose. Given these circumstances, it is hard to escape the conclusion that scarcely surprising that they should have taken an interest in reports about cosmetic mutilation, polygamy, infanticide, ritual murder, and the like. In addition, reports about "savages" began arriving at a time when Englishmen very much needed to be able to translate their apprehensive interest in an uncontrollable world out of medieval religious terms. The discovery of savages overseas enabled them to make this translation easily, to move from miracles to verifiable monstrosities, from heaven to earth.

As with skin color, English reporting of African customs was partly an exercise in self-inspection by means of comparison. The necessity of continuously measuring African practices with an English yardstick of course tended to emphasize the differences between the two groups, but it also made for heightened sensitivity to instances of similarity. Thus the Englishman's ethnocentrism tended to distort his perception of African culture in two opposite directions. While it led him to emphasize differences and to condemn deviations from the English norm, it led him also to seek out similarities. Particularly, Englishmen were inclined to see the structures of African societies as analogous to their own, complete with kings, counselors, gentlemen, and the baser sort. Here especially they found Africans like themselves, partly because they know no other way to describe any society and partly because there was actually good basis for such a view of the social organization of West African communities.

Despite the fascination and self-instruction Englishmen derived from discussing the savage behavior of Africans, they never felt that savagery was as important a quality in Africans as it was in the American Indians. As was the case with heathenism, contrasting social contexts played an important role in shaping the English response to savagery in the two peoples. Inevitably, the savagery of the Indians assumed a special significance in the minds of those actively engaged in a program of planting civilization in the American wilderness. The case with the African was different; the English errand into Africa was not a new or a perfect community but a

business trip. No hope was entertained for civilizing the Negro's steaming continent, and Englishmen therefore lacked compelling reason to develop a program for remodeling the African natives.

From the beginning, also, the importance of the Negro's savagery was muted by the Negro's color. Englishmen could go a long way toward expressing their sense of being different from Africans merely by calling them "black." By contrast, the aboriginals in America did not have the appearance of being radically distinct from Europeans except in religion and savage behavior. English voyagers placed much less emphasis upon the Indian's color than upon the Negro's, and they never permitted the Indian's physiognomy to distract their attention from what they regarded as his essential quality, his savagery.

It would be a mistake, however, to slight the importance of what was seen as the African's savagery, since it fascinated Englishmen from the very first. English observers in West Africa were sometimes so profoundly impressed by the Negro's behavior that they resorted to a powerful metaphor with which to express their own sense of difference from him. They knew perfectly well that Negroes were men, yet they frequently described the Africans as "brutish" or "bestial" or "beastly." The supposed hideous tortures, cannibalism, rapacious warfare, revolting diet (and so forth page after page) seemed somehow to place the Negro among the beasts. The eventual circumstances of the Englishman's contact with Africans served to strengthen this feeling. *Slave* traders in Africa necessarily handled Negroes the same way men in England handled beasts, herding and examining and buying, as with any other animals which were products of commerce.

The Apes of Africa

If Negroes were likened to beasts, there was in Africa a beast which was likened to men. It was a strange and eventually tragic happenstance of nature that Africa was the habitat of the animal which in appearance most resembles man. The animal called "orang-outang" by contemporaries (actually the chimpanzee) was native to those parts of western Africa where the early slave trade was heavily concentrated. Though Englishmen were acquainted (for the most part vicariously) with monkeys and baboons, they were unfamiliar with tail-less apes who walked about like men. Accordingly, it happened that Englishmen were introduced to the anthropoid apes and to Negroes at the same time and in the same place. The startlingly human appearance and movements of the "ape"—a generic term though often used as a synonym for the "orang-outang"—aroused some curious speculations.

In large measure these speculations derived from traditions which had been accumulating in Western culture since ancient times. Medieval books on animals contained rosters of strange creatures who in one way or another seemed disturbingly to resemble men. There were the *simia* and the *cynocephali* and the *satyri* and the others, all variously described and related to one another, all jumbled in a characteristic blend of ancient reports and medieval morality. The confusion was not easily nor rapidly dispelled, and many of the traditions established by this literature were very much alive during the seventeenth century.

The section on apes in Edward Topsell's *Historie of Foure-Footed Beastes* (1607) serves to illustrate how certain seemingly trivial traditions and associations persisted in such form that they were bound to affect the way in which Englishmen would perceive the inhabitants of Africa. Above all, according to Topsell, "apes," were venerous. The red apes were "so venerous that they will ravish their Women." Baboons were "as lustful and venerous as goats"; a baboon which had been "brought to the French king . . . above all loved the companie of women, and young maidens; his genitall member was greater than might match the quantity of his other parts." Pictures of two varieties of apes, a "Satyre" and an "Ægopithecus," graphically emphasized the "virile member."

In addition to stressing the "lustful disposi-tion" of the ape kind, Topsell's compilation contained suggestions concerning the character of simian facial features. "Men that have low and flat nostrils," readers were told in the section on apes, "are Libidinous as Apes that attempt women. . . ." There also seemed to be some connection between apes and devils. In a not altogether successful attempt to distinguish the "Satyre-apes" from the mythical creatures of that name, Topsell straightened everything out by explaining that it was "probable, that Devils take not any dænomination or shape from Satyres, but rather the Apes themselves from Devils whome they resemble, for there are many things common to the Satyre-apes and devilish Satyres." Association of apes and/or satyrs with devils was common in England: the inner logic of this association derived from uneasiness concerning the ape's "indecent likenesse and imitation of man"; it revolved around evil and sexual sin; and, rather tenuously, it connected apes with blackness.

Given this tradition and the coincidence of contact, it was virtually inevitable that Englishmen should discern similarity between the manlike beasts and the beastlike men of Africa. A few commentators went so far as to suggest that Negroes had sprung from the generation of ape-kind or that apes were themselves the offspring of Negroes and some unknown African beast. These contentions were squarely in line with the ancient tradition that Africa was a land "bringing dailie foorth newe monsters" because, as Aristotle himself had suggested, many different species came into proximity at the scarce watering places. Jean Bodin, the famous sixteenth-century French political theorist, summarized this wisdom of the ages with the categorical remark that "promiscuous coition of men and animals took place, wherefore the regions of Africa produce for us so many monsters." Despite all these monsters out of Africa, the notion that Negroes stemmed from beasts in a literal sense was not widely believed. It simply floated about, available, later, for anyone who wanted it.

Far more common and persistent was the notion that there sometimes occurred "a beastly copulation or conjuncture" between apes and Negroes, and especially that apes were inclined wantonly to attack Negro women. The very explicit idea that apes assaulted female human beings was not new; Africans were merely being asked to demonstrate what Europeans had known for centuries. As late as the 1730's a well-traveled, well-educated, and intelligent naval surgeon, John Atkins, was not at all certain that the stories were false: "At some Places the *Negroes* have been suspected of Bestiality with them [apes and monkeys], and by the Boldness and Affection they are known under some Circumstances to express to our Females; the Ignorance and Stupidity on the other side, to guide or control Lust; but more from the near resemblance [of apes] . . . to the Human Species would tempt one to suspect the Fact."

By the time Atkins addressed himself to this evidently fascinating problem, some of the confusion arising from the resemblance of apes to men had been dispelled. In 1699 the web of legend and unverified fact was disentangled by Edward Tyson, whose comparative study of a young "orang-outang" was a masterwork of critical scientific investigation. Throughout his dissection of the chimpanzee, Tyson meticulously compared the animal with human beings in every anatomical detail, and he established beyond question both the close relationship and the non-identity of ape and man. Here was a step forward; the question of the ape's proper place in nature was now grounded upon much firmer knowledge of the facts. Despite their scientific importance, Tyson's conclusions did nothing to weaken the vigorous tradition which linked the Negro with the ape. The supposed affinity between apes and men had as frequently been expressed in sexual as in anatomical terms, and his findings did not effectively rule out the possibility of unnatural sexual unions. Tyson himself remarked that orangs were especially given to venery.

The sexual association of apes with Negroes had an inner logic which kept it alive: sexual union seemed to prove a certain affinity without going so far as to indicate actual identity—which was what Englishmen really thought was the case. By forging a sexual link between Negroes and apes, furthermore, Englishmen were able to give vent to their feeling that Negroes were a lewd, lascivious, and wanton people.

Libidinous Men

Undertones of sexuality run throughout many English accounts of West Africa. To liken Africans—any human beings—to beasts was to stress the animal within the man. Indeed the sexual connotations embodied in the terms *bestial* and *beastly* were considerably stronger in Elizabethan English than they are today, and when the Elizabethan traveler pinned these epithets upon the behavior of Africans he was more frequently registering a sense of sexual shock than describing swinish manners.

Lecherousness among Africans was at times for Englishmen merely another attribute which one would expect to find among heathen, savage, beastlike men. One commentator's remarks made evident how closely interrelated all these attributes were in the minds of Englishmen: "They have no knowledge of God . . . they are very greedie eaters, and no lesse drinkers, and very lecherous, and theevish, and much addicted to uncleanenesse: one man hath as many wives as hee is able to keepe and maintaine." Sexuality was what one expected of savages.

Clearly, however, the association of Africans with potent sexuality represented more than an incidental appendage to the concept of savagery. Long before first English contact with West Africa, the inhabitants of virtually the entire continent stood confirmed in European literature as lustful and venerous. About 1526 Leo Africanus (a Spanish Moroccan Moor converted to Christianity) supplied an influential description of the little-known lands of "Barbary," "Libya," "Numedia," and "Land of Negroes"; and Leo was as explicit as he was imaginative. In the English translation (1600) readers were informed concerning the "Negroes" that "there is no Nation under Heaven more prone to Venery." Leo disclosed that "the Negroes . . . leade a beastly kind of life, being utterly destitute of the use of reason, of dexteritie of wit, and of all arts. Yea, they so behave themselves, as if they had continually lived in a Forrest among wild beasts. They have great swarmes of Harlots among them; whereupon a man may easily conjecture their manner of living." Nor was Leo Africanus the only scholar to elaborate upon the ancient classical sources concerning Africa. In a highly eclectic work first published in 1566, Jean Bodin sifted the writings of ancient authorities and concluded that heat and lust went hand in hand and that "in Ethiopia . . . the race of men is very keen and lustful." Bodin announced in a thoroughly characteristic sentence, "Ptolemy reported that on account of southern sensuality Venus chiefly is worshiped in Africa and that the constellation of Scorpion, which pertains to the pudenda, dominates that continent."

Depiction of the Negro as a lustful creature was not radically new, therefore, when Englishmen first met Africans face to face. Seizing upon and reconfirming these long-standing and apparently common notions, Elizabethan travelers and literati dwelt explicitly with ease upon the especial sexuality of Africans. Othello's embraces were "the gross clasps of a lascivious Moor." Francis Bacon's *New Atlantis* (1624) referred to "an holy hermit" who "desired to see the Spirit of Fornication; and there appeared to him a little foul ugly Æthiop." Negro men, reported a seventeenth-century traveler, sported "large Propagators." In 1623 Richard Jobson, a sympathetic observer, reported that Mandingo men were "furnisht with such members as are after a sort burthensome unto them." Another commentator thought Negroes "very lustful and impudent, especially, when they come to hide their nakedness, (for a *Negroes* hiding his Members, their extraordinary greatness) is a token of

their Lust, and therefore much troubled with the Pox." By the eighteenth century a report on the sexual aggressiveness of African women was virtually required of European commentators. By then, of course, with many Englishmen actively participating in the slave trade, there were pressures making for descriptions of "hot constitution'd Ladies" possessed of a "temper hot and lascivious, making no scruple to prostitute themselves to the *Europeans* for a very slender profit, so great is their inclination to white men."

While the animus underlying these and similar remarks becomes sufficiently obvious once Englishmen began active participation in the slave trade, it is less easy to see why Englishmen should have fastened upon Negroes a pronounced sexuality virtually upon first sight. The ancient notions distilled by Bodin and Leo Africanus must have helped pattern initial English perceptions. Yet clearly there was something in English culture working in this direction. It is certain that the presumption of powerful sexuality in black men was far from being an incidental or casual association in the minds of Englishmen. How very deeply this association operated is obvious in *Othello,* a drama which loses most of its power and several of its central points if it is read with the assumption that because the black man was the hero English audiences were indifferent to his blackness. Shakespeare was writing both *about* and *to* his countrymen's feelings concerning physical distinctions between peoples; the play is shot through with the language of blackness and sex. Iago goes out of his way to talk about his own motives: "I hate the Moor,/ And it is thought abroad that 'twixt my sheets/ He has done my office." Later, he becomes more direct, "For that I do suspect the lusty Moor hath leaped into my seat." It was upon this so obviously absurd suspicion that Iago based his resolve to "turn her virtue into pitch." Such was his success, of course, that Othello finally rushes off "to furnish me with some means of death for the fair devil." With this contorted denomination of Desdemona, Othello unwittingly revealed how deeply Iago's promptings about Desdemona's "own clime, complexion, and degree" had eaten into his consciousness. Othello was driven into accepting the premise that the physical distinction *matters*: "For she had eyes," he has to reassure himself, "and chose me." Then, as his suspicions give way to certainty, he equates her character with his own complexion:

> Her name, that was as fresh,
> As Dian's visage, is now begrim'd and black
> As mine own face.

This important aspect of Iago's triumph over the noble Moor was a subtly inverted reflection of the propositions which Iago, hidden in darkness, worked upon the fair lady's father. No one knew better than Iago how to play upon hidden strings of emotion. Not content with the straightforward crudity that "your daughter and the Moor are now making the beast with two backs," Iago told the agitated Brabantio that "an old black ram/Is tupping your white ewe" and alluded politely to "your daughter cover'd with a Barbary horse." This was not merely the language of (as we say) a "dirty" mind: it was the integrated imagery of blackness and whiteness, of Africa, of the sexuality of beasts and the bestiality of sex. And of course Iago was entirely successful in persuading Brabantio, who had initially welcomed Othello into his house, that the marriage was "against all rules of nature." Eventually Brabantio came to demand of Othello what could have brought a girl "so tender, fair, and happy"

> To incur a general mock
> Run from her guardage to the sooty bosom
> Of such a thing as thou.

Altogether a curious way for a senator to address a successful general.

These and similar remarks in the play *Othello* suggest that Shakespeare and his audiences were not totally indifferent to the sexual union of "black" men and "white" women. Shakespeare did not condemn such union; rather, he played upon an inner theme of black and white sexuality, showing how the poisonous mind of a white man perverted and destroyed the noblest of loves by means of bringing to the surface (from the darkness, whence Iago spoke) the lurking shadows of animal sex to assault the whiteness of chastity. Never did "dirty" words more dramatically "blacken" a "fair" name. At the play's climax, standing stunned by the realization that the wife he has murdered was innocent, Othello groans to Emilia, " 'Twas I that killed her"; and Emilia responds with a torrent of condemnation: "O! the more angel she,/ And you the blacker devil." Of Desdemona: "She was too fond of her filthy bargain." To Othello: "O gull! O dolt!/ As ignorant as dirt!" Shakespeare's genius lay precisely in juxtaposing these two pairs: inner blackness and inner whiteness. The drama meant little if his audiences had felt no response to this cross-inversion and to the deeply turbulent double meaning of black *over* white.

It required a very great dramatist to expose some of the more inward biocultural values which led—or drove—Englishmen to accept readily the notion that Negroes were peculiarly sexual men. Probably these values and the ancient reputation of Africa upon which they built were of primary importance in determing the response of Englishmen to Africans. Whatever the importance of biologic elements in these values—whatever the effects of long northern nights, of living in a cool climate, of possessing light-colored bodies which excreted contrasting lumps of darkness—these values by Shakespeare's time were interlocked with English history and culture and, more immediately, with the circumstances of contact with Africans and the social upheaval of Tudor England.

STUDY QUESTIONS

1. How might the sixteenth-century define "black"? How did their concept of blackness influence their attitude toward Africans?

2. What different theories were advanced to explain the reasons why Africans were black? What do these theories indicate about the attitude of the English toward the Africans?

3. How did Englishmen regard African religions? Why didn't the English try to convert Africans to Christianity?

4. How did the behavior and social customs of Africans reinforce English prejudice toward blacks?

5. How did Englishmen interpret African sexual behavior? Did their interpretation strengthen or weaken their prejudice toward Africans?

6. How did the formation of prejudice lead to the development of the institution of slavery?

BIBLIOGRAPHY

Historians have written more about slavery than any other aspect of Southern life. They have debated both the origins and developments of the institution. Those interested in the origins of slavery should read Winthrop Jordan, *White Over Black: American Attitudes Toward the Negro, 1550–1812* (1968); David B. Davis, *The Problem of Slavery in Western Culture* (1966); and Oscar and Mary Handlin, "The Origins of the Southern Labor System," *William and Mary Quarterly,* 3rd Ser., 7 (1950). In order to gauge the severity of slavery in the United States, historians have taken a comparative approach. Frank Tannenbaum, *Slave and Citizen: The Negro in the Americas* (1947), began the debate over theory and practice of slavery. Other important studies in this field are H. S. Klein, *Slavery in the Americas: A Comparative Study of Virginia and Cuba* (1967); Carl N. Degler, *Neither Black nor White: Slavery and Race Relations in Brazil and the United States* (1971); Philip D. Curtin, *The Atlantic Slave Trade: A Census* (1969); and Stanley M. Elkins, *Slavery: A Problem in American Institutional and Intellectual Life* (1959).

TOBACCO IN FOLK CURES IN WESTERN SOCIETY

Katharine T. Kell

Although tobacco consumption is clearly unhealthy, Americans continue their love affair with the substance. Capitalizing on the American male's unstable image of himself, cigarette advertisers stress the masculine qualities of smoking. In the 1940s the cigarette became a surrogate women whose possession came cheap. The motto, "So Round, So Firm, So Fully Packed. So Free and Easy on the Draw," was printed on every Lucky Strike pack. Today the Marlboro man—cowboy, truck driver, construction worker—casts his lean, masculine gaze from thousands of billboards and magazine advertisements. Next to these men the Surgeon General of the United States seems like a sissy worrywart.

Folklorist Katharine T. Kell shows that tobacco was not always regarded as unhealthy. For hundreds of years people used it to cure respiratory, head, internal, and skin ailments, and for a brief time Europeans viewed it as a medical panacea. Indeed, the student of colonial America can better comprehend the spectacular rise of the tobacco culture by understanding the seventeenth-century attitudes toward the leaf. After reading the essay, you'll see how the emergence of the gentry class and the development of slavery influenced the history of tobacco in America.

Perhaps the most important aspect about the folklore of tobacco is that the white man did not know about it until after the discovery of the Western Hemisphere, although smoke-usage and even smoking of a sort had a faint parallel in Europe. Europeans had used smoke in the form of incense at least since the days of the Egyptians, and the Scythians and Thracians discovered early the narcotic effect of burning hemp seed. Hippocrates prescribed the inhalation of smoke for "female diseases," and Pliny later recommended sucking-up the smoke from burning coltsfoot through reeds as a cure for coughs (a cure which lasted into modern times), but these usages were isolated and limited. Smoking as we know it did not exist, and tobacco itself, all-pervasive as it is in contemporary times, had to wait until that day in 1492 before Europeans became aware of it. Thus, any European folklore about tobacco is no more than four hundred and seventy-two years old—an important fact for the folklorist, for it means that he sometimes can trace usages to their origins instead of having to conjecture about them in remote antiquity. It means further that if he would understand those usages, he would do well to look at the intellectual climate of Europe in the late fifteenth and early sixteenth centuries.

Early European Attitudes Toward The Indians

The most important fact to understand about the intellectual climate surrounding Europeans in the early days of contact is that they had no accurate concept of human behavior other than their own and of course no correct idea of the structures of American Indian aboriginal societies. They saw Indian customs as astonishing, and in order to understand them at all, the Euro-

"Tobacco in Folk Cures in Western Society" by Katharine T. Kell. Reproduced by permission of the American Folklore Society from *Journal of American Folklore* 78(308): 99–112, 1965. Not for further reproduction.

peans had to understand them in terms of their own, however invalid this process might be. Therefore they created anthropomorphic gods and put them in celestial heavens. Accordingly their observations—and those of some modern writers who base their works uncritically upon the early accounts of explorers—are more accurate a description of how the Indians looked to Europeans than how the Indians looked to themselves. But in this paper we are concerned not with ethnography but with folklore, which moves far more freely in fantasy than in fact.

We know that the Indians used tobacco ritually both in religion and medicine—which were seldom separable, since illness was thought to be spiritual in origin. The Mayans offered smoke to the sky gods by blowing it toward the sun and the four points of the earth—a custom paralleled among the Canalino Indians along the Pacific coast, though in the latter case the smoke was blown to the four points of the compass and over the dead.

Before recapitulating Indian usage generally, we might consider here the tangential question of how it was used, for usage methods bear upon a question of anthropological interest—how the tobacco habit was passed from the aborigines of America to native peoples in other parts of the world. Pipe-smoking natives of the Pacific, for example, were by this trait identified as having been contacted first by the British, who got the habit from the pipe-smoking Indians of Virginia, though as in most ethnographic problems, the evidence is somewhat hazy, for the pipe was almost universal among tobacco-smoking tribes of both North and South America. All five forms of tobacco consumption existed throughout most of the Western Hemisphere in pre-Columbian times, though different areas favored one method above the others. Snuff was used in the West Indies, along the Amazon basin, in Mexico, and in Peru. In western South America near the Andes and along the northwest coast Indians chewed but did not smoke. In the West Indies, Panama, and in the northern part of South America generally, cigars were favored by shamans. Corn-husk cigarettes existed in Mexico, Central America, and the northern part of South America. The Mayans of western Guatemala treated colds by applying hot snake-fat wrapped in tobacco leaves. Medicine men in some of the northern Andean regions had their patients snuff tobacco or swallow tobacco pellets to bring about relaxation when broken and dislocated bones had to be set. Tobacco smoke was (and still is) blown over the bodies of parturient women generally in Central American and Costa Rica. The Aztecs made a panacea from tobacco mixed with water, soot, living insects, and the ashes of scorpions, spiders, worms, small vipers, and other creatures, which had been burned ritually—certainly a challenge to modern sotweed factors whose filter-tipped cigarettes crowd more and more extraneous materials into the product; moreover, the Aztecs used this particular concoction extra-somatically—they presented it symbolically to the gods and then smeared their bodies with it. We should expect such complexity from the Aztecs, for they thought all plants possessed animate spirits, and that of tobacco was a deity of great importance. An Aztec medicine man used tobacco in rituals in which he recited allegorical invocations: "Help thou," he might say, referring to tobacco, "for now is the time, thou, the nine times beaten one, the one nine times rubbed between the hands, holy green one, my father and mother, son of the Milky Way . . . "

Other tobacco practices even now unfamiliar to ourselves were reported for the Indians. East of the Rockies propitiary offerings of tobacco were made when plants were gathered for medicine; tobacco might be left in the hole from which another root had been dug, or it might be sprinkled on the stems of plants from which leaves or bark had been taken. The Onondagas scattered it around the first plant found, which would be left untouched, and then others of its kind would be gathered. Onondagas also chewed tobacco leaves and applied them to facial inflammations such as erysipelas. Before a curing ritual Seneca medicine men would cast

pinches of tobacco into fires—an action that appealed to the early observers as a savage parallel of the church use of incense, smoke lifting the words to the gods. Iroquois healers threw tobacco into fires, and at large gatherings rubbed the ashes on the heads of people sick with any number of disease. The Iroquois also used tobacco to soothe angry spirits; De Cost Smith in the 1800's mentioned that while he was on an Iroquois reservation he was given a tribal mask, and when he was about to leave, a tribesman asked him for some tobacco, half of which was wrapped in a calico bag and attached to the mask, and the other half of which was thrown into a fire every second or two. The Indian told Smith to repeat this action every three months in order to be free of the "frights and illnesses" which the mask would otherwise bring him because of being deprived of the feasting and dancing. In the southern part of North America the Creeks ate green tobacco during their midsummer Busk festivals to "afflict their souls" and purify themselves. The Mississaguans of Ontario offered tobacco to water gods, and if one of their people drowned, they considered him accursed. Such a man would be buried on a remote island and his spirit would be given periodic tributes of food, tobacco, and gunpowder. The neighboring Indians of the Bay of Quinté left tobacco near the mouth of the Moira River when they sailed up it on their annual hunting expeditions.

But Europeans did not understand these usages. They knew little about the Indians' various religious and medical systems, and still less about the interrelations between the two; and even those observers who showed signs of trying to understand did not avoid applying European standards of judgment at least to the religious practices. Thomas Hariot, one of the men who returned from Raleigh's ill-fated Virginia expedition in the 1580's, wrote that the Indians threw tobacco on angry waters during a storm or cast it into the air after an escape from danger, but that they did it with strange gestures, "stamping, sometimes dauncing, clapping of hands, holding up of hands, and staring up into the heavens, uttering therewithal and chattering strange words and noises." Captain Archer, also commenting on the Virginian Indians, noted that they saluted daybreak and sunset by outlining a circle on the ground with dried tobacco and "making many Devillish gestures, with a Hellish noise, wagging their heades and handes. . . ." Nor were the earlier Spanish observers in South America much more discerning. Francisco López de Gómara, writing about the shamans in the West Indies, said that they smoked to the point of senselessness so that after they had regained consciousness they might tell the people what the gods had said and say that "God's will will be done." Also Ramón Pané, probably the first to write about the Indians, said of the Haitian Caribs that their *bubuitihus* (doctors) "purged" themselves by snuffing *cohoba* (tobacco) in order to effect cures. This intoxicated the doctors so much that they uttered "many senseless things," later claiming to have communicated with the *cemíes* who had revealed the cause of the sickness. Even Bishop Bartolomé de las Casas, who became noted for his defense of the Indians, showed a lack of basic understanding. He wrote about a ceremony in which a chief in Cuba first snuffed *cohoba*, then began to speak certain words which must have been a prayer to the "true God," "or whatever god they had," and the people answered him "almost as we do when we say Amen. . . ." John Gerard, the late sixteenth-century British herbalist who had never been to America, spoke of the "priests and enchanters of hot countries" who became drunk on smoking, "that after they have lien for dead three or foure houres, they may tell the people what wonders, visions, or illusions they have seen. . . ."

Nor did Europeans fully perceive the relation of religion and medicine in the tobacco complex. They tended to separate the two, discounting the religion, but giving tentative consideration to the medical uses. Las Casas, in observing what may have been ritualistic vomiting and purgation rites, said that the Indians did this in order to relieve themselves and "live more healthfully."

Other writers, commenting on customs in South and Central America, said that the Indians in general smoked, chewed, snuffed, or applied tobacco in some manner to cure indigestion, asthma and catharrh, snakebite, pulmonary diseases, headaches, open wounds, and swellings. John Josselyn, a French traveler in New England, reported that the Indians there made a strong decoction of *pooke* (tobacco) to cure burns and scalds. Gradually South American whites, while scourging the Indians' religious practices, began to think of tobacco in medical terms. One early usage as reported by the renowned Oviedo, was the adoption of smoking to combat syphilis. Oviedo said that the Christians in the New World had taken up smoking because "in the state of ecstasy" brought about by the habit, syphilitic sufferers thought they no longer felt pain.

The Humours Theory

Not so gradually in Europe, however, people began to think of tobacco in medical terms. The word was out that the Indians used tobacco in medicine, and ambassadors and merchants flocked to Portugal awaiting the new imports. One such ambassador was the Frenchman Jean Nicot, from whom tobacco's scientific name subsequently came, and who convinced himself that a poultice of tobacco juice and leaves had relieved his headaches and cured one of his acquaintances of the cancerous face ulcer, *nolí-mē-tangère*. Nicot's cook also used the poultice to heal the near amputation of his thumb with a knife. Nicot sent samples of the plant to a number of people, including the Queen Mother, Catherine de' Medici. He gave it a singing recommendation, and Catherine, ever interested in new medicines, decided that tobacco relieved not only her own headaches but her colds as well. . .

Tobacco soon cropped up in gardens, drawings of it appeared in herbals, and in an amazingly short time it became the rage in medicine. From the time of its first European mention as a cure by a professor at the University of Salamanca in 1543 until some thirty years later when Monardes wrote about its all-healing properties, the number of ailments it was supposed to cure grew from a tentative handful to literally every sickness known to man. It became a true panacea. Monardes made no mention of tobacco in the first edition of his book (1565), but in the second (1571), he included a long list of diseases it would cure, including cancer, headaches, coughs, asthma, stomach cramps, gout, intestinal worms, and female disease. Monardes's Latin translator, Charles Clusius, added goitre to the list, and finally concluded that the plant was in fact a heal-all.

Physicians of the calibre of Ziegler, Vittich, Neander, and Franken concurred, and the famous Dutch physician Everard even called his book *De herba panacea* (1587). Their only point of disagreement was how the tobacco should be prescribed. Some felt their patients should smoke it, others ordered chewing. Some would make an infusion of the leaves and have their patients drink that. Some maintained that the leaves should be dry; others, fresh and green. Some said that the tobacco should be hot, others cold. Some would use it in its pure state, others mixed it with herbs. One would make a salve out of it, another a syrup, another an oil, another a powder. Still others would use just the smoke, especially to cure heavy coughs or delirium. Only two things were clear: No ailment could resist tobacco if the doctors prescribe it properly, and smoking itself was excellent because it expelled superfluous moisture and became a preventive for all sorts of ills.

This blanket acceptance of tobacco as the panacea for which the medieval alchemists had long sought leads us to another important understanding we must have of the climate of intellectual opinion in the fifteenth and sixteenth centuries: the reason for the rapidity of European acceptance of tobacco as medicine was the basic medical theory itself, the theory of humours. Fundamentally this was the belief that only four elements (air, fire, earth, and water) composed all things, including the human body and its illnesses. These elements were capable of much interfunctioning, but ideally they balanced one another. They had four basic properties which occurred in combinations (moist, hot, dry, and cold—that is, water has the combined properties of moist and cold, fire of hot and dry, and so forth); and they corresponded to the four seasons of the year (spring, summer, fall, and winter). They appeared in the human body, together with their properties, in the forms of four humours—blood, yellow bile, black bile, and phlegm—and when the humours balanced, the human being was healthy. Sickness resulted from an imbalance of these humours—from either an improper mixture, or a dearth or superfluity of one or more of them—and the indicated approach in cures, therefore, was to reestablish the balance. Individuals differed, however, because each individual had a dominant humour which governed his whole being. Thus, a man might be predominantly sanguine (blood), choleric or bilious (yellow bile), melancholy (black bile), or phlegmatic (phlegm)—terms still in use today.

The humours theory was neither simple nor totally without merit. For one thing, many variants of interbalance were possible among the humours, this complicating the theory considerably. For another, during the Middle Ages the implicatoin of the four seasons brought in the whole field of medieval astrology (Christianity and pagan mythology also became mixed up in it), thus making the theory even more complex. For still another, erroneous though the theory may be, the concept that health is a state of bodily equilibrium and that sickness is a departure from this norm is a valid one today. It began in Ancient Greece, being sanctioned by Hippocrates and Aristotle, and it lasted unquestioned through the medieval period, not seriously to be challenged until the seventeenth and eighteenth centuries with the findings of William Harvey, Robert Boyle, Herman Boerhaave, and others. Even in the seventeenth century itself, most practicing physicians took the theory for granted. The famous Dr. Sydenham, for example, who was a friend of Boyle, stated his dedication to the principles of Hippocrates (as would any other reputable doctor at the time), and wrote that diseases resulted either from harmful particles of the air which "insinuate themselves" into the blood and whole frame, thus upsetting it, or from "different kinds of fermentation and putrefactions of humours detained too long in the body." Sydenham's mid-eighteenth century editor, John Swan, apparently saw no reason to emend this statement, although he emended many others. As a matter of fact, some medical historians find that traces of the theory have lasted until almost within living memory. Singer and Underwood say it lingered in dermatology into the mid-nineteenth century, or until Ferdinand von Hebra found new classifications for skin diseases. Douglas Guthrie says the theory did not receive its death blow until Rudolf Virchow published his book on cellular structure in 1858. Logan Clendening remarks that the theory survives today in our doctrines of constitutions (constitutional inadequacy, etc.), and in our references to psychological types (sanguine, phlegmatic, etc.).

At any rate, this was the theory with which sixteenth- and seventeenth-century Europeans approached tobacco and by which they sought to explain it as the panacea long searched for. By means of this theory they concluded that tobacco, properly applied, must somehow dry up superfluous moisture, counter the cold elements in the body, and establish the all-important balance between the humours. As Kemp said, it could warm a man if he felt cold, yet cool him if he felt hot; it could give him a good appetite, yet abate his hunger; it could keep him awake if he felt sleepy, yet could give him a good night's sleep; for above all it stabilized the humours—the corrupt humours were drawn from every part of the body to the mouth and "voided and spitten out." Smoking caused the brain to contract and shrink "just like a sponge" when superfluous water is squeezed out of it, Bartolomaus Schimper wrote enthusiastically in 1660.

And Vittich wrote that there could be no doubt about tobacco's ability to "cleanse all impurities" and do away with "every gross and viscous humour." One observer in England, where the people as a whole adopted smoking sooner than did people on the continent, wrote that the English smoked because they thought they could not "live" in England otherwise; they said smoking "dissipates the evil humours of the brain.

Even the few debunkers in the sixteenth century thought tobacco benefited the humours in some way. André Thevet wrote that it was nonsense to think that the Indians used tobacco for diverse illnesses, but that smoking nevertheless did have a certain efficacy—namely, in clearing the head of superfluous humours or in sustaining one when hungry or thirsty. Thevet also implied that the Indians themselves had said that tobacco was good to "cleanse" and do away with the "superfluous humours of the brain." It is doubtful that the Indians ever said anything of the sort, because even after the whites had fairly well inundated Indian cultures with their own, the Indians never adopted the humours theory widely. I am in fact aware of only one reminder of it: William Madsen wrote in 1955 that in San Francisco Tecospa, a valley of Mexico (where Spanish influence is still apparent), the Nahuatl Indians believe that all things, including illnesses, are either hot or cold. Tobacco is hot because fire consumes it, and it therefore is good for cold ailments such as dislocated bones and heart attacks. On the other hand, although typhoid fever and typhus are hot, the Nahuatls also treat them with tobacco, rubbing it on the patient's legs and feet to draw fever out of the trunk. But this is only a modern reminder of the humours concept, probably mirroring early white influence. The theory itself was European, not Indian; and although Thevet was right in asserting that tobacco was no panacea, he assumed too much when he implied that the Indians used tobacco to do away with superfluous humours. Nevertheless it is significant that even Thevet, debunker though he was in the tobacco-as-panacea period, obviously took the humours theory for granted.

By the mid and late years of the seventeenth century, however, Europeans had very much tried tobacco, and their common sense told almost all of them that it was not the panacea they had hoped for. In addition, the Thirty Years War had brought about a great increase in smoking itself (not just of tobacco in cures) and the various European governments greeted this increase with strong opposition, sometimes vicious, always vigorous. Generally, the debunkers attacked smoking on the grounds that it was filthy, ungodly, and a fire hazard. The concept that tobacco was a panacea also infuriated them. James I, who headed the pre-war opposition in England (the English smoked earlier), wrote sarcastically that tobacco was supposed to cure gout in the feet, and at the same time clear the head; the smoke, being light, "flies up into the head," while its virtue, being heavy, "runs downe to the little toe." In addition, he noted that although tobacco clearly did not cure the newly introduced syphylis, that some of its panegyrists had asserted that this was because it cured only the Indians of the disease, not the whites. In England, James sneered, tobacco is "refined," "and will not deigne to cure heere any other than cleanly and gentlemanly diseases."

But although tobacco was no longer a panacea, the humours theory remained, and one other approach for attack, therefore, was by way of the theory itself. Debunkers said that smoking upset the humours, drying out the body or dissipating natural heat, and resulting in premature old age, impotence, and sterility. (They later attacked snuff on the ground that it brought the brain to a dry, sooty state.) Old people were told not to smoke because they were naturally dried up anyway. Catholic priests, on the other hand, should do so because it helped them maintain chastity. In 1602 there appeared a pamphlet called *Work for Chimney Sweeps: A Warning Against Tobacco* in which the writer argued that smoking "withereth our unctuous and radical moisture," to the danger of the "continuance of

mankind." Smoking, he said, made the humours "crude and raw," and the "sperm and seed of man" were "greatly altered and decayed." This concept tended to spread. As early as the sixteenth century in Ceylon, Portuguese soldiers resisted their officers' orders to smoke as a cure for beri-beri (the officers also prescribed pork and palm-wine) because of the rumor that smoking led to impotence. The concept also tended to last even after the humours theory itself fell into disrepute. In nineteenth-century England a Mr. Turton presented a paper to the Royal Medical Society in which he cited several cases to prove that smoking causes sterility. One of them was that of a "popular" writer who, after his marriage, turned out to be impotent because he had "long been an inveterate smoker." (So his wife divorced him, remarried, and "after the ordinary time she became a mother.") Also, the powerful nineteeth-century American Anti-Tobacco League often warned against sterility, and any woman who smoked came under special fire. Aside from the fact that she "tacitly admitted that she had relinquished her chastity," as Brooks puts it, she might develop a mustache and would probably become sterile—or if she did reproduce, her offspring would die before the age of two.

But even after the humours theory died, the belief lived on. Possibly the folksay that smoking stunts a child's growth or intelligence reflects this; also, Roland M. Harper in a pamphlet entitled *Some Social and Moral Effects of Tobacco* (1938) veils that charge somewhat by saying that smokers seem to have more daughters than sons—if they have any children at all. But Dr. Alton Ochsner, a present-day anti-tobacconist, returns to the theme in full. He says many doctors think that decreased sexual activity in thirty- to fifty-year-old men is due to excessive smoking, adding that a recent German study of over five thousand women showed a "greater incidence of frigidity, sterility," and other disorders among the smokers.

But nineteenth and early twentieth century anti-tobacconists listed many other disorders than impotency and sterility as resulting from smoking, such as mental perversion and exhaustion, drug addiction, drunkenness, blindness, cancer of the lips and tongue, heart disease, tuberculosis, carbon-monoxide poisoning, delirium tremens, epilepsy, slavering, hemorrhoids, rheumatism, and gout.

Tobacco As a Disinfectant

Certainly by the mid and late years of the seventeenth century the concept of tobacco as a panacea had perished, although occasional eighteenth-century reminders of it cropped up. There were certain snuffs which their promoters said would clear the head of "all humours" or would cure "all disorders of body and mind." Even the nineteenth century echoed the idea when the Clingman Tobacco Cure company of Durham advertised tobacco cakes and ointments for bunions, snakebites, scarlet fever, lockjaw, and "other ailments." But these uses were rare, and people as a whole by the seventheeth century no longer seriously took tobacco as a panacea. The humours theory was not yet dead at that time, but passing out through the question of how one should apply it. The debunkers had said among other things that smoking upset the humours, but the great majority of people believed not only that smoking benefited the humours in some way, but also that it probably prevented illnesses from ever arising. Smokers and those who kept tobacco shops were healthier than non-smokers, they said, and this must have been because tobacco was a kind of prophylactic or disinfectant. Probably no other concept in the history of tobacco cures has had more influence than the idea of tobacco as a disinfectant; it has survived the various periods of opposition and lasted at least in folk thinking down to the present time.

At first the belief settled in the idea that tobacco, habitually smoked or chewed, would keep one from getting the plague—a belief which many doctors endorsed. The famous William Barclay stated this at the outset of the London plague of 1614, and so did Isbrand von Diemerbroek following the Dutch epidemic in 1636. By the time of the Great Plague of 1665 the belief had established itself well. Kemp wrote that tobacco was a fine fumigation for "bad air"—it cleaned the air and choked, suppressed, and dispersed any "venemous vapour"—and he prescribed that it be smoked either in its pure state or mixed with shredded nutmeg and rue seeds. Tobacco-prohibiting countries sold it on doctors' prescriptions—prescriptions designed not only to prevent people from getting the plague, but also for curing them if they got it. In England authorities at Eton forced the boys to smoke. One of them recalled later that he had never been so whipped in his life as he was one day for not doing so. Pepys also showed the belief in his *Diary* (June 7, 1665) when he wrote that the sight of two or three houses with red crosses marked on the doors had frightened him so much that he felt compelled to buy a roll of tobacco "to smell to and chew" as a protection against the plague.

Probably this concept also partly accounted for the great increase of tobacco consumption during the seventeenth century. When excavations of English cemetaries took place early in the twentieth century, pipe after pipe turned up. (They were tiny clays. The English later called them "fairy" pipes, the Scottish "Celtic" or "elfin," and both peoples adopted them as luck pieces. But the Irish said they belonged to the *cluricaunes,* and destroyed them.) These plague-pipes emerged in such numbers, however, that H. Syer Cuming observed that everyone who went outdoors must have "invoked the protection of tobacco." Tobacco itself took on an undefined but implied role of a charm. We must "wear it about our clothes and about our coaches," William Byrd exhorted fellow Virginians—"hang bundles of it round our beds." No one who kept a tobacconist's shop, other people said, ever caught the disease.

So thoroughly did the belief entrench itself in folk thinking, that it survived intact into the nineteenth century and disguised in variants into

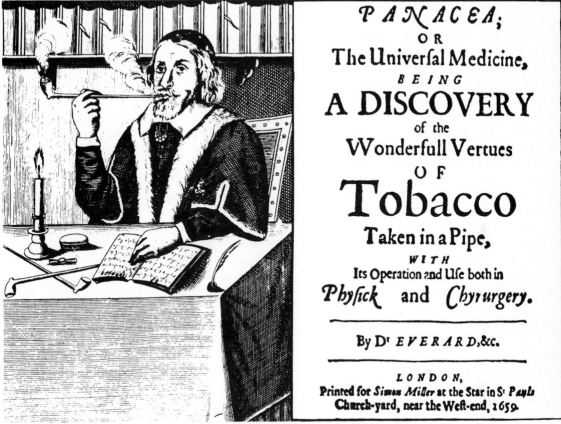

▪▪▪ *In America and England, tobacco became known as a medical panacea. Right is the title page from the 1659 printing of Dr. Gilles Everard's book about the leaf, entitled* Panacea. *At left is the author practicing what he preaches.*

the present time. In the eighteenth century churchmen commonly used it to disinfect holy buildings. In the nineteenth, the various cholera epidemics again evoked statements that no tobacconist ever died of the disease, and that everyone should therefore be allowed to smoke in restricted areas. In Berlin, where the government banned public smoking, a man wrote a letter to the city officials which argued that not only did tobacco purify the air, but also that smoking itself made people feel "secure against infection." In the 1822 cholera epidemic a picture appeared in London which showed women smoking cigars as a protection. Again, in 1901–1902, Penn wrote that tobacco was "unequal-

led" as a disinfectant: It was deadly to all sorts of germs and bacteria, and scientists forbade its use in laboratories because it destroyed the bacilli. Smoke also slowed the growth of many kinds of microbes, he said, while destroying many others, particularly those of Asiatic cholera.

In the 1918 influenza epidemic, the belief reared up again. Doctors are said to have smoked heavily while on their rounds, and they advised train travelers to ride only in smoking cars. A woman whose husband died in that epidemic told me that her husband's nurse once said, "Have you ever noticed how a doctor will light a cigarette after he leaves a home which has an infection of this kind?" Even as late as 1927

Pierre Schrumpf-Pierron in a book which dealt with the medical properties of tobacco, cited almost as many doctors who believed in its disinfectant qualities as those who did not. But the belief did not confine itself only to doctors. Brooks says that present day respiratory epidemics in parts of England will increase snuff-consumption and sooner or later will result in a letter to a newspaper praising snuff's prophylactic qualities. A man who works in a chemical factory told me his co-workers believe pipe-smoking is a protection: "The guys will say, 'I know why you smoke a pipe. It's because you're around chemicals all the time.' Like you should breathe through a pipe and then you wouldn't get the chemicals in your lungs."

Probably the popular practice of rubbing tobacco and ashes into rugs and other woolen articles for moth prevention is a variant of the belief in tobacco's disinfectant properties. Another practice is that of applying tobacco in some way to potted plants "to make them grow." Another informant put it this way: "Papa used to put cigar ashes on the house ferns. Mom raised her eyebrows. But Papa said, 'Now, Mamma, that's good for the plants.'" Three other informants, all with a Slavic background, said that the best way to apply tobacco to house plants is to soak cigar or cigarette ashes or butts in water, and use the nicotinized liquid as a bug-killing bath or spray. The Slavic background of these informants suggests that the practice may occur more often in this culture group, at least in the Detroit area, than in others.

The Specifics

No serious student of tobacco can underestimate the importance of it as a disinfectant, for this is probably the most pervasive single belief in the whole system of tobacco cures. But other cures exist. Sometimes the humours theory and the idea of tobacco-as-disinfectant are still apparent in the specifics—for example in the use of tobacco to cure respiratory ailments and headaches. Then again, the humours theory seems hardly

present at all as in the nineteenth-century idea that a local application of tobacco would relieve the pain of hernia or post-operative cases. Sir Astley Cooper, the respected British physician, also recommended tobacco wine to reduce hernia—a wine made by steeping an ounce of tobacco in a pound of Spanish wine.

Respiratory ailments. But perhaps the tobacco-as-disinfectant theory is most apparent in the various cures for throat and respiratory ailments—that is, since respiratory ailments resulted from breathing "bad air," the fumigating properties of tobacco would therefore cure the respiratory ailments. This idea was corroborated by the testimony of early American explorers, who thought that the Indians in general smoked to cure pulmonary diseases and asthma. They also said that the Indians used snuff to relieve head colds, a remedy which Catherine de' Medici adopted. Thus, seventeenth-century Europeans, convinced that American aborigines had a panacea, and also applying the period's accepted medical theory, pronounced tobacco to be an ineffable cure for all respiratory ills. Some, like Catherine, snuffed it—a cure which lasted at least until the end of the nineteenth century; Yeats says that his maternal grandfather never smoked nor drank, but that he took snuff when he had a cold. Others would smoke not only as a cure but also as a protection against "certain rheums and catarrhs," as Lord Herbert of Cherbury put it. Still others would drink some sort of distillation such as that mixed with "water of euphoria." Jean Liebault said that the Lord of Jarnac, a friend of Nicot, concocted this and wrote that he had "wondrously cured" an acquaintance's asthmatic condition (1570).

This specific survived in folklore. Modern folk-cure collections often mention that people employ tobacco for certain throat and respiratory diseases. Doering in 1944 observed that Canadians living in Wentworth County, Ontario, used snuff for allergies of the nasal passages such as rose fever and hay fever. The Fowlers in 1950 said that Kentuckians recommended smoking a pipe to cure phthisic. In 1937 Emelyn Elizabeth

Gardner said that the New Yorkers of Schoharie Hills brewed tobacco tea for asthma, colds, croup, "and so on." Finally in Michigan, informant Vera Brady recently said that smoking cured her tonsillitis. "This gal," she said, meaning herself, "who was a chronic 'tonsillitiser,' has never had another attack since [first] smoking a cigarette. I used to have a sore throat every morning. At eighteen they even took my tonsils out. Since then I started to smoke. I've never had an inside sore throat—the inside swallowing soreness which we used to know as tonsillitis—I've never had an inside sore throat since I became a heavy smoker."

Head ailments. Peripheral to the belief that tobacco would cure throat and respiratory ailments were the ones that it could deal with various illnesses involving the head. The use of tobacco to cure headaches was one such example. Not only Catherine de' Medici and Nicot so employed it, but also famous doctors such as Monardes prescribed it. Another ailment was giddiness. The renowned doctor, William Barclay, advised tobacco for this (and may therefore have been a forerunner in nineteenth-century homeopathic medicine). Quickening the understanding, strengthening the memory, and improving the eyesight were three additional reasons why people smoked or snuffed—as one enthusiastic patron of Schneeberger's [snuff] Powder said he did.

Occasionally one runs across modern references to tobacco for headaches. Ortiz says that Cuban countrymen sometimes put tobacco leaves on their temples as a cure for this; and Professor Greenway says that Spanish Americans of rural New Mexico paste cigarette-tax stamps on their foreheads as a similar cure. I have also learned recently that a "well known Parisian medical doctor" recommends smoking for migraine and "tired nerves." In addition, this doctor says that smoking feeds the red blood cells and relieves suffering from gall stones. But aside from this, I have found few modern tobacco cures for headaches or "tired nerves." Instead, so far as the head is concerned, people seem to use tobacco chiefly for ears or teeth.

Earache remedies involving tobacco abound. Most sources agree that the usual way to apply it is to blow tobacco smoke in the ear either to cure an earache or to relieve its pain. Vance Randolph mentions this in his *Ozark Superstitions* and adds that if this remedy fails, the "yarb doctors" intermittently apply in the ear a few drops of warm water which the doctors have nicotinized by blowing smoke through it with a reed or pipe stem. Another source says that the act of chewing tobacco will relieve an earache—this same informant adds that people who chew never get cancer.

Tobacco in toothache remedies as well as in dentifrices has a similarly large currency. Here again is a time-honored usage, for this was one of the first "observed" Indian practices. Early explorers thought that the Venezuelan natives chewed tobacco for dental purposes, and that the Indians of the Andean highlands mixed tobacco leaves with lime and pulverized shells or other substances to use as a dental powder. They also reported that the Panamanian Indians dug out pipe dottle for the same purpose. In tobacco's initial European history, therefore, one of the claims made for smoking was that it was excellent not only for toothaches but also for caries prevention. Somewhat later, in the time of Queen Caroline, doctors recommended that women and children chew. Chroniclers say that Caroline herself did so.

This belief also survived the various periods of debunking. Ortiz says that present-day Cubans sometimes use snuff for this purpose, and that in the early nineteenth century, they exported a combination of powdered tobacco and red clay to England as a dentifrice. Also in the mid-nineteenth century antiquarian James Eccleston made the mistake (for the time) of writing that the women of Elizabeth's court had "generally black and rotten" teeth, which probably was due, he said, "to their frequent habit of taking the Nicotian weed to excess." Fellow antiquarians attacked him vigorously; they said everyone knows that tobacco strengthens rather than weakens the teeth. Again in the mid-nineteenth century, German and Swiss folklorists reported smoking for toothaches–the Germans said that people smoked a mixture of tobacco and shavings from the bony knuckle of a mare. In 1896 John Bain reaffirmed the belief in *Tobacco in Song and Story* and recommended a mixture of cigar ashes and camphorated chalk as "an excellent tooth-powder." Today, tobacco chewing for the teeth appears in collections of folk cures from as separated areas as Ontario, South Carolina, Kentucky, New England, and the "Dutch" area of Pennsylvania. This latter source adds that "the cud placed on inflamed parts is considered healing." In Michigan an informant told me that he once knew a girl who saved tobacco ashes (any kind), then mixed them to a paste with lemon juice and used the mixture to brush her teeth. "She said it would shine up the teeth."

Internal ailments. The subject of internal ailments is another large area in which the folk use tobacco remedies. The humours theory most likely is also behind these. Cuban Indians used tobacco in what were probably purgation rites, but which the Europeans took to be health measures for the purpose of expelling superfluous humours, and Camden later wrote that the West Indians taught Drake and his men to use tobacco for "crudityes." Hence throughout the sixteenth, seventeenth, and eighteenth centuries we find some form of tobacco being recommended for numerous internal ailments ranging from purgation to ague—Defoe showed Robinson Crusoe curing his ague by smoking tobacco and drinking an infusion of the leaves. More pointedly, however, Europeans also often used it as a purgative. Henry Buttes wrote in 1599 that drinking four ounces of the juice would "purgeth up down." In the eighteenth century the famous Dr. Sydenham cured what he called the "iliac passion" (probably severe intestinal influenza) with a tobacco-smoke enema, no water added. In the nineteenth century Zak Nielsen in his *Terkel Stenhugger; i "To Landsby-historier"* (Copenhagen, 1889) reported that Danish farmers used this same tobacco-smoke enema for horses that needed laxatives. Frank G. Speck found that modern Catawba Indians used commercial tobacco as a horse cure, but he did not say what ailment it was supposed to remedy.

Nowadays people seem to believe in tobacco more as an emetic than as a cathartic. Ortiz says that for this purpose the Cubans sometimes drink an infusion such as that made from tobacco and sugar (although they also use it as a cathartic), and he quotes J. M. Dalziel as saying that the emetic qualities of tobacco are so great that if someone applies the bruised leaves to a wound, "the toxic effects of nausea with vomiting and prostration are soon felt." Daniel and Lucy Thomas say that Kentuckians induce vomiting by putting a wet tobacco leaf under the foot, in the armpit, or on the stomach. Also in this connection, I recently came upon an item in hobo lore: A friend told me that she had heard Art Linkletter comment on a TV program that hoboes "teach a greenhorn a lesson" by rubbing chewing tobacco between his big and second toes in order to induce vomiting (Unfortunately, a letter to Linkletter earned me only a postcard thanking me for being a fan.)

But also in modern times, people use tobacco for any number of internal purposes, not just as an emetic. They may use it for ailments ranging all the way from hiccups (which the Pennsylvania Dutch cure by placing a tobacco poultice on the stomach) to severe abdominal pain, later diagnosed as appendicitis and cured by surgery. Randolph says that he has seen this illness seemingly relieved instantly upon the application of a poultice of hot water-soaked tobacco leaves. In Germany people have applied a honey-smeared tobacco leaf to a stitch in the side. In southern Indiana they sometimes take tobacco seeds in molasses to cure intestinal worms.

Colic is another internal ailment believed unable to resist the healing powers of tobacco. Randolph says that one Ozark mother who never used tobacco ordinarily, chewed it constantly during the months she was nursing to "purify" her milk. This seems to combine colic prevention with the disinfectant theory. Other Ozark mothers squeeze some of their breast milk into a cup, blow tobacco smoke through it with a reed pipe stem, and feed it to their colicky babies. Still others blow the smoke under the child's clothing. Randolph comments: "I have seen this done several times, and it really did seem to relieve the pain—or at least to distract the child's attention for the moment." The Thomases say that Kentuckians blow smoke on the baby's bare stomach to relieve colic.

Recently I have found two colic recipes: Put half a gill of good rye whiskey into a bottle; blow tobacco smoke from a pipe into the bottle; shake it well, and drink it. Or, pound to a fine powder a white-clay pipe which has turned blackish from smoking, and take it.

The source of these recipes is one of two paperbacks which I acquired not long ago from a Detroit teacher who in turn bought them from a ninth grade Negro student who said he had found them in his attic. The first, the source of the recipes above, is *John George Hohman's Long Lost Friend, or Pow-Wows; a Collection of Mysterious and Invaluable Arts and Remedies for Man as Well as Animals* (n. p., 1938). The second is *Albertus Magnus; Being the Approved, Verified, Sympathetic and Natural Egyptian Secrets; or White and Black Art for Man and Beast* (n. p., n. d.). The material in the two books ranges from dyes for "fine, scarlet reds" to incantations which guarantee that "no person will deny anything to you." Both books, abundant in cures as well as charms, make interesting reading for the folklorist. Tobacco is mentioned eight times as an ingredient in a cure—particularly in a concoction to be given to a farm animal. For a horse swollen from overeating: Mix a few pinches of black snuff tobacco in four or five pounds of fresh milk, give it to the horse, and drive him around slowly. For distempered horses: Mix one ounce of rhubarb, antimonium, and a quarter ounce of black snuff into a glassful of wine and vinegar and pour this three or four times into the horse's nostrils. For biliousness in cattle: Give each animal a handful of oats first thing in the morning, and nothing more for one hour. "This will take

the bile off." Then put woodworm (sic), rue, assafoedita, juniper berries, juniper wood, garlic, and black tobacco into an old earthen pot, under which coals are burning, and let the fumes go directly under the nostrils and belly of the animal. "Probatum."

Skin ailments. All of the above five recipes pertain to internal ailments, which seems to testify again to the importance of tobacco for this type of upset in man and beast. In addition to these, however, three other recipes appear for skin ailments, only one of which is for animals. For mange or itch in sheep: Grease them with an ointment made of equal parts of tobacco, fir wood, linden wood, pigeon manure, chicken fat, aquafortis, oil of turpentine, rapeseed oil, and aloes. A salve for wounds: Fry in butter two ounces of dry tobacco (or a handful of green) together with a handful of elder leaves, and press the mixture through a cloth. Another salve or plaster: Boil a pound of tobacco in a pound of cider "till the strength is out"; strain it; add a pound each of beeswax and sheep tallow, and stir it over a slow fire until everything dissolves. This plaster "cured the sore leg of a woman who for eighteen years had used the prescriptions of doctors in vain."

It is not surprising that these two books contain recipes for skin ailments, for skin-ailment specifics make up another large area in the system of tobacco cures. It is again an area time-honored because Indians apparently sanctioned it. Cortez said that the Mexicans applied warm fresh leaves to swellings and open wounds. Cochet, a French traveler, wrote that Peruvian Indians did similarly for snakebite, adding that each year they observed a festival day for the plant. A later writer, John Josselyn, said that the New England Indians used a strong decoction of *"pooke"* (tobacco) to cure burns and scalds. Early European scientists therefore experimented with tobacco in this cure and concluded that it was highly efficacious.

The belief spread as rapidly as did tobacco usage. Jonson had Bobadilla comment that "for your green wound, your *Balsamum* and your St.

John's *woort* are all mere gulleries and trash to it, especially your *Trinidado; your Nicotian* is good too'' (*Every Man in His Humour*, III. ii). Spenser, apparently seeking clemency for Sir Walter Ralegh, called it ''divine tobacco'' and had Belphoebe apply it to the wounded Timias:

The soveraine weede betwixt two marbles plaine
Shee pownded small, and did in veeces bruze,
And then atweene her lilly handes twaine
Into his wound the juice thereof did scruze

In the late seventeenth century doctors almost invariably praised tobacco for this usage. Vittich wrote that it would heal all sores and wounds of ''however long standing'' and he recommended that the sore first be bathed with white wine or urine, wiped with a clean sponge or rag, then covered with a white napkin containing one or two freshly-pounded tobacco leaves together with their juice. Sydenham's eighteenth-century editor, Dr. John Swan, also gave a complicated recipe for a salve, including tobacco, hog's grease, red or claret wine, turpentine, birthwort roots, and wax, all of which had to go through various stages of marination and boiling. Swan ended by saying, ''So thou has made an accurate Oyntment or Salve for Wounds, or for old Ulcers of the Legs, &c.'' Even the debunkers praised tobacco for skin ailments. One such disbeliever, Tobias Venner, wrote a tract (1637) which he entitled *A Brief and Accurate Treatise Concerning the Taking of the Fume of Tobacco, Which Very Many, In These Dayes doe too too Licenciously Use.* While he denounced the use of tobacco as a panacea in this work, he nevertheless praised it strongly for the healing of wounds, ulcers, scabs, and the like.

Tobacco remedies for ailments of the skin have survived in folklore almost as persistently as those for ears and teeth. They can be found everywhere in America, in urban as well as rural areas, in eastern as well as western. Generally people apply the tobacco externally. Occasionally, however, one comes across a recommendation that the tobacco be used in liquid form and taken internally. Stout reports that ringworm sufferers in Iowa sometimes drink a tea made from tobacco juice. B. A. Botkin comments that New Englanders drink a similar brew to ''deaden pain''—although he does not indicate what kind of pain. One informant says that a friend advised her mother to smoke cigarettes to cure an arm rash. Another says that habitual tobacco chewers will not be affected by snakebite: ''A guy gets bitten by a snake. You get two holes where the snake bit. You cut an X on each hole. You suck the blood out. It wouldn't hurt you if you [habitually] chewed tobacco.'' This cure seems to have overtones of the tobacco-as-prophylaxis theory.

In most cases, however, people apply the tobacco externally, often in the forms of chewed poultices. This is the usual treatment not only for snakebite but also for infected cuts to draw out the poison, as well as for felons, boils, carbuncles, and bee stings. In addition people lay on other kinds of tobacco poultices. The nineteenth-century Danish writer, Zak Nielsen, said that village blacksmiths in Denmark (who were also local veterinarians) would paste tobacco leaves on any kind of sores on horses. Randolph says that Ozark mountaineers apply tobacco leaves and cold water to boils, and tobacco leaves and hot water to cuts, stings, bites, bruises, and bullet wounds. Roxie Martin reports that Blue Ridge mountaineers apply a poultice of tobacco leaves and sugar to cuts in order to stop bleeding. Even Hawaiians practice the custom. They treat a cut either by breaking a cigarette in half and applying the tobacco, or, as a German-Hawaiian girl advised, putting on a mixture of mashed tobacco leaves and salt. Farther out in the Pacific the natives of Luzon have used tobacco against leeches. While on the march they formerly carried sticks split at the ends to hold dry tobacco leaves. If they felt a leech, they applied the leaves to it.

People also use tobacco wrappings. Germans apply pieces of paper from tobacco sacks to bleeding cuts and some Americans, at least in the

Detroit area, wrap minor burns tightly in the inner wrappings of cigarette packages, the metallic side to the skin. This latter item may or may not be folklore; I first learned about it from a man who said he had heard that the Army Medical Department experimented with this for field use during World War II. I have used this cure personally, however, and find that it works.

Warts are not forgotten among tobacco cures for skin ailments. In Kentucky people cure warts with tobacco juice. In Ontario people chew tobacco, break the "chaw" into pieces, apply the pieces to the warts, wrap up the pieces, and throw them away. Whoever picks them up will get the warts. An Ozark mountaineer woman waits until she dreams of some man. She then asks that man to spit tobacco juice on a penny so that she might rub it on her warts. She gives the penny to the man, and when he spends it the warts fall off.

Love philters. Finally, not only have voodoo doctors carried tobacco in their charm bags, but also people who concoct charms have used it in love philters. Strictly speaking, love philters probably do not come under the heading of tobacco in cures. But the spirit behind them is pleasant to consider, though the items in the philters themselves may not be; and if love is the mighty conqueror after all, then we might even put them under the heading of tobacco-as-panacea. In South Carolina Negroes are said to eat tobacco seeds, one at a time, as an aphrodisiac. And around the Rio Grande a would-be lover is advised to kill a jack rabbit, take out its eyes, dry them, grind them to a powder, roll them in a cigarette, and "give to the young lady to smoke."

■ ■ ■

STUDY QUESTIONS

1. How did the pre-Columbian Indians use tobacco? Why didn't the Europeans fully understand the Indians' uses of tobacco?

2. What was the humours theory of medicine? How was tobacco used by those who believed in and practiced humours-based medicine?

3. What attitude did James I have about tobacco?

4. What accounts for the rise in tobacco consumption during the seventeenth century?

5. How was tobacco used in folk medicine?

BIBLIOGRAPHY

Tobacco was essential to the development of the Chesapeake colonies. Wesley F. Craven, *The Southern Colonies in the Seventeenth Century, 1607–1689* (1949) and Gloria L. Main, *Tobacco Colony, Life in Early Maryland, 1650–1720* (1982) provide useful discussions of the topic. Thad W. Tate and David L. Ammerman, eds., *The Chesa-*

peake in the Seventeenth Century (1979) discusses the recent research trends for the region.

Historians and social scientists similarly have studied the pattern and significance of tobacco use. Robert Sobel, *They Satisfy: The Cigarette in American Life* (1978) is a lively look at the subject. Michael E. Starr, "The Marlboro Man: Cigarette Smoking and Masculinity in America," *Journal of Popular Culture,* XIII (1984) examines the reasons for the shift in the form of tobacco consumption in America.

HORSES AND GENTLEMEN

T. H. Breen

Traditional lines between history and the social sciences, and history and the humanities have largely melted in the past generation. Historians have employed sociological, psychological, and anthropological theories and techniques to better uncover the richness of the past. In the following essay, T. H. Breen demonstrates in an exciting and provocative fashion the uses of anthropological techniques for the historian. Breen particularly was influenced by the ground-breaking work of anthropologist Clifford Geertz, who used cockfighting as a text for interpreting Balinese society. In "Notes on the Balinese Cockfight," Geertz writes, "In the cockfight . . . the Balinese forms and discovers his temperament and his society's temper at the same time."

Breen is interested in the temperament of the aristocratic Virginian and the temper of his society. In horse racing, a passion for the wealthy of Virginia, he hoped to expose the core values of colonial society. As he illustrates, horse racing involved more than simply wagering money, creating excitement, and aping English aristocratic manners: "By promoting horse racing the great planters legitimized the cultural values which racing symbolized—materialism, individualism, and competitiveness. . . . The wild sprint down the dirt track served the interests of Virginia's gentleman better than they imagined."

In the fall of 1686 Durand of Dauphiné, a French Huguenot, visited the capital of colonial Virginia. Durand regularly recorded in a journal what he saw and heard, providing one of the few firsthand accounts of late seventeenth-century Virginia society that has survived to the present day. When he arrived in Jamestown the House of Burgesses was in session. "I saw there fine-looking men," he noted, "sitting in judgment booted and with belted sword." But to Durand's surprise, several of these Virginia gentlemen "started gambling" soon after dinner, and it was not until midnight that one of the players noticed the Frenchman patiently waiting for the contest to end. The Virginian—obviously a veteran of long nights at the gaming table—advised Durand to go to bed. " 'For,' said he, 'it is quite possible that we shall be here all night,' and in truth I found them still playing the next morning."

The event Durand witnessed was not unusual. In late seventeenth- and early eighteenth-century Virginia, gentlemen spent a good deal of time gambling. During this period, in fact, competitive gaming involving high stakes became a distinguishing characteristic of gentry culture. Whenever the great planters congregated, someone inevitably produced a deck of cards, a pair of dice, or a backgammon board; and quarter-horse racing was a regular event throughout the colony. Indeed, these men hazarded money and tobacco on almost any proposition in which there was an element of chance. Robert Beverley, a member of one of Virginia's most prominent families, made a wager "with the gentlemen of the country" that if he could produce seven hundred gallons of wine on his own plantation, they would pay him the handsome sum of one thousand guineas. Another leading planter offered six-to-one odds that Alexander Spots-

"Horses and Gentlemen: The Cultural Significance of Gambling among the Gentry of Virginia" by T. H. Breen in *The William and Mary Quarterly*, XXXIV, April 1977, pp. 239–257. Reprinted by permission of the author.

swood could not procure a commission as the colony's governor. And in 1671 one disgruntled gentleman asked a court of law to award him his winnings from a bet concerning "a Servant maid." The case of this suspect-sounding wager—unfortunately not described in greater detail—dragged on until the colony's highest court ordered the loser to pay the victor a thousand pounds of tobacco.

The great planters' passion for gambling, especially on quarter-horse racing, coincided with a period of far-reaching social change in Virginia. Before the mid-1680s constant political unrest, servant risings both real and threatened, plant-cutting riots, and even a full-scale civil war had plagued the colony. But by the end of the century Virginia had achieved internal peace. Several elements contributed to the growth of social tranquility. First, by 1700 the ruling gentry were united as they had never been before. The great planters of the seventeenth century had been for the most part aggressive English immigrants. They fought among themselves for political and social dominance, and during Bacon's Rebellion in 1676 various factions within the gentry attempted to settle their differences on the battlefield. By the end of the century, however, a sizable percentage of the Virginia gentry, perhaps a majority, had been born in the colony. The members of this native-born elite—one historian calls them a "creole elite"—cooperated more frequently in political affairs than had their immigrant fathers. They found it necessary to unite in resistance against a series of interfering royal governors such as Thomas Lord Culpeper, Francis Nicholson, and Alexander Spotswood. After Bacon's Rebellion the leading planters—the kind of men whom Durand watched gamble the night away—successfully consolidated their control over Virginia's civil, military, and ecclesiastical institutions. They monopolized the most important offices; they patented the best lands.

A second and even more far-reaching element in the creation of this remarkable solidarity among the gentry was the shifting racial composition of the plantation labor force. Before the

1680s the planters had relied on large numbers of white indentured servants to cultivate Virginia's sole export crop, tobacco. These impoverished, often desperate servants disputed their masters' authority and on several occasions resisted colonial rulers with force of arms. In part because of their dissatisfaction with the indenture system, and in part because changes in the international slave trade made it easier and cheaper for Virginians to purchase black laborers, the major planters increasingly turned to Africans. The blacks' cultural disorientation made them less difficult to control than the white servants. Large-scale collective violence such as Bacon's Rebellion and the 1682 plant-cutting riots consequently declined markedly. By the beginning of the eighteenth century Virginia had been transformed into a relatively peaceful, biracial society in which a few planters exercised almost unchallenged hegemony over both their slaves and their poorer white neighbors.

The growth of gambling among the great planters during a period of significant social change raises important questions not only about gentry values but also about the social structure of late seventeenth-century Virginia. Why did gambling, involving high stakes, become so popular among the gentlemen at precisely this time? Did it reflect gentry values or have symbolic connotations for the people living in this society? Did this activity serve a social function, contributing in some manner to the maintenance of group cohesion? Why did quarter-horse racing, in particular, become a gentry sport? And finally, did public displays such as this somehow reinforce the great planters' social and political dominance?

In part, of course, gentlemen laid wagers on women and horses simply because they enjoyed the excitement of competition. Gambling was a recreation, like a good meal among friends or a leisurely hunt in the woods—a pleasant pastime when hard-working planters got together. Another equally acceptable explanation for the gentry's fondness for gambling might be the transplanting of English social mores. Certainly,

the upper classes in the mother country loved betting for high stakes, and it is possible that the all-night card games and the frequent horse races were staged attempts by a provincial gentry to transform itself into a genuine landed aristocracy. While both views possess merit, neither is entirely satisfactory. The great planters of Virginia presumably could have favored less risky forms of competition. Moreover, even though several planters deliberately emulated English social styles, the widespread popularity of gambling among the gentry indicates that this type of behavior may have had deeper, more complex cultural roots than either of these explanations would suggest.

In many societies competitive gaming is a device by which the participants transform abstract cultural values into observable social behavior. In his now-classic analysis of the Balinese cockfight Clifford Geertz describes contests for extremely high stakes as intense social dramas. These battles not only involve the honor of important villagers and their kin groups but also reflect in symbolic form the entire Balinese social structure. Far from being a simple pastime, betting on cocks turns out to be an expression of the way the Balinese perceive social reality. The rules of the fight, the patterns of wagering, the reactions of winners and losers—all these elements help us to understand more profoundly the totality of Balinese culture.

The Virginia case is analogous to the Balinese. When the great planter staked his money and tobacco on a favorite horse or spurred a sprinter to victory, he displayed some of the central elements of gentry culture—its competitiveness, individualism, and materialism. In fact, competitive gaming was for many gentlemen a means of translating a particular set of values into action, a mechanism for expressing a loose but deeply felt bundle of ideas and assumptions about the nature of society. The quarter-horse races of Virginia were intense contests involving personal honor, elaborate rules, heavy betting, and wide community interest; and just as the cockfight opens up hidden dimensions of Balinese culture, gentry gambling offers an opportunity to improve our understanding of the complex interplay between cultural values and social behavior in Virginia.

Gambling reflected core elements of late seventeenth- and early eighteenth-century gentry values. From diaries, letters, and travel accounts we discover that despite their occasional cooperation in political affairs, Virginia gentlemen placed extreme emphasis upon personal independence. This concern may in part have been the product of the colony's peculiar settlement patterns. The great planters required immense tracts of fresh land for their tobacco. Often thousands of acres in size, their plantations were scattered over a broad area from the Potomac River to the James. The dispersed planters lived in their "Great Houses" with their families and slaves, and though they saw friends from time to time, they led for the most part isolated, routine lives. An English visitor in 1686 noted with obvious disapproval that "their Plantations run over vast Tracts of Ground . . . whereby the Country is thinly inhabited; the Living solitary and unsociable." Some planters were uncomfortably aware of the problems created by physical isolation. William Fitzhugh, for example, admitted to a correspondent in the mother country, "Society that is good and ingenious is very scarce, and seldom to be come at except in books."

Yet despite such apparent cultural privation, Fitzhugh and his contemporaries refused to alter their life styles in any way that might compromise their freedom of action. They assumed it their right to give commands, and in the ordering of daily plantation affairs they rarely tolerated outside interference. Some of these planters even saw themselves as lawgivers out of the Old Testament. In 1726 William Byrd II explained that "like one of the Patriarchs, I have my Flocks and my Herds, my Bond-men and Bondwomen, and every Soart of Trade amongst my own Servants, so that I live in a kind of Independence on every one but Providence." Perhaps Byrd exaggerated for literary effect, but forty years earlier Durand had observed, "There are no lords [in Virginia], but each is sovereign on his own plantation." Whatever the origins of this independent spirit, it bred excessive individualism in a wide range of social activities. While these powerful gentlemen sometimes worked together to achieve specific political and economic ends, they bristled at the least hint of constraint. Andrew Burnaby later noted that "the public or political character of the Virginians corresponds with their private one: they are haughty and jealous of their liberties, impatient of restraint, and can scarcely bear the thought of being controuled by any superior power."

The gentry expressed this uncompromising individualism in aggressive competitiveness, engaging in a constant struggle against real and imagined rivals to obtain more lands, additional patronage, and high tobacco prices. Indeed, competition was a major factor shaping the character of face-to-face relationships among the colony's gentlemen, and when the stakes were high the planters were not particular about the methods they employed to gain victory. In large part, the goal of the competition within the gentry group was to improve social position by increasing wealth.

Some gentlemen believed that personal honor was at stake as well. Robert "King" Carter, by all accounts the most successful planter of his generation, expressed his anxiety about losing out to another Virginian in a competitive market situation. "In discourse with Colonel Byrd, Mr. Armistead, and a great many others," he explained, "I understand you [an English merchant] had sold their tobaccos in round parcels and at good rates. I cannot allow myself to come behind any of these gentlemen in the planter's trade." Carter's pain arose not so much from the lower price he had received as from the public knowledge that he had been bested by respected peers. He believed he had lost face. This kind of intense competition was sparked, especially among the less affluent members of the gentry, by a dread of slipping into the ranks of what one eighteenth-century Virginia historian called the "common Planters." Gov. Francis Nicholson, an

A notice of a horce race in Anne Arundel County, Maryland, as seen in The Maryland Gazette, May 17, 1745.

acerbic English placeman, declared that the ordinary sort of planters" knew full well "from whence these mighty dons derive their originals." The governor touched a nerve; the efforts of "these mighty dons" to outdo one another were almost certainly motivated by a desire to disguise their "originals," to demonstrate anew through competitive encounters that they could legitimately claim gentility.

Another fact of Virginia gentry culture was materialism. This certainly does not mean that the great planters lacked spiritual concerns. Religion played a vital role in the lives of men like Robert Carter and William Byrd II. Nevertheless, piety was largely a private matter. In public these men determined social standing not by a man's religiosity or philosophic knowledge but by his visible estate—his lands, slaves, buildings, even by the quality of his garments. When John Bartram, one of America's first botanists, set off in 1737 to visit two of Virginia's most influential planters, a London friend advised him to purchase a new set of clothes, "for though I should not esteem thee less, to come to me in what dress thou will,—yet these Virginians are a very gentle, well-dressed people—and look, perhaps, more at a man's outside than his inside." This perception of gentry values was accurate. Fitzhugh's desire to maintain outward appearances drove him to collect a stock of monogrammed silver plate and to import at great expense a well-crafted, though not very practical, English car-

riage. One even finds hints that the difficulty of preserving the image of material success weighed heavily upon some planters. When he described local Indian customs in 1705, Robert Beverly noted that native Americans lived an easy, happy existence "without toiling and perplexing their mind for Riches, which other people often trouble themselves to provide for uncertain and ungrateful Heirs."

The gentry were acutely sensitive to the element of chance in human affairs, and this sensitivity influenced their attitudes toward other men and society. Virginians knew from bitter experience that despite the best-laid plans, nothing in their lives was certain. Slaves suddenly sickened and died. English patrons forgot to help their American friends. Tobacco prices fell without warning. Cargo ships sank. Storms and droughts ruined the crops. The list was endless. Fitzhugh warned an English correspondent to think twice before allowing a son to become a Virginia planter, for even "if the best husbandry and the greatest forecast and skill were used, yet ill luck at Sea, a fall of a Market, or twenty other accidents may ruin and overthrow the best Industry." Other planters, even those who had risen to the top of colonial society, longed for greater security. "I could wish," declared William Byrd I in 1685, "wee had Some more certain Commodity [than tobacco] to rely on but see no hopes of itt." However desirable such certainty may have appeared, the planters always put their labor and money into tobacco, hoping for a run of luck. One simply learned to live with chance. In 1710 William Byrd II confided in his secret diary, "I dreamed last night . . . that I won a tun full of money and might win more if I had ventured."

Gaming relationships reflected these strands of gentry culture. In fact, gambling in Virginia was a ritual activity. It was a form of repetitive, patterned behavior that not only corresponded closely to the gentry's values and assumptions but also symbolized the realities of everyday planter life. This congruence between actions and belief, between form and experience, helps to account for the popularity of betting contests. The wager, whether over cards or horses, brought together in a single, focused act the great planters' competitiveness, independence, and materialism, as well as the element of chance. It represented a social agreement in which each individual was free to determine how he would play, and the gentleman who accepted a challenge risked losing his material possessions as well as his personal honor.

The favorite household or tavern contests during this period included cards, backgammon, billiards, nine-pins, and dice. The great planters preferred card games that demanded skill as well as luck. Put, piquet, and whist provided the necessary challenge, and Virginia gentlemen— Durand's hosts, for example—regularly played these games for small sums of money and tobacco. These activities brought men together, stimulated conversation, and furnished a harmless outlet for aggressive drives. They did not, however, become for the gentry a form of intense, symbolic play such as the cockfight in Bali. William Byrd II once cheated his wife in a game of piquet, something he would never have dared to do among his peers at Williamsburg. By and large, he showed little emotional involvement in these types of household gambling. The exception here proves the rule. After an unusually large loss at the gaming tables of Williamsburg, Byrd drew a pointed finger in the margin of his secret diary and swore a "solemn resolution never at once to lose more than 50 shillings and to spend less time in gaming, and I beg the God Almighty to give me grace to keep so good a resolution . . ." Byrd's reformation was short-lived, for within a few days he dispassionately noted losing another four pounds at piquet.

Horse racing generated far greater interest among the gentry than did the household games. Indeed for the great planters and the many others who came to watch, these contests were preeminently a social drama. To appreciate the importance of racing in seventeenth-century Virginia, we must understand the cultural significance of horses. By the turn of the century pos-

session of one of these animals had become a social necessity. Without a horse, a planter felt despised, an object of ridicule. Owning even a slow footed saddle horse made the common planter more of a man in his own eyes as well as in those of his neighbors; he was reluctant to venture forth on foot for fear of making an adverse impression. As the Rev. Hugh Jones explained in 1724, "almost every ordinary Person keeps a Horse; and I have known some spend the Morning in ranging several Miles in the Woods to find and catch their Horses only to ride two or three Miles to Church, to the Court-House, or to a Horse-Race, where they generally appoint to meet upon Business." Such behavior seems a waste of time and energy only to one who does not comprehend the symbolic importance which the Virginians attached to their horses. A horse was an extension of its owner; indeed, a man was only as good as his horse. Because of the horse's cultural significance, the gentry attempted to set its horsemanship apart from that of the common planters. Gentlemen took better care of their animals, and, according to John Clayton, who visited Virginia in 1688, they developed a distinctive riding style. "They ride pretty sharply," Clayton reported; "a Planter's Pace is a Proverb, which is a good sharp hand-Gallop." A fast-rising cloud of dust far down a Virginia road probably alerted the common planter that he was about to encounter a social superior.

The contest that generated the greatest interest among the gentry was the quarter-horse race, an all-out sprint by two horses over a quarter-mile dirt track. The great planters dominated these events. In the records of the country courts—our most important source of information about specific races—we find the names of some of the colony's most prominent planter families—Randolph, Eppes, Jefferson, Swan, Kenner, Hardiman, Parker, Cocke, Batte, Harwick (Hardidge), Youle (Yowell), and Washington. Members of the House of Burgesses, including its powerful speaker, William Randolph, were frequently mentioned in the contests that came before the courts. On at least one occasion the Rev. James Blair, Virginia's most eminent clergyman and a founder of the College of William and Mary, gave testimony in a suit arising from a race run between Capt. William Soane and Robert Napier. The tenacity with which the gentry pursued these cases, almost continuations of the race itself, suggests that victory was no less sweet when it was gained in court.

Many elements contributed to the exclusion of lower social groups from these contests. Because of the sheer size of wagers, poor freemen and common planters could not have participated regularly. Certainly, the members of the Accomack County Court were embarrassed to discover that one Thomas Davis, "a very poore Man," had lost 500 pounds of tobacco or a cow and calf in a horse race with an adolescent named Mr. John Andrews. Recognizing that Davis bore "a great charge of wife and Children," the justices withheld final judgment until the governor had an opportunity to rule on the legality of the wager. The Accomack court noted somewhat gratuitously that if the governor declared the action unlawful, it would fine Davis five days' work on a public bridge. In such cases country justices ordinarily made no comment upon a plaintiff's or defendant's financial condition, assuming, no doubt, that most people involved in racing were capable of meeting their gaming obligations.

The gentry actively enforced its exclusive control over quarter-horse racing. When James Bullocke, a York County tailor, challenged Mr. Mathew Slader to a race in 1674, the county court informed Bullocke that it was "contrary to Law for a Labourer to make a race being a Sport for Gentlemen" and fined the presumptuous tailor two hundred pounds of tobacco and cask. Additional evidence of exclusiveness is found in early eighteenth-century Hanover County. In one of the earliest issues of the colony's first newspaper, the *Virginia Gazette,* an advertisement appeared announcing that "some merry-dispos'd gentlemen" in Hanover planned to celebrate St. Andrew's Day with a race for quarter-milers. The Hanover gentlemen explained in a later, fuller description that "all Persons resorting there are desir'd to behave themselves with Decency and Sobriety, the Subscribers being resolv'd to discountenance all Immorality with the utmost Rigour." The purpose of these contests was to furnish the county's "considerable Number of Gentlemen, Merchants, and credible Planters" an opportunity for "cultivating Friendship." Less affluent persons apparently were welcome to watch the proceedings provided they acted like gentlemen.

In most match races the planter rode his own horse, and the exclusiveness of these contests meant that racing created intensely competitive confrontations. There were two ways to set up a challenge. The first was a regularly scheduled affair usually held on Saturday afternoon. By 1700 there were at least a dozen tracks, important enough to be known by name, scattered through the counties of the Northern Neck and the James River valley. The records are filled with references to contests held at such places as Smith's Field, Coan Race Course, Devil's Field, Yeocomico, and Varina. No doubt, many races also occurred on nameless country roads or convenient pastures. On the appointed day the planter simply appeared at the race track and waited for a likely challenge. We know from a dispute heard before the Westmoreland County Court in 1693 that John Gardner boldly "Challeng'd all the horses then upon the ground to run with any of them for a thousand pounds of Tobo and twenty shillings in money." A second type of contest was a more spontaneous challenge. When gentlemen congregated over a jug of hard cider or peach brandy, the talk frequently turned to horses. The owners presumably bragged about the superior speed of their animals, and if one planter called another's bluff, the men cried out "done, and done," marched to the nearest field, and there discovered whose horse was in fact the swifter.

Regardless of the outcome, quarter-horse races in Virginia were exciting spectacles. The crowds of onlookers seem often to have been fairly large, as common planters, even servants, flocked to the tracks to watch the gentry challenge one another for what must have seemed immense amounts of money and tobacco. One witness before a Westmoreland County Court reported in 1674 that Mr. Stone and Mr. Youle had run a challenge for £10 sterling "in sight of many people." Attendance at race days was sizable enough to support a brisk trade in cider and brandy. In 1714 the Richmond County Court fined several men for peddling liquors "by Retaile in the Race Ground." Judging from the popularity of horses throughout planter society, it seems probable that the people who attended these events dreamed of one day riding a local champion such as Prince or Smoaker.

The magnitude of gentry betting indicates that racing must have deeply involved the planter's self-esteem. Wagering took place on two levels. The contestants themselves made a wager on the outcome, a main bet usually described in a written statement. In addition, side wagers were sometimes negotiated between spectators or between a contestant and spectator. Of the two, the main bet was far the more significant. From accounts of disputed races reaching the county courts we know that gentlemen frequently risked very large sums. The most extravagant contest of the period was a race run between John Baker and John Haynie in Northumberland County in 1693, in which the two men wagered 4000 pounds of tobacco and 40 shillings sterling on the speed of their sprinters, Prince and Smoaker. Some races involved only twenty or thirty shillings, but a substantial number were run for several pounds sterling and hundreds of pounds of tobacco. While few, if any, of the seventeenth-century gentlemen were what we would call gambling addicts, their betting habits seem irrational even by the more prudential standards of their own day: in conducting normal business transactions, for example, they would never have placed so much money in such jeopardy.

To appreciate the large size of these bets we must interpret them within the context of Vir-

ginia's economy. Between 1660 and 1720 a planter could anticipate receiving about ten shillings per hundredweight of tobacco. Since the average grower seldom harvested more than 1500 pounds of tobacco a year per man, he probably never enjoyed an annual income from tobacco in excess of eight pounds sterling. For most Virginians the conversion of tobacco into sterling occurred only in the neat columns of account books. They themselves seldom had coins in their pockets. Specie was extremely scarce, and planters ordinarily paid their taxes and conducted business transactions with tobacco notes—written promises to deliver to the bearer a designated amount of tobacco. The great preponderance of seventeenth-century planters were quite poor, and even the great planters estimated their income in hundreds, not thousands, of pounds sterling. Fitzhugh, one of the wealthier men of his generation, described his financial situation in detail. "Thus I have given you some particulars," he wrote in 1686, "which I thus deduce, the yearly Crops of corn and Tobo, together with the surplusage of meat more than will serve the family's use, will amount annually to 60000lb. Tobo wch. at 10 shilling per Ct. is 300£ annum." These facts reveal that the Baker-Haynie bet—to take a notable example—amounted to approximately £22 sterling, more than 7 percent of Fitzhugh's annual cash return. It is therefore not surprising that the common planters seldom took part in quarter-horse racing: this wager alone amounted to approximately three times the income they could expect to receive in a good year. Even a modest wager of a pound or two sterling represented a substantial risk.

Gentlemen sealed these gaming relationships with a formal agreement, either a written statement laying out the terms of the contest or a declaration before a disinterested third party of the nature of the wager. In either case the participants carefully stipulated what rules would be in effect. Sometimes the written agreements were quite elaborate. In 1698, for example, Richard Ward and John Steward, Jr., "Covenanted and agreed" to race at a quarter-mile track in Henrico County known as Ware. Ward's mount was to enjoy a ten-yard handicap, and if it crossed the finish line within five lengths of Stewards' horse, Ward would win five pounds sterling; if Steward's obviously superior animal won by a greater distance, Ward promised to pay six pounds sterling. In another contest William Eppes and Stephen Cocke asked William Randolph to witness an agreement for a ten-shilling race: "each horse was to keep his path, they not being to crosse unlesse Stephen Cocke could gett the other Riders Path at the start at two or three Jumps."

Virginia's county courts treated race covenants as binding legal contracts. If a gentleman failed to fulfill the agreement, the other party had legitimate grounds to sue; and the county justices' first consideration during a trial was whether the planters had properly recorded their agreement. The Henrico court summarily dismissed one gambling suit because "noe Money was stacked down nor Contract in writing made[,] one of wch in such cases is by the law required." Because any race might generate legal proceedings, it was necessary to have a number of people present at the track not only to assist in the running of the contest but also to act as witnesses if anything went wrong. The two riders normally appointed an official starter, several judges, and someone to hold the stakes.

Almost all of the agreements included a promise to ride a fair race. Thus two men in 1698 insisted upon "fair Rideing"; another pair pledged "they would run fair horseman's play." By such agreements the planters waived their customary right to jostle, whip, or knee an opponent, or to attempt to unseat him. During the last decades of the seventeenth century the gentry apparently attempted to substitute riding skill and strategy for physical violence. The demand for "fair Rideing" also suggests that the earliest races in Virginia were wild, no-holds-barred affairs that afforded contestants ample opportunity to vent their aggressions.

The intense desire to win sometimes under-mined a gentleman's written promise to run a fair race. When the stakes were large, emotions ran high. One man complained in a York County court that an opponent had interfered with his horse in the middle of the race, "by meanes whereof the s[ai]d Plaintiff lost the said Race." Joseph Humphrey told a Northumberland County court that he would surely have come in first in a challenge for 1500 pounds of tobacco had not Capt. Rodham Kenner (a future member of the House of Burgesses) "held the defendt horses bridle in running his race." Other riders testified that they had been "Josselled" while the race was in progress. An unusual case of interference grew out of a 1694 race which Rodham Kenner rode against John Hartly for one pound sterling and 575 pounds of tobacco. In a Westmoreland County court Hartly explained that after a fair start and without using "whipp or Spurr" he found himself "a great distance" in front of Kenner. But as Hartly neared the finish line, Kenner's brother, Richard, suddenly jumped onto the track and "did hollow and shout and wave his hat over his head in the plts [plaintiff's] horse's face." The animal panicked, ran outside the posts marking the finish line, and lost the race. After a lengthy trial a Westmoreland jury decided that Richard Kenner "did no foule play in his hollowing and waveing his hatt." What exactly occurred during this race remains a mystery, but since no one denied that Richard acted very strangely, it seems likely that the Kenner brothers were persuasive as well as powerful.

Planters who lost large wagers because an opponent jostled or "hollowed" them off the track were understandably angry. Yet instead of challenging the other party to a duel or allowing gaming relationships to degenerate into blood feuds, the disappointed horsemen invariably took their complaints to the courts. Such behavior indicates not only that the gentlemen trusted the colony's formal legal system—after all, members of their group controlled it—but also that they were willing to place institutional limitations on their own competitiveness. Gentlemen who felt they had been cheated or abused at the track immediately collected witnesses and brought suit before the nearest county court. The legal machinery available to the aggrieved gambler was complex; and no matter how unhappy he may have been with the final verdict, he could rarely claim that the system had denied due process.

The plaintiff brought charges before a group of justices of the peace sitting as a county court; if these men found sufficient grounds for a suit, the parties—in the language of seventeenth-century Virginia—could "put themselves upon the country." In other words, they could ask that a jury of twelve substantial freeholders hear the evidence and decide whether the race had in fact been fairly run. If the sums involved were high enough, either party could appeal a local decision to the colony's general court, a body consisting of the governor and his council. Several men who hotly insisted that they had been wronged followed this path. For example, Joseph Humphrey, loser in a race for 1500 pounds of tobacco, stamped out of a Northumberland County court, demanding a stop to "farther proceedings in the Common Law till a hearing in Chancery." Since most of the General Court records for the seventeenth century were destroyed during the Civil War, it is impossible to follow these cases beyond the county level. It is apparent from the existing documents, however, that all the men involved in these race controversies took their responsibilities seriously, and there is no indication that the gentry regarded the resolution of a gambling dispute as less important than proving a will or punishing a criminal. It seems unlikely that the colony's courts would have adopted such an indulgent attitude toward racing had these contests not in some way served a significant social function for the gentry.

Competitive activities such as quarter-horse racing served social as well as symbolic functions. As we have seen, gambling reflected core elements of the culture of late seventeenth-century Virginia. Indeed, if it had not done so, horse racing would not have become so popular among the colony's gentlemen. These contests also helped the gentry to maintain group cohesion during a period of rapid social change. After 1680 the great planters do not appear to have become significantly less competitive, less individualistic, or less materialistic than their predecessors had been. But while the values persisted, the forms in which they were expressed changed. During the last decades of the century unprecedented external pressures, both political and economic, coupled with a major shift in the composition of the colony's labor force, caused the Virginia gentry to communicate these values in ways that would not lead to deadly physical violence or spark an eruption of blood feuding. The members of the native-born elite, anxious to preserve their autonomy over local affairs, sought to avoid the kinds of divisions within their ranks that had contributed to the outbreak of Bacon's Rebellion. They found it increasingly necessary to cooperate against meddling royal governors. Moreover, such earlier unrest among the colony's plantation workers as Bacon's Rebellion and the plant-cutting riots had impressed upon the great planters the need to present a common face to their dependent laborers, especially to the growing number of black slaves who seemed more and more menacing as the years passed.

Gaming relationships were one of several ways by which the planters, no doubt unconsciously, preserved class cohesion. By wagering on cards and horses they openly expressed their extreme competitiveness, winning temporary emblematic victories over their rivals without thereby threatening the social tranquility of Virginia. These non-lethal competitive devices, similar in form to what social anthropologists have termed "joking relationships," were a kind of functional alliance developed by the participants themselves to reduce dangerous, but often inevitable, social tensions.

Without rigid social stratification racing would have lost much of its significance for the gentry. participation in these contests publicly identified a person as a member of an elite group. Great planters raced against their social peers. They certainly had no interest in competing with social inferiors, for in this kind of relationship victory carried no positive meaning: the winner gained neither honor nor respect. By the same token, defeat by someone like James Bullocke, the tailor from York, was painful, and to avoid such incidents gentlemen rarely allowed poorer whites to enter their gaming relationships—particularly the heavy betting on quarter horses. The common planters certainly gambled among themselves. Even the slaves may have laid wagers. But when the gentry competed for high stakes, they kept their inferiors at a distance, as spectators but never players.

The exclusiveness of horse racing strengthened the gentry's cultural dominance. By promoting these public displays the great planters legitimized the cultural values which racing, symbolized—materialism, individualism, and competitiveness. These colorful, exclusive contests helped persuade subordinate white groups that gentry culture was desirable, something worth emulating; and it is not surprising that people who conceded the superiority of this culture readily accepted the gentry's right to rule. The wild sprint down a dirt track served the interests of Virginia's gentlemen better than they imagined.

■■■

STUDY QUESTIONS

1. Breen notes that the "great planter's passion for gaming . . . coincided with a period of far-reaching social change in Virginia." How was Virginia changing?

2. Why did the Virginia gentry feel the need to display solidarity in the face of their social and economic inferiors? Why were members of the gentry reluctant to compete against social inferiors?

3. How important was excitement in work and play for the Virginia gentry?

4. What were the "core values" of Virginia society, and how did gambling illustrate those values?

5. What does Breen mean by the "role of chance" in colonial Virginia?

6. How did a member of the Virginia gentry view his best horse as an extension of himself? What were the symbolic aspects of horse racing in colonial Virginia?

7. How do sports and games illustrate the "core values" of American society?

BIBLIOGRAPHY

Clifford Geertz's masterful essay "Deep Play: Notes on the Balinese Cockfight," *Daedalus*, 101 (1972) demonstrates the relationships between how people play and how they live. Recently sports historians have continued Geertz's line of investigation. They have shown that sports and games play important roles in society. Benjamin G. Rader, *American Sports: From the Age of Folk Games to the Age of Spectators* (1983) presents a balanced and insightful overview of the subject.

Several historians have studied English sports and pastimes of the seventeenth and eighteenth centuries. Among the better studies are Roger Longrigg, *The English Squire and His Sport* (1977); Patricia Ann Lee, "Play and the English Gentleman in the Early Seventeenth Century," *Historian,* 31 (1969); Dennis Brailsford, *Sport and Society: Elizabeth to Anne* (1969); Robert W. Malcolmson, *Popular Recreations in English Society, 1700–1850,* (1980); and E. P. Thompson, "Patrician Society, Plebian Culture," *Journal of Social History,* 7 (1974). For American attitudes toward sports and games see Winton V. Salberg, *Redeem the Times: The Puritan Sabbath in Early America,* (1977); Nancy L. Struna, "Sport and Societal Values: Massachusetts Bay," *Quest,* 27 (1977); and C. Robert Barnett, "Recreational Patterns of the Colonial Virginia Aristocrat," *Journal of the West Virginia Historical Association,* 2 (1978).

SWILLING THE PLANTERS WITH BUMBO

Charles S. Sydnor

During the eighteenth century, colonial American assemblies gained strength and expanded their jurisdiction. Aggressively independent, the popularly elected colonial legislatures jealously guarded their rights and frequently opposed the governors appointed by the Crown. Although in theory the governors enjoyed broad privileges, in practice the local leaders in the assemblies wielded considerable power. According to Jack P. Greene, the leading authority on the subject, by the middle of the century the royal governors were on the defensive.

Many historians have held up the assemblies as examples of the early success of democracy in America. But if they are correct, it was a form of democracy that few contemporary Americans would recognize. In the South, the men elected to the assemblies were from the rich and powerful colonial families. Poorer landowners deferred to their economic superiors in politics as naturally as they did in literature or science.

Charles Sydnor takes a hard look at the election process in colonial Virginia. He demonstrates that a candidate's position on an important issue and even his character were often less important than the quality and quantity of the rum he passed out on election day. As James Madison learned when he ran for office without distributing free liquor, the ''voter preferred free rum to the high ideals of a young reformer.''

It would be pleasant to think that voters were good and wise in the bright, beginning days of the American nation; that in Jefferson's Arcadia, to use a popular euphemism, the sturdy, incorruptible freeholders assembled when occasion demanded and, with an eye only to the public good and their own safety, chose the best and ablest of their number to represent them in the Assembly. It is true that the voters of early Virginia chose their representatives and that often they chose remarkably well; but it is an error to think that the voters were the only positive active force at work in elections. For good or ill, the candidates and their friends also played an important part by using many forms of persuasion and pressure upon the voters.

A play called *The Candidates; or, the Humours of a Virginia Election,* written about 1770 by Colonel Robert Munford of Mecklenburg County, Virginia, provides valuable insight into the part played by candidates in the elections of eighteenth-century Virginia. In this play one of the former delegates to the Assembly, Worthy by name, has decided not to stand for reelection. The other, Wou'dbe, offers himself once more "to the humours of a fickle croud," though with reluctance, asking himself: "Must I again resign my reason, and be nought but what each voter pleases? Must I cajole, fawn, and wheedle, for a place that brings so little profit?" The second candidate, Sir John Toddy, "an honest blockhead," with no ability except in consuming liquor and no political strength except his readiness to drink with the poor man as freely as with the rich, looks for support among the plain people who like him because he "wont turn his back upon a poor man, but will take a chearful cup with one as well as another." Scorned by the leading men of the county, the other two candidates, Smallhopes and Strutabout, a vain, showy fellow, are adept in the low arts of winning the

support of ignorant men.

Each of these candidates had some influence, following, or support which, in the language of that day, was known as his interest. It was common practice at this time for two candidates to join interests, as the phrase went, in hopes that each could get the support of the friends of the other. When Sir John suggests to Wou'dbe a joining of interests by asking him "to speak a good word for me among the people," Wou'dbe refuses and tells him plainly "I'll speak a good word to you, and advise you to decline" to run. Because Wou'dbe could not, from principle, join interests with any one of the three other candidates, he loses votes by affronting first one and then another of them. Just in the nick of time, Wou'dbe's colleague Worthy descends from the upper reaches of respectability and greatness to save Wou'dbe from defeat and political virtue from ruin. With stilted phrase Worthy denounces "the scoundrels who opposed us last election" and directs Wou'dbe to "speak this to the people, and let them know I intend to stand a poll." The good men of the county rally to the side of righteousness; Sir John (between alcoholic hiccoughs) announces "I'm not so fitten" as "Mr. Worthy and Mr. Wou'dbe"; Strutabout and Smallhopes, looking as doleful as thieves upon the gallows, are ignominiously defeated; and Worthy and Wou'dbe are triumphantly reelected.

Among the more important of the unwritten rules of eighteenth-century Virginia politics, a rule which the candidates and their advisers often mentioned was the necessity for candidates to be present at elections. Judge Joseph Jones, out of his ripe experience, wrote in 1785 to his young nephew James Monroe, "respecting your offering your service for the County the coming year, . . . it would be indispensabily necessary you should be in the County before the election and attend it when made." In 1758 several of Washington's friends wrote him to "come down" from Fort Cumberland, where he was on duty with his troops, "and show your face" in Frederick County where he was a candidate for

---

"Swilling the Planters with Bumbo" by Charles S. Sydnor in *Gentlemen Freeholders.* Copyright 1952 by The University of North Carolina Press. Reprinted by permission.

burgess. One of his supporters warned him that "you being elected absolutely depends on your presence." Thanks to the hard work of his friends and the patriotic circumstances of his absence, Washington was elected; but it is evident that the absence of a candidate from the county before and during the taking of the poll was regarded as a distinct handicap.

Fifty years later Henry St. George Tucker, who planned to stand for election at Winchester, was delayed by bad weather and other circumstances at Staunton. He wrote to his father: "I shall not be able to reach Winchester time enough for the election and I presume I shall be withdrawn in consequence of what I have written to my friends in Winchester." But by hard driving he made it, arriving "a few moments before the polls were opened"; and he was elected. As late as 1815 Tucker continued to place himself personally before the people while the voting was in process. Even though he was "still very weak" from illness, he played his part in an election of that year while the enormous number of 737 votes was polled until, as he wrote his father, "fatigue well nigh overcame me."

A sharp distinction must be made between election-day and pre-election behavior of the candidate toward the voter. The code of the times required that in the days before the election the candidate maintain a dignified aloofness from the voters; however, this rule was broken perhaps as often as it was observed. The tipsy Sir John Toddy, in *The Candidates*, assisted by his henchman Guzzle, tries unabashedly to work himself into the good graces of three freeholders named Prize, Twist, and Stern. As they and their wives are sitting on a rail fence, with other freeholders standing about, Sir John comes up to a group. At his shoulder stands Guzzle to whisper the names of the prospective voters to him.

SIR JOHN: *Gentlemen and ladies, your servant, hah! my old friend Prize, how goes it? how does your wife and children do?*

SARAH: *At your service, sir.* (making a low courtsey.)

PRIZE: *How the devil come he to know me so well, and never spoke to me before in his life?* (aside.)

GUZZLE: (whispering to Sir John) *Dick Stern.*

SIR JOHN: *Hah! Mr. Stern, I'm proud to see you; I hope your family are well; how many children? does the good woman keep to the told stroke?*

CATHARINE: *Yes, an't please your honour, I hope my ladys' well, with your honour.*

SIR JOHN: *At your service, madam.*

GUZZLE: (whispering [to] Sir John) *Roger Twist.*

SIR JOHN: *Hah! Mr. Roger Twist! your servant, sir. I hope your wife and children are well.*

TWIST: *There's my wife. I have no children, at your service.*

James Littlepage, a candidate for burgess in Hanover County in 1763, practiced nearly every art known to his generation for getting his candidacy before the people and winning their support. The gathering of worshippers at church services afforded him an opportunity to meet people; but unfortunately, he could not be at two churches at the same time. Deciding that it was more important to go to a dissenting congregation, he prepared the way by letters to two freeholders in which he announced that he would "be at your Church To-morrow Se'nnight," and asked their support, setting forth the platform on which he was campaigning and circulating the false rumor that his opponent had "declined serving this County."

To take care of matters at the other church which he was unable to attend personally, he sent a letter to three freeholders for them to read and pass about among those in attendance. As one of those who saw the letter recalled its substance, Littlepage wrote that he "was that Day gone to the lower Meeting House of the Dissenters, to know their Sentiments whether they would submit to the damned Tobacco Law, and desired to know whether they also would submit to it; that if they would send him Burgess he would be hanged, or burnt (or Words to that Effect) if he did not get that Part of it, directing a

■ ■ *Spirits were often responsible for bringing men together for the sake of politics. Depicted above is an eighteenth-century political club, where we get the impression that men met not for the sake of philosophy, but for their love of revelry.*

Review of Tobacco, repealed, as being an Infringement on the Liberty of the Subjects, the Inspectors being so intimidated by it that they refused the greater Part of their Tobacco; and that he would endeavor to have the Inspectors chosen by the People."

To meet the voters who could not be found in assemblies, Littlepage went on a house-to-house canvass. After discussing his chances in one part of the county with his friend John Boswell, and being assured that "he might have a good Chance, if he would go up amongst them," Littlepage "accordingly went up, and the said *Boswell* rode about with him among the People." He was the soul of hospitality, inviting those who lived at some distance from the courthouse to spend the night with him on their way to the poll. Littlepage was elected.

James Madison in his old age recalled that

when he entered politics it was "the usage for the candidates to recommend themselves to the voters . . . by personal solicitation." Madison thoroughly disliked this practice. Shortly before the election of representatives to the first Congress of the United States he wrote from Philadelphia to George Washington: "I am pressed much in several quarters to try the effect of presence on the district into which I fall, for electing a Representative; and am apprehensive that an omission of that expedient, may eventually expose me to blame. At the same time I have an extreme distate to steps having an electioneering appearance, altho' they should lead to an appointment in which I am disposed to serve the public; and am very dubious moreover whether any step which might seem to denote a solicitude on my part would not be as likely to operate against as in favor of my pretensions."

Colonel Landon Carter, writing in 1776, said that he had once been "turned out of the H. of B." because "I did not familiarize myself among the People," whereas he well remembered his "son's going amongst them and carrying his Election." The contrasting experiences of father and son suggest that going among the people was important to get a man elected. However, the son, Robert Wormeley Carter, lost his seat in an election in Richmond County in 1776 even though, according to his father, he had "kissed the———of the people, and very seriously accommodated himself to others." With mounting anger the Colonel wrote: "I do suppose such a Circumstance cannot be parallelled, but it is the nature of Popularity. She, I long discovered to be an adultress of the first order." The son was likewise displeased with the decision of the voters, but he naturally thought that his campaign methods were above reproach. He wrote in his diary "as for myself I never ask'd but one man to vote for me since the last Election; by which means I polled but 45. votes an honorable number."

Father and son were miles apart in describing what the son had done; but they were in complete agreement as to what he ought to have done. Both thought that candidates should not solicit votes, and there were other men who thought exactly as they did. Henry St. George Tucker wrote to his father before an election to be held on April 6, 1807, "Please to take notice also, that I am no *electionerer.*" "I have studiously avoided anything like canvassing. . . . My opponents are sufficiently active I learn." Of his victory he wrote: "it has been entirely without solicitation on my part." Eight years later he was again elected though he declared that he had "never attended a public meeting or been at the home of a single individual, and though my adversary and his friends had ransacked the county in the old Electioneering Style."

The contrast between ideal and reality was well illustrated by statements made during an election quarrel in Accomac County. The following advice was given to the freeholders: "If a man sollicits you earnestly for your vote, avoid him; self-interest and sordid avarice lurk under his forced smiles, hearty shakes by the hand, and deceitfully enquires after your wife and family." However, it was said, referring to the candidates, that "every person who observes the two gentlemen, allows that the smiles of Mr. S.——h are more forced than Mr. H——ry's, and of this Mr. S——h himself is so conscious that he has declared, he would give an Hundred Pounds could he shake hands with the freeholders, and smile in their faces with as good a grace as Col. Pa——e, that he might be more equally match'd."

Some candidates sought to injure a rival by starting the rumor that he was withdrawing from the race, that he had joined interests with an unpopular man, that he was a common drunkard, that he despised poor folks, or that "It's his doings our levies are so high." If the rumor was false, it was better for the candidate to keep silent and let one of his supporters circulate it. More often, the candidate, with the help of his friends, undertook to set himself and his views on current issues in a favorable light.

Sir John Toddy, whose supporters were great lovers of rum, promised to get the price of that article reduced, and it is said of Strutabout that "he'll promise to move mountains. He'll make the rivers navigable, and bring the tide over the tops of the hills, for a vote." The noble Worthy promised no more than to "endeavour faithfully to discharge the trust you have reposed in me." And Wou'dbe answered the questions of the voters with carefully measured words. When asked if he would reduce the price of rum and remove an unpopular tax, he answered, "I could not," explaining that it would be beyond his power to accomplish these things. His position on other matters is set forth in the following dialogue.

STERN. *Suppose, Mr. Wou'dbe, we that live over the river, should want to come to church on this side, is it not very hard we should pay ferryage; when we pay as much to the church as you do?*

WOU'DBE. *Very hard.*

STERN. *Suppose we were to petition the assembly could you get us clear of that expense?*

WOU'DBE. *I believe it to be just; and make no doubt but it would pass into a law.*

STERN. *Will you do it?*

WOU'DBE. *I will endeavour to do it.*

STERN. *Huzza for Mr. Wou'dbe! Wou'dbe forever!*

PRIZE. *Why don't you burgesses, do something with the damn'd pickers? If we have a hogshead of tobacco refused, away it goes to them; and after they have twisted up the best of it for their own use, and taken as much as will pay them for their trouble, the poor planter has little for his share.*

WOU'DBE. *There are great complaints against them; and I believe the assembly will take them under consideration.*

PRIZE. *Wil you vote against them?*

WOU'DBE. *I will, if they deserve it.*

Littlepage, it will be recalled, promised to fight the existing system of tobacco inspection, and thereby was said to have gained much favor with the people. He also proposed to have the inspectors chosen yearly by the freeholders of the county, an extension of democracy which must have seemed radical to some men of the time. Friends of George Wythe, appealing to those who felt burdened by taxes, declared that "he would serve as Burgess for the said County for nothing," and they offered to "give Bond to repay any Thing that should be levied on the county for him." A rival candidate, William Wager, realizing that he must follow suit, immediately upon "hearing this Declaraion, came up and said, he would serve on the same terms."

There is some evidence that the House of Burgesses frowned upon campaign commitments by candidates, especially upon those which reflected upon the prerogative of the House by promising that it would act according to the will of a single member. The powerful Committee of Privileges and Elections investigated the making of campaign promises by some of the candidates, and the committee gave detailed reports to the House of its findings. Perhaps it was to protect himself against the disapproval of the House that Littlepage, who had promised much during his campaign, "Just before the Poll was opened . . . publickly and openly declared, in the Court House, before a great Number of People, that he did not look upon any of the Promises he had made to the People as binding on him, but that they were all void."

There is no way of knowing how many of the candidates followed the rule approved by the Carters, Tucker, and Munford's character Wou'dbe: "never to ask a vote for myself," and how many of them followed the example of Littlepage in unashamedly and energetically courting the voters wherever they could find them, even going on house-to-house canvasses. Most of the candidates seem to have operated between these extremes. While they did not insulate themselves from the voters before elections, they avoided unseemly and ostentatious activity in their mingling with the people. The distinction between approved and disapproved conduct was close, and it is easier to be sure that a line was drawn than to be sure just where it was drawn. A man was likely to shift it a bit, depending on whether he was judging his own actions or those of his rival. John Clopton once gave his candidate son shrewd advice about cultivating the people and tricking a rival at the very time that he was fulminating against the tricks, deceptions, and intimidations practiced by the son's opponents!

Whether the candidates actively campaigned or not, a good many votes were committed before the election. The Quakers or the Presbyterians, the men along the south side of a river or in the northern corner of a county—these and other groups might discuss the candidates and decide which of them to support. Similarly, powerful men would let their friends, relatives, and dependents know how they stood toward the candidates. Thus, elections were often settled before they were held. A curious attempt to hold back this natural operation of democracy was made in a brief notice published in the *Virginia Gazette*. It was addressed "To the free and independent ELECTORS of the borough of NORFOLK," and it desired them "not to engage your votes or interest until the day of election, as a Gentleman of undoubted ability intends to declare himself as a candidate on that day, and hopes to succeed.

From these cases it is evident that although many candidates entered the race several weeks before election day, a few of them, like the unnamed gentleman of Norfolk or like Worthy in Munford's play, waited until the last minute before announcing their decision to stand a poll. John Marshall recalled in his old age that he had had the unusual experience of being made a candidate contrary to his wishes. He described the event, which occurred at Richmond during an election to the Virginia legislature in the spring of 1795, in the following words.

"I attended at the polls to give my vote early & return to the court which was then in session at the other end of the town. As soon as the election commenced a gentleman came forward and demanded that a poll should be taken for me. I was a good deal surprised at this entirely unexpected proposition & declared my decided dissent. I said that if my fellow citizens wished it I would become a candidate at the next succeeding election, but that I could not consent to serve this year because my wishes & my honour were engaged for one of the candidates. I then voted for my friend & left the polls for the court which was open and waiting for me. The gentleman said that he had a right to demand a poll for whom he pleased, & persisted in his demand that one should be opened for me—I might if elected refuse to obey the voice of my constituents if I chose to do so. He then gave his vote for me.

"As this was entirely unexpected—not even known to my brother who though of the same political opinions with myself was the active & leading partisan of the candidate against whom I voted, the election was almost suspended for ten or twelve minutes, and a consultation took place among the principal freeholders. They then came in and in the evening information was brought me that I was elected. I regretted this for the sake of my friend. In other respects I was well satisfied at being again in the assembly."

Many of the candidates may have been perfectly circumspect in their pre-election behavior, but all of them, with hardly an exception, relied on the persuasive powers of food and drink dispensed to the voters with open-handed liberality. Theoderick Bland, Jr., once wrote with apparent scorn that "Our friend, Mr. Banister, has been very much ingaged ever since the dissolution of the assembly, in swilling the planters with bumbo." When he supplied the voters with liquor Banister was in good company; it included Washington, Jefferson, and John Marshall.

The favorite beverage was rum punch. Cookies and ginger cakes were often provided, and occasionally there was a barbecued bullock and several hogs. The most munificent as well as democratic kind of treat was a public occasion, a sort of picnic, to which the freeholders in general were invited. George Washington paid the bills for another kind of treat in connection with his Fairfax County campaigns for a seat in the House of Burgesses. It consisted of a supper and ball on the night of the election, replete with fiddler, "Sundries &ca." On at least one occasion he shared the cost of the ball with one or more persons, perhaps with the other successful candidate, for his memorandum of expenses closes with the words: "By Cash paid Captn. Dalton for my part of ye Expense at the Election Ball. £ 8.5.6."

A supper and ball of this kind was probably more exclusive than a picnic-type of treat. Hospitality was often shown also to small groups, usually composed of important and influential men. Mumford describes a breakfast given the morning of the election by Wou'dbe for the principal freeholders. Worthy was the guest of honor; fine salt shad, warm toast and butter, coffee, tea, or chocolate, with spirits for lacing the chocolate, were set before the guests; and although it was said that "we shall have no polling now," it was understood that all were for Worthy and Wou'dbe.

It was a common practice for candidates to keep open house for the freeholders on their way to the election, and it is a marvel where space was found for all to sleep. When Littlepage heard that some of the voters who lived more than twenty-five miles from the courthouse were unwilling to ride so far in cold weather, he invited them to call at his house which was about five miles from the courthouse. Some ten of them came and were hospitably entertained, "though their Entertainment was not more than was usual with him." Some of the company "were pretty merry with Liquor when they came" to his home. That evening "they chiefly drank Cider." "Some of them drank Drams in the Morning, and went merry to the Court House."

Candidates frequently arranged for treats to be given in their names by someone else. Lieutenant Charles Smith managed this business for George Washington during a campaign in Frederick County in 1758. Two days after the election, which Washington had not been able to attend, Smith sent him receipts for itemized accounts that he had paid to five persons who had supplied refreshments for the voters. A year or two earlier in Elizabeth City County Thomas Craghead sought to repay William Wager, a candidate for burgess, for help he had once received in time of distress. He invited several people to

Wager's house and out of his own purse entertained them with "Victuals and Drink." He also had a share in treating all who were present at a muster of Captain Wager's militia company, after which they drank Wager's health.

Samuel Overton, a candidate in Hanover County, directed Jacob Hundley "to prepare a Treat for some of the Freeholders of the said County at his House." Later, Overton withdrew from the race, but a group of freeholders, perhaps ignorant of Overton's withdrawal, came to Hundley's house. He thereupon sent a messenger, desiring Overton's "Directions whether they were to be treated at his Expense," and Overton ordered him "to let them have four Gallons of Rum made into punch, and he would pay for it."

At this juncture some of the finer points of campaigning begin to appear. Littlepage, an active candidate, was among those present at Hundley's house; and Littlepage had agreed in return for Overton's withdrawal to reimburse Overton the sum of £ 75, which was the expense he had incurred in this and a previous election. As a codicil it was agreed that Littlepage would pay only £ 50 in case "Mr. Henry," presumably Patrick Henry, should enter the race and be elected. While the treat was in progress Hundley told Littlepage "that the Liquor was all drank." He immediately ordered two gallons more, telling Hundley that he supposed Overton would pay for it. Whether any of the company heard this conversation is in doubt; but this much is clear, that Littlepage paid Overton to withdraw, that Littlepage attended a treat for Overton's friends, and that Littlepage succeeded, according to the testimony of one of the guests, in winning "the Interest" of most of them.

On election day the flow of liquor reached high tide. Douglas S. Freeman calculated that during a July election day in Frederick County in the year 1758, George Washington's agent supplied 160 gallons to 391 voters and "unnumbered hangers-on." This amounted to more than a quart and a half a voter. An itemized list of the refreshments included 28 gallons of rum, 50 gallons of rum punch, 34 gallons of wine, 46 gal-

lons of beer, and 2 gallons of cider royal. During the close and bitter struggle between John Marshall and John Clopton for a seat in Congress in 1799, a "barrel of whiskey . . . with the head knocked in" was on the courthouse green.

Defeated candidates often complained of the wrongdoing of their successful opponents. George Douglas of Accomac County alleged before the Committee of Privileges and Elections that Edmund Scarburgh, shortly before the issuance of the writ of election, had twice given "strong Liquors to the People of the said County; once at a Race, and the other Time at a Muster; and did, on the Day of Election cause strong Liquor to be brought in a Cart, near the Courthouse Door, where many People drank thereof, whilst the Polls of the Election were taking; and one Man in particular, said, *Give me a Drink, and I will go and vote for Col. Scarburgh,* . . . and drink was accordingly given him out of the said Cart, where several People were merry with Drink: But it doth not appear, whether that Person voted for the said *Scarburgh,* or not; or was a Freeholder." Contrary to the recommendation of the Committee, Scarburgh was seated.

Captain Robert Bernard was charged with intimidation as well as improper treating in his efforts to help Beverley Whiting win an election in Gloucester County. He attended a private muster of Captain Hayes' men and solicited the freeholders among them to vote for Whiting. "And the next Day, at a Muster of his own Company, the said *Bernard* brought 40 Gallons of Cyder, and 20 Gallons of Punch into the Field, and treated his Men, solliciting them to vote for Mr. *Whiting,* as they came into the Field; and promised one *James Conquest,* to give him Liquor, if he would vote for Mr. *Whiting,* which *Conquest* refused; and then *Bernard* said he should be welcome to drink, tho' he would not vote for him: That the said *Bernard* promised one *Gale,* a Freeholder to pay his Fine, if he would stay from the Election; which *Gale* accordingly did: That the Day of Election, the said *Bernard* treated several Freeholders, who said they would vote for Mr. *Whiting,* at one *Sewell's* Ordinary: And that, at the Election, one of the Freeholders said, he was going to vote for Mr. *Whiting*, because he had promised Capt. *Bernard* so to do; but that he had rather give Half a Pistole than do it: And other Freeholders, who were indebted to Col. *Whiting*, said, that Capt. *Bernard* told them, that Col. *Whiting* would be angry with them if they voted against Mr. *Whiting;* which the said *Bernard* denied, upon his Oath, before the Committee.''

The House of Burgesses compelled Bernard to acknowledge his offense, to ask the pardon of the House, and to pay certain fees; and it requested the Governor to issue a writ for a new election in Gloucester County.

The law strictly prohibited any person ''directly or indirectly'' from giving ''money, meat, drink, present, gift, reward, or entertainment . . . in order to be elected, or for being elected to serve in the General Assembly''; but in one way or another nearly all the candidates gave treats, and seldom was a voice raised in protest. One of the rare protests was adopted at a general meeting of the citizens of Williamsburg two years before the Declaration of Independence. In an address to Peyton Randolph, who was a candidate for reelection to the House of Burgesses, the townsmen declared themselves to be ''greatly scandalized at the Practice which has too much prevailed throughout the Country of entertaining the Electors, a Practice which even its Antiquity cannot sanctify; and being desirous of setting a worthy Example to our Fellow Subjects, in general, for abolishing every Appearance of Venality (that only Poison which can infect our happy Constitution) and to give the fullest Proof that it is to your singular Merit alone you are indebted for the unbought Suffrages of a free People; moved, Sir, by these important Considerations, we earnestly request that you will not think of incurring any Expense or Trouble at the approaching Election of a Citizen, but that you will do us the Honour to partake of an Entertainment which we shall direct to be provided for the Occasion.''

Three years later young James Madison, feeling that ''the corrupting influence of spiritous liquors, and other treats,'' was ''inconsistent with the purity of moral and republican principles,'' and wishing to see the adoption of ''a more chaste mode of conducting elections in Virginia,'' determined ''by an example, to introduce it.'' He found, however, that voters preferred free rum to the high ideals of a young reformer; ''that the old habits were too deeply rooted to be suddenly reformed.'' He was defeated by rivals who did not scruple to use ''all the means of influence familiar to the people.'' For many years to come liquor had a large part in Virginia elections. In 1795 Jefferson wrote that he was in despair because ''the low practices'' of a candidate in Albermarle County were ''but too successful with the unthinking who merchandize their votes for grog.'' In 1807 Nathaniel Beverley Tucker, writing from Charlotte Court House, informed his father, St. George Tucker, that ''In this part of the state . . . every decent man is striving to get a seat in the legislature. There are violent contests every where that I have been, to the great anoyance of old John Barleycorn, who suffers greatly in the fray.''

Although the custom of treating was deeply ingrained, the law was not entirely disregarded. It did not prohibit a man's offering refreshment to a friend; it only prohibited treating ''in order to be elected.'' Through various interpretations of these words most of the candidates found ways of dispensing largess to the freeholders without incurring the censure of the House of Burgess and perhaps without suffering from an uneasy conscience. Everyone would agree that it was wrong to give liquor to ''one *Grubbs*, a Freeholder,'' who announced at an election that ''he was ready to vote for any one who would give him a Dram.'' Neither should a candidate ask votes of those whom he was entertaining though it was perhaps all right for him to make the general remark ''that if his Friends would stand by him he should carry his Election.'' Some men thought that there should be no treating after the election writ was issued until the poll had been taken. James Littlepage ''expressly ordered'' Paul Tilman, whom he had employed ''to prepare his Entertainment at the Election . . . not to give the Freeholders any Liquor until after the closing of the Poll," and Littlepage produced evidence to show that "none of them had any Liquor, except some few who insisted on it, and paid for it themselves."

To avoid the appearance of corruption, it was well for the candidate to have the reputation of being hospitable at all times. When William Wager's campaign was under investigation, especially in the matter of the treat given in his home by one of his friends and another treat given in his honor to his militia company, Wager introduced evidence to show that he customarily entertained all who came to his house, strangers as well as freeholders, and that he usually treated the members of his militia company with punch after the exercises were over. "They would after that come before his Door and fire Guns in Token of their Gratitude, and then he would give them Punch 'til they dispersed, and that this had been a frequent Practice for several Years."

To avoid the reality as well as the appearance of corruption, the candidates usually made a point of having it understood that the refreshments were equally free to men of every political opinion. If a candidate's campaign was under investigation, it was much in his favor if he could show that among his guests were some who had clearly said that they did not intend to vote for him. Washington reflected an acceptable attitude when he wrote while arranging for the payment of large bills for liquor consumed during a Frederick County election: "I hope no Exception were taken to any that voted against me but that all were alike treated and all had enough; it is what I much desir'd." Washington seems to have followed this policy in subsequent elections. A young Englishman, who witnessed an election at Alexandria in 1774 when Washington was one of the two successful candidates, wrote: "The Candidates gave the populace a Hogshead of Toddy (what we call Punch in England). In the evening the returned Member gave a Ball to the Freeholders and Gentlemen of the town. This was conducted with great harmony. Coffee and Chocolate, but no Tea. This Herb is in disgrace among them at present."

Bountiful supplies of free liquor were responsible for much rowdiness, fighting, and drunkenness, but the fun and excitement of an election and the prospect of plentiful refreshments of the kind customarily consumed in that day helped to bring the voters to the polls. Thus in a perverse kind of way treating made something of a contribution to eighteenth-century democracy. Although one sometimes found a man who lived by the rule, "never to taste of a man's liquor unless I'm his friend," most of the voters accepted such refreshments as were offered. As they drank, they were less likely to feel that they were incurring obligations than that the candidate was fulfilling his obligation. According to the thinking of that day, the candidate ought to provide refreshments for the freeholders. His failure to fulfill this obligation would be interpreted as a sign of "pride or parsimony," as a "want of respect" for the voters, as James Madison found to his sorrow.

The Virginia voter expected the candidate to be manly and forthright, but he wanted the candidate to treat him with due respect. He had the power to approve and reject, and the sum total of this consciousness of power among the voters was a strong and significant aspect of the democratic spirit in eighteenth-century Virginia.

■ ■ ■

STUDY QUESTIONS

1. How were candidates for office supposed to behave during the preelection weeks and on election day? How in reality did they behave?

2. What was the fate of candidates who tried to reform election practices?

3. Did "treating" the voters promote or retard the development of a democratic election process?

4. How did the normal election practices affect the deferential pattern of relations in colonial Virginia?

5. How did eighteenth-century elections differ from modern elections? What brought the eighteenth-century voter to the polls? What brings the twentieth-century voter to the election booth?

BIBLIOGRAPHY

The above essay is from Charles Sydnor, *Gentlemen Freeholders: Political Practices in Washington's Virginia* (1952). The classic work on the growth of American assemblies in the Southern colonies is Jack P. Greene, *The Quest for Power: The Lower Houses of Assembly in the Southern Royal Colonies, 1689–1776* (1963). The question of who could vote is ably discussed in Chilton Williamson, *American Suffrage from Property to Democracy, 1760–1860* (1960).

The kinds of men who filled the colonial assemblies is treated in Carl Bridenbaugh, *Seat of Empire: The Political Role of Eighteenth-Century Williamsburg* (1950); Jack P. Greene, "Foundations of Political Power in the Virginia House of Burgesses, 1720–1776," *William and Mary Quarterly*, 3rd Ser., 16 (1959); and R. M. Zemsky, *Merchants, Farmers, and River Gods: An Essay on Eighteenth-Century American Politics* (1971). All three works trace the upper-class character of colonial Virginia leadership.

Part Three

THE
REVOLUTIONARY
GENERATION

W hen Thomas Jefferson proclaimed in the Declaration of Independence that people had the right to dissolve their government when it ceased to protect their "unalienable rights," he helped set in motion a crusade against European imperialism which lasted well into the twentieth century. Beginning with the "shot heard 'round the world" at Lexington, Massachusetts, on April 19, 1775, colonial rebellions swept through Latin America early in the nineteenth century and Africa and Asia in the twentieth century. By 1776, after nearly 170 years in the New World, the American colonists were ready for independence. With an English heritage and experience from trial and error, they had developed a political culture which emphasized localism, representative government, popular sovereignty, and individual rights. They had also acquired an American identity clearly distinguishing them from their English cousins. When the French and Indian War initiated changes in British imperial policy, colonists rebelled in a desperate, and ultimately successful attempt to preserve a moral order.

But the destruction of one set of political relationships did not automatically create new ones. In the summer of 1776, the Second Continental Congress was a government without constitutional authority. The colonies were at best a loose alliance of competing states with limited resources, trying to make war against a major world power. The war also revealed strains between the rich and poor. The Continental Army, for example, was periodically weakened by the struggles for power between well-to-do officers and enlisted men, as well as by the lack of support from civilians and politicians. The colonists triumphed by winning the war in

the court of world opinion and by draining England of its financial and emotional resources. Their first attempt at constitution-making, the Articles of Confederation, ended in failure. Although that government managed to bring the Revolution to a successful conclusion, Americans realized that a central government had to be able to support itself economically and maintain public order. When Shays' Rebellion in 1786 raised doubts about the latter, the Founding Fathers gathered in Philadelphia in the summer of 1787 to try again.

They were eminently successful. The Constitution was a model political document, even though it represented the vested interests of a conservative minority. After its ratification in 1788, the Constitution became the symbol of the new republic. Americans considered themselves a free people blessed with a fundamental consensus about politics and power. They took their place among independent nations of the world confident that God had destined them for greatness.

Life was not easy. Older rivalries between the lower and upper classes, as well as between the seaboard region and the frontier, still manifested themselves. In 1794, a rebellion of poor farmers in western Pennsylvania challenged the authority of the new government. There were also political tensions within the ruling elite. During the 1790s a two party system gradually emerged in the United States. George Washington, Alexander Hamilton, and John Adams led the Federalist Party, and Thomas Jefferson and James Madison headed the Democratic-Republicans. Both parties struggled for power throughout the 1790s and early 1800s. Despite the challenges, the new nation survived.

A "MOST UNDISCIPLINED, PROFLIGATE CREW"

James Kirby Martin

Few events in United States history have generated as much mythical rhetoric as the American Revolution. The struggle to separate from the British empire spawned an intense debate about freedom, equality, opportunity, and patriotic loyalty. Historians, usually servants of the status quo, then transformed the American Revolution into a crusade for liberty, creating an image of unity and commitment which never really existed. History has a way of telescoping reality, sometimes to distortion. The American Revolution was a complicated phenomenon of diverse groups competing for influence and power; it was hardly a unified crusade. Most people were not directly engaged in the conflict, and those who were had a variety of motivations. Many slaves, for example, saw the Revolution as an opportunity to secure freedom. Some poor people hoped to acquire land of their own and to enjoy full civil rights. Western land developers and eastern merchants believed the Revolution would eliminate British commercial restrictions. Some Virginia planters hoped to avoid repaying debts to London tobacco brokers. And many colonists, but certainly not a majority, genuinely wanted the Revolution to restore their civil liberties—to return the divinely-guaranteed rights so recently taken from them by an autocratic king and an arbitrary Parliament. Amidst such contrary goals, as well as concerted opposition to the Revolution from many other colonists, the 1770s and 1780s constituted an era of conflict and competition in American history.

In "Protest and Defiance in the Ranks," James Kirby Martin surveys the public mood during the American Revolution by looking at the morale problems of the Continental Army. Traditionally, historians studying the American Revolution have focused their attention on elites—wealthy businessmen, educated philosophers, prosperous planters, and Continental congressmen—to determine public attitudes. By looking at different groups, such as army officers and enlisted personnel, Martin sees different forces at work during the Revolution. Instead of finding a unified country engaged in a righteous crusade against evil, Martin describes dissension and mutiny in the army, with enlisted men alienated from officers and all of them alienated from the society at large. Plagued by shortages of food, clothing, and pay, the soldiers felt abandoned by an apathetic public. Their protests became a minor rebellion against social customs in the larger struggle against the British Empire.

Asequence of events inconceivable to Americans raised on patriotic myths about the Revolution occurred in New Jersey during the spring of 1779. For months the officers of the Jersey brigade had been complaining loudly about everything from lack of decent food and clothing to pay arrearages and late payments in rapidly depreciating currency. They had petitioned their assembly earlier, but nothing had happened. They petitioned again in mid-April 1779, acting on the belief that the legislature should "be informed that our pay is now only *minimal*, not *real*, that four months' pay of a private will not procure his wretched wife and children a single bushel of wheat." Using "the most plain and unambiguous terms," they stressed that "unless a speedy and ample remedy be provided, the total dissolution of your troops is inevitable." The Jersey assembly responded to this plea in its usual fashion—it forwarded the petition to the Continental Congress without comment. After all, the officers, although from New Jersey, were a part of the Continental military establishment.

The assembly's behavior only further angered the officers, and some of them decided to demonstrate their resolve. On May 6 the brigade received orders to join John Sullivan's expedition against the Six Nations. That same day, officers in the First Regiment sent forth yet another petition. They again admonished the assembly about pay and supply issues. While they stated that they would prepare the regiment for the upcoming campaign, they themselves would resign as a group unless the legislators addressed their demands. Complaints had now turned into something more than gentlemanly protest. Protest was on the verge of becoming nothing less

than open defiance of civil authority, and the Jersey officers were deadly serious. They had resorted to their threatened resignations to insure that the assembly would give serious attention to their demands—for a change.

When George Washington learned about the situation, he was appalled. "Nothing, which has happened in the course of the war, . . . has given me so much pain," the commander in chief stated anxiously. It upset him that the officers seemingly had lost sight of the "principles" that governed the cause. What would happen, he asked rhetorically, "if their example should be followed and become general?" The result would be the "ruin" and "disgrace" of the rebel cause, all because these officers had *"reasoned wrong about the means of obtaining a good end."*

So developed a little known but highly revealing confrontation. Washington told Congress that he would have acted very aggressively toward the recalcitrant officers, except that "the causes of discontent are too great and too general and the ties that bind the officers to the service too feeble" to force the issue. What he did promise was that he would not countenance any aid that came "in [such] a manner extorted." On the other hand, the officers had been asking the assembly for relief since January 1778, but to no avail. They, too, were not about to be moved.

The New Jersey legislature was the political institution with the ability to break the deadlock. Some of the legislators preferred disbanding the brigade. The majority argued that other officers and common soldiers might follow the First Regiment's lead and warned that the war effort could hardly succeed without a Continental military establishment. The moment was now ripe for compromise. The assemblymen agreed to provide the officers with whatever immediate relief could be mustered in return for the latter calling back their petitions. That way civil authorities would not be succumbing to intimidation by representatives of the military establishment, and the principle of subordination of military to civil authority would remain inviolate. The assembly thus provided an immediate

"A 'Most Undisciplined, Profligate Crew': Protest and Defiance in the Continental Ranks, 1776–1783" by James Kirby Martin in *Arms and Independence: The Military Character of the American Revolution,* edited by Ronald Hoffman and Peter J. Albert, 1984. Reprinted by permission of the publisher, The University Press of Virginia.

payment of £200 to each officer and $40 to each soldier. Accepting the compromise settlement as better than nothing, the brigade moved out of its Jersey encampment on May 11 and marched toward Sullivan's bivouac at Easton, Pennsylvania. Seemingly, all now had returned to normal.

The confrontation between the New Jersey officers and the state assembly serves to illuminate some key points about protest and defiance in the Continental ranks during the years 1776–83. Most important here, it underscores the mounting anger felt by Washington's regulars as a result of their perceived (and no doubt very real) lack of material and psychological support from the society that had spawned the Continental army. It is common knowledge that Washington's regulars suffered from serious supply and pay shortages throughout the war. Increasingly, historians are coming to realize that officers and common soldiers alike received very little moral support from the general populace. As yet, however, scholars have not taken a systematic look at one product of this paradigm of neglect, specifically, protest and defiance. The purpose of this essay is to present preliminary findings that will facilitate that task.

Given that there was a noticeable relationship between lack of material and psychological support from the civilian sector and mounting protest and defiance in the ranks, it is also important to make clear that patterns of protest were very complex. A second purpose of this essay is to outline those basic patterns and to indicate why protest and defiance did not result in serious internal upheaval between army and society in the midst of the War for American Independence. To begin this assessment, we must bring Washington's Continentals to the center of the historical arena.

During the past twenty years, historians have learned that there were at least two Continental armies. The army of 1775–76 might be characterized as a republican constabulary, consisting of citizens who had respectable amounts of property and who were defending hearth and home. They came out for what they believed would be a rather short contest in which their assumed virtue and moral commitment would easily carry the day over seasoned British regulars not necessarily wedded to anything of greater concern than filling their own pocketbooks as mercenaries.

The first army had a militialike appearance. Even though phrases of commitment were high sounding, there was not much discipline or rigorous training. These early soldiers had responded to appeals from leaders who warned about "our wives and children, with everything that is dear to us, [being] subjected to the merciless rage of uncontrolled despotism." They were convinced that they were "engaged . . . in the cause of virtue, of liberty, of *God*." Unfortunately, the crushing blows endured in the massive British offensive of 1776 against New York undercut such high-sounding phrases about self-sacrifice. The message at the end of 1775 had been "Persevere, ye guardians of liberty." They did not.

The second Continental establishment took form out of the remains of the first. Even before Washington executed his magnificent turnabout at Trenton and Princeton, he had called for a "respectable army," one built on long-term enlistments, thorough training, and high standards of discipline. The army's command, as well as many delegates in Congress, now wanted soldiers who could stand up against the enemy with more than notions of exalted virtue and moral superiority to upgird them. They called for able-bodied men who could and would endure for the long-term fight in a contest that all leaders now knew could not be sustained by feelings of moral superiority and righteousness alone.

To assist in overcoming manpower shortages, Congress and the states enhanced financial promises made to potential enlistees. Besides guarantees about decent food and clothing, recruiters handed out bounty moneys and promises of free land at war's end (normally only for long-term service). Despite these financial incentives, there was no great rush to the Continental banner. For the remainder of the war, the army's command, Congress, and the states struggled to maintain minimal numbers of Continental soldiers in the ranks.

In fact, all began to search diligently for new recruits. Instead of relying on propertied freeholders and tradesmen of the ideal citizen-soldier type, they broadened the definition of what constituted an "able-bodied and effective" recruit. For example, New Jersey in early 1777 started granting exemptions to all those who hired substitutes for long-term Continental service—and to masters who would enroll indentured servants and slaves. The following year Maryland permitted the virtual impressment of vagrants for nine months of regular service. Massachusetts set another kind of precedent in 1777 by declaring blacks (both slave and free) eligible for the state draft. Shortly thereafter, Rhode Islanders set about the business of raising two black battalions. Ultimately, Maryland and Virginia permitted slaves to substitute for whites. The lower South, however, refused to do so, even in the face of a successful British invasion later in the war.

The vast majority of Continentals who fought with Washington after 1776 were representative of the very poorest and most repressed persons in Revolutionary society. A number of recent studies have verified that a large proportion of the Continentals in the second establishment represented ne'er-do-wells, drifters, unemployed laborers, captured British soldiers and Hessians, indentured servants, and slaves. Some of these new regulars were in such desperate economic straits that states had to pass laws prohibiting creditors from pulling them from the ranks and having them thrown in jail for petty debts. (Obviously, this was not a problem with the unfree.)

The most important point to be derived from this dramatic shift in the social composition of the Continental army is that few of these new common soldiers had enjoyed anything close to economic prosperity or full political (or legal) liberty before the war. As a group, they had

something to gain from service. If they could survive the rigors of camp life, the killing diseases that so often ravaged the armies of their times, and the carnage of skirmishes and full-scale battles, they could look forward to a better life for themselves at the end of the war. Not only were they to have decent food and clothing and regular pay until the British had been irrevocably beaten, they had also been promised free land (and personal freedom in the cases of indentured servants, black slaves, and criminals). Recruiters thus conveyed a message of personal upward mobility through service. In exchange for personal sacrifice in the short run, there was the prospect of something far better in the long run, paralleling and epitomizing the collective rebel quest for a freer political life in the New World.

To debate whether these new Continentals were motivated to enlist because of crass materialism or benevolent patriotism is to sidetrack the issue. A combination of factors was no doubt at work in the mind of each recruit or conscript. Far more important, especially if we are to comprehend the ramifications of protest and defiance among soldiers and officers, we must understand that respectably established citizens after 1775 and 1776 preferred to let others perform the dirty work of regular, long-term service on their behalf, essentially on a contractual basis. Their legislators gave bounties and *promised* many other incentives. Increasingly, as the war lengthened, the civilian population and its leaders did a less effective job in keeping their part of the agreement. One significant outcome of this obvious civilian ingratitude, if not utter disregard for contractual promises, was protest and defiance coming from Washington's beleaguered soldiers and officers.

That relations between Washington's post-1776 army and Revolutionary society deteriorated dramatically hardly comes as a surprise to those historians who have investigated surviving records. Widespread anger among the rank and file became most demonstrable in 1779 and 1780, at the very nadir of the war effort. Pvt.

Protest among the ranks stemmed from the poor conditions of camp life, bad food, irregular pay, and a lack of clothing.

Joseph Plumb Martin captured the feelings of his comrades when he reflected back on support for the army in 1780. He wrote: "We therefore still kept upon our parade in groups, venting our spleen at our country and government, then at our officers, and then at ourselves for our imbecility in staying there and starving in detail for an ungrateful people who did not care what became of us, so they could enjoy themselves while we were keeping a cruel enemy from them." Gen. John Paterson, who spoke out in March 1780, summarized feelings among many officers when he said, "It really gives me great pain to think of our public affairs; where is the public spirit of the year 1775? Where are those flaming *patriots* who were ready to sacrifice their lives, their fortunes, their all, for the public?" Such thoughts were not dissimilar from those of "A Jersey Soldier" who poured his sentiments into an editorial during May 1779 in support of those regimental officers who were trying to exact some form of financial justice from their state legislature. The army, he pointed out, had put up with "a load . . . grown almost intolerable." "It must be truly mortifying to the virtuous soldier to observe many, at this day, displaying their cash, and sauntering in idleness and luxury," he went on, including "the gentry . . . [who] are among the foremost to despise our poverty and laugh at our distress." He certainly approved the actions of his comrades because he resented "the cruel and ungrateful disposition of the people in general, in withholding from the army even the praise and glory justly due to their merit and services," just as he resented society's failure to live up to its contract with the soldiers. These statements, which are only a representative sampling, indicate that the army had come to believe that Revolutionary civilians had taken advantage of them—and had broken their part of the contract for military services.

There were real dangers hidden behind these words. With each passing month beginning in 1777, Washington's regulars, especially that small cadre that was signing on for the long-term fight, became more professional in military demeanor. Among other things, including their enhanced potential effectiveness in combat, this meant that soldiers felt the enveloping (and reassuring) bonds of "unit cohesion." The immediate thoughts of individual soldiers, whether recruited, dragooned, or pressed into service, became attached to their respective primary units in the army, such as the particular companies or regiments in which they served. The phenomenon was nothing more than a developing comradeship in arms. Any threat or insult thus became an assault on the group, especially if that threat or insult were directed at all members of the group. The bonding effect of unit cohesion suggests that collective protest and defiance would become more of a danger to a generally unsupportive society with each passing month, unless civilians who had made grand promises started to meet their contractual obligations more effectively.

Indeed, the most readily observable pattern in Continental army protest and defiance was that it took on more and more of a collective (and menacing) character through time. At the outset, especially beginning in 1776, most protest had an individual character. Frequently it was the raw recruit, quite often anxious for martial glory but quickly disillusioned with the realities of military service once in camp, who struck back against undesirable circumstances. Protest could come through such diverse expressions as swearing, excessive drinking, assaulting officers, deserting, or bounty jumping. One source of such behavior was the dehumanizing, even bru-

tal nature of camp life. Another had to do with broken promises about pay, food, and clothing. A third was a dawning sense that too many civilians held the soldiery in disregard, if not utter contempt.

It must be remembered that middle- and upper-class civilians considered Washington's new regulars to be representative of the "vulgar herd" in a society that still clung to deferential values. The assumption was that the most fit in terms of wealth and community social standing were to lead while the least fit were to follow, even when that meant becoming little more than human cannon fodder. Perhaps James Warren of Massachusetts summarized the social perceptions of "respectable" citizens as well as any of the "better sort" when he described Washington's troops in 1776 as "the most undisciplined, profligate Crew that were ever collected" to fight a war.

While civilians often ridiculed the new regulars as riffraff, troublemakers, or mere hirelings (while conveniently ignoring the precept that military service was an assumed obligation of all citizens in a liberty-loving commonwealth), individual soldiers did not hold back in protesting their circumstances. In many cases, they had already acknowledged the personal reality of downtrodden status before entering the ranks. Acceptance of these circumstances and the conditions of camp life did not mean, however, that these new soldiers would be passive. Thus it may be an error to dismiss heavy swearing around civilians or repeated drunkenness in camp as nothing more than manifestations of "time-honored military vices," to borrow the words of one recent student of the war period.

At least in some instances, individual soldiers could have been making statements about their sense of personal entrapment. Furthermore, protest through such methods as drunkenness (this was a drinking society but not one that condoned inebriety) was a defensive weapon. One of Washington's generals, for instance, bitterly complained in 1777 that too many soldiers consistently made it "a practice of getting drunk . . .

once a Day and thereby render themselves unfit for duty." To render themselves unfit for duty was to give what they had received—broken promises. Defiance that came in the form of "barrel fever" for some soldiers thus translated into statements about how society looked upon and treated them.

Only over time did individual acts of protest take on a more collective character. That transition may be better comprehended by considering the phenomenon of desertion. While it is true that a great many soldiers did not think of desertion as a specific form of protest, they fled the ranks with greater frequency when food and clothing were in very short supply or nonexistent, as at Valley Forge. However, primary unit cohesion worked to militate against unusually high desertion levels. Sustained involvement with a company or regiment reduced the likelihood of desertion. Hence as soldiers came to know, trust, and depend upon one another, and as they gained confidence in comrades and felt personally vital to the long-term welfare of their primary group, they were much less likely to lodge a statement of individual protest through such individualized forms as desertion.

So it appears to have been with Washington's new regulars. Thad W. Tate discovered that, in the regiments of New York, Maryland, and North Carolina, about 50 percent of all desertions occurred within six months of enlistments. Mark Edward Lender, in studying New Jersey's Continentals, also found that the rate of desertion dropped off dramatically for those soldiers who lasted through just a few months of service. The first few days and weeks in the ranks were those in which these poor and desperate new regulars asked themselves whether vague promises of a better lot in life for everyone, including themselves, in a postwar republican polity was worth the sacrifice now being demanded. Many enlistees and conscripts concluded that it was not, and they fled. Since they had little proof that they could trust the civilian population and its leaders, they chose to express their defiance through desertion. Unit cohesion, in turn,

helped sustain those who read the equation differently, and it eased the pain of enduring a long war in return for the remote prospect of greater personal freedom, opportunity, and prosperity.

Then there were those individuals who neither deserted nor became hard-core regulars. By and large, this group defied civil and military authority through the practice of bounty jumping. The procedure, which Washington once referred to as "a kind of business" among some soldiers, was straightforward. It involved enlisting, getting a bounty, and deserting, then repeating the same process with another recruiting agent in another location. Some of the most resourceful bounty jumpers got away with this maneuver seven, eight, or even nine times, if not more. Most jumpers appear to have been very poor young men without family roots. The most careful of them went through the war unscathed. Bounties thus provided a form of economic aggrandizement (and survival) in a society that generally treated its struggling classes with studied neglect. To accept a bounty payment, perhaps even to serve for a short period, and then to run off, was a strongly worded statement of personal defiance.

Bounty jumping was invariably the act of protesting individuals; looting and plundering (like desertion) combined individual with collective protest. Certainly there were numerous occasions when hungry soldiers looted by themselves. Just as often, groups of starving men "borrowed" goods from civilians. Even before the second establishment took form, looting had become a serious problem. Indeed, it probably abetted unit cohesion. One sergeant, for example, described how he and his comrades, searching desperately for food, "liberated" some geese belonging to a local farmer in 1776 and devoured them "Hearty in the Cause of Liberty of taking what Came to their Hand." Next "a sheep and two fat turkeys" approached this band of hungry soldiers, but "not being able to give the countersign," they were taken prisoner, "tried by fire and executed" for sustenance "by the whole Division of the freebooters."

When army looting of civilian property continued its unabated course in 1777, General Washington threatened severe penalties. He emphasized that the army's "business" was "to give protection, and support, to the poor, distressed Inhabitants; not to multiply and increase their calamities." These pleas had little impact. Incident after incident kept the commander in chief and his staff buried in a landslide of civilian complaints. Threats of courts martial, actual trials, and severe punishments did not deter angry, starving, protesting soldiers. In 1780 and 1781 Washington was still issuing pleas and threats, but to little avail. Not even occasional hangings contained an increasingly defiant and cohesive soldiery that wondered who the truly poor and distressed inhabitants were—themselves or civilians ostensibly prospering because of the army's travail. To strike back at hoarding, unsupportive citizens, as they had come to perceive the populace whom they were defending, seemed only logical, especially when emboldened by the comaraderie of closely knit fellow soldiers.

Above all else, two patterns stand out with respect to common soldier protest. First, as the war effort lengthened, defiance became more of a collective phenomenon. Second, such protest had a controlled quality. While there was unremitting resentment toward civilians who were invariably perceived as insensitive and unsupportive, protest rarely metamorphosed into wanton violence and mindless destruction. Soldiers may have looted and pillaged, they may have grabbed up bounties, and they may have deserted. But they rarely maimed, raped, or murdered civilians. Pvt. Joseph Plumb Martin attempted to explain why. Even though "the monster Hunger, . . . attended us," he wrote, and the new regulars "had borne as long as human nature could endure, and to bear longer we considered folly," he insisted that his comrades had become, in the end, "truly patriotic." They were persons who "loved their country, and they had already suffered everything short of death in its cause." The question by 1779 and 1780 was whether these hardened, cohesive veterans would be willing to endure even more privation.

In reflecting positively on the loyalty of his comrades, Martin was commenting on a near mutiny of the Connecticut Line in 1780. Indeed, the specter of collective defiance in the form of line mutinies had come close to reality with the near insubordination of the New Jersey officers in 1779. They had not demonstrated in the field, but they had made it clear that conditions in the army were all but intolerable—and that civil society, when desperate to maintain a regular force in arms, could be persuaded to concede on basic demands. Washington had used the phrase "extorted"; he had also pointed out that, "notwithstanding the expedient adopted for a saving appearances," this confrontation "cannot fail to operate as a bad precedent." The commander in chief was certainly right about the setting of precedents.

Among long-term veterans, anger was beginning to overwhelm discipline. There had been small-scale mutinies before, such as the rising of newly recruited Continentals at Halifax, North Carolina, in February 1776. In 1779 Rhode Island and Connecticut regiments threatened mutinies, but nothing came of these incidents. Then in 1780 another near uprising of the Connecticut Line occurred. Invariably, the issues had the same familiar ring: lack of adequate civilian support as demonstrated by rotten food, inadequate clothing, and worthless pay (when pay was available). On occasion, too, the heavy hand of company- and field-grade officers played its part. The near mutiny of the Connecticut Line in 1780 had been avoided by a fortuitous shipment of cattle and by promises from trusted officers of better treatment. In the end, the Connecticut Line calmed itself down, according to Martin, because the soldiery was "unwilling to desert the cause of our country, when in distress." Nevertheless, he explained that "we knew her cause involved our own, but what signified our perishing in the act of saving her, when that very act would inevitably destroy us, and she must finally perish with us."

By the end of 1780, there were some veterans who would have disputed Martin's reasoning. They had all but given up, let come what might for the glorious cause. On January 1, 1781, the Pennsylvania Line proved that point. Suffering through yet another harsh winter near Morristown, New Jersey, the Pennsylvanians mutinied. Some one thousand determined comrades in arms (about 15 percent of the manpower available to Washington) ostensibly wanted nothing more to do with fighting the war. On a prearranged signal, the Pennsylvanians paraded under arms, seized their artillery, and marched south toward Princeton, their ultimate target being Philadelphia. These veterans had had their fill of broken promises, of the unfulfilled contract. They maintained that they had signed on for three years, not for the duration. If they were to stay in the ranks, then they wanted the same benefits (additional bounty payments, more free land, and some pay in specie) that newer enlistees had obtained.

Formal military discipline collapsed as the officers trying to contain the mutineers were brushed aside. The soldiers killed one and wounded two other officers, yet their popular commander, Anthony Wayne, trailed along, attempting to appeal to their sense of patriotism. Speaking through a committee of sergeants, the soldiers assured Wayne and the other officers that they were still loyal to the cause, and they proved it by handing over two spies that Sir Henry Clinton had sent out from New York to monitor the situation. Moreover, the mutineers, despite their anger and bitterness, behaved themselves along their route and did not unnecessarily intimidate civilians who got in their way.

Later checking demonstrated that many of the mutineers were duration enlistees, yet that was a moot point. When the soldiers reached Trenton, representatives of Congress and the Pennsylvania government negotiated with them and agreed to discharge any veteran claiming three years in rank. Also, they offered back pay and new clothing along with immunity from prose-

cution for having defied their officers in leaving their posts. Once formally discharged, the bulk of the mutineers reenlisted for a new bounty. By late January 1781 the Pennsylvania Line was once more a functioning part of the Continental army.

These mutineers won because Washington was in desperate need of manpower and because they had resorted to collective defiance, not because their society wanted to address what had been grievances based on the contract for service. Unlike their officers, who had just won a major victory in driving for half-pay pensions, they were not in a position to lobby before Congress. Hence they employed one of the most threatening weapons in their arsenal, collective protest against civil authority, but only after less extreme measures had failed to satisfy their claims for financial justice. They were certainly not planning to overthrow any government or to foment an internal social revolution against better-placed members of their society. They had staked their hopes on a better life in the postwar period and had already risked their lives many times for the proposed republican polity. All told, the extreme nature of this mutiny demonstrated, paradoxically, both that Washington's long-term Continentals were the most loyal and dedicated republican citizens in the new nation, and that they were dangerously close to repudiating a dream that far too often had been a personal nightmare because of the realities of societal support and of service in the Continental army.

More worrisome in January 1781 than the matter of appropriate appreciation of the soldiers' actions was whether this mutiny, and its stillborn predecessors, would trigger further turbulence in the ranks. Also camped near Morristown during the winter of 1780–81 were veteran soldiers of the New Jersey Line. Their officers were aware that the Jersey regulars sympathized with the Pennsylvanians and had been in constant communication with them. Then, on January 20, 1781, the New Jersey Line, having witnessed the success of its comrades, also mutinied. The soldiers had each recently received $5 in specie as a token toward long overdue pay, but they were bothered by the better bounties and terms of enlistment offered newer recruits. Their leaders urged them on by shouting: "Let us go to Congress who have money and rum enough but won't give it to us!"

Within a few days, the Jersey Line had won acceptable concessions and was back under control. Washington, however, had decided that enough was enough. "Unless this dangerous spirit can be suppressed by force," he wrote to Congress, "there is an end to all subordination in the Army, and indeed to the Army itself." To back up his strong words, the commander ordered Gen. Robert Howe and about five hundred New England troops near West Point to march to the Jersey camp at Pompton to make sure that the mutineers were back in line and summarily to execute the most notorious leaders. Howe did as instructed. He reached Pompton on January 27, three days after grievances had been redressed. Deploying his men around the campsite just before dawn, Howe caught the Jersey soldiers off guard. He ordered them to fall in without arms, then singled out three ringleaders and ordered their summary execution, to be shot to death by nine of their comrades. A Jersey officer intervened in one case, but the other two were put to death by firing squad.

It was a brutal ending for men who had dreamed of a better future despite all of society's violations of the contract. Perhaps because of the calculated coldheartedness of Washington's orders, or perhaps because the war picture began to brighten in 1781, there were no major uprisings among Washington's regulars after the mutiny of the New Jersey Line. Then again, the soldiery may have been too worn down physically and mentally to continue their protest and defiance in the name of financial justice, humane treatment, and psychological support. They may have passed beyond the point of despair to that of quiet acceptance of whatever came their way, whether just or unjust.

An important question that must be raised in conclusion has to do with political perceptions and fears: given real concerns in Revolutionary society that a regular army could obtain too much power, could corrupt the political system, and could threaten the civilian sector with some form of tyranny, such as a military dictatorship, why did officers and soldiers never unite effectively and put maximum pressure on the frail Revolutionary political structure by protesting in unison? They could have easily played on fears of a coup. But about the closest such union was the Jersey officers' defiance of 1779. Thus, while common soldiers got drunk, deserted, looted, or mutinied, officers pursued their own (and largely separate) avenues of protest. This is curious, especially since the officers too worried about the personal financial cost of service; they too came to resent civilian indifference, ineptitude, and greed; and they too were dismayed over society's inability to treat them with respect. They feared that their virtuous behavior and self-sacrifice would go unappreciated if not completely unrecognized and unrewarded. Having so much in common with their brethren in the rank and file, then, it is worth considering why the officers almost never aligned with them. For if they had, the alliance might have been powerful enough to have fomented something truly menacing to the vitals of Revolutionary society.

The officer corps developed its own forms of protest, and the pattern paralleled that of the common soldiers. The movement was from a dominant expression of individual defiance (resignations in 1776 and 1777) to collective protest (the drive for half-pay pensions which began in earnest during the fall of 1777 and climaxed with the Newburgh Conspiracy of 1782–83). Like common soldiers, the officers had collectivized their protest. In that sense, unit cohesion among comrades had come into play, but such cohesion never broke through the vertical hierarchy of military rank.

Part of the reason lay in the social gulf separating the two groups. As befit the deferential nature of their times as well as their concern for maintaining sharp distinctions in rank as a key to a disciplined fighting force, officers, many of whom were drawn from the "better sort" in society, expected nothing less than steady, if not blind obedience to their will from the rank and file. In their commitment to pursuing the goals of the Revolution, the officers were anything but social levelers. Indeed, many of them feared that the Revolution might get out of hand and lead to actual internal social upheaval, particularly if the "vulgar herd" gained too much influence and authority, whether in or out of the army. They hesitated to turn their troops against society because these same soldiers could always turn against them as well and, through brute force, undermine all assumed claims to economic and social preeminence in Revolutionary America.

Washington's veteran officers, even though they complained and protested with vehemence, also willingly accepted their responsibilities as the army's leadership cadre. The officers administered harsh discipline to deserters, looters, bounty jumpers, and mutineers whenever it seemed necessary—and sometimes when it was not. They generally supported Washington's desire to set the legal limit for lashes at 500 strokes, and many of them often sanctioned whippings of more than 100 lashes, despite the Articles of War of 1776. For example, officers took with relish to Washington's general orders at Morristown in 1780 to inflict 100 to 500 lashes on duly tried plunderers and to administer up to 50 lashes on the spot, even before formal hearings, when soldiers were caught breaking military laws.

Many officers thus used their authority with impunity and rarely expressed sympathy for the plight of common soldiers in the ranks. They were much more concerned with societal stability and the protection of property, as well as with military decorum and hierarchy, all of which precluded the officer corps from working in harmony with the soldiery when protesting common grievances against the civilian sector.

Washington's officers, in reality, were caught between the rank and file, for which they had little sympathy, and the larger society, which had little sympathy for them. They pursued their half-pay pension demands, resorting to such defiant acts as threatening to resign en masse during the late summer of 1780. Later they became even more extreme as some toyed with the idea of a full mutiny, if not the possibility of a coup, during the Newburgh crisis. In the end, they failed in their short-term quest for pensions or commutation, as the soldiery fell short in its drive for minimal levels of respectable support. Perhaps those quests would have been more successful had officers and regulars been able to unite in a common bond transcending social class and military rank. If they had, the story of the Revolution might have been quite different. Recalling the common well of bitterness, the ending might well have had more of a Napoleonic cast to it.

That it did not is more than a mere testament to class, hierarchy, and rank. It is also a statement about the evolving feelings among both hard-core officers and regulars, regardless of the multifold reasons that brought them to the service in the first place, that they were fighting for something worthwhile, something of consequence for their particular lives. If they protested, they still maintained residual faith in their personal dreams. They also came to comprehend that, for all of the pain and suffering that was their lot, they could make a lasting contribution. Henry Knox stated the proposition aptly in 1783 when he noted that there was "a favorite toast in the army," that of " 'A hoop to the barrel,' or 'Cement to the Union.' " That is the way that these protesting, defying, long-term Continentals should be remembered, not as a "most undisciplined, profligate Crew," but as individuals who, for all of their defiance, made the necessary personal sacrifice to insure that the Revolution and its ideals would succeed when so many about them in their society did not.

■ ■ ■

STUDY QUESTIONS

1. Despite the desire of many colonists to separate from Great Britain, there was not much unanimity among Americans. Why? How would you explain the dissension?

2. Historians have frequently looked back on American society in the colonial period as the least aristocratic in the world. Do you agree? Were there any aristocratic values in colonial America? Describe them. How does class conflict in the Continental Army expose those aristocratic values?

3. In the 1770s, soldiers complained that the public really did not care much about what was happening to them. Do you agree that the public was apathetic toward the soldiers in the 1770s? Why or why not?

BIBLIOGRAPHY

For a standard treatment of the military dimension of the American Revolution, see J. R. Alden, *A History of the American Revolution* (1969). More analytical treatments can be found in Don Higginbotham, *The War of American Independence: Military Attitudes, Policies and Practice, 1763–1789* (1971) and John Shy's *A People Numerous and Armed: Reflections on the Military Struggle for American Independence* (1976). For the classic study of social change during the Revolution, see J. Franklin Jamison, *The American Revolution Considered as a Social Movement* (1926). A more recent, though still supportive, interpretation of the social dimension of the revolutionary era is Jackson T. Main's *The Social Structure of Revolutionary America* (1969). Jesse Lemisch's article "Listening to the 'Inarticulate': William Widger's Dream and the Loyalties of American Revolutionary Seamen in British Prisons," *Journal of Southern History*, 35 (1969) offers an additional look at the feelings of lower-class Americans. Finally, for an excellent description of American attitudes toward the Revolution over the past two hundred years, see Michael Kammen, *A Season of Youth: The American Revolution and the Historical Imagination* (1978).

THE CONSTITUTION:
WAS IT AN ECONOMIC
DOCUMENT?

Henry Steele Commager

When the Puritans left England for Massachusetts in 1629, they were dedicated to reforming the Church of England. Their goal was to build a model city in Boston where a perfect social, economic, and political order would be home for God's elect. This Puritan sense of mission came to permeate American culture and eventually created a profound vision of historical destiny. By the early nineteenth century, most Americans, including intellectuals like historian George Bancroft, were looking back on the American Revolution and the Constitutional Convention as handiworks of God, the fulfillment of a divinely preordained plan. The Founding Fathers were seen as inspired men implementing a cosmic will, and the government they created seemed a model of democracy, freedom, and restraint.

In 1913, when Charles Beard wrote *An Economic Interpretation of the Constitution of the United States,* he challenged not only the academic world but the national identity as well. By arguing that the Founding Fathers were motivated by greed in their constitution-making, Beard was simultaneously assaulting the idea of destiny. The Founding Fathers were not agents of God, just ordinary people promoting their own economic self-interest. The strong central government they wanted so desperately would stabilize the economy, reduce inflation, improve the trade balance, and suppress political insurgency. Despite the academic and public controversy surrounding Beard's interpretation, the book quickly became the standard in the field, the reference against which all interpretations of the Constitution were measured. Never again would the Founding Fathers enjoy reputations as demigods, and never again would Americans look back on their own history with the naivete they once had. In "The Constitution: Was It An Economic Document?" historian Henry Steele Commager takes a critical look at the debate Charles Beard initiated.

By June 26, 1787, tempers in the Federal Convention were already growing short, for gentlemen had come to the explosive question of representation in the upper chamber. Two days later Franklin moved to invoke divine guidance, and his motion was shunted aside only because there was no money with which to pay a chaplain and the members were unprepared to appeal to Heaven without an intermediary. It was not surprising that when James Madison spoke to the question of representation in the proposed legislature, he was conscious of the solemnity of the occasion. We are, he said, framing a system "which we wish to last for ages" and one that might "decide forever the fate of Republican Government."

It was an awful thought, and when, a few days later, Gouverneur Morris spoke to the same subject he felt the occasion a most solemn one; even the irrepressible Morris could be solemn. "He came here," he observed (so Madison noted),

as a Representative of America; he flattered himself he came here in some degree as a Representative of the whole human race; for the whole human race will be affected by the proceedings of this Convention. He wished gentlemen to extend their views beyond the present moment of time: beyond the narrow limits . . . from which they derive their political origin. . . .

Much has been said of the sentiments of the people. They were unknown. They could not be known. All that we can infer is that if the plan we recommend be reasonable & right; all who have reasonable minds and sound intentions will embrace it . . .

These were by no means occasional sentiments only. They were sentiments that occurred again and again throughout the whole of that long hot summer, until they received their final,

"The Constitution: Was It An Economic Document?" by Henry Steele Commager in *American Heritage*, December 1958, Volume X, Number 1. Reprinted by permission of the author.

eloquent expression from the aged Franklin in that comment on the rising, not the setting, sun. Even during the most acrimonious debates members were aware that they were framing a constitution for ages to come, that they were creating a model for people everywhere on the globe; there was a lively sense of responsibility and even of destiny. Nor can we now, as we contemplate that Constitution which is the oldest written national constitution, and that federal system which is one of the oldest and the most successful in history, regard these appeals to posterity as merely rhetorical.

That men are not always conscious either of what they do or of the motives that animate them is a familar rather than a cynical observation. Some 45 years ago Charles A. Beard propounded an economic interpretation of the Constitution—an interpretation which submitted that the Constitution was *essentially* (that is a crucial word) an economic document—and that it was carried through the Convention and the state ratifying conventions by interested economic groups for economic reasons. "The Constitution," Mr. Beard concluded, "was essentially an economic document based upon the concept that the fundamental private rights of property are anterior to government and morally beyond the reach of popular majorities."

At the time it was pronounced, that interpretation caused something of a sensation, and Mr. Beard was himself eventually to comment with justifiable indignation on the meanness and the vehemence of the attacks upon it—and him. Yet the remarkable thing about the economic interpretation is not the criticism it inspired but the support it commanded. For within a few years it had established itself as the new orthodoxy, and those who took exception to it were stamped either as professional patriots—perhaps secret Sons or Daughters of the Revolution—or naïve academicians who had never learned the facts of economic life.

The attraction that the economic interpretation had for the generation of the twenties and thirties—and that it still exerts even into the fifties—is one of the curiosities of our cultural history, but it is by no means an inexplicable one. To a generation of materialists Beard's thesis made clear that the stuff of history was material. To a generation disillusioned by the exploitations of big business it discovered that the past, too, had been ravaged by economic exploiters. To a generation that looked with skeptical eyes upon the claims of Wilsonian idealism and all but rejoiced in their frustration, it suggested that all earlier idealisms and patriotisms—even the idealism and patriotism of the framers—had been similarly flawed by selfishness and hypocrisy.

Yet may it not be said of *An Economic Interpretation of the Constitution* that it is not a conclusion but a point of departure? It explains a great deal about the forces that went into the making of the Constitution, and a great deal, too, about the men who assembled in Philadelphia in 1787, but it tells us extraordinarily little about the document itself. And it tells us even less about the historical meaning of that document.

What were the objects of the Federal Convention? The immediate objects were to restore order; to strengthen the public credit; to enable the United States to make satisfactory commercial treaties and agreements; to provide conditions in which trade and commerce could flourish; to facilitate management of the western lands and of Indian affairs. All familiar enough. But what, in the light of history, were the grand objects of the Convention? What was it that gave Madison and Morris and Wilson and King and Washington himself a sense of destiny?

There were two grand objects—objects inextricably interrelated. The first was to solve the problem of federalism, that is, the problem of the distribution of powers among governments. Upon the wisdom with which members of the Convention distinguished between powers of a general and powers of a local nature, and assigned these to their appropriate governments, would depend the success or failure of the new experiment.

But it was impossible for the children of the eighteenth century to talk or think of powers without thinking of power, and this was a healthy realism. No less troublesome—and more fundamental—than the problem of the distribution of powers, was the problem of sanctions. How were they to enforce the terms of the distribution and impose limits upon all the governments involved? It was one thing to work out the most ideal distribution of general and local powers. It was another thing to see to it that the states abided by their obligations under the Articles of Union and that the national government respected the autonomy of the states and the liberty of individuals.

Those familiar with the Revolutionary era know that the second of these problems was more difficult than the first. Americans had, indeed, learned how to limit government: the written constitutions, the bills of rights, the checks and balances, and so forth. They had not yet learned (nor had anyone) how to "substitute the mild magistracy of the law for the cruel and violent magistracy of force." The phrase is Madison's.

Let us return to the *Economic Interpretation*. The correctness of Beard's analysis of the origins and backgrounds of the membership of the Convention, of the arguments in the Convention, and of the methods of assuring ratification, need not be debated. But these considerations are, in a sense, irrelevant and immaterial. For though they are designed to illuminate the document itself, in fact they illuminate only the processes of its manufacture.

The idea that property considerations were paramount in the minds of those assembled in Philadelphia is misleading and unsound and is borne out neither by the evidence of the debates in the Convention nor by the Constitution itself. The Constitution was not *essentially* an economic document. It was, and is, *essentially* a political document. It addresses itself to the great and fundamental question of the distribution of powers between governments. The Constitution was—and is—a document that attempts to provide sanctions behind that distribution; a document that sets up, through law, a standing rule to live by and provides legal machinery for the enforcement of that rule. These are political, not economic functions.

Not only were the principles that animated the framers political rather than economic; the solutions that they formulated to the great questions that confronted them were dictated by political, not by economic considerations.

Here are two fundamental challenges to the Beard interpretation: first, the Constitution is primarily a document in federalism; and second, the Constitution does not in fact confess or display the controlling influence of those who held that "the fundamental private rights of property are anterior to government and morally beyond the reach of popular majorities."

Let us look more closely at these two contentions. The first requires little elaboration or vindication, for it is clear to all students of the Revolutionary era that the one pervasive and over-branching problem of that generation was the problem of imperial organization. How to get the various parts of any empire to work together for common purposes? How to get central control—over war, for example, or commerce or money—without impairing local autonomy? How, on the other hand, preserve personal liberty and local self-government without impairing the effectiveness of the central government? This was one of the oldest problems in political science, and it is one of the freshest—as old as the history of the Greek city-states; as new as the recent debate over Federal aid to education or the Bricker amendment.

The British failed to solve the problem of imperial order; when pushed to the wall they had recourse to the hopelessly doctrinaire Declaratory Act, which was, in fact, a declaration of political bankruptcy; as Edmund Burke observed, no people is going to be argued into slavery. The Americans then took up the vexatious problem. The Articles of Confederation were satisfactory enough as far as the distribution of powers was concerned, but wholly wanting in sanctions. The absence of sanctions spelled the failure of the Articles—and this failure led to the Philadelphia Convention.

Now it will be readily conceded that many, if not most, of the questions connected with federalism were economic in character. Involved were such practical matters as taxation, the regulation of commerce, coinage, western lands, slavery, and so forth. Yet the problem that presented itself to the framers was not whether government should exercise authority over such matters as these; it was *which* government should exercise such authority—and how should it be exercised?

There were, after all, no anarchists at the Federal Convention. Everyone agreed that *some* government had to have authority to tax, raise armies, regulate commerce, coin money, control contracts, enact bankruptcy legislation, regulate western territories, make treaties, and do all the things that government must do. But where should these authorities be lodged—with the state governments or with the national government they were about to erect, or with both?

This question was a political, not an economic, one. And the solution at which the framers arrived was based upon a sound understanding of politics, and need not be explained by reference to class attachments or security interests.

Certainly if the framers were concerned primarily or even largely with protecting property against popular majorities, they failed signally to carry out their purposes. It is at this point in our consideration of the *Economic Interpretation of the Constitution* that we need to employ what our literary friends call *explication du texte*. For the weakest link in the Beard interpretation is precisely the crucial one—the document itself. Mr. Beard makes amply clear that those who wrote the Constitution were members of the propertied classes, and that many of them were personally involved in the outcome of what they were about to do; he makes out a persuasive case that the division over the Constitution was along economic lines. What he does not make clear is how or where the Constitution itself reflects all these economic influences.

Much is made of the contract clause and the paper money clause of the Constitution. No state may impair the obligations of a contract—whatever those words mean, and they apparently did not mean to the framers quite what Chief Justice Marshall later said they meant in *Fletcher v. Peck* or *Dartmouth College v. Woodward.* No state may emit bills of credit or make anything but gold and silver coin legal tender in payment of debts.

These are formidable prohibitions, and clearly reflect the impatience of men of property with the malpractices of the states during the Confederation. Yet quite aside from what the states may or may not have done, who can doubt that these limitations upon the states followed a sound principle—the principle that control of coinage and money belonged to the central, not the local governments, and the principle that local jurisdictions should not be able to modify or overthrow contracts recognized throughout the Union?

What is most interesting in this connection is what is so often overlooked: that the framers did not write any comparable prohibitions upon the United States government. The United States was not forbidden to impair the obligation of its contracts, not at least in the Constitution as it came from the hands of its property-conscious framers. Possibly the Fifth Amendment may have squinted toward such a prohibition; we need not determine that now, for the Fifth Amendment was added by the *states* after the Constitution had been ratified. So, too, the emission of bills of credit and the making other than gold and silver legal tender were limitations on the states, but not on the national government. There was, in fact, a lively debate over the question of limiting the authority of the national government in the matter of bills of credit. When the question came up on August 16, Gouverneur Morris threatened that "The Monied interest will oppose the plan of Government, if paper emissions be not prohibited." In the end the Convention dropped out a specific authorization to emit bills of credit, but pointedly did not prohibit such

action. Just where this left the situation troubled Chief Justice Chase's Court briefly three-quarters of a century later; the Court recovered its balance, and the sovereign power of the government over money was not again *successfully* challenged.

Nor were there other specific limitations of an economic character upon the powers of the new government that was being erected on the ruins of the old. The framers properly gave the Congress power to regulate commerce with foreign nations and among the states. The term commerce—as Hamilton and Adair (and Crosskey, too!) have made clear—was broadly meant, and the grant of authority, too, was broad. The framers gave Congress the power to levy taxes and, again, wrote no limitations into the Constitution except as to the apportionment of direct taxes; it remained for the most conservative of Courts to reverse itself, and common sense, and discover that the framers had intended to forbid an income tax! Today, organizations that invoke the very term "constitutional" are agitating for an amendment placing a quantitative limit upon income taxes that may be levied; fortunately, Madison's generation understood better the true nature of governmental power.

The framers gave Congress—in ambiguous terms, to be sure—authority to make "all needful Rules and Regulations respecting the Territory or other Property" of the United States, and provided that "new states may be admitted." These evasive phrases gave little hint of the heated debates in the Convention over western lands. Those who delight to find narrow and undemocratic sentiments in the breasts of the framers never cease to quote a Gouverneur Morris or an Elbridge Gerry on the dangers of the West, and it is possible to compile a horrid catalogue of such statements. But what is significant is not what framers said, but what they did. They did not place any limits upon the disposition of western territory, or establish any barriers against the admission of western states.

The fact is that we look in vain *in the Constitution itself* for any really effective guarantee for

■■ *The above ''Representation of the Federal Chariot'' shows Washington and Frankin, with the Constitution and the Cap of American Freedom in hand, being pulled by thirteen freemen to ratification and the country's political salvation.*

property or any effective barriers against what Beard calls ''the reach of popular majorities.''

It will be argued, however, that what the framers feared was the *states,* and that the specific prohibitions against state action, together with the broad transfer of economic powers from state to nation, were deemed sufficient guarantee against state attacks upon property. As for the national government, care was taken to make that sufficiently aristocratic, sufficiently the representative of the propertied classes, and sufficiently checked and limited so that it would not threaten basic property interests.

It is at this juncture that the familiar principle of limitation on governmental authority commands our attention. Granted the wisest distribution of powers among governments, what guarantee was there that power would be properly exercised? What guarantees were there against the abuse of power? What assurance was

there that the large states would not ride rough-shod over the small, that majorities would not crush minorities or minorities abuse majorities? What protection was there against mobs, demagogues, dangerous combinations of interests or of states? What protection was there for the commercial interest, the planter interest, the slave interest, the securities interests, the land speculator interests?

It was Madison who most clearly saw the real character of this problem and who formulated its solution. It was not that the people as such were dangerous; ''The truth was,'' he said on July 11, ''that all men having power ought to be distrusted to a certain degree.'' Long before Lord Acton coined the aphorism, the Revolutionary leaders had discovered that power corrupts. They understood, too, the drive for power on the part of individuals and groups. All this is familiar to students of *The Federalist,* No. 10. It should be familiar to students of the debates in Philadelphia, for there, too, Madison set forth his theory and supported it with a wealth of argument. Listen to him on one of the early days of the Convention, June 6, when he is discussing the way to avoid abuses of republican liberty—abuses which "prevailed in the largest as well as the smallest [states] . . ."

. . . And were we not thence admonished [he continued] to enlarge the sphere as far as the nature of the Government would admit. This was the only defence against the inconveniences of democracy consistent with the democratic form of Government [our italics]. All civilized Societies would be divided into different Sects, Factions & interests, as they happened to consist of rich & poor, debtors and creditors, the landed, the manufacturing, the commercial interests, the inhabitants of this district or that district, the followers of this political leader or that political leader, the disciples of this religious Sect or that religious Sect. In all cases where a majority are united by a common interest or passion, the rights of the minority are in danger. . . . In a Republican Govt. the Majority if united have always an opportunity [to oppress the minority. What is the remedy?] The only remedy is to enlarge the sphere, & thereby divide the community into so great a number of interests & parties, that in the first place a majority will not be likely at the same moment to have a common interest separate from that of the whole or of the minority; and in the second place, that in case they should have such an interest, they may not be apt to unite in the pursuit of it. It was incumbent on us then to try this remedy, and . . . to frame a republican system on such a scale & in such a form as will controul all the evils which have been experienced.

This long quotation is wonderfully eloquent of the attitude of the most sagacious of the framers. Madison, Wilson, Mason, Franklin, as well as Gerry, Morris, Pinckney, and Hamilton feared power. They feared power whether exercised by a monarch, an aristocracy, an army, or a majority, and they were one in their determination to write into fundamental law limitations on the arbitrary exercise of that power. To assume, as Beard so commonly does, that the fear of the misuse of power by majorities was either peculiar to the Federalists or more ardent with them than with their opponents, is mistaken. Indeed it was rather the anti-Federalists who were most deeply disturbed by the prospect of majority rule; they, rather than the Federalists, were the "men of little faith." Thus it was John Lansing, Jr., of New York (he who left the Convention rather than have any part in its dangerous work) who said that "all free constitutions are formed with two views—to deter the governed from crime, and the governors from tyranny." And the ardent Patrick Henry, who led the attack on the Constitution in the Virginia Convention—and almost defeated it—complained not of too little democracy in that document, but too much.

The framers, to be sure, feared the powers of the majority, as they feared all power unless controlled. But they were insistent that, in the last analysis, there must be government by majority; even conservatives like Morris and Hamilton made this clear. Listen to Hamilton, for example, at the very close of the Convention. Elbridge Gerry, an opponent of the Constitution, had asked for a reconsideration of the provision for calling a constitutional convention, alleging that this opened the gate to a majority that could "bind the union to innovations that may subvert the State-Constitutions altogether." To this Hamilton replied that

There was no greater evil in subjecting the people of the U.S. to the major voice than the people of a particular State. . . . It was equally desirable now that an easy mode should be established for supplying defects which will probably appear in the New System. . . . There could be no danger in giving this power, as the people would finally decide in the case.

And on July 13, James Wilson, another staunch Federalist, observed that "The majority of people wherever found ought in all questions to govern the minority."

But we need not rely upon what men said; there is too much of making history by quotation anyway. Let us look rather at what men did. We can turn again to the Constitution itself. Granted the elaborate system of checks and balances: the separation of powers, the bicameral legislature, the executive veto, and so forth—checks found in the state constitutions as well, and in our own democratic era as in the earlier one—what provision did the framers make against majority tyranny? What provisions did they write into the Constitution against what Randolph called "democratic licentiousness"?

They granted equality of representation in the Senate. If this meant that conservative Delaware would have the same representation in the upper chamber as democratic Pennsylvania, it also meant that democratic Rhode Island would have the same representation as conservative South Carolina. But the decision for equality of representation was not dictated by considerations either economic or democratic, but rather by the recalcitrance of the small states. Indeed, though it is difficult to generalize here, on the whole it is true that it was the more ardent Federalists who favored proportional representation in both houses.

They elaborated a most complicated method of electing a Chief Executive, a method designed to prevent the easy expression of any majority will. Again the explanation is not simple. The fact was that the framers did not envision the possibility of direct votes for presidential candidates which would not conform to state lines and interests and thus lead to dissension and confusion. Some method, they thought, must be designated to overcome the force of state prejudices (or merely of parochialism) and get an election; the method they anticipated was a preliminary elimination contest by the electoral college and then eventual election by the House.

This, said George Mason, was what would occur nineteen times out of twenty. There is no evidence in the debates that the complicated method finally hit upon for electing a President was designed either to frustrate popular majorities or to protect special economic interests; its purpose was to overcome state pride and particularism.

Senators and Presidents, then, would not be the creatures of democracy. But what guarantee was there that senators would be representatives of property interests, or that the President himself would recognize the "priority of property"? Most states had property qualifications for office holding, but there are none in the Federal Constitution. As far as the Constitution is concerned, the President, congressmen, and Supreme Court justices can all be paupers.

Both General Charles Cotesworth Pinckney and his young cousin Charles, of South Carolina, were worried about this. The latter proposed a property qualification of $100,000 (a tidy sum in those days) for the Presidency, half that for the judges, and substantial sums for members of Congress. Franklin rebuked him. He was distressed, he said, to hear anything "that tended to debase the spirit of the common people." More surprising was the rebuke from that stout conservative, John Dickinson. "He doubted," Madison reports, "the policy of interweaving into a Republican constitution a veneration for wealth. He had always understood that a veneration for poverty & virtue were the objects of republican encouragement." Pinckney's proposal was overwhelmingly rejected.

What of the members of the lower house? When Randolph opened "the main business" on May 29 he said the remedy for the crisis that men faced must be "the republican principle," and two days later members were discussing the fourth resolution, which provided for election to the lower house by the people. Roger Sherman of Connecticut thought that "the people should have as little to do as may be about the Government," and Gerry hastened to agree in words now well-worn from enthusiastic quotation that

"The evils we experience flow from the excess of democracy." These voices were soon drowned out, however. Mason "argued strongly for an election . . . by the people. It was to be the grand depository of the democratic principle of the Govt." And the learned James Wilson, striking the note to which he was to recur again and again, made clear that he was for "raising the federal pyramid to a considerable altitude, and for that reason wished to give it as broad a basis as possible." He thought that both branches of the legislature—and the President as well, for that matter—should be elected by the people. "The Legislature," he later observed, "ought to be the most exact transcript of the whole Society."

A further observation is unhappily relevant today. It was a maxim with John Adams that "where annual elections end, there tyranny begins," and the whole Revolutionary generation was committed to a frequent return to the source of authority. But the framers put into the Constitution no limits on the number of terms which Presidents or congressmen could serve. It was not that the question was ignored; it received elaborate attention. It was rather that the generation that wrote the Constitution was better grounded in political principles than is our own; that it did not confuse, as we so often do, quantitative and qualitative limitations; and that—in a curious way—it had more confidence in the intelligence and the good will of the people than we seem to have today. It is, in any event, our own generation that has the dubious distinction of writing into the Constitution the first quantitative limitation on the right of the majority to choose their President. It is not the generation of the framers that was undemocratic; it is our generation that is undemocratic.

It is relevant to note, too, that the Constitution contains no property qualification for voting. Most states, to be sure, had such qualifications—in general a freehold or its equivalent—and the Constitution assimilated such qualifications as states might establish. Yet the framers, whether for reasons practical or philosophical

we need not determine, made no serious efforts to write any property qualifications for voting into the Constitution itself.

The question of popular control came up clearly in one other connection as well: the matter of ratification. Should the Constitution be ratified by state legislatures, or by conventions? The practical arguments for the two methods were nicely balanced. The decisive argument was not, however, one of expediency but of principle. "To the people with whom all power remains that has not been given up in the Constitutions derived from them" we must resort, said Mason. Madison put the matter on principle, too. "He considered the difference between a system founded on the Legislatures only, and one founded on the people, to be the true difference between a *league* or *treaty* and a *Constitution.*" Ellsworth's motion to refer the Constitution to legislatures was defeated by a vote of eight to two, and the resolution to refer it to conventions passed with only Delaware in the negative.

Was the Constitution designed to place private property beyond the reach of majorities? If so, the framers did a very bad job. They failed to write into it the most elementary safeguards for property. They failed to write into it limitations on the tax power, or prohibitions against the abuse of the money power. They failed to provide for rule by those whom Adams was later to call the wise and the rich and the wellborn. What they did succeed in doing was to create a system of checks and balances and adjustments and accommodations that would effectively prevent the suppression of most minorities by majorities. They took advantage of the complexity, the diversity, the pluralism, of American society and economy to encourage a balance of interests. They worked out sound and lasting political solutions to the problems of class, interest, section, race, religion, party.

Perhaps the most perspicacious comment on this whole question of the threat from turbulent popular majorities against property and order came, *mirabile dictu,* from the dashing young Charles Pinckney of South Carolina—he of the "lost" Pinckney Plan. On June 25 Pinckney made a major speech and thought it important enough to write out and give to Madison. The point of departure was the hackneyed one of the character of the second branch of the legislature, but the comments were an anticipation of De Tocqueville and Lord Bryce. We need not, Pinckney asserted, fear the rise of class conflicts in America, nor take precautions against them.

The genius of the people, their mediocrity of situations & the prospects which are afforded their industry in a Country which must be a new one for centuries are unfavorable to the rapid distinction of ranks. . . . If equality is . . . the leading feature of the U. States [he asked], where then are the riches & wealth whose representation & protection is the peculiar province of this permanent body [the Senate]. Are they in the hands of the few who may be called rich; in the possession of less than a hundred citizens? certainly not. They are in the great body of the people . . . [There was no likelihood that a privileged body would ever develop in the United States, he added,

either from the landed interest, the moneyed interest, or the mercantile.] Besides, Sir, I apprehend that on this point the policy of the U. States has been much mistaken. We have unwisely considered ourselves as the inhabitants of an old instead of a new country. We have adopted the maxims of a State full of people . . . The people of this country are not only very different from the inhabitants of any State we are acquainted with in the modern world; but I assert that their situation is distinct from either the people of Greece or of Rome . . . Our true situation appears to me to be this—a new extensive Country containing within itself the materials for forming a Government capable of extending to its citizens all the blessings of civil & religious liberty—capable of making them happy at home. This is the great end of Republican Establishments. . . .

Not a government cunningly contrived to protect the interests of property, but one capable of extending to its citizens the blessings of liberty and happiness—was that not, after all, what the framers created?

■ ■ ■

STUDY QUESTIONS

1. What was the essence of Beard's argument about the Founding Fathers and the making of the Constitution? How does Commager feel about Beard's interpretation?

2. Why did the economic interpretation of the Constitution gain such credence in the United States during the 1920s and 1930s?

3. At the Constitutional Convention, what were the two major objectives of the Founding Fathers, and how does the Beard interpretation coincide with those objectives?

4. When finally completed and ratified, did the Constitution provide specific protections for propertied interests against the whim of popular majorities? Explain your answer.

5. As far as Commager is concerned, what was the real motivation behind the Constitution? How would you evaluate his point of view? Explain your answer.

BIBLIOGRAPHY

The now classic view of the Constitution as a reactionary document enabling an economic elite to control the new federal government is Charles Beard's *An Economic Interpretation of the Constitution of the United States* (1913). During the 1950s, two historians took great exception to Beard's arguments, claiming that his evidence did not really hold up to careful scrutiny. See Robert E. Brown, *Charles Beard and the Constitution* (1956) and Forrest McDonald, *We the People: The Economic Origins of the Constitution* (1958). For a view of the years preceding the Constitutional Convention as a time of great crisis, see John Fiske, *The Critical Period of American History* (1888). Merrill Jensen's *The New Nation* (1950) and *The Articles of Confederation* (1958) generally endorse the Beard interpretation, as does Jackson T. Main's *The Antifederalists* (1961).

WATERMELON ARMIES AND WHISKEY BOYS

Gerald Carson

When the Constitution was finally ratified in 1788, a new nation entered the arena of world politics. After more than a decade of debate over political philosophy, which included a violent revolution as well as the failure of one federal government, the Founding Fathers tried again. This time they committed themselves to a stronger central government with the power to tax and levy tariffs, as well as a more powerful executive branch. The experience of Shays' Rebellion in western Massachusetts in 1786 frightened conservatives with the specter of anarchy and class warfare. Since the Articles of Confederation government had been powerless to suppress the tax rebellion, people like James Madison, Alexander Hamilton, and George Washington decided that a more concentrated political power was necessary for national stability. They had convened the Constitutional Convention at Philadelphia in the summer of 1787 to generate the power which would provide that stability. George Washington was elected president in the election of 1788 and the new government went into operation in the spring of 1789.

President Washington selected Alexander Hamilton to serve in his cabinet as secretary of the treasury, and Hamilton quickly developed a financial program which included funding of the national debt, assumption of state debts, protective tariffs, a national bank, and a tax on the grain mash of western farmers. This "Whiskey Tax" triggered intense opposition along the agricultural frontier. A new tax rebellion, not unlike that of Daniel Shays in 1786, erupted in western Pennsylvania. It was a major test of the new federal government. In "Watermelon Armies and Whiskey Boys," historian Gerald Carson describes the confrontation which eventually proved that the Constitution and the federal government were here to stay.

When one recalls that the President of the United States, the Secretary of War, the Secretary of the Treasury and the governors of four states once mobilized against the farmers of western Pennsylvania almost as large an army as ever took the field in the Revolutionary War, the event appears at first glance as one of the more improbable episodes in the annals of this country. Thirteen thousand grenadiers, dragoons, foot soldiers and pioneers, a train of artillery with six-pounders, mortars and several "grass-hoppers," equipped with mountains of ammunition, forage, baggage and a bountiful stock of tax-paid whiskey, paraded over the mountains to Pittsburgh against a gaggle of homespun rebels who had already dispersed.

Yet the march had a rationale. President George Washington and his Secretary of the Treasury, Alexander Hamilton, moved to counter civil commotion with overwhelming force because they well understood that the viability of the United States Constitution was involved. Soon after he assumed his post at the Treasury, Hamilton had proposed, to the astonishment of the country, that the United States should meet fully and promptly its financial obligations, including the assumption of the debts contracted by the states in the struggle for independence. The money was partly to be raised by laying an excise tax upon distilled spirits. The tax, which was universally detested in the West—"odious" was the word most commonly used to describe it—became law on March 3, 1791.

The news of the passage of the measure was greeted with a roar of indignation in the back country settlements. The duty was laid uniformly upon all the states, as the Constitution provided. If the West had to pay more, Secretary Hamilton explained, it was only because it used more whiskey. The East could, if it so desired, forgo

beverage spirits and fall back on cider and beer. The South could not. It had neither orchards nor breweries. To Virginia and Maryland the excise tax appeared to be as unjust and oppressive as the well-remembered Molasses Act and the tea duties of George III. "The time will come," predicted fiery James Jackson of Georgia in the House of Representatives, "when a shirt shall not be washed without an excise."

Kentucky, then thinly settled, but already producing its characteristic hand-made, whole-souled liquor from planished copper stills, was of the opinion that the law was unconstitutional. Deputy revenue collectors throughout the Bluegrass region were assaulted, their papers stolen, their horses' ears cropped and their saddles cut to pieces. On one wild night the people of Lexington dragged a stuffed dummy through the streets and hanged in effigy Colonel Thomas Marshall, the chief collector for the district.

Yet in no other place did popular fury rise so high, spread so rapidly, involve a whole population so completely, express so many assorted grievances, as in the Pennsylvania frontier counties of Fayette, Allegheny, Westmoreland and Washington. In these counties, around 1791, a light plume of wood smoke rose from the chimneys of no less than five thousand log stillhouses. The rates went into effect on July first. The whiskey-maker could choose whether he would pay a yearly levy on his still capacity or a gallonage tax ranging from nine to eleven cents on his actual production.

Before the month was out, "committees of correspondence," in the old Revolutionary phrase, were speeding horsemen over the ridges and through the valleys to arouse the people to arm and assemble. The majority, but not all, of the men who made the whiskey decided to "forbear" from paying the tax. The revenue officers were thoroughly worked over. Robert Johnson, for example, collector for Washington and Allegheny counties, was waylaid near Pigeon Creek by a mob disguised in women's clothing. They cut off his hair, gave him a coat of tar and feathers and stole his horse.

The Pennsylvania troubles were rooted in the economic importance and impregnable social position of mellow old Monongahela rye whiskey. In 1825, for instance, when the Philadelphia Society for Promoting Agriculture offered a gold medal to the person in Pennsylvania who carried on large-scale farming operations without providing ardent spirits for his farm workers, the medal could not be awarded. There were no entries for the uncoveted honor.

The frontier people had been reared from childhood on the family jug of farmer whiskey. They found the taste pleasant, the effect agreeable. Whiskey was usually involved when there was kissing or fighting. It beatified the rituals of birth and death. The doctor kept a bottle in his office for his own use under the deceptive label "Arsenic—Deadly poison." The lawyer produced the bottle when the papers were signed. Whiskey was available in the prothonotary's office when the trial-list was made up. Jurors got their dram, and the constable drew his ration for his services on election day. The hospitable barrel and the tin cup were the mark of the successful political candidate. The United States Army issued a gill to a man every day. Ministers of the gospel were paid in rye whiskey, for they were shepherds of a devout flock, Scotch Presbyterians mostly, who took their Bible straight, especially where it said: "Give strong drink unto him that is ready to perish, and wine unto those that be of heavy hearts."

With grain the most abundant commodity west of the mountains, the farmers could eat it or drink it, but they couldn't sell it in distant markets unless it was reduced in bulk and enhanced in value. A Pennsylvania farmer's "best holt," then, was whiskey. A pack-horse could move only four bushels of grain. But it could carry twenty-four bushels if it was condensed into two kegs of whiskey slung across its back, while the price of the goods would double when they reached the eastern markets. So whiskey became the remittance of the fringe settlements for salt, sugar, nails, bar iron, pewter plates, powder and shot. Along the Western rivers where men saw

few shilling pieces, a gallon of good, sound rye whiskey was a stable measure of value.

The bitter resistance of the Western men to the whiskey tax involved both practical considerations and principles. First, the excise payment was due and must be paid in hard money as soon as the water-white distillate flowed from the condensing coil. The principle concerned the whole repulsive idea of an internal revenue levy. The settlers of western Pennsylvania were a bold, hardy, emigrant race who brought with them bitter memories of oppression under the excise laws in Scotland and Ireland, involving invasion of their homes, confiscation of their property and a system of paid informers. Revenue collectors were social outcasts in a society which warmly seconded Doctor Samuel Johnson's definition of excise: "a hateful tax levied upon commodities, and adjudged not by the common judges of property, but wretches hired by those to whom excise is paid."

The whiskey boys of Pennsylvania saw it as simply a matter of sound Whig doctrine to resist the exciseman as he made his rounds with Dicas' hydrometer to measure the proof of the whiskey and his marking iron to brand the casks with his findings. Earlier, Pennsylvania had taxed spirits. But whiskey produced for purely private use was exempt. William Findley of Westmoreland County, a member of Congress at the time and a sympathetic interpreter of the Western point of view, looked into this angle. To his astonishment, he learned that all of the whiskey distilled in the West was for purely personal use. So far as the state's excise tax was concerned, or any other tax, for that matter, the sturdy Celtic peoples of the Monongahela region had cheerfully returned to nature: they just didn't pay. About every sixth man made whiskey. But all were involved in the problem, since the other five took their grain to the stillhouse where the master distiller turned it into liquid form.

The state had been lenient. But now matters had taken a more serious turn. The new federal government in Philadelphia was dividing the whole country up into "districts" for the purpose

Although the excise tax on distilled spirits was laid on all states, the back country settlements were the most affected. Above, Whiskey Rebels tar and feather a federal tax collector as his house is being burned.

of collecting the money. And the districts were subdivided into smaller "surveys." The transmontane Pennsylvanians found themselves in the grip of something known as the fourth survey, with General John Neville, hitherto a popular citizen and leader, getting ready to enforce the law, with a reward paid to informers and a percentage to the collectors, who appeared to be a rapacious set.

The first meeting of public protest against the 1791 federal tax was held at Redstone Old Fort, now Brownsville. The proceedings were moderate on that occasion, and scarcely went beyond the right of petition. Another meeting in August, more characteristic of others which were to follow, was radical in tone, disorderly, threatening. It passed resolves to the effect that any person

taking office under the revenue law was an enemy of society.

When warrants were issued in the affair of Robert Johnson, the process server was robbed, beaten, tarred and feathered and left tied to a tree in the forest. As the inspectors' offices were established, they were systematically raided. Liberty poles reappeared as whiskey poles. The stills of operators who paid the tax were riddled with bullets in attacks sardonically known as "mending" the still. This led to a popular description of the Whiskey Boys as "Tom the Tinker's Men," an ironical reference to the familiar, itinerant repairer of pots and kettles. Notices proposing measures for thwarting the law, or aimed at coercing the distillers, were posted on trees or published in the *Pittsburgh Gazette* over the signature, "Tom the Tinker," nom de plume of the insurgent John Holcroft and other anti-tax agitators. Findley, who tried to build a bridge of understanding between the backwoodsmen and the central government, described the outbreak as not the result of any concerted plan, but rather as a flame, "an infatuation almost incredible."

An additional grievance grew out of the circumstance that offenders were required to appear in the federal court at Philadelphia, three hundred miles away. The whiskey-makers saw this distant government as being no less oppressive than one seated in London, and often drew the parallel. The Scotch-Irish of western Pennsylvania were, in sum, anti-federalist, anti-tax, and it may be added, anti-Indian. West of Pittsburgh lay Indian country. The men of the west held to a simple concept of how to solve the Indian problem: extermination. The Indians had the same program, in reverse, and were getting better results. The bungling campaigns which generals Hamar and St. Clair had conducted in the early 1790's made the people of the fringe settlements despair of the ability of the Union to protect them.

Congress amended the excise tax law in 1792 and again in 1794 to lighten the burden on country distillers. A further conciliatory step was taken. To ease the hardships of the judicial process, Congress gave to the state courts jurisdiction in excise offenses so that accused persons might be tried in their own vicinity. But some fifty or sixty writs already issued and returnable at Philadelphia resulted in men being carried away from their fields during harvest time. This convinced the insurgents that the federalist East was seeking a pretext to discipline the democratic West.

One day in July, while the papers were being served, William Miller, a delinquent farmer-distiller, and political supporter of General Neville, saw the General riding up his lane accompanied by a stranger who turned out to be a United States marshal from Philadelphia. The marshal unlimbered an official paper and began to read a summons. It ordered said Miller peremptorily to "set aside all manner of business and excuses" and appear in his "proper person" before a Philadelphia judge. Miller had been planning to sell his property and remove to Kentucky. The cost of the trip to Philadelphia and the fine for which he was liable would eat up the value of his land and betterments. The farm was as good as gone.

"I felt my blood boil at seeing General Neville along to pilot the sheriff to my very door," Miller said afterward. "I felt myself mad with passion."

As Neville and the marshal rode away, a party from the county militia which was mustered at Mingo Creek fired upon them, but there were no casualties. When the General reached Bower Hill, his country home above the Chartiers Valley, another party under the command of John Holcroft awaited him there and demanded his commission and official papers. The demand was refused and both sides began to shoot. As the rebels closed in on the main house, a flanking fire came from the Negro cabins on the plantation. The Whiskey Boys were driven off with one killed and four wounded.

The next day, Major James McFarlane, a veteran of the Revolution, led an attack in force upon Neville's painted and wall-papered mansion, furnished with such marvels as carpets, mirrors, pictures and prints and an eight-day clock. The house was now defended by a dozen soldiers from Fort Fayette at Pittsburgh. A firefight followed during which a soldier was shot and McFarlane was killed—by treachery, the rebels said, when a white flag was displayed. The soldiers surrendered and were either released or allowed to escape. Neville was not found, but his cabins, barns, outbuildings and finally the residence were all burned to the ground. Stocks of grain were destroyed, all fences leveled, as the victors broke up the furniture, liberated the mirrors and clock, and distributed Neville's supply of liquor to the mob.

The funeral of McFarlane caused great excitement. Among those present were Hugh Henry Brackenridge, author, lawyer and one of the western moderates, and David Bradford, prosecuting attorney for Washington County. The former wished to find ways to reduce the tension; the latter to increase it. Bradford was a rash, impetuous Marylander, ambitious for power and position. Some thought him a second-rate lawyer. Others disagreed. They said he was third-rate. But he had a gift for rough mob eloquence. Bradford had already robbed the United States mails to find out what information was being sent east against the conspirators. He had already called for the people to make a choice of "submission or opposition . . . with *head, heart, hand* and *voice.*"

At Major McFarlane's funeral service Bradford worked powerfully upon the feelings of his sympathizers as he described "the murder of McFarlane." Brackenridge also spoke, using wit and drollery to let down the pressure and to make palatable his warning to the insurgents that they were flirting with the possibility of But the temper of the throng was for Bradford, clearly revealed in the epitaph which was set over McFarlane's grave. It said "He fell . . . by the hands of an unprincipled villain in the support of what he supposed to be the rights of his country."

The high-water mark of the insurrection was the occupation of Pittsburgh. After the fight and the funeral, Bradford called out the militia regiments of the four disaffected counties. They were commanded to rendezvous at Braddock's Field, near Pittsburgh, with arms, full equipment and four days' rations. At the field there was a great beating of drums, much marching and countermarching, almost a holiday spirit. Men in hunting shirts practiced shooting at the mark until a dense pall of smoke hung over the plain, as there had been thirty-nine years before at the time of General Braddock's disaster. There were between five and seven thousand men on the field, many meditating in an ugly mood upon their enemies holed up in the town, talking of storming Fort Fayette and burning Pittsburgh as "a second Sodom."

Bradford's dream was the establishment of an independent state with himself cast as a sort of Washington of the West. Elected by acclaim as Major General, he dashed about the field on a superb horse in a fancy uniform, his sword flashing, plumes floating out from his hat. As he harangued the multitude, Bradford received applications for commissions in the service of—what? No one quite knew.

Marching in good order, strung out over two and a half miles of road, the rebels advanced on August first toward Pittsburgh in what was hopefully intrepreted as a "visit," though the temper of the whiskey soldiers was perhaps nearer to that of one man who twirled his hat on the muzzle of his rifle and shouted, "I have a bad hat now, but I expect to have a better one soon." While the panic-stricken burghers buried the silver and locked up the girls, the mob marched in on what is now Fourth Avenue to the vicinity of the present Baltimore and Ohio Railroad station. A reception committee extended nervous hospitality in the form of hams, poultry, dried venison, bear meat, water and whiskey. They agreed to banish certain citizens obnoxious to the insurrectionists. One building on a suburban farm was burned. Another attempt at arson failed to come off. The day cost Brackenridge four barrels of prime Monongahela. It was better, he reflected, "to be employed in extinguishing the fire of their thirst than of my house." Pittsburgh was fortunate in getting the main body in and then out again without a battle or a burning.

All through the month of August armed bands continued to patrol the roads as a "scrub Congress," in the phrase of one scoffer, met at Parkinson's Ferry, now Monongahela, to debate, pass resolutions and move somewhat uncertainly toward separation from the United States. Wild and ignorant rumors won belief. It was said that Congress was extending the excise levy to plows at a dollar each, that every wagon entering Philadelphia would be forced to pay a dollar, that a tax was soon to be established at Pittsburgh of fifteen shillings for the birth of every boy baby, and ten for each girl.

With the terrorizing of Pittsburgh, it was evident that the crisis had arrived. The President requisitioned 15,000 militia from Pennsylvania, New Jersey, Virginia and Maryland, of whom about 13,000 actually marched. Would the citizens of one state invade another to compel obedience to federal law? Here one gets a glimpse of the larger importance of the affair. Both the national government and the state of Pennsylvania sent commissioners to the West with offers of pardon upon satisfactory assurances that the people would obey the laws. Albert Gallatin, William Findley, Brackenridge and others made a desperate effort to win the people to compliance, though their motives were often questioned by both the rebels and the federal authorities. The response to the offer of amnesty was judged not to be sufficiently positive. Pressed by Hamilton to have federal power show its teeth, Washington announced that the troops would march.

The army was aroused. In particular, the New Jersey militia were ready for lynch law because they had been derided in a western newspaper as a "Water-mellon Army" and an uncomplimentary estimate was made of their military capabilities. The piece was written as a take-off on the kind of negotiations which preceded an Indian treaty. Possibly the idea was suggested by the fact that the Whiskey Boys were often called "White Indians." At any rate, in the satire the Indians admonished the great council in Philadelphia: ". . . Brothers, we have that powerful monarch, Capt. Whiskey, to command us. By the power of his influence, and a love to *his person* we are compelled to every great and heroic act. . . . We, the Six United Nations of White Indians . . . have all imbibed his principles and passions—that is a love of whiskey. . . . Brothers, you must not think to frighten us with . . . infantry, cavalry and artillery, composed of your water-mellon armies from the Jersey shores; they would cut a much better figure in warring with the crabs and oysters about the Capes of Delaware."

Captain Whiskey was answered hotly by "A Jersey Blue." He pointed out that "the water-

mellon army of New Jersey" was going to march westward shortly with "ten-inch howitzers for throwing a species of melon very useful for curing a *gravel occasioned by whiskey!*" The expedition was tagged thereafter as the "Watermelon Army."

The troops moved in two columns under the command of General Henry (Light Horse Harry) Lee, Governor of Virginia. Old Dan Morgan was there and young Meriwether Lewis, five nephews of President Washington, the governors of Pennsylvania and New Jersey, too, and many a veteran blooded in Revolutionary fighting, including the extraordinary German, Captain John Fries of the Bucks County militia, and his remarkable dog to which the Captain gave the name of a beverage he occasionally enjoyed—Whiskey.

The left wing marched west during October, 1794, over General Braddock's old route from Virginia and Maryland to Cumberland on the Potomac, then northwest into Pennsylvania, to join forces with the right wing at Union Town. The Pennsylvania and New Jersey corps proceeded via Norristown and Reading to Harrisburg and Carlisle. There, on October 4th, President Washington arrived, accompanied by Colonel Hamilton. The representatives of the disaffected counties told the President at Carlisle that the army was not needed but Hamilton convinced him that it was. Washington proceeded with the troops as far as Bedford, then returned to Philadelphia for the meeting of Congress. Hamilton ordered a roundup of many of the rebels and personally interrogated the most important ones. Brackenridge, incidentally, came off well in his encounter with Hamilton, who declared that he was satisfied with Brackenridge's conduct.

By the time the expedition had crossed the mountains, the uprising was already coming apart at the seams. David Bradford, who had been excluded from the offer of amnesty, fled to Spanish Louisiana. About two thousand of the best riflemen in the West also left the country, including many a distiller, who loaded his pot still on a pack horse or a keel boat and sought asylum in Kentucky where, hopefully, a man could make "the creature" without giving the public debt a lift.

The punitive army moved forward in glorious autumn weather, raiding chicken coops, consuming prodigious quantities of the commodity which lay at the heart of the controversy. Richard Howell, governor of New Jersey and commander of the right wing, revived the spirits of the Jersey troops by composing a marching song, "Dash to the Mountains, Jersey Blue":

To arms once more, our hero cries,
Sedition lives and order dies;
To peace and ease then bid adieu
And dash to the mountains, Jersey Blue.

Faded diaries, old letters and orderly books preserve something of the gala atmosphere of the expedition. At Trenton a Miss Forman and a Miss Milnor were most amiable. Newton, Pennsylvania, was ticketed as a poor place for hay. At Potts Grove a captain of the cavalry troop got kicked in the shin by his horse. Among the Virginians, Meriwether Lewis enjoyed the martial excitement, wrote to his mother in high spirits of the "mountains of beef and oceans of Whiskey"; sent regards "to all the girls" and announced that he would bring "an Insergiant Girl to se them next fall bearing the title of Mrs. Lewis." If there was such a girl, he soon forgot her.

Yet where there is an army in being there are bound to be unpleasant occurrences. Men were lashed. Quartermasters stole government property. A soldier was ordered to put a Scotch-Irish rebel under guard. In execution of the order, he ran said insurgent through with his bayonet, of which the prisoner died. At Carlisle a dragoon's pistol went off and hit a countryman in the groin; he too died. On November 13, long remembered in many a cabin and stump-clearing as "the dismal night," the Jersey horse captured various citizens whom they described grimly as "the whiskey pole gentry," dragging them out of bed, tying them back to back. The troopers held their prisoners in a damp cellar for twenty-four hours without food or water, before marching them off at gun point to a collection center at Washington, Pennslyvania.

In late November, finding no one to fight, the army turned east again, leaving a volunteer force under General Morgan to conciliate and consolidate the position during the winter. Twenty "Yahoos" were carried back to Philadelphia and paraded by the Philadelphia Horse through the streets of the city with placards marked "Insurrection" attached to their hats, in an odd federalist version of a Roman triumph. The cavalry was composed, as an admirer said, of "young men of the first property of the city," with beautiful mounts, uniforms of the finest blue broadcloth. They held their swords elevated in the right hand while the light flashed from their silver stirrups, martingales and jingling bridles. Stretched over half a mile they came, first two troopers abreast, then a pair of Yahoos, walking; then two more mounted men, and so on.

The army, meditating upon their fatigues and hardships, called for a substantial number of hangings. Samuel Hodgson, Commissary-general of the army, wrote to a Pittsburgh confidant, "We all lament that so few of the insurgents fell—such disorders can only be cured by copious bleedings. . . ." Philip Freneau, friend and literary colleague of Brackenridge, suggested in retrospect—ironically, of course—the benefits which would have accrued to the country "if Washington had drawn and quartered thirty or forty of the whiskey boys." Most of the captives escaped any punishment other than that of being held in jail without a trial for ten or twelve months. One died. Two were finally tried and sentenced to death. Eventually both were let off.

Gradually the bitterness receded. In August, 1794, General Anthony Wayne had crushed the Indians at the Battle of Fallen Timbers. A treaty was concluded with Spain in October, 1795, clearing the Mississippi for Western trade. The movement of the army into the Pennsylvania hinterland, meanwhile, brought with it a flood of cash which furnished the distillers with currency for paying their taxes. These events served to produce a better feeling toward the Union.

If the rising was a failure, so was the liquor tax. The military adventure alone, without ordinary costs of collection, ran up a bill of $1,500,000, or about one third of all the money that was realized during the life of the revenue act. The excise was quietly repealed during Jefferson's administration. Yet the watermelon armies and the Whiskey Boys made a not inconsiderable contribution to our constitutional history. Through them, the year 1794 completed what 1787 had begun; for it established the reality of a federal union whose law was not a suggestion but a command.

■■■

STUDY QUESTIONS

1. How important was whiskey as an agricultural product to western farmers? Why did they so greatly resent the federal government's tax?

2. In what ways did the farmers of western Pennsylvania compare the Whiskey Tax to the actions of the English Parliament during the 1760s and 1770s? How did their own response to the Whiskey Tax resemble the actions of the leaders of the American Revolution in resisting English oppression?

3. Why did the Whiskey Rebellion fail to achieve its goals?

4. Some historians believe President George Washington and Alexander Hamilton overreacted to the Whiskey Rebellion. Do you agree? What was Washington's major objective in organizing an expeditionary force to crush the rebellion?

5. How was the Whiskey Rebellion a test for the new federal government?

BIBLIOGRAPHY

The best survey of the 1790s is John C. Miller, *The Federalist Era, 1789–1801* (1960). Also see Leonard D. White, *The Federalists* (1948). For histories of the two presidential administrations, see Forrest McDonald, *The Presidency of George Washington* (1974) and Ralph Adams Brown, *The Presidency of John Adams* (1975). John C. Miller's biography *Alexander Hamilton* (1959) is excellent. Robert W. Buel, Jr., *Securing the Revolution: Ideology in American Politics, 1789–1815* (1972) deals with the challenges the young nation faced in guaranteeing its survival. For a study of the Whiskey Rebellion, see Leland D. Baldwin, *The Whiskey Rebels* (1939).

THE ADAMS–JEFFERSON CORRESPONDENCE, 1812–1826

Rush Welter

On July 4, 1826, within a few hours of each other, John Adams and Thomas Jefferson died, ending a political and personal relationship which had stretched fifty years, fluctuating between friendship, political rivalry, alienation, and again back to friendship. The two men had seemed so different. Born in New England and shaped intellectually by the philosophical residue of Puritanism, John Adams was a committed man who distrusted human nature and found compromise and accommodation difficult. Jefferson, on the other hand, found compromise easy and preferable to confrontation. With an Enlightenment-based rationalism, he had high hopes for the human race. While Adams had economic values based on the interests of New England's commercial elite, Jefferson's were tied to the landed Virginia aristocracy. In terms of political philosophy, Adams believed in a strong central government willing to subsidize commercial and industrial interests, while Jefferson became an advocate of states' rights and laissez-faire. While Adams became an ardent Federalist, Jefferson emerged as the leading Democratic-Republican.

During the 1770s and early 1780s, the overwhelming challenge of separating the colonies from England and establishing an independent government blurred these differences. Adams and Jefferson were colleagues in revolution. But in the 1790s, with the Revolution receding into history, their differences steadily became more clear. Adams defeated Jefferson for the presidency in 1796, but in 1800 Jefferson got his revenge, expelling Adams from office after only one term. Their friendship died. The silence between them continued until 1812, when they cautiously initiated a correspondence. Over the next fourteen years, they restored their personal relationship, becoming even more intimate than during the Revolution. In "The Adams-Jefferson Correspondence," Rush Welter describes their letters and the opinions they revealed.

"You and I ought not to die before we have explained ourselves to each other" wrote John Adams to his new-old friend, Thomas Jefferson, in July of 1813. For fifteen years, from 1812 to 1826, the "two ancient servants" of the people explained themselves. Each had become in the past a symbolic figure around which partisans rallied; to the comtemporary observer the breach between them in the 1790s must have seemed final, but to these giants living out their days after the passing of the heroic age it was not. Most of their public papers are oriented in the contrasts between them: in political disagreements, in personal quarrels, in controversy over hasty legislation, in arguments which were usually over means rather than ends. But in their correspondence they regained the intimacy which had cooled during their years of national political activity, and the interplay of their minds, reflected in their letters, sums up better than anything else the coincidence of their inmost thoughts.

The reconciliation of 1812 was effected by their mutual friend Benjamin Rush. Adams, with a characteristic mixture of shrewdness and petulance, betrayed that he was ready for it in the famous letter to Rush dated December 25, 1811. After a list of inconsequential symbolic grievances ("Jefferson and Rush were for liberty and straight hair. I thought curled hair was as republican as straight"), he concluded:

I have nothing to say to him, but to wish him an easy journey to heaven, when he goes, which I wish may be delayed, as long as life shall be agreeable to him. And he can have nothing to say to me, but to bid me make haste and be ready. Time and chance, however, or possibly design, may produce ere long a letter between us.

From "The Adams–Jefferson Correspondence, 1812–1826" by Rush Welter in *American Quarterly,* II, Fall 1950, pp. 234–250.

Before Rush could answer, Adams opened the correspondence on New Year's Day, 1812.

It is not possible to understand the letters that followed without recalling something about the principals. John Adams had retired to his Quincy farm to bask in the occasional homage offered him by Massachusetts, and to still the unrest of the proud, lonely soul which had so suffered from the ineptitudes of his outspoken tongue. Now, virtually alone, without an equal to whom he could talk freely, he submerged himself in his books, reading over those which bitter experience had taught him were close to the truth, seeking still to find a writer who could systematize his own impressions, or support them from antiquity. As it had always been, his ideal was that of the just view of man, and it was natural that in the end he should turn to Jefferson to round out his knowledge. As he wrote in 1816, ". . . I am not acquainted with any man on this side of Monticello who can give me any information upon subjects that I am now *analyzing* and *investigating*, if I may be permitted to use the pompous words now in fashion."

The Jefferson to whom he turned was in many ways his antithesis. Jefferson lacked the insistent devotion to "cause" that Adams felt, preferring to avoid many painful issues that he might face the major ones. Without his tolerance, born (as Boorstin shows) of a composite of humility before, and dogma about, the order of nature, the correspondence could never have occurred. Psychologically an optimist where Adams could be one only intellectually, the cultured Virginia gentleman was to fend off many of Adams' most bitter remarks rather than try to answer them. But when in retirement he came to distill his wide-ranging ideas and to extract therefrom the essence, he found that at base they were more frequently similiar to Adams' than different.

The tenor of the letters marks the difference between personalities. Adams' letters are each intended to fill a gap in his knowledge, or to track down a wandering principle and tie it into the whole. Enthusiastically the older man wrote letters whenever struck by an idea, at one time writing eleven to Jefferson's one. Vigorous, with scorching passages relieved by long-winded anecdotes and a fleeting Yankee earthiness of expression, his letters acted as a safety valve until he relaxed in the formality of a felicitous eighteenth-century conclusion. One receives the impression that for him the letters and the friendship were often most important for their forensic opportunities.

Jefferson answered him with all the traditional graciousness of the Virginia aristocrat, and as a result his letters frequently seem overshadowed. Not so deadly serious, he gently pricked Adams' speculative bubbles, and to delight him indulged in his own occasional fanciful dreams. Patiently he answered exacting queries—for instance, what became of the Wollaston who moved to Virginia after founding Merry Mount?—and always his friendship for the "patriarch of Quincy" was more important than the ideas in his letters. His very phrases were, as Adams described them, "sweet simplicity":

And shall you and I, my dear Sir, at our age, like Priam of old, gird on the "arma, diu desueta, trementibus aevo humeris"? *Shall we, at our age, become the Athletae of party, and exhibit ourselves as gladiators in the arena of the newspapers? Nothing in the universe could induce me to it.*

Only rarely could Adams reply in kind, and then self-consciously.

As the participants grew older the letters grew generally briefer and further apart, although the intervals were as irregular and unpredictable as ever. Their ideas flowed only intermittently, most of the letters being merely affirmations of friendship. Jefferson gradually gave up writing, and after January 1819 Adams followed suit because he had to resort to an amanuensis. As a result his later letters are sketchy, hung together by the merest threads, as if to follow the flickerings of his intellect; one can see the irascible grandfather fuming over his incapacity and his dependence on other hands. During the last years, the correspondence was virtually dead,

only occasionally bursting forth fruitfully, and it ended in 1826, as it were, in the middle of a sentence.

One must approach the letters not as systematic treatises but as flashes of wisdom arising from the lurking desire both men felt to search life out on its fundamental terms. In their investigations Adams, although older, almost invariably led the way. For him the problem of man was threefold, and each of the three aspects must be analyzed dispassionately: the nature of man; the civil state of man; and the extent and uses of men's learning. Around these three considerations Adams grouped his other inquiries and concerns: his faith, his personal antipathies, his experience in the past; the nature of revolution, the nature of progress, man's hope for the future. Jefferson, although his ideas were more evanescent and he tended to evade some of the issues, followed the pattern. Focusing on first one and then another problem, together they pushed back the frontiers of their knowledge with all the equipment the eighteenth century possessed.

The Nature of Man

"Know thyself, human Nature," Adams cautioned himself after describing to Jefferson the intolerant attitudes of the trinitarian church-militant in New England. "Man is limited" was the lesson he had learned; limited by two factors, his own nature and external circumstances over which he has no control. Among themselves men are factious, passionate and unreasoning, gullible and self-deceiving, and capable of only limited self-improvement. As to faction, Jefferson had always been in agreement. In answer to Adams' letter concerning the "spiritual tyranny" of churches as the inevitable outcome of factious divisions, he wrote at length describing parties as having existed through all time, ranging on each side individual human beings, each of whom "takes his side in favor of the many, or of the few, according to his constitution, and the circumstances in which he is placed . . ." To both men the world was a battleground; in 1822 Jefferson remarked that ". . . the Cannibals of

Europe are going to eating one another again," and Adams responded with a characteristically farfetched naturalistic analogy, discovering in vinegar and in pepper-water among the "eeels" and "animalcules" the same turmoil which agitated the world.

Eels and animalcules could hardly be given credit for the power of reason, but neither Adams nor Jefferson could discover overwhelming evidence that man used what superior gifts he had. Adams put it in 1817:

[Destutt de Tracy] all along supposes that Men are rational and consciencious Creatures. I say so too; but I say at the Same time that their passions and Interests generally prevail over their Reason and their consciences: and if Society does not contrive some means of contracting and restrain[in]g the former the World will go on as it has done.

The most rational man seldom acts it, and Adams must be given credit for seeing in himself in 1823 the same dangerous conflict between reason and passion: "My old imagination is kindling into a kind of missionary enthusiasm for the cause of the Greeks. . . . But after all they are feelings rather than reasonings." Meanwhile Jefferson, observing the irrational turmoil threatened by the Missouri controversy, came to marvel "What a Bedlamite is man?" For them both there was only the hope that out of bedlam would come a better era—but bedlam must be lived through first.

If man is factious, unreasoning, and fallible even when reasonable, the doctrine of his perfectibility is likely to falter. Adams worried the point, off and on, during the correspondence, and each time Jefferson ignored the thrust. In the end, however, and without significant dissent, Adams succeeded in defining man's potential as an "improvability" which could never attain perfection. To him the millennium was a mockery, no less than a neo-Platonic misuse of the power of reason, a sort of wishful thinking; and as Plato's "disciples" he enlisted Rousseau and Tom Paine! Rather, "Our hopes . . . of sudden tranquillity ought not to be too sanguine." To his own question as to when the hope for perfect freedom might be fulfilled on earth, he finally replied with a direct "never" until man himself reached perfection:

I cannot contemplate human affairs, without laughing or crying. I choose to laugh. When People talk of the Freedom of Writing speaking or thinking, I cannot choose but laugh. No such thing ever existed, no such thing now exists; but I hope it will exist.

Such is the nature of man's self-limiting factors. Even, however, were men to prove completely virtuous in any one country or any one age, the two old men could not believe perfection itself enough. Perhaps this was a reflection of the frustrations of each in dealing with his own countrymen; at any rate they agreed that the times have some effect on men. Adams, proprietor of the estate on which Merry Mount had been established, wrote to Jefferson condemning Thomas Morton for his part in it, yet concluded: "The Character of the Miscreant, however, is not wholly contemptible. It marks the Complextion of the Age in which he lived. How many such Characters could you and I enumerate, who in our times have had a Similar influence on Society!" To him, the "wave" of public opinion had at times swept all before it—into the crusades, into the Reformation, into revolution—and man was incapable of stemming the tide. Jefferson tacitly consented to this interpretation of history in a late letter, asking Adams whether his study of history indicated that Brutus and Cicero could possibly have succeeded in reforming Rome, given only their lifetimes and the state of the empire, and concluded that it was an insoluble "enigma."

But these men had not become determinists; the "wave" was not so irresistible as Adams had said in his exuberance over discovering a word which fitted his sense of history. It is significant, in view of his apparent devotion to classical political theorists, that in several contexts he rejected also the idea that history follows a cyclical pattern; rather, it has an epidemic nature, and he followed the metaphor out: Epidemics can sometimes be cured by man. Jefferson struck

 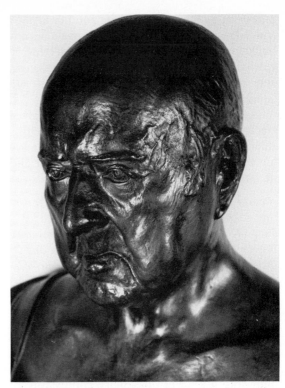

■ ■ ■ *Above are John Browere's 1825 life masks of Thomas Jefferson, 82, and John Adams, 90.*

even closer at the heart of determinism (in the form peculiar to New England) when he caught up a casual remark of Adams, to remind him that Calvinism is "daemonism." Adams had already tried to find his way out; according to his logic at one point, either man controls his destinies or he does not. If he does not, "liberty" has no meaning. In this mood, he stated the balance, and it is clear which alternative he preferred.

When Adams came, as he said, after thirty years of thinking on the subject, to sum up the relative worth of individual men, he opened a discussion with Jefferson which has since become famous. Adams characteristically opened his attack with a categorical statement of the problem: Who are the aristocrats? Who shall choose them—particularly when "birth and wealth together have prevailed over virtue and talents in all ages. The many will acknowledge no other *aristoi.* " Not content with waiting for a reply, he scouted about in his classical authors

until he found in Theognis the summation he wanted, and retranslating him to prove his point (Grotius having distorted the meaning) he challenged Jefferson to disprove it. Another letter put it in a more practical light:

And is this great fact in the natural history of man, this unalterable principle . . . and daily experience from the creation, to be overlooked, forgotten, neglected, or hypocritically waved out of sight, by a legislator, by a professed writer upon civil government[?] . . .

Before Jefferson had time to answer, Adams wrote again to ask him whether he could deny the existence of a "hereditary aristocracy of merino sheep" and an "aristocracy of land-jobbers and stock-jobbers."

In answer, Jefferson refused to meet the point directly. First he questioned Adams as to what Theognis had meant, insisting in his famous letter "For I agree with you that there is a natural aristocracy among men" that a moral aristocracy was meant, to which Adams replied that Theognis' remarks were based primarily in experience and not in ethics. When Jefferson tried to question the fact of ascendancy of birth and wealth, Adams cogently reminded him of a local whispering campaign maligning Mrs. Bowdoin, widow of the well-known New Englander; at the time, people had said that she could not be guilty of bringing disgrace to her name. What was this, but aristocratic feeling in a republic? Jefferson tried to distinguish between a "true" and a "false" aristocracy, exulting that in Virginia the false aristocracy had not survived the laws of entail and primogeniture. Adams remarked that Jefferson's was a distinction without a difference and told him to look again into the history of Virginia as well as Massachusetts for "romances" of the growth of an aristocracy of wealth. Furthermore, he said, a really false aristocracy cannot survive, but one of wealth and birth will, and the question is not what is an aristocrat, but what to do with him. "Your distinction between the *aristoi* and *pseudo-aristoi* will not help the matter. I would trust one as soon as the other with unlimited power."

Adams had borne down Jefferson's air castles under the weight of reality, and all that survived of Jefferson's view was the point that historically the invention of gunpowder had helped destroy what he called "false" aristocracy. Logically, this very fact tended to prove Adams' point, and Adams concluded the discussion: "You suppose a difference of opinion between you and me, on the subject of aristocracy. I can find none." There the matter rested, although he was to return to it indirectly, estimating the total worth of man he had so criticized in a memorable credo:

The vast prospect of mankind, which these books have passed in review before me, from the most ancient records, histories, traditions, and fables that remain to us, to the present day, has sickened my very soul, and almost reconciled me to Swift's travels among the Yahoos. Yet I never can be a misanthrope. Homo sum. I must hate myself before I can hate my fellow-men, and that I cannot and will not do.

Man, by implication in all these letters, is worth saving, true aristocrat or no, and the question of whether he can be answers itself: Why else spend so much time on him? There was no need for explicit statement, but Adams phrased it for both of them: "The question before the human race is, Whether the God of nature shall govern the World by his own laws, or whether Priests and Kings shall rule it by fictitious Miracles?" For "God of nature" read "human nature," as Adams intended, and his dichotomy breaks down; between the extremes of the "Platonic" millennium on the one hand, and determinism on the other, is a realm in which human nature can operate for its own good. "You and I hope for splendid improvements in human society, and vast ameliorations in the condition of mankind. Our faith may be supported by more rational arguments than any of the former." Still, the "improvability" of man did not establish the outlines of Adams' basic triangle: What was the present state of man, from which to work forward; and what was the state of his knowledge, by which to work forward?

The Civil State of Man

Both Jefferson and Adams saw that in the present civil state of man were the roots of the future, and in their views of contemporary events they were in surprisingly close agreement. For both, also, the present was the logical outcome of events in which they had participated, and which could now be looked at in a reflective mood. An admitted devotee of the "maxims" of "history" and "practice," Adams dissected the American past and held it to the clear light of time, examining some of its heroes with considerable bitterness. On John Dickinson's conservative myopia he and Jefferson agreed, and Hamilton, to Adams the "bastard Bratt of a Scotch Pedlar," was no one for whom Jefferson felt inclined to battle. Paine, Jefferson did not mention after Adams' scathing attacks.

When they turned to contemplate the contemporary scene their comments were more analytical but no less striking than Adams' offhand epithets. Despite their own efforts, and those of their successors, the faction Adams and Jefferson worried about continued to run rampant, causing the former to comment in 1813, "There is virtually a white rose and a red rose, a Caesar and a Pompey, in every state in this union, and contests and dissensions will be as lasting." More and more, however, faction was overshadowed by a fundamental cleavage between North and South; the split terrified both Adams and Jefferson. As early as February 1812 Adams observed:

. . . the Prospect of the Future, will depend on the Union: and how is that Union to be preserved [?] . . . Our Union is an immense structure . . . But the first Week, if not the first day of the Debacle would melt all the cement . . .

The War of 1812 brought "terrorism" between the sections; Massachusetts would indulge in a "civil war" in the middle of a national one:

I know not whether we have ever seen any moments more serious than the present. The Northern States are now retaliating, upon the Southern States, their conduct from 1797 to 1800. It is a mortification to me, to see, how servile Mimicks they are.

And as the Missouri question crystallized, the two were in complete agreement. It foreshadowed the possible separation of the states, said Adams in 1819, to which Jefferson shrewdly replied a year later, ". . . it is only the John Doe or the Richard Roe of the ejectment." He had already commented, "I thank God that I shall not live to witness its issue."

With their own union threatening to dissolve around them, what hope could the two old men have for progress in less favored lands? Jefferson, the pragmatist of 1822, was to urge his country to benefit from the quarrels of "the Cannibals of Europe"; the "pugnacious humor of mankind" would properly serve to balance the birth rate in Europe. Adams concurred, but as a matter of fact neither looked at it so simply. As the Napoleonic era waned, to be succeeded by Bourbon reaction and the ascendancy of the Holy Alliance, Jefferson and Adams debated the eddies in European history while agreeing about its main direction; its progress had everywhere been cruelly stopped by the excesses of the French Revolution, and a growing sense of responsibility among the ruling classes wiped out. It was Jefferson who defended Napoleon in 1815 as the only hope of the French as a nation, but the supposed Anglophile Adams who pointed out that England was worse than Napoleon in the struggle.

In their common concern for France, the two overstated the case against England, and elsewhere they admitted to each other that they were worried about her future. Adams offered a discreet hope for the welfare of the "old lady" in 1816, fearing revolution might wipe her out. When, however, Jefferson sought to hold out hope for a democratic reform, Adams dogmatically denied that in its present state England could afford a democratic regime. Power was too deeply entrenched in a small class, and the habits of the people were too undemocratic and factious.

Although they disagreed about England's capacity for democracy, both thought that most of the rest of the world was not ready for it. Partly as a result of their opposition to all forms of Catholic thought, they could not believe that revolutionary Spain or Latin America could establish successful republics. To this proposition Adams adduced his inevitable insistence on their failure to adopt the necessary checks and balances, while at his most optimistic all Jefferson could say was, ". . . I wish, moreover, that our ideas may be erroneous, and theirs prove well founded."

Man's Learning

The present seemed to offer little hope to declining patriots, and it was in a sort of passive withdrawal from the world's problems that the two undertook a sometimes miscellaneous study of learning for its own sake. From the very first their letters were those of seekers after knowledge: Adams sending Jefferson a book; Jefferson critically describing a translation he had recently read; Adams asking a question about the Indians of Virginia; Jefferson wanting to know whether it was in 1774 or 1775 that Dickinson spoke as described. But at the same time their exercises in knowledge were a fundamental part of their mutual outlook, for learning was more than a passion of retirement; it was the third structural key to the future. Despite their discouragements, within the boundaries circumscribing man's powers the two saw a vast area of knowledge which might become useful to him if wisely cultivated.

The problem was to discover which of the many sources of knowledge were reliable. As he had mocked the "millennium" of certain French ideologues like Tracy, so Adams mocked false prophets of every description, eclectically including in one of his letters an attack on the Prophet of the Wabash, Tecumseh's brother. Mocking the "prophets," Adams did not fear their influence so much as that of false systems of thought; to him, the abuse of reason, of which Plato provided the chief example, was willful destruction of the foundations of the future, and of course Platonism was in equal disfavor with Jefferson. Adams was being bitterly satirical when he commented on "systems" which proved the Indians to be the seven lost tribes or the special children of God, "I could make a system too," and proceeded, by false analogy (that is, Platonism), to make several.

Adams and Jefferson investigated each book they read in terms of their search for an undefiled source of knowledge. They tried to root out its "truths" and to slough off its "artificial vestments." Frequently they discovered perversions of the past; some accidental (like a significant mistranslation of *ancien scripture* as "Holy Scripture"), but many intentional, and all corrupting. For Adams the greatest crime of the past was that "the documents are destroyed"—". . . the destruction of the library at Alexandria is all the answer we can obtain to these questions. I believe that Jews, Grecians, Romans and Christians all conspired or connived at that savage catastrophe."

As they extended their knowledge to its limits both men became increasingly aware of their own fallibility as to learning, and by reflection, of the inevitability of fallibility among human beings, however learned. It was a sobering experience for Adams when, in a letter denouncing banks as the source of tyranny, he propounded something he could not understand: Why should Amsterdam, the home of banks, have been the center of European religious liberty and political economy ". . . more honestly practised in that Frog land, than any other country in the World?" Long before, in discussing the origin of the American Indian, he and Jefferson had taken final refuge in an "*Ignoro*," but at that time their ignorance had been more a convention than a philosophical conviction. A month after his query about Amsterdam, Adams declared of the true meaning of "liberty," "Human understanding will never dive in this state of existence to such depths," and in the next year proposed to add to the faculty of Jefferson's university

. . . *Professorships of the Philosophy of the human Understanding—whose object should be to ascertain the Limits of human knowledge already acquired . . . though I suppose you will have doubts of the propriety of setting any limits, or thinking of any limits of human Power, or human Wisdom, or human Virtue.*

But his challenge to Jefferson was a challenge to a straw man, for the latter observed that there were things beyond finite comprehension.

And yet both continued to believe that enough study and reflection on man's total accumulation of learning could unearth the knowledge necessary to his self-improvement. Adams was acutely interested in the founding of the University of Virginia and happily suggested books and courses to Jefferson, who responded with frequent reports on the progress of university bills through the state legislature. The implicit idea, that the function of education is to prepare man for a greater destiny on earth, echoes from one of Adams' earliest letters: "The human Mind is awake," he wrote in 1813. "Let it not sleep. Let it however consider. Let it think, let it pause." In suggesting a curriculum he was to include even writers with whom he could not agree, in the anticipation that the waking, cautious mind might draw added knowledge even from prejudiced writers.

Indeed, knowledge was the strongest reason for optimism about man's future. Because of this, as much as any religious attitude, it was with vehement disapproval that the two educators watched the revival of the Inquisition and the resurgence of Catholicism after the Napoleonic era. "All will depend on the progress of knowledge," wrote Adams in 1816, to which Jefferson added hopefully in later years:

The light which has been shed on mankind by the art of printing, has eminently changed the condition of the world. As yet, that light has dawned on the middling classes only of the men of Europe. The kings and the rabble, of equal ignorance, have not yet received its rays; but it continues to spread, and while printing is preserved, it can no more recede than the sun return on his course.

The Summing-up

Assuming man's "improvability," without relying on a deterministic philosophy, it was still necessary to find a way of effecting change in the face of vested interests. In their own past, the American Revolution seemed to Adams and Jefferson to have been a supremely natural way of engineering change, and although both tried occasionally to get behind the superficial incidents and discuss the basic events in its progress, they assumed that its methods had been both necessary and successful. But in spite of Jefferson's celebrated theory of successive revolutionary generations, revolution as a creed no longer appealed to either of them; for example, they agreed in retrospect that the French Revolution had been at best ill conceived. To Adams, the worst thing that could be said of revolution was that it tended to become a gross "ideology," as

misleading as any millennial expectation, or for that matter any hope that Catholic peoples could become democrats. In the minds of both men there was an insecure balance between revolutionary and peaceful change; at best they could only "hope" that other revolutions might work out.

Their failure to set up any vehicle for radical change necessarily made impossible any systematic idea of how man might shape the future. Social progress was possible, and by some alchemy therefore probable, but that was virtually all. Lacking an "ideology" the patriarchs tended to leave the problems they stated to solution by younger men, and in the end, as their letters show, the times passed them by. Their early formal protests that they had retired from the world became comfortable convictions. To resign oneself to the feeling that every fact is an imponderable became the easier way out, and in the surrender Jefferson led:

You see, my dear Sir, how easily we prescribe for others a cure for their difficulties, while we cannot cure our own. We must leave both, I believe, to heaven, and wrap ourselves up in the mantle of resignation, and of that friendship of which I tender to you the most sincere assurances.

He supplemented this later in 1821: "Yet I will not believe our labors are lost. I shall not die without a hope that light and liberty are on steady advance." It was now mainly a matter of wish rather than conviction, and the creed had become as "scanty" as Adams had once called Priestley's Unitarianism.

The last four letters are in a sense a summing-up. Adams, hearing of Jefferson's willingness "to go again over the scenes of past life," said he chose to die forever. Jefferson answered in his own defense, "And why not? . . . Why not then taste them again, fat and lean together[?]" Unanswered, he wrote to introduce Thomas Jefferson Randolph:

Like other young people he wishes to be able in the winter nights of old age to recount to those around him what he has heard and learnt of the Heroic age preceding his birth, and which of the Argonauts individually he was in time to have seen.

To these last letters of Jefferson, with their rather soft optimism, Adams' reply is a counterbalance. Virtually his last words were: "Public affairs go on pretty much as usual, perpetual chicanery and rather more personal abuse than there used to be . . ."

Yet, with the aged personalities which they convey, the last letters contain little of the vitality of the earlier, and the lasting quality of the correspondence is independent of the phase of easy resignation. That lasting quality is epitomized in what one might anticipate as an "Emersonian" strain—an unsystematic affirmation, an exuberance and earthiness combined, an assumption the Americans are chosen people. There are grounds for the analogy in the language itself. Witness Jefferson's dictum in 1821:

In short, the flames kindled on the 4th of July, 1776, have spread over too much of the globe, to be extinguished by the feeble engines of despotism; on the contrary, they will consume these engines and all who work them,

and Adams' "A few American steam boats and our Quincy stone cutters would soon make the Nile as navigable as our Hudson, Potomac, or Mississippi." Succinctly and concretely in such phrases both men had stated the buoyant optimism and faith in America that has characterized the longest traditions of American thought. The future belonged in 1826, as in 1776, to those who made it their own.

■■■

STUDY QUESTIONS

1. How would you compare the personality of John Adams with that of Thomas Jefferson? How might personality differences have affected their political careers and the degeneration of their friendship?

2. From the points of view expressed in the correspondence, what were the major differences in political philosophy between the two men?

3. The author implies that as a result of their correspondence between 1812 and 1826, Adams and Jefferson discovered that they had much in common. What exactly did they have in common? Why, for so long, did their differences overpower their similarities?

BIBLIOGRAPHY

For general discussions of the 1790s and early 1800s, when the two-party system emerged, see John C. Miller, *The Federalist Era, 1789–1801* (1960) and Marshall Smelser, *The Democratic Republic, 1801–1815* (1968). The standard biography of Thomas Jefferson is Dumas Malone's *Jefferson and His Times* (5 vols., 1948–1974). For a shorter, more manageable biography, see Merrill D. Peterson, *Thomas Jefferson and the New Nation: A Biography* (1970). On John Adams, see Page Smith, *John Adams* (2 vols., 1960) and S. G. Kurtz, *The Presidency of John Adams* (1957).

Part Four

ADJUSTING TO AMERICA

The nineteenth century was a time of extraordinary social and economic upheaval in the Western world, even though the historic forces at work were subtle and evolutionary in their impact. For a number of reasons—the absence of war in Europe after the Napoleonic era, improved sanitation and public health, the smallpox vaccine, and the dissemination of the potato and mass-produced grains —population growth was extraordinary. The European population exploded from 140 million people in 1750, to 260 million in 1850, to 400 million in 1914. Farm sizes dwindled, and younger sons and laborers began moving to cities to look for work. The industrial economy was also changing, destroying home production in favor of mass-produced factory goods. Traditional village lifestyles were altered forever. The Atlantic economy was slowly integrating America and Western Europe.

In the United States, a tremendous demand for labor attracted millions of those European peasants. Rapid industrialization, unprecedented economic growth, tremendous population increases, and steady expansion into the western territories created a dynamic society. At the same time, more and more workers were moving into the great American cities to work on the assembly lines. Never before in human history had the way people made their livings undergone more dramatic change.

Within that larger economy, there were many distinct cultures of people trying to cope with the changes around them. Minority groups were especially vulnerable to social and economic change because they usually had little political power to control the forces affecting their lives. In the South, millions of black slaves were managing to develop a unique Afro-American culture that sustained them emotionally amidst gross discrimination and exploitation. They substituted cultural vitality for political power and succeeded in surviving psychologically and ordering their lives. In the Southwest, acquired from Mexico in 1848, perhaps 80,000 Hispanics were engaged in a similar struggle, frustrated about being under Anglo power and struggling to retain their land and culture. Throughout the United States, women too were trying to cope with changing circumstances. People, confused by the social changes accompanying the Industrial Revolution, tried to preserve a sense of the mythical past by creating a "cult of domesticity" for women. In addition, hundreds of thousands of Native Americans were finding their way of life incompatible with the growth-oriented, materialistic economy of industrial America. For all these people, the changing nature of American society was an extraordinary challenge, one that required adjustment and accommodation.

THE CULT OF
TRUE WOMANHOOD:
1820–1860

Barbara Welter

In a recent interview with the Public Broadcasting System, American feminist Gloria Steinem was asked if her opinions about the women's movement had changed at all in the last twenty years. After reflecting for a moment, she remarked that over the years she had become increasingly aware that the problem of sexism was rooted more deeply than she had first assumed. One look at public policy debates in the United States during the 1980s confirms her belief. Most of the major domestic public policy questions in the United States today directly involve the place of women in the society: wage discrimination, affirmative action and promotion, abortion and freedom of choice, Social Security and retirement benefits, child care, the Equal Rights Amendment, pornography and censorship, rape and sexual abuse, insurance and annuity rate differentials, divorce and child support, poverty and welfare, and gay rights. Virtually all of these problems have their roots in the sexual stereotyping so common in American culture. This sexual stereotyping is a residue from before the industrial and even modern eras when divisions of labor in society were directly tied to pregnancy, birthing, nursing, and child-rearing. Although the economic institutions dictating such divisions of labor are rapidly disappearing in modern society, the sexual stereotypes have lives of their own, continuing to shape public expectations of men and women.

In "The Cult of True Womanhood, 1820–1860," historian Barbara Welter looks at the antebellum decades of the nineteenth century and describes an important stage in the public expression of sexual sterotypes. By making virtues of domesticity, submissiveness, passivity, and chastity for women, and leaving men free to exhibit a much wider range of behaviors, American culture hoped to promote industrialization while preserving some semblance of premodern values. The irony, of couse, was that the relevance of the "cult of womanhood" declined in direct proportion to the pace of industrialization. Women gradually became confined to an increasingly unreal world of impossible expectations; the underside of domesticity and submissiveness, for many women, was anger, guilt, and extraordinary frustration. Even after the ratification of the Nineteenth Amendment in 1920, the "cult of womanhood" still influenced American attitudes, and the modern feminist movement had to turn its attention to changing those attitudes as a prerequisite to the realization of freedom and equality for both sexes.

The nineteenth-century American man was a busy builder of bridges and railroads, at work long hours in a materialistic society. The religious values of his forebears were neglected in practice if not in intent, and he occasionally felt some guilt that he had turned this new land, this temple of the chosen people, into one vast countinghouse. But he could salve his conscience by reflecting that he had left behind a hostage, not only to fortune, but to all the values which he held so dear and treated so lightly. Woman, in the cult of True Womanhood presented by the women's magazines, gift annuals and religious literature of the nineteenth century, was the hostage in the home. In a society where values changed frequently, where fortunes rose and fell with frightening rapidity, where social and economic mobility provided instability as well as hope, one thing at least remained the same—a true woman was a true woman, wherever she was found. If anyone, male or female, dared to tamper with the complex of virtues which made up True Womanhood, he was damned immediately as an enemy of God, of civilization and of the Republic. It was a fearful obligation, a solemn responsibility, which the nineteenth-century American woman had—to uphold the pillars of the temple with her frail white hand.

The attributes of True Womanhood, by which a woman judged herself and was judged by her husband, her neighbors and society could be divided into four cardinal virtues—piety, purity, submissiveness and domesticity. Put them all together and they spelled mother, daughter, sister, wife—woman. Without them, no matter whether there was fame, achievement or wealth, all was ashes. With them she was promised happiness and power.

"The Cult of True Womanhood: 1820–1860" by Barbara Welter from *American Quarterly*, XVIII, Summer 1966, pp. 151–174. Published by the American Studies Association. Copyright © 1966. Reprinted by permission of American Quarterly and the author.

Religion or piety was the core of woman's virtue, the source of her strength. Young men looking for a mate were cautioned to search first for piety, for if that were there, all else would follow. Religion belonged to woman by divine right, a gift of God and nature. This "peculiar susceptibility" to religion was given her for a reason: "the vestal flame of piety, lighted up by Heaven in the breast of woman" would throw its beams into the naughty world of men. So far would its candle power reach that the "Universe might be Enlightened, Improved, and Harmonized by WOMAN!!" She would be another, better, Eve, working in cooperation with the Redeemer, bringing the world back "from its revolt and sin." The world would be reclaimed for God through her suffering, for "God increased the cares and sorrows of woman, that she might be sooner constrained to accept the terms of salvation." A popular poem by Mrs. Frances Osgood, "The Triumph of the Spiritual Over the Sensual" expressed just this sentiment, woman's purifying passionless love bringing an erring man back to Christ.

Dr. Charles Meigs, explaining to a graduating class of medical students why women were naturally religious, said that "hers is a pious mind. Her confiding nature leads her more readily than men to accept the proffered grace of the Gospel." Caleb Atwater, Esq., writing in *The Ladies' Repository,* saw the hand of the Lord in female piety: "Religion is exactly what a woman needs, for it gives her that dignity that best suits her dependence." And Mrs. John Sandford, who had no very high opinion of her sex, agreed throughly: "Religion is just what woman needs. Without it she is ever restless or unhappy. . . ." Mrs. Sandford and the others did not speak only of that restlessness of the human heart, which St. Augustine notes, that can only find its peace in God. They spoke rather of religion as a kind of tranquilizer for the many undefined longings which swept even the most pious young girl, and about which it was better to pray than to think.

One reason religion was valued was that it did

not take a woman away from her "proper sphere," her home. Unlike participation in other societies or movements, church work would not make her less domestic or submissive, less a True Woman. In religious vineyards, said the *Young Ladies' Literary and Missionary Report,* "you may labor without the apprehension of detracting from the charms of feminine delicacy." Mrs. S. L. Dagg, writing from her chapter of the Society in Tuscaloosa, Alabama, was equally reassuring: "As no sensible woman will suffer her intellectual pursuits to clash with her domestic duties" she should concentrate on religious work "which promotes these very duties."

The women's seminaries aimed at aiding women to be religious, as well as accomplished. Mt. Holyoke's catalogue promised to make female education "a handmaid to the Gospel and an efficient auxiliary in the great task of renovating the world." The Young Ladies' Seminary at Bordentown, New Jersey, declared its most important function to be "the forming of a sound and virtuous character." In Keene, New Hampshire, the Seminary tried to instill a "consistent and useful character" in its students, to enable them in this life to be "a good friend, wife and mother" but more important, to qualify them for "the enjoyment of Celestial Happiness in the life to come." And Joseph M. D. Mathews, Principal of Oakland Female Seminary in Hillsborough, Ohio, believed that "female education should be preeminently religious."

If religion was so vital to a woman, irreligion was almost too awful to contemplate. Women were warned not to let their literary or intellectual pursuits take them away from God. Sarah Josepha Hale spoke darkly of those who, like Margaret Fuller, threw away the "One True Book" for others, open to error. Mrs. Hale used the unfortunate Miss Fuller as fateful proof that "the greater the intellectual force, the greater and more fatal the errors into which women fall who wander from the Rock of Salvation, Christ the Saviour. . . ."

One gentleman, writing on "Female Irreligion" reminded his readers that "Man may make himself a brute, and does so very often, but can woman bruitfy herself to his level—the lowest level of human nature—without exerting special wonder?" Fanny Wright, because she was godless, "was no woman, mother though she be." A few years ago, he recalls, such women would have been whipped. In any case, "woman never looks lovelier than in her reverence for religion" and, conversely, "female irreligion is the most revolting feature in human character."

Purity was as essential as piety to a young woman, its absence as unnatural and unfeminine. Without it she was, in fact, no woman at all, but a member of some lower order. A "fallen woman" was a "fallen angel," unworthy of the celestial company of her sex. To contemplate the loss of purity brought tears; to be guilty of such a crime, in the women's magazines at least, brought madness or death. Even the language of the flowers had bitter words for it: a dried white rose symbolized "Death Preferable to Loss of Innocence." The marriage night was the single great event of a woman's life, when she bestowed her greatest treasure upon her husband, and from that time on was completely dependent upon him, an empty vessel, without legal or emotional existence of her own.

Therefore all True Women were urged, in the strongest possible terms, to maintain their virtue, although men, being by nature more sensual than they, would try to assault it. Thomas Branagan admitted in *The Excellency of the Female Character Vindicated* that his sex would sin and sin again, they could not help it, but woman, stronger and purer, must not give in and let man "take liberties incompatible with her delicacy." "If you do," Branagan addressed his gentle reader, "You will be left in silent sadness to bewail your credulity, imbecility, duplicity, and premature prostitution."

Mrs. Eliza Farrar, in *The Young Lady's Friend,* gave practical logistics to avoid trouble: "Sit not with another in a place that is too narrow; read not out of the same book; let not your eagerness to see anything induce you to place your head close to another person's."

If such good advice was ignored the consequences were terrible and inexorable. In *Girlhood and Womanhood: Or Sketches of My Schoolmates,* by Mrs. A. J. Graves (a kind of mid-nineteenth-century *The Group*), the bad ends of a boarding school class of girls are scrupulously recorded. The worst end of all is reserved for "Amelia Dorrington: The Lost One." Amelia died in the almshouse "the wretched victim of depravity and intemperance" and all because her mother had let her be "high-spirited not prudent." These girlish high spirits had been misinterpreted by a young man, with disastrous results. Amelia's "thoughtless levity" was "followed by a total loss of virtuous principle" and Mrs. Graves editorializes that "the coldest reserve is more admirable in a woman a man wishes to make his wife, than the least approach to undue familiarity."

A popular and often-reprinted story by Fanny Forester told the sad tale of "Lucy Dutton." Lucy "with the seal of innocence upon her heart, and a rose-leaf on her cheek" came out of her vine-covered cottage and ran into a city slicker. "And Lucy was beautiful and trusting, and thoughtless: and he was gay, selfish and profligate. Needs the story to be told? . . . Nay, censor, Lucy was a child—consider how young, how very untaught—oh! her innocence was no match for the sophistry of a gay, city youth! Spring came and shame was stamped upon the cottage at the foot of the hill." The baby died; Lucy went mad at the funeral and finally died herself. "Poor, poor Lucy Dutton! The grave is a blessed couch and pillow to the wretched. Rest thee there, poor Lucy!" The frequency with which derangement follows loss of virtue suggests the exquisite sensibility of woman, and the possibility that, in the women's magazines at least, her intellect was geared to her hymen, not her brain.

If, however, a woman managed to withstand man's assaults on her virtue, she demonstrated her superiority and her power over him. Eliza Farnham, trying to prove this female superiority, concluded smugly that "the purity of women is the everlasting barrier against which the tides of man's sensual nature surge."

A story in *The Lady's Amaranth* illustrates this dominance. It is set, improbably, in Sicily, where two lovers, Bianca and Tebaldo, have been separated because her family insisted she marry a rich old man. By some strange circumstance the two are in a shipwreck and cast on a desert island, the only survivors. Even here, however, the rigid standards of True Womanhood prevail. Tebaldo unfortunately forgets himself slightly, so that Bianca must warn him: "We may not indeed gratify our fondness by caresses, but it is still something to bestow our kindest language, and looks and prayers, and all lawful and honest attentions on each other." Something, perhaps, but not enough, and Bianca must further remonstrate: "It is true that another man is my husband, but you are my guardian angel." When even that does not work she says in a voice of sweet reason, passive and proper to the end, that she wishes he wouldn't but "still, if you insist, I will become what you wish; but I beseech you to consider, ere that decision, that debasement which I must suffer in your esteem." This appeal to his own double standards holds the beast in him at bay. They are rescued, discover that the old husband is dead, and after "mourning a decent season" Bianca finally gives in, legally.

Men could be counted on to be grateful when women thus saved them from themselves. William Alcott, guiding young men in their relations with the opposite sex, told them that "Nothing is better calculated to preserve a young man from contamination of low pleasures and pursuits than frequent intercourse with the more refined and virtuous of the other sex." And he added, one assumes in equal innocence, that youths should "observe and learn to admire, that purity and ignorance of evil which is the characteristic of well-educated young ladies, and which, when we are near them, raises us above those sordid and sensual considerations which hold such sway over men in their intercourse with each other."

The Rev. Jonathan F. Stearns was also impressed by female chastity in the face of male passion, and warned woman never to compromise the source of her power: "Let her lay aside delicacy, and her influence over our sex is gone."

Women themselves accepted, with pride but suitable modesty, this priceless virtue. *The Ladies' Wreath,* in "Woman the Creature of God and the Manufacturer of Society" saw purity as her greatest gift and chief means of discharging her duty to save the world: "Purity is the highest beauty—the true pole-star which is to guide humanity aright in its long, varied, and perilous voyage."

Sometimes, however, a woman did not see the dangers to her treasure. In that case, they must be pointed out to her, usually by a male. In the nineteenth century any form of social change was tantamount to an attack on woman's virtue, if only it was correctly understood. For example, dress reform seemed innocuous enough and the bloomers worn by the lady of that name and her followers were certainly modest attire. Such was the reasoning only of the ignorant. In another issue of *The Ladies' Wreath* a young lady is represented in dialogue with her "Professor." The girl expresses admiration for the bloomer costume—it gives freedom of motion, is healthful and attractive. The "Professor" sets her straight. Trousers, he explains, are "only one of the many manifestations of that wild spirit of socialism and agrarian radicalism which is at present so rife in our land." The young lady recants immediately: "If this dress has any connexion with Fourierism or Socialism, or fanaticism in any shape whatever, I have no disposition to wear it at all . . . no true woman would so far compromise her delicacy as to espouse, however unwittingly, such a cause."

America could boast that her daughters were particularly innocent. In a poem on "The American Girl" the author wrote proudly:

Her eye of light is the diamond bright,
Her innocence the pearl,
And these are ever the bridal gems
That are worn by the American girl.

Lydia Maria Child, giving advice to mothers, aimed at preserving that spirit of innocence. She regretted that "want of confidence between mothers and daughters on delicate subjects" and

suggested a woman tell her daughter a few facts when she reached the age of twelve to "set her mind at rest." Then Mrs. Child confidently hoped that a young lady's "instinctive modesty" would "prevent her from dwelling on the information until she was called upon to use it." In the same vein, a book of advice to the newly-married was titled *Whisper to a Bride.* As far as intimate information was concerned, there was no need to whisper, since the book contained none at all.

A masculine summary of this virtue was expressed in a poem "Female Charms":

I would have her as pure as the snow on the
mount—
As true as the smile that to infamy's given—
As pure as the wave of the crystalline fount,
Yet as warm in the heart as the sunlight of
heaven.
With a mind cultivated, not boastingly wise,
I could gaze on such beauty, with exquisite
bliss;
With her heart on her lips and her soul in her
eyes—
What more could I wish in dear woman than
this.

Man might, in fact, ask no more than this in woman, but she was beginning to ask more of herself, and in the asking was threatening the third powerful and necessary virtue, submission. Purity, considered as a moral imperative, set up a dilemma which was hard to resolve. Woman must preserve her virtue until marriage and marriage was necessary for her happiness. Yet marriage was, literally, an end to innocence. She was told not to question this dilemma, but simply to accept it.

Submission was perhaps the most feminine virtue expected of women. Men were supposed to be religious, although they rarely had time for it, and supposed to be pure, although it came awfully hard to them, but men were the movers, the doers, the actors. Women were the passive, submissive responders. The order of dialogue was, of course, fixed in Heaven. Man was "woman's superior by God's appointment, if not in intellectual dowry, at least by official decree." Therefore, as Charles Elliott argued in *The Ladies' Respository*, she should submit to him "for the sake of good order at least." In *The Ladies Companion* a young wife was quoted approvingly as saying that she did not think woman should "feel and act for herself" because "When, next to God, her husband is not the tribunal to which her heart and intellect appeals—the golden bowl of affection is broken." Women were warned that if they tampered with this quality they tampered with the order of the Universe.

The Young Lady's Book summarized the necessity of the passive virtues in its readers' lives: "It is, however, certain, that in whatever situation of life a woman is placed from her cradle to her grave, a spirit of obedience and submission, pliability of temper, and humility of mind, are required from her."

Woman understood her position if she was the right kind of woman, a true woman. "She feels herself weak and timid. She needs a protector," declared George Burnap, in his lectures on *The Sphere and Duties of Woman*. "She is in a measure dependent. She asks for wisdom, constancy, firmness, perseverance, and she is willing to repay it all by the surrender of the full treasure of her affections. Woman despises in man every thing like herself except a tender heart. It is enough that she is effeminate and weak; she does not want another like herself." Or put even more strongly by Mrs. Sandford: "A really sensible woman feels her dependence. She does what she can, but she is conscious of inferiority, and therefore grateful for support."

Mrs. Sigourney, however, assured young ladies that although they were separate, they were equal. This difference of the sexes did not imply inferiority, for it was part of that same order of Nature established by Him "who bids the oak brave the fury of the tempest, and the alpine flower lean its cheek on the bosom of eternal snows." Dr. Meigs had a different analogy to make the same point, contrasting the anatomy of the Apollo of the Belvedere (illustrating the male principle) with the Venus de Medici (illustrating the female principle). "Woman," said the physician, with a kind of clinical gallantry, "has a head almost too small for intellect but just big enough for love."

This love itself was to be passive and responsive. "Love, in the heart of a woman," wrote Mrs. Farrar, "should partake largely of the nature of gratitude. She should love, because she is already loved by one deserving her regard."

Woman was to work in silence, unseen, like Wordsworth's Lucy. Yet, "working like nature, in secret" her love goes forth to the world "to regulate its pulsation, and send forth from its heart, in pure and temperate flow, the life-giving current." She was to work only for pure affection, without thought of money or ambition. A poem, "Woman and Fame," by Felicia Hemans, widely quoted in many of the gift books, concludes with a spirited renunciation of the gift of fame:

Away! to me, a woman, bring
Sweet flowers from affection's spring.

"True feminine genius," said Grace Greenwood (Sara Jane Clarke) "is ever timid, doubtful, and clingingly dependent; a perpetual childhood." And she advised literary ladies in an essay on "The Intellectual Woman"—"Don't trample on the flowers while longing for the stars." A wife who submerged her own talents to work for her husband was extolled as an example of a true woman. In *Women of Worth: A Book for Girls*, Mrs. Ann Flaxman, an artist of promise herself, was praised because she "devoted herself to sustain her husband's genius and aid him in his arduous career."

Caroline Gilman's advice to the bride aimed at establishing this proper order from the beginning of a marriage: "Oh, young and lovely bride, watch well the first moments when your will conflicts with his to whom God and society have given the control. Reverence his *wishes* even when you do not his *opinions*."

Mrs. Gilman's perfect wife in *Recollections of a Southern Matron* realizes that "the three golden

■■ *Domesticity was a virtue and the true woman stayed at home to serve her family.*

threads with which domestic happiness is woven'' are ''to repress a harsh answer, to confess a fault, and to stop (right or wrong) in the midst of self-defense, in gentle submission.'' Woman could do this, hard though it was, because in her heart she knew she was right and so could afford to be forgiving, even a trifle condescending. ''Men are not unreasonable,'' averred Mrs. Gilman. ''Their difficulties lie in not understanding the moral and physical nature of our sex. They often wound through ignorance, and are surprised at having offended.'' Wives were advised to do their best to reform men, but if they couldn't, to give up gracefully. ''If any habit of his annoyed me, I spoke of it once or twice, calmly, then bore it quietly.''

A wife should occupy herself ''only with domestic affairs—wait till your husband con-

fides to you those of a high importance—and do not give your advice until he asks for it,'' advised the *Lady's Token.* At all times she should behave in a manner becoming a woman, who had ''no arms other than gentleness.'' Thus ''if he is abusive, never retort.'' *A Young Lady's Guide to the Harmonious Development of a Christian Character* suggested that females should ''become as little children'' and ''avoid a controversial spirit.'' *The Mother's Assistant and Young Lady's Friend* listed ''Always Conciliate'' as its first commandment in ''Rules for Conjugal and Domestic Happiness.'' Small wonder that these same rules ended with the succinct maxim: ''Do not expect too much.''

As mother, as well as wife, woman was required to submit to fortune. In *Letters to Mothers* Mrs. Sigourney sighed: ''To bear the evils and sorrows which may be appointed us, with a patient mind, should be the continual effort of our sex. . . . It seems, indeed, to be expected of us; since the passive and enduring virtues are more immediately within our province." Of these trials "the hardest was to bear the loss of children with submission" but the indomitable Mrs. Sigourney found strength to murmur to the bereaved mother: "The Lord loveth a cheerful giver." *The Ladies' Parlor Companion* agreed thoroughly in "A Submissive Mother," in which a mother who had already buried two children and was nursing a dying baby saw her sole remaining child "probably scalded to death. Handing over the infant to die in the arms of a friend, she bowed in sweet submission to the double stroke." But the child "through the goodness of God survived, and the mother learned to say 'Thy will be done.' "

Woman then, in all her roles, accepted submission as her lot. It was a lot she had not chosen or deserved. As *Godey's* said, "the lesson of submission is forced upon woman." Without comment or criticism the writer affirms that "To suffer and to be silent under suffering seems the great command she has to obey." George Burnap referred to a woman's life as "a series of suppressed emotions." She was, as Emerson said, "more vulnerable, more infirm, more mortal than man." The death of a beautiful woman, cherished in fiction, represented woman as the innocent victim, suffering without sin, too pure and good for this world but too weak and passive to resist its evil forces. The best refuge for such a delicate creature was the warmth and safety of her home.

The true woman's place was unquestionably by her own fireside—as daughter, sister, but most of all as wife and mother. Therefore domesticity was among the virtues most prized by the women's magazines. "As society is constituted," wrote Mrs. S. E. Farley, on the "Domestic and Social Claims on Woman," "the true dignity and beauty of the female character seem to consist in a right understanding and faithful and cheerful performance of social and family duties." Sacred

Scripture re-enforced social pressure: "St. Paul knew what was best for women when he advised them to be domestic," said Mrs. Sandford. "There is composure at home; there is something sedative in the duties which home involves. It affords security not only from the world, but from delusions and errors of every kind."

From her home woman performed her great task of bringing men back to God. *The Young Ladies' Class Book* was sure that "the domestic fireside is the great guardian of society against the excesses of human passions." *The Lady at Home* expressed its convictions in its very title and concluded that "even if we cannot reform the world in a moment, we can begin the work by reforming ourselves and our households—It is woman's mission. Let her not look away from her own little family circle for the means of producing moral and social reforms, but begin at home."

Home was supposed to be a cheerful place, so that brothers, husbands and sons would not go elsewhere in search of a good time. Woman was expected to dispense comfort and cheer. In writing the biography of Margaret Mercer (every inch a true woman) her biographer (male) notes: "She never forgot that it is the peculiar province of woman to minister to the comfort, and promote the happiness, first, of those most nearly allied to her, and then of those, who by the Providence of God are placed in a state of dependence upon her." Many other essays in the women's journals showed woman as comforter: "Woman, Man's Best Friend," "Woman, the Greatest Social Benefit," "Woman, A Being to Come Home To," "The Wife: Source of Comfort and the Spring of Joy."

One of the most important functions of woman as comforter was her role as nurse. Her own health was probably, although regrettably, delicate. Many homes had "little sufferers," those pale children who wasted away to saintly deaths. And there were enough other illnesses of youth and age, major and minor, to give the nineteenth-century American woman nursing experience. The sickroom called for the exercise of her higher qualities of patience, mercy and gentleness as well as for her housewifely arts. She could thus fulfill her dual feminine function—beauty and usefulness.

The cookbooks of the period offer formulas for gout cordials, ointment for sore nipples, hiccough and cough remedies, opening pills and refreshing drinks for fever, along with recipes for pound cake, jumbles, stewed calves head and currant wine. *The Ladies' New Book of Cookery* believed that "food prepared by the kind hand of a wife, mother, sister, friend" tasted better and had a "restorative power which money cannot purchase."

A chapter of *The Young Lady's Friend* was devoted to woman's privilege as "ministering spirit at the couch of the sick." Mrs. Farrar advised a soft voice, gentle and clean hands, and a cheerful smile. She also cautioned against an excess of female delicacy. That was all right for a young lady in the parlor, but not for bedside manners. Leeches, for example, were to be regarded as "a curious piece of mechanism . . . their ornamental stripes should recommend them even to the eye, and their valuable services to our feelings." And she went on calmly to discuss their use. Nor were women to shrink from medical terminology, since "If you cultivate right views of the wonderful structure of the body, you will be as willing to speak to a physician of the bowels as the brains of your patient."

Nursing the sick, particularly sick males, not only made a woman feel useful and accomplished, but increased her influence. In a piece of heavy-handed humor in *Godey's* a man confessed that some women were only happy when their husbands were ailing that they might have the joy of nursing him to recovery "thus gratifying their medical vanity and their love of power by making him more dependent upon them." In a similar vein a husband sometimes suspected his wife "almost wishes me dead—for the pleasure of being utterly inconsolable."

In the home women were not only the high-

est adornment of civilization, but they were supposed to keep busy at morally uplifting tasks. Fortunately most of housework, if looked at in true womanly fashion, could be regarded as uplifting. Mrs. Sigourney extolled its virtues: "The science of housekeeping affords exercise for the judgment and energy, ready recollection, and patient self-possession, that are the characteristics of a superior mind." According to Mrs. Farrar, making beds was good exercise, the repetitiveness of routine tasks inculcated patience and perseverance, and proper management of the home was a surprisingly complex art: "There is more to be learned about pouring out tea and coffee than most young ladies are willing to believe." Godey's went so far as to suggest coyly, in "Learning vs. Housewifery" that the two were complementary, not opposed: chemistry could be utilized in cooking, geometry in dividing cloth, and phrenology in discovering talent in children.

Women were to master every variety of needlework, for, as Mrs. Sigourney pointed out, "Needle-work, in all its forms of use, elegance, and ornament, has ever been the appropriate occupation of woman." Embroidery improved taste; knitting promoted serenity and economy. Other forms of artsy-craftsy activity for her leisure moments included painting on glass or velvet, Poonah work, tussy-mussy frames for her own needlepoint or water colors, stands for hyacinths, hair bracelets or baskets of feathers.

She was expected to have a special affinity for flowers. To the editors of *The Lady's Token* "A Woman never appears more truly in her sphere, than when she divides her time between her domestic avocations and the culture of flowers." She could write letters, an activity particularly feminine since it had to do with the outpourings of the heart, or practice her drawingroom skills of singing and playing an instrument. She might even read.

Here she faced a bewildering array of advice. The female was dangerously addicted to novels, according to the literature of the period. She should avoid them, since they interfered with "serious piety." If she simply couldn't help herself and read them anyway, she should choose edifying ones from lists of morally acceptable authors. She should study history since it "showed the depravity of the human heart and the evil nature of sin." On the whole, "religious biography was best."

The women's magazines themselves could be read without any loss of concern for the home. *Godey's* promised the husband that he would find his wife "no less assiduous for his reception, or less sincere in welcoming his return" as a result of reading their magazine. *The Lily of the Valley* won its right to be admitted to the boudoir by confessing that it was "like its namesake humble and unostentatious, but it is yet pure, and, we trust, free from moral imperfections."

No matter what later authorities claimed, the nineteenth century knew that girls *could* be ruined by book. The seduction stories regard "exciting and dangerous books" as contributory causes of disaster. The man without honorable intentions always provides the innocent maiden with such books as a prelude to his assault on her virtue. Books which attacked or seemed to attack woman's accepted place in society were regarded as equally dangerous. A reviewer of Harriet Martineau's *Society in America* wanted it kept out of the hands of American women. They were so susceptible to persuasion, with their "gentle yielding natures" that they might listen to "the bold ravings of the hard-featured of their own sex." The frightening result: "such reading will unsettle them for their true station and pursuits, and they will throw the world back again into confusion."

The debate over women's education posed the question of whether a "finished" education detracted from the practice of housewifely arts. Again it proved to be a case of semantics, for a true woman's education was never "finished" until she was instructed in the gentle science of homemaking. Helen Irving, writing on "Literary Women," made it very clear that if women invoked the muse, it was as a genie of the household lamp. "If the necessities of her position require these duties at her hands, she will perform them nonetheless cheerfully, that she knows herself capable of higher things." The literary woman must conform to the same standards as any other woman: "That her home shall be made a loving place of rest and joy and comfort for those who are dear to her, will be the first wish of every true woman's heart." Mrs. Ann Stephens told women who wrote to make sure they did not sacrifice one domestic duty. "As for genius, make it a domestic plant. Let its roots strike deep in your house. . . ."

The fear of "blue stockings" (the eighteenth-century male's term of derision for educated or literary women) need not persist for nineteenth-century American men. The magazines presented spurious dialogues in which bachelors were convinced of their fallacy in fearing educated wives. One such dialogue took place between a young man and his female cousin. Ernest deprecates learned ladies ("A *Woman* is far more lovable than a *philosopher*") but Alice refutes him with the beautiful example of their Aunt Barbara who "although she *has* perpetrated the heinous crime of writing some half dozen folios" is still a model of "the spirit of feminine gentleness." His memory prodded, Ernest concedes that, by George, there was a woman: "When I last had a cold she not only made me a bottle of cough syrup, but when I complained of nothing new to read, set to work and wrote some twenty stanzas on consumption."

The magazines were filled with domestic tragedies in which spoiled young girls learned that when there was a hungry man to feed French and china painting were not helpful. According to these stories many a marriage is jeopardized because the wife has not learned to keep house. Harriet Beecher Stowe wrote a sprightly piece of personal experience for *Godey's*, ridiculing her own bad housekeeping as a bride. She used the same theme in a story "The Only Daughter," in which the pampered beauty learns the facts of domestic life from a rather difficult source, her mother-in-law. Mrs. Hamilton tells Caroline in the sweetest way possible to shape up in the kitchen, reserving her rebuke for her son: "You are her husband—her guide—her protector—now see what you can do," she admonishes him. "Give her credit for every effort: treat her faults with tenderness; encourage and praise whenever you can, and depend upon it, you will see another woman in her." He is properly masterful, she properly domestic and in a few months Caroline is making lumpless gravy and keeping up with the darning. Domestic tranquillity has been restored and the young wife moralizes: "Bring up a girl to feel that she has a responsible part to bear in promoting the happiness of the family, and you make a reflecting being of her at once, and remove that lightness and frivolity of character which makes her shrink from graver studies." These stories end with the heroine drying her hands on her apron and vowing that *her* daughter will be properly educated, in piecrust as well as Poonah work.

The female seminaries were quick to defend themselves against any suspicion of interfering with the role which nature's God had assigned to women. They hoped to enlarge and deepen that role, but not to change its setting. At the Young Ladies' Seminary and Collegiate Institute in Monroe City, Michigan, the catalogue admitted few of its graduates would be likely "to fill the learned professions." Still, they were called to "other scenes of usefulness and honor." The average woman is to be "the presiding genius of love" in the home, where she is to "give a correct and elevated literary taste to her children, and to assume that influential station that she ought to possess as the companion of an educated man."

At Miss Pierce's famous school in Litchfield, the students were taught that they had "attained the perfection of their characters when they could combine their elegant accomplishments with a turn for solid domestic virtues." Mt. Holyoke paid pious tribute to domestic skills: "Let a young lady despise this branch of the duties of woman, and she despises the appointments of her existence." God, nature and the Bible "enjoin these duties on the sex, and she cannot vio-

late them with impunity." Thus warned, the young lady would have to seek knowledge of these duties elsewhere, since it was not in the curriculum at Mt. Holyoke. "We would not take this privilege from the mother."

One reason for knowing her way around a kitchen was that America was "a land of precarious fortunes," as Lydia Maria Child pointed out in her book *The Frugal Housewife: Dedicated to Those Who Are Not Ashamed of Economy.* Mrs. Child's chapter "How To Endure Poverty" prescribed a combination of piety and knowledge—the kind of knowledge found in a true woman's education, "a thorough religious *useful* education." The woman who had servants today, might tomorrow, because of a depression or panic, be forced to do her own work. If that happened she knew how to act, for she was to be the same cheerful consoler of her husband in their cottage as in their mansion.

An essay by Washington Irving, much quoted in the gift annuals, discussed the value of a wife in case of business reverses: "I have observed that a married man falling into misfortune is more apt to achieve his situation in the world than a single one . . . it is beautifully ordained by Providence that woman, who is the ornament of man in his happier hours, should be his stay and solace when smitten with sudden calamity."

A story titled simply but eloquently "The Wife" dealt with the quiet heroism of Ellen Graham during her husband's plunge from fortune to poverty. Ned Graham said of her: "Words are too poor to tell you what I owe to that noble woman. In our darkest seasons of adversity, she has been an angel of consolation—utterly forgetful of self and anxious only to comfort and sustain me." Of course she had a little help from "faithful Dinah who absolutely refused to leave her beloved mistress," but even so Ellen did no more than would be expected of any true woman.

Most of this advice was directed to woman as wife. Marriage was the proper state for the exercise of the domestic virtues. "True Love and a Happy Home," an essay in *The Young Ladies'*

Oasis, might have been carved on every girl's hope chest. But although marriage was best, it was not absolutely necessary. The women's magazines tried to remove the stigma from being an "Old Maid." They advised no marriage at all rather than an unhappy one contracted out of selfish motives. Their stories showed maiden ladies as unselfish ministers to the sick, teachers of the young, or moral preceptors with their pens, beloved of the entire village. Usually the life of single blessedness resulted from the premature death of a fiancé, or was chosen through fidelity to some high mission. For example, in "Two Sisters," Mary devotes herself to Ellen and her abandoned children, giving up her own chance for marriage. "Her devotion to her sister's happiness has met its reward in the consciousness of having fulfilled a sacred duty." Very rarely, a "woman of genius" was absolved from the necessity of marriage, being so extraordinary that she did not need the security or status of being a wife. Most often, however, if girls proved "difficult," marriage and a family were regarded as a cure. The "sedative quality" of a home could be counted on to subdue even the most restless spirits.

George Burnap saw marriage as "that sphere for which woman was originally intended, and to which she is so exactly fitted to adorn and bless, as the wife, the mistress of a home, the solace, the aid, and the counsellor of that ONE, for whose sake alone the world is of any consequence to her." Samuel Miller preached a sermon on women: "How interesting and important are the duties devolved on females as WIVES . . . the counsellor and friend of the husband; who makes it her daily study to lighten his cares, to soothe his sorrows, and to augment his joys; who, like a guardian angel, watches over his interests, warns him against dangers, comforts him under trials; and by her pious, assiduous, and attractive deportment, constantly endeavors to render him more virtuous, more useful, more honourable, and more happy." A woman's whole interest should be focused on her husband, paying him "those numberless attentions

to which the French give the title of *petits soins* and which the woman who loves knows so well how to pay . . . she should consider nothing as trivial which could win a smile of approbation from him."

Marriage was seen not only in terms of service but as an increase in authority for woman. Burnap concluded that marriage improves the female character "not only because it puts her under the best possible tuition, that of the affections, and affords scope to her active energies, but because it gives her higher aims, and a more dignified position." *The Lady's Amaranth* saw it as a balance of power: "The man bears rule over his wife's person and conduct. She bears rule over his inclinations: he governs by law; she by persuasion. . . . The empire of the woman is an empire of softness . . . her commands are caresses, her menaces are tears."

Woman should marry, but not for money. She should choose only the high road of true love and not truckle to the values of a materialistic society. A story "Marrying for Money" (subtlety was not the strong point of the ladies' magazines) depicts Gertrude, the heroine, rueing the day she made her crass choice: "It is a terrible thing to live without love. . . . A woman who dares marry for aught but the purest affection, calls down the just judgments of heaven upon her head."

The corollary to marriage, with or without true love, was motherhood, which added another dimension to her usefulness and her prestige. It also anchored her even more firmly to the home. "My Friend," wrote Mrs. Sigourney, "If in becoming a mother, you have reached the climax of your happiness, you have also taken a higher place in the scale of being . . . you have gained an increase of power." The Rev. J. N. Danforth pleaded in *The Ladies' Casket,* "Oh, mother, acquit thyself well in thy humble sphere, for thou mayest affect the world." A true woman naturally loved her children; to suggest otherwise was monstrous.

America depended upon her mothers to raise up a whole generation of Christian statesmen who could say "all that I am I owe to my angel mother." The mothers must do the inculcating of virtue since the fathers, alas, were too busy chasing the dollar. Or as *The Ladies' Companion* put it more effusively, the father "weary with the heat and burden of life's summer day, or trampling with unwilling foot the decaying leaves of life's autumn, has forgotten the sympathies of life's joyous springtime. . . . The acquisition of wealth, the advancement of his children in worldly honor—these are his self-imposed tasks." It was his wife who formed "the infant mind as yet untainted by contact with evil . . . like wax beneath the plastic hand of the mother."

The Ladies' Wreath offered a fifty-dollar prize to the woman who submitted the most convincing essay on "How May An American Woman Best Show Her Patriotism." The winner was Miss Elizabeth Wetherell who provided herself with a husband in her answer. The wife in the essay of course asked her husband's opinion. He tried a few jokes first—Call her eldest son George Washington," "Don't speak French, speak American"—but then got down to telling her in sober prize-winning truth what women could do for their country. Voting was no asset, since that would result only in "a vast increase of confusion and expense without in the smallest degree affecting the result." Besides, continued this oracle, "looking down at their child," if "we were to go a step further and let the children vote, their first act would be to vote their mothers at home." There is no comment on this devastating male logic and he continues: "Most women would follow the lead of their fathers and husbands," and the few who would "fly off on a tangent from the circle of home influence would cancel each other out."

The wife responds dutifully: "I see all that. I never understood so well before." Encouraged by her quick womanly perception, the master of the house resolves the question—an American woman best shows her patriotism by staying at home, where she brings her influence to bear "upon the right side for the country's weal." That woman will instinctively choose the side of

right he has no doubt. Besides her "natural refinement and closeness to God" she has the "blessed advantage of a quiet life" while man is exposed to conflict and evil. She stays home with "her Bible and a well-balanced mind" and raises her sons to be good Americans. The judges rejoiced in this conclusion and paid the prize money cheerfully, remarking "they deemed it cheap at the price."

If any woman asked for greater scope for her gifts the magazines were sharply critical. Such women were tampering with society, undermining civilization. Mary Wollstonecraft, Frances Weight and Harriet Martineau were condemned in the strongest possible language—they were read out of the sex. "They are only semi-women, mental hermaphrodites." The Rev. Harrington knew the women of America could not possibly approve of such perversions and went to some wives and mothers to ask if they did want a "wider sphere of interest" as these nonwomen claimed. The answer was reassuring. " 'NO!' they cried simultaneously, 'Let the men take care of politics, *we will take care of the children!'* " Again female discontent resulted only from a lack of understanding: women were not subservient, they were rather "chosen vessels." Looked at in this light the conclusion was inescapable: "Noble, sublime is the task of the American mother."

"Women's Rights" meant one thing to reformers, but quite another to the True Woman. She knew her rights,

The right to love whom others scorn,
The right to comfort and to mourn,
The right to shed new joy on earth,
The right to feel the soul's high worth . . .
Such women's rights, and God will bless
And crown their champions with success.

The American woman had her choice—she could define her rights in the way of the women's magazines and insure them by the practice of the requisite virtues, or she could go outside the home, seeking other rewards than love. It was a decision on which, she was told, everything in her world depended. "Yours it is to determine," the Rev. Mr. Stearns solemnly warned from the pulpit, "whether the beautiful order of society . . . shall continue as it has been" or whether "society shall break up and become a chaos of disjointed and unsightly elements." If she chose to listen to other voices than those of her proper mentors, sought other rooms than those of her home, she lost both her happiness and her power—"that almost magic power, which, in her proper sphere, she now wields over the destinies of the world."

But even while the women's magazines and related literature encouraged this ideal of the perfect woman, forces were at work in the nineteenth century which impelled woman herself to change, to play a more creative role in society. The movements for social reform, westward migration, missionary activity, utopian communities, industrialism, the Civil War—all called forth responses from woman which differed from those she was trained to believe were hers by nature and divine decree. The very perfection of True Womanhood, moreover, carried within itself the seeds of its own destruction. For if woman was so very little less than the angels, she should surely take a more active part in running the world, especially since men were making such a hash of things.

Real women often felt they did not live up to the ideal of True Womanhood: some of them blamed themselves, some challenged the standard, some tried to keep the virtues and enlarge the scope of womanhood. Somehow through this mixture of challenge and acceptance, of change and continuity, the True Woman evolved into the New Woman—a transformation as startling in its way as the abolition of slavery or the coming of the machine age. And yet the sterotype, the "mystique" if you will, of what woman was and ought to be persisted, bringing guilt and confusion in the midst of opportunity.

The women's magazines and related literature had feared this very dislocation of values and blurring of roles. By careful manipulation and interpretation they sought to convince woman that she had the best of both worlds—power and virtue—and that a stable order of society depended upon her maintaining her traditional place in it. To that end she was identified with everything that was beautiful and holy.

"Who Can Find a Valiant Woman?" was asked frequently from the pulpit and the editorial pages. There was only one place to look for her—at home. Clearly and confidently these authorities proclaimed the True Woman of the nineteenth century to be the Valiant Woman of the Bible, in whom the heart of her husband rejoiced and whose price was above rubies.

■■■

STUDY QUESTIONS

1. Summarize the "cult of true womanhood" and the behavioral expectations it imposed on American women.

2. Welter argues that the "cult of true womanhood" was an attempt to preserve premodern values in the industrial age. What did she mean? In what sense was industrialization incompatible with the "cult of true womanhood?" Why did the "cult of true womanhood" often leave nineteenth century women feeling guilty?

3. To what extent was the "cult of true womanhood" simply an attempt by chau-

vinist men in literary circles to prevent women from taking advantage of new opportunities provided by the rise of an industrial society? Was this a conspiracy or an unconscious cultural attempt to prevent change?

4. If the "cult of true womanhood" was indeed an attempt to retard modernization, what were people worried about? If they demanded domesticity, submissiveness, and chastity of women, why did they so fear professionalism, assertiveness, and sexual freedom?

BIBLIOGRAPHY

For general histories of the women's movement in the United States, see Andrew Sinclair, *The Better Half* (1965) and Page Smith, *Daughters of the Promised Land* (1970). Important scholarly work has been done on the origins of the feminist movement in early American history. See Barbara J. Berg, *The Remembered Gate: Origins of American Feminism—The Woman and the City, 1800–1860* (1977); Ann Douglas, *The Feminization of American Culture* (1977); and Nancy F. Cott, *The Bonds of Womanhood: "Women's Sphere" in New England, 1780–1835* (1977). Ellen DuBois's *Feminism and Suffrage. The Emergence of an Independent Women's Movement in America, 1848–1869* (1978) deals with the early years of the crusade for the right to vote and how it led to a much broader demand for equality. Philip Greven's *The Protestant Temperament* (1977) analyzes family roles and religious training in early America.

THE ANIMAL
TRICKSTER

Lawrence W. Levine

For more than 350 years, Americans have debated the questions of slavery, arguing continually over the nature of slavery and the black personality, but always agreeing that the unique relationship between black and white people has had an enormous impact on United States history. An early generation of historians looked upon the slaves as genetically inferior people—lazy, childlike, obsequious, and quite incapable of dealing independently with civilized society. By the 1950s, historians were rejecting the idea of genetic inferiority, but they were still looking back on slavery with a white perspective. While one group argued that the viciousness of slavery had transformed black people into a frightened, weak mass, another group claimed that blacks were rebellious and bitterly unhappy, always trying to undermine plantation slavery. But in recent years, historians have taken a more complex approach to the history of black slavery, arguing that a delicate and symbiotic relationship existed between whites and blacks in the antebellum South, and that the slaves developed a rich Afro-American culture, despite the pains of bondage, which provided them fulfillment, power, and a sense of self-worth. Lawrence W. Levine's book *Black Culture and Black Consciousness: Afro-American Folk Thought from Slavery to Freedom* (1977) is a major contribution to the contemporary interpretation of slavery. The following selection, "The Animal Trickster," clearly illustrates how slaves developed a folk culture enabling them to interpret their environment, vent frustration, and provide forms of symbolic association necessary to group survival.

Although the range of slave tales was narrow in neither content nor focus, it is not surprising or accidental that the tales most easily and abundantly collected in Africa and among Afro-Americans in the New World were animal trickster tales. Because of their overwhelmingly paradigmatic character, animal tales were, of all the narratives of soical protest or psychological release, among the easiest to relate both within and especially outside the group.

The propensity of Africans to utilize their folklore quite consciously to gain psychological release from the inhibitions of their society and their situation . . . needs to be reiterated here if the popularity and function of animal trickster tales is to be understood. After listening to a series of Ashanti stories that included rather elaborate imitations of afflicted people—an old woman dressed in rags and covered with sores, a leper, an old man suffering from the skin disease yaws—which called forth roars of laughter from the audience, the English anthropologist R. S. Rattray suggested that it was unkind to ridicule such subjects. "The person addressed replied that in everyday life no one might do so, however great the inclination to laugh might be. He went on to explain that it was so with many other things: the cheating and tricks of priests, the rascality of a chief—things about which every one knew, but concerning which one might not ordinarily speak in public. These occasions gave every one an opportunity of talking about and laughing at such things; it was 'good' for every one concerned, he said." Customs such as these led Rattray to conclude "beyond a doubt, that West Africans had discovered for themselves the truth of the psychoanalysts' theory of 'repressions,' and that in these ways they sought an outlet for what might otherwise become a dangerous complex."

Certainly this was at the heart of the popularity of animal trickster tales. Whether it is accurate to assert, as Rattray has done, that the majority of "beast fables" were derived from the practice of substituting the names of animals for the names of real individuals whom it would have been impolitic or dangerous to mention, there can be no question that the animals in these tales were easily recognizable representations of both specific actions and generalized patterns of human behavior. "In the fable," Léopold Senghor has written, "the animal is seldom a totem; it is this or that one whom every one in the village knows well: the stupid or tyrannical or wise and good chief, the young man who makes reparation for injustice. Tales and fables are woven out of everday occurrences. Yet it is not a question of anecdotes or of 'material from life.' The facts are images and have paradigmatic value." The popularity of these tales in Africa is attested to by the fact that the Akan-speaking peoples of the West Coast gave their folk tales the generic title *Anansesem* (spider stories), after the spider trickster Anansi, whether he appeared in the story or not, and this practice was perpetuated by such New World Afro-American groups as the South American Negroes of Surinam who referred to all their stories, whatever their nature, as *Anansitori*, or the West Indian blacks of Curaçao who called theirs *Cuenta de Nansi*.

For all their importance, animals did not monopolize the trickster role in African tales; tricksters could, and did, assume divine and human form as well. Such divine tricksters as the Dahomean Legba or the Yoruban Eshu and Orunmila did not survive the transplantation of Africans to the United States and the slaves' adaptation to Christian religious forms. Human tricksters, on the other hand, played an important role in the tales of American slaves. By the nineteenth century, however, these human tricksters were so rooted in and reflective of their new cultural and social setting that outside of function they bore increasingly little resemblance to their African counterparts. It was in the animal trickster that the most easily perceivable correspondence in form and usage between African and Afro-American tales can be found. In both cases the primary trickster figures of animal tales were weak, relatively powerless creatures who attain their ends through the application of native wit and guile rather than power or authority: the Hare or Rabbit in East Africa, Angola, and parts of Nigeria; the Tortoise among the Yoruba, Ibo, and Edo peoples of Nigeria; the Spider throughout much of West Africa including Ghana, Liberia, and Sierra Leone; Brer Rabbit in the United States.

In their transmutation from their natural state to the world of African and Afro-American tales, the animals inhabiting these tales, though retaining enough of their natural characteristics to be recognizable, were almost thoroughly humanized. The world they lived in, the rules they lived by, the emotions that governed them, the status they craved, the taboos they feared, the prizes they struggled to attain were those of the men and women who lived in this world. The beings that came to life in these stories were so created as to be human enough to be identified with but at the same time exotic enough to allow both storytellers and listeners a latitude and freedom that came only with much more difficulty and daring in tales explicitly concerning human beings.

This latitude was crucial, for the one central feature of almost all trickster tales in their assault upon deeply ingrained and culturally sanctioned values. This of course accounts for the almost universal occurrence of trickster tales, but it has not rendered them universally identical. The values people find constraining and the mechanisms they choose to utilize in their attempts at transcending or negating them are determined by their culture and their situation. "It is very well to speak of 'the trickster,' " Melville and Frances Herskovits have noted, "yet one need but compare the Winnebago trickster [of the North American Indians] . . . with Legba and Yo in Dahomey to find that the specifications for the first by no means fit the second." The same may be said of the slave trickster in relation to the trickster figures of the whites around them. Although animal trickster tales do not seem to have caught a strong hold among American whites during the eighteenth and the first half of the nineteenth century, there were indigenous American tricksters from the tall, spare New Englander Jonathan, whose desire for pecuniary gain knew few moral boundaries, to the rough roguish confidence men of southwestern tales. But the American process that seems to have been most analogous in function to the African trickster tale was not these stories so much as the omnipresent tales of exaggeration. In these tall tales Americans were able to deal with the insecurities produced by forces greater than themselves not by manipulating them, as Africans tended to do, but by overwhelming them through the magnification of the self epitomized in the unrestrained exploits of a Mike Fink or Davy Crockett. "I'm . . . half-horse, half-alligator, a little touched with the snapping turtle; can wade the Mississippi, leap the Ohio, ride upon a streak of lightning, and slip without a scratch down a honey locust; can whip my weight in wildcats, . . . hug a bear too close for comfort, and eat any man opposed to Jackson," the latter would boast.

It is significant that, with the exception of the stories of flying Africans, mythic strategies such as these played almost no role in the lore of nineteenth-century slaves; not until well after emancipation do tales of exaggeration, with their magnification of the individual, begin to assume importance in the folklore of Afro-Americans. Nor did the model of white trickster figures seem to have seriously affected the slaves, whose own tricksters remained in a quite different mold— one much closer to the cultures from which they had come. In large part African trickster tales revolved around the strong patterns of authority so central to African cultures. As interested as they might be in material gains, African trickster figures were more obsessed with manipulating the strong and reversing the normal structure of power and prestige. Afro-American slaves, cast into a far more rigidly fixed and certainly a more alien authority system, could hardly have been expected to neglect a cycle of tales so ideally suited to their needs.

This is not to argue that slaves in the United States continued with little or no alteration the trickster lore of their ancestral home. The divergences were numerous: divine trickster figures disappeared; such important figures as Anansi the spider were at best relegated to the dim background; sizable numbers of European tales and themes found their way into the slave repertory. But we must take care not to make too much of these differences. For instance, the fact that the spider trickster retained its importance and its Twi name, Anansi, among the Afro-Americans of Jamaica, Surinam, and Curaçao, while in the United States Anansi lived only a peripheral existence in such tales as the Aunt Nancy stories of South Carolina and Georgia, has been magnified out of proportion by some students. "The sharp break between African and American tradition," Richard Dorson has written, "occurs at the West Indies, where Anansi the spider dominates hundreds of cantefables, the tales that inclose songs. But no Anansi stories are found in the United States." The decline of the spider trickster in the United States can be explained by many factors from the ecology of the United States, where spiders were less ubiquitous and important than in either Africa or those parts of the New World in which the spider remained a central figure, to the particular admixture of African peoples in the various parts of the Western Hemisphere. Anansi, after all, was but one of many African tricksters and in Africa itself had a limited influence. Indeed, in many parts of South America where aspects of African culture endured overtly with much less alteration than occurred in the United States, Anansi was either nonexistent or marginal.

What is more revealing than the life or death of any given trickster figure is the retention of the trickster tale itself. Despite all of the changes that took place, there persisted the mechanism, so well developed throughout most of Africa, by

means of which psychic relief from arbitrary authority could be secured, symbolic assaults upon the powerful could be waged, and important lessons about authority relationships could be imparted. Afro-Americans in the United States were to make extended use of this mechanism throughout their years of servitude.

In its simplest form the slaves' animal trickster tale was a cleanly delineated story free of ambiguity. The strong assault the weak, who fight back with any weapons they have. The animals in these tales have an almost instinctive understanding of each other's habits and foibles. Knowing Rabbit's curiosity and vanity, Wolf constructs a tar-baby and leaves it by the side of the road. At first fascinated by this stranger and then progressively infuriated at its refusal to respond to his friendly salutations, Rabbit strikes at it with his hands, kicks it with his feet, butts it with his head, and becomes thoroughly enmeshed. In the end, however, it is Rabbit whose understanding of his adversary proves to be more profound. Realizing that Wolf will do exactly what he thinks his victim least desires, Rabbit convinces him that of all the ways to die the one he is most afraid of is being thrown into the briar patch, which of course is exactly what Wolf promptly does, allowing Rabbit to escape.

This situation is repeated in tale after tale: the strong attempt to trap the weak but are tricked by them instead. Fox entreats Rooster to come down from his perch, since all the animals have signed a peace treaty and there is no longer any danger: "I don't eat you, you don' boder wid me. Come down! Le's make peace!" Almost convinced by this good news, Rooster is about to descend when he thinks better of it and tests Fox by pretending to see a man and a dog coming down the road. "Don' min' fo' comin' down den," Fox calls out as he runs away. "Dawg ain't got no sense, yer know, an' de man got er gun." Spotting a goat lying on a rock, Lion is about to surprise and kill him when he notices that Goat keeps chewing and chewing although there is nothing there but bare stone. Lion reveals himself and asks Goat what he is eating. Overcoming the momentary paralysis which afflicts most of the weak animals in these tales when they realize they are trapped, Goat saves himself by saying in his most terrifying voice: "Me duh chaw dis rock, an ef you dont leff, wen me done . . . me guine eat you."

At its most elemental, then, the trickster tale consists of a confrontation in which the weak use their wits to evade the strong. Mere escape, however, does not prove to be victory enough, and in a significant number of these tales the weak learn the brutal ways of the more powerful. Fox, taking advantage of Pig's sympathetic nature, gains entrance to his house during a storm by pleading that he is freezing to death. After warming himself by the fire, he acts exactly as Pig's instincts warned him he would. Spotting a pot of peas cooking on the stove, he begins to sing:

Fox and peas are very good,
But Pig and peas are better.

Recovering from his initial terror, Pig pretends to hear a pack of hounds, helps Fox hide in a meal barrel, and pours the peas in, scalding Fox to death.

In one tale after another the trickster proves to be as merciless as his stronger opponent. Wolf traps Rabbit in a hollow tree and sets it on fire, but Rabbit escapes through a hole in the back and reappears, thanking Wolf for an excellent meal, explaining that the tree was filled with honey which melted from the heat. Wolf, in his eagerness to enjoy a similar feast, allows himself to be sealed into a tree which has no other opening, and is burned to death. "While eh duh bun, Buh Wolf bague an pray Buh Rabbit fuh leh um come out, but Buh Rabbit wouldnt yeddy [hear] um." The brutality of the trickster in these tales was sometimes troubling ("Buh Rabbit . . . hab er bad heart," the narrator of the last story concluded), but more often it was mitigated by the fact that the strong were the initial aggressors and the weak really had no choice. The characteristic spirit of these tales was one not of moral judgment but of vicarious triumph. Storytellers allowed their audience to share the heartening spectacle of a lion running in terror from a goat or a fox fleeing a rooster; to experience the mocking joy of Brer Rabbit as he scampers away through the briar patch calling back to Wolf, "Dis de place me mammy fotch me up,—dis de place me mammy fotch me up"; to feel the joyful relief of Pig as he turns Fox's song upside down and chants:

Pigs and peas are very good,
But Fox and peas are better.

Had self-preservation been the only motive driving the animals in these stories, the trickster tale need never have varied from the forms just considered. But Brer Rabbit and his fellow creatures were too humanized to be content with mere survival. Their needs included all the prizes human beings crave and strive for: wealth, success, prestige, honor, sexual prowess. Brer Rabbit himself summed it up best in the tale for which this section is named:

De rabbit is de slickest o' all de animals de Lawd ever made. He ain't de biggest, an' he ain't de loudest but he sho' am de slickest. If he gits in trouble he gits out by gittin' somebody else in. Once he fell down a deep well an' did he holler and cry? No siree. He set up a mighty mighty whistling and a singin', an' when de wolf passes by he heard him an' he stuck his head over an' de rabbit say, "Git 'long 'way f'om here. Dere ain't room fur two. Hit's mighty hot up dere and nice an' cool down here. Don' you git in dat bucket an' come down here." Dat made de wolf all de mo' onrestless and he jumped into the bucket an' as he went down de rabbit come up, an' as dey passed de rabbit he laughed an' he say, "Dis am life; some go up and some go down."

There could be no mistaking the direction in which Rabbit was determined to head. It was in his inexorable drive upward that Rabbit emerged not only as an incomparable defender but also as a supreme manipulator, a role that complicated the simple contours of the tales already referred to.

In the ubiquitous tales of amoral manipulation, the trickster could still be pictured as much on the defensive as he was in the stories which had him battling for his very life against stronger creatures. The significant difference is that now the panoply of his victims included the weak as well as the powerful. Trapped by Mr. Man and hung from a sweet gum tree until he can be cooked, Rabbit is buffeted to and fro by the wind and left to contemplate his bleak future until Brer Squirrel happens along. "This yer my cool air swing," Rabbit informs him. "I taking a fine swing this morning." Squirrel begs a turn and finds his friend surprisingly gracious: "Certainly, Brer Squirrel, you do me proud. Come up here, Brer Squirrel, and give me a hand with this knot" Tying the grateful squirrel securely in the tree, Rabbit leaves him to his pleasure—and his fate. When Mr. Man returns, "he take Brer Squirrel home and cook him for dinner."

It was primarily advancement not preservation that led to the trickster's manipulations, however. Among a slave population whose daily rations were at best rather stark fare and quite often a barely minimal diet, it is not surprising that food proved to be the most common symbol of enhanced status and power. In his never-ending quest for food the trickster was not content with mere acquisition, which he was perfectly capable of on his own; he needed to procure the food through guile from some stronger animal. Easily the most popular tale of this type pictures Rabbit and Wolf as partners in farming a field. They have laid aside a tub of butter for winter provisions, but Rabbit proves unable to wait or to share. Pretending to hear a voice calling him, he leaves his chores and begins to eat the butter. When he returns to the field he informs his partner that his sister has just had a baby and wanted him to name it. "Well, w'at you name um?" Wolf asks innocently. "Oh, I name um Buh Start-um," Rabbit replies. Subsequent calls provide the change for additional assaults on the butter and additional names for the nonexistent babies: "Buh Half-um," "Buh Done-um," After

work, Wolf discovers the empty tub and accuses Rabbit, who indignantly denies the theft. Wolf proposes that they both lie in the sun, which will cause the butter to run out of the guilty party. Rabbit agrees readily, and when grease begins to appear on his own face he rubs it onto that of the sleeping wolf. "Look, Buh Wolf," he cries, waking his partner, "de buttah melt out on you. Dat prove you eat um." "I guess you been right," Wolf agrees docilely, "I eat um fo' trute." In some versions the animals propose a more hazardous ordeal by fire to discover the guilty party. Rabbit successfully jumps over the flames but some innocent animal—Possum, Terrapin, Bear—falls in and perishes for Rabbit's crime.

In most of these tales the aggrieved animal, realizing he has been tricked, desperately tries to avenge himself by setting careful plans to trap Rabbit, but to no avail. Unable to outwit Rabbit, his adversaries attempt to learn from him, but here too they fail. Seeing Rabbit carrying a string of fish, Fox asks him where they came from. Rabbit confesses that he stole them from Man by pretending to be ill and begging Man to take him home in his cart which was filled with fish. While riding along, Rabbit explains, he threw the load of fish into the woods and then jumped off to retrieve them. He encourages Fox to try the same tactic, and Fox is beaten to death, as Rabbit knew he would be, since Man is too shrewd to be taken in the same way twice.

And so it goes in story after story. Rabbit cheats Brer Wolf out of his rightful portion of a cow and a hog they kill together. He tricks Brer Fox out of his part of their joint crop year after year "until he starved the fox to death. Then he had all the crop, and all the land too." He leisurely watches all the other animals build a house in which they store their winter provisions and then sneaks in, eats the food, and scares the others, including Lion, away by pretending to be a spirit and calling through a horn in a ghostly voice that he is a "better man den ebber bin yuh befo." He convinces Wolf that they ought to sell their own grandparents for a

Although the animals in the trickster tales were physically recognized as animals, they were thoroughly human in their actions.

"You is my master many a day on land, Brer Rabbit," Frog tells him just before killing and eating him, "but I is you master in the water."

It is significant that when these defeats do come, most often it is not brute force but even greater trickery that triumphs. Normally, however, the trickster has more than his share of the food. And of the women as well, for sexual prowess is the other basic sign of prestige in the slaves' tales. Although the primary trickster was occasionally depicted as a female—Ol' Molly Hare in Virginia, Aunt Nancy or Ann Nancy in the few surviving spider stories—in general women played a small role in slave tales. They were not actors in their own right so much as attractive possessions to be fought over. That the women for whom the animals compete are frequently the daughters of the most powerful creatures in the forest makes it evident that the contests are for status as well as pleasure. When Brer Bear promises his daughter to the best whistler in the forest, Rabbit offers to help his only serious competitor, Brer Dog, whistle more sweetly by slitting the corner of his mouth, which in reality makes him incapable of whistling at all. If Rabbit renders his adversaries figuratively impotent in their quest for women, they often retaliate in kind. In the story just related, Dog chases Rabbit, bites off his tail, and nothing more is said about who wins the woman.

More often than not, though, Rabbit is successful. In a Georgia tale illustrating the futility of mere hard work, Brer Wolf offers his attractive daughter to the animal that shucks the most corn. Rabbit has his heart set on winning Miss Wolf but realizes he has no chance of beating Brer Coon at shucking corn. Instead, he spends all of his time during the contest singing, dancing, and charming Miss Wolf. At the end he sits down next to Coon and claims that he has shucked the great pile of corn. Confused, Wolf leaves the decision up to his daughter:

Now Miss Wolf she been favoring Brer Rabbit all the evening. Brer Rabbit dancing and singing

tub of butter, arranges for his grandparents to escape so that only Wolf's remain to be sold, and once they are bartered for the butter he steals that as well.

The many tales of which these are typical make it clear that what Rabbit craves is not possession but power, and this he acquires not simply by obtaining food but by obtaining it through the manipulation and deprivation of others. It is not often that he meets his match, and then generally at the hands of an animal as weak as himself. Refusing to allow Rabbit to cheat him out of his share of the meat they have just purchased, Partridge samples a small piece of liver and cries out, "Br'er Rabbit, de meat bitter! Oh, 'e bitter, bitter! bitter, bitter! You better not eat de meat," and tricks Rabbit into revealing where he had hidden the rest of the meat. "You is a damn sha'p feller," Partridge tells him. "But I get even wid you." Angry at Frog for inviting all the animals in the forest but him to a fish dinner, Rabbit frightens the guests away and eats all the fish himself. Frog gives another dinner, but this time he is prepared and tricks Rabbit into the water.

plum turned Miss Wolf's head, so Miss Wolf she say, "It most surely are Brer Rabbit's pile." Miss Wolf she say she "plum 'stonished how Brer Coon can story so." Brer Rabbit he take the gal and go off home clipity, lipity. Poor old Brer Coon he take hisself off home, he so tired he can scarcely hold hisself together.

In another Georgia tale the contest for the woman seems to be symbolically equated with freedom. Fox promises his daughter to any animal who can pound dust out of a rock.

Then Brer Rabbit, he feel might set down on, 'cause he know all the chaps can swing the stone hammer to beat hisself, and he go off sorrowful like and set on the sand bank. He sat a while and look east, and then he turn and set a while and look west, but may be you don't know, sah, Brer Rabbit sense never come to hisself 'cepting when he look north.

Thus inspired, Rabbit conceives of a strategy allowing him to defeat his more powerful opponents and carry off the woman.

In the best known and most symbolically interesting courting tale, Rabbit and Wolf vie for the favors of a woman who is pictured as either equally torn between her two suitors or leaning toward Wolf. Rabbit alters the contest by professing surprise that she could be interested in Wolf, since he is merely Rabbit's riding horse. Hearing of this, Wolf confronts Rabbit, who denies ever saying it and promises to go to the woman and personally refute the libel as soon as he is well enough. Wolf insists he go at once, and the characteristic combination of Rabbit's deceit and Wolf's seemingly endless trust and gullibility allows Rabbit to convince his adversary that he is too sick to go with him unless he can ride on Wolf's back with a saddle and bridle for support. The rest of the story is inevitable. Approaching the woman's house Rabit tightens the reins, digs a pair of spurs into Wolf, and trots him around crying, "Look here, girl! what I told you? Didn't I say I had Brother Wolf for my riding-horse?" It

was in many ways the ultimate secular triumph in slave tales. The weak doesn't merely kill his enemy: he mounts him, humiliates him, reduces him to servility, steals his woman, and, in effect, takes his place.

Mastery through possessing the two paramount symbols of power—food and women—did not prove to be sufficient for Rabbit. He craved something more. Going to God himself, Rabbit begs for enhanced potency in the form of a larger tail, greater wisdom, bigger eyes. In each case God imposes a number of tasks upon Rabbit before his wishes are fulfilled. Rabbit must bring God a bag full of blackbirds, the teeth of a rattlesnake or alligator, a swarm of yellowjackets, the "eyewater" (tears) of a deer. Rabbit accomplishes each task by exploiting the animals' vanity. He tells the blackbirds that they cannot fill the bag and when they immediately prove they can, he traps them. He taunts the snake, "dis pole *swear* say you ain't long as him." When Rattlesnake insists he is, Rabbit ties him to the stick, ostensibly to measure him, kills him, and takes his teeth. Invariably Rabbit does what is asked of him but finds God less than pleased. In some tales he is chased out of Heaven. In others God counsels him, "Why Rabbit, ef I was to gi' you long tail aint you see you'd 'stroyed up de whol worl'? Nobawdy couldn' do nuttin wid you!" Most commonly God seemingly complies with Rabbit's request and gives him a bag which he is to open when he returns home. But Rabbit cannot wait, and when he opens the bag prematurely "thirty bull-dawg run out de box, an' bit off Ber Rabbit tail again. An' dis give him a short tail again."

The rabbit, like the slaves who wove tales about him, was forced to make do with what he had. His small tail, his natural portion of intellect—these would have to suffice, and to make them do he resorted to any means at his disposal—means which may have made him morally tainted but which allowed him to survive and even to conquer. In this respect there was a direct relationship between Rabbit and the slaves, a relationship which the earliest collectors and interpreters of these stories understood well. Joel Chandler Harris, as blind as he could be to some of the deeper implications of the tales he heard and retold, was always aware of their utter seriousness. "Well, I tell you dis," Harris had Uncle Remus say, "ef deze yer tales wuz des fun, fun, fun, en giggle, giggle, giggle, I let you know I'd a-done drapt um long ago." From the beginning Harris insisted that the animal fables he was collecting were "thoroughly characteristic of the negro," and commented that "it needs no scientific investigation to show why he selects as his hero the weakest and most harmless of all animals, and brings him out victorious in contests with the bear, the wolf, and the fox.

Harris' interpretations were typical. Abigail Christensen noted in the preface to her important 1892 collection of black tales: "It must be remembered that the Rabbit represents the colored man. He is not as large nor as strong, as swift, as wise, nor as handsome as the elephant, the alligator, the bear, the deer, the serpent, the fox, but he is 'de mos' cunnin' man dat go on fo' leg' and by this cunning he gains success. So the negro, without education or wealth, could only hope to succeed by stratagem." That she was aware of the implications of these strategies was made evident when she remarked of her own collection: "If we believe that the tales of our nurseries are as important factors in forming the characters of our children as the theological dogmas of maturer years, we of the New South cannot wish our children to pore long over these pages, which certainly could not have been approved by Froebel." In that same year Octave Thanet, in an article on Arkansas folklore, concluded, "Br'er Rabbit, indeed, personifies the obscure ideals of the negro race. . . . Ever since the world began, the weak have been trying to outwit the strong; Br'er Rabbit typifies the revolt of his race. His successes are just the kind of successes that his race have craved."

These analyses of the animal trickster tales have remained standard down to our own day.

They have been advanced not merely by interpreters of the tales but by their narrators as well. Prince Baskin, one of Mrs. Christensen's informants, was quite explicit in describing the model for many of his actions:

You see, Missus, I is small man myself; but I aint nebber 'low no one for to git head o' me. I allers use my sense for help me 'long jes' like Brer Rabbit. 'For de wah ol' Marse Heywood mek me he driber on he place, an' so I aint hab for work so hard as de res'; same time I git mo' ration ebery mont' an' mo' shoe when dey share out de cloes at Chris'mus time. Well, dat come from usin' my sense. An' den, when I ben a-courtin' I nebber 'lowed no man to git de benefit ob me in dat. I allers carry off de purties' gal, 'cause, you see, Missus, I know how to play de fiddle an' allers had to go to ebery dance to play de fiddle for dem.

More than half a century later, William Willis Greenleaf of Texas echoed Baskin's admiration: "De kinda tales dat allus suits mah fancy de mo'es' am de tales de ole folks used to tell 'bout de ca'iens on of Brothuh Rabbit. In de early days Ah heerd many an' many a tale 'bout ole Brothuh Rabbit what woke me to de fac' dat hit tecks dis, dat an' t'othuh to figguh life out—dat you hafto use yo' haid fo om'n a hat rack lack ole Brothuh Rabbit do. Ole Brothuh Rabbit de smaa'tes' thing Ah done evuh run 'crost in mah whole bawn life."

This testimony—and there is a great deal of it—documents the enduring identification between black storytellers and the central trickster figure of their tales. Brer Rabbit's victories became the victories of the slave. This symbolism in slave tales allowed them to outlive slavery itself. So long as the perilous situation and psychic needs of the slave continued to characterize large numbers of freedmen as well, the imagery of the old slave tales remained both aesthetically and functionally satisfying. By ascribing actions to semi-mythical actors, Negroes were able to overcome the external and internal censorship that their hostile surroundings imposed upon them. The white master could believe that the rabbit stories his slaves told were mere figments of a childish imagination, that they were primarily humorous anecdotes depicting the "roaring comedy of animal life." Blacks knew better. The trickster's exploits, which overturned the neat hierarchy of the world in which he was forced to live, became their exploits; the justice he achieved, their justice; the strategies he employed, their strategies. From his adventures they obtained relief; from his triumphs they learned hope.

To deny this interpretation of slave tales would be to ignore much of their central essence. The problem with the notion that slaves completely identified with their animal trickster hero whose exploits were really protest tales in disguise is that it ignores much of the complexity and ambiguity inherent in these tales. This in turn flows from the propensity of scholars to view slavery as basically a relatively simple phenomenon which produced human products conforming to some unitary behavioral pattern. Too frequently slaves emerge from the pages of historians' studies either as docile, accepting beings or as alienated prisoners on the edge of rebellion. But if historians have managed to escape much of the anarchic confusion so endemic in the Peculiar Institution, slaves did not. Slaveholders who considered Afro-Americans to be little more than subhuman chattels converted them to a religion which stressed their humanity and even their divinity. Master who desired and expected their slaves to act like dependent children also enjoined them to behave like mature, responsible adults, since a work force consisting only of servile infantiles who can make no decisions on their own and can produce only under the impetus of a significant other is a dubious economic resource, and on one level or another both masters and slaves understood this. Whites who considered their black servants to be little more than barbarians, bereft of any culture worth the name, paid a fascinated and flattering attention to their song, their dance, their tales, and their forms of religious exercise. The life of every slave could be altered by the most arbitrary and amoral acts. They could be whipped, sexually assaulted, ripped out of societies in which they had deep roots, and bartered away for pecuniary profit by men and women who were also capable of treating them with kindness and consideration and who professed belief in a moral code which they held up for emulation not only by their children but often by their slaves as well.

It would be surprising if these dualities which marked the slaves' world were not reflected in both the forms and the content of their folk culture. In their religious songs and sermons slaves sought certainty in a world filled with confusion and anarchy; in their supernatural folk beliefs they sought power and control in a world filled with arbitrary forces greater than themselves; and in their tales they sought understanding of a world in which, for better or worse, they were forced to live. All the forms of slave folk culture afforded their creators psychic relief and a sense of mastery. Tales differed from the other forms in that they were more directly didactic in intent and therefore more compellingly and realistically reflective of the irrational and amoral side of the slaves' universe. It is precisely this aspect of the animal trickster tales that has been most grossly neglected.

Although the vicarious nature of slave tales was undeniably one of their salient features, too much stress has been laid on it. These were not merely clever tales of wish-fulfillment through which slaves could escape from the imperatives of their world. They could also be painfully realistic stories which taught the art of surviving and even triumphing in the face of a hostile environment. They underlined the dangers of acting rashly and striking out blindly, as Brer Rabbit did when he assaulted the tar-baby. They pointed out the futility of believing in the sincerity of the strong, as Brer Pig did when he allowed Fox to enter his house. They emphasized the necessity of comprehending the ways of the powerful, for only through such understanding could the weak endure. This lesson especially was repeated endlessly. In the popular tales featuring a race between a slow animal and a swifter opponent, the former triumphs not through persistence, as does his counterpart in the Aesopian fable of the Tortoise and the Hare, but by outwitting his opponent and capitalizing on his weaknesses and short-sightedness. Terrapin defeats Deer by placing relatives along the route with Terrapin himself stationed by the finish line. The deception is never discovered, since to the arrogant Deer all terrapins "am so much like anurrer you cant tell one from turrer." "I still t'ink Ise de fas'est runner in de worl'," the bewildered Deer complains after the race. "Maybe you air," Terrapin responds, "but I kin head you off wid sense." Rabbit too understands the myopia of the powerful and benefits from Mr. Man's inability to distinguish between the animals by manipulating Fox into taking the punishment for a crime that Rabbit himself commits. "De Ole Man yent bin know de diffunce tween Buh Rabbit an Buh Fox," the storyteller pointed out. "Eh tink all two bin de same animal." For black slaves, whose individuality was so frequently denied by the whites above them, this was a particularly appropriate and valuable message.

In many respects the lessons embodied in the animal trickster tales ran directly counter to those of the moralistic tales considered earlier. Friendship, held up as a positive model in the moralistic tales, was pictured as a fragile reed in the trickster tales. In the ubiquitous stories in which a trapped Rabbit tricks another animal into taking his place, it never occurs to him simply to ask for help. Nor when he is being pursued by Wolf does Hog even dream of asking Lion for aid. Rather he tricks Lion into killing Wolf by convincing him that the only way to cure his ailing son is to feed him a piece of half-roasted wolf liver. The animals in these stories seldom ask each other for disinterested help. Even more rarely are they caught performing acts of altruism—and with good reason. Carrying a string of fish he has just caught, Fox comes upon the prostrate form of Rabbit lying in the middle of the road moaning and asking for a doctor. Fox

lays down his fish and hurries off to get help— with predictable results: "Ber Fox los' de fish. An' Ber Rabbit got de fish an' got better. Dat's da las' of it." Brer Rooster learns the same lesson when he unselfishly tries to help a starving Hawk and is rewarded by having Hawk devour all of his children.

Throughout these tales the emphasis on the state of perpetual war between the world's creatures revealed the hypocrisy and meaninglessness of their manners and rules. Animals who called each other brother and sister one moment were at each other's throats the next. On his way to church one Sunday morning, Rabbit meets Fox and the usual unctuous dialogue begins. "Good-mornin', Ber Rabbit!" Fox sings out. "Good-mornin', Ber Fox!" Rabbit sings back. After a few more pleasantries, the brotherliness ends as quickly as it had begun and Fox threatens: "Dis is my time, I'm hungry dis mornin'. I'm goin' to ketch you." Assuming the tone of the weak supplicant, Rabbit pleads: "O Ber Fox! leave me off dis mornin'. I will sen' you to a man house where he got a penful of pretty little pig, an' you will get yer brakefus' fill." Fox agrees and is sent to a pen filled not with pigs but hound dogs who pursue and kill him. Reverting to his former Sabbath piety, Rabbit calls after the dogs: "Gawd bless yer soul! dat what enemy get for meddlin' Gawd's people when dey goin' to church." "I was goin' to school all my life," Rabbit mutters to himself as he walks away from the carnage, "an learn every letter in de book but *d*, an' D was death an' death was de en' of Ber Fox."

Such stories leave no doubt that slaves were aware of the need for role playing. But animal tales reveal more than this; they emphasize in brutal detail the irrationality and anarchy that rules Man's universe. In tale after tale violence and duplicity are pictured as existing for their own sake. Rabbit is capable of acts of senseless cruelty performed for no discernible motive. Whenever he comes across an alligator's nest "didn' he jes scratch the aigs out fur pure meaness, an' leave 'em layin' around to spile." In an extremely popular tale Alligator confesses to Rabbit that he doesn't know what trouble is. Rabbit offers to teach him and instructs him to lie down on the broom grass. While Alligator is sleeping in the dry grass, Rabbit sets it on fire all around him and calls out: "Dat's trouble, Brer 'Gator, dat's trouble youse in." Acts like this are an everyday occurrence for Rabbit. He sets Tiger, Elephant, and Panther on fire, provokes Man into burning Wolf to death, participates in the decapitation of Raccoon, causes Fox to chop off his own finger, drowns Wolf and leaves his body for Shark and Alligator to eat, boils Wolf's grandmother to death and tricks Wolf into eating her. These actions often occur for no apparent reason. When a motive is present there is no limit to Rabbit's malice. Nagged by his wife to build a spring house, Rabbit tricks the other animals into digging it by telling them that if they make a dam to hold the water back they will surely find buried gold under the spring bed. They dig eagerly and to Rabbit's surprise actually do find gold. "But Ole Brer Rabbit never lose he head, that he don't, and he just push the rocks out the dam, and let the water on and drown the lastest one of them critters, and then he picks up the gold, and of course Ole Miss Rabbit done get her spring house." It is doubtful, though, that she was able to enjoy it for very long, since in another tale Rabbit coolly sacrifices his wife and little children in order to save himself from Wolf's vengeance.

Other trickster figures manifest the identical amorality. Rabbit himself is taken in by one of them in the popular tale of the Rooster who tucked his head under his wing and explained that he had his wife cut his head off so he could sun it. "An' de rabbit he thought he could play de same trick, so he went home an' tol' his ol' lady to chop his head off. So dat was de las' of his head." All tricksters share an incapacity for forgetting or forgiving. In a North Carolina spider tale, Ann Nancy is caught stealing Buzzard's food and saves herself only by obsequiously comparing her humble lot to Buzzard's magnifi-

cence, stressing "how he sail in the clouds while she 'bliged to crawl in the dirt," until he takes pity and sets her free. "But Ann Nancy ain't got no gratitude in her mind; she feel she looked down on by all the creeters, and it sour her mind and temper. She ain't gwine forget anybody what cross her path, no, that she don't, and while she spin her house she just study constant how she gwine get the best of every creeter." In the end she invites Buzzard to dinner and pours a pot of boiling water over his head, "and the poor old man go baldheaded from that day." At that he was lucky. When Rabbit's friend Elephant accidentally steps on Rabbit's nest, killing his children, Rabbit bides his time until he catches Elephant sleeping, stuffs leaves and grass in his eyes, and sets them on fire. Hare, unable to forgive Miss Fox for marrying Terrapin instead of himself, sneaks into her house, kills her, skins her, hangs her body to the ceiling, and smokes her over hickory chips.

The unrelieved violence and brutality of these tales can be accounted for easily enough within the slave-as-trickster, trickster-as-slave thesis. D. H. Lawrence's insight that "one sheds one's sicknesses in books" is particularly applicable here. Slave tales which functioned as the bondsmen's books were a perfect vehicle for the channelization of the slaves' "sicknesses": their otherwise inexpressible angers, their gnawing hatreds, their pent-up frustrations. On one level, then, the animal trickster tales were expressions of the slaves' unrestrained fantasies: the impotent become potent, the brutalized are transformed into brutalizers, the undermen inherit the earth. But so many of these tales picture the trickster in such profoundly ambivalent or negative terms, so many of them are cast in the African mold of not depicting phenomena in hard-and-fast, either-or, good-evil categories, that it is difficult to fully accept Bernard Wolfe's argument that it is invariably "the venomous American slave crouching behind the Rabbit." Once we relax the orthodoxy that the trickster and the slave are necessarily one, other crucial levels of meaning and understanding are revealed.

"You nebber kin trus Buh Rabbit," a black storyteller concluded after explaining how Rabbit cheated Partridge. "Eh all fuh ehself; an ef you listne ter him tale, eh gwine cheat you ebry time, an tell de bigges lie dout wink eh yeye." Precisely what many slaves might have said of their white masters. Viewed in this light, trickster tales were a prolonged and telling parody of white society. The animals were frequently almost perfect replicas of whites as slaves saw them. They occasionally worked but more often lived a life filled with leisure-time activities: they fished, hunted, had numerous parties and balls, courted demure women who sat on verandas dressed in white. They mouthed lofty platitudes and professed belief in noble ideals but spent much of their time manipulating, oppressing, enslaving one another. They surrounded themselves with meaningless etiquette, encased themselves in rigid hierarchies, dispensed rewards not to the most deserving but to the most crafty and least scrupulous. Their world was filled with violence, injustice, cruelty. Though they might possess great power, they did not always wield it openly and directly but often with guile and indirection. This last point especially has been neglected; the strong and not merely the weak could function as trickster. Jenny Proctor remembered her Alabama master who was exceedingly stingy and fed his slaves badly: "When he go to sell a slave, he feed that one good for a few days, then when he goes to put 'em pu on the auction block he takes a meat skin and greases all around that nigger's mouth and makes 'em look like they been eating plenty meat and such like and was good and strong and able to work." Former slaves recalled numerous examples of the master as trickster:

There was one old man on the plantation that everybody feared. He was a good worker but he didn't allow anybody to whip him. Once he was up for a whipping and this is the way he got it. Our young master got a whole gang of paddy-rollers and hid them in a thicket. Then he told old man Jack that he had to be whipped. "I won't hit you but a few licks," he told him, "Papa is going away and he sent me to give you that whipping he told you about." Old man Jack said, "Now, I won't take nairy a lick." Young master took out a bottle of whiskey, took a drink and gave the bottle to old man Jack and told him to drink as much as he wanted. Old man Jack loved whiskey and he drank it all. Soon he was so drunk he couldn't hardly stand up. Young Mars called to the men in hiding, "Come on down, I got the wild boar." They whipped the old man almost to death. This was the first and last time he ever got whipped.

Slave tales are filled with instances of the strong acting as tricksters: Fox asks Jaybird to pick a bone out of his teeth, and once he is in his mouth, Fox devours him; Buzzard invites eager animals to go for a ride on his back, then drops them to their deaths and eats them; Wolf constructs a tar-baby in which Rabbit almost comes to his end; Elephant, Fox, and Wolf all pretend to be dead in order to throw Rabbit off guard and catch him at their "funerals"; Fox tells Squirrel that he had a brother who could jump from the top of a tall tree right into his arms, and when Squirrel proves he can do the same, Fox eats him. Tales like these, which formed an important part of the slaves' repertory, indicate that the slave could empathize with the tricked as well as the trickster. Again the didactic function of these stories becomes apparent. The slaves' interest was not always in being like the trickster but often in avoiding being like his victims from whose fate they could learn valuable lessons. Although the trickster tales could make a mockery of the values preached by the moralistic tales—friendship, hard work, sincerity—there were also important lines of continuity between the moralistic tales and the trickster stories. Animals were taken in by the trickster most easily when they violated many of the lessons of the moralistic tales: when they were too curious, as

Alligator was concerning trouble; too malicious, as Wolf was when he tried to kill Rabbit by the most horrible means possible; too greedy, as Fox and Buzzard were when their hunger for honey led to their deaths; overly proud and arrogant, as Deer was in his race with Terrapin; unable to keep their own counsel, as Fox was when he prematurely blurted out his plans to catch Rabbit; obsessed with a desire to be something other than what they are, as the Buzzard's victims were when they allowed their desire to soar in the air to overcome their caution.

The didacticism of the trickster tales was not confined to tactics and personal attributes. They also had important lessons to teach concerning the nature of the world and of the beings who inhabited it. For Afro-American slaves, as for their African ancestors, the world and those who lived in it were pictured in naturalistic and unsentimental terms. The vanity of human beings, their selfishness, their propensity to do anything and betray anyone for self-preservation, their drive for status and power, their basic insecurity, were all pictured in grim detail. The world was not a rational place in which order and justice prevailed and good was dispensed. The trickster, as Louise Dauner has perceived, often functioned as the eternal "thwarter," the symbol of "the irrational twists of circum-stance." His remarkably gullible dupes seldom learned from their experience at his hands any more than human beings learn from experience. There was no more escape from him than there is escape from the irrational in human life. The trickster served as agent of the world's irrationality and as reminder of man's fundamental helplessness. Whenever animals became too bloated with their power or importance or sense of control, the trickster was on hand to remind them of how things really were. No animal escaped these lessons; not Wolf, not Lion, not Elephant, indeed, not the trickster himself. Throughout there is a latent yearning for structure, for justice, for reason, but they are not to be had, in this world at least. If the strong are not to prevail over the weak, neither shall the weak dominate the strong. Their eternal and inconclusive battle served as proof that man is part of a larger order which he scarcely understands and certainly does not control.

If the animal trickster functioned on several different symbolic levels—as black slave, as white master, as irrational force—his adventures were given coherence and continuity by the crucial release they provided and the indispensable lessons they taught. In the exploits of the animal trickster, slaves mirrored in exaggerated terms the experiences of their own lives.

■■■

STUDY QUESTIONS

1. Animal trickster tales were common features of European and African folk culture. What is a "trickster," and how did the Afro-American trickster stories differ from their European and African counterparts?

2. When southern whites living in the antebellum plantation society heard the slave trickster tales, how did they interpret them? How did the slaves interpret them?

3. To what extent did the trickster tales offer slaves a form of power as well as a means of releasing the frustrations of bondage? What did the trickster tales reveal about Afro-American slave culture?

4. How might a contemporary feminist interpret the slave trickster tales of the eighteenth and nineteenth centuries?

BIBLIOGRAPHY

For the most traditional, and now classic, interpretation of slavery and the slave personality, see Ulrich B. Phillips's *American Negro Slavery* (1918). The major revision of Phillips's work came in Herbert Aptheker's *American Negro Slave Revolts* (1943) and especially Kenneth Stampp's *The Peculiar Institution* (1956). Both books emphasize the constant rebelliousness of black slaves in the United States. In 1959, Stanley B. Elkins wrote *Slavery: A Problem in American Intellectual and Institutional Life,* where he argued that the brutality of slavery had transformed black people into an infantile generation, plagued by laziness, confusion, and ineptitude. For more recent works which emphasize the strength and complexity of Afro-American slave culture, see John H. Blassingame, *The Slave Community* (1972); Gerald W. Mullin, *Flight and Rebellion* (1972); Leslie Howard Owen, *This Species of Property* (1976); George P. Rawick, *From Sundown to Sunup* (1972); Eugene D. Genovese, *Roll, Jordan, Roll: The World the Slaves Made* (1974); and Herbert Gutman, *The Black Family in Slavery and Freedom, 1750–1925* (1976).

FOLKLORE AND LIFE EXPERIENCE

Arnoldo De Leon
and Saul Sanchez

Although Hispanic values are deeply rooted in American culture, more than three centuries of contact in the Southwest have produced little understanding between Anglos and their Spanish-speaking neighbors. A tenuous accomodation has replaced the violence of the nineteenth century, but an enormous gulf of suspicion, ignorance, and confusion still divides Anglos and Mexican Americans. Historians and anthropologists, until recently, have reinforced the misunderstanding by giving ethnocentrism an intellectual legitimacy. Writing always from an Anglo perspective, albeit a liberal one, they have described Mexicans as a pleasant but inscrutable people, blessed with a love of life but cursed with a cultural malaise, a fatalism enabling them to survive tragedy but crippling any hope for triumph. Passive and childlike, ready to accept the course of history and quietly absorb stress, Mexicans were, according to the scholarly stereotype, unwilling and incapable of influencing their environment. Success, vertical mobility, and entrepreneurial opportunity were hopelessly beyond them.

But just as a new generation of historians have rewritten the Afro-American past, so too have young scholars taken another look at Mexican-American ethnicity. The foremost revisionary work is Arnoldo De Leon's *The Tejano Community, 1836–1900,* a study of Spanish-speaking people in nineteenth-century Texas. Combining the research techniques of history and anthropology with an Hispanic perspective, De Leon rejects the long-held notion of Mexican passivity and fatalism. Instead, he discovered and portrays a people who confidently exercised great control over their cultural and physical world through hard work, a vibrant folk culture and ethnoreligion, and strong extended families. They were hardly the hapless and helpless people of so many scholarly discourses. This selection from De Leon's work clearly illustrates the richness and vitality of Tejano culture.

Historians searching for the role of folklore in the lives of Tejanos confront serious difficulties. Generally speaking, Mexicanos, like other poor and illiterate classes, did not record their lore; historians who seek access to this oral tradition have to rely upon what Mexicanos related to inquisitive whites. Although these compilations are reliable, what Mexicans relayed to these collectors must be scrutinized rigorously. It it possible, for instance, that Mexicanos did not trust the interviewers and told them only what they wanted to hear. In addition, Tejanos may have been reluctant to relate tales that verged on the pornographic or those that revealed intimate feelings about race and other features of Mexican American culture that they believed whites could not comprehend. The tales, moreover, surely lost something in the cultural and linguistic translation. Anglo folklorists could not have captured the teller's intonation, stress, chants, and mimicking, all of which are common to Mexican American storytelling traditions.

Equally disturbing for the historian and folklorist is that these legends, myths, and other tales, collected in the twentieth century, forfeited the flavor of their nineteenth century milieu. Yet, grouped together from different sources and different times, they give a clearer indication of the part folklore played in the belief system and world view that characterized nineteenth century Mexican Americans.

In Texas, itinerants, historians, journalists, and other observers recorded the folklore of the state's Spanish-speaking community. But all historians owe a debt to the Texas Folklore Society for its indefatigable efforts in collecting Mexican American materials. Organized in 1909, issuing its first volume in 1916, and continuing until the present, the Society regularly published scores of items relating to Tejano life. Long uninterpreted

or simply ignored, these and other collections reveal the views of a preindustrial folk as they came into contact with the predominantly agrarian society. They reveal not the behavior of a people living in the culture of poverty, but rather the culture of Tejanos who just happened to be poor. They identify the autonomous spirit of a community socialized, partly by choice, partly by force, as Mexican American.

Folklore provided an intrinsic survival tool for Tejanos; it identified them with the past and thus with an experience at once contiguous and familiar. It gave them a sense of history and thus the psychological affirmation necessary to endure in a setting that constantly reminded them that they came from practically nothing.

Because Tejano folklore was firmly planted in the Texas pre-Revolutionary War experience, it lent a profound sense of cultural continuity traceable to Mexico's colonial period. Legends about buried treasures, the naming of places, the origin of certain plants, miracles, and events involving the presence of Spaniards all related to Spanish themes, settings, characters, and the like.

No other aspects of folklore revealed the legacy of the Spanish experience as much as the legends about buried treasurers. Spanish *entradas* into Texas and searches by Spanish-Mexicans in later decades engendered a rich lore about mythical wealth and tales of hidden treasures. According to legends told by nineteenth century Tejanos, Spaniards had hidden fortunes in moments of crises (usually Indian attacks) only to be prevented by some happenstance from returning at a later date to retrieve them. Thus, precious treasures lay hidden in diverse areas of the state from El Paso to East Texas. This folklore passed on to Anglo Americans who migrated to the state in later generations, became part of the fantasy of the new arrivals.

The Spanish past manifested itself in many other ways. Such folktales as that of "Pedro de Urdemalas" for example, revealed the presence of Spanish characters. Border *corridos* (ballads) that appeared around the 1860s were a link to Spanish *romances*, although their subject matter and structure belonged to the New World, while the *tragedia* (a ballad of tragedy) tended to resemble the epics of Medieval France and Spain *(La Chanson de Roland* and *El Cantar de Mío Cid)* in origin and theme.

When Spanish domination ended for Tejanos in 1821, the post-Spanish experience threaded its way into folklore as had the colonial historical past. Thus an evolving and unfolding experience embraced tales of buried treasures left in Texas by Antonio López de Santa Anna or by *bandidos* and *rancheros.* For varied reasons associated with accidents, the law, or Indian attacks, Mexicans had left their goods at various points in McMullen County in hopes of returning some day. Tejanos related these legends to whites who themselves continued the search for the elusive treasure in following generations.

Also, folklore exposed Tejanos as the bicultural people they became after the Texas Revolution. On the one hand, it displayed the interest that Mexican Americans still retained in affairs that occurred in the mother country. Through songs, for example, they eulogized Mexican heroes: with the *coplas* of *los franceses,* Tejanos of the lower border hailed the exploits of Mexican president Benito Juárez in his struggle against the French imperialists of the 1860s. Corridos praised the victory of Texas-born Ignacio Zaragoza over the French at Puebla on May 5, 1862, and immortalized Catarino Garza for his revolution of 1891–92 against Mexican President Porfirio Díaz. Social types, settings, traditions, and other elements similarly pointed to the Mexican cultural presence. On the other hand, as a folklore in flux, it displayed the Tejano's familiarity with the people who controlled Texas politics, economics, and society. Old legends about buried treasures, for one, showed a modification that included the presence of the *americanos.* In legends surrounding the battles of Palo Alto and Resaca de la Palma (May 8 and 9, 1846), the Mexican Army, pressed by Zachary Taylor's troops, lightened the retreat by burying its pay money and other valuables in the battlefield. Other tales had Anglos, rather than Spaniards or Mexicans, burying treasure and then, because of

unforeseen contingencies, never returning to retrieve it. Still others had the ghosts of white men guarding buried treasures, instead of the ghosts of Mexicans or Spaniards who had protected them before white men became part of the life experience of Tejanos.

Similarly, corridos reflected the Tejano adaptation to the American setting and their evolving nature as a bicultural people. While the *corridos* about Ignacio Zaragoza celebrated the exploits of a Mexican national hero, it also celebrated the fame of a native Tejano *(general de la frontera).* And surely, Mexicanos would not have eulogized the exploits of Ulysses S. Grant in song (or even have been aware of him) had they retained immutable ties to Mexico and repudiated all interest in the United States. Because those two corridos were sung during the same period, they indicated the familiarity of the border people with the significance of the two men and the fact that the Tejano mind naturally identified with both. Additionally, the corridos about the Catarino Garza revolution of 1891–92 displayed a Tejano familiarity with both Texan and Mexican events. *El Corrido de los Pronunciados* eulogized the attack of Garza upon Mexican territory, while the *Corrido de Capitán Jol* depicted Texas Ranger Captain Lee Hall as a coward and an ineffective fighter compared to the *pronunciados* that defeated him. This type of ethnocentrism attested to a way of life on the border colored by the interaction between Mexican Americans and white Texans.

More aspects of folklore pointed to an experience of Tejanos well acquainted both with their past and their present. Folkloric themes indicated familiarity with time, featured settings, characters, and stylistic arrangements intimate to the narrator. Place names like Presidio, San Elizario, and San Antonio, ranchos belonging to well-to-do families, the Big Bend, and the *chaparral* country of South Texas, local flora like *el cenizo* and the *guadalupana* vine, all permeated the folklore and thus revealed the Tejano's closeness to his environment. Allusions to personalities like the widow Doña Fidencia Ortega of San Elizario, Bartolo Mendoza of El Paso County, the

Cantú family of South Texas, to the peasant José Dias and to the rich Don Pedro Carrasco, similarly reflected the reality of their daily experience. Descriptive detail, symbolism, and other stylistic forms added specificity and a localized frame of reference, more plausible characters, strength of purpose, and a more meaningful and convincing portrait to that folklore.

The benevolence of a Christian God, common to folklore universally, was also shown in the religious dimension of their folk stories. In their case, He was an altruistic God seemingly an integral part of a world of disadvantaged people. A beneficient God took care of His people, intervened on their behalf in desperate moments, and fought off evil forces. He was a concerned God who intervened directly in order to give Tejanos relief from natural calamities. *Kineños* (residents of the King Ranch of South Texas), for example, related the story of a compassionate God bursting into tears that became the rain which brought relief to the drought-stricken countryside and His suffering people.

Also, folklore revealed a protective God who intervened in times of great desperation. Time after time, He had come to the assistance of the legendary Father Antonio Margil de Jesús, the ubiquitous folkloric figure. Nineteenth century folklore credited Margil, accompanying the Domingo Ramón expedition in 1716, with working a miracle through the agency of prayer by turning an attacking "swarm of savages" near San Antonio into inoffensive deer. Then, as the expedition approached the city, Margil again rescued the thirsty party through another miracle that begot the San Antonio River. That same year, he delivered another thirsty missionary party from its plight near Nacogdoches by a miracle that produced a living stream of cool water from a site that came to be called the Holy Springs of Father Margil.

Folktales such as "El Cenizo" (which explained the creation of the cenizo shrub) and "La Guadalupana Vine" (which related how the *guadalupana* vine acquired its medicinal value) and the song "Nuestra Señora de los Dolores" (which recounted the powers of such a statue in

Webb County) likewise revealed a faith, a moral uprightness, and a humility that testified to the privileged status and special relationship that Tejano vaqueros understood themselves to have with their Creator. In each, the miraculous intervention of the Divine warded off imminent catastrophe. In "El Cenizo," vaqueros arose on Ash (cenizo) Wednesday to rejoice over the desperately needed rain sent to them in response to their prayers. Likewise, the Virgen de Guadalupe had intervened directly to teach vaqueros that the guadalupana vine dipped in *mescal* had extraordinary medicinal values. And "Nuestra Señora de los Dolores," an old statue of the Virgin Mary kept at La Becerra Ranch in Webb County, invariably responded to the pleas of drought-stricken *rancheros* in the latter half of the century. During dry spells they carried the unprepossessing image in solemn procession while mothers marched praying the rosary and chanting "Nuestra Señora de los Dolores" (the song relating in ten assonantal *cuartetas* the affliction of the Virgin upon learning of the imminent crucifixion of the Lord). Legend had it that rain fell within days after the marchers arrived at the drought-stricken ranch.

In each case, the Divine had intervened to bestow His blessings, not in behalf of one individual, but characteristically for the benefit of an entire community or group. In the legend of "La Guadalupana Vine" the Virgin intended the gift, in the form of the medicinal vine, for Mexicanos in general and the vaquero specifically. The wooden statue of the Virgin Mary ("of a dark color" and its paint "a kind of sticky-looking clay") to which Tejanos sang the verses of "Nuestra Señora de los Dolores," ostensibly represented God's people, the Mexicanos. In the legend of "El Cenizo," a considerate God delivered His blessings to *la gente* in the form of the rain.

A guardian God similarly defended His people from evil forces. In the legend of "The Devil's Grotto," a priest used the holy cross to overcome Satan and deliver the pagan people of Presidio, Texas, from the havoc wreaked upon them by the Devil. Converted to the Christian faith, the people thenceforth enjoyed good health, their crops grew abundantly, and they no longer feared Satan's evil designs. Similarly, a legend concerning the old Mission de Nuestra Señora de la Purísima Concepción de Acuña supposed that the Virgin, responding to the prayers of a supplicating *padre* seeing his neophytes retreating into the safety of the Mission with Comanches close on their heels, had interceded at the gates and somehow held back the "wild tribes" at the very lintel as the neophytes rushed into the safety of the Mission just as the gates closed behind them. In another legend, San Miguel, the patron saint of Socorro (in the El Paso Valley) came to the aid of the community when, during the Civil War, wild marauders from Major T. T. Teel's command commenced bombarding the old church at Socorro. San Miguel appeared in the tower waving a flaming sword and thus held them in check until the Major arrived from Ysleta to end the indiscriminate attack.

Likewise, Tejanos carried on their traditional world view that explained the mysteries of nature and the universe. *Kineños,* for example, employed folk yarns to explain astronomical phenomena. They borrowed freely from Catholic theology and their experiences as vaqueros at the King Ranch in giving subjective renditions of the arrangements of the heavenly bodies. For others, a similar world perception begot explanations of such things as the origin of the Earth's inhabitants, their place in the world order, their functions, and so on. Explanatory stories about birds especially followed such a scheme. Through folktales, Tejanos explained the mysteries in the *aves* (birds): the *paisano* (roadrunner) ran among the chaparral in order to hide his shame and disgrace after being punished for his vanity and arrogance; the owl called "Cú, Cú, Cú, Cú, Cú," as he searched for the Pájaro Cú who had become arrogant after receiving a coat of feathers from other birds that had clothed his naked body (the owl had posted bond that the Pájaro Cú would remain humble after receiving the coat); the male cardinal was beautiful while the female was a wonderful singer because the spirit of the plains could give only one gift to

each; and, the song of the dove was a sob because she never saw the Christ Child when all the other creatures of the world came to worship Him (the dove was so humble and unassuming that no one thought of telling her the wonderful news). Similarly, *la cigarra* (locust or *cicada*) achieved its ugly form when his wife called upon the eagle, the monarch of all birds, to check the *cigarra's* roaming ways. The *cigarra's* eyes thus became popped and round and his colored wings turned an ashy gray (his wife, then wanting to be happy with the ugly creature, asked the eagle to make her like her husband).

Hence, by borrowing from their theology and everyday experiences and then combining that with their worldly wisdom, Tejanos rendered seemingly rational explanations of phenomena with which they had daily contact. Structured around such a prosaic framework, the explanations achieved credibility. Folklore provided a vehicle through which rational explanations untangled the supernatural, be it prairie lights, ghosts and spirits, mysterious lakes, physical ailments, or psychological states of mind. Thus, in explaining *la luz del llano,* that mysterious red light that appears at night on the prairie, which scientists believe is caused by peculiar atmospheric conditions, Kineño folklore held that it originated out of a covenant between an old woman and an old wizard. In exchange for food for her starving girls, the woman had agreed to surrender them to the wizard four years later. When the wizard took them the mother was so disconsolate that she set out searching for them, risking the wizard's warning that she not hunt for them on the penalty of immolation. Finally caught and burned alive, the old woman nevertheless kept up the search. Hence, *la duz del llano* was a bundle of fire held together by the spirit of the old woman who still traversed the llanos seeking her lost daughters. Unexplainable lights at night often were believed to indicate precious metals underground. Thus, legend held that the lights about Fort Ramírez (on Ramireño Creek in Nueces County) pointed to the money Ramírez had buried before Indians killed him in the early part of the century. Strange and unexplainable

■ ■ ■ *A strong sense of filial responsibility permeated nineteenth-century Mexican-American life.*

events such as those occurring at Rancho El Blanco, an old Spanish ranch in what is now Jim Hogg County, could be explained similarly—for ghosts and spirits in different forms haunted buried treasures. The appearance of a wraith at San Pedro's sparkling springs in San Antonio also signified the spirit of the tragic Francisco Rodríguez family that guarded the family's hidden treasure. Anyone daring to search for it confronted the specter of Don Francisco or his son or daughter, or the daughter's lover, who had, during Texas' colonial period, been part of a tragic scenario that had led to the treasure's burial. Likewise the feared presence at Espantosa (part of a multiplicity of pools—*tinajas*—and small lakes situated for many miles up and down the west side of the Nueces River and fifteen to twenty miles back) of huge alligators with a horn on their noses, was a result of God's wrath upon

Mexican robbers who had once upon a time enticed the most beautiful señoritas to the lake's banks and kidnapped them. In his terrible vengence, God created the reptiles to prey on the children, the women, and the bandits. But after exterminating the band, the monsters still craved for human flesh and, hence, Tejanos in the 1870s still dreaded the Espantosa.

Tejanos also used folk tales as a means of explaining physical or psychological ailments. Such was the case concerning the robust young Eutiquio Holguín of nineteenth century San Elizario who suffered from a strange malady that rendered him paralytic. After all remedies failed, it became obvious he was the victim of the local witch of Cenecú. Traumatized nightly by the *bruja* (witch), Eutiquio finally managed to grab her hand and struggle with her one night. He gradually recovered after that and, when fully recuperated, paid a visit to the *bruja*. Finding all her *monos* (figurines), he threw them into the fire, and with that the witch of Cenecú lost her powers.

And not illogically, a particularly distressing psychological state of mind caused by shock or tragedy found convenient explanation through folklore, as in the case of Elisa Váldez of San Antonio in 1888. A widow, she reluctantly consented to marry a second time. Still harboring feelings of guilt about infidelity to her dead husband, she had wandered away from the wedding festivity to be alone. Then she heard the musicians sing:

Toma el arpa con que canto Las hazañas de los reyes y de amor las dulces leyes De tu imperio seductor

At that moment she felt something pulling on her dress and, turning around, she saw a turkey. Frightened, the conviction forced itself upon her that the turkey was her dead husband coming to upbraid her for her forgetfulness and faithlessness to his memory. She knew then that her marriage could not be consummated, and, indeed, all Eliza did after that was wander around Mission Espada tending to her goat and her pet, the large turkey over which she sang Mexican love songs.

The strength, the durability, and the phenomenal endurance of the mortar of which the Mission de Nuestra Señora de la Purísima Concepción de Acuña in San Antonio consisted, also found its explanation in folklore. It was as strong as brass and had resisted the effects of time because, according to legend, the priest had explained to the Indian workers that as the mission and church were to be erected in honor of the Virgin who was without sin, the mortar was to be mixed each day with fresh pure milk as a tribute to her purity. So also could the beneficient properties of particular plants that rendered Tejanos so much curative services he explained.

Stylized romantic tales and legends, ballads and *canciones* (songs), fables, and other folkloric stories focused on the notions Tejanos held about disenchantment with the opposite sex, fil-

ial responsibility, friendships, and other special relationships. The theme of love—especially between sweethearts—persisted in such tragic romances as the one involving María Morales and Alfonso Salinas. Legend held that María had defied her betrothal to a man of her father's choice by marrying Alfonso secretly. But as the newly wedded pair rowed along the San Antonio River, a deep whirlpool caught and swallowed them. So profound was their love that, when their lifeless bodies were found, they were clasped inseparably in each other's arms and had to be buried in the same casket. Similarly, nineteenth century vaqueros and *campesinos* (farm workers) expressed their feelings of endearment toward special ladies in such canciones as "Adelita" and "La Trigueña."

Folklore also employed elements of the supernatural to show the power of love over evil. In the tale of "Blanca Flor," the gambler Juan had given his soul to the Devil in exchange for five years of good luck. At the end of the period, Juan went to the Devil's retreat at the Hacienda of Qui-quiri-qui to fulfill his commands. While there he fell in love with the Devil's beautiful daughter, Blanca Flor, and through her help escaped his commitment to the Devil. Upon marrying Blanca Flor, the legend held, he renounced his former evil ways and both lived happily ever after. Love had redeemed the former gambler.

Tejanos expressed the intimacy of filial relationships through folklore as well. In the tale of "La Luz de Llano," the mother's love for her daughters had been so eternal that the spirit of the old woman in the form of "la luz del llano" still searched for her lost daughters. In contrast, the wrath of God visited the childbeater or unprincipled parent who abused little *inocentes* (innocents). In the "Devil on the Border," Tejanos related the story of a child-beating father who took his newborn baby from his wife to starve it. She cursed the brute: "May the Devil get you." About midnight a terrific whirlwind enveloped the rancho; the smell of sulfur became suffocating, and a dust of ashes choked the people. At daylight, the people hurried toward the place where the father had taken the baby. There they found the dead child, a white dove hovering over its corpse. All that remained of the father was a heap of greenish yellow sulfur.

Filial responsibility necessarily included socializing the young, and nineteenth-century Tejano folklore contained abundant tales on morals, lessons, and good examples to be imitated by the young. Advice, counsel, and admonitions played prominent roles in these stories. Among the many tales told to impatient children was the story of King Solomon, the wise man who had discovered the secret of returning from death. Telling his most faithful servant that he would die on a certain day, he instructed him further on how to wrap his body, how to dig it up after three weeks, and how to unwrap it so that it would be resurrected. The servant was to tell no one. But people soon started wondering about Solomon's disappearance and threatened the servant with death. Realizing that if he talked, Solomon would never return but that, if he did not, both he and Solomon would be dead forever, the servant revealed the story. "They had not been patient with time, and just for that the secret of returning alive from death was lost forever."

Another didactic story concerned a little boy with three bad habits: aimlessness, asking about people's affairs, and not controlling his temper. One day while running away from home he encountered an old man who gave him three pieces of advice for his last three *pesos:* don't leave a highway for a trail; don't ask about things that don't concern you; and don't lose your temper. Leaving empty handed and feeling swindled, the boy soon encountered three crises to which the *viejito's* (old man) advice applied. By following it, he came into a thriving business and a lovely wife as rewards.

Other tales, such as "Baldheads," were intended to warn the young of certain deceptive types. A country boy had entrusted his money to a bald-headed man who owned a *Casa de Encargos,* which the boy thought to be a bank. Returning a few hours later, he was told that he had

deposited nothing. To recover the money, his father designed a plan. He took a bag full of buttons and washers to the *Casa de Encargos* and as he arranged for its deposit, the son entered asking for his money. The clerk, fearing to lose the larger sum the old man possessed, returned the boy's cash. The father then revealed the plot and, turning to his son, advised him: "Keep an eye on bald-heads."

And a tale of the Alamo sought to inculcate children with the value of courtesy by alerting them that someday they might meet the *"padre."* According to this legend, the *padre* rewarded courtesy with gifts.

As a cultural form, folklore defined the Tejano sense of values, ideals, and collective behavior. Those folktales that articulated the theme of retributive justice, for example, contained a repugnant, sometimes grotesque manifestation of supernatural evil that dramatized the consequences of unacceptable behavior. In the legend of "The Devil's Grotto," Satan arrived to bring all manner of distress to the unconverted people of the Presidio, Texas, area and left them in peace only after they were converted. In the legend of "La Casa de la Labor," Doña Fidencia Ortega of San Elizario refused the parish priest Father Pedro a little wine to celebrate the feast of San Isidro and saw her beautiful ranch burn down the next day; the smouldering remains gave "testimony of the wrath of God." Shortly afterward she was seen "riding to the *laguna* on a bull that snorted fire" and plunged into the water never to be seen again. More terrestrial though no less gruesome as symbols of punishment for bad behavior were "two slender hands" that drove Don Miguel mad for killing his lover's fiancé in the tale of "The Little White Dog." Similarly, in the tale "A Boom in Guarache Leather," a set of mean-looking bandits met their punishment at the hands of the destitute José Días, who, sharing their camp overnight, innocently placed an ugly devil's mask over his face as protection from the bitter night's cold. Waking to find what they thought to be the very devil, the malefactors fled the campsite, scrambling over a cliff to their deaths.

Stories that dramatized the favorable outcome of retributive justice, as adduced by the rewards granted the obedient in recompense for their desirable behavorial traits, were as common. In "A Hanged Man Sends Rain," Bartolo Mendoza, a convict destined for execution on a day that "seemed to grow hotter with each moment that passed," repented of his crime before God and thus summoned Providence to send relief to drought-stricken San Elizario. Upon expiring on the gallows, he sent rain from Heaven. In a legend of the Big Bend country told by Natividad Luján in the early 1880s, his uncle Santiago had been killed by Indians sometime around mid-century and became "among the blessed who died for the Faith among the heathens" and his soul had journeyed to purgatory, there to be rescued by prayers said by his faithful descendants.

Folktales featuring the compensation of those who lived acceptably and the punishment of those who lived unacceptably were as frequent. Juan Verdadero was one person whose exemplary behavior resulted in his being handsomely rewarded. According to the story, Juan never lied. But he became an innocent pawn between his *patrón* (boss) and a neighboring landowner who bet his farm that "any man under the urge of necessity will lie." Certain that Juan could be induced into a falsehood, the neighbor sent his daughter to Juan with an offer to exchange her valuable ring for the heart of the prize bull Juan herded. After an excrutiatingly difficult decision, Juan killed the bull for the ring. As he approached the ranch house, his *patrón* queried:

"Juan Verdadero, how is the herd?" "Some fat, some poor, upon my word." "And the white and greenish-colored bull?" "Dead, señor, dead," replied Juan.

Juan had not lied, so his *patrón* made him the administrator of the new estate that the neighbor surrendered. But the case of Doña Carolina who lived in the mid-century El Paso Valley was different. She was haughty and arrogant until she suffered a harrowing experience while searching for her absent husband. After the ordeal, she was no longer the supercilious woman of former days, and everyone noticed her new behavior. *Desobedientes* (disobedients), *malcriados* (ill-bred persons), *sinvergüenzas* (no 'counts) and other nonconformists recieved the severest castigations. Tejanos had little tolerance for culprits who abused their children or their spouses. One wife-beater was Don Paniqua, a magically powerful person everyone feared. One day his wife gave birth to a devil-baby who prophesied various horrors, both for the world and Don Paniqua. The raging Don Paniqua took the baby into the thicket and returned without it. No one knew what happened, but, when Don Paniqua died, the Kineños said, he became the foreman of the *infierno's* (hell) *corrida*. Other evil men, the Kineños maintained, went to work in Don Paniqua's outfit.

Brief and pithy animal tales that took the form of fables focused on deviant and unacceptable behavior. For being too proud, the mockingbird had suffered the loss of part of his beautiful feathers; for being audacious in addressing his superiors as cousins, the *paisano* had been condemned to forget to fly and to feed on unclean things; for growing overbearing and cruel toward his ugly and less gifted wife, the male cardinal suffered the loss of his wife's respect; and, for being a spirited adventurer who ignored his mate, the *cicada* incurred its repugnant appearance.

Like fables, corridos pointed to the Tejano value system. Lyrics often extolled the deeds of such great men as Ignacio Zaragoza, Ulysses Grant, and Catarino Garza, heroes who Tejanos looked upon as the personification of courage, liberty, and justice. The corridos not only exalted the adventures of those who challenged the powerful through defiance or confrontation, but they expressed delight in seeing the antagonist demeaned or denigrated—especially if he represented injustice and oppression.

Folktales also expressed a reality in which Tejanos could poke fun at the world, at its inhabitants, and at themselves. They ridiculed the Devil in a tale involving Pedro de Urdemañas (or

Urdemalas), a well-traveled and much-experienced *cabellero* who arrived in hell to regale the Devil with the wonders of Texas. Hastening to see the marvels of Texas first hand, the Devil arrived in the state only to face a series of calamities with chili peppers, prickly pears, and an unruly cow. Returning swiftly to hell, he expelled Urdemañas who happily returned to Texas to pursue the life style of his former days.

Also popular was the tale of Chano Calanche, who, for a bottle of wine, agreed to help some bandits rid themselves of a priest's body. Tricked by the killers into thinking that he had not buried the corpse—each time he returned to claim the bottle, he found the body of the *padrecito,* not knowing that the bandits had actually killed three priests—the drunken Chano finally decided to dispose of it once and for all. Lighting fire to the corpse, he stayed with it until he fell asleep. He awoke, however to find the padrecito at his campfire; it was actually a traveling priest that happened to stop to warm his morning meal. After the incident, the story held, Chano never claimed the wine and it was said that the prize occupied a place of esteem in the *cantina* (bar) for years after that and was never put up for sale.

In a tale with a more universal theme, Tejano common folks mocked female curiosity. "My wife is not inquisitive," retorted a husband to his friend's suggestion that "all women are curious." But, when his partner took a box to the first man's wife with instructions to keep it sealed, the wife could not resist her curiosity. Upon opening the box, she unwittingly allowed the bird inside to fly away, thereby ridiculing the husband and her own ineptness at keeping secrets.

And they could demean themselves, as in the song of "Coplas del Payo," which portrayed in a jesting manner the general misfortune of their lives. In this story, an overseer encouraged a forlorn lover—an ordinary worker like the narrator—to jump over a cliff.

As poor and disadvantaged people, Tejanos employed folklore as a means of expressing wish

fulfillment, wishful fantasizing, and ambitiousness. Such tales generally expressed expectations of winning against misfortune. One of those tales involved a poor, elderly couple who owned a miraculous dog capable of acting as a beast of burden, a hunter, and a racer. One day, a stranger arrived in a nearby town with a very swift horse that made short work of the local opposition. With a chance to make $10,000, the poor man matched his dog against the visiting steed. The dog won easily—in fact did not stop at the finish line but ran all the way to the moon—and the poor, elderly couple had gained their ambition to be wealthy. Another tale involved a *conducta* (convoy) of weary, hungry men preparing to cook their meager meal at the end of the day. At that point Agapito Cercas spoke up: "Don't bother to cook anything. This very day a hog was slaughtered at my home. Just wait and I will bring you *carne adobada, chile con asadura,* and *tortillas calientes.*" He withdrew from the group, and, according to a witness, took off his clothes and disappeared. In a while, he called for his clothes and reappeared with the food he had promised. Some of the men started eating the appetizing meal they wished for, but others refused it suspecting the work of the supernatural.

As an ambitious people not fatalistically resigned to their lot, Tejanos used folklore to constantly question their social condition. They displayed confidence in themselves and showed that they regarded themselves to be as good as the next man and that, if granted more favorable circumstances, they could overcome their problems. Further revealed was the high regard Tejanos had of themselves: that they were good enough to outwit more formidable antagonists, whether it be a wily coyote, a rich *compadre,* or a more fortunate neighbor.

This displayed itself conspicuously in several of the trickster tales. As a genre, these tales include the antagonistic forces of the weak (the underdog) and the strong (the opposer) with a scenario in which the weak used their wit to overcome the powerful. Such was the case of the innocent man outsmarted by a wily coyote who had rescued him from a snake; the man had originally rescued the snake from a trap where-upon the snake had turned on him because "to repay good with evil" was *la costumbre*—the custom. Beholden to the coyote, the man compensated the animal "with good" (contrary to custom). The man soon learned that he had been too generous, for the coyote kept increasing the payment. Tricking the coyote, he finally unleashed his dog upon the opportunist. "It isn't right to repay good with evil," called the outwitted coyote. "Perhaps," answered the man, "*pero es la costumbre.*"

Commonly, the antagonist was a compadre, for Tejanos spoke in terms of their own culture and social conditions as ordinary people. One tale involved two compadres—one rich and the other poor, and the former arrogant and snobbish toward the latter. One day the poor man was so desperate for survival that he schemed to extract money from his more affluent compadre. But his rich compadre grew so angry at his tricks that he finally sought to drown his nemesis by putting him in a bag and dumping him in the sea. But the poor compadre slyly escaped the bag and surfaced to report that he had recovered the rich man's lost pearls at the bottom of the water. Eager to retrieve more jewels, the rich compadre persuaded the poor man to tie him in a sack and dump him in the ocean—all his worldly goods would be put in trust to the poor man for the favor. The poor man did as his compadre wished and became wealthy and was held in great esteem by the people of the town for his innocent little pranks.

In a similar tale, a poor man sought to get even with a rich compadre who looked condescendingly upon him because of his poverty. He succeeded in convincing the rich man of the powers of a newly purchased cap. All that was necessary to obtain items at the store was to say "*Debo de gorra*" (put it on the cap, cuff). "What a marvelous cap," said the rich man, "Sell it to me for $30,000." Feigning reluctance, the poor man surrendered it. But when the rich man attempted to buy an expensive diamond necklace with it, he found himself in jail for failing to pay. The poor man went on to live a life of lux-

ury, while the rich fellow wound up in the mad house.

A tale indicating the awareness Tejanos felt concerning social distance involved Don Pedro Carrasco, the owner of many cattle, and José Días, the owner of a single but fat and very productive cow. Jealous of José, Don Pedro tricked José into killing his only cow, telling him of the high price *guarache* leather was bringing in the neighboring town of Aldama. Disappointed at being tricked into killing his only cow (the price of leather at Aldama was rock bottom), José was making his way slowly homeward when he came upon some money left by bandits. Taking his new found wealth, he arrived home to show the people the money which, he said, he had made off his cow. Don Pedro, thinking that the price of *guarache* leather was indeed high, killed his herd, only to find himself tricked by his sly compadre. Now José and his family became wealthy and gave money to the *santitos* (saints) and the poor. Such trickster tales allowed Tejanos to engage the enemy and triump over him. It also permitted the psychic relief from oppressive conditions.

Nineteenth-century Texas folklore revealed an aspiring, scheming, dreaming, and changing people concerned with a multiplicity of things affecting them both as human beings and as an oppressed people. Like dependent classes elsewhere, Tejanos employed folklore to question their existence, to explain it, and to satisfy the mind as to the universe about them; but folklore was not limited to that. It also functioned as entertainment, as a way of eulogizing heroes and expressing discontent with "no 'counts," a means of expressing kinship, a vehicle for inculcating values and behavior patterns, a mode of teaching the lessons of acceptable ideals both to adults and the young, an art of poking fun at themselves, a manner of engaging in wishful fantisizing, and, much more importantly, a technique for passing on survival skills through fictionalized accounts where the weak could indeed triumph over powerful forces. Folklore, encompassing all these functions, acted not only to give identity and solidarity to a community that shared a similar experience, but it also provided them with a covert and subconscious form of resistance to oppression.

Folklore, of course, is a universal cultural feature among all classes, and it was present long before Tejanos met Anglos in the 1820s. It persisted as a vital force of the Tejano nineteenth century experience, and it continued long after 1900. Indeed, it was in the first four or five decades of the twentieth century that the aforementioned Texas Folklore Society collected most of its materials. Primarily the tales and legends of Tejanos from the rural areas, that folklore, while manifesting the changes of the twentieth century, reflected themes, settings, and stylistic forms similar to the folklore of nineteenth century agrarian Texas. It continued being a part of the intimate side of the Texas Mexican experience— like that of raising families, worshipping in particular ways, and maintaining a language. That folklore thrived meant it was part of an expressive culture defined from within but that also took and rejected from outside standards, observances, and patterns as it saw fit.

■■■

STUDY QUESTIONS

1. De Leon argues that Tejano culture was a fusion of Mexican and Anglo experiences. Do you agree? Why or why not?

2. Evaluate the traditional Anglo argument that Tejano culture was passive and fatalistic, with Tejanos taking a negative view of themselves and assuming they had little power over their own lives.

3. How did the Anglo view of Tejanos reinforce the existing social and economic institutions of nineteenth century Anglo society?

4. Modern societies have increasingly distinguished between magic and formal religion. Can such distinctions be made for Tejano culture? Why or why not?

BIBLIOGRAPHY

For portraits of Mexican-Americans as passive and fatalistic people, see William Madsen, *Mexican-Americans of South Texas* (1964) or Norman D. Humphrey, "The Cultural Background of the Mexican Immigrant," *Rural Sociology*, 13 (1948). More recent treatments of Mexican-American history which employ liberal outrage over past discrimination as their major focus include Rodolfo Acuña, *Occupied America: The Chicano's Struggle for Liberation* (1972) and Carey McWilliams, *North from Mexico* (1968). For the best treatments of Mexican-American ethnicity, which transcend the Anglo perspective, see Arnoldo De Leon, *The Tejano Community, 1836–1900* (1982); Leonard Pitt, *The Decline of the Californios: A Social History of Spanish-Speaking Californians, 1848–1890* (1966); and Louise Ano Nuevo Kerr, "Mexican Chicago: Chicano Assimilation Aborted, 1939–1952," in Melvin G. Holli and Peter d'A. Jones, *The Ethnic Frontier: Group Survival in Chicago and the Midwest* (1977).

THE WORLD OF NATIVE AMERICANS

James S. Olson and Raymond Wilson

It is a matter of considerable controversy among scholars, but most archaeologists believe there were one to two million Native Americans living in the United States when the Pilgrims landed at Plymouth Rock in 1621. By the time of the American Revolution, the native population had dropped to 600,000. It fell to approximately 350,000 by the time of the Civil War, and bottomed out at about 225,000 in 1910. European civilization—its diseases, technology, and bureaucracies—almost annihilated the Native American population. Dependent on subsistence agriculture, hunting, and fishing, tuned to the rhythms of nature on sacred land, and divided into hundreds of premodern cultures, Native Americans could not have been more different from the white settlers. Their views of life, death, time, land, and the environment clashed sharply, and over the course of three hundred years confrontations between Europeans and Native Americans occurred again and again. Functioning in separate cultural worlds, they never understood each other.

Throughout United States history, a tragic cycle repeated itself. Hordes of European settlers on their way to new farms in the West encountered the Native American tribes, pushed them off valuable land onto land no whites wanted, and then promised peace between the two peoples. But in another generation, more white settlers would find value in previously "worthless" land, and once again the Native Americans would find themselves on the move. Before the Civil War, this cycle of dispossession focused on the tribes of the eastern woodlands. Congress passed the Indian Removal Act in 1830, forcing the eastern tribes to abandon their ancestral homelands and move across the Mississippi River. Their trek would eventually become known as "The Trail of Tears." In "The World of Native Americans," James S. Olson and Raymond Wilson describe the life-styles and cultural values of Native Americans, and discuss how those values set them on a collision course with European civilization.

In September of 1953, several of us left our second-grade class for morning recess and discovered a strange commotion out on the playground. Children were milling about in small groups, buzzing with excitement about the "Indian"—a real Indian—who was going to our school—Hollydale Elementary in South Gate, California. Jerry Pete was a Navajo, and as he rocked back and forth on the playground swing he seemed a bit surprised about and perhaps suspicious of all the attention. I still remember thinking as I watched him that he was rather ordinary for a real Indian; he was not doing anything spectacular, at least not compared to television images of screaming warriors killing innocent pioneers. Jerry Pete rode my bus home that afternoon, disembarked at my stop, and ran into the neighbor's house. A real Indian was living next door, right in the middle of a white working-class suburb.

Our neighbors were Mormons who, through a church program, had entered into an arrangement with Jerry's parents whereby he would spend the school year with that family in California and return each summer to his home on the Navajo Reservation in Arizona. Jerry Pete, a Navajo, and I, a grandson of Norwegian and Swedish immigrants, became fast friends. We played baseball, basketball, flag football, Monopoly, crazy-eights, and over-the-line together; went to cub scouts and boy scouts; watched situation comedies and game shows on hot summer afternoons; and rode our bicycles through the streets and paved riverbeds of south Los Angeles. During two summers I was a guest in his home in Arizona. We swam in the Colorado River, slept at night in an old hogan, hunted rabbits and snakes, and wandered daily through the Navajo community. Once I watched in total fascination as an old man worked on an

James S. Olson and Raymond Wilson. "The World of Native Americans," from *Native Americans in the Twentieth Century*. Urbana: University of Illinois Press, 1984, pp. 1–24. © 1984 by the Board of Trustees of the University of Illinois.

elaborate sand painting. On graduation night Jerry and I went to the all-night party in the high school gymnasium and then went to Laguna Beach to bodysurf at the "wedge." The next afternoon, Jerry Pete packed his bags and returned to the reservation. He still lives there.

His decision to trade life in the city suburbs for what I considered the quaint but abject poverty of an Arizona reservation shocked me terribly—perhaps even angered me, as if in some way he had passed judgment on my way of life. What had happened? Had he encountered some discrimination? Had someone been thoughtless or ugly? Perhaps the Mormon family had tired of him? But none of these was true. I insisted on looking for what had "pushed" Jerry back to the reservation, some visible crisis driving or expelling him from the prosperity of my world. Years later, as I came to appreciate Native American history, I realized that Jerry had been pulled, not pushed. Celsa Apapas, a Cupeño woman from California, eloquently described her feelings in 1965:

You asked us to think what place we like next best to this place, where we always lived. You see that graveyard out there? There are our fathers and our grandfathers. You see that Eagle-nest Mountain and that Rabbit-hole Mountain? When God made them, He gave us this place. We have always been here. We do not care for any other place. . . . If you give us the best place in the world, it is not so good for us as this. This is our home. . . . If we cannot live here, we want to go into the mountain and die. We do not want any other home.

With hindsight, I remembered that Jerry Pete had always seemed a little shy around European Americans. He was rarely excited about our ambitions and curiously quiet about his own—as much an observer of my childhood as he was a participant. On the reservation, around his own people, Jerry was always more relaxed and animated, as if invisible restraints on his feelings had disappeared. And on the reservation, despite gracious hospitality, I often felt like an outsider—a sojourner—which is exactly what I was. Despite ten years of companionship, I never really made the cultural jump from my world to his. A barrier existed between the two societies, and neither one of us was ever able to cross it, despite the innocence of boyhood friendship. It was not a question of either self-righteousness or self-consciousness, but simply a set of different expectations buried deep in our psyches. In this sense, I was symbolic of American history, for most European Americans never crossed that cultural barrier either; rather, they spent hundreds of years viewing Native American society from a very distorted perspective. Ever since 1607, when the English colonists first settled along the James River in Virginia, a profound veil divided the two peoples; and more than three centuries later, after countless contacts and confrontations, the veil is still intact, still preventing much understanding.

In the 1960s and 1970s curiosity about Native Americans increased dramatically, becoming almost a fascination born of guilt about the past and a nostalgia for earlier times. Best-selling books such as Vine Deloria's *Custer Died for Your Sins*, Dee Brown's *Bury My Heart at Wounded Knee*, and Ruth Beebe Hill's *Hanta Yo*, and movies such as *Little Big Man* and *A Man Called Horse* symbolized the growing interest, as did the increased popularity of such Native American writers as N. Scott Momaday, Alonzo Lopez, and James Welch. For the first time people were beginning to discard a few of their traditional stereotypes, and they were just beginning to sense the distinctiveness of Native American culture—its holistic independence from the assumptions of Western civilization. Jerry Pete, of course, along with hundreds of thousands of other Native Americans, had realized this all along; but it has taken all of United States history for non–Native Americans even to approach the same idea. In the process, Native Americans have suffered.

A recent television commercial illustrates not only a Native American vision of contemporary America but the consuming interest Americans of European descent have in Native American values today. Produced by the Advertising Council, the commercial pictures Iron Eyes Cody, a lone and proud Native American astride a horse, looking out over a freeway somewhere in the United States. Cody is painfully reviewing the blacktop, traffic jams, heat, noise, litter, pollution, blinking lights, crowding, and mounting frustration—the more debilitating consequences of a modern technological society. In the closing scene, the camera pans back and focuses on Cody again, particularly on the tear he is shedding for the condition of his country. For perhaps forty thousand years Native Americans lived and traveled throughout the continent without significantly altering its environmental heritage or balance; they were at peace with their surroundings. But only four centuries of European civilization seemingly had changed the country forever. The traditional faith in "Manifest Destiny," with its emphasis on expansion, progress, unbridled growth, as well as racial superiority, had a new generation of critics in the 1960s and 1970s. As modern society began to choke on its own materialism, and as Americans suffered through inflation, unemployment, pollution, and chronic energy shortages, the world of Native Americans suddenly took on a new meaning; to some it even became an appealing alternative to the endless series of crises. Perhaps the Native Americans had been right all along in their approach to life, death, and change. Even then, of course, most non–Native Americans had no appreciation for the structure and complexity of Native American values; but they did, for the first time, realize that Native Americans were indeed different (but not necessarily different in the sense of being inferior), that their vision of living and dying was not at all like that of Europeans, and (perhaps most important) that they were not likely to change easily or quickly.

When Columbus waded through the surf at San Salvador on October 12, 1492, he looked upon the natives with curious delight, a euphoria based on relief and a sense of fulfillment after a long and sometimes difficult voyage. Convinced that he had reached the East Indies, that he was close to Japan and China, Columbus named the natives Indians, a historical misnomer born of geographical ignorance which stuck. Years later, as Europeans came to realize that they had not reached Asia but had accidentally discovered a "new world," they began to wonder about the "Indians." If not Asians, then who were these strange people? And where did they come from? Few other questions so obsessed European explorers or intrigued generations of American folklorists. Some Europeans argued that the "Indians" were long-lost descendants of ancient Celtic, Nordic, Phoenician, Carthaginian, or Chinese travelers, while others believed them to be a remnant of the ten tribes of Israel or of the mysterious city of Atlantis. Millions of Mormons believe that Native Americans are descendants of three separate migrations from the Middle East between 2000 and 400 B.C. Some people have even held to an independent creation idea—that is, that God engaged in co-creations of humans in the Old World and in the New World. Among scholars, the consensus is that most Native Americans migrated to the New World from Siberia during the last two ice ages.

There was a time, almost forty thousand years ago, when the New World really was a vast island, empty of human beings and completely isolated from Europe and Asia. Exchanges of plants and animals had not occurred since before the great continental drifts. But then, slowly and almost imperceptibly, the native migrations commenced. As strange as it seems, these journeys of prehistoric people were unplanned and unconscious, not at all like the usual movement of immigrants. The wandering hunters never decided, once and for all, to leave for America, nor did they ever understand the significance of their migration—that they had traveled to a new continent. Indeed the migrations were generational and not individual; only over the course of hundreds of generations and thousands of years can they be considered as migrations at all. Of the nomadic hunters leaving Siberia on the trail of bison, musk ox, mammoth, moose, and caribou, no single individual, family, or even group ever completed the entire journey; the immigrants were ignorant of their own migration.

According to most New World archaeologists and anthropologists, the first Americans left Siberia sometime between forty and twenty-five thousand years ago. Sometime around 40,000 B.C., the onset of an ice age depressed general temperature levels around the world. Huge glaciers gradually covered all of Canada and the northern United States, freezing up millions of cubic miles of ocean water. The sea level dropped hundreds of feet as ocean water was absorbed into glacial ice, and the continental shelves around the world surfaced. Land masses became much more extensive. The shallow Bering Sea, North Pacific Ocean, and Arctic Ocean floors appeared, and a land bridge, known now as Beringia, connected Siberia with Alaska. The stage was set for the journey of the Siberian hunters.

At an evolutionary pace, vegetation slowly rooted and thrived in Beringia; and as the big game headed east from Siberia, small game such as foxes and woodchucks headed west from Alaska. Each season the temporary villages of Siberian families and tribes moved further east in the eternal quest for big game until, after thousands of years, the Asians had reached Alaska. And as thousands more years passed, the hunters slowly moved down through the Yukon and Mackenzie river valleys and the slopes of the Rocky Mountains. Around 13,000 B.C. the Ice Age ended, the great glaciers slowly melted back into the oceans, and Beringia submerged again under three hundred feet of water. Unknowingly, the Siberians had now become Americans.

For the next fifteen thousand years the Native American hunters settled throughout the New World, from the Arctic in North America to Tierra del Fuego in South America and from the Atlantic to the Pacific. The diaspora across the two New World continents was another unplanned journey of extended families splitting off from one another every generation. The passage of time and the need to adjust to new environments resulted in a kaleidoscope of cultures in America. When the European explorers first arrived in the 1490s, those wandering bands of Siberian hunters had become hundreds of separate ethnic groups, as independent from one another as they were distinct from the European invaders to come.

But Europeans were blind to that diversity and insisted on viewing Native American culture through a single lens, as if all Native Americans could somehow be understood in terms of a few monolithic assumptions. Social life in colonial and frontier America was terribly complex—a cauldron of competing racial, religious, and linguistic groups—and settlers saw Native Americans as just one more group among many. The Europeans should have known better. They were divided too—Sephardic, German, and Ashkenazi Jews; Baptist, Methodist, Congregational, Presbyterian, Pietistic, Lutheran, and Reformed Protestants; Roman and Uniate Catholics; Russian, Greek, Bulgarian, Syrian, Armenian, and Rumanian Orthodox; and Anglo-Saxon, German, Scandinavian, Magyar, Italian, Celtic, and Slavic ethnics. It is an irony that probably *because* of their own diversity, Europeans were unable to see Native Americans as anything more than a single group. Unlike black Africans, who came from diverse tribal backgrounds but were formed into a single, highly integrated African American slave culture, Native Americans were divided tribally by economic organization, language, religion, and political loyalty.

As the earliest hunters spread across the two continents, they adapted their lives to the land. Whether the environment included arctic ice, frozen tundra, mountains, oceans, forests, deserts, or jungles, they were remarkably successful in adjusting to it. A subsistence people in a rich and varied land, they developed hundreds of separate economic styles and technologies, and economic life became uniquely important to

tribal identities. At first, they were big-game hunters, and until perhaps 9000 B.C. they organized life around the bison, caribou, mammoth, moose, or musk ox. Long before agriculture developed or foraging became important, they spent the spring and summer killing the game, drying the meat, and making clothes and stone tools. Then, during the late fall and winter, they retreated into protective valleys to wait out the harsh northern cold. For thousands of years this remained the predominant life-style.

When the Europeans arrived, many Native Americans were still living as big-game hunters. Along the edges of the Arctic Ocean and in the northern tundra, Eskimo hunters went after whales, walruses, sea lions, seals, and polar bears. Living in igloo ice houses, venturing out on the ocean in umiak canoes, or hunting in the tundra with ivory goggles and harpoons, they adapted successfully to one of the world's most inhospitable regions. Farther south, the Chipewyans followed the caribou. Caribou meat and fat fed them, caribou skins clothed and housed them, and caribou bones provided their tools. On the Great Plains, tribes such as the Comanches, Arapahos, Cheyennes, and Sioux hunted the buffalo. Always on the move with portable tipis and horses, the Plains tribes pursued the buffalo with a passion. The buffalo served them as the caribou served the Chipewyan: buffalo meat, fat, skin, and bones supplied their material world. From the buffalo carcass they took fresh meat and dried the rest into jerky. Buffalo skins gave them their blankets, moccasins, clothes, and covering for their tipi homes. Buffalo hair and tendons became thread and strings for their bows. Buffalo horns were used as cups and spoons, and they even turned buffalo tongues into hairbrushes and buffalo fat into hair oil. The buffalo hunt was central to the tribal identity.

As most Native Americans scattered out over the continent and learned more about the nature of their surroundings, they began to rely less on big game and more on a wider variety of exploitable resources. Wood, ground stone, and chipped stone provided axes, drills, scrapers, spears, fishhooks, and harpoons. When the Great Lakes tribes invented the lightweight birchbark canoe, which was ideal for navigating shallow streams and easy portaging, their range and mobility increased enormously. For some tribes the end of the big-game hunts relieved them of their nomadism; they could establish semipermanent villages as long as the supply of fish, small animals, and plants held out. When, after a while, these resources became more scarce, tribes simply relocated their villages. The big-game hunters had always relied to an extent on plants and small animals, primarily as dietary supplements; but by 4000 B.C. most Native Americans (the Plains tribes being the major exception) had completed the transition to a new economy in which foraging for small game, fish, and plants filled all material needs.

There was a great deal of variety to the foraging economies. Coastal tribes in California, like the Costanoans south of San Francisco, lived off sea snails, shrimp, mussels, oysters, crabs, and abalone. Because of the abundant oak trees, many California tribes used the acorn as a dietary staple. They gathered, shelled, and pounded the acorns into flour and were able to store grain surpluses for long periods of time. To collect and carry the acorns and flour, they developed elaborate techniques of basketmaking. Along the Northwest Coast, from Oregon through British Columbia, the richest foraging economies appeared. Forests abounded in bear, deer, elk, and moose, while the mountains were full of mountain sheep and goats. The sea delivered whales, dolphins, seals, salmon, halibut, sturgeon, smelt, and grunion, as well as crabs, oysters, and clams, to the Yurok, Coo, Umpqua, Chinook, Chehalis, and Makah tribes. And other tribes such as the Klamaths, Cayuse, Yakimas, and Walla Wallas occupied the major rivers and streams in the spring and summer, organizing economic life around the giant salmon, returned from the sea, which they speared, hooked, netted, or trapped and then dried for the future. In the Great Basin—the arid, hot, and economically austere deserts of Nevada, Utah, and eastern California—such tribes as the Utes, Paiutes, Paviotsos, and Shoshones lived a marginal existence, perpetually hunting for rabbits, snakes, insects, roots, berries, seeds, nuts, and green leaves. Starvation was often close at hand, although these people developed a splendid desert lore. And throughout the upper Midwest, Native Americans traveled in their canoes along the rivers and streams, catching lake trout, pike, and pickerel and hunting small game. For all these various tribes, the foraging process created a distinct form of economic life which shaped their outlook on the world.

Finally, beginning more than five thousand years ago, many Native Americans, especially the tribes east of the Mississippi River and in the southwestern deserts, made the transition to agriculture. It was a small move at first: simply a collective discovery at different times and in different places of how to plant and harvest the wild beans, squash, and corn they had been gathering for thousands of years. The tribes still hunted and foraged for food, but at least part of their nutritional needs were now filled by farming. Gradually, over the course of hundreds of years, farming techniques grew more sophisticated as the Native Americans discovered the best times to plant and harvest, how to rotate crops, how to fertilize the land with animal wastes or dead fish, and how to irrigate the land. When they learned how to preserve crops through the winter and spring, they were able to settle into permanent villages and then cities, and farming became the basis of their entire economy. Hunting and foraging became purely supplementary in importance, providing additions to their diet rather than the foundation.

Beans, squash, and corn became staple crops for all Native American agricultural societies, but the conditions for farming varied according to region. Among the early Hohokam people of southern Arizona, where rainfall was limited and often confined to summer thunderstorms, irrigation was essential. They constructed small dams and ditches to trap rainfall or tilled their gardens on hillsides where the runoff from melting snow would water the plants. Later tribes adopted and further developed Hohokam techniques for irrigating crops. The Havasupais, whose home was the Grand Canyon in northwestern Arizona, constructed large irrigation ditches to water their fields. On the Gila and Salt rivers in Arizona, the Pimas built elaborate canal systems to trap flood water for irrigating their plants. In the Eastern Woodlands, because of the discovery of agriculture, the now-famous Moundbuilder societies appeared more than a thousand years ago. Native Americans there lived in cities with substantial, permanent housing, religious temples, community centers, communal fields, and unique burial grounds. Later, such northeastern tribes as the Mohawks, Senecas, Menominees, and Sacs and Foxes lived in settled agricultural villages, cultivating corn, beans, and squash in communal gardens. Their wigwams or bark houses were separated by streets and surrounded by protective stockades. In the Southeast, the Five Civilized Tribes (Cherokee, Choctaws, Chickasaws, Creeks, and Seminoles) lived in similarly well-developed farming villages. Their way of life was completely different from the wandering nomadism of the big-game hunters. Perhaps the most striking example of the early agricultural society is that of the several Pueblo tribes, whose unique multistory rock-and-stucco villages are still in use after as long as a thousand years.

Today, the values associated with work, education, status, and class create powerful group identities; out of those identities, as well as self-perceptions based on language, national origins, race, and religion, emerges ethnicity. A steelworker living in a working-class suburb in Youngstown, Ohio, identifies closely with other blue-collar workers rather than with a wealthy physician living in a well-to-do suburb of Long Island, New York. Or a wheat farmer in the Texas Panhandle would likely feel more comfortable with other farmers than with a group of Greenwich Village artists. Economic identities

were similarly important to Native Americans. With such vast differences between the hunting, fishing, and farming economies, as well as between the different technologies of different regions, it is no wonder that economic organization became an important part of Native American ethnicity. Identity is closely related to the way people feed and clothe themselves, so ethnic loyalties naturally cluster around those feelings.

But technology and economic organization are only part of ethnicity. Indeed, compared to Native American linguistic differences, the varieties of tribal economic life seem relatively minor, at least as far as ethnicity is concerned. Because the New World was settled by several waves of migrating people who spread across two enormous land-masses over the course of perhaps four hundred centuries, linguistic development was amazingly diverse, a "Tower of Babel" in its own right. When two tribal languages were completely different, mutually unintelligible to one another, it is clear that the two tribal groups were totally unrelated or related only in the very distant past. And, of course, when two tribes spoke similar languages, their common histories in the Americas were more recent and their origins in time and space more common.

European languages are classified into such major groups as Romance, Germanic, Slavic, and Uralo-Altaic, and each of these groups is then subdivided into specific languages. The Romance languages, for example, consist of Spanish, Portuguese, French, Italian, Latin, and Rumanian, while Russian, Czech, Polish, Slovakian, Serbo-Croatian, Slovenian, Bulgarian, Rusin, and Ukrainian are Slavic languages. Individual languages, then, can be subdivided again into dialects, remnants of different origins. Although most people in the United States speak English, there are immediately recognizable differences between a Southern "drawl," a New England "brogue," or "Brooklynese." Ethnic loyalties group around languages as well as dialects. Native American languages were similarly diverse and complex, and tribal identities were closely related to them.

Although historians, anthropologists, and linguists are still debating the structure of Native American languages, many now agree that there were thirteen major native language groups in what is now the United States: Eskimo-Aleut, Na-Dene, Algonquian-Ritwan-Kutenai, Iroquois-Caddoan, Gulf, Siouan-Yuchi, Utaztecan-Tanoan, Mosan, Penutian, Yukian, Hokaltecan, Keres, and Zuñi. Except for the Yukian and Zuñi groups, each of these can be divided into many different languages. Yukian is one language and one language group spoken only by the Yuki tribe of California, as is the Zuñi group, spoken by the Zuñis of the Southwest. But the Iroquois-Caddoan group, on the other hand, is divided into the Iroquois group of languages and the Caddoan group. The Iroquois group consists of the Erie, Huron, Iroquois, Neutral, Susquehannock, and Tionontati languages, spoken by the northeastern tribes, and the Cherokee, Nottoway, and Tuscarora languages in the Carolinas. Caddo, Kichai, Tawakoni, Waco, and Wichita are Caddo languages spoken on the southeastern plains, as are the Arikara and Pawnee languages on the eastern plains. The Algonquian-Ritwan-Kutenai language group was even more complex, indicating the vast tribal migrations that had once occurred in North America. The Algonquian group consisted of the Cree, Montagnais, and Naskapi languages in the subarctic regions of North America; the Abnaki, Chickahominy, Delaware, Lumbee, Malecite, Massachuset, Mattapony, Micmac, Mohegan, Nanticoke, Narraganset, Nipmuc, Pamlico, Pamunkey, Pennacook, Passamaquoddy, Penobscot, Pequot, Powhatan, Shawnee, Wampanoag, and Wappinger languages in the Eastern Woodlands; the Illinois, Kickapoo, Menominee, Miami, Ojibwa, Ottawa, Peoria, Potawatomi, Sac, and Fox languages in the Midwest; and the Arapaho, Astina, Blackfoot, Cheyenne, and Plains Cree languages on the Great Plains. The related Ritwan group languages consisted of the Wiyot and Yurok languages in northern California, and the Kutenai group consisted of the Kutenai language in northern Montana and Idaho. At one time, thousands of years ago, all of these tribes were a closely related people, and only over the course of hundreds of generations did they scatter across the continent and develop into dozens of independent groups. In all there were more than two hundred separate languages spoken by the Native Americans of what is now the United States when the European settlers began arriving in the seventeenth century.

In many cases, these languages contained different dialects. The Santee, Teton, and Yankton Sioux all spoke slightly different versions of their language, and the Blood, Piegan, and Siksika Blackfeet spoke different versions of the Blackfoot language. All of this made for an enormous linguistic diversity. In a stretch of only three hundred miles along the Pacific Coast between northern California and Washington, dozens of languages were spoken, including Bella Coola, Chehalis, Coast Salish, Tillamook, Makah, Wiyot, Haida, Hupa, and Mattole, as well as several dialects of each. It was the same in southern Alaska, where Native Americans spoke nineteen versions of the Athapascan language. Sometimes small groups lived next to one another without being able to communicate except through interpreters or sign language. For example, the Tanoans and Keresans, who lived side by side in the Rio Grande Valley, could only communicate by sign language (and, later, Spanish). Although identity and dialect are close kin, if only because communication and problem resolution depend so directly on linguistic tools, language of the early migrants diversified to reach a state of bewildering variety in America, as complex as anywhere on earth.

Beyond economic organization and language, for most societies the marrow of ethnicity is religion, and Native American cultures were certainly no exception. But like the economies and the languages, Native American religions were hardly monolithic; instead, they were characterized by a rich variety of theological assumptions and ceremonial rituals. The theologies provided them with a common tribal perspective on the purpose of life and the operation of the cosmos, and the ceremonial rituals became forms of symbolic association in which members of the tribes expressed and acknowledged a common heritage and a common future. Out of common faiths and symbolic associations emerged the religious dimension of Native American ethnicity.

Still, there were some major religious characteristics common to many tribal groups. Most indigents of North America were polytheistic, believing in many gods and many levels of deity. At the basis of most Native American beliefs in the supernatural was a profound conviction that an invisible force, a powerful spirit, permeated the entire universe and ordered the cycles of birth and death for all living things. The Iroquois called this spirit the *Orenda*, the Algonquins *Manitu*, the Cayuse *Honeawoat*, the Ojibwa *Gitchimanidu*, and the Sioux *Wakan Tanka*. European Christians and Jews incorrectly tried to equate this "Great Spirit" with the God of their own religious views. But for Native Americans the *Orenda* or *Manitu* or *Wakan Tanka* or *Honeawoat* was more pantheistic—a fusion of matter, spirit, time, and life, a divine energy unifying all of the universe. It was not at all a personal being presiding omnipotently over the salvation or damnation of individual people.

Beyond this belief in a universal spirit, most Native Americans attached supernatural qualities to animals, heavenly bodies, the seasons, dead ancestors, the elements, and geologic formations. In short, their world was infused with the divine.

Common characteristics essentially ended there. Most other beliefs and practices were amazingly and colorfully diverse. The Pawnees, for example, believed that the wind, sun, and stars were all divine spirits but that they were ruled by an even higher god called *Tirawahat*, "The Expanse of the Heavens." Eskimo and Aleut tribes worshipped *Sedna*, the sea goddess who directed their hunts, as well as the "Mother

of the Caribou" and the "Moon Man." The Pomos of California believed in the coyote god. Paiutes in the Great Basin had various plant spirits they tried to please, and the Yumans accepted predestination at face value. The Navajos had well-developed fears of witches dressed like wolves. Each tribe also had unique views of the creation and their own origins. The Cayuses in Oregon and Washington believed they sprang originally from the heart of a giant beaver trapped in the Palouse River. Tribal legend had the Kiowas emerging eons ago from a hollow cottonwood log at the command of a supernatural being, while the Navajos believed mankind slowly evolved from four underworlds beneath the surface of the earth. Or among the California Luiseños, "the people" came from two supernatural parents, floating in the sky, who united and created all the "thoughts" of what was to come in the world. So each Native American tribe possessed its own pantheon of deities and theologies.

The abundance of divinities, however, was nothing compared to the array of ceremonial rituals designed to propitiate them. In their ceremonialism Native Americans were even more diverse, and that diversity was linked directly to economic organization and population. Among the Native Americans of the northwestern plateau and the Great Basin, ceremonialism was limited, often being confined to simple individual rites. Among the Pueblos of the Southwest, on the other hand, where people lived settled, agrarian lives in urban concentrations, ceremonial rituals were far more elaborate, sometimes consuming more than a hundred days each year. Among many of the California tribes also, ceremonialism was very elaborate because they had the time necessary for such devotions; food was plentiful and economic survival almost guaranteed. Hunting and foraging societies prayed for good hunts and abundant food supplies. The Tlingits performed salmon rites to guarantee the return of the salmon each year, while the Mandans on the Great Plains performed the Okipa ceremony to

■ ■ *An 1834 sketch depicts Mandan Indians doing a bison dance, part of the Okipa ceremony. Two select warriors, who thenceforward never dare to fly from the enemy, use real skin and horns to create a perfect imitation of the buffalo's head.*

guarantee successful buffalo hunts. Farming societies, on the other hand, prayed for benign weather conditions to bring good harvests. The Pomos, for example, believed the Kuksu Dance would bring rain. The Iroquois tribes of New York had maple syrup, wild strawberry, corn, bean, and harvest ceremonies, and the Choctaws of the Southeast performed the Great Corn Dance.

Native American religious ceremonies also revolved around the relationship between the individual, the community, and the cosmos; mystical rituals were performed to reveal universal truth; sharpen individual understanding; and acknowledge birth, puberty, marriage, and death. The Yuroks of northern California had

"World Renewal" ceremonies each year involving the Jumping Dance and the Deerskin Dance, both designed to preserve harmony in nature. In southern California, the Luiseños held the Toloache Ceremony every few years. Men would consume a narcotic drink from the Jimsonweed to induce visions of life and the world. It was also an initiation rite into manhood for young boys, who had to fast, take the narcotic, and endure several minutes lying on top of a red ant bed. The Pueblos performed curing and cleansing rituals, initiation into secret societies, and the prayer vigils in underground kivas. Once a year, for example, the Hopis initiated young men and women into the Katcina Cult, symbolic of adulthood. On the Great Plains, Native

Americans went on "vision quests" through dancing, prayer, fasting, and even self-mutilation to establish contact with the invisible power of the universe. Many tribes, such as the Arapahos and Cheyennes, sought their vision through the Sun Dance ceremony. Although the Sun Dance varied from tribe to tribe, it usually took place in the summer and lasted for seven days. Tribesmen erected a central pole, danced around it, and stared at it in trancelike concentration for hours on end. In some tribes a young man would cut the skin of his chest, insert leather strips through the wounds, secure the strips to the pole, and then dance until the strips tore through his skin—all this acted as a measure of his sincerity and dedication. In the 1880s the Ghost Dance spread to the Great Plains; it was a "vision quest" too, in which the participants, wearing what they considered to be protective garments, danced in anticipation of the transformation of the earth, the disappearance of white people, and the return of all the dead buffalo and dead Native Americans. To all tribes, such rituals were of great importance; even the fierce Chiricahua Apaches, though in their last years of freedom perpetually at war with Mexicans and Americans alike, would risk death or capture to observe Ceremonials for the Maidens when one of the girls reached maturity. So throughout Native America, religious rituals were as much an ingredient of ethnic identity as language and economic organization, and they were diverse enough to divide Native Americans into hundreds of religious communities.

Finally, Native American culture in the United States involved complex forms of political authority and loyalty, some very parochial in scope and others quite broad and inclusive. Political organizations helped guarantee internal order and govern external relations; and even though some Native Americans might have shared economic organization and technology, language, and religion, they could still have been divided by conflicting political loyalties. In areas such as the Great Basin, where food was scarce and population dispersed, political loyalty often did not transcend small groups of extended families. The Paiutes wandered the Great Basin in small bands of perhaps one hundred people and met just once a year with other Paiute bands to hunt antelope and arrange marriages. For Paiutes, political loyalty did not extend beyond the band. Tribal authority, on the other hand, was more extensive and usually involved more people, often including many bands or clans. On the Great Plains, the Comanches and the Cheyennes hunted buffalo in bands, but governing warrior societies or councils had members from all the bands. Political loyalty here transcended the clan or band to include the entire tribe. And in a few instances, political loyalty even transcended the tribe. The Senecas, Cayugas, Onondagas, Oneidas, Mohawks, and, later, Tuscaroras were members of the Iroquois League, a political confederation formed to resolve disputes and promote peace between the tribes.

In addition to different levels of political loyalty, Native American society was characterized by different forms of political sovereignty, with the source of political power flowing from a number of individuals or groups. Most bands were quite egalitarian, with several heads of families making most decisions. Many small California tribes functioned without central leadership at all. Other Native American groups were quite the opposite. The Natchez of the Southeast were ruled by a powerful chief called the "Great Sun." In Virginia, Powhatan was the great leader of several tribes when the English colonists established Jamestown in 1607. Where political power was centralized, the tribal chief shared power with war chiefs and religious chiefs, shamans, and priests. The Cheyennes had a council of forty-four men who advised the chief, and the Iroquois League chiefs worked with a council of fifty other men. Political sovereignty was as diverse as political loyalty, varying from tribe to tribe and ranging from the early pure democracy of nomadic foraging bands to the centralized autocracy of the Natchez.

Before the arrival of Europeans, Native America was actually hundreds of Native Americas, a kaleidoscope of ethnic groups, each unique because of its combination of economic organization and technology, language, religion, and political values. It is almost impossible to describe with any meaningful accuracy this ethnic diversity. In California, for example, there were nearly three hundred separate tribes, each with a distinct identity. The Sioux on the Great Plains were actually from many different tribes. The Western Sioux were nomadic hunters and consisted of the Brulé, Hunkpapa, Two Kettles, Blackfeet Sioux, Sans Arcs, Miniconjou, and Oglala tribes. The Yankton and Yanktonai Sioux lived in eastern South Dakota, and the Santee Sioux of Minnesota consisted of the Sisseton, Wahpeton, Mdewakanton, and Wahpekute tribes. In the Southwest, the Apaches consisted of the Jicarillas of northeastern New Mexico, the Mescaleros of southern New Mexico, the Chiricahuas of southeastern Arizona, the Western Apaches of eastern Arizona, and the Lipans and Kiowa-Apaches of the Great Plains. And there were, for example, the River Crow and the Mountain Crow; the Northern Cheyenne and the Southern Cheyenne; the Siksika, Piegan, and Blood Blackfeet; the Northern Paiutes and the Southern Paiutes in the Great Basin; and in California the Pit River Achomawais and the Pit River Atsugewis. The list could go on and on, but the reality is quite clear: Native American society was neither monolithic nor highly integrated, contrary to what many non–Native Americans have believed. It was, instead, hundreds of ethnic groups, each characterized by a high degree of independence and cultural integrity as well as a highly developed sense of tribal loyalty.

Not surprisingly, it is difficult, even intellectually dangerous, to generalize about Native American culture. Few, if any, descriptions of "Native American values" apply to all North American tribal groups. There was simply too much diversity. But in a number of ways, most Native American tribes interpreted life from a certain common perspective, employing a set of values sharply at odds with the assumptions of European civilization. When compared to one another, the tribes are highly diverse; but when all of them are compared to European society, a Native American culture becomes discernible—one that revolved around Native American visions of life, time, community, and the environment. Because most of these values contrasted sharply with European assumptions, nearly four hundred years of intense controversy between Americans of European extraction and Native Americans has resulted—a struggle which today is not at all ready to end.

During the fifteenth and sixteenth centuries in Europe, when religious faith and science were still closely fused, scholars neatly classified all of existence into a "great chain of being," a hierarchical order of life placing God and angels at the top, human beings just below the angels, and all other forms of life in a descending priority of importance, from the great apes to the tiniest insects. Poor people were not equal to rich people, nor were animals equal to any people at all; a divinely imposed hierarchy fixed the ranks of life according to natural, inflexible inequalities. The grace of God extended only to the higher forms of life: human beings and angels. To the European, humanity unquestionably represented the highest form of life, as humans were the only beings on earth possessing immortal souls with the prospects of eternal existence and thus the only forms of life deserving serious ethical consideration. And even then, some groups of people were more deserving of ethical consideration than others, particularly white Europeans when compared to the black and brown peoples in other parts of the world. God looked upon white people, they assumed, with special favor.

But while Europeans placed all things into this fixed, eternal hierarchy of categories, most Native Americans were just as certain that all of creation—animals, plants, insects, lakes, mountains, rivers, oceans, stars, the sun, the moon, and the wind—had souls of their own of some spiritual essence imparted from the source of all life. Man was not unique and transcendent but only part of a larger, eternal whole. The human place in the scheme of things had no special, predestined significance. Indeed, man was usually no better or worse than anything else; he was merely different, as all things were unique and different. Not only did all things have spirits which gave them life, but all spirit was basically of the same essence, different only in degree and not in kind; and through discipline, observation, and personal tranquility, individuals could learn from the world and make contact with the soul of the universe or any of its creations. There was no "great chain of being" relegating most forms of life to eternal insignificance. For most Native Americans there was a unity to the universe which European society little appreciated.

For example, while Europeans respected animals only for their size and ferocity—bears, wolves, and mountain lions, for instance—Native Americans generally felt that every animal had a special gift which humans could cultivate by imitation. Vultures, though repulsive to Europeans, were admired by Native Americans for their keen sight and ability to live their entire lives without ever directly consuming water. Native Americans respected such a gift. Mountain lions, just before a kill, exhibited extraordinary stealth and patience, talents which people could use as well. Beavers were industrious, otters playful, salmon relentless, wolves cooperative, and dogs loyal. All living things were useful and necessary—for food, information, and worship. And all living things deserved respect and ethical consideration. Many tribes even required ceremonial apologies to game animals about to be killed—an expression of sorrow for terminating their stay on earth. Every form of life was equal in its divinely appointed sphere and fitted perfectly into the natural whole.

Because of this pantheism, most Native American tribes felt comfortable with the environment, close to the moods and rhythms of nature, in tune with the living planet. Europeans were quite different, viewing the earth itself as lifeless and inorganic, subject to any kind of manipulation or alteration. Europeans tended to be alienated from nature and came to the New World to use the wilderness, to conquer and exploit its natural wealth for private gain. Theirs was an aggressive, acquisitive culture set on converting nature into money, property, and security. For most of them, the environment was not sacred and the earth had no transcendent meaning in itself. Even the Christian heaven, with its gold-paved streets and perpetual rest, was distant and otherworldly, as if for heaven to be heaven it had to be far away.

But for Native Americans, the environment was sacred, possessing a cosmic significance equal to its material riches. The earth was sacred—a haven for all forms of life—and it had to be protected, nourished, and even worshipped. For the Plains Indians, the cottonwood tree was special. Even the slightest breeze set the cottonwood branches and leaves in motion, so they felt that the cottonwood was especially close to the spirit of the universe, a barometer of the "Great Spirit." They burned logs from the cottonwood tree only in religious ceremonies. Because of their belief that the earth in spring was pregnant and ready to issue forth new life, the Taos of New Mexico removed hard shoes from their horses and walked about barefoot or in soft moccasins themselves, hesitant to disturb the "mother" of everything. Chief Smohalla of the Wanapun tribe illustrated Native American reverence for the earth when he said in 1885:

God said he was the father and earth was the mother of mankind; that nature was the law; that the animals, and fish, and plants obeyed nature, and that man only was sinful.

You ask me to plow the ground! Shall I take a knife and tear my mother's bosom? Then when I die she will not take me to her bosom to rest.

You ask me to dig for stone! Shall I dig under her skin for her bones? Then when I die I cannot enter her body to be born again.

You ask me to cut grass and make hay and sell it, and be rich like white men! But how dare I cut off my mother's hair?

Many Native Americans had a compelling, religious loyalty to place—the space from which man and spirit flowed. For the Taos, Blue Lake in northwest New Mexico was an ancient holy place, a religious shrine, the source of life and a manifestation of the great spirit of the universe. Economically and spiritually, Blue Lake was the center of their lives. For the Shoshone in eastern California, Coso Hot Springs was a sacred place of healing and worship, a living well to which they talked, sang, and prayed. For the Sioux tribes, the Black Hills of South Dakota were sacred as the home of Wakan Tanka, the burial ground of the dead, and the place where "vision quests" took place. In their simple economies and reverence for land and space, Native Americans lived tens of thousands of years in a symbiotic relationship with the earth, using resources without exhausting them, prospering without destroying. Celsa Apapas, therefore, could have been speaking for Native Americans of many tribes throughout the land.

The Native Americans' approach to individual time, as well as their attachment to space, set them apart from Europeans, creating a cultural gap which four centuries have still not bridged. People of European background viewed time in linear terms as a consecutive, sequential commodity against which the individual measured a life. "Life" for them was inextricably linked to "time," a series of goals between birth and death—childhood, adolescence, young adulthood, middle age, and old age as well as schooling, career, and retirement. All these were "passages," different stages of "times" of life people experienced before death. Death too, then, was linked with time. Early death seemed especially tragic to them because of what the deceased had *not* been able to achieve and what "passages" of life had been missed. Time was precious and fleeting, something not to be wasted—like health and money. Time was a commodity, an economic good for sale or rent; most of European society was dedicated to its full employment.

Except in their sense of childhood, most Native Americans had little sense of such "passages." Adulthood itself implied fulfillment, and there was no feeling of wasting life, of not having done or experienced enough, of having dissipated time. Nor did they think of "having their whole lives ahead of them." The past and the future, for individuals at least, were vague concepts, and Native Americans usually functioned in what might more properly be called an "expanded present." In the Hopi language there was no word for "time," no vehicle for expressing a concept the Hopis did not possess. Time was not a commodity occurring between two fixed points, not a tangible product that could be measured and manipulated. Above all else, time was intangible, a natural process in which all living things fulfilled the promise of their creation—the stages of the moon, the rising and setting of the sun, the seasons of the year, the blooming and withering of flowers, the greening and browning of grasses, the hibernation of bears, the hatching of doves, and the births and deaths of people. Theirs was a life without clocks, deadlines, or rigid schedules. Time was not an enemy.

The individual relationship to the community among Native Americans was just as unique as their view of the cosmos and time, at least when compared to European values. Ever since the Reformation, English intellectuals and philosophers had separated individuals from society, lifting them out of a community context. The more traditional, corporate assumption that individual goals were subordinate to community needs—the collective view of the medieval world—was replaced by a competitive individualism, the view that community needs were best served by the aggressive assertion of individual self-interest. Only in individual, worldly success, the Puritans claimed, could people assure themselves of divine approbation; and success was interpreted as the accumulation of material wealth, especially when compared to the wealth of friends and peers. The almighty God, in other words, revealed his will through the successes and failures of in-dividual people. Europeans were capitalists, and the true measure of a person—temporal as well as spiritual—was economic, a function of monetary status.

In a way, most Native Americans maintained a corporate view of society, even though the intricacies of that perspective made it quite different from the concept in European medieval thought. Native Americans managed, at once, to encourage individuality without worshipping individualism. Many tribes tried to avoid com-petitive, self-centered attitudes in children. With little or no sense of time in individual terms, parents did not pressure children into weaning, bowel or bladder control, walking, or talking before they were ready. Society offered no par-ticular status or reward for such early childhood development, and trying to hasten it along would have been considered as ludicrous as making an egg hatch or a flower blossom early. Parents were rather permissive, content to let children learn and grow at a natural, individual pace. The ultimate values to be given children were self-confidence, tranquility, and emotional security, not a compulsive need to be materially richer than the neighbors. Most tribal cultures also encouraged people to seek an individual accommodation with the universe, a personal bond of trust with the earth and all living things. Individuality—not necessarily individual success—was the measure of social status in Native America.

The result was a culture which venerated individuality while nurturing community needs. Native Americans expected human society to function harmoniously, just as nature did; and even though occasional shocks might upset the natural balance, stability would always return. Even nature rebelled into tornadoes, hurricanes, earthquakes, floods, and droughts, only to revert quickly to its usual predictability. While the European settlers needed lawyers to resolve disputes in court, Native Americans expected earlier settlement of disputes, long before they disrupted tribal harmony. A complex web of intellectual, economic, and social networks bound individuals into a morally integrated so-ciety, one which venerated community and group survival.

Intellectually, Native Americans were care-fully bound into communities by history as well as by the oral traditions conveying the past to each new generation. If Native Americans pos-sessed only vague notions of time in individual terms, they were more conscious of historical time, at least as it affected their own community. Major events of the past—a tribal move to new territory, a natural disaster, a military defeat or victory—were all remembered; it was the prac-tice of passing on these and other traditions to young people though oral history which sus-tained Native American communalism. In the written world of Europeans, where knowledge was visual through the printed page, the indi-vidual could independently acquaint himself with the community in the solitude of a library. Indeed, learning could be a solitary experience, simply absorbing knowledge from inanimate books. But in nonliterate societies, history and its conveyance were of necessity a community experience in which the storyteller created men-tal images or "pictures" of the past, intelligible to all, and passed them on to members of the tribe during ceremonial rituals. Generation after generation, the same "pictures" were handed down with remarkable consistency to young people, each time explaining the origins and history of the tribe. To begin their tribal history, for example, many of the Sioux went back to the beginning of time when Wakan Tanka was walking through the Black Hills of South Da-kota. Surveying the fruits of his creations, he was pleased. He gloried in the gifts he had given to the animals: strength to the bear, swiftness to the hawk, grace to the deer, perseverance to the turtle, and majesty to the eagle. He had but one more gift to impart, and that was love; so Wakan Tanka joined with the Earth Mother and created the first man, right there in the Black Hills. This story was the very fabric of Sioux life. In the visual, literate world of the Europeans, where authors and publishers printed words and distributed books, people interpreted them on their own, according to their own prejudices, and there was rarely agreement on the meaning or significance of history. But in the oral traditions of such Native American societies as the Sioux, where group interaction with the storyteller occurred constantly and where individuals were forced to interpret the storyteller's message immediately and in the presence of the group, history became a community constant, a source of unanimity, security, and agreement. Unlike Europeans, the Sioux and many other Native Americans enjoyed a communality of knowledge binding the tribes into tightly knit groups.

Native American economic life in most instances served to melt individual interests into those of the larger community. Despite vast differences in organization and technology, Native American economic life operated on a subsistence level, with most people engaged directly in the pursuit of food, whether hunting, foraging, or farming. Until the Industrial Revolution and the commercialization of agriculture, the peasant and small farming economies of Europe and America had been much the same. But by 1800 more and more people were able to live off the agricultural production of relatively few, and each year tens of thousands of people were released for industrial or service occupations. It is not coincidental that the rise of liberal individualism accompanied the Industrial Revolution, for the economic activities of most people became indirectly related to the production of living necessities. For most Native Americans, however, where a subsistence economy prevailed, divisions of labor were minimal and accumulation of surpluses problematical; the cooperation of everyone in the community was a prerequisite to survival. Individual economic independence is a function of prosperity, of guaranteed material security. Most Native Americans, too close to the potential disasters of nature, never enjoyed such a luxury, at least in the United States. Whether in the buffalo hunts on the Great Plains, the communal corn gardens

of the Southeast, or the irrigation projects of the Southwest, survival demanded community cooperation, a submersion of individualistic compulsions to group necessities. Most Native Americans maintained an overpowering concern for community welfare, for the economic survival of everyone. The gap between the rich and the poor was far less pronounced than among Europeans; the capriciousness of subsistence living generated a moral dynamic to assist neighbors. The willingness to share, to part with material security, was often considered a personal asset, a sure sign of status and nobility. Christianity, of course, preached a similar message but ran up against the pressures of competitive, entrepreneurial individualism. Most Native American societies proved far more successful implementing those values.

Finally, the Native American social structure helped create an atmosphere in which individual interests fused with those of the larger community. The building blocks of all Native American societies were kinship groups, even though family authority could be patrilineal or matrilineal and genealogies real or imagined. Among the Hopis, for example, men joined their wives' households after marriage, supporting them economically but maintaining very passive roles in terms of authority and discipline. From the nuclear or small extended families of the most primitive Great Basin tribes to the elaborate clans and clan alliances of the Iroquois tribes, Native Americans tended to view authority in family or clan terms; and different positions within a family implied different roles. In a patrilineal family, for example, "grandfather" offered wisdom to everyone; "father" offered authority and responsibility; "uncle" offered assistance; "children" offered obedience; and "brother" offered equality. Since everyone understood the behavior associated with these roles, and most people occupied several roles simultaneously, family values actually governed society, providing direct moral restraints on individual deviancy. The pull of family loyalty, perhaps the most powerful governing force in human society, was overwhelming in Native America, guaranteeing reciprocal devotions among individuals and the group.

Native American views of life, earth, individuality, and community all merged in their approach to land ownership, and it was this issue which lay at the heart of the Native American–European conflict in the United States, directly precipitating most of the violent confrontations. From 1607, when the English colonists first arrived, right through the controversies ongoing in the 1980s, the issue has always been land, with European and American settlers seizing it throughout United States history and Native Americans fighting to keep it from individual ownership historically and wanting it back today. Europeans wanted the land—all the land—and were never satisfied as long as Native Americans possessed any of it that was worthwhile. This was because they were frustrated by the subsistence economies of Native Americans, considering their land-use methods inefficient and incapable of extracting the most from the soil. The Native Americans were not concerned with extracting everything from the soil, but only enough for them to live in the present. That fact alone, some settlers believed, justified taking the land, peacefully if possible (whether by fair trading or trickery), but violently if necessary. Year after year they moved Native Americans to worthless land, promising them permanent control of it, only to move them again once better reconnaissance, technology, and/or population expansion had rendered the land valuable.

Convinced that the land there was useless, the Virginia settlers pushed the Powhatan Indians north of the York River after 1644 but had to move them again after settlers began pouring into the area a few years later. President Andrew Jackson was sure that much of the land west of the Mississippi River would forever be useless for agriculture, so he signed the Indian Removal Act of 1830, pushing the eastern tribes onto the Great Plains, erroneously called the "Great American Desert." By the 1850s settlers were pouring into Kansas and Nebraska. The federal government relocated the Five Civilized Tribes to Indian Territory, now Oklahoma, only to violate their land titles and civil rights again when "sooners" and then oil speculators settled there. Allotment, termination, and relocation, major policies toward Native Americans in the twentieth century, all had as their rationale the "protection" of Native Americans from encroaching civilization by moving them off land they had inhabited for as far back as tribal memory extended.

The most fundamental question involved ownership of land. The idea of private property—in which one man or one group possessed eternal, exclusive control of a piece of land—was foreign and confusing to most Native Americans, who had long ago adopted communal land systems. Giving one person exclusive, perpetual control of land was as inconceivable as distributing the sky. Like time, land was not a commodity—not a tangible, lifeless item to be measured and sold. It was, instead, a living thing in its own right, imbued with a soul and held in trust by all the living for their use and the use of their children. The Reverend John Heckewelder, a Moravian minister, recalled a Native American's reaction to his complaint about the Native American's horses eating grass on his land:

My friend, it seems you lay claim to the grass my horses have eaten, because you had enclosed it with a fence: now tell me, who caused the grass to grow? Can you make the grass grow? I think not, and no body can except the great Manni-to. He it is who causes it to grow for both my horses and for yours! See, friend! The grass which grows out of the earth is common to all; the game in the woods is common to all. Say, did you never eat venison and bear's meat? . . . Well, and did you ever hear me or any other Indian complain about that? No; then be not disturbed at my horses having eaten only once, of what you call your grass, though the grass my horses did eat, in like manner as the meat you did eat, was given to the Indians by the Great Spirit. Besides, if you will but consider, you will find that my horses did not eat all your grass.

Private property seemed ridiculous, insanely selfish, even sacrilegious to most Native Americans. Throughout the history of the United States, they could not understand or accept the European approach to the land; and out of this conflicting perspective came centuries of violence.

But questions of private property were only part of the larger cultural autonomy common to most Native American societies. Europeans failed to understand the dynamics of those cultures, seeing them as nothing more than a pathology, a deviant life-style badly in need of reform. Europeans were dangerously ethnocentric—self-righteously convinced of their own religious, political, and economic superiority. They approached Native America from two different but equally damaging perspectives. Some Europeans denied even the humanity of Native Americans and created powerful negative stereotypes about them, justifying the conflict necessary to drive them off the land. If Indians really were bloodthirsty savages, society was better off without them. The notion that "the only good Indian is a dead Indian," begun by Puritan colonials, peaked late in the nineteenth century with a nearly genocidal assault on Native American civilization.

The other perspective seemed more humane, superficially, and grew out of a combination of liberal guilt and missionary zeal. Dismayed about the violence inflicted upon Native Americans, these Europeans wanted to protect them, to insulate them from the more aggressive, less morally restrained settlers. But beyond these feelings of guilt, they also wanted to change the Native Americans. They accepted their humanity—as well as their cultural inferiority—but instead of annihilating them to clear the land, liberals and missionaries sought to assimilate them into the European culture. That is, they sought to remake the Native Americans' society, transforming them into "law-abiding" farmers who believed in property and Jesus Christ. The irony is that although the methods of the assimilationists were far more

benign than the genocidal ravages of Indian haters, the results were the same: the virtual elimination of much of Native American civilization. The land would be cleared of Native American society after all.

The debate between the Indian haters and the liberal assimilationists persisted throughout United States history, shaping Native American policy at every turn and governing all relations between the European and Native American cultures; but the debate exposed the moral shortcomings of European expectations. To most Native Americans, the assimilationists were little better than the genocidal maniacs; for, although they did not hate individual Native Americans, they did hate their culture and were committed to tearing individuals from their cultural moorings. Indeed, they may have been more destructive than the Indian haters, for at least Native Americans always knew where their more overt enemies stood on the issues. Assimilationists always blanketed their ideas in the rhetoric of love, peace, and harmony, making it easy for Native Americans to take them at their word. Off their guard temporarily, Native Americans lost time after time, especially when Indian haters joined forces with the assimilationists, as they did with the Indian Removal Act of 1830 and the Dawes Severalty Act of 1887. Liberals saw in both instances an opportunity to protect Native Americans, while Indian haters saw a clear opportunity to clear Native Americans off valuable land. This unique coalition of liberals and reactionaries proved to be one of the great political ironies of the nineteenth century. United States Native American policy, therefore, was basically an incestuous political struggle among non–Native Americans, with each side promoting a set of ideas out of touch with Native American values but commonly dedicated, consciously and unconsciously, to the destruction of their culture.

In the twentieth century the trumpets of genocide stopped sounding, as did the "cant of conquest," but the assimilationist refrain became louder than ever. Most non–Native

Americans, ignorant of Native American needs, applauded the triumph, seeing real progress each time in the allotment program of the Dawes Severalty Act of 1887, the Indian Citizenship Act of 1924, the modified tribalism of the Indian Reorganization Act of 1934, the termination and relocation policies of the 1950s, the antipoverty programs of the 1960s, and the self-determination policies of the 1970s and 1980s. Although some of these programs were better than others—or, at least, less destructive—the federal government still failed to come to grips with Native American culture.

The allotment programs—institutionalized in the Dawes Act of 1887, the Curtis Act of 1898, the Dead Indian Land Act of 1902, and the Burke Act of 1906—succeeded in taking over ninety million acres of land from Native Americans by 1932, all to eliminate "retarded" tribal loyalties and to transform individual Native Americans into family farmers. The allotment program was formally criticized as recently as 1981, when a U.S. District Court decision branded it as "probably one of the best-intended grievous errors in the history of American policy-making." In the end, most Native Americans did not become successful commercial farmers and still lost their land. The Indian Citizenship Act of 1924, designed as a reward for the loyal service of thousands of Native Americans in World War I and as an attempt to integrate them legally into the polity, did nothing to ameliorate their economic problems or restore tribal sovereignty and culture. The Indian Reorganization Act of 1934, ending allotment and presumably restoring tribal authority, only replaced direct Bureau of Indian Affairs supervision of the tribes with indirect BIA supervision of all tribal decisions through tribal councils. Also, by providing for election of tribal leaders and majority rule in tribal decisions, the Indian Reorganization Act undermined the hereditary rule and consensus politics common to many Native American tribes. In some ways, the

act actually insulated BIA officials from Native American criticism by redirecting their anger toward the tribal officials implementing federal policies. Native Americans still did not really enjoy self-determination.

After World War II Congress resurrected earlier attempts to clear Native Americans off the land. Once again assimilationists triumphed, sending thousands to live in the cities and trying to end federal supervision of the tribes altogether, all with the intention of incorporating individual Native American families into the larger United States population. Termination and relocation were not much different from the allotment programs, being merely a twentieth-century version of them. During the 1960s federal antipoverty programs trained Native Americans for jobs in an industrial economy—as welders, auto and diesel mechanics, machinists, construction workers, secretaries, and heavy equipment operators. But to make full use of these skills, Native Americans would have had to relocate to the cities where most of the jobs existed. The result of many antipoverty programs were thousands of culturally alienated Native Americans living in the cities and thousands of unemployed, skilled Native American workers living on the reservations. High-minded liberals in the Department of Justice promoted the civil rights movement, often assuming that Native Americans wanted integration as much as blacks did. They were bewildered and sometimes angry when tribal leaders scoffed at the whole idea of integration, preferring the isolation of their people from "white" values. Even the Indian Self-Determination Act of 1975, designed to shift more authority to tribal councils, left the Bureau of Indian Affairs in a position to approve all tribal decisions, an arrangement Native American activists greatly resented. After more than 350 years of contact, the political relationship between Native Americans and non–Native Americans was still a tenuous one, marked by mutual suspicion and enormous cultural differences.

■ ■ ■

STUDY QUESTIONS

1. Where did the Native Americans come from, and how did they arrive on the North American continent? Over what period of time did they arrive?

2. Describe the economic life of the Native Americans. What were the major differences among the hunting, farming, and foraging economies? Use examples to illustrate your answers.

3. How would you compare the linguistic diversity of the Native Americans of North America to that of the non–Native American population? Why was there so much linguistic diversity among Native Americans?

4. What was the source of Native American tribalism?

5. Although there was a great diversity to Native American religious rituals, some fundamental religious concepts were common to most tribes. What were those basic assumptions?

6. Compare and contrast the Native American view of living things with the European notion of "the great chain of being."

7. How did the Native Americans view the environment, and how did their point of view clash with that of most Europeans?

8. How did most Native Americans view land ownership? Why did that point of view lead to so much conflict with whites?

BIBLIOGRAPHY

For general histories of Native Americans in the United States, see Alvin M. Josephy, Jr., *The Indian Heritage of America* (1970) and Wilcomb E. Washburn, *The Indian in America* (1975). The best general survey is Arrell Morgan Gibson's *The American Indian: Prehistory to the Present* (1980). For ethnic and cultural history, see Robert F. Spencer, *The Native Americans: Ethnology and Backgrounds of the North American Indians* (1977); Shirley Hill Witt and Stan Steiner, *The Way: An Anthology of American Indian Literature* (1972); and Symmes C. Oliver, *Ecology and Cultural Continuity as Contributing Factors in the Social Organization of the Plains Indians* (1962). For Native American history before the arrival of the Europeans, see Robert Claiborne, *The First Americans* (1973); William Denevan, *The Native Population of the Americas in 1492* (1976); Howard S. Russell, *Indian New England before the Mayflower* (1980); and Paul S. Martin, *Indians before Columbus: Twenty Thousand Years of North American History Revealed by Archaeology* (1947). Whites' attitudes toward Native Americans are described in Roy Harvey Pearce, *Savagism and Civilization: A Study of the Indian and the American Mind* (1965) and J. E. Chamberlain, *The Harrowing of Eden: White Attitudes toward North American Natives* (1975).

Part Five

THE AGE
OF
IMAGINATION

For more than a century, historians have described the era of the 1830s and 1840s as "The Age of Jackson" or "The Age of Democracy." It was a propitious time for the young nation. A vast hinterland of apparently limitless resources beckoned to a generation of land-hungry settlers from both the Old World and the New. Two oceans protected them from the threats of foreign powers. With traditions vastly overwhelmed by expectations, it was the "age of imagination"—a time when Americans saw themselves as the hope of the world, and their country as the place where mankind's potential would ultimately be fulfilled. Such vision translated into "Manifest Destiny," a slogan capturing the national imagination in the 1840s and justifying the march across the continent. A generation of Americans believed that God intended that they assume sovereignty over North America. It was also their intention to obliterate any vestige of aristocratic privilege, governmental oppression, or corporate hegemony. "Young America" glorified individual rights, common people, and popular sovereignty.

The origins of democratic individualism were buried deep in the European past and the American environment. From their English ancestors, the American colonists had inherited Lockean values—the belief that government was designed to protect individual rights, primarily life, liberty, and property. The settlers themselves were young, adventurous, ambitious, and unwilling to tolerate the status quo. Had they been otherwise, they would have stayed forever in the Old World. In America, they encountered the harsh frontier wilderness where individualism, self-reliance, and hard work were taken for granted. Unencumbered by aristocratic privilege and

free to establish their own political institutions, the settlers of the United States accepted democratic individualism as the natural order of things.

Andrew Jackson personified the age of democracy. His humble roots in the Tennessee frontier gave poverty a certain social status, at least among politicians. In his assault on the Second Bank of the United States, Jackson stood as an enemy of economic privilege and as a friend of competition and laissez-faire. Impatient with those who prized wealth and social standing, Jackson inspired an unprecedented national infatuation with the democratic ideal. He was a politician of extraordinary charisma.

The national preoccupation with democracy also inspired a wide variety of reform movements during the 1830s and 1840s. Led by Horace Mann of Massachusetts, educational reformers campaigned for a public school system where the future of democracy could be guaranteed by a literate electorate. Dorothea Dix led a crusade for mental health reform, primarily in the treatment of emotional illnesses. During the age of Andrew Jackson, the last property requirements for holding public office disappeared. William Ladd spearheaded a drive for international peace. Bible tract and temperance societies campaigned across the nation to purify society through the abolition of alcohol. And the great crusade of the antebellum period, led by people like William Lloyd Garrison and Theodore Dwight Weld, was the assault on slavery, a bitter issue which eventually tore the nation apart in a civil war. But that was only a distant threat in the 1830s and 1840s. Confidence and hope were the symbols of Jacksonian America.

MAN OF IRON

John William Ward

For generations philosophers have debated the role of the individual in history—whether the force of historical events automatically produces "the great man or woman" or whether great individuals actually shape the course of history. Because they have traditionally worshipped at the altar of individualism and created a political culture to match, Americans have always preferred the latter interpretation, the one allowing great people to affect destiny. At best, historical greatness is an ephemeral blessing, frequently bestowed too quickly and always subject to the capricious mood of public opinion. Those who achieve it are usually lucky to have their personal skills tested by some great national crisis. Any list of the "great presidents" will include George Washington, Abraham Lincoln, and Franklin D. Roosevelt, primarily because they had to confront the founding of the nation or a civil war or a great depression and global war. Others who aspire to greatness try to link their careers to some great test, such as Theodore Roosevelt and the charge up San Juan hill in 1898 or John F. Kennedy and the exploits of PT-109. Carved out of an enormous, forbidding wilderness by restless immigrants assuming tremendous risks, American society placed a great premium on individual determination, courage, and perseverence.

In "The Man of Iron," John William Ward looks at Andrew Jackson as a "great man" whose overpowering personality, at least in the minds of his contemporaries, helped establish the roots of a democratic revolution. By the mid-1820s, Jackson seemed the perfect man to lead the young nation. In his exploits against the British at New Orleans in 1815, the Creek Indians in the frontier wars, or his famous duel with Charles Dickinson, Andrew Jackson had demonstrated an unrivaled determination to achieve whatever he wanted, regardless of human and even supernatural opposition. For a young country preoccupied with its own identity, Andrew Jackson was indeed the "symbol for an age"—a man whose own skills were complemented by the forces of history.

In the two versions of the Battle of New Orleans that attributed American success to nature or to God, Andrew Jackson, although important, was not quite at the center of attention; he functioned as the representative of a more basic force. Thus, in the Abbé Dubourg's address quoted before, when the Abbé says to Jackson, 'we extol that fecundity of genius, by which, in an instant of the most discouraging distress, you created unforeseen resources, raised as it were from the ground, hosts of intrepid warriors, and provided every vulnerable point with ample means of defence,' the significant point of reference is *'Him'* who outfitted Jackson as *'the man of his right hand.'* There was a third explanation, however, of the American victory that was ready to make Jackson himself the center of focus, dispensing with the beneficence of nature or the providence of God. The shift in emphasis may be observed by comparing the Abbé's speech with one at Jackson's death by a eulogist who lifted the Abbé's words but in doing so left God behind. 'Not one in a whole generation could be found [said Hugh A. Garland] with [Jackson's] powers of command, that fecundity of genius, by which, under the most trying circumstances, he created unforeseen resources—raised, as it were, from the ground, hosts of intrepid warriors, and provided every vulnerable point with ample means of defence.' In the Abbé's address, the next words are: 'To *Him* we trace that instinctive superiority of your mind, which at once rallied around you universal confidence.' But in Garland's eulogy, the following words are: 'that instinctive superiority, self-reliance, and impulsive energy, which at once rallied around him universal confidence.' Although the priest's language with its suggestion of the miraculous is retained, the thought is radically different.

Andrew Jackson, as the self-reliant man, had no need of God.

1

From the day of the Battle of New Orleans, the idea that the victory was due to Jackson alone was widely entertained. *The Enquirer* printed a letter from New Orleans to a gentleman in Congress which held that 'to Jackson every credit is due, for inspiring general confidence, uniting our scattered efforts, for calling forth our dormant strength.' A more widely printed letter said, 'the glorious result is principally attributable to the wisdom, prudence, decision and personal example of General Jackson, which really seemed to instil into every breast his own patriotism and heroic courage. He is truly a great man.' As Major Latour, Jackson's engineer, expressed it: 'Although his body was ready to sink under the weight of sickness, fatigue and continued watching, his mind nevertheless, never lost for a moment that energy which he knew well how to communicate to all that surrounded him . . . the energy manifested by General Jackson spread, as it were, by contagion, and communicated itself to the whole army.' Latour dedicated his study of the Battle of New Orleans to Jackson, saying, 'The voice of the whole nation has spared me the task of showing how much of these important results are due to the energy, ability and courage of a single man.'

In making Jackson the cause of victory, the ground taken was that he communicated his own will to win to his comrades in arms. As one said, 'his master-spirit pervaded every bosom.' A contemporary history of the United States recorded that 'undismayed by the difficulties which surrounded him, General Jackson . . . mingled with the citizens and infused into the greater part of his own spirit and energy.' Biographers of Jackson borrowed the sentiment from one another. With only minor variations, three separate works on Jackson carried the words: *'Before him was an army proud of its name, and* distinguished for its deeds of valour—an army, the finest that ever appeared on our shores,—one that had driven the warriors of France, the conquerors of continental Europe, from the pillars of Hercules to the Pyrenees. *Opposed to this was his own unbending spirit, and an inferior, undisciplined, and half-armed force.'* The militia victory at New Orleans was compared to the militia disaster at Washington by pointing out that 'there was unmistakeable evidence of the presence [at New Orleans] of a chief, who inspired confidence, courage and determination in all under his command.' The difference made by a resolute commander was emphasized by the *New-York Evening Post:* 'If we had a Jackson everywhere we should succeed everywhere.' Charles Jared Ingersoll deduced a general law from Jackson's victory at New Orleans. Quoting Voltaire, Ingersoll remarked that 'seldom . . . is anything great done in the world, except by the genius and firmness of some one man, contending with the prejudices of the multitude, and overcoming them.'

As the years passed, the thesis which held Jackson's master-spirit to be cause of victory was more clearly defined. In 1827, a poet wrote of Jackson at New Orleans:

His eye shows openness and seems to speak,
But nothing's there that shows a woman's freak,
His will *chains every nerve—none durst betray*
The secret feeling he would hide from day—
But when he wills, *his every look takes fire*
And flames to view the hidden soul's desire.

Against seemingly insuperable obstacles, upon which every chronicler of the Battle of New Orleans loved to dwell, Jackson's will was sufficient. It was said of Jackson at New Orleans, 'In an instant he resolved; and his resolutions, let me tell you were as firm as the decrees of Heaven . . . never were the words of the poet more applicable, than to him—

From orbs convulsed, should all the planets fly,
World crush on world, and ocean mix with sky;

Above is an indication that some believed Jackson was taken too seriously as the Man of Iron.

He, unconcerned, would view the falling world,
And still maintain the purpose of his soul.'

Finally, an account of the battle published in a magazine just before Jackson's death said, 'Nothing was ready except the General—Andrew Jackson. . . he had already evinced that iron energy, indomitable perseverance and ceaseless activity, so necessary. . . Not one of the wavering, but a man who could keep his object as steadily before him as the mariner his port, and trample them down and crush without remorse whoever barred the path.'

As used in the last quotation, 'iron' was the key word in most appraisals of Andrew Jackson. Throughout his career, Jackson was lauded as a man of iron; his iron will was central to innumerable descriptions of his character. Even before the news of his victory at New Orleans reached the northern cities, the word 'iron' had been applied to him. In *The Enquirer* of January 28, 1815, one week before the *National Intelligencer, Extra* announced the outcome of the battle of January 8, a writer offered a curious nation some notice 'of the life and character of . . . a man whose life will constitute, and has constituted already, an important epoch in the history of our country.' After describing the bare biographical items of Jackson's career up to 1815, the account took notice of his person: 'He is tall, thin and spare, but muscular and hardy, with an eye quick and penetrating—I have frequently seen Gen. Jackson, and such was the impression his appearance made on my mind, that I have said to myself he is a man of Iron. Adversity can make no impression on a bosom braced by such decision and firmness as is visible in his face and manners.' Their appetite further whetted by the news of Jackson's glorious victory, the people eagerly read this account which was copied by nearly every newspaper in the nation. It proved so popular that when Jackson entered the political scene it appeared as campaign literature and was even reprinted in eulogy at his death.

2

From the time of his victory in 1815 to his death in 1845, Jackson was constantly before the American imagination as the embodiment of the success that awaits the man of iron will, the man who can overcome insuperable opposition simply by determination. At the end of Jackson's life, eulogists across the nation reminded the American people of his 'inflexibility of purpose, the indomitable will,' the character 'run in that iron mould.' One recalled the compliment paid by the French to the ' "tete de fer," ' the iron will of the stern old man.' During his life, visitors to Jackson came away and recorded that they 'had seen and scanned the Man of Iron will.' Not only

was there general agreement that Jackson's 'well known inflexibility of purpose was, unquestionably, one of his most remarkable characteristics,' but nearly every commentator on Andrew Jackson sought the adjective 'Iron' to describe his self-reliance.

As did the description in the *Enquirer*, which noted Jackson's 'quick and penetrating' eye, accounts which dwelt on Jackson's extraordinary will power usually noted his flashing eye, which was, of course, the physical sign of the spirit within, or as the anonymous poet quoted above put it, 'But when he *wills*, his every look takes fire / And flames to view the hidden soul's desire.' An historian of the Battle of New Orleans described Jackson's entry into the city in this fashion: 'The chief of the party . . . was a tall, gaunt man, of very erect carriage, with a countenance full of stern decision and fearless energy, but furrowed with care and anxiety. His complexion was sallow and unhealthy; his hair was iron grey, and his body thin and emaciated. . . But the fierce glare of his bright and hawk-like grey eye, betrayed a soul and a spirit which triumphed over all the infirmities of the body.' Jackson's infirmity some years later caused young Josiah Quincy in Boston to make a similar observation: 'But the spirit in Jackson was resolute to conquer physical infirmity. His eyes seemed brighter than ever, and all aglow with the mighty will which can compel the body to execute his behests.' The President nearly collapsed on his tour of New England and Quincy elaborated his remark: 'No person who had seen the collapsed condition in which the President was deposited at the hotel would have imagined that he could resume his travels the next day; and it was, undoubtedly, by an exertion of the will of which only the exceptional man is capable that he was able to do so. But the art of mastering the physical nature was familiar to Jackson. . . An immaterial something flashed through his eye as he greeted us in the breakfast room, and it was evident that the faltering body was again held in subjection.' The belief that the spirit of man was to be apprehended in the expression of the eye led Clark Mills in a wood carving of Jackson's head to accentuate the eyes so that the sculpture verges toward caricature.

Andrew Jackson's constant ill-health provided admirers of his will power many opportunities to elaborate upon the superiority of mind over matter. As one biographer wrote of Jackson during the Creek War, 'his mind arose in majesty as his body was emaciated by toil.' Alexander Walker observed that at New Orleans 'his body was sustained alone by the spirit within.' Now there was, to be sure, greater justification for lauding Jackson's will power in the matter of his physical condition than (say) in his victory over the British at New Orleans, but Jackson's contemporaries were more concerned with proving the efficacy of the will than making valid descriptive statements. In the important struggle against the Second Bank of the United States, which occupied so much of Jackson's political life, the social and economic complexity of the problem was naïvely reduced to a dramatic struggle between the Hero and the Monster. George Lippard remembered that when the proponents of the bank suggested that rebellion might follow if the bank was crushed old Andrew Jackson rose from his seat in anger.

I can see him yet [wrote Lippard]. 'Come!' he shouted in a voice of thunder, as his clutched hand was raised above his white hairs, 'come with bayonets in your hands instead of petitions, surround the White House with your legions. I am ready for you all! With the people at my back, whom your gold can neither buy nor awe, I will swing you up around the capitol, each rebel of you—on a gibbet—high as Haman's!'

When I think . . . of that ONE MAN, standing there at Washington, battling with all the powers of Bank and panic combined, betrayed . . . assailed . . . when I think of that one man placing his back against the rock, and folding his arms for the blow, while he uttered his vow, 'I will not swerve one inch from the course I have chosen!' I

must confess that the records of Greece and Rome— nay, the proudest days of Napoleon, cannot furnish an instance of a WILL like that of ANDREW JACKSON.

Still another said that in the bank controversy it required Andrew Jackson's 'amazing inflexibility of will' to put down the monster of corruption. George Bancroft made the point with great flourish:

The storm [against Jackson] rose with unexampled vehemence . . . the impetuous swelling wave rolled on, without one sufficient obstacle, till it reached his presence; but as it dashed in its highest fury at his feet, it broke before his firmness. The commanding majesty of his will appalled his opponents and revived his friends. He, himself, had a proud consciousness that his will was indomitable. . . he stood erect, like a massive column, which the heaps of falling ruins could not break, nor bend, nor sway from its fixed foundation.

The belief that Andrew Jackson was able to put down the Second Bank of the United States solely because he willed its destruction was so widespread that when James Parton assembled materials for the first scholarly (and still the best) biography of Jackson he concluded the description of the bank crisis with the observation that 'never was there exhibited so striking an illustration of the maxim, that WILL, not talent, governs the world. The will of one man, Andrew Jackson . . . carried the day against the assembled talent and the interested capital of the country.' The degree of Jackson's appeal to the imagination of his contemporaries as the embodiment of the power of the will is suggested by the motto that Parton found appropriate for his three-volume study: 'Desperate Courage Makes One a Majority.'

In other controversies besides the bank fight Jackson's opponents, as well as his supporters, testified to the esteem in which the self-reliant man was held in the United States. The testimony of the opposition was, of course, negative. They attacked Jackson on the ground that he was weak-willed. During the struggle over the bank, the anti-Jacksonians castigated the President as a weakling led by 'advisers who are goading him on.' The same accusation was made in connection with the removal of office-holders. It was said that Jackson was 'scarcely a free agent,' that 'he has been ruled, against his better judgment, by a combination of interest and prejudice, by which he was surrounded from the moment of reaching the seat of government.' In the election of 1824, the editor of the *Richmond Enquirer*, then in opposition to Jackson, had written that he would be too much exposed to other men, shrewder statesmen than himself. *'They* will probably govern more than he will—they will generally be the power behind the throne greater than the throne itself.' In similar vein, Duff Green was represented as 'the Dictator at Washington,' with Jackson as his pliant tool. It was admiration for the self-reliant man that gave emotional force to the characterization of Martin Van Buren as the 'little magician' and that informed the attacks on Jackson's 'Kitchen Cabinet.' In both cases Jackson was made to appear as the object of manipulation; stress on the roles of the foxy Vice-President and the back-stairs politicians made Jackson seem to be the will-less leader. Americans agreed with Fanny Kemble who, knowing nothing of Jackson's measures, asserted that 'firmness, determination, decision, I respect above all things; and if the old general is, as they say, very obstinate, why obstinacy is so far more estimable than weakness, *especially* in a ruler, that I think he sins on the right side of the question.' The majority of Americans seemed to agree, and the importance of will power is suggested by the attempt of Jackson's opponents to strip him of that attribute.

3

Of the many incidents in Jackson's life that provided material for the glorification of the man of iron will, the most notorious was, perhaps, Andrew Jackson's famous duel with Charles Dickinson. Jackson's quarrel with Dickinson was of long standing and its origin does not concern us here as much as its result. The result was a duel with pistols at twenty-four feet. Dickinson was a skilled pistol shot. Tradition has it that on the way to the site of the duel he delighted those who accompanied him by placing four shots from a distance of twenty-four feet into an area that could be covered by a silver dollar. He was even supposed to have cut a string at that distance and left it as mute evidence for Jackson of the fate that was in store for him. Because of Dickinson's excellence as a duelist Andrew Jackson decided that his only course was to allow Dickinson to fire first; then Jackson, if not dead, would be able to place his shot unhurriedly. However, there was a good chance that Jackson would be dead. To shorten the odds against such a possibility, Jackson dressed himself in a loose-fitting cloak which disguised his extremely slender figure hoping to deceive Dickinson and mislead his aim.

On the dueling ground John Overton, Jackson's friend, gave the command to fire. Jackson deliberately took Dickinson's shot which hit him in the breast. Then, calmly and decidedly, he waited until Dickinson was brought back to the mark from which he had recoiled in horror at the thought he had missed. Jackson levelled his pistol and fired; the pistol stopped at half-cock. Under the rules of the occasion, this was not considered a fire. Jackson recocked his pistol, aimed, and shot Dickinson fatally through the groin.

In the company of Overton, Jackson left the field without disclosing the fact that he had been seriously wounded himself. A friend of the general wrote later to Parton that Jackson did not want the dying Dickinson to have even the gratification of knowing that he had not missed. Dickinson's bullet had lodged near Jackson's heart; it pained and troubled him all his life and was probably the source of the pulmonary disorders which Jackson usually attributed to tuberculosis.

One must admit that Jackson's conduct in the duel provides an example of animal courage of an intense degree. But in telling the story, admirers added the final touch: 'His astonishing self-command appeared almost superhuman to his friends who witnessed the scene; to one of whom he declared, that so fixed was his resolution, that he should have killed his antagonist, had he himself been shot through the brain.' In this embellishment, Jackson is presented as able to put aside death itself until his object is achieved. Another anecdote to the same end concerns a conversation supposed to have occurred in a New York omnibus between a merchant and a broker, whose speculative occupation makes him an appropriate adversary of Jackson.

MERCHANT *(with a sigh): 'Well, the old General is dead.'*

BROKER *(with a shrug): 'Yes, he's gone at last.'*

MERCHANT *(not appreciating the shrug): 'Well, sir, he was a good man.'*

BROKER *(with a shrug more pronounced): 'I don't know about that.'*

MERCHANT: *(energetically): 'He was a good man, sir. If any man has gone to heaven, General Jackson has gone to heaven.'*

BROKER *(doggedly): 'I don't know about that.'*

MERCHANT: *'Well, sir, I tell you that if Andrew Jackson has made up his mind to go to heaven, you may depend upon it he's there.'*

The tradition that glorified Jackson as the man of iron will not only found God to be unnecessary, it asserted that the intensity of Jackson's determination was sufficient to set aside the very judgment of God. As we shall see, this was not a typical attitude, but it represents the extreme of the admiration for Jackson as a symbol of the success that inevitably awaits the man of sufficient determination.

■ ■ ■

STUDY QUESTIONS

1. What exactly did the concept of the "man of iron" mean to most Americans in the 1820s and 1830s? How did Andrew Jackson's prepresidential career seem to embody those virtues?

2. The "man of iron" image was obviously important enough to the American identity to become part of the political culture. Why were Americans so impressed with the "man of iron" image? At that point in American history, how did the faith in determination and self-reliance serve the emerging national identity?

3. John William Ward states that the "man of iron" image was compelling enough to let many Americans assume Andrew Jackson could even transcend the will of God. Why was that an important assumption?

4. Are there other people in United States history whose political careers were propelled by similar images held by the American people? Can you explain some examples?

BIBLIOGRAPHY

For an introduction to the age of Jackson, see Glyndon G. Van Deusen, *The Jacksonian Era, 1828–1848* (1959). Also see Edward Pessen, *Jacksonian America: Society, Personality, and Politics* (1978). A dated but still important interpretation of the phenomenon of Jacksonian democracy is Arthur M. Schlesinger, Jr., *The Age of Jackson* (1945). For a brief biography of Andrew Jackson, see Robert V. Remini, *Andrew Jackson* (1966). For a longer and eminently readable biography, see Marquis James, *The Life of Andrew Jackson* (1937). Finally, see John William Ward, *Andrew Jackson: Symbol for an Age* (1955) and Marvin Meyers, *The Jacksonian Persuasion* (1957) for analyses of the culture of Jacksonian democracy.

PANACEAS IN THE AGE OF DEMOCRACY

Few decades in American history can rival the 1980s for mass preoccupation with looking and feeling good. A cult of physical fitness and youthful vigor, which started gaining momentum in the 1960s, became a virtual obsession in the 1980s, spawning new growth industries and capturing the popular imagination. Jogging, weightlifting, aerobics, cycling, swimming, plastic surgery, and fat farms, along with a host of therapeutic systems to achieve emotional health, dominated American popular culture in the 1980s. But it wasn't the first time the country had been obsessed with how people looked and felt. The age of Jacksonian democracy had generated similar concerns.

"It is a woman's *business* to be beautiful," an editor for *Godey's Lady's Magazine* wrote at the tail end of the Jacksonian era. The maxim was almost equally true for men. The nineteenth century witnessed a growing interest in books about beauty, advice on how to become beautiful, and aids that enhanced beauty. Just as reformers attempted to perfect human institutions, men and women labored to perfect their looks with new hairstyles and cosmetics. And just as men competed in the commercial world, women competed in the fashion world. According to Harriet Beecher Stowe, to be a Southern "belle" was a full-time "profession."

Feeling good was just as important as looking good. Americans also sought personal fulfillment and a better life through patent medicines. In the age of democracy, medicine was democratized, and men became physicians simply by proclaiming themselves such. Like P. T. Barnum, these new "doctors" were often more professional hucksters than physicians. In the following essays Estelle Kleiger and Martin Kaufman take a look at fashion and health in nineteenth-century America.

Vanity in the 19th Century
by Estelle Kleiger

George Washington wore a perfumed, powdered wig at his inauguration, and very likely rouge as well. Most of the other men present were similarly bedecked; it was standard fashion for upper-class men of that period. Women of the same class were more elaborately adorned and went to greater extremes to be fashionable. Their ghostly pallor was not always due to delicate health, but to ceruse, a white lead paint, known to be toxic. In spite of the horror stories about the slow death and ruined complexions of its users, some women braved the consequences. They used rouge, too, and their hair—real and false, powdered and pomaded—reached heights of a foot or more above their heads. A Philadelphia newspaper of that time advertised hair dressing with "construction of rolls" to raise heads to the desired "pitch." No attempt was made by either sex to conceal the wearing of cosmetics, since their use was the mark of the aristocrat.

Of course, such fashions were not for rural New Englanders, whose intense concern was with the state of their souls and with eking a living from the land, and whose moral codes forbade such frivolities. Those who used these artificialities were plantation owners, wealthy residents of Southern cities, especially New Orleans where the extravagant French influence was very strong, and some in the upper classes of New York, Boston, and Philadelphia.

Americans copied European styles, but they usually ran a year or so behind the times because of slow communications. Also, the most extreme fashions were shunned because they did not suit the temper of the country. The "macaronis," whose fashion originated in Italy and spread to other European countries, affected an exaggerated, heavily made-up style, and wore tiny hats atop enormous powdered wigs. Although they were severely criticized in Europe, they had some adherents. In the colonies they were merely ridiculed and gained fame through "Yankee Doodle."

Yet, Americans were surely fashion conscious. Most wealthy homes reserved a special room or closet for hair powdering, a distinctly messy process. The powder was distributed by means of a bellows which dusted the hair and everything else in sight. Two people were involved: the subject of the powdering, who kept a cone or similar object over his eyes, nose, and mouth; and a second person, usually a valet or a barber, who operated the bellows. Many men had their hair powdered and curled daily, but women whose elaborate coiffures took many hours to complete had their hair arranged only once in several months, and neither combed nor washed their heads between times. When one considers the infrequency of shampoos and the fact that powder was applied over oil or pomade to make it stick, the charm of this fashion rapidly fades. Wigs, powdered or not, were much easier to maintain, and were as popular here as in England.

The French Revolution sent tremors throughout the Western World. Here, our own Revolution began a leveling process, with political power slowly slipping from the hands of the aristocrats who founded the country. One by one the states discarded property qualifications for voting and moved toward universal suffrage for white men. The old guard was dying off and being replaced by men of the people. By the beginning of the 19th century, as part of the growing resentment against class distinctions, there was a gradual building of social pressures against the use of cosmetics.

Carry-overs from previous years, however, persisted, and despite warnings of the hazards of white paint containing bismuth and lead, some women still used it. Hair styles for the upper classes of both sexes became simpler, although

Estelle Kleiger, "Vanity in the 19th Century." From *American History Illustrated* 14 (August 1979), pp. 24–27, 30–31. Reprinted through the courtesy of Cowles Magazines, publisher of AMERICAN HISTORY ILLUSTRATED.

men, even more than women, continued to be perfumed and powdered. Describing her husband's appearance at James Monroe's Inaugural Ball, Mrs. Robert Goodloe Harper wrote in a letter that he had been "perfumed like a milliner." The North was more restrictive about the use of cosmetics than the South, where the wealthy clung to aristocratic ways for a longer period. Before John Adams' Administration, Philadelphia was the nation's Capital, and when it moved to Washington, a change in decor was evident. State entertaining became more elaborate and the wealthy Southerners who flocked there were more heavily made up, their clothes showing the French influence. Eight years later when the gay and beautiful Dolley Madison moved into the White House, the use of cosmetics throughout the country was already more subdued. Tongues wagged about whether or not the first lady "rouged," but the momentous question was never really settled.

The voice of the common man grew louder as the century progressed and the modes and manners of the aristocrats were more roundly criticized. Andrew Jackson, a Westerner whose cruder speech and bearing dismayed his predecessors, was elected President. Men who used cosmetics were ridiculed and labeled effeminate. President Martin Van Buren's career suffered even when a political opponent revealed that he installed a bathtub in the White House. A President who insisted on "the pleasures of a warm or tepid bath" might also perfume his whiskers with "Double Extract of Queen Victoria"! The mere mention of this toilet preparation in connection with President Van Buren was enough to make him a laughingstock.

The stress on respectability during Queen Victoria's reign extended to this country, and cosmetics for women, too, fell into disfavor. Some older women, set in their habits, continued to paint and also to powder their hair. The writer of a mid-century book on perfumes, while conceding that it was passé, nevertheless stated his belief that powder imparted "a degree of softness to the features."

Occasionally during the early years of the Victorian era, articles appeared urging the use of cosmetics, at least for the elderly, but most commentators took the opposite view, as did Mrs. Merrifield in a mid-century *Godey's Lady's Magazine*. She berated the attempt to conceal or repair the "ravages of time" with paint and false hair, calling it a violation of the "laws of nature," and, as if that were not enough, "a positive breach of sincerity." Besides, she continued, this "acting a lie" deceives nobody but "the unfortunate perpetrator of the would-be deceit." Lip rouge was condemned to an even greater degree than cheek rouge. M. M. Marberry wrote that Victoria Woodhull, the notorious 19th-century free-wheeler, was accused by some of using lipstick, but that most people refused to believe she would go *that* far. Cheek rouge ("false bloom") was permissible under certain very special circumstances, such as the case of a pale invalid who wished to spare the feelings of loved ones. For the rest, women could go on pinching their cheeks and biting their lips to give them color.

In spite of public censure, cosmetics were still used, but furtively, and to avoid scorn they were often invested with health-giving or healing qualities. For example, an 1853 *Godey's* gave a formula for "Carnation Lip Salve" with alkanet root as a coloring agent. Ostensibly designed to prevent or soothe chapped lips, that it also reddened them was only incidental. "Tri-cosian Fluid," imported from England, was a hair dye for women, and aside from its primary purpose, it was advertised as being "highly beneficial in nervous headaches or weakness of the eyes." Some cosmetic preparations appeared in pharmacies and barbershops, and these included Pearl Powder, Florida Water, Orange Flower Water, Bear's Oil, and Macassar Oil. The last two were hair dressings for men, Bear's Oil being used mostly by frontiersmen, with Macassar Oil the preference of the wealthy. Both were greasy and antimacassars (doilies to protect the backs of chairs) soon became popular.

■ ■ *An 1875 artist illustrates* Godey's *fashions of the day. A Sears, Roebuck catalogue of the time declared that it is "in the nature of the human family . . . to use the best means obtainable, [to] render themselves more pleasing and attractive to others."*

Hair dye for men was also available. An 1897 Sears, Roebuck catalogue advertised "Old Reliable Hair and Whisker Dye" which, it claimed, had been in use since 1860. The price was forty cents a bottle.

Until the last quarter of the 19th century, however, most cosmetic preparations were made in the home. Women concocted all sorts of mixtures, some of them sounding good enough to eat. Fresh strawberries steeped for seven days in white wine produced a solution which was supposed to make the skin firmer. Cucumber juice rubbed on the face and left there to dry would keep the complexion soft and white. New milk, skimmed milk, and buttermilk each had special healing and beautifying effects

(some of the claims are still in favor), but a 19th-century author was quick to specify that he referred only to the "milk of healthy, grass-fed cows, not the washy, unwholesome liquid given by the stall fed animals kept in the crowded districts of large cities."

The editor of *Godey's Lady's Magazine*, Sarah Josepha Hale, shared with her readers her special beauty secret: She believed that brown butcher's paper soaked in fresh apple vinegar, applied to the temples and left there overnight, would prevent crow's-feet. Freckles were considered a bane and attempts at erasing them ranged from frequent applications of lemon juice to powerful lotions containing hydrochloric and sulphuric acid. *Godey's* stated that the favorite

Parisian lotion for removing freckles was "an ounce of alum and an ounce of lemon juice in a pint of rose water."

For men, beards and mustaches were the fashion news of the 19th century. Following a long period of relative beardlessness, facial hair burst into view in a profusion of styles and shapes, from the trim goatee to the long and flowing full beard. Side whiskers appeared first in the early part of the century, gradually becoming longer and fuller. The American army, disapproving of the lack of uniformity, issued a directive in 1835 forbidding side whiskers that extended below the ear lobe. For the most part the order was not strictly enforced and in 1840, in an effort to go along with the times, the army issued another one permitting the wearing of mustaches. Each commanding officer was to set his own fashion rules. But this, again, proved to be too restrictive, and in 1853 the army threw up its hands: Beards, too, were declared within regulations, and all objection on the army's part had to be set aside when President Lincoln decided to join the ranks of the bearded. Just why he did so has often been a matter of speculation. A young woman urged him "for heaven's sake, to raise side-whiskers to fill out the lantern jaw," but Carl Sandburg suggested that a desire to appear graver and more responsible may have been the reason. But for whatever reason, the President did grow a beard—and set a style.

Lincoln's results were so successful that a cartoon appeared advertising jars of "Lincoln Whiskeropherous," guaranteed to grow whiskers in a few weeks. Actually, the selling of unguents to stimulate the growth of facial hair was a thriving business, and full-grown beards and mustaches were lovingly rubbed with oils and pomades. In addition to those purchased in the store, many preparations for men came from home, made by the housewife along with her own toiletries. The famous Macassar Oil consisted chiefly of oil of almonds, colored red with alkanet root and scented with oil of cassia. It could be made at home for a fraction of its barbershop price. Nitrate of silver was used to dye hair black, but it had the disadvantage of imparting a tell-tale iridescent quality which resembled, according to one description, the feathers on "the neck of a pigeon."

After the Civil War the mood of the country changed. Many of those who found themselves in a better financial position, stressed frivolities. The old families looked down upon these *nouveau riche* who, in many cases, had made their money through unscrupulous means. They were offended by the lavish entertaining of this group. Suffragette Matilda Joslyn Gage blasted politicians in the Grant Administration for giving parties which, she said, rivaled foreign ones. The wealthy traveled in greater numbers to Europe and returned home with the latest in fashion and beauty aids. There was a brief revival of hair powdering for women, only now gold and silver dust were used. Some of the more daring used mascara which, it is believed, Empress Eugenie introduced. At about this time a new method of making face powder was discovered. Previously, it had been made with chloride of bismuth, arsenic salts, or lead, the constant use of which was harmful. The new powder had a zinc oxide base, was harmless, and did not discolor. Also it was cheap, and women of limited means could purchase it.

In the 1880s, the glamorous Harriet Hubbard Ayer, with an estranged husband, two children, and no money, began to sell a face cream that she said she herself had been using for many years. She wrote and publicized the story that originally the cream had been made for Julie Récamier, a great French beauty, and that she, Mrs. Ayer, had come upon it quite by accident. She explained that while in Europe she suffered a severe sunburn and believed that her complexion was "irretrievably injured." An unidentified countess, sympathizing with her predicament, gave her a pot of the cream. The improvement it brought about was almost miraculous, Mrs. Ayer wrote, thus stressing the curative powers of the cream as well as its beautifying effects.

From the start, the cream sold well here and in England, and soon Mrs. Ayer hit on another advertising scheme, one that started a whole new trend: She asked famous beauties to endorse her cream—for a consideration, of course. At first only actresses, who were on the far side of respectability anyway, would agree to do so, but eventually Mrs. James Brown Potter of Tuxedo Park, a socialite, lent her name to Mrs. Ayer's product. Her testimonial, the first to feature a name from the Social Register, caused a storm of consternation among members of that group, but it was not long before others entered the field, making certain to let it be known that the proceeds from such arrangements went to charity.

The Victorian era was drawing to a close. A few older men kept their beards, though no longer fashionable. A highly imaginative variety of styles in mustaches flourished in the 1890s, but at the turn of the century they, too, vanished and men became clean shaven once again. Women were still surreptitious about their use of cosmetics. The dictates of respectability decreed that soap and water were sufficient to keep their complexions glowing and to allow their inner beauty to shine. Despite the scandals of the period and the effective and growing political activity of the suffragists, mawkish sentimentality, at least in song and verse, kept women on their pedestals.

Then bleached blonde hair became popular with actresses, and the term "peroxide blonde" came into being, but no "nice" woman succumbed to this fashion, or, as a writer in an 1892 *Ladies Home Journal* grimly put it, "It goes without saying that a well-bred woman does not dye her hair." Yet a sizable number of them did, though they often tried to avoid detection by taking months to complete the process. Harriet Hubbard Ayer placed the blame for the blonde craze on the men who, "from the beginning of the world," have sung of the beauty of golden-haired women. She discouraged bleaching of the hair because, she wrote, it never remains the same color and because a woman with bleached hair is "regarded lightly." But for those who "hurl anathemas" at the artful use of cosmetics, she wrote, let men show their devotion and loyalty to "sallow-faced, pale-lipped, dull, thin-haired women," and the application of these substances would soon cease.

Advertisers played on people's natural desire to improve their appearance. The 1897 Sears, Roebuck catalogue declared that it is

in the nature of the human family from the savage to the most civilized to use the best means obtainable, by which they can render themselves more pleasing and attractive to others. It is almost a duty and a pleasure we owe to one another. It is almost criminal to go about with a repulsive complexion, etc., when the means to render yourself attractive are so easily obtainable.

In spite of this and similar rhetoric, and the great increase in commercial preparations available, the social attitude toward cosmetics remained restrictive. Not until after World War I was there general acceptance of their use.

"Step Right Up, Ladies and Gentlemen": Patent Medicines in 19th-Century America

by Martin Kaufman

The band was playing a familiar melody and hundreds of local residents were attracted to the wagon that had been converted to a stage. When enough people had gathered, the show began. It might have been magic, sleight-of-hand, puppets, blackface minstrels, or dancing and chanting Indians. When the mood was right, the pitchman began his spiel: "Do you ever get a rundown feeling? Do you ever find it hard to get out of bed in the morning? Do you ever lose your appetite?"

Nearly every member of the audience nodded at least once.

The pitchman continued. "Well," he exclaimed dramatically, "those are the first signs of galloping consumption!" A wave of panic swept through the audience, but the pitchman would not stop until he had everyone scared to death.

"Maybe next week you'll see the next sign," he warned ominously. "You'll begin to cough until you cough every minute of the day and night. Then, you'll begin to spit blood." "Finally," he said in a lowered voice, "your loved ones will be measuring you for a coffin." Now the audience was scared to death. The pitchman suddenly turned savior: "But, there's still hope, my friends. The hope is right here in this little bottle." Then he described the miracle cure he was offering at a "special low introductory price." As the mood darkened and fear tugged at the listeners' imaginations, they pushed toward the stage waving fists full of dollars to exchange for the hawker's magic, health-giving wares.

Martin Kaufman, " 'Step Right Up, Ladies and Gentlemen': Patent Medicines in 19th-Century America." From *American History Illustrated* 16 (August 1981), pp. 38–45. Reprinted through the courtesy of Cowles Magazines, publisher of AMERICAN HISTORY ILLUSTRATED.

A scene like this was all too familiar to small town and rural Americans in the late 19th century. It was a time when Americans were being deluged with claims that this elixir, that panacea, would cure everything from cancer to bad breath.

America's patent medicine industry began as did the nation itself, made in England. Some of the colonists probably brought bottles of Daffy's Elixir with them or boxes of Anderson's or Lockyer's Pills, early British remedies that were advertised as being superior to anything dispensed by local practitioners. Concocters of Anderson's Pills, produced in the 1630s, said their cure-all had been formulated by a physician to King Charles I, based on a recipe he had learned in Venice. Since few Englishmen could afford the fees charged by university-trained physicians, the claims for Anderson's Pills set that product far above the medications dispensed by local apothecaries, who had neither been to Venice nor served the King.

During the colonial period Americans suffered from a wide variety of ailments. There were the common problems—respiratory infections, dysentery, and fevers of various kinds. In addition, there were periodic epidemics of disease, especially smallpox and yellow fever.

The American scene was perfectly suited for the arrival of British patent medicines. Too many people practiced medicine in the colonies with inadequate training and limited ability. Only a small number of physicians graduated from medical colleges; the first American school did not open its doors until 1765. Most practitioners had learned their craft through apprenticeship, and not many American physicians had the time, the teaching ability, the library, or sufficient scientific knowledge to share with their students. In addition, physicians expected to be paid for their services, and most Americans were yeoman farmers who could not afford to summon a doctor for every problem. Instead the farmers turned to do-it-yourself guides to self-medication, like William Buchan's *Domestic Medicine; Or the Family Physician*, first published in

Edinburgh in 1769, and they supplemented the self-help prescriptions with relatively inexpensive patent medicines, especially those that promised to cure a wide variety of ailments.

The colonial American medical scene was a varied one. The era itself was an age of discovery, and challenging traditional ideas about the healing arts led to a number of alternatives to Galen's old humoral system, which had dominated western medicine since the second century A.D. Sidestepping the old philosophy, physicians generally believed that medicines had to taste horrible in order to drive disease from the body, so they searched for ingredients that not only tasted horrible, but also were repugnant in other ways. Obnoxious substances like flies' wings, wood lice, and even dung and urine were extolled for their medicinal qualities. And people assumed that the larger the number of ingredients in a medication, the more likely it would be as a curative. This belief in polypharmacy led to the development of medicines containing forty, fifty, or even sixty ingredients.

Nature, too, promised the key to healing, infecting many practitioners with the idea that in every geographical area grew herbs, roots, and barks which if properly used could cure the sicknesses peculiar to the region. Such thinking encouraged a great interest in medical botany, and Americans and others began to search for plants they could use to heal the sick. On the opposite side of the theoretical scale were practitioners convinced that people in other lands were healthier than Americans, and that exotic medical secrets could cure local ailments. Thus, they searched for oriental treatments, and even tried to pry "botanical secrets from Indian medicine men."

Well before the Revolution some Americans were compounding and selling their own medications. "The Widow Read," Benjamin Franklin's mother-in-law, was one. In 1731 she advertised her "well-known Ointment for the ITCH." Widow Read's Ointment promised to perform the cure, and as a bonus, to drive away "all Sorts of Lice. . . ."

Ironically, the first patent medicine to stress an American origin was actually made in England. Dr. John Hill's American Balsam, marketed in 1770, proclaimed to cure everything from whooping cough to "*hypochondriacal disease.*" During the 1760s the same Dr. Hill had assured a receptive public that his "Balsamic Addition" could transform water into "the Nature and Quality of Asses Milk."

When the Revolution severed trade with England, Americans could no longer get their supplies of Turlington's Balsam, Bateman's Pectoral Drops, and other British patent medicines. After the war ended in 1783 British-made medications never returned to their prewar eminence. America was a "brave new world," and Americans were anxious to declare independence not only in terms of political leadership but in other areas as well. In a tremendous outpouring of cultural nationalism, American theologians broke away from their British leaders, and Noah Webster preached the glories of a distinctive "American" language. American physicians began to work on an American Pharmacopoeia, and Americans looked to American cures for American ailments. In effect, they were declaring independence from British treatments and from British patent-medicines. By 1804 a New York drug catalog included eighty to ninety nostrums, most of them native in origin.

The first American to receive a patent for a medicine was Samuel Lee, Jr. of Windham, Connecticut. In 1796 Lee patented his Bilious Pills, which he said cured a wide variety of ailments including yellow fever, dysentery, dropsy, worms, and female complaints. Before long three other Lees were marketing their own Bilious pills, causing tremendous animosity among nostrum venders named Lee.

The turn of the century brought a new era in the history of American medicine, a period known as "The Age of Heroic Medicine." Based on the theories of Dr. Benjamin Rush, a signer of the Declaration of Independence and a professor of medicine at the University of Pennsylvania, heroic medicine called for massive bloodletting and administering large doses of purgatives, especially calomel, a mercury compound. Patients with virtually every ailment were subjected to giving up several pints of blood and were dosed with emetics, which caused vomiting, and with cathartics, which caused the patient to purge from the other end.

During the same period new medical schools opened promiscuously throughout the nation, but standards for admission and graduation fell to a pathetic low. Every year thousands of new doctors were "turned loose on the community, to cure or to kill, as the case may be."

With the age of heroic medicine and the decline of standards within the medical profession came competition from alternative schools of medical practice, most notably the Thomsonians and eclectics, who depended upon botanical remedies, and the homeopaths, who dispensed infinitesimal doses of drugs. These developments made self-medication an even more desirable alternative. When physicians could not agree, and when patients were being charged high fees for the heroic treatments of the day, it was natural for the average citizen to try to cure himself before resorting to professional care.

At the same time, there were major changes taking place in American life. The public school movement was providing education for the average man, and an abundance of newspapers kept him up-to-date on current events. In those newspapers the reader was subjected to numerous advertisements for patent medicines that offered alternatives to depending on physicians, at a much cheaper price. Furthermore, America was becoming more of a democracy. Voting restrictions withered and a mass of semi-literate voters elected that great champion of the Common Man, Andrew Jackson, to the presidency. Americans demanded medical democracy as well: In state after state, laws governing the licensing of physicians were repealed. Medical sects competed with orthodox practitioners, confusing patients with claims and counterclaims tossed about by professional physicians.

Later, Lemuel Shattuck wrote in his celebrated *Report of the Sanitary Commission of Massachusetts:* "Any one, male or female, learned or ignorant, an honest man or a knave, can assume the name of physician, and 'practice' upon any one, to cure or to kill, as either may happen, without accountability. It's a free country!" The declining prestige of the medical profession created a vacuum that William Swaim stepped in to fill in 1820.

Swaim was a New York bookbinder who had learned from a physician the recipe for the medication that cured his own illness. He moved to Philadelphia and began manufacturing a substance he called Swaim's Panacea. It was a syrup of sarsaparilla and considered by medical men as a wonder cure for syphilis, scrofula, and skin ailments. Swaim sold it at less than half the price of the French variety. The recipe included sarsaparilla, oil of wintergreen (which made his medication more delectable), and mercury, which was used to treat skin problems. Swaim managed to get testimonials from some leading physicians, including Dr. Nathaniel Chapman, a professor at the University of Pennsylvania Medical School and a man who later became the first president of the American Medical Association. Swaim published books extolling the virtues of his Panacea, and he promised that it would cure a number of ailments, including cancer, rheumatism, gout, hepatitis, and syphilis.

By 1827 the medical profession had begun to question the benefits of this Panacea. Committees of the Medical Society of the City of New York and of the Philadelphia Medical Society reported the drug to be dangerous. Swaim's Panacea, claimed spokesmen, had been the primary cause of death in many cases. Physicians retracted their glowing testimonials of the medicinal stuff and admitted they were wrong. Their experience with the Panacea convinced them to abandon its use.

But non-professionals did not read medical journals, and even if they did, would not have believed these same physicians they accused of seeking to destroy competition to improve their economic position. Despite medical opposition, sales of Swaim's Panacea soared. By 1850 Swaim was a wealthy man worth approximately $500,000. Swaim's Panacea continued to be manufactured and sold well into the 20th century.

Another leader in the patent medicine industry was Benjamin Brandreth, born in England, the grandson of a Liverpool physician who had devoted years to developing a recipe for the perfect purgative. Brandreth inherited the recipe and in 1835 came to America determined to produce his Vegetable Universal Pills. He set up shop in the village of Sing Sing (now Ossining) up the Hudson from New York City and turned out pills by the thousands. Brandreth was so successful that within five years his wealth was estimated at more than $200,000. Brandreth's Pills were composed of sarsaparilla as well as aloes, gamboge, and colocynth, all powerful cathartics. In a day and age when the American diet consisted of salted meats, fat-fried foods, and virtually no fresh fruits or vegetables except during the summer months, such a product could hardly miss as a money-maker. Indigestion was a national problem, and physicians responded by prescribing purgatives for stomach and bowel ailments.

Brandreth's advertisement insisted that the body was a battlefield between the forces of life and death. Good health demanded that "pollutions" and "decompositions" be removed, and of course, Brandreth's Universal Vegetable Pills were the fastest and best way to rid oneself of the forces of death. Brandreth even published a 224-page book, intending to prove that "Purgation Is the Cornerstone of All Curatives." His newspaper advertisements boasted that people in the West rode sixty miles through the woods for their supply of Brandreth's Pills. Needless to say, residents of the city did not have to go quite so far for their favorite purgative.

In 1853 Doctor Hostetter's Celebrated Stomach Bitters Tonic made its appearance. Produced in Pittsburgh by the doctor's son David

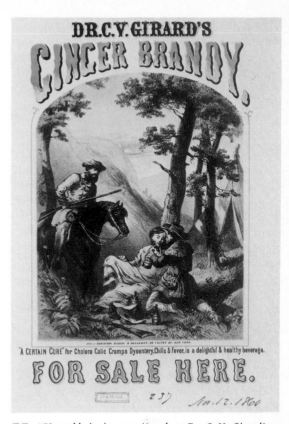

■ ■ *"Vegetable invigorants," such as Dr. C. V. Girard's Ginger Brandy, were not subject to liquor license laws—even though they were often sold by the drink because they were so potent.*

Hostetter, this new medicine took advantage of changes in medical thought. By the 1850s purging and bloodletting were being abandoned by physicians, and the trend was toward vegetable (and safer) remedies. Hostetter's advertisements emphasized *"vegetable curatives,* and more especially, *vegetable invigorants."*

As it turned out, Hostetter's Bitters were a bit more than a "vegetable invigorant." They contained 32 percent alcohol, 64 percent water, and only 4 percent herbs. Although so potent that in some places they were sold by the drink, Hostetter's Bitters was a medicine and not a beverage; nor did they require a state or federal license. Yet, Carl Sandburg wrote how America's youth "heard that you could get drunk on one bottle of

Hostetter's.'' Interestingly, Hostetter not only defended the alcoholic content but declared that it contained 39 percent alcohol rather than the 32 percent found by a government chemist. He insisted that his medication contained ''the pure Essence of Rye.''

Hostetter's was not the only bitters on the market. The bitters trade grew in direct response to the success of the temperance movement. The enactment of license laws and the legal and moral condemnation of drinking easily could be surmounted if the alcohol was a medicine rather than a drink. Ironically, some patent medicine manufacturers sought acceptance from temperance advocates by producing temperance bitters with no alcoholic content. Analysis, however, proved that in some temperance bitters the alcoholic content ranged from 40 to 80 percent. Hostetter's Bitters was the most successful of a large number of similar ''medications,'' and from the 1860s to the 1880s Hostetter's had annual sales above one million dollars.

America's patent medicine makers used different methods to sell their wares to an unsuspecting public. They reached their largest market through newspaper advertising—virtually every 19th-century newspaper was filled with columns of advertisements for various patent medicines and miracle cures for every known ailment. One editor declared that without nostrum advertising his paper would require a tenfold increase in circulation in order to make the same profits. As a result, it was rare for any editor to criticize a patent medicine industry helping to make his paper financially successful. Some newspapers did draw the line when it came to advertisements for abortionists or for venereal cures, but those same papers were filled with notices for remedies for consumption, cancer, piles, painful menstruation, and falling of the womb.

Advertisements changed to meet changing circumstances. During the Civil War the patent medicine makers took careful aim at the newly developing military market. Brandreth's Pills claimed to protect soldiers from ''the arrows of disease, usually as fatal to Soldiers as the bullets

of the foe.'' Hostetter's Bitters, which undoubtedly brought warmth to Yankee soldiers and reduced the army's effectiveness in the process, was promoted as a ''positive protective against the fatal maladies of the Southern swamps and the poisonous tendency of the impure rivers and bayous.'' In the South, intense nationalism manifested itself in antagonism toward Yankee cures. ''Southern preparations'' were widely advertised in Southern papers—the makers of Broom's Anti-Hydropic Tincture declared: ''Dropsy Cured! No Yankee Humbug!''

Before long patent medicine could be advertised from coast to coast, with outdoor signs as well as with newspaper notices. Henry T. Hembold, the manufacturer of Extract of Buchu, took the lead in outdoor advertising. His remedy was made from an African plant that physicians used as a gentle stimulant, especially in bladder and urinary ailments. Hembold insisted that Buchu was a cure-all for diseases of the sexual organs, but as time passed he became more confident that Buchu could conquer other illnesses, too. He advertised Buchu as a cure for general debility, mental and physical depression, imbecility, confused ideas, sleeplessness, hysteria, low spirits, and of course, ''Disorganization or Paralysis of the Organs of Generation.''

Hired agents posted his advertisements on trees, walls, and rocks from coast to coast. The New York *Herald* complained that nostrum sellers had ''crossed the continent and laid their unclean paws on the Rocky Mountains and the Sierra Nevada.'' Everyone in the nation had to have heard of Buchu: ''this magic word adorns every dead wall, fence, rock, and telegraph pole from the Atlantic to the Pacific.'' Even apparently inaccessible and insurmountable sections of the Rocky Mountains, some said, were plastered with advertisements for Hembold's Buchu. Unfortunately for Henry Hembold, Buchu could not cure his ailments; he drank to excess and eventually was confined to an asylum.

Nostrum literature abounded in 19th-century America. Various manufacturers produced advertising cards listing the virtues and portraying the benefits of their nostrum, often with testimonials from satisfied customers. The card for Dr. Thomas's Eclectic Oil claimed to "positively cure" toothache in five minutes, backache in two days. At fifty cents a bottle, could one go wrong?

The card for Ayer's Cathartic Pills demonstrated that it was "a safe, pleasant and reliable Family Medicine." Indeed, it was so safe, pleasant, and reliable that the card featured naked babies packaging the pills. Any member of the family suffering from "Costiveness, Jaundice, Indigestion, Headache, Biliousness, and all other diseases resulting from a disordered state of the Digestive Apparatus" could benefit from Ayer's Cathartic Pills.

During the 1840s some patent medicine makers began to publish almanacs to praise the benefits of their nostrums and to provide potential customers with an entire year of astronomical information, cooking recipes, household hints, and other useful advice. Of course, the most important information in them was the medical advice which was always concluded by extolling Ayer's Cherry Pectoral or whatever other nostrum was highlighted in the almanac. By the end of the 19th century James C. Ayer's *American Almanacs* cost his company $120,000 a year to print sixteen million copies. Ayer printed almanacs in over twenty languages, not only for immigrants in the United States, but also for potential customers around the world. Each year just before Christmas storekeepers throughout the country received their supplies of the books to distribute to friends and customers. The almanac was a combination of a calendar, a reference work, and a source of entertainment complete with cartoons, stories, and jokes. Ayer's *Almanac* declared that it was "second only to the Bible in circulation," which probably was not an overstatement.

Another advertising ploy was the traveling medicine show. According to James Harvey Young, the historian who devoted his life to chronicling the story of patent medicines in America, the "grandest spectacle of all" was the Indian show of John E. Healy and "Texas Charley" Bigelow. In 1882 Healy and Bigelow joined "Nevada Ned" Oliver to form the Kickapoo Indian Medicine Company. Then, they organized traveling medicine shows to sell Kickapoo Indian Sagwa, a remedy made of herbs and alcohol. They hired hundreds of Indians, "none of them Kickapoo," and some seventy-five Kickapoo Medicine Shows toured the country at the same time.

The "standard" show began with the Indians sitting in a semi-circle, in front of a painted Indian scene. "Nevada Ned" or another "scout" introduced the Indians, each of whom responded with a grunt—except the last, who delivered what seemed to be "an impassioned oration in his native tongue." The scout served as interpreter, describing the fabulous remedy "which had saved countless Indian lives" and which now was being offered to save the white man as well. When the show ended, the Indians and the whites in the company sold bottles of Kickapoo Indian Sagwa.

After the show, whether it was a blackface minstrel comedy, a magic act, or a songfest, the pitchman started the most important part of the program, at least from the perspective of the nostrum vender. His job was to "scare the living daylights out of the people in his audience," making them "sick and frightened enough" to buy the remedy. He might describe some common ailment and then declare it to be the first sign of some dreaded disease. He might exclaim that "the seeds of disease" were within every member of the audience. Would they die of cancer, consumption? Perhaps some unknown malady?

The pitchman often provided visible evidence of his product's healing powers. One hawker asked a husky man from the audience to blow through a straw into a "sensitive diagnostic liquid." When he did, the fluid (which was really limewater) turned milky, sure "evidence" of consumption or some other ailment. And if a strapping, healthy fellow was so afflicted, the lesson was apparent—every member of the audience might be sick as well. Then, a few drops of the medicine's "active ingredient" (vinegar) cleared the liquid, "demonstrating" the potency of the medication. At this point the selling began; invariably the eager audience bought the nostrum so vividly demonstrated before its very eyes.

For the members of the audience it was a spectacle—a band, a show, a circus—helping to relieve the isolation and perhaps the boredom inherent in rural and small town America. Yet, it was a costly moment of excitement, relieving them not only of feelings of isolation and boredom, but also of their hard-earned money.

Moreover, the medication they purchased promised to cure everything from halitosis to sore feet, but it was much more likely to be ineffective and in some cases positively dangerous. Being dependent on laxatives was certainly not beneficial, and many of the patent medicines were laxatives intended to purge the body of the "agents of death." In addition, some remedies included a significant amount of alcohol and many people who relied on these became alcoholics. Finally, some remedies contained opium and many people dependent on them to relieve minor symptoms of illness ended up being addicted to narcotics. Aside from the dangers of laxatives, alcohol, or opium, relying on nostrums kept genuinely sick patients from consulting physicians who might have been able to help them.

The medicine show was a symbol of an age, but happily that age was reaching its end. Medical science had improved substantially from the days when physicians dispensed calomel and bloodletting for every ailment. Now medicine was based more firmly on science, and physicians were better able to treat the ill. Moreover, with the turn of the 20th century America was entering its Progressive Era, with its emphasis on protection of the public. In the early years of the 20th century came a major attack on the patent-medicine frauds of the day.

The assault began in the *Ladies Home Journal* and in *Collier's Magazine,* where Samuel Hopkins Adams exposed what he called "The Great American Fraud." Then came the work of Dr. Harvey W. Wiley, chief chemist of the United States Department of Agriculture, who became the leading "muckraker" in a campaign against impure food and drugs. This movement led to passage of the Pure Food and Drug Act of 1906, which forced drug manufacturers to truthfully list on their labels the presence and amounts of dangerous substances.

Medical quackery did not die when the Pure Food and Drug Act passed, but the legislation marked the first step toward governmental protection of the health and well being of an American public that for over a century had been subjected to uncontrolled, ineffective, and too often dangerous medications that were promoted indiscriminately.

■ ■ ■

STUDY QUESTIONS

1. How did Americans in the eighteenth century regard wigs, powders, and rouge? Did their views demonstrate a class attitude?

2. What role did fashion journals play in the fashion industry?

3. How did fashions change during the nineteenth century?

4. How did nineteenth-century medicine differ from colonial medicine?

5. In the age of Jacksonian democracy who protected the consumer from bad or worthless medicines?

BIBLIOGRAPHY

Two popular books on fashion are Richard Corson, *Fashions in Makeup* (1972) and *Fashions in Hair* (1965). More scholarly and insightful are Lois W. Banner, *American Beauty* (1983), Valerie Steele, *Fashion and Eroticism* (1985), and Alison Lurie, *The Language of Clothes* (1981). Michael and Ariane Batterbery, *Mirror, Mirror: A Social History of Fashion* (1977) is also valuable for understanding change over time. Karen Halttunen, *Confident Men and Painted Women* (1982) offers a new interpretation of Jacksonian popular culture. On patent medicines see James Harvey Young, *The Toadstool Millionaires: A Social History of Patent Medicines in America Before Federal Regulation* (1961).

THE GREAT ONEIDA
LOVE-IN

Morris Bishop

By the early nineteenth century, the Puritan impulse to change the world was still alive, but its energies were now dissipated in a multitude of crusades. One of them was the utopian movement. Blessed with few class distinctions or entrenched traditions, as well as with abundant land and space, America became a laboratory for dramatic social exchange. Periodically, utopian idealists consciously tried to start society anew—creating social institutions from scratch instead of dealing with normal conventions. Most of those proved to be feeble attempts destined for historical oblivion, but a few succeeded, not so much because they changed but because they managed to stimulate debate about fundamental American values. The most unique of the utopian experiments took place at Oneida Lake, New York, and it also provoked bitter controversy in American society.

Morris Bishop's ''The Great Oneida Love-in'' describes the dream and the reality of John Humphrey Noyes's utopian community. While American culture placed a premium on private property and individual progress, Noyes preached a socialistic gospel of group property and community progress. In a society worshipping monogamy and sexual propriety, Noyes called for ''complex marriage'' where all men and women were united together sexually. In a country where religious sectarianism was the norm, Noyes worked for a ''community of believers'' without churches and denominational competition. Despite his dreams, Noyes failed to reform American society; indeed, American culture eventually transformed the Oneida community.

S in, the conviction of sin, the assurance of punishment for sin, pervaded pioneer America like the fever and ague, and took nearly as many victims. Taught that in Adam's fall we had sinned all, threatened with hell-fire by revivalist preachers, tortured by the guilt of intimate offenses, earnest youths whipped themselves into madness and suicide, and died crying that they had committed the sin against the Holy Ghost, which is unforgivable, though no one knows quite what it is.

The year 1831 was known as the Great Revival, when itinerant evangelists powerfully shook the bush and gathered in a great harvest of sinners. In September of that year John Humphrey Noyes, a twenty-year-old Dartmouth graduate and a law student in Putney, Vermont, attended such a revival. He was in a mood of metaphysical despair, aggravated by a severe cold. During the exhortings the conviction of salvation came to him. Light gleamed upon his soul. "Ere the day was done," he wrote later, "I had concluded to devote myself to the service and ministry of God."

Noyes was a young man of good family. His father was a Dartmouth graduate, a successful merchant in Putney, and a congressman. John was a bookish youth, delighting in history, romance, and poetry of a martial character, such as lives of Napoleon or of the Crusaders or Sir Walter Scott's *Marmion.* He was red-haired and freckled, and thought himself too homely ever to consider marriage. But when he began preaching his face shone like an angel's: one of his sons later averred that "there was about him an unmistakable and somewhat unexpected air of spiritual assurance." According to his phrenological analysis, his bumps of amativeness, combativeness, and self-esteem were large, his

benevolence and philoprogenitiveness very large. His life confirmed these findings.

After his mystical experience in Putney, Noyes spent a year in the Andover Theological Seminary (Congregational). He found his teachers and companions lukewarm in piety, and devoted himself to an intensive study of the New Testament, most of which he could recite by heart. A divine direction—"I know that ye seek Jesus which was crucified. He is not here"—sent him from Andover to the Yale Theological Seminary in New Haven. There he came in contact with the doctrine of perfectionism and was allured by it.

Perfectionism asserted that men may be freed from sin and attain in this life the perfect holiness necessary to salvation. It rejected therefore the consequences of original sin and went counter to the Calvinistic dogma of total depravity. Perfectionism took shape early in the nineteenth century and found lodgment among adventurous groups in New Haven, Newark, Albany, and in villages of central New York, "the burned-over district," where religion smote with a searing flame. Perfectionism was likely to develop into antinomianism, the contention that the faithful are "directly infused with the holy spirit" and thus free from the claims and obligations of Old Testament moral law. And antinomianism led readily to scandal, as when three perfectionist missionaries, two men and a sister of one of them, were tarred and feathered for sleeping together in one bed.

Though suspected of perfectionist heresy, Noyes was licensed to preach in August, 1833. At about the same time, he made a sensational discovery: Jesus Christ had announced that He would return during the lifetime of some of His disciples. Jesus could not have been mistaken; therefore the Second Coming of Christ had taken place in A.D. 70. The "Jewish cycle" of religious history then ended and a "Gentile cycle" began, in which the Church has improperly usurped the authority of the apostles. We live no longer in an age of prophecy and promise, but in an age of fulfillment. Perfect holiness is attainable in this

"The Great Oneida Love-in" by Morris Bishop. Copyright © 1969 American Heritage Publishing Co., Inc. Reprinted by permission from *American Heritage* (February 1969).

life, as well as guaranteed deliverance from sin.

Noyes found this revelation by fasting, prayer, and diligent search of the Scriptures. At divine command he announced it in a sermon to the Free Church of New Haven on February 20, 1834. "I went home with a feeling that I had committed myself irreversibly, and on my bed that night I received the baptism which I desired and expected. Three times in quick succession a stream of eternal love gushed through my heart, and rolled back again to its source. 'Joy unspeakable and full of glory' filled my soul. All fear and doubt and condemnation passed away. I knew that my heart was clean, and that the Father and the Son had come and made it their abode."

This was all very well, but next day the word ran through New Haven, "Noyes says he is perfect!" with the inevitable corollary, "Noyes is crazy!" The authorities promptly expelled him from the seminary and revoked his license to preach. But the perfect are proof against imperfect human detractors. "I have taken away their license to sin, and they keep on sinning," said Noyes. "So, though they have taken away my license to preach, I shall keep on preaching." This he did, with some success. His first convert was Miss Abigail Merwin of Orange, Connecticut, with whom he felt himself sealed in the faith.

Nevertheless his way was far from smooth. He had yet to pass through what he called "the dark valley of conviction." He went to New York and wandered the streets in a kind of frenzy, catching a little sleep by lying down in a doorway, or on the steps of City Hall, or on a bench at the Battery. He sought the most ill-famed regions of the city. "I descended into cellars where abandoned men and women were gathered, and talked familiarly with them about their ways of life, beseeching them to believe on Christ, they might be saved from their sins. They listened to me without abuse." Tempted by the Evil One, he doubted all, even the Bible, even Christ, even Abigail Merwin, whom he suspected to be Satan in angelic disguise. But after drinking the dregs

of the cup of trembling he emerged purified and secure. He retreated to Putney for peace and shelter. His friends, even his sister, thought him deranged. But such was the power of his spirit that he gathered a little group of adepts, relatives, and friends to accept his revelation.

Miss Abigail Merwin, however, took fright, married a schoolteacher, and removed to Ithaca, New York. Noyes followed her there—a rather ungentlemanly procedure. After a few months she left her husband, but not for Noyes's arms—only to return to her father in Connecticut.

Noyes was delighted with the pretty village of Ithaca, with his lodging in the Clinton House, and especially with the broad-minded printers, unafraid of publishing heresies and liberal with credit. On August 20, 1837, he established a periodical, the *Witness*, for a subscription rate of one dollar; or, if a dollar should be inconvenient, for nothing. The issue of September 23 reverberated far beyond the subscription list of faithful perfectionists. Noyes had written a private letter expressing his radical views on marriage among the perfect. By a violation of confidence, this had reached the free-thinking editor of a paper called the *Battle-Axe*. Noyes, disdaining evasion, acknowledged in the *Witness* his authorship of the letter and reiterated his startling conclusions. The essential of "the *Battle-Axe* letter" lies in the concluding words: "When the will of God is done on earth as it is in heaven, *there will be no marriage.* The marriage supper of the Lamb is a feast at which *every dish is free to every guest.* Exclusiveness, jealousy, quarreling, have no place there, for the same reason as that which forbids the guests at a thanksgiving dinner to claim each his separate dish, and quarrel with the rest for his rights. In a holy community, there is no more reason why sexual intercourse should be restrained by law, than why eating and drinking should be—and there is as little occasion for shame in the one as in the other. . . . The guests of the marriage supper may each have his favorite dish, each a dish of his own procuring, and that without the jealousy of exclusiveness."

Ungallant as this statement is in its characterization of women as dishes to pass, it states a reasonable protest against the egotisms of marriage. One may readily perceive in it also a secret resentment against the unfaithful Abigail Merwin. One may even interpret it as the erotic outburst of repressed impulse. Noyes, an impassioned, amorous type, was still a virgin.

Noyes was soon vouchsafed a sign, almost a miracle. When he was eighty dollars in debt to an Ithaca printer, he received from a disciple in Vermont, Miss Harriet A. Holton of Westminster, a letter enclosing a gift of exactly eighty dollars. He paid his bill, returned to Putney, and after a decent interval, forgetting the perfectionist views of the *Battle-Axe* letter, proposed exclusive marriage to Miss Holton. The two were formally united in Chesterfield, New Hampshire, on June 28, 1838. For a honeymoon they drove to Albany to buy a second-hand printing press, with more of Harriet's money.

Thus began the Putney Community, which at first consisted only of Noyes and his wife, several of his brothers and sisters, and a small cluster of converts from the neighborhood. They lived in a group, sharing possessions and duties. Their chief occupations were spiritual exercises in pursuit of holiness and the printing of the *Witness* on their own press. Noyes had no great liking for sheer honest toil for its own sake; he wished to secure for all the freedom for spiritual development. The women prepared one hot meal a day—breakfast. Thereafter the hungry had to help themselves in the kitchen.

Noyes was restless in the monotonous peace of Putney. His wife inherited $9,000 in 1844; Noyes was provoked to fantastic visions. He wrote his wife: "In order to subdue the world to Christ we must carry religion into money-making." He proposed first a theological seminary for perfectionism, then agencies in Boston and New York to distribute their spiritual goods. "Then we must advance into foreign commerce, and as our means enlarge we must cover the ocean with our ships and the whole world with the knowledge of God. This is a great scheme, but not too great for God. . . . Within ten years we will plant the standard of Christ on the highest battlements of the world."

Though allured by such shimmering visions, he had to deal with present problems. An urgent personal problem was that of sex. His wife was pregnant five times in six years. She endured long agonies ending in four stillbirths. The only surviving child was Theodore, born in 1841. John Noyes suffered with his wife, and he protested against cruel nature, perhaps against God. Surely women were not made to suffer so. Surely there was a better way. A perfectionist could not brook flagrant imperfection. Noyes's habit was to seek and find a better way, and then sanctify it. The better way turned out to be male continence.

Noyes had been trained in the Puritan ethic, which did not regard marital sex as unholy. Nevertheless the consequences of male egotism horrified him. "It is as foolish and cruel to expend one's seed on a wife merely for the sake of getting rid of it," he wrote, "as it would be to fire a gun at one's best friend merely for the sake of unloading it." After his wife's disasters he lived for a time chaste by her side. But chastity proving to be no solution at all, he embraced male continence, of which the definition embarrasses the chaste pen. When embarrassed, the chaste pen may decently quote. One of the community disciples, H. J. Seymour, thus defined the practice: "checking the flow of amative passion before it reaches the point of exposing the man to the loss of virile energy, or the woman to the danger of undesired child-bearing." Or, with Latin decorum, *coitus reservatus;* or, more colloquially, everything but.

This was not actually the beginning of birth-control advocacy. In 1832 a Boston physician, Charles Knowlton, published *The Fruits of Philosophy; or the Private Companion of Young Married People,* pointing to the menace of excessive child-bearing and eventual overpopulation, and recommending contraception. Dr. Knowlton and his publisher were accused of blasphemy. Their case was carried to the Supreme Court, and they were condemned to several months in jail. Robert Dale Owen, the reformer of New Harmony, Indiana, supported by Miss Frances Wright, "the Priestess of Beelzebub," carried on the work. In his *Moral Physiology* (1836), Owen recommended *coitus interruptus,* which Noyes scored as substituting self-indulgence for self-control.

"Amativeness is to life as sunshine is to vegetation," wrote Noyes twelve years later in his *Bible Argument Defining the Relation of the Sexes in the Kingdom of Heaven.* "Ordinary sexual intercouse (in which the amative and propagative functions are confounded) is a momentary affair, terminating in exhaustion and disgust. . . . Adam and Eve . . . sunk the spiritual in the sensual in their intercourse with each other, by pushing prematurely beyond the amative to the propagative, and so became ashamed." In the future society, "as propagation will become a science, so amative intercourse will become one of the 'fine arts.' Indeed it will rank above music, painting, sculpture, &c.; for it combines the charms and the benefits of them all."

All this is very noble and high-minded; but we are trained to look for—and we usually find—a casuistical serpent in the gardens, who is able to transform impulse into ideals, even into new theologies. The serpent in this case was Mary Cragin, who with her husband, George, had joined the Putney Community. Mary was a charmer, and, to put it baldly, sexy. (Do not condemn her; some are, some aren't. This is a well-known fact.) Noyes feared that she might "become a Magdalene" if he did not save her. One evening in the woods, Noyes and Mary discovered that they were united by a deep spiritual bond. "We took some liberty of embracing, and Mrs. George distinctly gave me to understand that she was ready for the full consummation." But Noyes insisted on a committee meeting with the respective spouses. "We gave each other full liberty, and so entered into marriage in quartette form. The last part of the interview was as amiable and happy as a wedding, and a full consummation . . . followed."

This was Noye's first infidelity, according to the world's idiom. He found a more grandilo-

quent term for it—complex marriage, to contrast with the restrictiveness of simple marriage. Heaven beamed on the participants. "Our love is of God; it is destitute of exclusiveness, each one rejoicing in the happiness of the others," said Mary. The Putney Community, in general, applauded; some, under direction, adopted the new cure for marital selfishness. It appears that some puritan wives, as well as husbands, were secretly weary of the "scanty and monotonous fare" provided by monogamy.

But righteous Putney soon had hints of the goingson and uprose in anger. On October 26, 1847, Noyes was arrested, charged with adultery, and released, pending trial, in $2,000 bail. Noyes declared himself guiltless, insisting that in common law no tort has been committed if no one is injured. "The head and front and whole of our offense is communism of love. . . . If this is the unpardonable sin in the world, we are sure it is the beauty and glory of heaven." But in fear of mob violence from "the barbarians of Putney" he thought it well to jump bail, following the counsel of the highest authority: "When they persecute you in this city, flee ye into another."

A refuge awaited the persecuted saints in the burned-over district of central New York, a region familiar to Noyes. A group of perfectionists offered the Putneyans a sawmill and forty acres of woodland on Oneida Creek, halfway between Syracuse and Utica. It was a bland, fertile, welcoming country, suitable for an Eden. By good omen, the spot was the exact geographical center of New York, if one overlooked Long Island.

In mid-February of 1848, "the year of the great change," the pilgrims began to arrive. Defying the upstate winter, lodging in abandoned cabins, they set to with a will to build a community dwelling and workshops. Some of the neighbors looked at them askance; most welcomed these honest, pious, industrious newcomers, and some even were converted to perfectionism and threw in their lot with the colony.

Members of the Oneida community standing outside the Mansion House. This community home, with its towers, mansard roofs, and tall French windows, carried a message of security, peace, and material comfort.

The early years were the heroic age of Oneida. All worked together, cutting and sawing timber, digging clay for bricks, building simple houses, clearing land for vegetable gardens. Everyone took his or her turn at the household tasks. All work was held in equal honor, without prestige connotations. Noyes recognized that most American experiments in communal life had foundered because they were established on the narrow base of agriculture; his communism would live on industry. Thus Oneida marketed canned fruits and vegetables, sewing silk, straw hats, mop sticks, travelling bags, and finally, silver tableware. Its traps for animals, from rodents to bears, became famous as far as Alaska and Siberia. The cruelty of traps seldom occurred to the makers, who were frontiersmen as well as perfectionists. Sympathy with suffering beasts and the conservation of wildlife were concepts still undeveloped. To a critic, Noyes replied that since God had covered the earth with vermin, Oneida simply helped to cleanse it. Salesmen, known only as peddlers, were sent out to market the wares. On their return, they were given a Turkish bath and a sharp examination on faith and practice a spiritual rubdown to expunge the stains of the unregenerate world.

The Oneida Community prospered. The numbers of the faithful rose. The great Mansion House, the community home, was begun in 1860 and completed a dozen years later. It is a far-wandering red-brick building or group of buildings, standing on a knoll amid magnificent fat trees. Harmoniously proportioned, with its towers, mansard roofs, and tall French windows, it is a superb example of mid-nineteenth-century architecture. Its message is security, peace, and material comfort. The interior is graced with fine woodwork and decorations. The parlors, the excellent library, the lovely assembly hall, are redolent with memories, jealously preserved and proudly recounted. Here live a number of descendants of the original Oneidans, together with some lodgers, still regarded with kindly pity as "foreign bodies."

The memories, second-hand though they are, are all of a happy time, of a golden age long lost. John Humphrey Noyes, affectionately referred to by his grandchildren as "the Honorable John," was a cheerful person, and imposed happiness on his great family. The story is told of a visitor who asked her guide: "What is the fragrance I smell here in this house?" The guide answered: "It may be the odor of crushed selfishness." There was no money within the Oneida economy, no private possession, no competition for food and shelter, and hence little rivalry.

All worked and played together. Whenever possible, work was done on the "bee" system; thus a party of men and women would make handbags on the lawn, while a dramatic voice read a novel aloud. Classes were conducted in such recondite subjects as Greek and Hebrew. Dances and respectable card games, like euchre and whist, were in favor. Amateur theatricals were a constant diversion. The productions of *The Merchant of Venice, The Merry Wives of Windsor*, and especially of *H.M.S. Pinafore*, were famous as far as Utica and Syracuse. Music was encouraged, with an orchestra and much vocalization. Music, Noyes mused, was closely related to sexual love; it was an echo of the passions. However, music contained a menace; it gave rise to rivalries, jealousies, and vanities, to what Noyes reproved as "prima donna fever."

Noyes had strong views on dress. He called the contrast of men's and women's costumes immodest, in that it proclaimed the distinction of sex. "In a state of nature, the difference between a man and a woman could hardly be distinguished at a distance of five hundred yards, but as men and women dress, their sex is telegraphed as far as they can be seen. Woman's dress is

a standing lie. It proclaims that she is not a two-legged animal, but something like a churn, standing on castors. . . . Gowns operate as shackles, and they are put on that sex which has most talent in the legs."

From the beginning at Oneida, a new dress for women was devised, loose skirts to the knee with pantalets below, thus approximating a gentleman's frock coat and trousers. Some visitors were shocked, some were amused; few were allured. Indeed the specimens remaining in the community's collections and the representations in photographs hardly seem beautiful. But the wearers rejoiced in their new freedom of movement. They cut their hair, in despite of Saint Paul. It was asserted they looked and felt younger.

For thirty years the community, a placid island amid the stormy seas of society, lived its insulated life. It numbered, at its peak, three hundred members. It was undisturbed, except by invasions of visitors brought on bargain excursions by the railroads. As many as a thousand appeared on a single day, picnicking on the grounds, invading the workshops and private quarters. They were welcomed; but on their departure all the Oneidans turned to in order to collect the scatterings, to scrub out the tobacco stains on the parquet floors.

The structure, the doctrine, the persistence of Oneida made a unique social phenomenon. It was consciously a family, with Noyes as father. As Constance Noyes Robertson says, it substituted "for the small unit of home and family and individual possessions the larger unit of group-family and group-family life." Its faith was "Bible Communism." Though it held aloof from all churches and deconsecrated the Sabbath, it was pietistic in demanding the regeneration of society by rejecting competition, a money economy, and private ownership, whether of goods or persons. But it was not Marxian, for it made no mention of class warfare, of a revolution to come, of proletarian dictatorship.

The internal organization of the community

was loose and vague, depending largely on the will of Noyes. Justice and discipline were administered informally, if at all. To provide correction, Noyes trusted chiefly to a procedure known as mutual criticism. Saint Paul had said: "Speak every man truth with his neighbor; for we are members one of another"; and the Apostle James: "Confess your faults one to another." When an individual offered himself for criticism, or was designated from above, a committee prepared his "trial," but any member might join in the proceedings. The trial was a game, though a serious one. The subject was informed of his secret faults, of shortcomings he had not suspected. He learned that his very virtues, on which he had flattered himself, were only disguised vices. The critics would pounce on an unpopular fellow-member with glee, seizing the opportunity to reveal to him some home truths, at the same time revealing their hidden rancors. A transcript of the proceedings was posted and often printed. The subject of this primitive psychoanalysis was likely to suffer dreadfully from his new self-knowledge. "I was shaken from center to circumference," said one. "I was metaphorically stood upon my head and allowed to drain until all the self-righteousness had dripped out of me." Afterward the subject felt enlightened, purified, happy. "Mutual criticism," said Noyes, "subordinates the I-spirit to the We-spirit." It also made the subjects, mostly brooding introspectives, for a time the center of interest and concern for the whole community. Mutual criticism, under the name of "krinopathy," was even used as a therapeutic device to cure children's colds, with, it was said, remarkable success.

Of the various Oneida institutions, the most fascinating to the prurient observer is the organization of sex behavior. Since the community was a single great family, there could be within it no marrying and giving in marriage. Each was married to all, Noyes insisted; every man was husband and brother to every woman. Love, far from being a sin, was holy, a sacrament; in the

sexual experience one escaped from egotism and selfhood into the ecstasy of communion. Every effort must be to "abound"—one of Noyes's favorite words. One must spend, not hoard. The human heart seldom realizes its possibilities; it "is capable of loving any number of times and any number of persons; the more it loves the more it can love." One had only to look at surrounding society to recognize the evils of exclusive marriage, the chains binding unmatched natures, the secret adulteries, actual or of the heart, the hate-filled divorces, women's diseases, prostitution, masturbation, licentiousness in general.

Noyes maintained that sexual love was not naturally restricted to pairs, that second marriages were often the happiest. "Men and women find universally (however the fact may be concealed) that their susceptibility to love is not burned out by one honeymoon, or satisfied by one lover." The body should assert its rights; religion should make use of the senses as helpers of devotion. Sexual shame, the consequence of the fall of man, was factitious and irrational. "Shame ought to be banished from the company of virtue, though in the world it has stolen the very name virtue. . . . Shame gives rise to the theory that sexual offices have no place in heaven. Anyone who has true modesty would sooner banish singing from heaven than sexual music." Beware, said Noyes, of one who proclaims that he is free from sexual desire, beware of religious teachers with fondling hands. Beware especially of Dr. Josiah Gridley of Southampton, Massachusetts, who boasts that he could carry a virgin in each hand without the least stir of passion. In short, "you must not serve the lusts of the flesh; if you do you will be damned. You must not make monks of yourself; if you do you will be damned."

One might suspect that these doctrines would have led to outright antinomianism and to general orgies. Nothing of the sort occurred, thanks to the watchful care of Noyes and thanks to the character of the Oneidans, devout and rather humorless seekers for perfection. The system of complex marriage, or pantagamy, begun in Putney, was instituted. A man might request the privilege of a private visit with a lady, or a lady might take the initiative, for "in all nature the female element invites and the male responds." The request was submitted to a committee of elders, headed by Noyes, who gave the final approval or disapproval. The mate besought had the right of refusal. It was recommended that older women initiate young men, and vice versa. Thus the young men were expertly guided in the practice of male continence, while the maturer men undertook without complaint the education of the maidens. The committee was also concerned to break up "exclusive and idolatrous attachments" of two persons of the same age, for these bred selfishness. We are assured that complex marriage worked admirably, and that for many life became a continuous courtship. "Amativeness, the lion of the tribe of human passions, is conquered and civilized among us." But the records are unwontedly reticent on the details of the system's operation. Only one scandal is remembered, when an unworthy recruit tried to force his attentions on the women, and was expelled through a window into a snowdrift. One suspects that in spite of all the spiritual training, there were heartaches and hidden anger, and much whispering and giggling at the sound of midnight footsteps on the stairs.

The flaw in the system of continence was the threatening sterilization of the movement—the fate of the Shakers. Noyes recognized the danger, and in his *Bible Argument* of 1848 had proposed scientific propagation to replace random or involuntary propagation. But the time was not yet ripe. In the difficult early years of Oneida, Noyes discouraged childbearing, and his docile followers produced only forty-four offspring in twenty years. Then increasing prosperity permitted him to take steps for the perpetuation of his community. Early in 1869, he proposed the inauguration of stirpiculture, or the scientific improvement of the human stock by breeding.

"Every race-horse, every straight-backed bull, every premium pig tells us what we can do and what we must do for men." Oneida should be a laboratory for the preparation of the great race of the future.

The Oneidans, especially the younger ones, greeted the proposal with enthusiasm. Fifty-three young women signed these resolutions:

1. *That we do not belong to ourselves in any respect, but that we do belong to God, and second to Mr. Noyes as God's true representative.*

2. *That we have no rights or personal feelings in regard to childbearing which shall in the least degree oppose or embarrass him in his choice of scientific combinations.*

3. *That we will put aside all envy, childishness and selfseeking, and rejoice with those who are chosen candidates; that we will, if necessary, become martyrs to science, and cheerfully resign all desire to become mothers, if for any reason Mr. Noyes deem us unfit material for propagation. Above all, we offer ourselves "living sacrifices" to God and true Communism.*

At the same time thirty-eight young men made a corresponding declaration to Noyes:

The undersigned desire you may feel that we most heartily sympathize with your purpose in regard to scientific propagation, an offer ourselves to be used in forming any combinations that may seem to you desirable. We claim no rights. We ask no privileges. We desire to be servants of the truth. With a prayer that the grace of God will help us in this resolution, we are your true soldiers.

Thus began the first organized experiment in human eugenics. For several years Noyes directed all the matings, on the basis of physical, spiritual, moral, and intellectual suitability. In 1875 a committee of six men and six women was formed to issue licenses to propagate. The selective process bore some bitter fruit. The eliminated males particularly were unhappy, unconsoled by the reflection that in animal breeding one superior stud may serve many females. Noyes relented in his scientific purpose so far as to permit one child to each male applicant. There was also some covert grumbling that Noyes, then in his sixties, elected himself to father nine children, by several mates. Eugenically, to be sure, he was entirely justified; there could be no doubt of his superiority.

The results of the stirpicultural experiment have not been scientifically studied, though an article by Hilda Herrick Noyes, prepared in 1921, offered some valuable statistical information. About one hundred men and women took part; eighty-one became parents, producing fifty-eight living children and four stillborn. No mothers were lost during the experiment; no defective children were produced. The health of the offspring was exceptionally good; their longevity has far surpassed the average expectations of life. The children, and the children's children, constitute a very superior group, handsome, and intelligent. Many have brilliantly conducted the affairs of their great manufacturing corporation; others have distinguished themselves in public service, the arts, and literature.

The integration of the children into the community caused some difficulties. The mother kept her child until he was weaned and could walk; then he was transferred to the Children's House, though he might return to his mother for night care. Noyes, with his ideal of the community family, disapproved of egotistic, divisive "special love"; the mothers were permitted to see their children only once or twice a week. The children were excellently educated in the nursery school, the kindergarten, and the grammar school, by teachers chosen for their competence and natural liking for the young. If the children cried for their mothers, they were severely reproved for "partiality" or "stickiness." One graduate of the Children's House remembered that when he was forbidden to visit his mother

he went berserk. Another recalled her agony when she caught sight of her mother after a fortnight's enforced separation. The child begged her mother not to leave her—and the mother fled for fear of a penalty of an additional week's separation from her child.

The atmosphere of the Children's House was, in short, that of a friendly orphanage. If the disruption of the family units had any bad psychic effects on the children, they have not been recorded. Children accept their world as it is; they know no other. The memories of the Oneida boys and girls are mostly of happy schooldays under kind teachers, days of laughter, play and delightful learning. The judgment of one eminent product, Pierrepont B. Noyes, is surely correct, that the community system was harder on the mothers than on the children.

The fathers were more remote from their children than were the mothers. Pierrepont Noyes admitted: "Father never seemed a father to me in the ordinary sense." The system reflected indeed the character of John Humphrey Noyes. He was the Father of his people, the semidivine begetter of a community, and he loved the community communally. He saw no reason to encourage family bonds, "partiality," among the faithful, at cost to the community spirit. He seems to have shown little personal affection for his sons after the flesh. No doubt a phrenologist would have noted that his bump of parental love was small. One is tempted to go further, to see in his disregard for his children a certain horror of paternity, a deep-implanted remembrance of his four stillborn babies, of his wife's sufferings and his own.

The rumors of strange sex practices roused the righteous and the orthodox, already angered by Oneida's nonobservance of the Sabbath and rejection of church affiliations. A professor at Hamilton College, John W. Mears, still the bogeyman of Oneida after a hundred years, began in 1873 a long campaign to destroy the community and its band of sinners. Though most of the inhabitants and newspaper editors of the region defended Noyes and his followers, though local justice could find no grounds for prosecution, the churches demanded action against "the ethics of the barnyard," and sought enabling legislation from the state. The menace mounted until, in June, 1879, Noyes fled to Canada, as, thirty-one years before, he had fled from Vermont. From a new home in Niagara Falls, Ontario, he continued to advise and inspire his old companions until his death, on April 13, 1886.

With the Father's departure the community system collapsed. In August, 1879, complex marriage was abandoned. Most of the Oneidans paired off and married, to legitimize their children. There were distressing cases of mothers whose mates were already taken, of the children of Noyes himself, left high and dry. In the reorganization into conventional families, it was necessary to establish rights of private property. As Noyes had foreseen, the demons of greed, self-seeking, jealousy, anger, and uncharitableness invaded the serene halls of the Mansion House.

The Oneida industries were converted into a joint-stock company, the shares distributed to the members of the community. After a period of drifting and fumbling, the widely varied enterprises came under the inspired management of Pierrepont Noyes and became models of welfare capitalism, or the partnership of owners and workers. To the present day, high wages are paid, profits are shared, schools, country clubs, aids for home-building, are provided. Oneida is the leading producer of stainless-steel flatware, the second largest producer of silver-plated ware in the United States. It has over three thousand employees in the Oneida plants, and many more in the factories in Canada, Mexico, and the United Kingdom. Its net sales in 1967 amounted to fifty-four million dollars, with net profits of two and a half million.

This outcome is not the least surprising feature of the Oneida story. Nearly all other communistic experiments in this country have long since disappeared, leaving nothing more than a tumble-down barracks or a roadside marker. Oneida found a transformation into the capitalist world. It did so at the cost of losing its religious and social doctrines; but it has never lost the idealism, the humanitarianism and the communitarian love of John Humphrey Noyes.

■ ■ ■

STUDY QUESTIONS

1. Some psychohistorians have argued that the early life of John Humphrey Noyes explains better than anything else the eccentric radicalism of his social philosophy. What is the basis for that argument? Do you agree? Why or why not?

2. Most Americans found Noyes's ideas to be outrageous at best and satanic at worst. Why? Is there any realistic hope that Noyes could have succeeded had he lived in our era? Why or why not?

3. Although Noyes set out to change America, his vision and community were eventually transformed by the environment. What went wrong with the Oneida experiment? What significance do you see in the change in Oneida from a socialist commune to a modern corporation?

BIBLIOGRAPHY

The classic study of reform movements during the Jacksonian period is Alice Felt Tyler's *Freedom's Ferment* (1944). Also see Ronald G. Walter, *American Reformers, 1815–1860* (1978) and William G. McLoughlin, *Revivals, Awakenings, and Reform* (1978). Arthur Bestor's *Backwoods Utopias: The Sectarian and Owenite Phases of Communitarian Socialism in America, 1663–1829* (1950) remains an excellent survey. For sexual radicalism in early America, see Raymond Muncy, *Sex and Marriage in Utopian Communities* (1950). The best studies of John Humphrey Noyes and Oneida are M. L. Carden, *Oneida: Utopian Community to Modern Corporation* (1971) and R. D. Thomas, *The Man Who Would Be Perfect: John Humphrey Noyes and the Utopian Impulse* (1977).

GOUGE AND BITE, PULL HAIR AND SCRATCH

Elliott J. Gorn

The tidewater aristocracy of Virginia enjoyed horse racing, "the sport of kings." If no kings could be found among the gentry, there was no lack of royal pretensions. Gentlemen raced their horses against other gentlemen, and at stake was more than just money or glory. Riding on the outcome was a gentlemen's sense of self-worth. Robert "King" Carter, the most successful planter of his time, believed that if he lost a race, he lost face in the eyes of his peers. As T. H. Breen demonstrated in an earlier selection, gambling and horse racing provide the keys for unlocking the planters' attitudes toward themselves and life in general.

In the following essay, historian Elliott Gorn examines the brutal pasttimes of the working class men of the South and West. In particular, he focuses on gouging matches, where the object was to pry your opponent's eye out of its socket using your own thumb as the fulcrum. Like Breen, Gorn uses this activity as a means for understanding the world of working class men in the southern and western back-country. He uncovers a world where violence was common, where "Indians, wild animals, lawless criminals, and natural forces threatened life." It was also a world where work was physically hard and dangerous, and where men spent more time in the company of other men than with women. In this environment, Gorn notes, "a man's role in the all-male society was defined less by his ability as a bread-winner than by his strength, skill and ferociousness. Violent sports, heavy drinking, impulsive pleasure-seeking made sense for men whose lives were hard, futures unpredictable, and opportunities limited."

"I would advise you when You do fight Not to act like Tygers and Bears as these Virginians do—Biting one anothers Lips and Noses off, and *gowging* one another—that is, thrusting out one anothers Eyes, and kicking one another on the Cods, to the Great damage of many a Poor Woman." Thus, Charles Woodmason, an itinerant Anglican minister born of English gentry stock, described the brutal form of combat he found in the Virginia backcountry shortly before the American Revolution. Although historians are more likely to study people thinking, governing, worshiping, or working, how men fight—who participates, who observes, which rules are followed, what is at stake, what tactics are allowed—reveals much about past cultures and societies.

The evolution of southern backwoods brawling from the late eighteenth century through the antebellum era can be reconstructed from oral traditions and travelers' accounts. As in most cultural history, broad patterns and uneven trends rather than specific dates mark the way. The sources are often problematic and must be used with care; some speculation is required. But the lives of common people cannot be ignored merely because they leave few records. "To feel for a feller's eyestrings and make him tell the news" was not just mayhem but an act freighted with significance for both social and cultural history.

As early as 1735, boxing was "much in fashion" in parts of Chesapeake Bay, and forty years later a visitor from the North declared that, along with dancing, fiddling, small swords, and card playing, it was an essential skill for all young Virginia gentlemen. The term "boxing," however, did not necessarily refer to the comparatively tame style of bare-knuckle fighting familiar to eighteenth-century Englishmen. In 1746, four

deaths prompted the governor of North Carolina to ask for legislation against "the barbarous and inhuman manner of boxing which so much prevails among the lower sort of people." The colonial assembly responded by making it a felony "to cut out the Tongue or pull out the eyes of the King's Liege People." Five years later the assembly added slitting, biting, and cutting off noses to the list of offenses. Virginia passed similar legislation in 1748 and revised these statutes in 1772 explicitly to discourage men from "gouging, plucking, or putting out an eye, biting or kicking or stomping upon" quiet peaceable citizens. By 1786 South Carolina had made premeditated mayhem a capital offense, defining the crime as severing another's bodily parts.

Laws notwithstanding, the carnage continued. Philip Vickers Fithian, a New Jerseyite serving as tutor for an aristocratic Virginia family, confided to his journal on September 3, 1774:

By appointment is to be fought this Day near Mr. Lanes two fist Battles between four young Fellows. The Cause of the battles I have not yet known; I suppose either that they are lovers, and one has in Jest or reality some way supplanted the other; or has in a merry hour called him a Lubber *or a* thick-Skull, *or a* Buckskin, *or a* Scotsman, *or perhaps one has mislaid the other's hat, or knocked a peach out of his Hand, or offered him a dram without wiping the mouth of the Bottle; all these, and ten thousand more quite as trifling and ridiculous are thought and accepted as just Causes of immediate Quarrels, in which every diabolical Strategem for Mastery is allowed and practiced.*

The "trifling and ridiculous" reasons for these fights had an unreal quality for the matter-of-fact Yankee. Not assaults on persons or property but slights, insults, and thoughtless gestures set young southerners against each other. To call a man a "buckskin," for example, was to accuse him of the poverty associated with leather clothing, while the epithet "Scotsman" tied him to the low-caste Scots-Irish who settled the southern highlands. Fithian could not understand how such trivial offenses caused the bloody bat-

"Gouge and Bite, Pull Hair and Scratch: Fighting in the Southern Back Country" by Elliott J. Gorn in *American Historical Review*, Vol. 90, No. 1, pp. 18–43, February 1985. Reprinted by permission of the author.

tles. But his incomprehension turned to rage when he realized that spectators attended these "odious and filthy amusements" and that the fighters allayed their spontaneous passions in order to fix convenient dates and places, which allowed time for rumors to spread and crowds to gather. The Yankee concluded that only devils, prostitutes, or monkeys could sire creatures so unfit for human society.

Descriptions of these "fist battles," as Fithian called them, indicate that they generally began like English prize fights. Two men, surrounded by onlookers, parried blows until one was knocked or thrown down. But there the similarity ceased. Whereas "Broughton's Rules" of the English ring specified that a round ended when either antagonist fell, southern bruisers only began fighting at this point. Enclosed not inside a formal ring—the "magic circle" defining a special place with its own norms of conduct—but within whatever space the spectators left vacant, fighters battled each other until one called enough or was unable to continue. Combatants boasted, howled, and cursed. As words gave way to action, they tripped and threw, gouged and butted, scratched and choked each other. "But what is worse than all," Isaac Weld observed, "these wretches in their combat endeavor to their utmost to tear out each other's testicles."

Around the beginning of the nineteenth century, men sought original labels for their brutal style of fighting. "Rough-and-tumble" or simply "gouging" gradually replaced "boxing" as the name for these contests. Before two bruisers attacked each other, spectators might demand whether they proposed to fight fair—according to Broughton's Rules—or rough-and-tumble. Honor dictated that all techniques be permitted. Except for a ban on weapons, most men chose to fight "no holts barred," doing what they wished to each other without interference, until one gave up or was incapacitated.

The emphasis on maximum disfigurement, on severing bodily parts, made this fighting style unique. Amid the general mayhem, however, gouging out an opponent's eye became the sine qua non of rough-and-tumble fighting, much like the knockout punch in modern boxing. The best gougers, of course, were adept at other fighting skills. Some allegedly filed their teeth to bite off an enemy's appendages more efficiently. Still, liberating an eyeball quickly became a fighter's surest route to victory and his most prestigious accomplishment. To this end, celebrated heroes fired their fingernails hard, honed them sharp, and oiled them slick. " 'You have come off badly this time, I doubt?' " declared an alarmed passerby on seeing the piteous condition of a renowned fighter. " 'Have I,' says he triumphantly, shewing from his pocket at the same time an eye, which he had extracted during the combat, and preserved for a trophy."

As the new style of fighting evolved, its geographical distribution changed. Leadership quickly passed from the southern seaboard to upcountry counties and the western frontier. Although examples could be found throughout the South, rough-and-tumbling was best suited to the backwoods, where hunting, herding, and semisubsistence agriculture predominated over market-oriented, staple crop production. Thus, the settlers of western Carolina, Kentucky, and Tennessee, as well as upland Mississippi, Alabama, and Georgia, became especially known for their pugnacity.

The social base of rough-and-tumbling also shifted with the passage of time. Although brawling was always considered a vice of the "lower sort," eighteenth-century Tidewater gentlemen sometimes found themselves in brutal fights. These combats grew out of challenges to men's honor—to their status in patriarchal, kin-based, small-scale communities—and were woven into the very fabric of daily life. Rhys Isaac has observed that the Virginia gentry set the tone for a fiercely competitive style of living. Although they valued hierarchy, individual status was never permanently fixed, so men frantically sought to assert their prowess—by grand boasts over tavern gaming tables laden with money, by whipping and tripping each other's horses in violent quarter-races, by wagering one-half year's earnings on the flash of a fighting cock's gaff. Great planters and small shared an ethos that extolled courage bordering on fool-hardiness and cherished magnificent, if irratio-nal, displays of largess.

Piety, hard work, and steady habits had their adherents, but in this society aggressive self-assertion and manly pride were the real marks of status. Even the gentry's vaunted hospitality demonstrated a family's community standing, so conviviality itself became a vehicle for rivalry and emulation. Rich and poor might revel together during "public times," but gentry patronage of sports and festivities kept the focus of power clear. Above all, brutal recreations toughened men for a violent social life in which the exploitation of labor, the specter of poverty, and a fierce struggle for status were daily reali-ties.

During the final decades of the eighteenth century, however, individuals like Fithian's young gentlemen became less inclined to engage in rough-and-tumbling. Many in the planter class now wanted to distinguish themselves from social inferiors more by genteel manners, gra-cious living, and paternal prestige than by patri-archal prowess. They sought alternatives to brawling and found them by imitating the English aristocracy. A few gentlemen took box-ing lessons from professors of pugilism or attend-ed sparring exhibitions given by touring expo-nents of the manly art. More important, dueling gradually replaced hand-to-hand combat. The code of honor offered a genteel, though deadly, way to settle personal disputes while demon-strating one's elevated status. Ceremony distin-guished antiseptic duels from lower-class brawls. Cool restraint and customary decorum proved a man's ability to shed blood while remaining emotionally detached, to act as mercilessly as the poor whites but to do so with chilling gentili-ty.

Slowly, then, rough-and-tumble fighting found specific locus in both human and geo-graphical landscapes. We can watch men grap-ple with the transition. When an attempt at a formal duel aborted, Savannah politician Robert Watkins and United States Senator James Jack-son resorted to gouging. Jackson bit Watson's finger to save his eye. Similarly, when "a low fellow who pretends to gentility" insulted a dis-tinguished doctor, the gentleman responded with a proper challenge. "He had scarcely uttered these words, before the other flew at him, and in an instant turned his eye out of the socket, and while it hung upon his cheek, the fellow was barbarous enough to endeavor to pluck it entirely out." By the new century, such ambiguity had lessened, as rough-and-tumble fighting was relegated to individuals in back-woods settlements. For the next several decades, eye-gouging matches were focal events in the culture of lower-class males who still relished the wild ways of old.

"I saw more than one man who wanted an eye, and ascertained that I was now in the region of 'gouging.'" reported young Timothy Flint, a Harvard educated, Presbyterian minister bound for Louisiana missionary work in 1816. His spirits buckled as his party turned down the Mis-sissippi from the Ohio Valley. Enterprising farm-ers gave way to slothful and vulgar folk whom Flint considered barely civilized. Only vicious fighting and disgusting accounts of battles past disturbed their inertia. Residents assured him that the "blackguards" excluded gentlemen from gouging matches. Flint was therefore per-plexed when told that a barbarous-looking man was the "best" in one settlement, until he learned that best in this context meant not the most moral, prosperous, or pious but the local champion who had whipped all the rest, the man most dexterous at extracting eyes.

Because rough-and-tumble fighting declined in settled areas, some of the most valuable accounts were written by visitors who penetrat-ed the backcountry. Travel literature was quite popular during America's infancy, and many profit-minded authors undoubtedly wrote with their audience's expectations in mind. Images of heroic frontiersmen, of crude but unencumbered natural men, enthralled both writers and readers. Some who toured the new republic in the decades following the Revolution had strong prejudices against America's democratic pretensions. English travelers in particular doubted that the upstart nation—in which the lower class shouted its equality and the upper class was unable or unwilling to exercise proper authority—could survive. Ironically, backcountry fighting became a symbol for both those who inflated and those who punctured America's expansive national ego.

Frontier braggarts enjoyed fulfilling visitors' expectations of backwoods depravity, pumping listeners full of gruesome legends. Their narratives projected a satisfying, if grotesque, image of the American rustic as a fearless, barbaric, larger-than-life democrat. But they also gave Englishmen the satisfaction of seeing their former countrymen run wild in the wilderness. Gouging matches offered a perfect metaphor for the Hobbesian war of all against all, of men tearing each other apart once institutional restraints evaporated, of a heart of darkness beating in the New World. As they made their way from the northern port towns to the southern countryside, or down the Ohio to southwestern waterways, observers concluded that geographical and moral descent went hand in hand. Brutal fights dramatically confirmed their belief that evil lurked in the deep shadows of America's sunny democratic landscape.

And yet, it would be a mistake to dismiss all travelers' accounts of backwoods fighting as fictions born of prejudice. Many sojourners who were sober and careful observers of America left detailed reports of rough-and-tumbles. Aware of the tradition of frontier boasting, they distinguished apocryphal stories from personal observation, wild tales from eye-witness accounts. Although gouging matches became a sort of literary convention, many travelers compiled credible descriptions of backwoods violence.

"The indolence and dissipation of the middling and lower classes of Virginia are such as to give pain to every reflecting mind," one anonymous visitor declared. "Horse-racing, cock-

fighting, and boxing-matches are standing amusements, for which they neglect all business; and in the latter of which they conduct themselves with a barbarity worthy of their savage neighbors." Thomas Anburey agreed. He believed that the Revolution's leveling of class distinctions left the "lower people" dangerously independent. Although Anburey found poor whites usually hospitable and generous, he was disturbed by their sudden outbursts of impudence, their aversion to labor and love of drink, their vengefulness and savagery. They shared with their betters a taste for gaming, horse racing, and cockfighting, but "boxing matches, in which they display such barbarity, as fully marks their innate ferocious disposition," were all their own. Anburey concluded that an English prize fight was humanity itself compared to Virginia combat.

Another visitor, Charles William Janson, decried the loss of social subordination, which caused the rabble to reinterpret liberty and equality as licentiousness. Paternal authority—the font of social and political order—had broken down in America, as parents gratified their children's whims, including youthful tastes for alcohol and tobacco. A national mistrust of authority had brought civilization to its nadir among the poor whites of the South. "The lower classes are the most abject that, perhaps, ever peopled a Christian land. They live in the woods and deserts and many of them cultivate no more land than will raise them corn and cabbages, which, with fish, and occasionally a piece of pickled pork or bacon, are their constant food. . . . Their habitations are more wretched than can be conceived; the huts of the poor of Ireland, or even the meanest Indian wig-wam, displaying more ingenuity and greater industry." Despite their degradation—perhaps because of it—Janson found the poor whites extremely jealous of their republican rights and liberties. They considered themselves the equals of their best-educated neighbors and intruded on whomever they chose. The gouging match this fastidious Englishman witnessed in Georgia was the epitome of lower-class depravity:

We found the combatants . . . fast clinched by the hair, and their thumbs endeavoring to force a passage into each other's eyes; while several of the bystanders were betting upon the first eye to be turned out of its socket. For some time the combatants avoided the thumb stroke with dexterity. At length they fell to the ground, and in an instant the uppermost sprung up with his antagonist's eye in his hand!!! The savage crowd applauded, while, sick with horror, we galloped away from the infernal scene. The name of the sufferrer was John Butler, a Carolinian, who, it seems, had been dared to the combat by a Georgian; and the first eye was for the honor of the state to which they respectively belonged.

Janson concluded that even Indian "savages" and London's rabble would be outraged by the beastly Americans.

While Janson toured the lower South, his countryman Thomas Ashe explored the territory around Wheeling, Virginia. A passage, dated April 1806, from his *Travels in America* gives us a detailed picture of gouging's social context. Ashe expounded on Wheeling's potential to become a center of trade for the Ohio and upper Mississippi valleys, noting that geography made the town a natural rival of Pittsburgh. Yet Wheeling lagged in "worthy commercial pursuits, and industrious and moral dealings." Ashe attributed this backwardness to the town's frontier ways, which attracted men who specialized in drinking, plundering Indian property, racing horses, and watching cockfights. A Wheeling Quaker assured Ashe that mores were changing, that the underworld element was about to be driven out. Soon, the godly would gain control of the local government, enforce strict observance of the Sabbath, and outlaw vice. Ashe was sympathetic but doubtful. In Wheeling, only heightened violence and debauchery distinguished Sunday from the rest of the week. The citizens' willingness to close up shop and neglect business on the slightest pretext made it a questionable residence for any respectable group of men, let alone a society of Quakers.

To convey the rough texture of Wheeling life, Ashe described a gouging match. Two men drinking at a public house argued over the merits of their respective horses. Wagers made, they galloped off to the race course. "Two thirds of the population followed:—blacksmiths, shipwrights, all left work: the town appeared a desert. The stores were shut. I asked a proprietor, why the warehouses did not remain open? He told me all good was done for the day: that the people would remain on the ground till night, and many stay till the following morning." Determined to witness an event deemed so important that the entire town went on holiday, Ashe headed for the track. He missed the initial heat but arrived in time to watch the crowd raise the stakes to induce a rematch. Six horses competed, and spectators bet a small fortune, but the results were inconclusive, Umpires' opinions were given and rejected. Heated words, then fists flew. Soon, the melee narrowed to two individuals, a Virginian and a Kentuckian. Because fights were common in such situations, everyone knew the proper procedures, and the combatants quickly decided to "tear and rend" one another—to rough-and-tumble—rather than "fight fair." Ashe elaborated: "You startle at the words tear and rend, and again do not understand me. You have heard these terms, I allow, applied to beasts of prey and to carnivorous animals; and your humanity cannot conceive them applicable to man: It nevertheless is so, and the fact will not permit me the use of any less expressive term."

The battle began—size and power on the Kentuckian's side, science and craft on the Virginian's. They exchanged cautious throws and blows, when suddenly the Virginian lunged at his opponent with a panther's ferocity. The crowd roared its approval as the fight reached its violent denouement:

The shock received by the Kentuckyan, and the want of breath, brought him instantly to the ground. The Virginian never lost his hold; like those bats of the South who never quit the subject on which they fasten till they taste blood, he kept his knees in his enemy's body; fixing his claws in his hair, and his thumbs on his eyes, gave them an instantaneous start from their sockets. The sufferer roared aloud, but uttered no complaint. The citizens again shouted with joy. Doubts were no longer entertained and bets of three to one were offered on the Virginian.

But the fight continued. The Kentuckian grabbed his smaller opponent and held him in a tight bear hug, forcing the Virginian to relinquish his facial grip. Over and over the two rolled, until, getting the Virginian under him, the big man "snapt off his nose so close to his face that no manner of projection remained." The Virginian quickly recovered, seized the Kentuckian's lower lip in his teeth, and ripped it down over his enemy's chin. This was enough: "The Kentuckyan at length *gave out,* on which the people carried off the victor, and he preferring a triumph to a doctor, who came to cicatrize his face, suffered himself to be chaired round the ground as the champion of the times, and the first *rougher-and-tumbler.* The poor wretch, whose eyes were started from their spheres, and whose lip refused its office, returned to the town, to hide his impotence, and get his countenance repaired." The citizens refreshed themselves with whiskey and biscuits, then resumed their races.

Ashe's Quaker friend reported that such spontaneous races occurred two or three times a week and that the annual fall and spring meets lasted fourteen uninterrupted days, "aided by the licentious and profligate of all the neighboring states." As for rough-and-tumbles, the Quaker saw no hope of suppressing them. Few nights passed without such fights; few mornings failed to reveal a new citizen with mutilated features. It was a regional taste, unrestrained by law or authority, an inevitable part of file on the left bank of the Ohio.

By the early nineteenth century, rough-and-tumble fighting had generated its own folklore. Horror mingled with awe when residents of the Ohio Valley pointed out one-eyed individuals to visitors, when New Englanders referred to an empty eye socket as a "Virginia Brand," when North Carolinians related stories of mass rough-and-tumbles ending with eyeballs covering the ground, and when Kentuckians told of battle-royals so intense that severed eyes, ears, and noses filled bushel baskets. Place names like "Fighting Creek" and "Gouge Eye" perpetuated the memory of heroic encounters, and rustic bombast reached new extremes with estimates from some counties that every third man wanted an eye. As much as the style of combat, the rich oral folklore of the backcountry—the legends, tales, ritual boasts, and verbal duels, all of them in regional vernacular—made rough-and-tumble fighting unique.

It would be difficult to overemphasize the importance of the spoken word in southern life. Traditional tales, songs, and beliefs—transmitted orally by blacks as well as whites—formed the cornerstone of culture. Folklore socialized children, inculcated values, and helped forge a distinct regional sensibility. Even wealthy and well-educated planters, raised at the knees of black mammies, imbibed both Afro-American and white traditions, and charismatic politicans secured loyal followers by speaking the people's language. Southern society was based more on personalistic, face-to-face, kin-and-community relationships than on legalistic or bureaucratic ones. Interactions between southerners were guided by elaborate rituals of hospitality, demonstrative conviviality, and kinship ties—all of which emphasized personal dependencies and reliance on the spoken word. Through the antebellum period and beyond, the South had an oral as much as a written culture.

Boundaries between talk and action, ideas and behavior, are less clear in spoken than in written contexts. Psychologically, print seems more distant and abstract than speech, which is inextricably bound to specific individuals, times, and places. In becoming part of the realm of sight rather than sound, words leave behind their personal, living qualities, gaining in fixity what they

A REGULAR ROW IN THE BACKWOODS.

■ ■ *Men in the primitive southern backcountry used violence in sports, jokes, and talk as a means of release from life's hardships.*

lose in dynamism. Literate peoples separate thought from action, pigeon-holing ideas and behavior. Nonliterate ones draw this distinction less sharply, viewing words and the events to which they refer as a single reality. In oral cultures generally, and the Old South in particular, the spoken word was a powerful force in daily life, because ideation and behavior remained closely linked.

The oral traditions of hunters, drifters, herdsmen, gamblers, roustabouts, and rural poor who rough-and-tumbled provided a strong social cement. Tall talk around a campfire, in a tavern, in front of a crossroads store, or at countless other meeting places on the southwestern frontier helped establish communal bonds between disparate persons. Because backwoods humorists possessed an unusual ability to draw people together and give expression to shared feelings, they often became the most effective leaders and

preachers. But words could also divide. Fithian's observation in the eighteenth century—that seemingly innocuous remarks led to sickening violence—remained true for several generations. Men were so touchy about their personal reputations that any slight required an apology. This failing, only retribution restored public stature and self-esteem. "Saving face" was not just a metaphor.

The lore of backwoods combat, however, both inflated and deflated egos. By the early nineteenth century, simple epithets evolved into verbal duels—rituals well known to folklorists. Backcountry men took turns bragging about their prowess, possessions, and accomplishments, spurring each other on to new heights of selfmagnification. Such exchanges heightened tension and engendered a sense of theatricality and display. But boasting, unlike insults, did not always lead to combat, for, in a culture that valued oral skills, the verbal battle itself—the contest over who best controlled the power of words—was a real quest for domination:

"I am a man; I am a horse; I am a team. I can whip any man in all Kentucky, by G—d!" The other replied, "I am an alligator, half man, half horse; can whip any man on the Mississippi, by G—d!" The first one again, "I am a man; have the best horse, best dog, best gun and handsomest wife in all Kentucky, by G—d." The other, "I am a Mississippi snapping turtle: have bear's claws, alligator's teeth, and the devil's tail; can whip any man, by G—d."

Such elaborate boasts were not composed on the spot. Folklorists point out that free-phrase verbal forms, from Homeric epics to contemporary blues, are created through an oral formulaic process. The singer of epics, for example, does not memorize thousands of lines but knows the underlying skeleton of his narrative and, as he sings, fleshes it out with old commonplaces and new turns of phrase. In this way, oral formulaic composition merges cultural continuity with individual creativity. A similar but simplified version of the same process was at work in backwoods bragging.

A quarter-century after the above exchange made its way into print, several of the same phrases still circulated orally and were worked into new patterns. " 'By Gaud, stranger,' said he, 'do you know me?—do you know what stuff I'm made of? Clear steamboat, sea horse, alligator—run agin me, run agin a snag—jam up—whoop! Got the prettiest sister, and biggest whiskers of any man hereabouts—I can lick my weight in wild cats, or any man in all Kentuck!' " Style and details changed, but the themes remained the same: compairing oneself to wild animals, boasting of possessions and accomplishments, asserting domination over others. Mike Fink, legendary keelboatman, champion gouger, and fearless hunter, put his own mark on the old form and elevated it to art:

"I'm a salt River roarer! I'm a ring tailed squealer! I'm a regular screamer from the old Massassip! Whoop! I'm the very infant that refused his milk before its eyes were open and called out for a bottle of old Rye! I love the women and I'm chockful o'fight! I'm half wild horse and half cock-eyed alligator and the rest o' me is crooked snags an' red-hot snappin' turtle. . . . I can out-run, out-jump, out-shoot, out-brag, out-drink, an' out-fight, rough-an'-tumble, no holts barred, any man on both sides the river from Pittsburgh to New Orleans an' back ag'in to St. Louiee. Come on, you flatters, you barger, you milk white mechanics, an' see how tough I am to chaw! I ain't had a fight for two days an' I'm spilein' for exercise. Cock-a-doodle-doo!"

Tall talk and ritual boasts were not uniquely American. Folklore indexes are filled with international legends and tales of exaggeration. But inflated language did find a secure home in American in the first half of the nineteenth century. Spread-eagle rhetoric was tailor-made for a young nation seeking a secure identity. Bombastic speech helped justify the development of unfamiliar social institutions, flowery oratory salved painful economic changes, and lofty words masked aggressive territorial expansion. In a circular pattern of reinforcement, heroic talk spurred heroic deeds, so that great acts found heightened meaning in great words. Alexis de Tocqueville observed during his travels in the 1830s that clearing land, draining swamps, and planting crops were hardly the stuff of literature. But the collective vision of democratic multitudes building a great nation formed a grand poetic ideal than haunted men's imaginations.

The gaudy poetry of the strapping young nation had its equivalent in the exaggeration of individual powers. Folklore placing man at the center of the universe buttressed the emergent ideology of equality. Tocqueville underestimated Americans' ability to celebrate the mundane, for ego magnification was essential in a nation that extolled self-creation. While America prided itself on shattering old boundaries, on liberating individuals from social, geographic, and cultural encumbrances, such freedom left each citizen frighteningly alone to succeed or fail in forging his own identity. To hyperbolize one's achievements was a source of power and control, a means of amplifying the self while bringing human, natural, and social obstacles down to size. The folklore of exaggeration could transform even the most prosaic commercial dealings into great contests. Early in the nineteenth century, legends of crafty Yankee peddlers and unscrupulous livestock traders abounded. A horse dealer described an animal to buyer in the 1840s: " 'Sir, he can jump a house or go through a pantry, as it suits him; no hounds are too fast for him, no day too long for him. He has the courage of a lion, and the docility of a lamb, and you may ride him with a thread. Weight did you say? Why, he would carry the national debt and not bate a penny.' " The most insipid marketplace transactions were transfigured by inflated language, legends of heroic salesmanship, and an ethos of contest and battle.

The oral narratives of the southern backcountry drew stength from these national traditions yet possessed unique characteristics. Above all, fight legends portrayed backwoodsmen reveling in blood. Violence existed for its own sake, unencumbered by romantic conventions and claiming no redeeming social or psychic value. Gouging narratives may have masked grimness with black humor, but they offered little pretense that violence was a creative or civilizing force. Thus, one Kentuckian defeated a bear by chewing off its nose and scratching out its eyes. "They can't stand Kentucky play," the settler proclaimed, "biting and gouging are too hard for them." Humor quickly slipped toward horror, when Davy Crockett, for example, coolly boasted, "I kept my thumb in his eye, and was just going to give it a twist and bring the peeper out, like taking up a gooseberry in a spoon." To Crockett's eternal chagrin, someone interrupted the battle just at this crucial juncture.

Sadistic violence gave many frontier legends a surreal quality. Two Mississippi raftsmen engaged in ritual boasts and insults after one accidentally nudged the other toward the water, wetting his shoes. Cheered on by their respective gangs, they stripped off their shirts, then pummeled, knocked out teeth, and wore skin from each other's faces. The older combatant asked if his opponent had had enough. "Yes," he was told, "when I drink your heart's blood, I'll cry enough, and not till then." The younger man gouged out an eye. Just as quickly, his opponent was on top, strangling his adversary. But in a final reversal of fortunes, the would-be victor cried out, then rolled over dead, a stab wound in his side. Protected by his clique, the winner jumped in the water, swam to a river island, and crowed: "Ruoo-ruoo-o! I can lick a steamboat. My fingernails is related to a sawmill on my mother's side and my daddy was a double breasted catamount! I wear a hoop snake for a neck-handkerchief, and the brass buttons on my coat have all been boiled in poison."

The danger and violence of daily life in the backwoods contributed mightily to sanguinary oral traditions that exalted the strong and deprecated the weak. Early in the nineteenth century, the Southwest contained more than its share of terrifying wild animals, powerful and well-organized Indian tribes, and marauding white outlaws. Equally important were high infant mortality rates and short life expectancies, agricultural blights, class inequities, and the centuries-old belief that betrayal and cruelty were man's fate. Emmeline Grangerford's graveyard poetry—set against a backdrop of rural isolation shattered by sadistic clan feuds—is but the best-known expression of the deep loneliness, death longings, and melancholy that permeated backcountry life.

At first glance, boisterous tall talk and violent legends seem far removed from sadness and alienation. Yet, as Kenneth Lynn has argued, they grew from common origins, and the former allowed men to resist succumbing to the latter. Not passive acceptance but identification with brutes and brawlers characterized frontier legendry. Rather than be overwhelmed by violence, acquiesce in an oppressive environment, or submit to death as an escape from tragedy, why not make a virtue of necessity and flaunt one's unconcern? To revel in the lore of deformity, mutilation, and death was to beat the wilderness at its own game. The storyteller's art dramatized life and converted nameless anxieties into high adventure; bravado helped men face down a threatening world and transform terror into power. To claim that one was sired by wild animals, kin to natural disasters, and tougher than steam engines—which were displacing rivermen in the antebellum era—was to gain a momentary respite from fear, a cathartic, if temporary, sense of being in control. Symbolically, wild boasts overwhelmed the very forces that threatened the backwoodsmen.

But there is another level of meaning here. Sometimes fight legends invited an ambiguous response, mingling the celebration of beastly acts with the rejection of barbarism. By their very nature, tall tales elicit skepticism. Even while men identified with the violence that challenged them, the folklore of eye gouging constantly tested the limits of credibility. "Pretty soon I got the squatter down, and just then he fixed his teeth into throte, and I felt my windpipe begin to loosen." The calculated coolness and understatement of this description highlights the outrageousness of the act. The storyteller has artfully maneuvered his audience to the edge of credulity.

Backwoodsmen mocked their animality by exaggerating it, thereby affirming their own humanity. A Kentuckian battled inconclusively from ten in the morning until sundown, when his wife showed up to cheer him on:

"So I gathered all the little strength I had, and I socked my thumb in his eye, and with my fingers took a twist on his snot box, and with the other hand, I grabbed him by the back of the head; I then caught his ear in my mouth, gin his head a flirt, and out come his ear by the roots! I then flopped his head over, and caught his other ear in my mouth, and jerked that out in the same way, and it made a hole in his head that I could have

rammed my fist through, and I was just goin' to when he hollered: 'Nuff!' "

More than realism or fantasy alone, fight legends stretched the imagination by blending both. As metaphoric statements, they reconciled contradictory impulses, at once glorifying and parodying barbarity. In this sense, gouging narratives were commentaries on backwoods life. The legends were texts that allowed plain folk to dramatize the tensions and ambiguities of their lives: they hauled society's-goods yet lived on its fringe; they destroyed forests and game while clearing the land for settlement; they killed Indians to make way for the white man's culture; they struggled for self-sufficiency only to become ensnared in economic dependency. Fight narratives articulated the fundamental contradiction of frontier life—the abandonment of "civilized" ways that led to the ultimate expansion of civilized society.

Foreign travelers might exaggerate and backwoods storytellers embellish, but the most neglected fact about eye-gouging matches is their actuality. Circuit Court Judge Aedamus Burke barely contained his astonishment while presiding in South Carolina's upcountry: "Before God, gentlemen of the jury, I never saw such a thing before in the world. There is a plaintiff with an eye out! A juror with an eye out! And two witnesses with an eye out!" If the "ring-tailed roarers" did not actually breakfast on stewed Yankee, washed down with spike nails and epsom salts, court records from Sumner County, Arkansas, did describe assault victims with the words "nose was bit." The gamest "gamecock of the wilderness" never really moved steamboat engines by grinning at them, but Reuben Cheek did receive a three-year sentence to the Tennessee penitentiary for gouging out William Maxey's eye. Most backcountrymen went to the grave with their faces intact, just as most of the southern gentry never fought a duel. But as an extreme version of the common tendency toward brawling, street fighting, and seeking personal vengeance, rough-and-tumbling gives us insight into the deep values and assumptions—the *mentalité*—of backwoods life.

Observers often accused rough-and-tumblers of fighting like animals. But eye gouging was not instinctive behavior, the human equivalent of two rams vying for dominance. Animals fight to attain specific objectives, such as food, sexual priority, or territory. Precisely where to draw the line between human aggression as a genetically programmed response or as a product of social and cultural learning remains a hotly debated issue. Nevertheless, it would be difficult to make a case for eye gouging as a genetic imperative, coded behavior to maximize individual or species survival. Although rough-and-tumble fighting appears primitive and anarchic to modern eyes, there can be little doubt that its origins, rituals, techniques, and goals were emphatically conditioned by environment; gouging was learned behavior. Humanistic social science more than sociobiology holds the keys to understanding this phenomenon.

What can we conclude about the culture and society that nourished rough-and-tumble fighting? The best place to begin is with the material base of life and the nature of daily work. Gamblers, hunters, herders, roustabouts, rivermen, and yeomen farmers were the sorts of persons usually associated with gouging. Such hallmarks of modernity as large-scale production, complex division of labor, and regular work rhythms were alien to their lives. Recent studies have stressed the premodern character of the southern uplands through most of the antebellum period. Even while cotton production boomed and trade expanded, a relatively small number of planters owned the best lands and most slaves, so huge parts of the South remained outside the flow of international markets or staple crop agriculture. Thus, backcountry whites commonly found themselves locked into a semisubsistent pattern of living. Growing crops for home consumption, supplementing food supplies with abundant game, allowing small herds to fatten in the woods, spending scarce money for essential staples, and bartering goods for the services of part-time or itinerant trades people, the upland folk lived in an intensely local, kin-based society. Rural hamlets, impassable roads, and provincial isolation—not growing towns, internal improvements, or international commerce—characterized the backcountry.

Even men whose livelihoods depended on expanding markets often continued their rough, premodern ways. Characteristic of life on a Mississippi barge, for example, were long periods of idleness shattered by intense anxiety, as deadly snags, shoals, and storms approached. Running aground on a sandbar meant backbreaking labor to maneuver a thirty-ton vessel out of trouble. Boredom weighed as heavily as danger, so tale telling, singing, drinking, and gambling filled the empty hours. Once goods were taken on in New Orleans, the men began the thousand-mile return journey against the current. Before steam power replaced muscle, bad food and whiskey fueled the gangs who day after day, exposed to wind and water, poled the river bottoms or strained at the cordelling ropes until their vessel reached the tributaries of the Missouri or the Ohio. Hunters, trappers, herdsmen, subsistence farmers, and other backwoodsmen faced different but equally taxing hardships, and those who endured prided themselves on their strength and daring, their stamina, cunning, and ferocity.

Such men played as lustily as they worked, counterpointing bouts of intense labor with strenuous leisure. What travelers mistook for laziness was a refusal to work and save with compulsive regularity. "I have seen nothing in human form so profligate as they are," James Flint wrote of the boatmen he met around 1820. "Accomplished in depravity, their habits and education seem to comprehend every vice. They make few pretensions to moral character; and their swearing is excessive and perfectly disgusting. Although earning good wages, they are in the most abject poverty; many of them being without anything like clean or comfortable clothing." A generation later, Mark Twain vividly remembered those who manned the great timber and coal rafts gliding past his boyhood home in Hannibal, Missouri: "Rude, uneducated, brave, suffering terrific hardships with sailor-like stoicism; heavy drinkers, course frolickers in moral sties like the Natchez-under-the-hill of the day, heavy fighters, reckless fellows, every one, elephantinely jolly, foul witted, profane; prodigal of their money, bankrupt at the end of the trip, fond of barbaric finery, prodigious braggarts; yet, in the main, honest, trustworthy, faithful to promises and duty, and often picaresquely magnanimous." Details might change, but penury, loose morality, and lack of steady habits endured.

Boatmen, hunters, and herdsmen were often separated from wives and children for long periods. More important, backcountry couples lacked the emotionally intense experience of the bourgeois family. They spent much of their time apart and found companionship with members of their own sex. The frontier town or crossroads tavern brought males together in surrogate brotherhoods, where rough men paid little deference to the civilizing role of women and the moral uplift of the domestic family. On the margins of a booming, modernizing society, they shared an intensely communal yet fiercely competitive way of life. Thus, where work was least rationalized and specialized, domesticity weakest, legal institutions primitive, and the market economy feeble, rough-and-tumble fighting found fertile soil.

Just as the economy of the southern backcountry remained locally oriented, the rough-and-tumblers were local heroes, renowned in their communities. There was no professionalization here. Men fought for informal village and county titles; the red feather in the champion's cap was pay enough because it marked him as first among his peers. Paralleling the primitive division of labor in backwoods society, boundaries between entertainment and daily life, between spectators and participants, were not sharply drawn. "Bully of the Hill" Ab Gaines from the Big Hatchie Country, Neil Brown of Totty's Bend, Vernon's William Holt, and Smithfield's Jim Willis—all of them were renowned Tennessee fighters, local heroes in their day. Legendary champions were real individuals, tested gang leaders who attained their status by being the meanest, toughest, and most ruthless fighters, who faced disfigurement and never backed down. Challenges were ever present; yesterday's spectator was today's champion, today's champion tomorrow's invalid.

Given the lives these men led, a world view that embraced fearlessness made sense. Hunters, trappers, Indian fighters, and herdsmen who knew the smell of warm blood on their hands refused to sentimentalize an environment filled with threatening forces. It was not that backwoodsmen lived in constant danger but that violence was unpredictable. Recreations like cockfighting deadened men to cruelty, and the gratuitous savagery of gouging matches reinforced the daily truth that life was brutal, guided only by the logic of superior nerve, power, and cunning. With families emotionally or physically distant and civil institutions weak, a man's role in the all-male society was defined less by ability as a breadwinner than by his ferocity. The touchstone of masculinity was unflinching toughness, not chivalry, duty, or piety. Violent sports, heavy drinking, and impulsive pleasure seeking were appropriate for men whose lives were hard, whose futures were unpredictable, and whose opportunities were limited. Gouging champions were group leaders because they embodied the basic values of their peers. The successful rough-and-tumbler proved his manhood by asserting his dominance and rendering his opponent "impotent," as Thomas Ashe put it. And the loser, though literally or symbolically castrated, demonstrated his mettle and maintained his honor.

Here we begin to understand the travelers' refrain about plain folk degradation. Setting out from northern ports, whose inhabitants were increasingly possessed by visions of godly perfection and material progress, they found southern upcountry people slothful and backward. Ashe's Quaker friend in Wheeling, Virginia, made the point. For Quakers and northern evangelicals, labor was a means of moral self-testing, and earthly success was a sign of God's grace, so hard work and steady habits became acts of piety. But not only Yankees endorsed sober restraint. A growing number of southern evangelicals also

embraced a life of decorous self-control, rejecting the hedonistic and self-assertive values of
old. During the late eighteenth century, as Rhys
Isaac has observed, many plain folk disavowed
the hegemonic gentry culture of conspicuous
display and found individual worth, group pride,
and transcendent meaning in religious revivals.
By the antebellum era, new evangelical waves
washed over class lines as rich and poor alike
forswore such sins as drinking, gambling, cursing, fornication, horse racing, and dancing. But
conversion was far from universal, and, for
many in backcountry settlements like Wheeling,
the evangelical idiom remained a foreign
tongue. Men worked hard to feed themselves
and their kin, to acquire goods and status, but
they lacked the calling to prove their godliness
through rigid morality. Salvation and self-denial
were culturally less compelling values, and the
barriers against leisure and self-gratification
were lower here than among the converted.

Moreover, primitive markets and the semisubsistence basis of upcountry life limited men's
dependence on goods produced by others and
allowed them to maintain the irregular work
rhythms of a precapitalist economy. The material
base of backwoods life was ill suited to social
transformation, and the cultural traditions of the
past offered alternatives to rigid new ideals.
Closing up shop in mid-week for a fight or horse
race had always been perfectly acceptable,
because men labored so that they might indulge
the joys of the flesh. Neither a compulsive need
to save time and money nor an obsession with
progress haunted people's imaginations. The
backcountry folk who lacked a bourgeois or
Protestant sense of duty were little disturbed by
exhibitions of human passions and were resigned to violence as part of daily life. Thus, the
relative dearth of capitalistic values (such as
delayed gratification and accumulation), the
absence of a strict work ethic, and a cultural tradition that winked at lapses in moral rigor limited society's demands for sober self-control.

Not just unconverted poor whites but also
large numbers of the slave-holding gentry still
lent their prestige to a regional style that favored
conspicuous displays of leisure. As C. Vann
Woodward has pointed out, early observers,
such as Robert Beverley and William Byrd, as
well as modern-day commentators, have described a distinctly "southern ethic" in American
history. Whether judged positively as leisure or
negatively as laziness, the southern sensibility
valued free time and rejected work as the consuming goal of life. Slavery reinforced this tendency, for how could labor be an unmitigated
virtue if so much of it was performed by despised
black bondsmen? When southerners did esteem
commerce and enterprise, it was less because piling up wealth contained religious or moral value
than because productivity facilitated the leisure
ethos. Southerners could therefore work hard
without placing labor at the center of their ethical universe. In important ways, then, the
upland folk culture reflected a larger regional
style.

Thus, the values, ideas, and institutions that
rapidly transformed the North into a modern
capitalist society came late to the South. Indeed,
conspicuous display, heavy drinking, moral
casualness, and love of games and sports had
deep roots in much of Western culture. As
Woodward has cautioned, we must take care not
to interpret the southern ethic as unique or aber-
rant. The compulsions to subordinate leisure to
productivity, to divide work and play into separate compartmentalized realms, and to improve
each bright and shining hour were the novel
ideas. The southern ethic anticipated human
evil, tolerated ethical lapses, and accepted the
finitude of man in contrast to the new style that
demanded unprecedented moral rectitude and
internalized self-restraint.

The American South also shared with large
parts of the Old World a taste for violence and
personal vengeance. Long after the settling of the
southern colonies, powerful patriarchal clans in
Celtic and Mediterranean lands still avenged
affronts to family honor with deadly feuds. Norbert Elias has pointed out that postmedieval
Europeans routinely spilled blood to settle private quarrels. Across classes, the story was the
same:

Two associates fall out over business; they quarrel, the conflict grows violent; one day they meet in a public place and one of them strikes the other dead. An innkeeper accuses another of stealing his clients; they become mortal enemies. Someone says a few malicious words about another; a family war develops. . . . Not only among the nobility were there family vengeance, private feuds, vendettas. . . . The little people too—the hatters, the tailors, the shepherds—were all quick to draw their knives.

Emotions were freely expressed: jollity and laughter suddenly gave way to belligerence; guilt and penitence coexisted with hate; cruelty always lurked nearby. The modern middle-class individual, with his subdued, rational, calculating ways, finds it hard to understand the joy sixteenth-century Frenchmen took in ceremonially burning alive one or two dozen cats every Midsummer Day or the pleasure eighteenth-century Englishmen found in watching trained dogs slaughter each other.

Despite enormous cultural differences, inhabitants of the southern uplands exhibited characteristics of their forebears in the Old World. The Scots-Irish brought their reputation for ferocity to the backcountry, but English migrants, too, had a thirst for violence. Central authority was weak, and men reserved the right to settle differences for themselves. Vengeance was part of daily life. Drunken hilarity, good fellowship, and high spirits, especially at crossroads taverns, suddenly turned to violence. Traveler after traveler remarked on how forthright and friendly but quick to anger the backcountry people were. Like European ancestors, they had not yet internalized the modern world's demand for tight emotional self-control.

Above all, the ancient concept of honor helps explain this shared proclivity for violence. According to the sociologist Peter Berger, modern men have difficulty taking seriously the idea of honor. American jurisprudence, for example, offers legal recourse for slander and libel because they involve material damages. But insult—publicly smearing a man's good name and besmirching his honor—implies no palpable injury and so does not exist in the eyes of the law. Honor is an intensely social concept, resting on reputation, community standing, and the esteem of kin and compatriots. To possess honor requires acknowledgment from others; it cannot exist in solitary conscience. Modern man, Berger has argued, is more responsive to dignity—the belief that personal worth inheres equally in each individual, regardless of his status in society. Dignity frees the evangelical to confront God alone, the capitalist to make contracts without customary encumbrances, and the reformer to uplift the lowly. Naked and alone man has dignity; extolled by peers and covered with ribbons, he has honor.

Anthropologists have also discovered the centrality of honor in several cultures. According to J. G. Peristiany, honor and shame often preoccupy individuals in small-scale settings, where face-to-face relationships predominate over anonymous or bureaucratic ones. Social standing in such communities is never completely secure, because it must be validated by public opinion whose fickleness compels men constantly to assert and prove their worth. Julian Pitt-Rivers has added that, if society rejects a man's evaluation of himself and treats his claim to honor with ridicule or contempt, his very identity suffers because it is based on the judgment of peers. Shaming refers to that process by which an insult or any public humiliation impugns an individual's honor and thereby threatens his sense of self. By risking injury in a violent encounter, an affronted man—whether victorious or not—restores his sense of status and thus validates anew his claim to honor. Only valorous action, not words, can redeem his place in the ranks of his peer group.

Bertram Wyatt-Brown has argued that his Old World ideal is the key to understanding southern history. Across boundaries of time, geography, and social class, the South was knit together by a primal concept of male valor, part of the ancient heritage of Indo-European folk cultures. Honor demanded clan loyalty, hospitality, protection of women, and defense of patriarchal prerogatives. Honorable men guarded their reputations, bristled at insults, and, where necessary, sought personal vindication through bloodshed. The culture of honor thrived in hierarchical rural communities like the American South and grew out of a fatalistic world view, which assumed that pain and suffering were man's fate. It accounts for the pervasive violence that marked relationships between southerners and explains their insistence on vengeance and their rejection of legal redress in settling quarrels. Honor tied personal identity to public fulfillment of social roles. Neither bourgeois self-control nor internalized conscience determined status; judgment by one's fellows was the wellspring of community standing.

In this light, the seemingly trivial causes for brawls enumerated as early as Fithian's time— name calling, subtle ridicule, breaches of decorum, displays of poor manners—make sense. If a man's good name was his most important possession, than any slight cut him deeply. "Having words" precipitated fights because words brough shame and undermined a man's sense of self. Symbolic acts, such as buying a round of drinks, conferred honor on all, while refusing to share a bottle implied some inequality in social status. Honor inhered not only in individuals but also in kin and peers; when members of two cliques had words, their tested leaders or several men from each side fought to uphold group prestige. Inheritors of primal honor, the southern plain folk were quick to take offense, and any perceived affront forced a man either to devalue himself or to strike back violently and avenge the wrong.

The concept of male honor takes us a long way toward understanding the meaning of eye-gouging matches. But backwoods people did not simply acquire some primordial notion without modifying it. Definitions of honorable behavior have always varied enormously across cultures. The southern upcountry fostered a particular style of honor, which grew out of the contradiction between equality and hierarchy. Honorific societies tend to be sharply stratified. Honor is apportioned according to rank, and men fight to maintain personal standing within their social categories. Because black chattel slavery was the basis for the southern hierarchy, slave owners had the most wealth and honor, while other whites scrambled for a bit of each, and bondsmen were permanently impoverished and dishonored. Here was a source of tension for the plain folk. Men of honor shared freedom and equality; those denied honor were implicitly less than equal—perilously close to a slave-like condition. But in the eyes of the gentry, poor whites as well as blacks were outside the circle of honor, so both groups were subordinate. Thus, a herdsman's insult failed to shame a planter since the two men were not on the same social level. Without a threat to the gentleman's honor, there was no need for a duel; horsewhipping the insolent fellow sufficed.

Southern plain folk, then, were caught in a social contradiction. Society taught all white men to consider themselves equals, encouraged them to compete for power and status, yet threatened them from below with the specter of servitude and from above with insistence on obedience to rank and authority. Cut off from upper-class tests of honor, backcountry people adopted their own. A rough-and-tumble was more than a poor man's duel, a botched version of genteel combat. Plain folk chose not to ape the dispassionate, antiseptic, gentry style but to invert it. While the gentleman's code of honor insisted on cool restraint, eye gougers gloried in unvarnished brutality. In contrast to duelists' aloof silence, backwoods fighters screamed defiance to the world. As their own unique rites of honor, rough-and-tumble matches allowed backcountry men to shout their equality at each other. And eye-gouging fights also dispelled any stigma of servility. Ritual boasts, soaring oaths, outrageous ferocity, unflinching bloodiness—all proved a man's freedom. Where the slave acted obsequiously, the backwoodsman resisted the slightest affront; where human chattels accepted blows and never raised a hand, plain folk celebrated violence; where blacks could not jeopardize their value as property, poor whites proved their autonomy by risking bodily parts. Symbolically reaffirming their claims to honor, gouging matches helped resolve painful uncertainties arising out of the ambiguous place of plain folk in the southern social structure.

Backwoods fighting reminds us of man's capacity for cruelty and is an excellent corrective to romanticizing premodern life. But a close look also keeps us from drawing facile conclusions about innate human aggressiveness. Eye gouging represented neither the "real" human animal emerging on the frontier, nor nature acting through man in a Darwinian struggle for survival, nor anarchic disorder and communal breakdown. Rather, rough-and-tumble fighting was ritualized behavior—a product of specific cultural assumptions. Men drink together, tongues loosen, a simmering old rivalry begins to boil; insult is given, offense take, ritual boasts commence; the fight begins, mettle is tested, blood redeems honor, and equilibrium is restored. Eye gouging was the poor and middling whites' own version of a historical southern tendency to consider personal violence socially useful—indeed, ethically essential.

Rough-and-tumble fighting emerged from the confluence of economic conditions, social relationships, and culture in the southern backcountry. Primitive markets and the semisubsistence basis of life threw men back on close ties to kin and community. Violence and poverty were part of daily existence, so endurance, even callousness, became functional values. Loyal to their localities, their occupations, and each other, men came together and found release from life's hardships in strong drink, tall talk, rude practical jokes, and cruel sports. They craved one another's recognition but rejected genteel, pious, or bourgeois values, awarding esteem on the basis of their own traditional standards. The glue that held men together was an intensely competitive status system in which the most prodigious drinker or strongest arm wrestler, the best tale teller, fiddle player, or log roller, the most daring gambler, original liar, skilled hunter, outrageous swearer, or accurate marksman was accorded respect by the others. Reputation was every-

thing, and scars were badges of honor. Rough-and-tumble fighting demonstrated unflinching willingness to inflict pain while risking mutilation—all to defend one's standing among peers—became a central expression of the all-male subculture.

Eye gouging continued long after the antebellum period. As the market economy absorbed new parts of the backcountry, however, the way of life that supported rough-and-tumbling waned. Certainly by mid-century the number of incidents declined, precisely when expanding international demand brought ever more up-country acres into staple production. Towns, schools, churches, revivals, and families gradually overtook the backwoods. In a slow and uneven process, keelboats gave way to steamers, then railroads; squatters, to cash crop farmers; hunters and trappers, to preachers. The plain folk code of honor was far from dead, but emergent social institutions engendered a moral ethos that warred against the old ways. For many individuals, the justifications for personal violence grew stricter, and mayhem became unacceptable.

Ironically, progress also had a darker side. New technologies and modes of production could enhance men's fighting abilities. "Birmingham and Pittsburgh are obliged to complete . . . the equipment of the "chivalric Kentuckian,' " Charles Agustus Murray observed in the 1840s, as bowie knives ended more and more rough-and-tumbles. Equally important, in 1835 the first modern revolver appeared, and manufacturers marketed cheap, accurate editions in the coming decade. Dueling weapons had been costly, and Kentucky rifles or horse pistols took a full minute to load and prime. The revolver, however, which fitted neatly into a man's pocket, settled more and more personal disputes. Raw and brutal as rough-and-tumbling was, it could not survive the use of arms. Yet precisely because eye gouging was so violent—because combatants cherished maimings, blindings, even castrations—it unleashed death wishes that invited new technologies of destruction.

With improved weaponry, dueling entered its golden age during the antebellum era. Armed combat remained both an expression of gentry sensibility and a mark of social rank. But in a society where status was always shifting and unclear, dueling did not stay confined to the upper class. The habitual carrying of weapons, once considered a sign of unmanly fear, now lost some of its stigma. As the backcountry changed, tests of honor continued, but gunplay rather than fighting tooth-and-nail appealed to new men with social aspirations. Thus, progress and technology slowly circumscribed rough-and-tumble fighting, only to substitute a deadlier option. Violence grew neater and more lethal as men checked their savagery to murder each other.

■■■

STUDY QUESTIONS

1. In which areas of the United States did gouging matches take place? Which class of men were most likely to be involved in such matches?

2. Why did the men fight? What distinguished between fighting "for real" and fighting "for fun"?

3. How did foreign travellers regard the fighting?

4. What does the language of the men in the backcountry tell us about their culture and attitude toward life?

5. How do the gouging matches reflect backcountry life? How did the backcountry environment affect the settlers of the region?

6. Which "manly" characteristics were most valued by the backcountry settlers?

7. Why did gouging matches eventually cease to be common?

BIBLIOGRAPHY

The work of modern social theorists is evident in Gorn's essay. Clifford Gretz, *The Interpretation of Culture* (1973); Norbert Elias, *The Civilizing Process* (1978); Richard G. Sipes, "War, Sports and Aggression: An Empirical Test of Two Rival Theories," *American Anthropoligist,* New Series, 75 (1973); and Peter Berger, et al., *The Homeless Man* (1973), present valuable insights. The nature of southern and western violence and society is discussed in Bertram Wyatt-Brown, *Southern Honor: Ethics and Behavior in the Old South* (1982); Arthur K. Moore, *The Frontier Mind* (1957); Sheldon Hackney, "Southern Violence," *American Historical Review,* 74 (1969); Richard Slotkin, *Regeneration Through Violence* (1973); James I. Robertson, Jr., "Frolics, Fights and Firewater in Frontier Tennessee," *Tennessee Historical Quarterly,* 17 (1958); and James Leyburn, *The Scotch-Irish: A Social History* (1962).

Part Six

AMERICANS
DIVIDED

In the aftermath of General Andrew Jackson's victory over the British in New Orleans in 1815, Americans temporarily sounded a harmonious note. Nationalism was the order of the day. Americans sang a new national anthem and joined together in national enterprises. They built roads and dug canals to tie the country together; they protected fledgling northern industries with a tariff; they hailed the end of political strife; and they boldly issued sweeping foreign policy measures. Americans proudly watched as government agents pushed the flag of the Republic north, south, and west.

Nationalism, however, was short-lived. As early as the Panic of 1819, observers of the national scene noticed fundamental divisions within America. A year later, during the Missouri controversy, those lines of division became clearer. In 1820 Thomas Jefferson denounced the Missouri Compromise restriction. It awoke him, he said, like "a fire-bell in the night" and sounded "the knell of the Union." If sectional tranquility was restored after the controversy, it lacked the optimism and giddiness of the earlier period.

Increasingly northerners and southerners found less common ground to stand upon and more issues that divided them. In the winter of 1832–33 a pall hung over the aristocratic festivities of Charleston, South Carolina. Led by the brilliant John C. Calhoun, South Carolina had nullified the tariffs of 1828 and 1832 and had forbidden the collection of customs duties within the state. The Union and the effectiveness of the Constitution swayed in balance. Again, the crisis passed. Politicians struck a compromise. But national unity was further weakened.

During the 1840s Americans looked westward toward vast expanses of land. Some saw opportunity and moved toward it. Others, like the Mormons, saw a chance to escape persecution, and they too packed up their belongings and headed West. Indians and Mexicans, who occupied much of the land, came face to face with a movement of people who were unconcerned with their plight. "Make way, I say, for the young American Buffalo," cried one Democratic orator, "—he has not yet got land enough."

In the spring of 1846, the United States declared war on Mexico. It was a war that unified many Americans—but only for a brief time. The war brought new lands, and the new lands revived old questions. What would be the status of the new lands? Would the new territories and states, once formed, be free or slave? Who would decide the answers to these questions, and how would they decide them?

During the 1850s politicians struggled over these questions. Ultimately they lost the struggle. One solution after another failed. The South, which had contributed greatly to the victory in the Mexican War, demanded the right to share in the fruits of the victory. They demanded the right to move into the newly annexed regions with their "peculiar institution" intact. Northerners were just as determined that the lands would be settled by free labor. By the mid-1850s the subject dominated the national political arena. The issue destroyed one political party, split another, and created yet another. Political rhetoric became increasingly more strident and vitriolic. In 1861 the politicians passed the issue on to the generals.

NOTES ON
MORMON POLYGAMY

Stanley S. Ivins

Upstate New York in the 1820s was a "burned-over district" according to one historian because of all the "hell-fire and damnation" preaching going on by competing Protestant denominations. Religion was a topic dear to most people's hearts as they contemplated the salvation or damnation of souls. Near Palmyra, New York, a confused young man, troubled by religious contention within his own family, decided to ask God for direct and complete answers to all of his questions about religion. After offering such a prayer, fifteen-year-old Joseph Smith, Jr., claimed to have been visited by two angelic beings. Identifying themselves as God the Father and Jesus Christ, they told him to join none of the churches and to wait for further instruction. Three years later Smith said he had been visited by an angel who had left him responsible for translating a historical record, engraved on golden plates, of the ancient inhabitants of the American continent. That translation was published in 1829 as the Book of Mormon, and the Church of Jesus Christ of Latter-day Saints was organized in 1830.

Under the charismatic leadership of Joseph Smith, the young church grew rapidly in the 1830s and 1840s, and encountered persecution in direct proportion to its success. Their internal cohesiveness and tendency to vote as a bloc usually embittered their neighbors and the practice of polygamy, introduced by Joseph Smith in the late 1830s, absolutely enraged American society. Driven from Ohio and Missouri, they settled in southern Illinois in 1839. Joseph Smith was assassinated in 1844. Brigham Young assumed leadership of the Mormons, and in 1846–47 he led them on an extraordinary journey across the continent to the valley of the Great Salt Lake in present-day Utah. Free of persecution, the Mormons thrived there, accepting tens of thousands of converts and colonizing new regions in southern Utah, Nevada, southern California, Idaho, Arizona, and Wyoming.

But for the next half-century, the practice of polygamy created a national uproar as well as a crusade against the Mormons involving an invasion of Utah by the United States Army in 1857, federal anti-polygamy laws, and mass jailings of Mormon leaders. In the process, a series of myths about the Mormon practice of polygamy became firmly entrenched in the public mind. In "Notes on Mormon Polygamy," Stanley Ivins describes polygamous marriages in Utah during the nineteenth century.

Time was when, in the popular mind, Mormonism meant only polygamy. It was assumed that every Mormon man was a practical or theoretical polygamist. This was a misconception, like the widespread belief that Mormons grew horns, for there were always many of these Latter-day Saints who refused to go along with the doctrine of "plurality of wives." It was accepted by only a few of the more than fifty churches or factions which grew out of the revelations of the prophet Joseph Smith. Principal advocate of the doctrine was the Utah church, which far outnumbered all other branches of Mormonism. And strongest opposition from within Mormondom came from the second largest group, the Reorganized Church of Jesus Christ of Latter-day Saints, with headquarters at Independence, Missouri.

This strange experiment in family relations extended over a period of approximately sixty-five years. It was professedly inaugurated on April 5, 1841, in a cornfield outside the city of Nauvoo, Illinois, with the sealing of Louisa Beeman to Joseph Smith. And it was brought to an official end by a resolution adopted at the seventy-fourth Annual Conference of the Utah church, on April 4, 1904. Since that time, those who have persisted in carrying on with it have been excommunicated. But the project was openly and energetically prosecuted during only about forty years. For the first ten years the new doctrine was kept pretty well under wraps, and it was not until the fall of 1852 that it was openly avowed and the Saints were told that only those who embraced it could hope for the highest exaltation in the resurrection. And during the fifteen years prior to 1904, there were only a few privately solemnized plural marriages. So it might be said that the experiment was ten years in embryo, enjoyed a vigorous life of forty years, and took fifteen years to die.

"Notes on Mormon Polygamy" by Stanley S. Ivins in *Western Humanities Review*, X, Summer 1956, pp. 229–239. Reprinted by permission of Western Humanities Review.

The extent to which polygamy was practiced in Utah will probably never be known. Plural marriages were not publicly recorded, and there is little chance that any private records which might have been kept will ever be revealed.

Curious visitors to Utah in the days when polygamy was flourishing were usually told that about one-tenth of the people actually practiced it. Since the abandonment of the principle this estimate has been revised downward. A recent official published statement by the Mormon church said: "The practice of plural marriage has never been general in the Church and at no time have more than 3 percent of families in the Church been polygamous." This estimate was apparently based upon testimony given during the investigation into the right of Reed Smoot to retain his seat in the United States Senate. A high church official, testifying there, referred to the 1882 report of the Utah Commission, which said that application of the antipolygamy laws had disfranchised approximately 12,000 persons in Utah. The witness declared that, since at least two-thirds of these must have been women, there remained no more than 4,000 polygamists, which he believed constituted less than 2 percent of the church population. The error of setting heads of families against total church membership is obvious. Using the same report, Senator Dubois concluded that 23 percent of Utah Mormons over eighteen years of age were involved in polygamy. Later on in the Smoot hearing the same church official testified that a careful census, taken in 1890, revealed that there were 2,451 plural families in the United States. This suggests that, at that time, 10 percent or more of the Utah Mormons might have been involved in polygamy.

Of more than 6,000 Mormon families, sketches of which are found in a huge volume published in 1913, between 15 and 20 percent appear to have been polygamous. And a history of Sanpete and Emery counties contains biographical sketches of 722 men, of whom 12.6 percent married more than one woman.

From information obtainable from all available sources, it appears that there may have been a time when 15, or possibly 20, percent of the Mormon families of Utah were polygamous. This leaves the great majority of the Saints delinquent in their obligation to the principle of plurality of wives.

While the small proportion of Mormons who went into polygamy may not necessarily be a true measure of its popularity, there is other evidence that they were not anxious to rush into it, although they were constantly reminded of its importance to their salvation.

A tabulation, by years, of about 2,500 polygamous marriages, covering the whole period of this experiment, reveals some interesting facts. It indicates that, until the death of prophet Joseph Smith in the summer of 1844, the privilege of taking extra wives was pretty well monopolized by him and a few of his trusted disciples. Following his death and the assumption of leadership by the Twelve Apostles under Brigham Young, there was a noticeable increase in plural marriages. This may be accounted for by the fact that, during the winter of 1845–1846, the Nauvoo Temple was finished to a point where it could be used for the performance of sacred rites and ordinances. For a few weeks before their departure in search of a refuge in the Rocky Mountains, the Saints worked feverishly at their sealings and endowments. As part of this religious activity, the rate of polygamous marrying rose to a point it was not again to reach for ten years. It then fell off sharply and remained low until the stimulation given by the public announcement, in the fall of 1852, that polygamy was an essential tenet of the church. This spurt was followed by a sharp decline over the next few years.

Beginning in the fall of 1856 and during a good part of the following year, the Utah Mormons were engaged in the greatest religious revival of their history. To the fiery and sometimes intemperate exhortations of their leaders, they responded with fanatical enthusiasm, which at times led to acts of violence against

those who were slow to repent. There was a general confession of sins and renewal of covenants through baptism, people hastened to return articles "borrowed" from their neighbors, and men who had not before given a thought to the matter began looking for new wives. And, as one of the fruits of the Reformation, plural marriages skyrocketed to a height not before approached and never again to be reached. If our tabulation is a true index, there were 65 percent more of such marriages during 1856 and 1857 than in any other two years of this experiment.

With the waning of the spirit of reformation, the rate of polygamous marrying dropped in 1858 to less than a third and in 1859 to less than a fifth of what it was in 1857. This decline continued until 1862, when Congress, responding to the clamor of alarmists, enacted a law prohibiting bigamy in Utah and other territories. The answer of the Mormons to this rebuke was a revival of plural marrying to a point not previously reached except during the gala years of the Reformation.

The next noticeable acceleration in the marriage rate came in 1868 and 1869 and coincided with the inauguration of a boycott against the Gentile merchants and the organization of an anti-Mormon political party. But this increased activity was short-lived and was followed by a slump lasting for a dozen years. By 1881 polygamous marrying had fallen to almost its lowest ebb since the public avowal of the doctrine of plurality.

With the passage of the Edmunds Act of 1882, which greatly strengthened the antipolygamy laws, the government began its first serious effort to suppress the practice of polygamy. The Mormons responded with their last major revival of polygamous activity, which reached its height in 1884 and 1885. But, with hundreds of polygamists imprisoned and most of the church leaders driven into exile to avoid arrest, resistance weakened and there was a sudden decline in marriages, which culminated in formal capitulation in the fall of 1890. This was the end, except for a

■ ■ *A Mormon family of the late 1860s—the husband, his five wives, and their children—posing for the camera in front of their home at Echo City, Utah.*

few undercover marriages during the ensuing fifteen years, while the experiment was in its death throes.

II

If there is any significance in this chronicle of polygamous marrying, it is in the lack of evidence that the steady growth of the Utah church was accompanied by a corresponding increase in the number of such marriages. The story is rather one of sporadic outbursts of enthusiasm, followed by relapses, with the proportion of the Saints living in polygamy steadily falling. And it appears to be more than chance that each outbreak of fervor coincided with some revivalist activity within the chuch or with some menace from without. It is evident that, far from looking upon plural marriage as a privilege to be made the most of, the rank and file Mormons accepted it as one of the onerous obligations of church membership. Left alone, they were prone to

neglect it, and it always took some form of pressure to stir them to renewed zeal.

The number of wives married by the men who practiced polygamy offers further evidence of lack of enthusiasm for the principle. A common mistaken notion was that most polygamists maintained large harems, an idea which can be attributed to the publicity given the few men who went in for marrying on a grand scale. Joseph Smith was probably the most married of these men. The number of his wives can only be guessed at, but it might have gone as high as sixty or more. Brigham Young is usually credited with only twenty-seven wives, but he was sealed to more than twice that many living women, and to at least 150 more who had died. Heber C. Kimball had forty-five living wives, a number of them elderly ladies who never lived with him. No one else came close to these three men in the point of marrying. John D. Lee gave the names of his nineteen wives, but modestly explained that, "as I was married to old Mrs. Woolsey for her soul's sake, and she was near sixty years old when I married her, I never considered her really a wife. . . . That is the reason that I claim only eighteen true wives." And by taking fourteen wives, Jens Hansen earned special mention in the *Latter-day Saint Biographical Encyclopedia,* which said: "Of all the Scandinavian brethren who figured prominently in the Church Bro. Hansen distinguished himself by marrying more wives than any other of his countrymen in modern times." Orson Pratt, who was chosen to deliver the first public discourse on the subject of plural marriage and became its most able defender, had only ten living wives, but on two days, a week apart, he was sealed for eternity to more than two hundred dead women.

But these men with many wives were the few exceptions to the rule. Of 1,784 polygamists, 66.3 percent married only one extra wife. Another 21.2 percent were three-wife men, and 6.7 percent went as far as to take four wives. This left a small group of less than 6 percent who married five or more women. The typical polygamist, far from being the insatiable male of popular fable, was a dispassionate fellow, content to call a halt after marrying the one extra wife required to assure him of his chance at salvation.

Another false conception was that polygamists were bearded patriarchs who continued marrying young girls as long as they were able to hobble about. It is true that Brigham Young took a young wife when he was sixty-seven years old and a few others followed his example, but such marriages were not much more common with Mormons than among other groups. Of 1,229 polygamists, more than 10 percent married their last wives while still in their twenties, and more than one half of them before arriving at the still lusty age of forty years. Not one in five took a wife after reaching his fiftieth year. The average age at which the group ceased marrying was forty years.

There appears to be more basis in fact for the reports that polygamists were likely to choose their wives from among the young girls who might bear them many children. Of 1,348 women selected as plural wives, 38 percent were in their teens, 67 percent were under twenty-five and only 30 percent over thirty years of age. A few had passed forty and about one in a hundred had, like John D. Lee's old Mrs. Woolsey, seen her fiftieth birthday.

There were a few notable instances of high-speed marrying among the polygamists. Whatever the number of Joseph Smith's wives, he must have married them all over a period of thirty-nine months. And Brigham Young took eight wives in a single month, four of them on the same day. But only a few enthusiasts indulged in such rapid marrying. As a rule it proceeded at a much less hurried pace. Not one plural marriage in ten followed a previous marriage by less than a year. The composite polygamist was first married at the age of twenty-three to a girl of twenty. Thirteen years later he took a plural wife, choosing a twenty-two-year-old girl. The chances were two to one that, having demonstrated his acceptance of the principle of plurality, he was finished with marrying. If, however, he took a third wife, he waited four years, then selected another girl of twenty-two. The odds were now three to one against his taking a fourth wife, but if he did so, he waited another four years, and once more chose a twenty-two-year-old girl, although he had now reached the ripe age of forty-four. In case he decided to add a fifth wife, he waited only two years, and this time the lady of his choice was twenty-one years old. This was the end of his marrying, unless he belonged to a 3 percent minority.

Available records offer no corroboration of the accusation that many polygamous marriages were incestuous. They do, however, suggest the source of such reports, in the surprisingly common practice of marrying sisters. The custom was initiated by Joseph Smith, among whose wives were at least three pairs of sisters. His example was followed by Heber C. Kimball, whose forty-five wives included Clarissa and Emily Cutler, Amanda and Anna Gheen, Harriet and Ellen Sanders, Hannah and Dorothy Moon, and Laura and Abigail Pitkin. Brigham Young honored the precedent by marrying the Decker sisters, Lucy and Clara, and the Bigelow girls, Mary and Lucy. And John D. Lee told how he married the three Woolsey sisters, Agatha Ann, Rachel, and Andora and rounded out the family circle by having their mother sealed to him for her soul's sake. Among his other wives were the Young sisters, Polly and Lovina, sealed to him on the same evening. The popularity of this custom is indicated by the fact that of 1,642 polygamists, 10 percent married one or more pairs of sisters.

While marrying sisters could have been a simple matter of propinquity, there probably was some method in it. Many a man went into polygamy reluctantly, fully aware of its hazards. Knowing that his double family must live in one small home, and realizing that the peace of his household would hinge upon the congeniality between its two mistresses, he might well hope that if they were sisters the chances for domestic tranquility would be more even. And a wife, consenting to share her husband with another, could not be blamed for asking that he choose her sister, instead of bringing home a strange woman.

III

The fruits of this experiment in polygamy are not easy to appraise. In defense of their marriage system, the Mormons talked much about the benefits it would bring. By depriving husbands of an excuse for seeking extramarital pleasure, and by making it possible for every woman to marry, it was to solve the problem of the "social evil" by eliminating professional prostitution and other adulterous activities. It was to furnish healthy tabernacles for the countless spirits, waiting anxiously to assume their earthly bodies. It was to build up a "righteous generation" of physically and intellectually superior individuals. It was to enhance the glory of the polygamist through a posterity so numerous that, in the course of eternity, he might become the god of a world peo-

pled by his descendants. And there was another blessing in store for men who lived this principle. Heber C. Kimball, Brigham Young's chief lieutenant, explained it this way:

I would not be afraid to promise a man who is sixty years of age, if he will take the counsel of brother Brigham and his brethren, that he will renew his age. I have noticed that a man who has but one wife, and is inclined to that doctrine, soon begins to wither and dry up, while a man who goes into plurality looks fresh, young and sprightly. Why is this? Because God loves that man, and because he honors His work and word. Some of you may not believe this; but I not only believe it—I also know it. For a man of God to be confined to one woman is small business; for it is as much as we can do now to keep up under the burdens we have to carry; and I do not know what we should do if we had only one wife apiece.

It does appear that Mormon communities of the polygamous era were comparatively free from the evils of professional prostitution. But this can hardly be attributed to the fact that a few men, supposedly selected for their moral superiority, were permitted to marry more than one wife. It might better be credited to the common teaching that adultery was a sin so monstrous that there was no atonement for it short of the spilling of the blood of the offender. It would be strange indeed if such a fearful warning failed to exert a restraining influence upon the potential adulterer.

There is, of course, nothing unsound in the theory that a community of superior people might be propagated by selecting the highest ranking males and having them reproduce themselves in large numbers. The difficulty here would be to find a scientific basis for the selection of the favored males. And there is no information from which an opinion can be arrived at as to the results which were obtained in this respect.

When it came to fathering large families and supplying bodies for waiting spirits, the polygamists did fairly well, but fell far short of some of their dreams. Heber C. Kimball once said of himself and Brigham Young: "In twenty-five or thirty years we will have a larger number in our two families than there now is in this whole Territory, which numbers more than seventy-five thousand. If twenty-five years will produce this amount of people, how much will be the increase in one hundred years?" And the *Millennial Star* reckoned that a hypothetical Mr. Fruitful, with forty wives, might, at the age of seventy-eight, number among his seed 3,508,441 souls, while his monogamous counterpart could boast of only 152.

With such reminders of their potentialities before them, the most married of the polygamists must have been far from satisfied with the results they could show. There is no conclusive evidence that any of Joseph Smith's many plural wives bore children by him. Heber C. Kimball, with his forty-five wives, was the father of sixty-five children. John D. Lee, with only eighteen "true wives," fell one short of Kimball's record, and Brigham Young fathered fifty-six children, approximately one for each wife.

Although the issue of the few men of many wives was disappointing in numbers, the rank and file of polygamists made a fair showing. Of 1,651 families, more than four-fifths numbered ten or more children. Half of them had fifteen or more and one-fourth, twenty or more. There were eighty-eight families of thirty or more, nineteen of forty or more, and seven of fifty or more. The average number of children per family was fifteen. And by the third or fourth generation some families had reached rather impressive proportions. When one six-wife elder had been dead fifty-five years, his descendants numbered 1,900.

While polygamy increased the number of children of the men, it did not do the same for the women involved. A count revealed that 3,335 wives of polygamists bore 19,806 children, for an average of 5.9 per woman. An equal number of wives of monogamists, taken from the same general group, bore 26,780 for an average of eight. This suggests the possibility that the overall production of children in Utah may have been less than it would have been without benefit of plurality of wives. The claim that plurality was needed because of a surplus of women is not borne out by statistics.

There is little doubt that the plural wife system went a good way toward making it possible for every woman to marry. According to Mormon teachings a woman could "never obtain a fullness of glory, without being married to a righteous man for time and all eternity." If she never married or was the wife of a Gentile, her chance of attaining a high degree of salvation was indeed slim. And one of the responsibilities of those in official church positions was to try to make sure that no woman went without a husband. When a widow or a maiden lady "gathered" to Utah, it was a community obligation to see to it that she had food and shelter and the privilege of being married to a good man. If she received no offer of marriage, it was not considered inconsistent with feminine modesty for her to "apply" to the man of her choice, but if she set her sights too high she might be disappointed. My grandmother, who did sewing for the family of Brigham Young, was fond of telling how she watched through a partly open doorway while he forcibly ejected a woman who was too persistent in applying to be sealed to him. Her story would always end with the same words: "And I just couldn't help laughing to see brother Brigham get so out of patience with that woman." However, if the lady in search of a husband was not too ambitious, her chances of success were good. It was said of the bishop of one small settlement that he "was a good bishop. He married all the widows in town and took good care of them." And John D. Lee was following accepted precedent when he married old Mrs. Woolsey for her soul's sake.

As for Mr. Kimball's claims concerning the spiritual uplift to be derived from taking a fresh, young wife, what man is going to quarrel with him about that?

IV

The most common reasons given for opposition to the plural wife system were that it was not compatible with the American way of life, that it debased the women who lived under it, and that it caused disharmony and unhappiness in the family. To these charges the Mormons replied that their women enjoyed a higher social position than those of the outside world, and that there was less contention and unhappiness in their families than in those of the Gentiles. There is no statistical information upon which to base a judgment as to who had the better of this argument.

In addition to these general complaints against polygamy, its critics told some fantastic stories about the evils which followed in its wake. It was said that, through some mysterious workings of the laws of heredity, polygamous children were born with such peculiarities as feeblemindedness, abnormal sexual desires, and weak and deformed bodies.

At a meeting of the New Orleans Academy of Sciences in 1861, a remarkable paper was presented by Dr. Samuel A. Cartwright and Prof. C. G. Forshey. It consisted mainly of quotations from a report made by Assistant Surgeon Robert Barthelow of the United States Army on the "Effects and Tendencies of Mormon Polygamy in the Territory of Utah." Barthelow had observed that the Mormon system of marriage was already producing a people with distinct racial characteristics. He said:

The yellow, sunken, cadaverous visage; the greenish-colored eye; the thick, protuberant lips; the low forehead; the light, yellowish hair, and the lank, angular person, constitute an appearance so characteristic of the new race, the production of polygamy, as to distinguish them at a glance. The older men and women present all the physical peculiarities of the nationalities to which they belong; but these peculiarities are not propagated and continued in the new race; they are lost in the prevailing type.

Dr. Cartwright observed that the Barthelow report went far "to prove that polygamy not only blights the physical organism, but the moral nature of the white or Adamic woman to so great a degree as to render her incapable of breeding any other than abortive specimens of humanity—a new race that would die out—utterly perish from the earth, if left to sustain itself."

When one or two of the New Orleans scientists questioned the soundness of parts of this paper, the hecklers were silenced by Dr. Cartwright's retort that the facts presented were not so strong as "those which might be brought in proof of the debasing influence of abolitionism on the moral principles and character of that portion of the Northern people who have enacted personal liberty bills to evade a compliance with their constitutional obligations to the Southern States, and have elevated the Poltroon Sumner into a hero, and made a Saint of the miscreant Brown."

Needless to say there is no evidence that polygamy produced any such physical and mental effects upon the progeny of those who practiced it. A study of the infant mortality rate in a large number of Mormon families showed no difference between the polygamous and monogamous households.

It is difficult to arrive at general conclusions concerning this experiment in polygamy, but a few facts about it are evident. Mormondom was not a society in which all men married many wives, but one in which a few men married two or more wives. Although plurality of wives was taught as a tenet of the church, it was not one of the fundamental principles of the Mormon faith, and its abandonment was accomplished with less disturbance than that caused by its introduction. The Saints accepted plurality in theory, but most of them were loath to put it into practice, despite the continual urging of leaders in whose divine authority they had the utmost faith. Once the initial impetus given the venture had subsided it became increasingly unpopular. In 1857 there were nearly fourteen times as many plural marriages for each one thousand Utah Mormons as there were in 1880. Left to itself, undisturbed by pressure from without, the church would inevitably have given up the practice of polygamy, perhaps even sooner than it did under pressure. The experiment was not a satisfactory test of plurality of wives as a social system. Its results were neither spectacular nor conclusive, and they gave little justification for either the high hopes of its promoters or the dire predictions of its critics.

■■■

STUDY QUESTIONS

1. List the basic myths surrounding the Mormon practice of polygamy and then describe the social reality of each idea.

2. Ivins feels that the practice of polygamy was really not that popular among the Mormons. What evidence does he use to support that idea?

3. How important was polygamy as a religious principle among the Mormons? What was the relationship between the "Reformation" and the practice of polygamy?

4. What did Mormons believe about the social and spiritual benefits of polygamy?

5. How did the non-Mormon public in the nineteenth century view polygamy? What did they believe about the consequences of polygamy? Why did they have such attitudes?

BIBLIOGRAPHY

The classic study of Mormon settlement in the Intermountain West is Leonard Arrington, *Great Basin Kingdom: An Economic History of the Latter-day Saints, 1830–1900* (1958). Still the best sociological study of the Mormon faith is Thomas F. O'Dea, *The Mormons* (1957). The best survey history of the Mormon Church is James B. Allen and Glen M. Leonard, *The Story of the Latter-day Saints* (1976). For background material to the founding of the Mormon Church, see Whitney Cross, *The Burned-over District* (1950). For biographies of Joseph Smith, see Fawn Brodie, *No Man Knows My History: The Life of Joseph Smith, the Mormon Prophet* (1946) and Donna Hill, *Joseph Smith. The Mormon Prophet* (1977). The drama of the trek west is described in Wallace R. Stegner, *The Gathering of Zion: The Story of the Mormon Trail* (1964). Robert Flanders, *Nauvoo: Kingdom on the Mississippi* (1965) is excellent. Leonard Arrington is now completing a biography of Brigham Young. A flawed work published in 1968 is Stanley Hirshon's *Lion of the Lord.*

THE SLAVE WAREHOUSE
from *Uncle Tom's Cabin*

Harriet Beecher Stowe

On meeting Harriet Beecher Stowe during the Civil War, President Abraham Lincoln remarked, "So this is the lady who made this big war!" To be sure, Stowe did not cause the Civil War, but her novel, *Uncle Tom's Cabin*, did arouse Northerners and anger Southerners. She portrayed slavery as a great moral evil—not at all the benign institution presented by Southern apologists. Unlike the abstract writings of some of her contemporaries, Stowe confirmed the reality of slavery to Northerners who had never seen a slave or ventured below the Mason–Dixon line. The novel gave Northern abolitionists a new rhetoric to use in condemning slavery, and it convinced the South that the North was bent on destroying the Southern way of life. State after state in the South banned the sale of the book, and Southern postmasters routinely intercepted it in the mail from Northern book distributors and destroyed all copies.

Published in 1852, *Uncle Tom's Cabin* became a runaway bestseller, a literary success on both sides of the Atlantic. Stowe's characters—Uncle Tom, Eliza, Simon Legree, and Little Eva—were hailed as universal types. In the following selection, "The Slave Warehouse," good-hearted Christian slaves are purchased at a slave auction by Simon Legree.

A slave warehouse! Perhaps some of my readers conjure up horrible visions of such a place. They fancy some foul, obscure den, some horrible *Tartarus "informis, ingens, cui lumen ademptum."* But no, innocent friend; in these days men have learned the art of sinning expertly and genteelly, so as not to shock the eyes and senses of respectable society. Human property is high in the market; and is, therefore, well fed, well cleaned, tended, and looked after, that it may come to sale sleek, and strong, and shining. A slave warehouse in New Orleans is a house externally not much unlike many others, kept with neatness; and where every day you may see arranged, under a sort of shed along the outside, rows of men and women, who stand there as a sign of the property sold within.

Then you shall be courteously entreated to call and examine, and shall find an abundance of husbands, wives, brothers, sisters, fathers, mothers, and young children, to be "sold separately, or in lots, to suit the convenience of the purchaser;" and that soul immortal, once bought with blood and anguish by the Son of God, when the earth shook, and the rocks were rent, and the graves were opened, can be sold, leased, mortgaged, exchanged for groceries or dry goods, to suit the phases of trade, or the fancy of the purchaser.

It was a day or two after the conversation between Marie and Miss Ophelia, that Tom, Adolph, and about half a dozen others of the St. Clare estate, were turned over to the loving kindness of Mr. Skeggs, the keeper of a depot on———street, to await the auction next day.

Tom had with him quite a sizable trunk full of clothing, as had most others of them. They were ushered, for the night, into a long room, where many other men, of all ages, sizes, and shades of complexion, were assembled, and from which roars of laughter and unthinking merriment were proceeding.

"Ah, ha! that's right. Go it, boys—go it!" said Mr. Skeggs, the keeper. "My people are always so merry! Sambo, I see!" he said, speaking approvingly to a burly Negro who was performing tricks of low buffoonery, which occasioned the shouts which Tom had heard.

As might be imagined, Tom was in no humor to join these proceedings; and, therefore, setting his trunk as far as possible from the noisy group, he sat down on it, and leaned his face against the wall.

The dealers in the human article make scrupulous and systematic efforts to promote noisy mirth among them, as a means of drowning reflection, and rendering them insensible to their condition. The whole object of the training to which the Negro is put, from the time he is sold in the northern market till he arrives south, is systematically directed towards making him callous, unthinking, and brutal. The slave-dealer collects his gang in Virginia or Kentucky, and drives them to some convenient, healthy place—often a watering-place,—to be fattened. Here they are fed full daily; and, because some incline to pine, a fiddle is kept commonly going among them, and they are made to dance daily; and he who refuses to be merry—in whose soul thoughts of wife, or child, or home, are too strong for him to be gay—is marked as sullen and dangerous, and subjected to all the evils which the ill-will of an utterly irresponsible and hardened man can inflict upon him. Briskness, alertness, and cheerfulness of appearance, especially before observers, are constantly enforced upon them, both by the hope of thereby getting a good master, and the fear of all that the driver may bring upon them, if they prove unsalable.

"What dat ar nigger doin' here?" said Sambo, coming up to Tom, after Mr. Skeggs had left the room. Sambo was a full black, of great size, very lively, voluble, and full of trick and grimace.

"What you doin' here?" said Sambo, coming up to Tom, and poking him facetiously in the side. "Meditatin', eh?"

"I am to be sold at the auction, to-morrow!" said Tom, quietly.

"The Slave Warehouse" from *Uncle Tom's Cabin* by Harriet Beecher Stowe. New York, 1852.

"Sold at auction—haw! haw! boys, an't this yer fun? I wish 't I was gwin that ar way!—tell ye, wouldn't I make 'em laugh? but how is it—dis yer whole lot gwine to-morrow?" said Sambo, laying his hand freely on Adolph's shoulder.

"Please to let me alone!" said Adolph, fiercely, straightening himself up, with extreme disgust.

"Law, now, boys! dis yer 's one o' yer white niggers—kind o' cream-color, ye know, scented!" said he, coming up to Adolph and snuffing. "O Lor! he'd do for a tobaccershop; they could keep him to scent snuff! Lor, he'd keep a whole shop agwine—he would!"

"I say, keep off, can't you?" said Adolph, enraged.

"Lor, now, how touchy we is—we white niggers! Look at us, now!" and Sambo gave a ludicrous imitation of Adolph's manner; "here's de airs and graces. We's been in a good family, I specs."

"Yes," said Adolph; "I had a master that could have bought you all for old truck!"

"Laws, now, only think," said Sambo, "the gentlemens that we is!"

"I belonged to the St. Clare family," said Adolph, proudly.

"Lor, you did! Be hanged if they aren't lucky to get shet of ye. Spects they 's gwine to trade ye off with a lot o' cracked teapots and sich like!" said Sambo, with a provoking grin.

Adolph, enraged at this taunt, flew furiously at his adversary, swearing and striking on every side of him. The rest laughed and shouted, and the uproar brought the keeper to the door.

"What now, boys? Order—order!" he said, coming in and flourishing a large whip.

All fled in different directions, except Sambo, who, presuming on the favor which the keeper had to him as a licensed wag, stood his ground, ducking his head with a facetious grin, whenever the master made a dive at him.

"Lor, Mas'r, 't an't us—we 's reg'lar stiddy—it's these yer new hands; they 's real aggravatin'—kinder pickin' at us, all time!"

The keeper, at this, turned upon Tom and Adolph, and distributing a few kicks and cuffs without much inquiry, and leaving general orders for all to be good boys and go to sleep, left the apartment.

While this scene was going on in the men's sleeping-room, the reader may be curious to take a peep at the corresponding apartment allotted to the women. Stretched out in various attitudes over the floor, he may see numberless sleeping forms of every shade of complexion, from the purest ebony to white, and of all years, from childhood to old age, lying now asleep. Here is a fine bright girl, of ten years, whose mother was sold out yesterday, and who to-night cried herself to sleep when nobody was looking at her. Here, a worn old Negress, whose thin arms and callous fingers tell of hard toil, waiting to be sold to-morrow, as a cast-off article, for what can be got for her; and some forty or fifty others, with heads variously enveloped in blankets or articles of clothing, lie stretched around them. But, in a corner, sitting apart from the rest, are two females of a more interesting appearance than common. One of these is a respectably dressed mulatto woman between forty and fifty, with soft eyes and a gentle and pleasing physiognomy. She has on her head a high-raised turban, made of a gay red Madras handkerchief, of the first quality, and her dress is neatly fitted, and of good material, showing that she has been provided for with a careful hand. By her side, and nestling closely to her, is a young girl of fifteen—her daughter. She is a quadroon, as may be seen from her fairer complexion, though her likeness to her mother is quite discernible. She has the same soft, dark eye, with longer lashes, and her curling hair is of a luxuriant brown. She also is dressed with great neatness, and her white, delicate hands betray very little acquaintance with servile toil. These two are to be sold to-morrow, in the same lot with the St. Clare servants; and the gentleman to whom they belong, and to whom the money for their sale is to be transmitted, is a member of a Christian church in New York, who will receive the money, and go thereafter to the sacrament of his Lord and theirs, and think no more of it.

These two, whom we shall call Susan and Emmeline, had been the personal attendants of an amiable and pious lady of New Orleans, by whom they had been carefully and piously instructed and trained. They had been taught to read and write, diligently instructed in the truths of religion, and their lot had been as happy an one as in their condition it was possible to be. But the only son of their protectress had the management of her property; and, by carelessness and extravagance, involved it to a large amount, and at last failed. One of the largest creditors was the respectable firm of B. & Co., in New York. B. & Co. wrote to their lawyer in New Orleans, who attached the real estate (these two articles and a lot of plantation hands formed the most valuable part of it), and wrote word to that effect to New York. Brother B., being, as we have said, a Christian man, and a resident in a free state, felt some uneasiness on the subject. He didn't like trading in slaves and souls of men—of course, he didn't; but, then, there were thirty thousand dollars in the case, and that was rather too much money to be lost for a principle; and so, after much considering, and asking advice from those that he knew would advise to suit him, Brother B. wrote to his lawyer to dispose of the business in the way that seemed to him the most suitable, and remit the proceeds.

The day after the letter arrived in New Orleans, Susan and Emmeline were attached, and sent to the depot to await a general auction on the following morning; and as they glimmer faintly upon us in the moonlight which steals through the grated window, we may listen to their conversation. Both are weeping, but each quietly, that the other may not hear.

"Mother, just lay your head on my lap, and see if you can't sleep a little," says the girl, trying to appear calm.

"I haven't any heart to sleep, Em; I can't; it's the last night we may be together!"

"Oh, mother, don't say so! perhaps we shall get sold together—who knows?"

"If 't was anybody's else case, I should say so, too, Em," said the woman; "but I'm so 'feared of losin' you that I don't see anything but the danger."

"Why, mother, the man said we were both likely, and would sell well."

Susan remembered the man's looks and words. With a deadly sickness at her heart, she remembered how he had looked at Emmeline's hands, and lifted up her curly hair, and pronounced her a first-rate article. Susan had been trained as a Christian, brought up in the daily reading of the Bible, and had the same horror of her child's being sold to a life of shame that any other Christian mother might have; but she had no hope—no protection.

"Mother, I think we might do first-rate, if you could get a place as cook, and I as chambermaid or seamstress, in some family. I dare say we shall. Let's both look as bright and lively as we can, and tell all we can do, and perhaps we shall," said Emmeline.

"I want you to brush your hair all back straight, to-morrow," said Susan.

"What for, mother? I don't look near so well, that way."

"Yes, but you'll sell better so."

"I don't see why!" said the child.

"Respectable families would be more apt to buy you, if they saw you looked plain and decent, as if you wasn't trying to look handsome. I know their ways better 'n you do," said Susan.

"Well, mother, then I will."

"And, Emmeline, if we shouldn't ever see each other again, after to-morrow—if I'm sold way up on a plantation somewhere, and you somewhere else—always remember how you've been brought up, and all Missis has told you; take your Bible with you, and your hymn-book; and if you're faithful to the Lord, he'll be faithful to you."

So speaks the poor soul, in sore discouragement; for she knows that to-morrow any man, however vile and brutal, however godless and merciless, if he only has money to pay for her, may become owner of her daughter, body and soul; and then, how is the child to be faithful? She thinks of all this, as she holds her daughter in her arms, and wishes that she were not handsome and attractive. It seems almost an aggravation to her to remember how purely and piously, how much above the ordinary lot, she has been brought up. But she has no resort but to *pray*; and many such prayers to God have gone up from those same trim, neatly arranged, respectable slave-prisons—prayers which God has not forgotten, as a coming day shall show; for it is written, "Whoso causeth one of these little ones to offend, it were better for him that a mill-stone were hanged about his neck, and that he were drowned in the depths of the sea."

The soft, earnest, quiet moonbeam looks in fixedly, marking the bars of the grated windows on the prostrate, sleeping forms. The mother and daughter are singing together a wild and melancholy dirge, common as a funeral hymn among the slaves:—

"Oh, where is weeping Mary?
Oh, where is weeping Mary?
 'Rived in the goodly land.
She is dead and gone to heaven;
She is dead and gone to heaven;
 'Rived in the goodly land.''

These words, sung by voices of a peculiar and melancholy sweetness, in an air which seemed like the sighing of earthly despair after heavenly hope, floated through the dark prison-rooms with a pathetic cadence, as verse after verse was breathed out—

"Oh, where are Paul and Silas?
Oh, where are Paul and Silas?
 Gone to the goodly land.
They are dead and gone to heaven;
They are dead and gone to heaven;
 'Rived in the goodly land.''

Sing on, poor souls! The night is short, and the morning will part you forever!

But now it is morning, and everybody is astir; and the worthy Mr. Skeggs is busy and bright, for a lot of goods is to be fitted out for auction. There is a brisk lookout on the toilet; injunctions passed around to every one to put on their best face and be spry; and now all are arranged in a circle for a last review, before they are marched up to the Bourse.

Mr. Skeggs, with his palmetto on and his cigar in his mouth, walks around to put farewell touches on his wares.

"How's this?" he said, stepping in front of Susan and Emmeline. "Where's your curls, gal?"

The girl looked timidly at her mother, who, with the smooth adroitness common among her class, answers—

"I was telling her, last night, to put up her hair smooth and neat, and not havin' it flying about in curls; looks more respectable so."

"Bother!" said the man, peremptorily, turning to the girl; "you go right along, and curl yourself real smart!" He added, giving a crack to a rattan he held in his hand, "And be back in quick time, too!"

"You go and help her," he added, to the mother. "Them curls may make a hundred dollars difference in the sale of her."

Beneath a splendid dome were men of all nations, moving to and fro, over the marble pave. On every side of the circular area were little tribunes, or stations, for the use of speakers and auctioneers. Two of these, on opposite sides of the area, were now occupied by brilliant and talented gentlemen, enthusiastically forcing up, in English and French commingled, the bids of connoisseurs in their various wares. A third one, on the other side, still unoccupied, was surrounded by a group, waiting the moment of sale to begin. And here we may recognize the St. Clare servants—Tom, Adolph, and others; and there, too, Susan and Emmeline, awaiting their turn with anxious and dejected faces. Various spectators, intending to purchase, or not intending, as the case might be, gathered around the group, handling, examining, and commenting on their various points and faces with the same freedom that a set of jockeys discuss the merits of a horse.

"Hulloa, Alf! what brings you here?" said a young exquisite, slapping the shoulder of a sprucely dressed young man, who was examining Adolph through an eye-glass.

"Well, I was wanting a valet, and I heard that St. Clare's lot was going. I thought I'd just look at his"—

"Catch me ever buying any of St. Clare's people! Spoilt niggers, every one. Impudent as the devil!" said the other.

"Never fear that!" said the first. "If I get'em, I'll soon have their airs out of them; they'll soon find that they've another kind of master to deal with than Monsieur St. Clare. 'Pon my word, I'll buy that fellow. I like the shape of him."

"You'll find it'll take all you've got to keep him. He's deucedly extravagant!"

"Yes, but my lord will find that he *can't* be extravagant with *me*. Just let him be sent to the calaboose a few times, and thoroughly dressed down! I'll tell you if it don't bring him to a sense of his ways! Oh, I'll reform him, up hill and down—you'll see. I buy him, that's flat!"

Tom had been standing wistfully examining the multitude of faces thronging around him, for one whom he would wish to call master. And if you should ever be under the necessity, sir, of selecting, out of two hundred men, one who was to become your absolute owner and disposer, you would, perhaps, realize, just as Tom did, how few there were that you would feel at all comfortable in being made over to. Tom saw abundance of men—great, burly, gruff men; little, chirping, dried men; long-favored, lank, hard men; and every variety of stubbed-looking, commonplace men, who pick up their fellow-men as one picks up chips, putting them into the fire or a basket with equal unconcern, according to their convenience; but he saw no St. Clare.

A little before the sale commenced, a short, broad, muscular man, in a checked shirt considerably open at the bosom, and pantaloons much

the worse for dirt and wear, elbowed his way through the crowd, like one who is going actively into a business; and, coming up to the group, began to examine them systematically. From the moment that Tom saw him approaching, he felt an immediate and revolting horror at him, that increased as he came near. He was evidently, though short, of gigantic strength. His round, bullet-head, large, light-grey eyes, with their shaggy, sandy eyebrows, and stiff, wiry, sunburned hair, were rather unprepossessing items, it is to be confessed; his large, coarse mouth was distended with tobacco, the juice of which, from time to time, he ejected from him with great decision and explosive force; his hands were immensely large, hairy, sunburned, freckled, and very dirty, and garnished with long nails, in a very foul condition. This man proceeded to a very free personal examination of the lot. He seized Tom by the jaw, and pulled open his mouth to inspect his teeth; made him strip up his sleeve, to show his muscle; turned him round, made him jump and spring, to show his paces.

"Where was you raised?" he added, briefly, to these investigations.

"In Kintuck, Mas'r," said Tom, looking about, as if for deliverance.

"What have you done?"

"Had care of Mas'r's farm," said Tom.

"Likely story!" said the other, shortly, as he passed on. He paused a moment before Dolph; then spitting a discharge of tobacco-juice on his well-blacked boots, and giving a contemptuous umph, he walked on. Again he stopped before Susan and Emmeline. He put out his heavy, dirty hand, and drew the girl towards him; passed it over her neck, and bust, felt her arms, looked at her teeth, and then pushed her back against her mother, whose patient face showed the suffering she had been going through at every motion of the hideous stranger.

The girl was frightened, and began to cry.

"Stop that, you minx!" said the salesman; "no whimpering here—the sale is going to begin." And accordingly the sale began.

This drawing of an 1861 Virginia slave auction shows the breaking up of families at a slave sale. Contrary to popular belief, slave markets were usually clean, well-tended warehouses. Slaves were fattened up and groomed before auctions in order to bring better prices.

Adolph was knocked off, at a good sum, to the young gentleman who had previously stated his intentions of buying him; and the other servants of the St. Clare lot went to various bidders.

"Now, up with you, boy! d 'ye hear?" said the auctioneer to Tom.

Tom stepped upon the block, gave a few anxious looks round; all seemed mingled in a common, indistinct noise—the clatter of the salesman crying off his qualifications in French and English, the quick fire of French and English bids; and almost in a moment came the final thump of the hammer, and the clear ring on the last syllable of the word *"dollars,"* as the auctioneer announced his price, and Tom was made over. He had a master.

He was pushed from the block; the short, bullet-headed man, seizing him roughly by the shoulder, pushed him to one side, saying, in a harsh voice, "Stand there, *you!*"

Tom hardly realized anything; but still the bidding went on—rattling, clattering, now French, now English. Down goes the hammer again—Susan is sold! She goes down from the block, stops, looks wistfully back—her daughter stretches her hands towards her. She looks with agony in the face of the man who has bought her—a respectable, middle-aged man, of benevolent countenance.

"Oh, Mas'r, please do buy my daughter!"

"I'd like to, but I'm afraid I can't afford it!" said the gentleman, looking, with painful interest, as the young girl mounted the block, and looked around her with a frightened and timid glance.

The blood flushes painfully in her otherwise colorless cheek, her eye has a feverish fire, and her mother groans to see that she looks more beautiful than she ever saw her before. The auctioneer sees his advantage, and expatiates volubly in mingled French and English, and bids rise in rapid succession.

"I'll do anything in reason," said the benevolent-looking gentleman, pressing in and joining with the bids. In a few moments they have run beyond his purse. He is silent; the auctioneer grows warmer; but bids gradually drop off. It lies now between an aristocratic old citizen and our bullet-headed acquaintance. The citizen bids for a few turns, contemptuously measuring his opponent; but the bullet-head has the advantage over him, both in obstinacy and concealed length of purse, and the controversy lasts but a moment; the hammer falls—he has got the girl, body and soul, unless God help her.

Her master is Mr. Legree, who owns a cotton plantation on the Red River. She is pushed along into the same lot with Tom and two other men, and goes off, weeping as she goes.

The benevolent gentleman is sorry; but, then, the thing happens every day! One sees girls and mothers crying, at these sales, *always*! it can't be helped, etc.; and he walks off, with his acquisition, in another direction.

Two days after, the lawyer of the Christian firm of B. & Co., New York, sent on their money to them. On the reverse of that draft, so obtained, let them write these words of the great Paymaster, to whom they shall make up their account in a future day: *"When he maketh inquisition for blood, he forgetteth not the cry of the humble!"*

"Thou art of purer eyes than to behold evil, and canst not look upon iniquity: wherefore lookest thou upon them that deal treacherously, and holdest thy tongue when the wicked devoureth the man that is more righteous than he?"—*Hab.* i. 13.

On the lower part of a small, mean boat, on the Red River, Tom sat—chains on his wrists, chains on his feet, and a weight heavier than chains lay on his heart. All had faded from his sky—moon and star; all had passed by him, as the trees and banks were now passing, to return no more. Kentucky home, with wife and children, and indulgent owners; St. Clare home, with all its refinements and splendors; the golden head of Eva, with its saint-like eyes; the proud, gay, handsome, seemingly careless, yet ever-kind St. Clare; hours of ease and indulgent leisure—all gone! and in place thereof, *what* remains?

It is one of the bitterest apportionments of a lot of slavery, that the Negro, sympathetic and assimilative, after acquiring, in a refined family, the tastes and feelings which form the atmosphere of such a place, is not the less liable to become the bond-slave of the coarsest and most brutal—just as a chair or table, which once decorated the superb saloon, comes, at last, battered and defaced, to the bar-room of some filthy tavern, or some low haunt of vulgar debauchery. The great difference is, that the table and chair cannot feel, and the *man* can; for even a legal enactment that he shall be "taken, reputed, adjudged in law, to be a chattel personal," cannot blot out his soul, with its own private little world of memories, hopes, loves, fears, and desires.

Mr. Simon Legree, Tom's master, had purchased slaves at one place and another, in New Orleans, to the number of eight, and driven them, handcuffed, in couples of two and two, down to the good steamer Pirate, which lay at the levee, ready for a trip up the Red River.

Having got them fairly on board, and the boat being off, he came round, with that air of efficiency which ever characterized him, to take a review of them. Stopping opposite to Tom, who had been attired for sale in his best broadcloth suit, with well-starched linen and shining boots, he briefly expressed himself as follows:

"Stand up."

Tom stood up.

"Take off that stock!" and, as Tom, encumbered by his fetters, proceeded to do it, he assisted him, by pulling it, with no gentle hand, from his neck, and putting it in his pocket.

Legree now turned to Tom's trunk, which, previous to this, he had been ransacking, and taking from it a pair of old pantaloons and a dilapidated coat, which Tom had been wont to put on about his stable-work, he said, liberating Tom's hands from the handcuffs, and pointing to a recess in among the boxes—

"You go there, and put these on."

Tom obeyed, and in a few moments returned.

"Take off your boots," said Mr. Legree.

Tom did so.

"There," said the former, throwing him a pair of course, stout shoes, such as were common among the slaves, "put these on."

In Tom's hurried exchange, he had not forgotten to transfer his cherished Bible to his pocket. It was well he did so; for Mr. Legree, having refitted Tom's handcuffs, proceeded deliberately to investigate the contents of his pockets. He drew out a silk handkerchief, and put it into his own pocket. Several little trifles, which Tom had treasured, chiefly because they amused Eva, he looked upon with a contemptuous grunt, and tossed them over his shoulder into the river.

Tom's Methodist hymn-book, which, in his hurry, he had forgotten, he now held up and turned over.

"Humph! pious, to be sure. So, what's yer name—you belong to the church, eh?"

"Yes, Mas'r," said Tom, firmly.

"Well, I'll soon have *that* out of you. I have none o' yer bawling, praying, singing niggers on my place; so remember. Now, mind yourself," he said, with a stamp and a fierce glance of his gray eye, directed at Tom, "*I'm* your church now! You understand—you've got to be as I say."

Something within the silent black man answered *No!* and, as if repeated by an invisible voice, came the words of an old prophetic scroll, as Eva had often read them to him, "Fear not! For I have redeemed thee. I have called thee by my name. Thou art MINE!"

But Simon Legree heard no voice. That voice is one he never shall hear. He only glared for a moment on the downcast face of Tom, and walked off. He took Tom's trunk, which contained a very neat and abundant wardrobe, to the forecastle, where it was soon surrounded by various hands of the boat. With much laughing, at the expense of niggers who tried to be gentlemen, the articles very readily were sold to one and another, and the empty trunk finally put up at auction. It was a good joke, they all thought, especially to see how Tom looked after his things, as they were going this way and that; and then the auction of the trunk, that was funnier than all, and occasioned abundant witticisms.

This little affair being over, Simon sauntered up again to his property.

"Now, Tom, I've relieved you of any extra baggage, you see. Take mighty good care of them clothes. It'll be long enough 'fore you get more. I go in for making niggers careful; one suit has to do for one year, on my place."

Simon next walked up to the place where Emmeline was sitting, chained to another woman.

"Well, my dear," he said, chucking her under the chin, "keep up your spirits."

The involuntary look of horror, fright, and aversion with which the girl regarded him, did not escape his eye. He frowned fiercely.

"None o' your shines, gal! you 's got to keep a pleasant face, when I speak to ye—'d ye hear? And you, you old yellow poco moonshine!" he said, giving a shove to the mulatto woman to whom Emmeline was chained, "don't you carry that sort of face! You 's got to look chipper, I tell ye!"

"I say, all on ye," he said, retreating a pace or two back, "look at me—look at me—look me right in the eye—*straight*, now!" said he, stamping his foot at every pause.

As by a fascination, every eye was now directed to the glaring greenish-gray eye of Simon.

"Now," said he, doubling his great, heavy fist into something resembling a blacksmith's hammer, "d' ye see this fist? Heft it!" he said, bringing it down on Tom's hand. "Look at these yer bones! Well, I tell ye this yer fist has got as hard as iron *knocking down niggers*. I never see the nigger, yet, I couldn't bring down with one crack," said he, bringing his fist down so near to the face of Tom that he winked and drew back. "I don't keep none o' yer cussed overseers; I does my own overseeing; and I tell you things *is* seen to. You 's every one on ye get to toe the mark, I tell ye; quick—straight—the moment I speak. That's the way to keep in with me. Ye won't find no soft spot in me, nowhere. So, now, mind yerselves; for I don't show no mercy!"

The women involuntarily drew in their breath, and the whole gang sat with downcast, dejected faces. Meanwhile, Simon turned on his heel, and marched up to the bar of the boat for a dram.

"That's the way I begin with my niggers," he said, to a gentlemanly man, who had stood by him during his speech. "It's my system to begin strong—just let 'em know what to expect."

"Indeed!" said the stranger, looking upon him with the curiosity of a naturalist studying some out-of-the-way specimen.

"Yes, indeed. I'm none o' yer gentlemen planters, with lily fingers, to slop round and be cheated by some old cuss of an overseer! Just feel of my knuckles, now; look at my fist. Tell ye, sir, the flesh on 't has come jest like a stone, practising on niggers—feel on it."

The stranger applied his fingers to the implement in question, and simply said,

"'T is hard enough; and, I suppose," he added, "practice has made your heart just like it."

"Why, yes, I may say so," said Simon, with a hearty laugh. "I reckon there's as little soft in me as in any one going. Tell you, nobody comes it over me! Niggers never gets round me, neither with squalling nor soft soap—that's a fact."

"You have a fine lot there."

"Real," said Simon. "There's that Tom, they telled me he was suthin uncommon. I paid a little high for him, 'tendin' him for a driver and a managing chap; only get the notions out that he's larnt by being treated as niggers never ought to be, he'll do prime! The yellow woman I got took in in. I rayther think she's sickly, but I shall put her through for what she's worth; she may last a year or two. I don't go for savin' niggers. Use up, and buy more, 's my way—makes you less trouble, and I'm quite sure it comes cheaper in the end;" and Simon sipped his glass.

"And how long do they generally last?" said the stranger. "Well, donno; 'cordin' as their constitution is. Stout fellers last six or seven years; trashy ones gets worked up in two or three. I used to, when I fust begun, have considerable trouble fussin' with 'em, and trying to make 'em hold out—doctorin' on 'em up when they 's sick, and givin' on 'em clothes and blankets, and what not, tryin' to keep 'em all sort o' decent and comfortable. Law, 't wasn't no sort o' use; I lost money on 'em, and 't was heaps o' trouble. Now, you see, I just put 'em straight through, sick or well. When one nigger's dead, I buy another; and I find it comes cheaper and easier, every way."

The stranger turned away, and seated himself beside a gentleman, who had been listening to the conversation with repressed uneasiness.

"You must not take that fellow to be any specimen of southern planters," said he.

"I should hope not," said the young gentleman, with emphasis.

"He is a mean, low, brutal fellow!" said the other.

"And yet your laws allow him to hold any number of human beings subject to his absolute will without even a shadow of protection; and, low as he is, you cannot say that there are not many such."

"Well," said the other, "there are also many considerate and humane men among planters."

"Granted," said the young man; "but, in my opinion, it is you considerate, humane men, that are responsible for all the brutality and outrage wrought by these wretches; because, if it were not for your sanction and influence, the whole system could not keep foothold for an hour. If there were no planters except such as that one," said he, pointing with his finger to Legree, who stood with his back to them, "the whole thing would go down like a mill-stone. It is your respectability and humanity that licenses and protects his brutality."

"You certainly have a high opinion of my good nature," said the planter, smiling; "but I advise you not to talk quite so loud, as there are people on board the boat who might not be quite so tolerant to opinion as I am. You had better wait till I get up to my plantation, and there you may abuse us all, quite at your leisure."

The young gentleman colored and smiled, and the two were soon busy in a game of backgammon. Meanwhile, another conversation was going on in the lower part of the boat, between Emmeline and the mulatto woman with whom she was confined. As was natural, they were exchanging with each other some particulars of their history.

"Who did you belong to?" said Emmeline.

"Well, my Mas'r was Mr. Ellis—lived on Levee Street. P'r'aps you've seen the house."

"Was he good to you?" said Emmeline.

"Mostly, till he tuk sick. He's lain sick, off and on, more than six months, and been orful oneasy. 'Pears like he warn't willin' to have nobody rest, day nor night; and got so curous, there couldn't nobody suit him. 'Pears like he just grew crosser, every day; kep me up nights till I got farly beat out, and couldn't keep awake no longer; and 'cause I got to sleep, one night, Lors, he talk so orful to me, and he tell me he'd sell me to just the hardest master he could find; and he'd promised me my freedom, too, when he died."

"Had you any friends?" said Emmeline.

"Yes, my husband—he's a blacksmith. Mas'r gen'ly hired him out. They took me off so quick, I didn't even have time to see him; and I's got four children. Oh, dear me!" said the woman, covering her face with her hands.

It is a natural impulse, in every one, when they hear a tale of distress, to think of something to say by way of consolation. Emmeline wanted to say something, but she could not think of anything to say. What was there to be said? As by a common consent, they both avoided, with fear and dread, all mention of the horrible man who was now their master.

True, there is religious trust for even the darkest hour. The mulatto woman was a member of the Methodist Church, and had an unenlightened but very sincere spirit of piety. Emmeline had been educated much more intelligently, taught to read and write, and diligently instructed in the Bible, by the care of a faithful and pious mistress; yet, would it not try the faith of the firmest Christians to find themselves abandoned, apparently, of God, in the grasp of ruthless violence? How much more must it shake the faith of Christ's poor little ones, weak in knowledge and tender in years.

The boat moved on—freighted with its weight of sorrow—up the red, muddy, turbid current, through the abrupt, tortuous windings of the Red River; and sad eyes gazed wearily on the steep red-clay banks, as they glided by in dreary sameness. At last the boat stopped at a small town, and Legree, with his party, disembarked.

■ ■ ■

STUDY QUESTIONS

1. How does Stowe convey the inhumanity of the slave auction?

2. How does Tom accept his fate?

3. How does Stowe portray the evil of Legree?

4. What reactions do you believe Stowe was trying to arouse in her readers?

BIBLIOGRAPHY

For studies of *Uncle Tom's Cabin* and Harriet Beecher Stowe see Charles A. Foster, *The Wrungless Ladder* (1954); Chester E. Jorgensen, ed., *Uncle Tom's Cabin as Book and Legend* (1952); Forrest Wilson, *Crusader and Crinoline* (1941); and Edmund Wilson, *Patriotic Gore* (1962). Anne Fields, *Life and Letters of Harriet Beecher Stowe* (1898), contains useful information on *Uncle Tom's Cabin*, and Herbert Ross Brown, *The Sentimental Novel in America 1789–1860)* (1940), puts the novel into its literary perspective.

THE SOUTHAMPTON SLAVE REVOLT

Henry F. Tragle

The need for some form of involuntary servitude was all but guaranteed in the American South. Land was abundant and cheap, but labor was limited and expensive. Unlike in England, where the opposite situation prevailed, in America the settlers found it fairly easy to acquire land of their own but practically impossible to find people to work it. If Southerners were going to get the most out of their land, they needed labor; if no volunteers were available, there would have to be slaves. They found their workers in West Africa, importing the first group of slaves to Virginia in 1619. By the time of the Civil War, that handful of blacks had become four million people.

Southern life was full of ambiguities, but none of them was more ironic than the role of those four million slaves. Whites needed blacks to plant their land, harvest their crops, clean their houses, cook their food, and suckle their children. Whites needed black slaves to thrive and prosper, so they imported more and more Africans, making black people a permanent, visible fixture in Southern life.

But the arrival of more and more blacks made Southern whites nervous. Despite the prevailing rationale that slavery benefitted all concerned, whites knew instinctively that the Africans resented their bondage and yearned to be free. Rumors of slave rebellions were rampant in the nineteenth century. Whites became paranoid about their blacks; they were always on guard, always searching for conspiracies, always afraid of a slave uprising. Then on the morning of August 22, 1831, their worst nightmares came true in Southampton, Virginia. There Nat Turner led a group of slaves on a bloody rampage through white farms and plantations. When the orgy of violence was over, sixty whites were dead, hacked apart by axes wielded by black hands. The South would never be the same again.

The voluminous histories of this country written in the 19th century, while admirable in many respects, are of little value to a student today who seeks reliable information on the institution of American slavery. Concerned primarily with slavery as a political question, or with its economic, social, and cultural impact on the white population, the historians rarely made any attempt to understand the black man as a human being.

One of the persistent themes pursued by those who have written recently on the subject of American slavery has been to ask why the slave was willing to tolerate his lot. Why, when in many sections of the South the slave population considerably outnumbered the white, was there no more evidence of unrest?

Actually, there was considerable. But one must look beyond the writings of the most respected of the 19th century historians in order to perceive this. The works of James Schouler, John Fiske, Hermann von Holst, John W. Burgess, James Ford Rhodes, and John Bach McMaster simply did not deal with the available evidence on this question. Satisfied to accept the stereotype of the American black man as docile, ignorant, and inherently inferior, they saw no reason to probe very deeply. Fiske did find that the absence of any insurrectionary spirit was, in itself, "one of the remarkable facts of American history," and Schouler, when considering the same question, wrote that American Negroes were "a black servile race, . . . brutish, obedient to the whip."

Yet, in order to see that all was not "sweetness and light" in the Southern states one can find countless instances of individual unrest and resistance, and a few uprisings organized on a sufficient scale to be called insurrections or revolts. The contemporary press and the historical archives of the states that were part of the slave-holding South are the best sources of such information. Despite the tendency of Southern newspapers to play down these stories, the back files of any such paper for the period from 1800 up to the time of the Civil War will reveal numerous accounts of homes or barns burned, of property damaged or destroyed, and instances of white masters beaten, or even murdered by their own slaves. A summary prepared by the state auditor of Virginia in 1831 shows that, between 1820 and 1831, the state paid out a total of $124,785 for 313 slaves who were either executed as criminals or were "transported" out of the state for acts judged to be criminal. Since, under existing law, the state was required to reimburse an owner for a slave executed or transported, and since neither of these actions could be taken without benefit of trial in a court of law, it can be assumed that the 313 slaves on the list had been judged guilty of serious crimes.

Three well-authenticated attempts at organized slave revolt took place in the first third of the 19th century. In 1800 there was the so-called "Gabriel's Insurrection" in Richmond. While the details of the plot have never been fully known, it is clear that a group of slaves living in and near the Virginia capital developed a plan to burn and sack the city and destroy its white inhabitants. Although discovered before any blow was actually struck, the conspiracy caused great excitement. Those believed to be the ringleaders were executed, the laws governing the conduct of slaves as well as of free black people were applied more severely, and the governor, James Monroe, wrote a special report on the matter for the Virginia Legislature.

In 1822 in Charleston, South Carolina, occurred what has come to be known as the "Denmark Vesey Plot." Vesey, who had been the slave of a sea-captain, had traveled abroad with his master and had learned to read and write. After purchasing his freedom, he became a respected black artisan in Charleston. In a plot that was revealed through slave informers,

Henry F. Tragle, "The Southampton Slave Revolt." From *American History Illustrated* 6 (November 1971), pp. 4–11, 44–47. Reprinted through the courtesy of Cowles Magazines, publisher of AMERICAN HISTORY ILLUSTRATED.

Vesey was accused along with a number of other black men, slave and free, of planning an insurrection and was executed. Again, no actual uprising took place, but it seems clear that plans had been laid to organize a black rebellion which would have extended well into the interior of the state.

The most famous instance of this sort, and the only one which actually resulted in the deaths of a sizable number of white people, took place in an obscure backwater of Virginia, Southampton County, in August of 1831. Generally referred to as "The Southampton Insurrection," or "the servile insurrection of 1831," it has been called by one historian the "single instance of sustained revolt of slaves against their masters in American history." Whether this description is justified or not depends on the criteria one uses, but there is no question that the revolt led by the slave Nat Turner had a powerful and lasting effect on the institution of slavery throughout the entire South.

Interest in Turner as an individual has recently been intensified by a highly successful fictionalized version of his exploits, as well as by the growing interest in serious study of the culture and history of the American black man as a hitherto neglected aspect of the American heritage. Nat Turner, as symbol and folk hero, has figured frequently in fiction, poetry, and drama in the 140 years since 1831. Harriet Beecher Stowe, in her novel, *Dred,* which she published in 1856, used what little was known of Turner in shaping her principal character, and included as an appendix to her book a portion of the "Confession" which he is supposed to have made while awaiting trial in the Southampton jail. George Payne Rainsford James, a prolific novelist of the 19th century and Historiographer Royal to King William IV of England, published a novel in 1853 which he called *The Old Dominion.* The plot is based on what had taken place in Southampton County some twenty years earlier, and Nat Turner emerges as a kind of black mystic. James had served for a short time as British Consul in Norfolk, Virginia, and it is possible that during this period he heard the actual event discussed.

It is possible to reconstruct from contemporary records and the news stories of the time a reasonably accurate account of what happened during the period August 21 through November 11, 1831, on which date Nat Turner was executed. But we know little about the man himself and even less about his basic motivation. He was born the slave of Benjamin Turner on October 2, 1800. The Turner home, located about fifteen miles southwest of Jerusalem, the county seat of Southampton, was characteristic of the style of life which prevailed in that part of Virginia. Most of Southampton's white male citizens farmed small holdings, and only a handful of its most prosperous citizens owned more than twenty-five slaves. In 1830 its population totaled 16,074 of which 6,573 were white and 9,501 black. Jerusalem, the main town, had but 175 inhabitants. The county was unusual in one particular: a relatively high proportion of its black population, 1,745, were what were then known as "free men (or women) of color." This exception from the prevailing pattern in Southside Virginia was due in large part to the activity of the Quakers and the Emancipating Baptists, both of which sects had flourished in the area in the years following the Revolutionary War. Both had taken strong stands against slavery. Little is known about these free black people and their way of life, but it is safe to assume that their existence was marginal at best. Of the fifty persons eventually tried on suspicion of having taken part in the revolt, five of those arraigned were free black men.

Since blacks lived under a legal system which made it a felony to teach a slave to read or write, it is not surprising that illiteracy among them was almost universal. Yet Nat Turner was not only literate, he was known, by black and white alike, for his profound knowledge of the Bible. As surprising as the possession of these skills is the fact that he avoided attracting the serious attention of white members of the community, whose suspicion and animosity could be readily aroused by any signs of intelligence or ability on the part of a slave. Yet the lawyer who recorded his "Confessions," Thomas R. Gray, wrote this evaluation in the concluding lines of his account:

It has been said that he was ignorant and cowardly, and his object was to murder and rob for the purpose of obtaining money to make his escape. It is notorious that he was never known to have a dollar in his life, to swear an oath, or drink a drop of spirits. As to his ignorance, he certainly never had the advantages of an education, but he can read and write (it was taught him by his parents) and for natural intelligence and quickness of apprehension, is surpassed by few men I have ever seen.

There is no evidence that Nat Turner was a pampered house servant, or that, except for the austerity of his personal life and his habit of reading the Bible in every free moment, he was outwardly much different from any other able-bodied male slave in the county. After the revolt he was characterized in news stories as a "Black Preacher," but white persons in the neighborhood who knew him denied that he had even attended church regularly. When Benjamin Turner died in 1810, Nat passed into the ownership of a younger brother, Samuel, and at his death in 1822, was sold to a neighbor, one Thomas Moore. In his "Confessions," he speaks of having revelations from Heaven, and is quoted as saying, "these confirmed me in the impression that I was ordained for some great purpose in the hands of the Almighty." Speaking further to Gray of the influence he realized that he had obtained over the minds of his fellows in bondage, he said, "I now began to prepare them for my purpose, by telling them that something was about to happen that would terminate in fulfilling the great promise that had been made to me." But he makes it clear that at this point he himself was not aware of the nature of his mission.

Finally, according to his account, he had a vision on May 12, 1828, in which he "heard a loud noise in the heavens, and the Spirit instantly appeared to me and said . . . the time was fast approaching when the first should be last and the last should be first." In the same vision he was told that "until the first sign appeared, I should conceal it from the knowledge of men."

In the meantime, the ordinary round of life went on in Southampton County. Nat Turner's third owner, Thomas Moore, died in 1828 and his nominal ownership passed to Moore's 9-year-old son, Putnam. Within two years the Widow Moore married a local wheelwright, Joseph Travis, who moved into her house and set up his business on the place.

On February 12, 1831, there occurred an eclipse of the sun, and this came to Nat Turner as the sign he had been awaiting. In his words, "the seal was removed from my lips, and I communicated the great work laid out for me to do, to four in whom I had the greatest confidence, (Henry, Hark, Nelson and Sam)." Slaves, of course, had no patronymic. Because many shared the same given name, they generally used the last name of their owner, and when they changed owners, they usually changed names. Hark (who had also belonged to Thomas Moore) subsequently was spoken of as Hark Travis. Yet Nat Turner seemed always to remain Nat Turner. Also, in the trials that eventually ensued, the arraignment usually read "Hark, or Sam, or Jack, a man slave belonging to" so and so. Nat Turner was arraigned as "Nat, alias Nat Turner." He was even mentioned in one news story in a Richmond paper (and not in a facetious manner) as "Mr. Turner."

The first date chosen for the beginning of his "mission of work" was July 4, 1831, but he tells in his "Confessions" that this date had to be abandoned because "I fell sick." Then on August 13 there occurred a day-long atmospheric phenomenon, during which the sun was seen but faintly and appeared to be of a greenish hue. This occurrence, which caused wide-spread consternation in many places in the eastern United States, was accepted by Nat Turner as a direct communication from God. After alerting those whom he had originally chosen as his primary lieutenants, and recruiting two more, he arranged a meeting for Sunday, August 21, deep in the woods near the Travis homestead at a place called Cabin Pond.

The followers met first and roasted a pig and drank brandy. Later in the day Nat Turner appeared and explained the nature of his mission. It is significant that he is also quoted in the "Confessions" as saying, "we expected . . . to concert a plan, as we had not yet determined on any." This, and the fact that no physical preparations, such as the prior secreting of weapons or supplies had been undertaken, gives the impression that Turner saw himself purely as an instrument acting for a higher power which would provide all that was necessary when the time came.

The gist of the plan which emerged was nothing less than the destruction of every white person within reach; again in the words of the "Confession," "we should commence at home (Mr. J. Travis') on that night, and until we had armed and equipped ourselves, and gathered sufficient force, neither age nor sex was to be spared. . . ."

Beginning at about 2 o'clock on the morning of Monday, August 22, the plan became reality. Leaving the site of the meeting, the group made its silent way through the woods to the Travis farm. Nat Turner ascended to a second-story window by means of a ladder, opened the door to the others, and they quickly disposed of Mr. and Mrs. Travis, their young child, Nat Turner's legal master, Putnam Moore, and a young apprentice, Joel Westbrook. Thus began the gory crusade, which was to lead in a long, S-shaped path toward the county seat. Having dispatched their first victims with axes and hatchets, they acquired weapons and horses as they went. By dawn, they had visited half a dozen homes and had killed more than twenty men, women, and children. Mounted now, they moved swiftly from house to house, gaining recruits as they went. But, probably to their surprise, many slaves on neighboring places either had to be

forced at gun-point to join them, and subsequently had to be guarded almost as hostages, or escaped and gave the alarm. When shortly after daybreak they began to find homes deserted, they realized that a warning had been spread.

The bloody details of the slayings which took approximately sixty lives were described at length in the Richmond and Norfolk newspapers in the days that followed. The stories appear to agree on several aspects which surprised the surviving white community; insofar as was ever known, no female victim was sexually molested, no wanton torture was inflicted, no buildings were burned, and—except for horses and weapons—relatively little in the way of personal property was taken.

At about 9 o'clock they arrived at the home of Captain Thomas Barrow, a veteran of the War of 1812. Disdaining to flee, the Captain held off the entire band long enough to permit his wife to escape. According to a local legend, Captain Barrow's determined resistance so impressed his slayers that, having finally killed him by cutting his throat, they wrapped the body in a quilt and placed a plug of tobacco on his chest.

From the gateway of his farm, Barrow had built a road eastward for about five miles to a junction with the highway that ran south from Jerusalem to the North Carolina line. Still known locally as Barrow Road (and officially as County Highway 658), this was one of the few real roads in the county. Nat Turner and his men now followed it eastward, sowing death as they went. They probably numbered between forty and fifty at their peak, and all were mounted. If there is a monument to the Southampton Revolt, it is the Barrow Road itself.

Apples were a principal product of the county, and almost every homestead had its own still where brandy was made. As the day wore on, this potent spirit took its toll of some, but it seemed not to affect the determination of the eight or ten leaders who were responsible for most of the killing. One of the recruits who had joined while still at the Cabin Pond, Will, appears to have been the principal executioner.

Most of his victims were decapitated by a razor-sharp axe. Strangely, according to Nat Turner's subsequent "Confessions," he dealt the death blow only once, and that to the young daughter of a Travis neighbor, Margaret Whitehead.

At Levi Waller's, the master of the house saw the band approaching and was able to conceal himself in a nearby field from which he watched the murder of his wife, his children, and a number of other children who attended a school at his homeplace. In all, eleven died at that one home, and their bodies were heaped in one room together. Levi Waller survived to appear as a witness at Nat Turner's trial. At William Williams' after killing the man of the house and his two children, the band caught Mrs. Williams and forced her to lie beside her dead husband, and then shot her. At Jacob Williams' house one of the original group, Nelson, was cheated of his intent to destroy his master, who was away from home, but Mrs. Williams, their two children, the wife of their overseer, Mrs. Caswell Worrell, and her child, as well as a visitor, Edwin Drewry, were left dead.

The final home visited, just about noontime, was that of Mrs. Rebecca Vaughan. Pleading vainly for her life, she was quickly dispatched, as were her niece, Eliza, her young son, Arthur, and their overseer. Although she did not know it, her older son, George, had fallen victim to the band when they encountered him earlier on the road leading to the Thomas Barrow homestead.

The Vaughan house lay close to the junction of the Barrow Road with the highway leading to the county seat, and again, in the words of Nat Turner's "Confessions," we learn that "here I determined on starting for Jerusalem." Presumably his goal was the local armory where weapons, powder, and shot were stored in abundance. In the aftermath, it was frequently speculated that Nat Turner intended to lead his band into the almost impenetrable fastness of the Dismal Swamp, some thirty miles distant; but this is never stated in his "Confessions."

Turning northeast at the crossroads, they rode toward Jerusalem. About half a mile from the junction lay the entrance to James Parker's farm. Some of the participants had friends here, who they thought would join them, and they probably also thought that weapons, and possibly additional brandy, could be obtained there. Apparently against his better judgment, Nat Turner had the party divide, some going toward the Parker house, from which the family had fled, while a small group including Turner himself stayed at the entrance to the farm.

Suddenly a detachment of militia rode into view. They had been tardily assembled when the alarm reached Jerusalem, and here, in Parker's cornfield, the first armed confrontation took place between the slaves in revolt and their embattled masters. Apparently there were no fatalities on either side, and after an exchange of shots, and a few wounds being inflicted, they broke off contact. But Nat Turner realized that the road to Jerusalem was effectively barred. His force was thrown into confusion by the encounter, was reduced in numbers, and now was much harder to manage. He resolved to try a crossing of the Nottaway River, which lay between him and the town, at a point to the east, Cypress Bridge, but a quick reconnaissance showed it to be well guarded.

Gathering the remnants of his force he turned south, seeking recruits. Discouraged by the obvious evidence that the countryside was now alarmed, he turned north again, crossed the path he had followed earlier, and holed up for the night, with a force of forty or fewer, near the Ridley plantation. During the night a false alarm scared off more than half of his remaining followers.

At dawn on Tuesday, August 23, the last blow of the revolt was struck. Probably believing that the residents had already fled "Belmont," the home of Dr. Simon Blunt, the band entered the lane leading from the main road. Close to the house they were met with withering fire from the doctor, his son, the overseer, and three white neighbors, who, rather than fleeing, had barricaded themselves in the house. At least one of Turner's men fell dead, and several including his principal lieutenant, Hark, were wounded. Blunt's own slaves, having hidden in an outbuilding, now rallied to the defense of their master and aided in the capture of the wounded and the unhorsed. Nat Turner escaped with a handful of the faithful.

Deciding to return to the vicinity of their starting point, they were met by militia along the Barrow Road. One or more were killed and by late afternoon, Nat Turner found himself alone, a fugitive pursued not only by the aroused citizenry of the county but by a horde of vigilantes from adjoining Virginia and North Carolina counties and by various military forces which had begun to arrive in response to appeals for help.

On Monday, when word of the trouble in the southwestern part of the county reached Jerusalem, the postmaster, James Trezevant, sent a letter by express rider to the mayor of Petersburg, some fifty miles away. This was relayed to Governor John Floyd in Richmond, who received it in the early morning hours of Tuesday, the 24th. He quickly ordered armed militia units to the scene, and arranged for weapons and supplies to be sent as rapidly as possible. Floyd, a veteran of the War of 1812 and a brigadier general in the militia, immediately considered the possibility that what was happening in Southampton could be the prelude to a general slave uprising. For this reason, together with others related to the prestige of the State, he refrained from asking for help from the Federal forces stationed at Fort Monroe, just across Hampton Roads from Norfolk.

However, word of what was happening had reached Norfolk by means of the regular stagecoach, and the mayor, backed by the city council, decided to call for Federal help. No possibility existed for communication with the state authorities in Richmond, so very soon a request had gone to Colonel House at Fort Monroe, to the commander of the United States Naval yard, and to two ships of war lying in the Roads. Within a matter of hours, a joint force of regular army troops, marines, and sailors was alerted

■ ■ *The use of bloodhounds for tracking runaway slaves was a common practice in states where slaves were numerous. Louisiana permitted anyone to shoot a fugitive slave who would not stop when ordered.*

and on their way to Southampton. As it turned out, the revolt was quelled before any of the Federal forces could participate and most were turned around and returned to their stations without reaching the site of the action. Governor Floyd, eventually learning of the precipitate action by Norfolk's mayor, was furious. He felt that the psychological impression which the call-out had created was bad. He also pointed out that, had the uprising been of a general character, drawing off the available Federal force from Fort Monroe would have left the area on the north bank of the James River, including numerous plantations and settlements where the blacks outnumbered the whites, entirely without possibility of reinforcement.

But the lot of the innocent blacks in Southampton County itself might have been better if Federal forces had taken charge. As it was, once the scare was over and the true nature of the threat ascertained, the life of every black person in the county was threatened. The spirit of revenge and retaliation ran wild. The editor of one Richmond newspaper, who went as a member of a militia troop of cavalry to the scene wrote:

It is with pain we speak of another feature of the Southampton Rebellion; for we have been most unwilling to have our sympathies for the sufferers diminished or affected by their misconduct. We allude to the slaughter of many blacks, without trial, and under circumstances of great barbarity.

The militia commander placed in charge by Governor Floyd, Brigadier General Richard Eppes, finally found it necessary to threaten to invoke the Articles of War to halt the indiscriminate slaughter.

Most of those involved were either killed or rounded up. In the meantime, the fear of an uprising had spread to neighboring counties in Virginia and North Carolina. It is impossible to estimate how many innocent blacks paid with their lives for no more than the merest suspicion. For example, a group of citizens from Sampson County in North Carolina, wrote to the governor to report that they had "ten or fifteen Negroes in Jail," and in passing noted that "the people of Duplin County have examined ten or fifteen Negroes, and found two guilty, and have put them to death." It was not even suggested that any of those jailed or executed were known to have participated in any type of threatening action.

Trials began in the Southampton Court of Oyer and Terminer on August 31 and continued into November. During this period more than twenty slaves, including one woman and three boys of less than fifteen years, were convicted and sentenced to death. Some of the sentences were subsequently reduced by the governor to transportation out of the state. All of those who

had been part of Nat Turner's original band were either killed in the aftermath of the revolt, or were subsequently executed. Estimates of the number who were killed without trial run to more than one hundred. In many instances, the only witnesses for the prosecution were fellow-slaves of the accused, some of whom were subsequently to go to the gallows.

Through all this, the question remained, "What had become of Nat Turner?" Despite search by several thousand militiamen, augmented by volunteer vigilantes from all over the area, the leader eluded capture. There were almost daily reports that he had been sighted; by one mail, the governor was informed that he had been taken prisoner in Washington; a few days later he was reported to have drowned while trying to escape capture in the western part of the state. On September 14, Floyd proclaimed a reward of $500 for his capture, and persons in the area increased this by another $600. Yet all this time "General Nat," as the papers frequently called him, was hiding no more than a mile from the place of original assembly at Cabin Pond. Having secured a small stock of food, he scratched a tiny "cave" under a pile of fence rails where he remained concealed for more than four weeks. Later, after two frightened slaves had stumbled onto this hiding place, he concealed himself in a haystack and then moved to the shelter of a hole beneath the branches of a fallen pine tree.

Finally, on October 30, when most of his companions had already been executed or shipped out of the state, he was discovered by a local white man, Benjamin Phipps. Armed only with a small sword, he surrendered and was turned over to the Southampton County jailor the next day. It was while awaiting trial that he agreed to talk with Thomas R. Gray. These "Confessions," which Gray is supposed to have taken down verbatim, were recorded on the 1st, 2d, and 3d of November. Gray is frequently referred to as Nat Turner's counsel at his trial, which took place on November 5. Actually he had no official connection with the case. It seems more likely that, as a local lawyer who had served as court-appointed counsel for some of those tried earlier, and who was familiar with all that had happened, he saw the considerable commercial possibilities in converting Nat Turner's story into a pamphlet. This is what he did, and very speedily. The twenty-three page document, authenticated by a certificate of the justices of the court, and containing lists of the white people who had been killed and all of the persons tried up to that time, was copyrighted by Gray in Washington on November 10, just one day before Nat Turner was, according to the sentence of the court, "taken by the Sheriff to the usual place of execution, and there . . . hanged by the neck until he be dead."

About ten days later the pamphlet was published in Baltimore, and the accuracy of Gray's estimate of public interest in the matter can be gauged by the fact that several other editions were subsequently printed, and it is said to have sold more than 40,000 copies. Yet today copies of the original pamphlet are very rare. A Norfolk newspaper wrote that a "portrait painter" of that town had made a likeness of Nat Turner while in jail. Pictures purporting to depict Nat Turner have been published, but it has never been established that any of these were drawn from life.

Governor Floyd was convinced, despite the lack of any real evidence, that the revolt was part of a larger plot which extended to many areas of the South. He also felt that the relative freedom which had been accorded black preachers as well as such abolitionist writings as Garrison's *Liberator* and Walker's *Appeal* had been part of the root cause. A resident of western Virginia, he favored the abolition of slavery, provided it was coupled with a removal of all black people from the state. His sentiments were not so much an expression of humanitarian feelings, as they were a conviction that Virginia could make no real economic progress while burdened with "the peculiar institution."

From letters to the newspapers during the fall of 1831, it can be readily seen that Floyd's views were widely shared. During November he wrote in his diary, "Before I leave this Government, I will have contrived to have a law passed gradually abolishing slavery in the State. . . ." Yet the message which he sent to the newly assembled legislature on December 6 contained no such proposal. Instead, after a lengthy review of the revolt and an analysis of what he believed to be its causes, he proposed the enactment of extremely stern laws which would apply to all of the state's black people, slave and free alike.

Between December 1831 and February 1832, the whole question of slavery was hotly debated by the legislature, and a resolution supporting emancipation failed by a very narrow margin. This debate, which engaged some of the best minds of the state, and which attracted wide attention, has been called the last free and uninhibited discussion of the question of slavery in any Southern legislative body. But once the vote was taken, those who had favored emancipation seemed to fade away. Floyd's biographer, Charles Ambler, explains the Governor's attitude in this way:

Absorbed as he was in national affairs, Floyd was perfectly willing to turn the whole subject of the state's proper policy regarding negro slavery over to the solution of a master who was at hand in the person of Thomas R. Dew of William and Mary College. . . . The able defense and justification of the institution of negro slavery which followed was accepted by Floyd and most other Virginians of whatever section as final.

In the end we are left with the question of the net effect of Nat Turner's actions on the institution of slavery itself. Did it hasten or retard the thrust toward emancipation? Herbert Aptheker, one of those who has written much on the subject concludes that "The Turner Revolt may be summed up by the one word accelerator." Probably the best assessment is that of John W. Cromwell, a black historian and lawyer, who saw the final results in this fashion:

Whether Nat Turner hastened or postponed the day of the abolition of slavery . . . is a question that admits of little or much discussion in accordance with opinions concerning the law of necessity and free will in national life. Considered in the light of its immediate effects upon its participants, it was a failure, an egregious failure, a wanton crime. Considered in its relation to slavery and as contributory to making it a national issue by deepening and stirring of the then weak local forces, that finally led to the Emancipation Proclamation and the Thirteenth Amendment, the insurrection was a moral success and Nat Turner deserves to be ranked with the great reformers of his day.

■ ■ ■

STUDY QUESTIONS

1. Nat Turner was not a "typical" Virginia slave. In what ways was he different?

2. In what ways was the black population of Southampton County unique? How might those unique demographic circumstances have contributed to white and black attitudes about slavery there?

3. In your opinion, was Nat Turner "crazy"? Explain your answer.

4. What was the white reaction to the slave uprising? How did the uprising affect the lives of the rest of the blacks—slave and free—in Southampton County?

5. Why did the slave uprising create an intense debate in Virginia about freeing all of the slaves? Why, in your opinion, did that emancipation movement fail?

BIBLIOGRAPHY

William Styron's *The Confessions of Nat Turner* (1968), a novel based on Turner's confession to Thomas Gray, remains a highly readable, if controversial, account of the 1831 rebellion. Herbert Aptheker's *American Negro Slave Revolts* (1943) provides a list of the antebellum slave revolts, but it is flawed by a highly polemical style. For more sophisticated accounts of slave resistance to bondage, see Gerald Mullin, *Flight and Rebellion: Slave Resistance in Eighteenth Century Virginia* (1972) and Kenneth M. Stampp, *The Peculiar Institution: Slavery in the Antebellum South* (1956). The best book on free blacks in the antebellum South is Ira Berlin, *Slaves Without Masters: The Free Negro in the Antebellum South* (1975). For outstanding descriptions of slave life and culture, see George Rawick, *From Sundown to Sunup: The Making of the Slave Community* (1972); John Blassingame, *The Slave Community: Plantation Life in the Antebellum South* (1972); and Lawrence W. Levine, *Black Culture and Black Consciousness: Afro-American Folk Thought from Slavery to Freedom* (1977).

JOHN BROWN AND THE PARADOX OF LEADERSHIP AMONG AMERICAN NEGROES

David Potter

John Brown was a man given to excess. He fathered twenty children, and in thirty-five years he engaged in more than twenty different businesses. When he was fifty-five, he radically changed professions. He became, in his mind and the minds of his devoted followers, a visionary and a modern-day prophet. His crusade and reason for living was the abolition of slavery. An utterly fearless man of action, he left talking to others and took matters into his own hands. On the night of May 24, 1856, John Brown, four of his sons, a son-in-law, and two other men left their bloodly imprint on history. At Pottawatomie Creek in Kansas, they murdered and mutilated five proslavery settlers. The action, Brown said, had been ''decreed by Almighty God, ordained from Eternity.''

In October 1859, Brown and a larger group of followers made a more daring raid. They were determined to capture the federal arsenal at Harpers Ferry, Virginia, and from there, to move South and liberate the slaves. The action failed and Brown was captured, tried, and executed. But his legacy lives on. As historian David Potter demonstrates in the following essay, Brown's raid on Harpers Ferry illustrated how far the North and South had grown apart and how much northern as well as southern whites were alienated from black people. In the North, the dead Brown became a sainted martyr. In the South he became a symbol of bloodthirsty northern aggression. Late in the 1850s, the two sections were speaking different languages as they marched toward civil war.

One of the anomalies in the history of American Negroes is that, as a group, they have had only very limited opportunity to choose their own leadership. Historians agree, more or less, on a selected list of men who have been Negro leaders—Frederick Douglass, Booker T. Washington, W. E. B. Du Bois, Marcus Garvey, Martin Luther King. Of course, there have also been other very distinguished figures—Thurgood Marshall, Ralph Ellison, James Baldwin, Walter White, Roy Wilkins, *et al.*, but they have not commanded large mass followings; and there have been still others like Elijah Muhammad, Malcolm X, and Stokeley Carmichael whose role is or was controversial even within the Negro community. But none of these men was ever chosen to leadership by an election in which the body of American Negroes voted for what might be called "the Negroes' choice." Despite the widespread growth of organized groups of Negro activists in recent years, there has never been an organization which we can designate with assurance as expressing the attitudes of the rank and file of American Negroes, unless it was Marcus Garvey's Universal Negro Improvement Association. Most of the others have appealed either to the middle class, as the NAACP has done, or to ideological radicals, and not to the run-of-the-mill American Negro.

This absence of an organizational basis for the selection of leaders has meant that the positions of leadership were gained in special ways, sometimes in arbitrary or, as it were, fictitious ways. For instance, Frederick Douglass received his license as spokesman for four million slaves from a small coterie of abolitionists who later quarrelled with him. True, he was an excellent choice and he proved a very able leader indeed—perhaps as able as any American Negro—but the choice was nevertheless a historical accident, as the choice of many excellent leaders has been.

Booker T. Washington, also an able man, did not owe his eminence to the recognition that Negroes gave him, but was appointed to the political leadership of American Negroes by Theodore Roosevelt, and to the economic leadership by Andrew Carnegie. W. E. B. Du Bois received his investiture in an especially ironical way—the anomaly of which he felt as keenly as anyone else. He was made the key figure in the NAACP by a wealthy, highly respectable, and I think one can say smug, self-appointed committee of upper-class white moderate reformers; later, he owed his more or less posthumous canonization to academic Marxist intellectuals whom most Negroes had never heard of. Today some of the militant types whose names flash like meteors across the headlines—Carmichael, Rap Brown, LeRoi Jones—have been fobbed off on American Negroes partly by social revolutionaries who care nothing for civil rights or Negro welfare within our existing society, and partly by the mass media which need sensational and extravagant material to galvanize the attention of a jaded public. If one looks for Negroes who owed their positions of leadership primarily to the support accorded them by other Negroes, the most authentic names are those of Marcus Garvey and Martin Luther King, and perhaps Roy Wilkins, despite the attacks which he has sustained from the left. At a more limited level, I think one should add Elijah Muhammad and Malcolm X.

These comments may seem extraneous indeed to a consideration of the career of John Brown, but indirectly they may have a certain pertinence because though Brown was not a Negro, he probably went farther in plans for launching a Negro revolution in the United States than anyone in history. He intended to become the commander-in-chief of an army of Negroes. Yet he had no Negro lieutenants; he took almost no advice from Negroes and acted in defiance of such advice as he did take; and most paradoxical of all, he completely concealed his intended insurrection from the Negroes who were expected to support it. His was the classic case of a man who acted in the name of American Negroes and relied upon them to follow him, but never really sought to represent them or to find out what they wanted their leader to do.

Historians of the antislavery movement have already complained, with considerable justice I think, that the Negro was neglected even by the abolitionists. Many abolitionists could not see the Negroes, as it were, for the slaves. Thus even the underground railroad became, historiographically, the first Jim Crow transportation in America. Traditional accounts pictured the railroad as an operation in which heroic white conductors braved dangers unspeakable in transporting fugitives from one hideout to the next, while the helpless and passive Negroes lay inert in the bottom of the wagon bed, concealed under a layer of hay. We now know that a good many respectable Yankee families who had never worked on the railroad later decided that they had intended to, or they would have if there had been a fugitive handy, and gradually translated this sentimental ex post facto intention into the legend of a fearless deed. But that is beside the point. What is relevant to the theme of this paper is that historically there was an anomalous relationship between the Negro slaves and their white sympathizers, and the paradox of this relationship shows up in its most striking form in the story of John Brown and Harpers Ferry. The paradox lay in the fact that the white abolitionists believed that the Negroes were all on the brink of a massive insurrection, yet they seldom consulted any Negro for corroboration and they conducted their own abolitionist activities—even John Brown's insurrectionary activities—as if Negroes could be regarded abstractly, like some sort of chemical element which at a certain heat would fuse into a new compound, and not concretely as a plurality of diverse men and women, each one with a temperament and aspirations of his own.

What were John Brown's specific relations with Negroes? It cannot be said that Negroes were entirely an abstraction to him, as they have been to some civil rights enthusiasts, for he knew Negroes, worked with them, and included them,

on terms of seeming familiarity, in the intimacy of his little band of followers. But let us examine the record in more detail.

John Brown was apparently reared from an early age to hate slavery. The details may have been overdramatized, as they have been in the story of the early life of Lincoln, but the fact appears clear. As early as the 1830's, he assisted in the escape of at least one fugitive; he made plans to rear a Negro child with his own children in his home; and he also thought of conducting a school for Negroes. His systematic activity in behalf of Negroes and his actual association with Negroes, however, began in the late 1840's when he agreed to move to North Elba, New York, where Gerrit Smith proposed to make him responsible for a colony of Negroes for which Smith was prepared to give 120,000 acres. At North Elba, Brown tried to help the Negro settlers, including at least one known fugitive. He gave them advice about farming and took some into his home, where they worked and shared the Spartan life of his family. But the North Elba project failed, primarily because the region never has been good farm country; it was frigid and rigorous in a way that made adaptation by Southern Negroes especially difficult. Moreover, Brown's own financial difficulties in the wool business made it impossible for him to stay at North Elba on a regular basis, and compelled him to spend much of his time at Springfield, Massachusetts, instead. At Springfield in 1847, he invited Frederick Douglass to visit him, and there he revealed to Douglass the first version of the plan which ultimately took him to Harpers Ferry. This was a scheme to organize a band of about twenty-five men, who would operate from hideouts in the Southern Appalachians. These men would induce slaves to run away and would assist them in their escape. Douglass had been a fugitive slave himself, had lived among slaves, had known the South at first hand; but there is no evidence that Brown asked him for his opinion about the practicability of the plan or about any aspect of the operations. Douglass probably knew a great deal that might have been useful to Brown, but Brown took no advantage of this potential information. This was characteristic of him throughout his life.

By the time of the enactment of the Fugitive Slave Act in 1850, Brown was in Springfield most of the time. In response to the act, he organized a League of Gileadites, as he called it, to offer physical resistance to the enforcement of the act. He drew up an "Agreement" and nine resolutions for the League, with an emphasis upon encouraging Negroes to be brave and not to resort to halfway measures: "When engaged, do not do your work by halves, but make clean work with your enemies and be sure you meddle not with any others. . . . All traitors must die, whenever caught and proven to be guilty." Brown wrote to his wife in November, 1850: "I, of course, keep encouraging my colored friends to 'trust in God and keep their powder dry.' I did so today at a Thanksgiving meeting, publicly." Forty-four black men and women of Springfield signed Brown's agreement, but their commitment was never put to the test, for no efforts were made by Federal officials to arrest fugitives in the Springfield area. Still, the League is of great interest, for it was the only case in which this man—who gave so much of his energy while living and finally his life itself to the Negro cause—relied primarily upon Negroes in his work.

As the focus of the slavery controversy shifted to Kansas, Brown shifted his activities to that arena, and the plans which he had revealed to Douglass fell into abeyance. But ultimately it was the Kansas diversion which led him back to the Virginia project. Kansas fed his impulse toward violence, his appetite for leadership, and his hatred of slavery. It also unfitted him for his former prosaic pursuits in the wool trade. If Kansas had continued as a scene of violence, he might have ended his career as a Jayhawker on the Kansas prairies, but by 1857 Kansas was becoming pacified. Robert J. Walker had replaced Geary as governor and was giving the Free-Soilers fair treatment; the Free-Soilers had won control of the legislature when Walker

threw out fraudulent proslavery votes. The antislavery party had nothing whatever to gain by a resumption of the border wars. They remembered, unpleasantly, the murders committed by Brown along Pottawatomie Creek (something which Easterners did not know about), and they regarded Brown as a troublemaker—triggerhappy and too much of a lone wolf. Brown began to perceive that his career as a Kansas guerrilla was played out, and though he still talked about organizing a crack military unit for Kansas, his thoughts were turning increasingly toward the old idea of some kind of operation in the Southern Appalachians.

Brown left Kansas twice, first in October, 1856, with a divided mind as to whether he ought to return and continue active in the border wars; and again in November, 1857, knowing that his path would lead to Virginia. It is significant that, on both occasions, he stopped off at Rochester to see Douglass (in December, 1856, and in January, 1858). What meaning the visit in 1856 may have had, no one now can tell; at least it showed, as Douglass testifies, that the relationship formed nine years previously had been kept very much alive. But the visit in 1858 lasted for three weeks, and during this time Brown unfolded in full, perhaps for the first time, his second version of a plan for operation in Virginia. Douglass did not, at that time, disassociate himself from the plan, and indeed he later helped Brown to raise funds among well-to-do Negroes. But having been both a slave and a fugitive, Douglass perceived defects in the realism of Brown's plan, and he warned Brown of the pitfalls which were involved. John Brown did with this advice what he always did with all advice—he ignored it.

An interval of twenty months was to elapse between these conferences with Douglass and the final action at Harpers Ferry. This represented a delay of over a year in Brown's original plans. The delay resulted from two things: first, lack of money; and second, the fact that a soldier of fortune named Hugh Forbes, whom Brown had taken on as a military adviser, became disaffected because he did not receive the pay which he thought he had been promised, broke confidence, and revealed much of the plot to Senators Henry Wilson and William H. Seward. This breakdown in security greatly alarmed Brown's financial supporters, who virtually ordered him to suspend his plans.

Thus, during most of 1858 and 1859, Brown, who wanted only to smite the slaveholders, discovered that he had to be a salesman and a fund-raiser first. So long as he was soliciting for funds for aid to Free-Soilers in Kansas, he was able to make public appeals. But as his insurrectionary scheme developed, it required the utmost secrecy, and he could appeal only to trusted sympathizers including principally the Secret Six— Gerrit Smith in Peterboro, New York, and five backers in Boston: George L. Stearns, Franklin B. Sanborn, Thomas Wentworth Higginson, Theodore Parker, and Samuel Gridley Howe. These men had been moderately generous since 1857, but they tended to want more action before they gave additional money, and Brown wanted additional money as a preliminary to the action. Often he was actually reduced to asking for handouts, and he never did obtain anything approaching the financial support which was needed for an operation on the scale which he projected.

Somehow, nevertheless, he weathered all these difficulties. Meanwhile, he had been looking to a means of formalizing his plans and raising recruits; and to this end he had made a curious pilgrimage with twelve of his followers, all of them white men except Richard Richardson, to Chatham, Ontario, in May, 1858. Ontario at that time had a population of upwards of thirty thousand Negroes, a vast proportion of whom were former slaves who might be expected to support a campaign against slavery in the South. Among these people, Brown had determined to make his appeal, to relax secrecy, and to seek the sanction and support of the Negro community for his daring plan. He had invited Gerrit Smith, Wendell Phillips, "and others of like kin" to be on hand.

Accordingly, on May 8, 1858, Brown presented to a secret "convention" at Chatham, consisting of twelve of his own followers and thirty-four resident Negroes, a plan of organization entitled "A Provisional Constitution and Ordinances for the people of the United States." This document condemned slavery, defined slavery as war, thus asserting for the slaves a legal status as belligerents, and provided for a provisional government, with a commander-in-chief of the army, an executive, a legislature, and a judiciary. This government was to act against slavery— indeed, to make war against it—and in explaining it Brown stated where the army would get its troops. "Upon the first intimation of a plan formed for the liberation of the slaves," he said, "they would immediately rise all over the Southern states." By "flocking to his standard" they would enable him to extend his operations outward and southward from the mountain country in which he would begin, until he could operate upon the plantations of the lower South. They could defeat any militia, or even Federal troops sent against them, and "then organize the freed blacks under this provisional Constitution." What John Brown was planning was not a raid but a revolution.

The convention politely voted for the proposed Constitution, and on the next day it elected John Brown commander-in-chief and members of his party Secretaries of State, of the Treasury, and of War. Two men were elected as members of Congress, and one of these, Osborn P. Anderson, was an Ontario Negro. All the others were whites.

But Gerrit Smith was not there; Frederick Douglass was not there; and Wendell Phillips was not there. And when John Brown left Ontario, only two new Negro recruits went with him, one of whom, fearing arrest, soon returned to Canada. This was the only real effort Brown ever made to organize Negro support, and it had failed completely. It indicated clearly that the most famous project for a Negro insurrection in the history of the United States did not have the full support of even a corporal's guard of

Negroes. There must have been hundreds of Negroes in Ontario who heard all about Brown's "secret" plan, but they had learned in a realistic school, and far more shrewdly than Emerson and Thoreau, and the litterateurs of Boston, they recognized that there was something unrealistic about this man. What was wrong was that he was recruiting members of a supporting cast for a theatrical melodrama in which the protagonist and principal actor was to be John Brown.

Only a month after the Chatham "convention" Brown sent one of his very earliest recruits, John E. Cook, to Harpers Ferry, Virginia, to live as a spy and to reconnoiter the environs. Cook found employment as a lock-tender on the canal and maintained his mission for over a year, but Brown was very apprehensive that he would talk too much, and this apprehension must have increased greatly when Cook married a local Harpers Ferry girl.

Fourteen months after the Chatham convention, Brown and a small band of followers began to converge on a farmhouse in Maryland which was to be their rendezvous. At first there were twenty of them, including sixteen whites and four Negroes—two of whom were born free and two of whom had run away from slavery. After they had gathered, Frederick Douglass came down to Chambersburg, Maryland, with a friend of his, Shields Green, who was, like himself, an escaped slave. Brown and Douglass had a final conference, which must have been a strained affair on both sides. Brown now revealed a new and even more alarming design—his purpose to seize the arsenal at Harpers Ferry. To this Douglass instantly took exception. He warned Brown that the position would be a trap from which escape would be impossible, and also that an attack on Federal property would turn the whole country against Brown's plans. He said that this was such a complete change of purpose that he would no longer participate. Brown urged him not to withdraw, saying, "I want you for a special purpose. When I strike, the bees will begin to swarm, and I shall want you to help me hive them." But Douglass still refused, and turning to

his friend he asked what Green intended to do. Green's reply was, "I b'lieve I'll go wid de ole man."

Green was later accused of lack of courage, but there was in fact something supremely heroic about his action. His remark showed little confidence in Brown's plan but much loyalty to Brown personally; and he later died on the gallows because he had subordinated his judgment to his sense of personal devotion.

On the evening of October 16, 1859, after waiting three months for additional men, money, and munitions, most of which never arrived, John Brown marched with nineteen of his band, now grown to twenty-two, down to Harpers Ferry. There he seized the Potomac River bridge, the Shenandoah River bridge, and the Federal armory and rifle works. He also sent out a detail to bring in two of the slaveholders of the neighborhood with their slaves. This mission was accomplished. Then he settled into the arsenal and waited, while first the local militia and later a small Federal force gathered to besiege him. Within thirty-six hours, his hopes were blasted and his force was destroyed—five men had escaped, but ten were dead or dying, and seven were in prison, all to die at the end of a rope.

Technically, Brown's operation had been such an unmitigated disaster that it has lent color to the belief that he was insane. Certain aspects were indeed incongruous. After making melodramatic gestures in the direction of secrecy, he had left behind him on the Maryland farm a large accumulation of letters which revealed all his plans and exposed all his secret supporters among the elite of Boston. As Hugh Forbes wrote, "the most terrible engine of destruction which he [Brown] would carry with him in his campaign would be a carpet-bag loaded with 400 letters, to be turned against his friends, of whom the journals assert that more than forty-seven are already compromised." After three and a half months of preparation, he marched at last without taking with him food for his soldiers' next meal, so that, the following morning, the Commander-in-Chief of the Provisional

Army of the North, in default of commissary, was obliged to order forty-five breakfasts sent over from the Wagner House. For the remaining twenty-five hours, the suffering of Brown's besieged men was accentuated by the fact that they were acutely and needlessly hungry. His liaison with allies in the North was so faulty that they did not know when he would strike, and John Brown, Jr., who was supposed to forward additional recruits, later stated that the raid took him completely by surprise. If this was, as is sometimes suggested, because of the disordered condition of young Brown's mind rather than because of lack of information from his father, it still leaves a question why such a vital duty should have been entrusted to one whose mental instability had been conspicuous ever since Pottawatomie. Finally, there was the seemingly incredible folly of seizing a Federal arsenal and starting a war against the state of Virginia with an army of twenty-two men. This latter folly was probably the strongest factor in the later contention that he was insane. In layman's terms, anybody who tried to conquer a state as large as one of the nations of Western Europe with less than two dozen troops might be regarded as crazy. Was John Brown crazy in these terms?

Without trying to resolve the insanity question, to which C. Vann Woodward, Allan Nevins, and others have given extensive attention, let me just make two brief comments: first, that insanity is a clear-cut legal concept concerning a psychological condition which is seldom clear-cut; second, that the insanity concept has been invoked too much by people whose ulterior purposes were too palpable—first by people who hoped to save Brown's life by proving him irresponsible; then by Republicans who wanted to disclaim his act without condemning him morally; and finally by adverse historians who wanted to discredit his deeds by saying that only a madman would do such things. The evidence shows that Brown was very intense and aloof, that he became exclusively preoccupied with his one grand design, that he sometimes behaved in a very confused way, that he alternated between brief periods of decisive action and long intervals when it is hard to tell what he was doing, that mental instability occurred with significant frequency in his family, and that some who knew him believed he had a vindictive or even a homicidal streak with strong fantasies of superhuman greatness. Also, Pottawatomie should be borne in mind. From all this, one may clearly infer that Brown was not, as we would now term it, a well-adjusted man.

But withal, the heaviest count in the argument against Brown's sanity is the seeming irrationality of the Harpers Ferry operation. Yet Harpers Ferry, it might be argued, was irrational if, and only if, the belief in a vast, self-starting slave insurrection was a delusion. But if this was a fantasy, it was one which Brown shared with Theodore Parker, Samuel Gridley Howe, Thomas Wentworth Higginson, and a great many others who have never been called insane. It was an article of faith among the abolitionists that the slaves of the South were seething with discontent and awaited only a signal to throw off their chains. It would have been heresy for an orthodox abolitionist to doubt this, quite as disloyal as for him to entertain the idea that any slave owner might be a well-intentioned and conscientious man. Gerrit Smith believed it, and two months before Brown's attempted coup he wrote, "The feeling among the blacks that they must deliver themselves gains strength with fearful rapidity." Samuel Gridley Howe believed it, and even after Brown's failure and when war came, he wrote that twenty to forty thousand volunteers could "plough through the South and be followed by a blaze of servile war that would utterly and forever root out slaveholding and slavery." Theodore Parker believed it, and wrote in 1850, "God forgive us our cowardice, if we let it come to this, that three millions of human beings . . . degraded by us, must wade through slaughter to their inalienable rights." After Harpers Ferry, Parker said, "The Fire of Vengeance may be waked up even in an African's heart, especially when it is fanned by the wickedness of a white man; then it runs from man to man, from town to town.

What shall put it out? The white man's blood." William Lloyd Garrison was apparently inhibited from making such statements by his opposition on principle to the use of violence, but his *Liberator* constantly emphasized the unrest and resentment among the slaves; and he had once declared that, but for his scruples, he would place himself "at the head of a black army at the South to scatter devastation and death on every side." As J. C. Furnas has expressed it, there was a widespread "Spartacus complex" among the abolitionists, a fascinated belief that the South stood on the brink of a vast slave uprising and a wholesale slaughter of the whites. "It is not easy, though necessary," says Furnas, "to grasp that Abolitionism could, in the same breath warn the South of arson, rape, and murder and sentimentally admire the implied Negro mob leaders brandishing axes, torches, and human heads." This complex arose from the psychological needs of the abolitionists and not from any evidence which Negroes had given to them. No one really asked the Negroes what they wanted, or just how bloodthirsty they felt. There is much evidence that they wanted freedom to be sure, but again there is not much evidence that anyone even asked them how they thought their freedom could best be gained, and how they would like to go about getting it. Certainly John Brown did not ask, when he had a really good opportunity at Chatham, Ontario. All he did was talk. He did not listen at all. In fact there is no evidence that he ever listened at anytime, and this is perhaps the most convincing proof that he lived in the "private world" of an insane man.

But Brown's idea that the South was a waiting torch, and that twenty-two men without rations were enough to put a match to it, far from being a unique aberration, was actually one of the most conventional, least original notions in his whole stock of beliefs. Thus the Boston *Post* spoke much to the point when it said, "John Brown may be a lunatic but if so, then one-fourth of the people of Massachusetts are madmen."

The *Post* certainly did not intend to shift the question from one concerning Brown's personal sanity to one concerning the mass delusions of the abolitionists. A historian may, however, regard the latter as a legitimate topic of inquiry. But if he should do so, he must recognize at once the further fact that the Spartacus delusion—if delusion it was—was not confined to the abolitionists. The Southerners, too, shared this concept, in the sense that they were ever fearful of slave insurrections and were immensely relieved to learn that the slaves had not flocked to Brown's support. Clearly they had felt no assurance that this would be the outcome.

This is no place for me to go into either the extent or the realism of Southern fears of slave insurrection. The only point to make here is that John Brown, believing in the potentiality of a slave insurrection, only believed what both abolitionist and slaveholders believed. But Brown needed to know the specifics of that potentiality as others did not. He needed to know how strong it was, how it could be cultivated, how it could be triggered. The lives of himself and his men depended upon knowing. Yet there is no evidence that he ever even asked the questions. He merely said, "When I strike, the bees will swarm." But Negroes are not bees, and when figures of speech are used in argumentation, they are usually a substitute for realistic thinking.

Brown may have been right, at a certain level and in a certain sense, in believing that the Negroes might revolt. But he was completely wrong in the literal-minded way in which he held the idea, and this indiscriminate notion about Negro reactions probably led him to what was really his supreme folly. He supposed that the Negroes of Jefferson County would instantly spring to the support of an insurrection of which they had not been notified—that they would, of their own volition, join a desperate coup to which they had not even been invited. Brown evidently thought of Negroes, as so many other people have done, as abstractions, and not as men and women.

It was not as if he had not been warned: his English soldier of fortune, Hugh Forbes, told him that even slaves ripe for revolt would not come in on an enterprise like this. "No preparatory notice having been given to the slaves," he said, "the invitation to rise might, unless they were already in a state of agitation, meet with no response, or a feeble one." But Brown brushed this aside: he was sure of a response, and calculated that on the first night of the revolt, between two hundred and five hundred slaves would rally to him at the first news of his raid. Again later, when John E. Cook was keeping his lonely and secret vigil for more than a year as Brown's advance agent at Harpers Ferry, and even after Brown had moved to the farm in Maryland, Cook pleaded to be allowed to give the slaves at least some inkling of what was afoot. But Brown sternly rejected this idea. Thus, when the "Negro insurrection" began, the Negroes were as unprepared for it, as disconcerted, and as mystified as anyone else.

Brown, in his grandiose way, boasted of having studied the slave insurrections of history—of Spartacus, of Toussaint. But one wonders what those two, or even Denmark Vesey, would have had to say about John Brown's mode of conducting an insurrection. Abraham Lincoln, with his usual talent for accuracy of statement, later said, "It was not a slave insurrection. It was an attempt by white men to get up a revolt among slaves, in which the slaves refused to participate." But in a way Lincoln understated the case. The slaves were never asked to participate. Brown's remarkable technique for securing their participation was to send out a detail in the middle of the night, kidnap them, thrust a pike into their hands, and inform them that they were soldiers in the army of emancipation. He then expected them to place their necks in a noose without asking for further particulars.

Yet he was so supremely confident of their massive support that all the strange errors of October 16 and 17 sprang from that delusion. This was why he marched without rations; it

American artist Thomas Hovenden's painting of The Last Moments of John Brown (1884) depicts a tender farewell from the most militant and controversial white champion of black freedom in the pre-Emancipation years.

was why thirteen of his twenty-one followers carried commissions as officers in their knapsacks, though none of his five Negro followers was included in this number—thirteen officers would hardly suffice to command the Negro troops who would swarm like bees to his headquarters; it was why he wanted the weapons at Harpers Ferry although he already had several times as many weapons as were needed for the men at the Maryland farm. Finally it was why he sat down at Harpers Ferry and waited while his adversaries closed the trap on him. He was still waiting for the word to spread and for the Negroes to come trooping in.

John Brown wanted to be a leader for the Negroes of America. He dwelled upon this idea almost to the exclusion of all others. Ultimately he died with singular bravery to vindicate his role. Yet he never thought to ask the Negroes if they would accept him as a leader, and if so, what kind of policy they wanted him to pursue. Of course he could not ask them all, but he never even asked Frederick Douglass or the gathering of Negroes at Chatham. He knew what he wanted them to do and did not really care what they themselves wanted to do. John Brown occupies and deserves a heroic place in the gallery of historic leaders of American Negroes. Yet, like many other prominent and less heroic figures in that gallery, he was a self-appointed savior, who was not chosen by the Negroes, who had no Negro following of any magnitude, and whose policies in the name of the Negro were not necessarily the policies of the Negroes themselves.

■ ■ ■

STUDY QUESTIONS

1. What is the "paradox of leadership among American Negroes"? What was the problem of the traditional relationship between black slaves and their white sympathizers?

2. During his childhood and early adulthood, what relationship did John Brown have with blacks?

3. What motivated John Brown to violently pursue the abolition of slavery? Was he a madman or a realistic reformer?

4. Before the raid on Harpers Ferry, what antislavery activities did Brown pursue? Would you consider him a "radical"?

5. How did Brown think he was going to lead a black rebellion without even consulting or informing blacks of his plans? What was the reason for such poor planning?

6. The raid on Harpers Ferry was an "unmitigated disaster" in Potter's opinion. Why?

7. In your opinion, was John Brown insane? Why or why not?

8. What was the "Spartacus complex"? Did it have any justification in reality? Why or why not?

BIBLIOGRAPHY

John Brown has not been forgotten—at least not by historians. In the 1970s, for example, he was the subject of four biographies. The most balanced biography of Brown is Stephen B. Oates, *To Purge This Land with Blood: A Biography of John Brown* (1970). Two older works that are also valuable are James C. Malin, *John Brown and* the Legacy of Fifty-Six (1942) and Garrison Villard, *John Brown, 1800–1859: A Biography Fifty Years After* (1910). James W. Davidson and Mark H. Lytle attempt a psychological interpretation of Brown in "The Madness of John Brown: The Uses of Psychohistory," *After the Fact: The Art of Historical Detection* (1982).

James A. Rawley, *Race and Politics: "Bleeding Kansas" and the Coming of the Civil War* (1969) presents a fine introduction to the section where Brown acquired his initial fame. Students interested in psychohistory should consult Robert J. Lifton, ed., *Explorations in Psychohistory* (1974) and Bruce Mazlish, *Psychoanalysis and History* (1971).

Part Seven

CIVIL WAR AND RECONSTRUCTION

It seemed impossible. Threats and rumors of civil war, rebellion, and secession had circulated throughout the 1850s, but most Americans had confidently assumed they were just talk, not descriptions of what really could come to pass. But when South Carolina military forces fired on Union vessels trying to resupply Fort Sumter in 1861, the rumors suddenly became reality. War was at hand—a war few people wanted. With an attempt at optimism, many people then decided the rebellion would be a short-run affair, decided quickly in the first major military engagement. The Confederate victory at the first battle of Bull Run dashed those hopes. Four years later, the Civil War would prove to have been the bloodiest, most costly conflict in American history.

The sectionalism that brought on the Civil War was evident from the very beginning of the republic. Southerners were devoted to slavery as a source of cheap labor. Southerners also saw slavery as an institution of social control, a way of managing a large, alien black population. To protect their economy and society, Southerners preached a loyalty to laissez-faire and states' rights.

As long as the nation was confined east of the Appalachian Mountains, the North and South were able to coexist peacefully because the two sections were relatively isolated from each other. But early in the nineteenth century, tens of thousands of Americans began pouring into the western territories each year, forcing new issues on the political system. After the War of 1812, a balance of power existed in the United States Senate between free states and slave states, but each time a new territory applied for statehood, its permanent status as a "slave state" or "free state" had to be decided. Most Northerners came to oppose the

expansion of slavery into the territories; Southerners believed the survival of their way of life depended on its expansion. Between 1820 and 1860, the country debated this fundamental issue repeatedly. The debate ultimately splintered the nation. Mainly because of their opposition to the expansion of slavery, the Republicans were anathema to the South, and when Abraham Lincoln won the presidency in 1860, the secession movement began.

Although the Civil War was not started as a crusade against slavery, it ended that way. The Emancipation Proclamation and the Thirteenth Amendment to the Constitution ended human bondage in the United States, and during Reconstruction Republicans worked diligently to extend full civil rights to Southern blacks. The Civil Rights Act of 1866 and the Fourteenth and Fifteenth Amendments to the Constitution were all to bring the emancipated slaves into the political arena and build a respectable Republican Party in the South.

Both goals were stillborn. When Congress removed the troops from the last Southern states in 1877, the old planter elite resumed control of Southern politics. They disenfranchised blacks and relegated them to second-class citizenship. The South became solidly "Democratic."

As Reconstruction was coming to an end, another era was beginning. Out west, ambitious farmers were rapidly settling the frontier, while cattlemen were forging their own empire by supplying the eastern demand for beef. Civilization was again replacing a wilderness mentality with familiar political, economic, and social institutions. America was trying to forget about the divisions of the past and get on with the business of building a new society.

JOHNNY REB AND BILLY YANK

Bell I. Wiley

General George S. Patton, famous commander of the United States Third and Seventh Armies in Europe during World War II, once remarked that "compared to war, all other forms of human endeavor pale into insignificance." For him, there was an inherent majesty in mobilizing people and resources, as if humanity resembled divinity only in the organized production of death. He undoubtedly looked at the Civil War in the same way.

By the late spring of 1861, throughout the United States—in the North and in the Confederate South—young men were kissing sweethearts good-bye, marching off to war in a mood of confidence, exhilaration, and moral certitude, embarking on a noble adventure. Usually carrying the family rifle and mustering together in neighborhood armies, these young soldiers were setting out as communities to right wrongs and implement the will of God. Each side underestimated its opponent, expected brief engagements where bravery and morality would prevail, and anticipated early, triumphant returns home. In a matter of months, sometimes only weeks, the smell of death and the sickening realization that war might last indefinitely crushed all naive assumptions of a quick victory.

Altogether, more than 600,000 soldiers died during the Civil War, and millions more were wounded. The soldiers of the United States of America and the Confederate States of America shared the suffering and misery of modern combat, spoke the same language, and worshipped the same ideals, but they were not necessarily the same people. Differences existed between the common soldiers of the two armies, and those differences eventually played a critical role in the outcome of the conflict. In "Johnny Reb and Billy Yank," Bell I. Wiley describes the lives and motivations of ordinary people caught up in extraordinary events.

The common soldiers of North and South during the American Civil War were very much alike. As a general rule they came from similar backgrounds, spoke the same language, cherished the same ideals, and reacted in like manner to the hardships and perils of soldiering. They hated regimentation, found abundant fault with their officers, complained often about army rations, and hoped earnestly for speedy return to civilian life. Even so, men of the opposing sides presented some notable and interesting differences.

In the first place, Billy Yanks were more often of foreign background than were their opposites in gray. During the decades preceding the Civil War several million Europeans migrated to America and because of convenience, economic opportunity, and other influences, most of them settled in the North. In 1861 there were about four million persons of alien birth living in the states adhering to the Union as against only about one fourth of a million residing in the Southern Confederacy. Because the immigrants tended to identify themselves with the section in which they settled, far more of them donned the Union blue than the Confederate gray. Probably one out of every four or five Billy Yanks was of foreign birth and only one out of every twenty or twenty-five Johnny Rebs.

On the Northern side the Germans, aggregating about 200,000, were the most numerous of the foreign groups. Next were the Irish, numbering about 150,000, then Canadians and Englishmen each totalling about 50,000 and, down the line, lesser numbers of Scandinavians, Frenchmen, Italians, and other nationalities.

It has been estimated that 15,000 to 20,000 Irishmen marched in Confederate ranks and they apparently outnumbered any other foreign group on the Southern side. But Canada, En-

gland, France, and Italy were well represented among wearers of the gray.

On both sides most of the foreigners were enlisted men, but many served as company and field grade officers and a considerable number attained the rank of general. Forty-five of the North's 583 general officers were of foreign birth, and among them were twelve Germans and twelve Irishmen. Among the Confederacy's 425 generals, there were nine foreigners of whom five were Irish.

In both armies the foreign groups added color and variety to camp life by singing their native songs, celebrating festive days, and observing customs peculiar to their homeland. St. Patrick's Day was always a great occasion among Irish units, featuring horse races, athletic contests, and consumption of large quantities of alcohol. As Pat and Mike lingered at flowing bowls their pugnacious tendencies were accentuated, and before night guardhouses were crowded with men suffering from cuts, bruises, or broken bones. Indeed, St. Patrick's Day sometimes produced more casualties among sons of Erin than did encounters on the battlefield.

In combat the foreigners gave a good account of themselves. Meagher's Irish Brigade was one of the best fighting units in the Civil War. Ezra J. Warner in *Generals in Blue* rates Prussian-born Peter J. Osterhaus as "certainly the most distinguished of the foreign-born officers who served the Union," and few, if any, division commanders of any nationality on either side had a better battle record than the Confederacy's beloved Irishman, Patrick R. Cleburne.

Among native participants two groups deserving special mention were the Indians and Negroes. The Confederacy had three brigades of [Indians], mostly Cherokees, Choctaws, and Seminoles. One of the Cherokees, Stand Watie, became a brigadier general. The Union Army had one brigade of Indians, most of whom were Creeks. Muster rolls of Indian units, filed in the National Archives, contain such names as Private Sweetcaller, Private Hog Shooter, Private Hog Toter, Private Flying Bird, and Lieutenant

Bell I. Wiley, "Johnny Reb and Billy Yank." From *American History Illustrated* 3 (April 1968), pp. 4–11, 44–47. Reprinted through the courtesy of Cowles Magazines, publisher of AMERICAN HISTORY ILLUSTRATED.

■ ■ *The differences between Johnny Rebs and Billy Yanks were sometimes difficult to see.* Left: *A group of the Irish Brigade, Union Army, resting during the 1862 Peninsular campaign.* Right: *Three Confederate soldiers ponder their fate after being captured at Gettysburg in 1863.*

Jumper Duck. At the Battle of Honey Springs in 1864, Yankee Indians fought Rebel Indians. In combat Indians acquitted themselves well, but between battles they were poor soldiers, since they had only vague ideas of discipline and regimentation.

On the Confederate side, Negroes served almost exclusively in accessory capacities, as cooks, hostlers, musicians, and body servants. On March 13, 1865, after prolonged and acrimonious discussion the Confederate Congress passed a law authorizing recruitment of 300,000 slaves to serve as soldiers. A few companies were organized but the war ended before any of them could get into combat. It seems unreasonable to think that slaves would have fought with any enthusiasm for the perpetuation of their bondage. More than 188,000 Negroes, most of whom were ex-slaves, wore the Union blue. Despite discriminations in pay, equipment, and association with fellow soldiers, and notwithstanding the fact that they had to do far more than their share of labor and garrison duty, Negro Yanks fought well at Port Hudson, Mil-

liken's Bend, Fort Wagner, the Crater, and other Civil War battles in which they participated.

Billy Yanks were better educated than Johnny Rebs, owing to the North's better schools and greater emphasis on public education. In some companies from the rural South, half of the men could not sign the muster rolls. Such companies were exceptional, but so were those that did not have from one to twenty illiterates. Sergeant Major John A. Cobb of the 16th Georgia Regiment wrote a kinsman on September 8, 1861: "Paying off soldiers is a good deal like paying off negroes their cotton money . . . about one third of the men in the regiment can't write their names, so the Pay Roll has a good many X (his mark) on it, and about one half of those that write them you can't read, nor could they themselves." Among Yanks the rate of illiteracy was highest in Negro units, but the typical Union regiment seems to have had no more than a half-dozen illiterates and many had none at all. On both sides, however, spelling and grammar frequently fell far below schoolroom standards. In soldier letters pneumonia sometimes appeared as *new mornion* or *new mony*, once as *wonst*, uneasy as *oneasy*, fought as *fit*, your as *yore* or *yorn*, and not any as *nary*. Other common usages were *tuck* for took, *purty* for pretty, *laig* for leg, and *shore* for sure. Long words were often divided, sometimes with strange results. One Reb complained about the "rashens" issued by the *comma sary*; another stated that he hoped to get a *fur low* when some more *volen teares* joined the *ridge ment*. A Yank wrote that he had been marching through mud that was *nea deap*. Another reported shortly after Lincoln ordered the organization of McClellan's forces into corps: "They are deviding the army up into corpses." While reading the letter of an Illinois soldier I was puzzled by the statement "I had the camp diary a few days ago," for I had not previously found indication that Civil War organizations kept unit journals. But my confusion was cleared up by the rest of the sentence which stated "but now I am about well of it." This soldier was suffering from a malady commonly known as the "Tennessee Quickstep."

A Yank who served under General Frederick Lander wrote in one of his letters: "Landers has the ganders." I read it just as it appeared, with a hard "g." On reflection I realized that the "g" was soft and that what the general really had was the jaundice. Landers was very unpopular with this particular Yank, so he added "I hope the old so and so dies." The next letter began: "Well old Landers is dead, and I'll bet he is down in hell pumping thunder at three cents a clap."

Soldiers in both armies frequently spelled hospital as "horsepittle," and that was a place which they abhorred almost as much as the devil himself. A Reb wrote that the hospital which served his unit "outstinks a ded horse."

Because of differences in Northern and Southern economy, Billy Yanks were more often town dwellers and factory workers than were Johnny Rebs. The contrast is vividly demonstrated in company descriptive rolls. The occupation columns on typical Southern rolls consist of a monotonous repetition of "farmer," while Northern rolls, except in the case of units recruited from agricultural communities, listed a wide assortment of occupations, including carpenters, clerks, coopers, shoemakers, bricklayers, printers, tinsmiths, mechanics, miners, plumbers, tailors, and boatmen. This diversity of skills among the rank and file gave the North a considerable advantage in what proved to be the first great modern war. It meant that if a wagon, steamboat, or locomotive broke down, or if a railroad needed rebuilding, or if a gun failed to function, a Northern commander could usually find close at hand soldiers who knew how to do the job.

Both during and after the war many people believed that the Confederate forces contained more boys and old men than did those of the Union. Study of descriptive rolls and other records indicates that this was an erroneous impression. There were many boys and old men on both sides. Charles Carter Hay enlisted in an Alabama regiment when he was 11 years old, and when four years later he surrendered at Appomattox he had not celebrated his 15th birthday. He had a counterpart on the Union side in the case of Johnny Clem, who began service as a drummer boy at age 9 in 1861, and who graduated to the fighting ranks after the Battle of Shiloh. E. Pollard enlisted in the 5th North Carolina Regiment at 73, but the oldest Civil War soldier apparently was 80-year-old Curtis King of the 37th Iowa, a non-combatant regiment known as the "Graybeards" because on its rolls there were 145 men who had passed their 60th birthday. But on both sides, most soldiers were neither very young nor very old. The largest single age group were the 18-year-olds, and three-fourths of the men fell in the age bracket 18–30.

Billy Yanks manifested a livelier interest in politics than did the men whom they opposed. This was due in part to the greater literacy of the Northern soldiers and their easier access to newspapers. On the national level the nature of politics was a contributing factor. Because the

Confederate Constitution provided a single term of six years for the Chief Executive, there was only one presidential campaign in the South during the war. This was a very dull affair because Jefferson Davis had no opposition. But in the North the campaign of 1864 between Lincoln and McClellan was a hard-fought contest, and most Yanks thought that the outcome would have a great impact on the prosecution of the war. Electioneering was lively in many units, and soldiers voted in impressive numbers. When ballots were tabulated it was found that the overwhelming majority had voted for "Uncle Abe" and continuance of war until the Union was restored.

Few, if any, other campaigns generated as much enthusiasm among Billy Yanks as did the Lincoln-McClellan contest, but even in the choice of governors, Congressmen, and lesser officials, the men in blue in their letters and diaries revealed considerably more interest than did wearers of the gray.

Billy Yanks' greater involvement in politics reflected a healthier interest in things intellectual. Owing to the North's better schools, the more cosmopolitan character of its population, the more varied pattern of its economy, the presence in its borders of more large cities, the greater prosperity of its citizens, better communication, easier access to books and papers, greater freedom of thought and discussion, and sundry other advantages. Union soldiers manifested greater curiosity about things past and present than their opposites in Confederate service. Common soldiers on either side who showed a deep concern for philosophic aspects of the conflict were rare. But the North appears to have had considerably more than its share of the exceptions.

In their religious attitudes and activities Billy Yanks and Johnny Rebs manifested some notable contrasts. Letters and diaries of Southern soldiers contain more references to religion than do those of the men in blue, and Rebs were more emotional in their worship than were Billy Yanks. During the last two years of the conflict,

great revivals swept over both the Eastern and Western armies of the Confederacy and men made open confessions of their sins, sought forgiveness at mourners' benches, and raised shouts of joy when relieved of the burden of guilt. Seasons of revival sometimes extended for several weeks as leading ministers from Richmond, New Orleans, Nashville, and other cities joined the army chaplains in promoting the cause of salvation. Revivals also took place in Northern units, but rarely did they extend beyond brigade or division. Certainly, the Union forces experienced no army-wide outbreaks of emotionalism such as occurred among Confederates.

The greater interest in religion manifested by Confederates and their greater susceptibility to revivalism was due to a combination of circumstances. The fact that Southerners were a more homogeneous people than Northerners and more often members of evangelistic sects made for greater religious zeal and emotionalism in Confederate camps. Another factor working to the same end was the South's greater ruralism. Still another factor was the example of high-ranking leaders. Robert E. Lee, Stonewall Jackson, and Leonidas Polk were deeply religious men and they showed far more interest in the spiritual welfare of their commands than did Grant, Sherman, and Sheridan. Jefferson Davis proclaimed more days of fasting and prayer and was more of a church man than was Abraham Lincoln.

The fortunes of war played a part in revivalism. The flood tides of emotionalism that swept over the Southern armies came after Vicksburg and Gettysburg, and to some extent they represent the tendency of a religiously rooted people in times of severe crises to seek supernatural deliverance from the woes that beset them.

The greater religiosity of the Confederates does not seem to have produced a higher level of morality in Southern camps. Comments of soldiers, complaints of chaplains, court-martial proceedings, and monthly health reports indicate that profanity, gambling, drunkenness, fornication, and other "sins" flourished as much among Rebs as among Yanks.

The Northern soldiers generally were of a more practical and prosaic bent of mind than were Johnny Rebs. This difference was reflected in the Northerners' greater concern for the material things of life. Billy Yanks more often engaged in buying and selling and other side activities to supplement their army pay. Their letters contain far more references to lending their earnings at interest, investing for profit, and other financial ventures than do those written by the men in gray. Admittedly, Yanks had more money to write about, but their better remuneration, important though it was, was not enough wholly to account for the difference.

Billy Yanks' letters were not so fanciful or poetic as those of Johnny Rebs, nor were they as rich in humor and banter. The Northerners did not so frequently address wives and sweethearts in endearing terms as did their Southern counterparts. Correspondence of the men in blue contains much delightful humor, but I have yet to find any matching that exemplified by the following selections from Confederate sources: A Georgia Reb wrote his wife after absence of about a year in Virginia: "If I did not write and receive letters from you, I believe that I would forgit that I was married. I don't feel much like a maryed man, but I never forgit it so far as to court enny other lady but if I should you must forgive me as I am so forgitful." Another Georgian while on tour of duty in East Tennessee wrote his spouse: "lis, I must tell you that I have found me a Sweat hart heare. . . . I had our pitures taken with her handen me a bunch of flowers . . . she lets on like she thinks a heep of me and when I told her I was marred she took a harty cry about it . . . she ses that she entends to live singel the balance of her days." A Tar Heel wrote a male friend at home: "Tommy I want you to be a good boy and tri to take cear of the wemmen and children tell I get home and we'll all have a chance. . . . I want you to go . . . and see my wife and children but I want you to take your wife with you [when you go]."

Billy Yanks' reasons for fighting were different from those of Johnny Rebs. Some Yanks went to war to free the slaves. One of these was Chauncey Cooke of the 25th Wisconsin Regiment, who wrote home before he heard of Lincoln's issuance of the Emancipation Proclamation: "I have no heart in this war if the slaves cannot be free." But Cooke represented a minority. The overwhelming majority of those who donned the blue did so primarily to save the imperilled Union. Devotion to the Union found eloquent expression in some of their letters. Private Sam Croft, a youth from Pennsylvania, wrote his homefolk about a hard march in September 1861: "I have never once thought of giving out. . . . I am well, hardy, strong, and doing my country a little service. I did not come for money and good living. My Heart beats high and I am proud of being a soldier. When I look along the line of glistening bayonets with the glorious Stars and Stripes floating over them . . . I am proud and sanquine of success." Croft died at Gettysburg.

Most Rebs who commented on their individual motivation indicated that they were fighting to protect their families and homes against foreign invaders and they envisioned the invaders as a cruel and wicked foe. "Teach my children to hate them with that bitter hatred that will never permit them to meet without seeking to destroy each other," wrote a Georgia Reb to his wife in 1862.

Many Confederates were fighting for slavery, though this was rarely indicated in their letters. Usually they represented themselves as fighting for self-government, state rights, or "the Southern way of life." There is no doubt in my mind that most Southerners, non-slaveholders as well as planters, were earnestly desirous of maintaining slavery, not primarily as an economic system, but rather as an established and effective instrument of social control. A North Carolina private wrote a friend in 1863: "You know I am a poor man having none of the property said to be the cause of the present war. But I have a wife and some children to rase in honor and never to be put on an equality with the African race." Thus did one Reb who owned no Negroes avow that he was fighting for slavery; there were many others like him.

Billy Yanks were better fed and better clothed than Johnny Rebs. In the latter part of the war they frequently were better armed. Each side experienced ups and downs of morale, but generally speaking Confederate morale was higher than that of the Northerners during the first half of the war and lower during the second half. The nadir of Union morale came early in 1863, in the wake of Grant's reverses in Mississippi and Burnside's bloody defeat at Fredericksburg. Confederate morale plummeted after Vicksburg and Gettysburg, rose slightly in the spring and summer of 1864 and began its final unabated plunge after the re-election of Lincoln.

What of the combat performance of Johnny Rebs and Billy Yanks? The Southerners apparently fought with more enthusiasm than their opponents; and, after battle, in letters to the folk at home, they wrote more vividly and in greater detail of their combat experiences. In a fight they demonstrated more of dash, elan, individual aggressiveness, and a devil-may-care quality than Billy Yanks. But the men in blue seemed to have gone about the business of fighting with greater seriousness than Johnny Rebs, and they manifested more of a group consciousness and team spirit. In other words, the Rebs thought a battle was a thrilling adventure in which each man was to a large extent on his own; to Yanks it was a formidable task requiring the earnest and coordinated exertion of all those involved— not a gameshooting experience as some Rebs seemed to regard it, but a grim and inescapable chore that ought to be performed with as much efficiency and expedition as possible.

These differences were reflected in the battle cheers of the opposing forces. Southerners charged with the "Rebel yell" on their lips. This was a wild, highpitched, piercing "holler," inspired by a combination of excitement, fright, anger, and elation. The standard Yankee cheer, on the other hand, was a regularly intoned huzza or hurrah. The contrast between Southern and Northern cheering was the subject of much comment by participants on both sides. A Federal officer observed after the second battle of Manassas: "Our own men give three successive cheers and in concert, but theirs is a cheering without any reference to regularity of form—a continual yelling." A Union surgeon who was in the Wilderness Compaign of 1864 stated: "On our side it was a resounding, continuous hurrah, while the famous dread-inspiring "Rebel yell" was a succession of yelps staccato and shrill."

Unquestionably Johnny Rebs made a better showing in combat during the first half of the war. This was due mainly to better leadership, particularly on the company and regimental levels. On both sides these officers were elected, and in the South, owing largely to the prevalence of the caste system, the successful candidates were usually planters or their sons—privileged persons, recognized community leaders, habituated to the direction of slaves, products of the military academies on which the region principally relied for education of its boys, and strongly indoctrinated with the spirit of *noblesse oblige*.

In the more democratic North, on the other hand, men were chosen as officers because of their effectiveness in persuading neighbors to sign up for military service. In many instances they were deficient in the essentials of leadership. By the summer of 1863, incompetent officers on both sides generally had been weeded out by resignation, dismissal, or hostile bullets. By that time also the Northerners had overcome the initial handicap of being less familiar with firearms than their opponents. During the last two years of the war, there was no discernible difference in the combat performance of Johnny Rebs and Billy Yanks. There was never any significant difference in their determination, pride, courage, devotion to cause, loyalty to comrades, and other basic qualities that go to make good soldiers. From the beginning to the end of the conflict the common soldiers of both sides acquitted themselves in a manner that merited the pride of their descendants and won for them a high standing among fighting men of all time.

■ ■ ■

STUDY QUESTIONS

1. What role did foreigners play in both armies? Why were foreigners more prominent in the Union Army? What impact might this have had on morale and organization?

2. To what extent did the South employ blacks as soldiers? Why were slaves not used more extensively as combat soldiers in the Confederate Army?

3. To what extent did Northern and Southern soldiers come from different demographic and economic backgrounds? What impact did those differences have on the outcome of the war?

4. Wiley claims that Southern soldiers were more religious than Northern soldiers. What evidence does he use to justify his claim?

5. When asked to describe their reasons for risking death in order to fight as soldiers, what explanations did Northern soldiers offer? How did their responses differ from those of Southern soldiers?

BIBLIOGRAPHY

For a general background study of American military history, see Walter Millis, *Arms and Men: A Study in American Military History* (1956) and Russell F. Weigley, *The American Way of War: A History of United States Military Strategy and Policy* (1973). A number of excellent works detail the history of the Civil War. One of the best general surveys is James G. Randall and David Donald, *The Civil War and Reconstruction* (1961). Also see Allan Nevins, *The War for the Union,* four volumes (1959–1972). Fred A. Shannon's *The Organization and Administration of the Union Army 1861–1865* (1928) and George W. Adams's *Doctors in Blue: The Medical History of the Union Army in the Civil War* (1952) both deal with the problems of mobilizing and caring for a modern army. Bell I. Wiley's *The Life of Johnny Reb* (1943) and *The Life of Billy Yank* (1952) describe the life of a typical soldier, as does Robert Cruden's *The War That Never Ended: The American Civil War* (1973). Stephen Crane's classic novel *The Red Badge of Courage* (1895) exposes the personal pain and tragedy of war.

MASTERS WITHOUT SLAVES

James L. Roark

Ever since the first Africans disembarked in Jamestown, Virginia, in 1617, white southerners have been trying to fathom the black personality. Confused by cultural differences, frightened by black skin, and guilt-ridden by the existence of slavery, they created an elaborate, sophisticated mythology about Africans, one which saw them as happy, irresponsible children destined to a life of cultural depravity until slave traders brought them to the New World. Here they enjoyed the opportunity of serving others in a civilized atmosphere. Although many whites worried about the stereotypes and suspected blacks of having hidden dreams and ambitions, they preferred to suppress such unsettling thoughts, hoping that the dynamics of bondage would continue to serve them forever. Emancipation in 1865 came as a shock to planters. With news of their freedom, tens of thousands of former slaves left the plantations in search of family members who had either been sold away or who had left for job opportunities, personal independence, or black companionship.

In "Masters Without Slaves," James L. Roark looks at the difficulties faced by southern whites who had lost their slaves. Exhilarated by their freedom and desperate for good jobs and a meaningful life, blacks left the rural South for cities, just as millions of white farmers and immigrants were doing. For southern whites still dependent on cheap labor and paranoid about large concentrations of free blacks, the exodus from the plantations was frightening. Not only were they dealing with the tremendous capital losses of emancipation, they were emotionally confronting the reality of a free black society. Instead of accepting the former slaves as members of a new society, southern whites continued to try to control black life. For many blacks, freedom still involved a constant struggle for acceptance and equality.

Like a blackened chimney standing amidst charred ruins, the proslavery ideology survived the destruction of the institution of slavery. Total continuity, like total change, does not occur in history, but this time, in the interplay between inertia and flux, clearly the traditional orthodoxies prevailed. Planters' basic ideas about slavery, blacks, agriculture, and Southern civilization revealed a remarkable resistance to change. Slaveholders had led the South into secession because they could not conceive of their social order without their peculiar labor system. When the war ended, they still were unable to imagine a decent and enduring Southern civilization without slavery.

Because ideological revolutions are rarely synchronized with social revolutions, dominant ideas can easily be out of phase with rapidly changing social environments. In the midst of disequilibrated systems, men and women often continue to operate within the confines of traditional ideas, though not without intense personal strain and tension. The anxiety which planters experienced during the war probably stemmed in part from their own private struggle to retain a set of ideas in the face of the destruction of the institution which had produced those ideas. Planters had little opportunity in the midst of war to construct an alternative ideology. Rather, their energies were consumed in a military struggle to preserve their peculiar society against an ideologically opposed enemy. They sought to deny the reality of the emerging, and still quite inconceivable, post-slavery world. Their Northern conquerors did not and really could not provide them with a convincing alternative ideology which would allow them to face their particular free-labor situation with any degree of confidence.

A large part of what planters witnessed during the war, moreover, served only to re-emphasize

the essential validity of their traditional assumptions. While a number of powerful forces were working to erode the planters' commitment to the slave-labor system, most of these could also have the reverse effect. War sometimes intensified doubt and guilt about slavery, for instance, but more often it operated to strengthen convictions about slavery's justice and utility. Direct contact with Northern soldiers convinced many planters of what they had always suspected. Despite their pieties, Yankees hated blacks, and the blacks' only salvation lay with protective Southerners. A Cobb County, Georgia, planter was appalled to hear a Union soldier say he was "willing the war should continue for 7 years longer if only to kill the Negroes off." Another Georgian declared, "If we are to judge of the future welfare of the colored race by what they have already experienced from the tender mercies of the Yankees, we cannot see that emancipation will be a blessing to them." Even Ella Clanton Thomas, who at the beginning of the war believed slavery was morally wrong, became "convinced the Negro *as a race* is better off with us as he has been than if he were made free. . . ."

While the "demoralization" of the slave population disillusioned some planters and soured them on slavery, black insubordination more often supplied planters with concrete, empirical evidence for slavery's indispensability. As their authority waned, planters learned that blacks often interpreted their new freedom as an opportunity to stop work and to look beyond the boundaries of the plantation. Planters could see that emancipation would mean the creation of millions of "shiftless black vagabonds" roaming the South. The lessons were all too clear—without subordination, blacks were irresponsible and destructive, and without coercion they would not work. When his slaves deserted, Louis Manigault cried out, "For my own part I am more than ever convinced that the only suitable occupation for the Negro is to be a Laborer of the Earth, and to work as a field hand upon a well ordered plantation."

RE-CONSTRUCTION,
OR "A WHITE MAN'S GOVERNMENT".

In this Currier & Ives print (1868) the offer of help from the freedman and the kindly advice from President Grant are angrily spurned by the representative of the planter class, who displays a passionate attachment to his basic proslavery beliefs.

War spawned reform movements to alleviate the worst aspects of slavery, but those efforts were rarely sponsored by the plantation gentry. Churchmen called for reform; plantation men demanded stricter slave codes. Planters pointed out that those gentlemen who had run the most permissive operations were the first to have trouble. One South Carolinian, for instance, said that it "has now been proven that those Planters who were the most indulgent to their Negroes when we were at peace, have since the commencement of the war encountered the greatest trouble in the management of this species of property." In the planters' eyes, mounting evidence pointed to the necessity for stricter laws, more rigid discipline, and less "petting," not a more humane slavery system. And certainly it was the planters and not the clergy who had their way during the war.

Moreover, churchmen themselves rarely had doubts about the essential justice of slavery, only about its practice. They were probably among the most ardent supporters of the Southern cause. They did, of course, have to deal with the problem of explaining how Southerners, a God-fearing people, could be getting whipped by those godless and sinful Yankees. And they found explanations that did not shake Southerners' faith in the cause. Clergymen could argue that the latest military defeat was but a temporary setback, that, as with Job, God was merely testing and tempering his people, or simply that the Almighty moved in mysterious ways. Some slaveholders, however, found their own answer to the puzzle. Dolly Burge, a slaveholder who had doubts about slavery, simply decided to put the entire question of right or wrong out of her mind and into God's hands. If the South was right, God would give it victory; if slavery was wrong, "I trust that He will show it unto us."

The nature of the evidence precludes a definitive answer to the question of whether the South was guilt-ridden over slavery, but my reading of it indicates that no more than a small fraction of Southern slaveholders felt even twinges of doubt and guilt. Most of those who did were women, who had a special perspective just because of their position as women in a slave society. They may have had special empathy for slaves because they subconsciously recognized the parallels between their positions, one as slave and the other as "Southern lady." More concretely, the existence of miscegenation undermined their faith in the institution. One woman thought that if the South were to lose the war, Southern women would have their revenge when Northern soldiers took the "bitter cup" of miscegenation back home. Their dedication to the institution was also challenged by the fact that as plantation mistresses they felt the burdens of slavery but few of the rewards. "I have never ceased to work," Dolly Burge declared, and "many a northern housekeeper has a much easier time than a Southern matron with her hundred slaves."

The vast majority of plantation men, and probably most plantation women, had no doubt about the morality and absolute necessity of slavery. Kenneth Stampp's assertion that one of the reasons the South lost the Civil War was that many Southerners were tormented by a moral crisis over slavery and saw in defeat a way of ridding themselves of a moral burden does not hold true for the planter class. As part of his evidence he points to the unwillingness of many Southerners to subordinate personal interests to the success of the Confederacy, and argues that had they seen the consequences of defeat as unbearable, they would have sacrificed more for victory. But planters had never been model citizens. A rural class, intensely individual and local in outlook, jealous of any intrusion into plantation affairs, planters had always tended to think of themselves as individual sovereigns who happened to give sustenance to the state. And in wartime, failure to give their all to the government in Richmond grew in part from the conviction that Richmond had proven almost as unfaithful to slavery as Washington. For four full years, by word and deed, the planter class proved that the slave-plantation system received their primary allegiance, and that its preservation was their first priority.

Other forces which worked to dissipate Southern attachment to slavery were localized or checked by more powerful counterthrusts. American patriotism and Southern nationalism were potent sentiments in the South, but they rarely dislodged planters from their primary commitment to slavery. Few planters ever entirely suppressed their national patriotism, but it was usually conditional, in 1865 as much as in 1861. If anything, war dampened warm feelings for the Union; it rarely fanned them. And Confederate policy, particularly where it touched slavery, undermined planters' allegiance to their government in Richmond. In addition, while slavery certainly grew less profitable, most planters ended the war still owning slaves, and most would have preferred to keep them. There was a substantial increase in cotton planting in the spring of 1865, and although slavery had not paid during the war, peace promised to end those conditions which had made it unprofitable.

It was probably the unusual combination of powerful forces and special circumstances that so completely shattered John Houston Bills's commitment to maintain slavery. First, this Tennessean was an ardent nationalist and a very reluctant Southern revolutionary. Second, living in a border state easily penetrated by Federal troops, he faced occupation earlier than most planters and endured the disruption of his plantations longer. Third, his plantations became definite economic liabilities, and his slaves grew particularly insubordinate. Fourth, unlike General Benjamin F. Butler and General Nathaniel Banks in Louisiana, General Lew Wallace did not demand *de facto* emancipation, and consequently, Bills lived with a malfunctioning slave system for three full years. Fifth, he had extensive business interests outside the South and was not totally dependent on slavery. Sixth, very early in the war, Bills came face to face with the reality of Northern power. And finally, he lived in an area in which significant numbers of people were reacting just as he was. Farther south, people looked more unfavorably upon taking loyalty oaths and fraternizing with the enemy.

For the majority of the planter class, the war served to reemphasize, not undermine, the validity of traditional beliefs. Wartime experiences were even powerful enough to transform the fundamental ideas of those who had earlier denied the logic of the proslavery argument. The metamorphosis of John Hartwell Cocke is a dramatic case in point. Clement Eaton describes this Virginian as one of the leading examples of liberalism in the antebellum South. Although he owned more than a hundred slaves, Cocke had called slavery "a curse on the land" and the proslavery argument "monstrous." He had been consistently willing to lay the blame for black backwardness on whites, arguing that slavery itself was the true cause of black inferiority. He had purchased two plantations in Alabama expressly to train and prepare his slaves for emancipation and freedom in Liberia. By the 1850s, Cocke was weakening in his conviction that slavery was an unmitigated evil, but still, on the eve of the war, he stood apart from his class, a lonely Jeffersonian in the age of Calhoun, a believer in the doctrines of equality and natural rights, an opponent of slavery, and an admirer of many things Yankee.

For John Hartwell Cocke, the war became

revelation. Unfortunately, we do not know how he arrived at his conclusions, but we do have a remarkable journal written in 1863 and 1864, in which he revealed that for him the war was a pilgrimage to slavery. He was struck, he said, with "the new light shed . . . over the Southern mind by the events of this war," and more pointedly, he declared that "the events of this war have developed the subject of slavery in a new light. . . ." Now he understood that "the institution of slavery [was] established by God himself" and had "been recognized & provided for by his Providential Government [in] every age down to the present time. . . ." From his fresh perspective, he could see that "the distinctions of colour" and "the different degrees of intelligence among men . . . stand as living monuments to the falsity of the modern doctrine that men are born equal." In truth, he declared, "God has made his creatures unequal—and fitted them to fill unequal lots—the madness of the French revolution and the puritanical fanaticism of the Yankees to the contrary notwithstanding." The "Golden Rule of God," he now believed, was "Subordination & Submission to Authority."

He was not willing to claim that all slavery was a positive good, but he did argue that what determined whether slavery was "a Blessing or a Curse" was "the characters of the heads of the tribes or families making up the Social Community." An "unregenerate master," he admitted, could be a "most prolific source of crime and wickedness," but "Human ingenuity may be challenged to conceive a more perfect & happy community than one made up of families" governed "by true Christian patriarchs." Wherever a master had received the grace of God, he argued, "the condition of the slaveholder on a Southern estate approaches more nearly to the covenant which God established with his servant Abraham than that of any other community." For on that plantation one could see the fulfillment of God's design—"the power of the Husband over his wife; the power of parents over their children; and . . . the power of Masters over their Slaves. . . ." After a lifetime of opposition, therefore, and ironically just as slavery was failing, this old Jeffersonian capitulated. He no longer stood apart from his class but accepted its fundamental social beliefs—in the divine sanction of slavery, natural inequality, the immutability of conservative, hierarchical principles, and the failure of an egalitarian Northern society.

But to talk in terms of either total continuity or absolute rupture in the planter mind is too neat and tidy. Most usual were intermediary positions characterized by confusion and tentativeness. The changes that swept the South were sometimes bewildering. "This is a strange world, anyway," Henry L. Graves said early in the war, "and these are strange times. One does not know what to beleive [*sic*], or what to think; things have all got into a sort of whirl wind, and are whirling and kicking & jumping around at such a rate, that half the time, a man hardly knows whether he is standing on his head or his feet. He does not know whether to laugh or cry." Rapid change was disorienting. "I feel as tho I held in my hands only broken threads, thwarted plans," Catherine Edmondston said. "My time seems like the fragments of a broken mirror. . . ." At the end of the war, a Virginia military hero explained that he felt "as does a soldier after a great battle or the explosion of a mine."

Despite some transformation and disorientation, however, plantation dwellers displayed a remarkable adherence to basic principles. The fundamental premises which underlay the proslavery ideology stood firm in the face of the deterioration and then the destruction of the peculiar institution itself. Blacks were inferior beings, planters agreed. Because they were not fit for free labor, it was both necessary and proper that they be kept in slavery. Only there would they remain productive and subordinate to whites. Slavery was, indeed, the sole solution to the problem posed by the massive presence of blacks and the enormous labor requirements of the South's vast plantations. Without slavery, the Charleston *Mercury* asserted in January, 1865, the South would become a *"most magnificent jungle."* Emancipation would mean that "our great productions, cotton, rice, and sugar, the basis upon which rest all other forms of

industry in the Cotton States, must quickly be swept away." And the destruction of plantation agriculture would mean the obliteration of Southern "civilization, society and government." Although the Confederacy was quickly passing into history, its ideological cornerstone had clearly survived. In 1861, Alexander Stephens had declared that slavery was the "natural and normal" condition for blacks, and four years and a war later Robert Barnwell Rhett, Sr., asserted that "it is absurd to suppose that the African will work under a system of voluntary labor. . . . the labor of the negro must be compulsory—he must be a slave."

The clearest and most graphic demonstration of the planters' loyalty to slavery was found in the final months of the war when the Confederate Congress debated a proposal to arm and free three hundred thousand Southern slaves. With Federal armies squeezing the life out of the Confederacy, President Jefferson Davis concluded that the South would probably have to sacrifice its peculiar institution in order to achieve independence. He proposed the beginning of emancipation as a means of gaining both manpower for the army and recognition by England and France. From the early months of the war, slaves had been used as government laborers, and free blacks had been enrolled as militia; and in February, 1864, the Confederate Congress had authorized the impressment of free blacks and slaves for noncombatant military roles. But in November, 1864, Davis proposed that the government commit itself to the gradual emancipation and military use of blacks, declaring to the Congress that if Southerners had to choose between "subjugation or . . . the employment of the slave as soldier, there seems no reason to doubt what should be our decision."

The proposal to free and arm slaves provoked an immediate reaction from planters and their spokesmen. Clearly, it was a major step in the destruction of slavery, one they refused to take. In July, 1864, Jefferson Davis had told a newspaper reporter, "We are not fighting for slavery. We are fighting for independence." But in the spring of 1865, the Charleston *Mercury* declared, *"We want no Confederate Government without our institutions."* Robert Barnwell Rhett, Sr., asked who gave Richmond the right "to destroy that which it was created to protect and perpetuate." Opponents in the Congress offered resolutions declaring the proposal unconstitutional, hazardous, and in violation of property rights and the Southern social system. Robert M. T. Hunter, a Confederate senator and prominent Virginia planter who had been a consistent supporter of the administration, broke with Davis on this issue. It was the "most pernicious idea that had been suggested since the war began," he declared. He reminded his fellow senators that the Confederacy had been born because Southerners feared that the Republican party "would emancipate the negroes in defiance of the constitution." "And now," he asserted, "it would be said that we had done the very thing . . . without any more constitutional rights." Representative James T. Leach of North Carolina, owner of nearly fifty slaves, was dumbfounded that any white Southerner would advocate putting guns into the hands of slaves and predicted that they would turn their weapons on their masters. A Mississippi planter-politician declared flatly that the idea was nothing less than a "proposition to subvert the labor system, the social system and the political system of our country."

Working planters reacted with almost universal horror. In January, 1865, Charles Ellis of Virginia reported that "public opinion is largely opposed to making any such concession to Yankee power and Yankee fanaticism, independent of the fact that such a measure plainly means the emancipation of every slave in the South." Planters recognized that the program contradicted fundamental principles. Crenshaw Hall of Alabama said in March, 1865, "many are bitterly, fiercely opposed to it—some from principle, others from meaner motives. It is argued that we yield in this great principle. . . ." And Catherine Edmondston of North Carolina was certain what that principle was. By offering emancipation as a

reward, she explained, the South was giving up everything, for Southerners had "hitherto contended that Slavery was Cuffee's normal condition, the very best position he could occupy, the one of all others in which he was the happiest, & to take him from that & give him what we think misery in the place of it, is to put ourselves in the wrong essentially." "No!" she cried, "freedom for whites, slavery for negroes, God has so ordained it!" Howell Cobb proclaimed the same message more succinctly. "If slaves will make good soldiers," he said, "our whole theory of slavery is wrong—but they won't make good soldiers."

In March, 1865, just weeks before the end of the war, the Confederate Congress authorized the president to enroll slaves in whatever military capacity he directed, but instead of calling for emancipation, it left ownership in the hands of the masters. Despite this touch of conservatism, the program was a radical one—to arm slaves. How could the Richmond government, once almost the agent of the planter class, have accepted a policy toward which planters were so hostile? Charged with the survival of the new nation, the Confederate Congress had from the beginning been compelled to adopt whatever means appeared necessary for victory. When pressed by an increasingly desperate military situation, the Congress had even been forced to rethink the issues of slavery and independence. The ultimate decision to arm slaves was also made easier by internal changes in the Congress. The elections of 1863 generally returned congressmen having less wealth and fewer slaves than their predecessors. Men who owned fewer than twenty slaves, for example, had made up less than half the first Congress but constituted more than half of the second. Even more important according to a recent analysis of the Confederate Congress was the fact that by November, 1864, a majority of congressmen came from areas occupied by Federal troops. Because any commitments called for by the Confederate Congress would be exacted only from those within the Confederacy's reach, the "external" members and their constituents were immune to the consequences of their own legislation. They were therefore more willing to sacrifice slavery. Even then, the Senate passed the bill by a bare majority, nine to eight; only one of the six planter-senators voluntarily supported the proposal, and he represented a district in occupied Mississippi. Congressional opposition was concentrated in those seaboard states where slavery still functioned, however poorly. In the end, of course, before slave soldiers could go into action, the war ended in a thumping Southern defeat.

Northern victory meant the final destruction of slavery. But emancipation was not always immediate. Planters occasionally released their slaves as soon as the news drifted to their estates, but just as often they refused to accept the verdict and sought to conceal the knowledge from their slaves. More than three months after Appomattox, a Terrell County, Georgia, planter wrote his wife that he was staying on the plantation, watching "the place and negroes," but expected to see her in the fall "if I can sell this place with *all* of them." The decision about when to free one's "freedmen" was often not a simple matter. Catherine Edmondston's family argued the issue at length. When she heard in May that her father planned to emancipate his slaves, she "could not understand it." "It seemed inexplicable to me," she said, "& suicidal in the last degree." She and her husband discussed emancipation late into the night, "viewing it in every point of view, as it bears upon our future life, upon our plans, & our property & talking over our fears for the terrible days which seem to be coming upon us. . . ." A week later they announced emancipation in the "slave quarters." It was often the arrival of Federal troops with the official proclamation that ended such debates. With only an occasional exception, by the beginning of summer even the most stubborn knew that slavery was dead.

The reactions of slaveholders to the final collapse of slavery are not as easily ascertained as might be thought. For Appomattox marked the

end of slavery, the end of the Confederacy, and the end of the war. Planters' responses to one of these events were intertwined with their responses to the others. Joy that the war was over can easily be mistaken for relief that slavery was gone, for instance. Those few who had expressed doubts about slavery during the war, of course, did feel genuine relief in 1865. Ella Clanton Thomas, for one, disliked "the loss of so much property" but concluded that abolition was to "some degree a great relief." Curiously, though, this woman who had once owned ninety slaves discovered different emotions by October. "I alone know the effect the abolition of slavery has had upon me," she said. "I did not know . . . how intimately my faith in revolution and faith in the institution of slavery had been woven together." That she actually suffered a loss of religious faith bears out her impression of slavery's hold on her.

Even the planters' direct statements about their reactions to emancipation can be misleading. A substantial proportion of those who expressed themselves on the subject after April, 1865, declared their satisfaction that slavery was gone. Scarcely a single memoir or autobiography written after the war defended slavery, except perhaps as a boon to blacks. Planters often said they welcomed the institution's destruction because of its heavy burdens. Joseph Buckner Killebrew of Tennessee went further to declare that "slavery was a great curse." He rejoiced that this "relic of barbarism" had been crushed.

Often, in fact, planters even denied that slavery had ever been central to Southern history. Thomas Watson had spoken for his class when he declared in June, 1864, "It was to save that Institution that we seceded, and braved the fanaticism of our northern foes. Our political organism is based on slavery." But after the war, planters could often be heard to argue that the Confederacy was founded on other principles— liberty, independence, and especially states' rights. One old planter remembered years later that "contrary to the opinions of many," the

Confederacy "had for its origin other aims & objects than to sustain a system of slavery." Rather, it was an example of the fealty of the "English race to constitutional liberty." The most striking recantation, however, was that of Alexander Stephens, who had once asserted that slavery was the cornerstone of the Confederacy, and who after the war declared that it "was not a contest between the advocates or opponents of that Peculiar Institution."

Kenneth Stampp has argued that the speed with which white Southerners dissociated themselves from slavery is an indication of how great a burden it had been for them before emancipation. More likely, it is evidence of a nearly universal desire to escape the ignominy attached to slavery in the postwar period. Certainly Stampp's thesis is rarely corroborated by evidence from the years *before* emancipation. Planters had not been elusive or ambiguous about the principles of the Confederacy during the secession debates, and the inescapable fact is that they engaged in one of the bloodiest wars of the century to protect their institutions. Most relinquished their bondsmen not with just perfunctory resistance, but only when Federal soldiers appeared at the gates of their plantations.

Our clearest evidence of how planters felt in 1865 about emancipation is found in their visions of the future. There were some, of course, who readily accepted the end of slavery and who were sanguine about the future of the South after the triumph of free labor. In June, a Georgian wrote to his sister to encourage her to continue to plant. He was confident that she had "the tact and ability for the Emergency," and was certain that she could "make money with free labor." The trick was simple: "Let the women and children go," and "Hire only those who are able bodied." "It is all over," he said pragmatically, "and we must make the best of it."

More representative, however, was the opinion of an Alabama gentleman. He had lost his masterhood, but he could not relinquish the attendant social perspective. "The Yankees have declared the Negroes all free," he began his report to his absent partner. "We have no authority to control them in any way, or even to defend ourselves except by military law." He predicted that murder and rapine would soon prevail. "Our country and town are filled with idle negroes, crops abandoned in many cases. On some plantations *all* the negroes have left. . . . The result will be that our whole country north and south will be impovished [*sic*] and ruined. Our situation will soon be like that of Jamaica." Try as he might, he could not find a single bright spot on the horizon. "In all our material interests, we are hopelessly ruined. The loss of our slaves, to a very great extent destroys the value of all other property, credits, etc." Everyone, he said, was trying to sell, but "no one wishes to buy. No one has money to buy with. All wish to sell and get out of the country. Many expect to go to South America, others will go to Misouri [*sic*] & Iowa. Many to Texas. The idea is to get away from the free Negro." What else was there to do? he asked. "Most of our people are entirely satisfied that they can not control the labour of the free negro."

Southern planters entered the Civil War convinced that plantations and slavery were one. Plantations would not have developed except for slavery, and without slavery they would die. The growers of sugar, rice, and cotton agreed that "this country without slave labor would be wholly worthless, a barren waste and desolate plain. Emancipation would mean not only that grass would envelop proud plantations but that it would grow in the streets of every Southern city as well. Without slavery, they believed, the South would experience racial warfare, social anarchy, and economic collapse. Because they identified their entire society with their labor system, they concluded that emancipation would mean the end of everything decent in the Southern life.

■ ■ ■

STUDY QUESTIONS

1. Roark argues that the proslavery ideology survived after the Civil War even though slavery was dead. Why?

2. How did planter experiences during the war actually reinforce, in their own minds, the validity of the proslavery ideology?

3. What did planters fear about emancipation? Were any of their fears realistic?

4. Were most southerners psychologically guilty about the institution of slavery? Why or why not?

5. Describe the main arguments of the proslavery ideology.

BIBLIOGRAPHY

For the best study of the immediate consequences of emancipation, see Leon F. Litwack, *Been in the Storm So Long: The Aftermath of Slavery* (1979). Herbert G. Gutman's *The Black Family in Slavery and Freedom, 1750–1925* (1976) provides an excellent description of the impact of emancipation on the black family. For a dated but still excellent summary of the aftermath of slavery, see Joel Williamson, *After Slavery: The Negro in South Carolina During Reconstruction, 1861–1877* (1965). Lawrence Levine's *Black Culture and Black Consciousness: Afro-American Folk Thought from Slavery to Freedom* (1977) is the best analysis of black society and its cultural values during and after slavery.

For a description of planter society during the Civil War, see James L. Roark, *Masters Without Slaves* (1977); Michael P. Johnson, *Toward a Patriarchal Republic* (1977); Emory Thomas, *The Confederate Nation* (1979); and Paul Escott, *After Secession* (1978).

THE KNIGHTS OF
THE
RISING SUN

Allen W. Trelease

The Civil War, which started in 1861 and ended in 1865, was like a nightmare come true for most Americans. More than 600,000 young men were dead, countless others wounded and permanently maimed, and the South a prostrate ruin. For the next twelve years, northern Republicans tried to "reconstruct" the South in a chaotic crusade mixing retribution, corruption, and genuine idealism. Intent on punishing white southerners for their disloyalty, northern Republicans, especially the Radicals, tried to extend full civil rights—via the Fourteenth and Fifteenth Amendments—to the former slaves. For a variety of reasons, the attempt at giving equality to southern blacks failed, and by 1877 political power in the South reverted to the white elite.

A major factor in the failure of Radical Republicans to "reconstruct" the South was the rise of the Ku Klux Klan. Enraged at the very thought of black political power, Klansmen resorted to intimidation and violence, punishing southern blacks even suspected of sympathizing with Radicals' goals for the South. In "The Knights of the Rising Sun," historian Allen W. Trelease describes Klan activities in Texas during the late 1860s. Isolated from the main theaters of the Civil War, much of Texas remained unreconstructed, and the old white elite, along with their Klan allies, succeeded in destroying every vestige of black political activity and in eliminating the Republican Party from the political life of the state.

Large parts of Texas remained close to anarchy through 1868. Much of this was politically inspired despite the fact that the state was not yet reconstructed and took no part in the national election. In theory the Army was freer to take a direct hand in maintaining order than was true in the states which had been readmitted, but the shortage of troops available for this duty considerably lessened that advantage. At least twenty counties were involved in the Ku Klux terror, from Houston north to the Red River. In Houston itself Klan activity was limited to the holding of monthly meetings in a gymnasium and posting notices on lampposts, but in other places there was considerable violence.

By mid-September disguised bands had committed several murders in Trinity County, where two lawyers and both justices of the peace in the town of Sumter were well known as Klansmen. Not only did the crimes go unpunished, but Conservatives used them to force a majority of the Negroes to swear allegiance to the Democratic party; in return they received the familiar protection papers supposedly guaranteeing them against further outrage. "Any one in this community opposed to the Grand Cyclops and his imps is in danger of his life," wrote a local Republican in November. In Washington County the Klan sent warning notices to Republicans and committed at least one murder. As late as January 1869 masked parties were active around Palestine, shaving heads, whipping, and shooting among the black population, as well as burning down their houses. The military arrested five or six men for these offenses, but the Klan continued to make the rounds of Negroes' and Union men's houses, confiscating both guns and money. Early in November General J. J. Reynolds, military commander in the state, declared in a widely quoted report that "civil law east of the Trinity river is almost a dead letter" by virtue

of the activities of Ku Klux Klans and similar organizations. Republicans had been publicly slated for assassination and forced to flee their homes, while the murder of Negroes was too common to keep track of. These lawless bands, he said, were "evidently countenanced, or at least not discouraged, by a majority of the white people in the counties where [they] are most numerous. They could not otherwise exist." These statements did not endear the general to Conservative Texans, but they were substantially true.

The worst region of all, as to both Klan activity and general banditry, remained northeast Texas. A correspondent of the Cincinnati *Commercial* wrote from Sulphur Springs early in January 1869:

Armed bands of banditti, thieves, cut-throats and assassins infest the country; they prowl around houses, they call men out and shoot or hang them, they attack travellers upon the road, they seem almost everywhere present, and are ever intent upon mischief. You cannot pick up a paper without reading of murders, assassinations and robbery. . . . And yet not the fourth part of the truth has been told; not one act in ten is reported. Go where you will, and you will hear of fresh murders and violence. . . . The civil authority is powerless—the military insufficient in number, while hell has transferred its capital from pandemonium to Jefferson, and the devil is holding high carnival in Gilmer, Tyler, Canton, Quitman, Boston, Marshall and other places in Texas.

Judge Hardin Hart wrote Governor Pease in September to say that on account of "a regularly organized band which has overrun the country" he could not hold court in Grayson, Fannin, and Hunt counties without a military escort.

Much of this difficulty was attributable to outlaw gangs like those of Ben Bickerstaff and Cullen Baker, but even their activities were often racially and politically inspired, with Negroes and Union men the chief sufferers. Army officers and soldiers reported that most of the population at Sulphur Springs was organized into Ku Klux clubs affiliated with the Democratic party and some of the outlaws called themselves Ku Klux Rangers. At Clarksville a band of young men calling themselves Ku Klux broke up a Negro school and forced the teacher to flee the state.

White Conservatives around Paris at first took advantage of Klan depredations among Negroes by issuing protection papers to those who agreed to join the Democratic party. But the marauding reached such proportions that many freedmen fled their homes and jobs, leaving the crops untended. When a body of Klansmen came into town early in September, apparently to disarm more blacks, some of the leading citizens warned them to stop. The freedmen were not misbehaving, they said, and if they needed disarming at a later time the local people would take care of it themselves. Still the raiding continued, and after a sheriff's posse failed to catch the culprits the farmers in one neighborhood banded together to oppose them by force. (Since the Klan had become sacred among Democrats, these men claimed that the raiding was done by an unauthorized group using its name. They carefully denied any idea of opposing the Klan itself.) Even this tactic was ineffective so far as the county as a whole was concerned, and the terror continued at least into November. The Freedmen's Bureau agent, Colonel DeWitt C. Brown, was driven away from his own farm thirty miles from Paris and took refuge in town. There he was subjected to constant threats of assassination by Klansmen or their sympathizers. From where he stood the Klan seemed to be in almost total command.

The Bureau agent at Marshall (like his predecessor in the summer) suspected that the planters themselves were implicated in much of the terrorism. By driving Negroes from their homes just before harvest time the Klan enabled many landowners to collect the crop without having to pay the laborers' share.

Jefferson and Marion County remained the center of Ku Klux terrorism, as the Cincinnati reporter pointed out. A garrison of twenty-six men under Major James Curtis did little to deter violence. Bands of hooded men continued to make nocturnal depredations on Negroes in the surrounding countryside during September and October as they had for weeks past. "Whipping the freedmen, robbing them of their arms, driving them off plantations, and murdering whole families are of daily, and nightly occurrence," wrote the local Bureau agent at the end of October, "all done by disguised parties whom no one can testify to. The civil authorities never budge an inch to try and discover these midnight marauders and apparently a perfect apathy exists throughout the whole community regarding the general state of society. Nothing but martial law can save this section as it is at present. . . ." Inside town, Republicans hardly dared go outdoors at night, and for several weeks the county judge, who was afraid to go home even in the daytime, slept at the Army post. The local Democratic newspapers, including the *Ultra Ku Klux*, encouraged the terror by vying with one another in the ferocity of their denunciations of Republicans.

Major Curtis confirmed this state of affairs in a report to General Reynolds:

Since my arrival at the Post . . . [in mid-September] I have carefully observed the temper of the people and studied their intentions. I am constrained to say that neither are pacific. The amount of unblushing fraud and outrage perpetrated upon the negroes is hardly to be believed unless witnessed. Citizens who are esteemed respectable do not hesitate to take every unfair advantage. My office is daily visited by large numbers of unfortunates who have had money owing them, which they have been unable to obtain. The moral sense of the community appears blunted and gray headed apologists for such men as Baker and Bickerstaff can be met on all the street corners. . . . The right of franchise in this section is a farce. Numbers of negroes have been killed for daring to be Radicals, and their houses have so often been broken into by their Ku Klux neighbors in search of arms that they are now

pretty well defenceless. The civil officers cannot
and will *not punish these outrages. Cavalry armed
with double barrelled shotguns would soon scour
the country and these desperadoes be met on their
own ground. They do not fear the arms that the
troops now have, for they shoot from behind
hedges and fences or at night and then run. No
more notice is taken here of the death of a Radical
negro than of a mad dog. A democratic negro
however, who was shot the other day by another
of his stripe, was followed to his grave through the
streets of this city by a long procession in carriages,
on horseback, and on foot. I saw some of the most
aristocratic and respectable white men in this city
in the procession.*

On the same night that Curtis wrote, the new
Grand Officers of the Knights of the Rising Sun
were installed in the presence of a crowd of
1,200 or 1,500 persons. "The town was beautifully illuminated," a newspaper reported, "and
the Seymour Knights and the Lone Star Club
turned out in full uniform, with transparencies
and burners, in honor of the occasion." Sworn
in as Grand Commander for the ensuing twelve
months was Colonel William P. Saufley, who
doubled as chairman of the Marion County
Democratic executive committee. Following the
installation "able and patriotic speeches" were
delivered by several notables, including a Democratic Negro.

As usual, the most hated Republican was the
one who had the greatest Negro following. This
was Captain George W. Smith, a young Union
army veteran from New York who had settled in
Jefferson as a merchant at the end of the war. His
business failed, but the advent of Radical Reconstruction opened the prospect of a successful
political career; at the age of twenty-four Smith
was elected to the state constitutional convention by the suffrage of the Negro majority around
Jefferson. At the convention, according to a perhaps overflattering posthumous account, he was
recognized as one of the abler members. "In his
daily life he was correct, almost austere. He never drank, smoked, chewed, nor used profane

language." However, "he was odious as a negro
leader, as a radical, as a man who could not be
cowed, nor scared away." Smith may also have
alienated his fellow townspeople by the strenuous efforts he made to collect debts they owed
him. Even a few native Republicans like Judge
Charles Caldwell, who was scarcely more popular with Conservatives, refused to speak from the
same platform with him. As his admirer pointed
out, Smith "was ostracized and his life often
threatened. But he refused to be scared. He sued
some of his debtors and went to live with colored
people." One day, as he returned from a session
of the convention, his carpetbag—perhaps symbolically—was stolen, its contents rifled, and a
list of them published in a local newspaper.

The beginning of the end for Smith came on
the night of October 3, after he and Anderson
Wright, a Negro, had spoken at a Republican
meeting. As he opened the door of a Negro cabin
to enter, Smith was fired upon by four men outside including Colonel Richard P. Crump, one of
Jefferson's leading gentry. Smith drew his
revolver and returned the fire, wounding two of
the assailants and driving them away. He then
went to Major Curtis at the Army post. Here
Crump, with the chief of police and others, soon
arrived bearing a warrant for his arrest on a
charge of assault. The attackers' original intention to kill Smith now assumed greater urgency
because he and several Negroes present had recognized their assailants. Smith objected strenu-
ously to their efforts to get custody of him, protesting that it was equivalent to signing his death
warrant. Nevertheless Curtis turned him over to
the civil authorities on their assurance of his
safety. Smith was taken off to jail and a small
civilian guard was posted around it. The major
was uneasy, however, and requested reinforcements from his superior, but they were
refused.

The next day there were signs in Jefferson of
an assembling of the Knights of the Rising Sun.
Hoping to head off a lynching, Curtis dispatched
sixteen soldiers (the greater part of his command) to help guard the jail. At 9 P.M., finally, a

Terrorist activities by Ku Klux Klansmen, such as those related in this article, convinced many Republicans that conditions for southern blacks and their white supporters were ''worse than slavery,'' as this cartoon from Harper's Weekly (October 26, 1874) graphically depicts.

signal was sounded—a series of strokes on a bell at the place where the Knights held their meetings. About seventy members now mobilized under the command of Colonel Saufley and proceeded to march in formation toward the jail; they were in disguise and many carried torches. The jail building lay in an enclosed yard where at that time four black men were confined for a variety of petty offenses. One of the prisoners was Anderson Wright, and apparently the real reason for their being there was that they had witnessed the previous night's attempt to murder Smith; they may even have been fellow targets at that time. When the Knights reached this enclosure they burst through it with a shout and overpowered the guard, commanded by a young Army lieutenant. The invaders then turned to the Negro prisoners and dragged them into some adjoining woods. Wright and a second man, Cornelius Turner, managed to escape from them, although Wright was wounded; the other

two prisoners were shot nearly to pieces. As soon as Major Curtis heard the shooting and firing he came running with his remaining soldiers; but they too were quickly overpowered. Repeatedly the major himself tried to prevent the mob from entering the jail building in which Smith was confined, only to be dragged away from the door each time. They had no trouble unlocking the door, for city marshall Silas Nance, who possessed the key, was one of the conspirators.

At first Smith tried to hold the door shut against their entry. Eventually failing at this, he caught the foremost man, pulled him into the room, and somehow killed him. ''It is common talk in Jefferson now,'' wrote a former Bureau agent some months later, ''that Capt. Smith killed the first man who entered—that the Knights of the Rising Sun afterward buried him secretly with their funeral rites, and it was hushed up, he being a man from a distance. It is an established fact that one Gray, a strong man, who ventured into the open door, was so beaten by Capt. Smith that he cried, 'Pull me out! He's killing me!' and he was dragged out backward by the leg.'' All this took place in such darkness that the Knights could not see their victim. Some of them now went outside and held torches up to the small barred window of Smith's cell. By this light they were able to shoot him four times. ''The door was burst open and the crowd surged in upon him as he fell, and then, man after man, as they filed around fired into the dying body. This refinement of barbarity was continued while he writhed and after his limbs had ceased to quiver, that each one might participate in the triumph.''

Once the mob had finished its work at the jail it broke up into squads which began patrolling the town and searching for other Republican leaders. County Judge Campbell had anticipated trouble earlier in the evening and taken refuge as usual at Major Curtis' headquarters. Judge Caldwell was hated second only to Smith after his well-publicized report as chairman of the constitutional convention's committee on lawlessness. Hearing the shooting around the jail, he fled from his home into the woods. In a few moments twenty-five or thirty Knights appeared at the house, looking for him. Some of the party were for killing him, and they spent two hours vainly trying to learn his whereabouts from his fifteen-year-old son, who refused to tell. Another band went to the house of G. H. Slaughter, also a member of the convention, but he too escaped.

The next day the few remaining white Republicans in town were warned by friends of a widely expressed desire to make a "clean sweep" of them. Most of them stayed at the Haywood House hotel the following night under a military guard. Meanwhile the KRS scoured the city looking for dangerous Negroes, including those who knew too much about the preceding events for anyone's safety. When Major Curtis confessed that the only protection he could give the white Republicans was a military escort out of town, most of them decided to leave. At this point some civic leaders, alarmed at the probable effects to the town and themselves of such an exodus under these circumstances, urged them to stay and offered their protection. But the Republicans recalled the pledge to Smith and departed as quickly as they could, some openly and others furtively to avoid ambush.

White Conservatives saw these events—or at least their background and causes—in another light. They regarded Smith as "a dangerous, unprincipled carpet-bagger" who "lived almost entirely with negroes, on terms of perfect equality." Whether there was evidence for it or not, they found it easy to believe further that this "cohabitation" was accompanied by "the most unbridled and groveling licentiousness"; according to one account he walked the streets with Negroes in a state of near-nudity. For at least eighteen months he had thus "outraged the moral sentiment of the city of Jefferson," defying the whites to do anything about it and threatening a race war if they tried. This might have been overlooked if he had not tried repeatedly to precipitate such a collision. As head of the Union League he deliverd inflammatory speeches and organized the blacks into armed mobs who com-

mitted assaults and robberies and threatened to burn the town. When part of the city did go up in flames earlier in the year Smith was held responsible. Overlooking the well-attested white terrorism which had prevailed in the city and county for months, a Democratic newspaper claimed that all had been peace and quiet during Smith's absence at the constitutional convention. But on his return he resumed his incendiary course and made it necessary for the whites to arm in self-defense.

According to Conservatives the initial shooting affray on the night of October 3 was precipitated by a group of armed Negroes with Smith at their head. They opened fire on Crump and his friends while the latter were on their way to protect a white man whom Smith had threatened to attack. Democrats did not dwell overlong on the ensuing lynching, nor did they bother to explain the killing of the Negro prisoners. In fact the affair was made deliberately mysterious and a bit romantic in their telling. According to the Jefferson *Times,* both the soldiers and the civilians on guard at the jail characterized the lynch party as "entirely sober and apparently well disciplined." (One of the party later testified in court that at least some of them had put on their disguises while drinking at a local saloon.) "After the accomplishment of their object," the *Times* continued, "they all retired as quietly and mysteriously as they came—none knowing who they were or from whence they came." (This assertion, it turned out, was more hopeful than factual.)

The *Times* deplored such proceedings in general, it assured its readers, but in this case lynching "had become . . . an unavoidable necessity. The sanctity of home, the peace and safety of society, the prosperity of the country, and the security of life itself demanded the removal of so base a villain." A month later it declared: "Every community in the South will do well to relieve themselves [*sic*] of their surplus Geo. Smiths, and others of like ilk, as Jefferson rid herself of hers. This is not a healthy locality for such incendiaries, and no town in the South should be." Democratic papers made much of Judge Caldwell's refusal to appear publicly with Smith—which was probably inspired by his Negro associations. They claimed that Smith's fellow Republicans were also glad to have him out of the way, and noted that the local citizens had assured them of protection. But there was no mention of the riotous search and the threats upon their lives which produced that offer, nor of their flight from the city anyway.

The Smith affair raises problems of fact and interpretation which appeared in almost every Ku Klux raid across the South. Most were not so fully examined or reported as this, but even here it is impossible to know certainly where the truth lay. Republican and Democratic accounts differed diametrically on almost every particular, and both were colored by considerations of political and personal interest. But enough detailed and impartial evidence survives to sustain the Republican case on most counts. Negro and Republican testimony concerning the actual events in October is confirmed by members of the KRS who turned state's evidence when they were later brought to trial. Smith's prior activities and his personal character are less clear. Republicans all agreed later that he was almost puritanical in his moral code and that he was hated because of his unquestioned social associations and political influence with the blacks. He never counseled violence or issued threats to burn the town, they insisted; on the contrary, the only time he ever headed a Negro crowd was when he brought a number of them to help extinguish the fire which he was falsely accused of starting.

As elsewhere in the South, the logic of some of the charges against Smith is not convincing. Whites had a majority in the city and blacks in the county. Theoretically each could gain by racial violence, offsetting its minority status. But Conservatives always had the advantage in such confrontations. They were repeatedly guilty of intimidating the freedmen, and in case of an open collision everyone (including Republicans) knew they could win hands down. Democrats were certainly sincere in their personal and political detestation of Smith; almost as certainly

they were sincere in their fears of his political activity and what it might lead to. From their viewpoint an open consorter with and leader of Negroes was capable of anything. It was easy therefore to believe the worst and attribute the basest motives without clear evidence. If some Negroes did threaten to burn the town—often this was a threat to retaliate for preceding white terrorism—it was easy to overlook the real cause and attribute the idea to Smith. The next step, involving hypocrisy and deliberate falsehood in some cases, was to charge him with specific expressions and activities which no other source substantiates and which the logic of the situation makes improbable. Men who practiced or condoned terrorism and murder in what they conceived to be a just cause would not shrink from character assassination in the same cause.

Interestingly enough, most of the character assassination—in Smith's case and generally—followed rather than preceded Ku Klux attacks. This did not arise primarily from a feeling of greater freedom or safety once the victim was no longer around to defend himself; some victims, unlike Smith, lived to speak out in their own behalf. Accusations after the fact were intended rather to rationalize and win public approval of the attack once it had occurred; since these raids were the product of at least semisecret conspiracy there was less need to win public approval beforehand. Sometimes such accusations were partially true, no doubt, and it was never easy for persons at a distance to judge them; often it is no easier now. Democrats tended to believe and Republicans to reject them as a matter of course. The *Daily Austin Republican* was typical of Radical papers in its reaction to Democratic newspaper slurs against Smith after his death: "We have read your lying sheets for the last *eighteen* months, and this is the first time you have made any such charges. . . ." It was surely justified in charging the Democratic editors of Texas with being accessories after the fact in Smith's murder.

The military authorities had done almost nothing to stop KRS terrorism among the Negroes before Smith's murder, and this violence continued for at least two months afterward. Similar conditions prevailed widely, and there were too few troops—especially cavalry—to patrol every lawless county. But the murder of a white man, particularly one of Smith's prominence and in such a fashion, aroused officials to unwonted activity. The Army recalled Major Curtis and sent Colonel H. G. Malloy to Jefferson as provisional mayor with orders to discover and bring to justice the murderers of Smith and the two freedmen killed with him. More troops were also sent, amounting ultimately to nine companies of infantry and four of cavalry. With their help Malloy arrested four of Jefferson's leading men on December 5. Colonel W. P. Saufley, whom witnesses identified as the organizer of the lynching, would have been a fifth, but he left town the day before on business, a Democratic newspaper explained, apparently unaware that he was wanted. (This business was to take him into the Cherokee Indian Nation and perhaps as far as New York, detaining him so long that the authorities never succeeded in apprehending him.) That night the KRS held an emergency meeting and about twenty men left town for parts unknown while others prepared to follow.

General George P. Buell arrived soon afterward as commandant, and under his direction the arrests continued for months, reaching thirty-seven by early April. They included by common repute some of the best as well as the worst citizens of Jefferson. Detectives were sent as far as New York to round up suspects who had scattered in all directions. One of the last to leave was General H. P. Mabry, a former judge and a KRS leader who was serving as one of the counsel for the defense. When a soldier revealed that one of the prisoners had turned state's evidence and identified Mabry as a leader in the lynching, he abruptly fled to Canada.

The authorities took great pains to recover Anderson Wright and Cornelius Turner, the Negro survivors of the lynching, whose testimony would be vital in the forthcoming trials. After locating Wright, General Buell sent him with an Army officer to find Turner, who had escaped to New Orleans. They traveled part of the way by steamboat and at one point, when the officer was momentarily occupied elsewhere, Wright was set upon by four men. He saved himself by jumping overboard and made his way to a nearby Army post, whence he was brought back to Jefferson. Buell then sent a detective after Turner, who eventually was located, and both men later testified at the trial.

The intention of the authorities was to try the suspects before a military commission, as they were virtually sure of acquittal in the civil courts. Defense counsel (who consisted ultimately of eleven lawyers—nearly the whole Jefferson bar) made every effort to have the case transferred; two of them even went to Washington to appeal personally to Secretary of War Schofield, but he refused to interfere. R. W. Loughery, the editor of both the Jefferson *Times* and the *Texas Republican* in Marshall, appealed to the court of public opinion. His editorials screamed indignation at the "terrible and revolting ordeal through which a refined, hospitable, and intelligent people are passing, under radical rule," continually subject to the indignity and danger of midnight arrest. He also sent requests to Washington and to Northern newspapers for intercession against Jefferson's military despotism. The prisoners, he said, were subject to brutal and inhuman treatment. Loughery's *ex parte* statement of the facts created a momentary ripple but no reversal of policy. In reality the prisoners were treated quite adequately and were confined in two buildings enclosed by a stockade. Buell released a few of them on bond, but refused to do so in most cases for the obvious reason that they would have followed their brothers in flight. Although they seem to have been denied visitors at first, this rule was lifted and friends regularly brought them extra food and delicacies. The number of visitors had to be limited, however, because most of the white community regarded them as martyrs and crowded to the prison to show their support.

After many delays the members of the military commission arrived in May and the trial got under way; it continued into September.

Although it proved somewhat more effective than the civil courts in punishing Ku Klux criminals, this tribunal was a far cry from the military despotism depicted by its hysterical opponents. The defense counsel presented their case fully and freely. Before long it was obvious that they would produce witnesses to swear alibis for most or all of the defendants. Given a general public conspiracy of this magnitude, and the oaths of KRS members to protect each other, this was easy to do; and given the dependence of the prosecution by contrast on Negro witnesses whose credibility white men (including Army officers) were accustomed to discounting, the tactic was all too effective. The results were mixed. At least fourteen persons arrested at one time or another never went to trial, either for lack of evidence or because they turned state's evidence. Seventeen others were tried and acquitted, apparently in most cases because of sworn statements by friends that they were not present at the time of the lynching. Only six were convicted. Three of these were sentenced to life terms, and three to a term of four years each in the Huntsville penitentiary. General Reynolds refused to accept the acquittal of Colonel Crump and three others, but they were released from custody anyway, and the matter was not raised again. Witnesses who had risked their lives by testifying against the terrorists were given help in leaving the state, while most of the defendants returned to their homes and occupations. The arrests and trials did bring peace to Jefferson, however. The Knights of the Rising Sun rode no more, and the new freedom for Radicals was symbolized in August by the appearance of a Republican newspaper.

Relative tranquillity came to northeast Texas generally during the early part of 1869. Some Republicans attributed this to the election of General Grant, but that event brought no such result to other parts of the South. Both Ben Bickerstaff and Cullen Baker were killed and their gangs dispersed, which certainly helped. The

example of military action in Jefferson likely played a part; it was accompanied by an increase of military activity throughout the region as troops were shifted here from the frontier and other portions of the state. Immediately after the Smith lynching in October, General Reynolds ordered all civil and military officials to "arrest, on the spot any person wearing a mask or otherwise disguised." Arrests did increase, but it was probably owing less to this order than to the more efficient concentration of troops. In December the Bureau agent in Jefferson had cavalry (for a change) to send out after men accused of Ku Klux outrages in Upshur County. Between October 1868 and September 1869 fifty-nine cases were tried before military commissions in Texas, chiefly involving murder or aggravated assault; they resulted in twenty-nine convictions. This record was almost breathtaking by comparison with that of the civil courts.

The Texas crime rate remained high after 1868. Organized Ku Klux activity declined markedly, but it continued in sporadic fashion around the state for several years. A new state government was elected in November 1869 and organized early the next year under Republican Governor E. J. Davis. In his first annual message, in April 1870, Davis called attention to the depredations of disguised bands. To cope with them he asked the legislature to create both a state police and a militia, and to invest him with the power of martial law. In June and July the legislature responded affirmatively on each count. The state police consisted of a mounted force of fewer than 200 men under the state adjutant general; in addition, all county sheriffs and their deputies and all local marshals and constables were considered to be part of the state police and subject to its orders. In November 1871 a law against armed and disguised persons followed. Between July 1870 and December 1871 the state police arrested 4,580 persons, 829 of them for murder or attempted murder. Hundreds of other criminals probably fled the state to evade arrest. This activity, coupled with occasional use of the governor's martial law powers in troubled local-ities, seems to have diminished lawlessness by early 1872. There still remained the usual prob-lems of prosecuting or convicting Ku Klux offenders, however, and very few seem to have been punished legally.

■■■

STUDY QUESTIONS

1. Why was Klan terrorism so rampant in Texas? Did the federal government pos-sess the means of preventing it?

2. What was the relationship between the Ku Klux Klan in Texas and the Demo-cratic Party?

3. How did well-to-do white planters respond to the Ku Klux Klan?

4. What were the objectives of the Ku Klux Klan in Texas?

5. Who were the White Conservatives? How did they interpret Klan activities?

6. Why did the state government try to curtail Klan activities in the early 1870s? Did state officials succeed?

BIBLIOGRAPHY

The standard work on Reconstruction, one which created two generations of ste-reotypes by vindicating the South and indicting the North, is William A. Dunning, *Reconstruction, Political and Economic* (1907). The first major dissent from Dunning was W. E. B. Du Bois's classic work *Black Reconstruction* (1935). It was not until the social changes of the 1960s, triggered by the civil rights movement, that historians took a new look at Reconstruction. John Hope Franklin's *Reconstruction After the Civil War* (1961) first questioned the Dunning view, arguing that northern inten-tions toward the South were humanitarian as well as political. Kenneth Stampp's *The Era of Reconstruction* (1965) carried that argument further, restoring the repu-tation of "carpetbaggers" and "scalawags," describing the successes of black poli-ticians, and criticizing the Ku Klux Klan. Also see Allen Trelease, *White Terror* (1967); Sarah Wiggins, *The Scalawag in Alabama Politics, 1865–1881* (1977); and L. N. Powell, *New Masters: Northern Planters During the Civil War and Reconstruction* (1980).

For studies of Andrew Johnson, see Howard K. Beale, *The Critical Year: A Study of Andrew Johnson and Reconstruction* (1930), which takes the traditional point of view. A very critical view is Eric McKitrick, *Andrew Johnson and Reconstruction* (1960). Also see Michael Benedict, *The Impeachment of Andrew Johnson* (1973).

DAY OF THE LONGHORNS

Dee Brown

The Texas Longhorn looked slightly unbalanced, as if it were about to fall over. Its body often appeared thin, and its horns stretched out like the curved balancing rod of a high-wire performer. And its face—only another Longhorn or a Texan could love it. Nevertheless, this rugged breed of steer was the focus of the long drives during the dusty, golden age of cowboys.

Ironically, this era of the cowboy was made possible by the westward push of railroad builders. After the Civil War, a three- or four-dollar Texas Longhorn could be sold in the upper Mississippi region for forty dollars. If Texas entrepreneurs could drive the steers to the railheads, they could earn a $100,000 profit from 3,000 head of cattle. And so the drive was on, first to Sedalia, Missouri, and later, as railways extended west, to the Kansas cowtowns of Newton, Abilene, Ellsworth, and Dodge City. During the late 1860s and 1870s, a total of over four million cattle survived the heat, dust, Indian attacks, and other problems and reached the Kansas railroads. Dee Brown describes the difficult journey and the Longhorns, and the cowboys who drove them to the railheads.

W hen Coronado marched northward from Mexico in 1540, searching for the mythical golden cities of Cibola, he brought with his expedition a number of Spanish cattle. These were the first of the breed to enter what is now the United States. Over the next century other Spanish explorers and missionaries followed, most of them bringing at least "a bull and a cow, a stallion and a mare." From these seed stocks, Longhorns and mustangs and cowboys and ranching slowly developed in the Southwest, the Spanish cattle mutating and evolving, the vaquero perfecting his costume and the tools of his trade.

The Longhorns, which also came to be known as Texas cattle, took their name from their wide-spreading horns which sometimes measured up to eight feet across, and there are legends of horn spreads even more extensive. From their mixed ancestry of blacks, browns, reds, duns, slates, and brindles the Longhorns were varicolored, the shadings and combinations of hues so differentiated that, as J. Frank Dobie pointed out, no two of these animals were ever alike in appearance. "For all his heroic stature," said Dobie, "the Texas steer stood with his body tucked up in the flanks, his high shoulder-top sometimes thin enough to split a hail stone, his ribs flat, his length frequently so extended that his back swayed."

Ungraceful though they were, the Longhorns showed more intelligence than domesticated cattle. They were curious, suspicious, fierce, and resourceful. After all, by the mid–19th century they were the survivors of several generations which had lived under wild or semiwild conditions. They possessed unusually keen senses of smell, sight, and hearing; their voices were powerful and penetrating; they could survive extreme heat or cold; they could exist on the sparest of vegetation and water; they could outwalk any other breed of cattle. It was this last attribute that brought the Texas Longhorns out of their native habitat and onto the pages of history to create the romantic era of the cowboys, the long drives, and riproaring trail towns of the Great Plains.

The drives began even before Texas became a state. A few enterprising adventurers occasionally would round up a herd out of the brush and drive them overland to Galveston or Shreveport where the animals were sold mainly for their hides and tallow. After the California gold rush of 1849 created a demand for meat, a few daring young Texans drove herds all the way to the Pacific coast. W. H. Snyder put together an outfit that moved out of Texas into New Mexico, and then crossed Colorado, Wyoming, Utah, and Nevada. After two years Snyder finally got his Longhorns to the miners. Captain Jack Cureton of the Texas Rangers followed a southern route across New Mexico and Arizona, dodging Apaches all the way, but from the meat-hungry goldseekers Cureton took a profit of $20,000, a considerable fortune in those days.

In the early 1850s a young English emigrant named Tom Candy Ponting probably established the record for the longest trail drive of Longhorns. Ponting was engaged in the livestock business in Illinois when he learned of the easy availability of Longhorns in Texas. Late in 1852 he and his partner traveled there on horseback, carrying a small bag of gold coins. They had no trouble assembling a herd of 700 bawling Longhorns at nine dollars or less a head. Early in 1853 they headed north for Illinois. It was a rainy spring and Ponting and his partner had to hire Cherokees to help swim the cattle across the Arkansas River. "I sat on my horse every night while we were crossing through the Indian country," said Ponting. "I was so afraid I could not sleep in the tent, but we had no stampede." Missouri was still thinly settled, and there was plenty of vegetation to keep the Longhorns from losing weight. At St. Louis the

Dee Brown, "Day of the Longhorns." From *American History Illustrated* 9 (January 1975), pp. 4–9, 42–48. Reprinted through the courtesy of Cowles Magazines, publisher of AMERICAN HISTORY ILLUSTRATED.

animals were ferried across the Mississippi, and on July 26, Ponting and his cattle reached Christian County, Illinois.

There through the winter months he fed them on corn, which cost him fifteen cents a bushel. He sold off a few scrubs to traveling cattle buyers, and then in the spring he cut out the best of the herd and started trail driving again, this time toward the East. At Muncie, Indiana, Ponting found that railroad cars were available for livestock transport to New York. "We made arrangements and put the cattle on the cars. We unloaded them at Cleveland, letting them jump out on the sand banks. We unloaded them next at Dunkirk, then at Harnesville, and then at Bergen Hill." On July 3, 1854, from Bergen Hill in New Jersey, Ponting ferried the much-traveled Longhorns across the Hudson to the New York cattle market, completing a two-year journey of 1,500 miles on foot and 600 miles by rail. They were the first Texas Longhorns to reach New York City.

"The cattle are rather long-legged though finehorned, with long taper horns, and something of a wild look," reported the New York *Tribune*. "The expense from Texas to Illinois was about two dollars a head, the owners camping all the way. From Illinois to New York, the expense was seventeen dollars a head." To the New York buyers the Longhorns were worth eighty dollars a head. Tom Ponting had more than doubled his investment.

About this same time another young adventurer from Illinois, Charles Goodnight, was trying to build up his own herd of Longhorns in the Brazos River country. As a young boy Goodnight had journeyed to Texas with his family, riding much of the way bareback. When he was 21, he and his stepbrother went to work for a rancher, keeping watch over 400 skittish Longhorns and branding the calves. Their pay for this work was one-fourth of the calves born during the year. "As the end of the first year's branding resulted in only thirty-two calves for our share," Goodnight recalled afterward, "and as the value was about three dollars per head, we figured out that we had made between us, not counting expenses, ninety-six dollars."

Goodnight and his partner persevered, however, and after four years of hard work they owned a herd of 4,000. Before they could convert many of their animals into cash, however, the Civil War began. Goodnight soon found himself scouting for a company of Confederate mounted riflemen and spent most of the war disputing control of the upper Brazos and Red River country with Comanches and Kiowas instead of with blue-coated Yankees. At the war's end his makeshift uniform was worn out, his Confederate money was worthless, and his Longhorn herd had virtually disappeared. "I suffered great loss," Goodnight said. "The Confederate authorities had taken many of my cattle without paying a cent. Indians had raided our herds and cattle thieves were branding them, to their own benefit without regard to our rights." He was 30 years old and financially destitute.

Almost every other Texan returning from the war found himself in the same situation. When rumors reached the cattle country early in the spring of 1866 that meat was in short supply in the North, hundreds of young Texans began rounding up Longhorns. Huge packing houses were being constructed in Northern cities, and on a 345-acre tract where nine railroads converged, the Chicago Union Stock Yards was opened for business. A Longhorn steer worth five dollars in useless Confederate money in Texas would bring forty dollars in good U.S. currency in the Chicago market.

From the brush country, the plains, and the coastal regions of Texas, mounted drivers turned herd after herd of cattle northward across Indian Territory. Their goal was the nearest railhead, Sedalia, in west-central Missouri. Following approximately the route used by Tom Ponting thirteen years earlier, the trail drivers forded Red River and moved on to Fort Gibson, where they had to cross the more formidable Arkansas. Plagued by unseasonable cold weather, stampedes, and flooded streams, they pushed their Longhorns on into southeastern Kansas.

Here they encountered real trouble. From Baxter Springs northward to Sedalia railhead, the country was being settled by small farmers, many of them recent battlefield enemies of the Texans. The settlers did not want their fences wrecked and their crops trampled, and they used force in stopping the Texans from driving cattle across their properties. By summer's end, over 100,000 stalled cattle were strung out between Baxter Springs and Sedalia. The grass died or was burned off by defiant farmers. Dishonest cattle buyers from the North bought herds with bad checks. The unsold cattle died or were abandoned, and the great drives of 1866 came to an end. For many of the Texans it had been a financial bust.

A less optimistic folk might have gone home defeated, but not the cattlemen of Texas. By the spring of 1867 many were ready to drive Longhorns north again. And in that year, thanks to an enterprising Yankee stockman, a convenient shipping point was waiting to welcome their coming. At the end of the Civil War, Joseph McCoy of Springfield, Illinois, had started a business of buying livestock for resale to the new packinghouses in Chicago. Appalled by the Baxter Springs–Sedalia debacle of 1866, McCoy was determined to find a railroad shipping point somewhere at the end of an open trail from Texas. He studied the maps of new railroads being built westward and chose a town in Kansas—Abilene, near the end of the Kansas Pacific Railroad.

"Abilene in 1867 was a very small, dead place," McCoy admitted. But it met all the requirements for a cattle-shipping town. It was west of the settled farming country; it had a railroad, a river full of water for thirsty steers, and a sea of grass for miles around for holding and fattening livestock at the end of the drives. And nearby was Fort Riley, offering protection from possible Indian raids.

Within sixty days McCoy managed to construct a shipping yard, a barn, an office, and a hotel. From the Kansas Pacific he wheedled railroad ties to build loading pens sturdy enough to hold wild Longhorns. Meanwhile, he had sent messengers southward to inform the cattlemen of Texas that Abilene was "a good safe place to drive to, where they could sell, or ship cattle unmolested to other markets."

Over what soon became known as the Chisholm Trail, thousands of Texas cattle began moving into Abilene. Although the 1867 season got off to a late start and rail shipments did not begin until September, 36,000 Longhorns were marketed that first year. In 1868 the number doubled, and in 1870 the Kansas Pacific could scarcely find enough cars to handle the 300,000 Longhorns sold to Northern packing houses. Abilene in the meantime had grown into a boom town of stores, hotels, saloons, and honkytonks where Texas cowboys celebrated the end of their trail drive and engendered the legends of gunmen, lawmen, shootouts, and exotic dance hall girls.

One Texas cowman who did not make the long drive north to Abilene was Charles Goodnight. Back in the spring of 1866 when most of his neighbors were driving herds across Indian Territory for the Sedalia railhead, Goodnight was still trying to round up his scattered Longhorns. By the time he was ready to move out, he suspected that there was going to be a glut of cattle in Kansas and Missouri. Instead of heading north, he combined his Longhorns with those of Oliver Loving and they started their herd of 2,000 west toward New Mexico. Cattle were reported to be in great demand there by government agents who bought them for distribution to reservation Indians.

To reach New Mexico, Goodnight and Loving followed the abandoned route of the Butterfield Overland Stage along which waterholes and wells had been dug by the stage company. For this arduous journey, Goodnight constructed what was probably the first chuckwagon. Obtaining an old military wagon, he rebuilt it with the toughest wood he knew, a wood used by Indians for fashioning their bows—Osage orange or *bois d'arc*. At the rear he built a chuckbox with a hinged lid to which a folding leg was attached so that when it was lowered it formed a cook's work table. Fastened securely in front of the wagon was a convenient spigot running through to a barrel of water. Beneath the driver's seat was a supply of necessary tools such as axes and spades, and below the wagon was a cowhide sling for transporting dry wood or buffalo chips to be used in making cooking fires. A generation of trail drivers would adopt Goodnight's chuckwagon for long drives and roundups, and variations of it are still in use today.

Goodnight's and Loving's first drive to New Mexico was uneventful until they began crossing the lower edge of the Staked Plains, where the water holes had gone dry. For three days the rangy Longhorns became almost unmanageable from thirst, and when they scented the waters of the Pecos they stampeded, piling into the river, some drowning under the onrush of those in the rear. The partners succeeded, however, in driving most of the herd into Fort Sumner, where several thousand Navajos confined in the Bosque Redondo were near starvation.

A government contractor took more than half the Longhorns, paying Goodnight and Loving $12,000 in gold. By the standards of that day they had suddenly become prosperous. While Loving drove the remainder of the cattle to the Colorado mining country, Goodnight returned to Texas to round up another herd of Longhorns.

In the years immediately following the disruptions of the Civil War, thousands of unbranded Longhorns roamed wild in the Texas brush country. The cowboys soon discovered that the easiest way to round up these cattle was to lure them out of the chaparral with tame decoys. James H. Cook, an early trail driver who later became a leading cattleman of the West, described such a wild Longhorn roundup:

"About sunrise we left the corral, taking with us the decoy herd, Longworth leading the way. After traveling a mile or more he led the herd into a dense clump of brush and motioned us to stop driving it. Then, telling two men to stay

with the cattle he rode off, signaling the other men and myself to follow him . . . in the brush ahead I caught a glimpse of some cattle. A few minutes later I heard voices singing a peculiar melody without words. The sounds of these voices indicated that the singers were scattered in the form of a circle about the cattle. In a few moments some of the cattle came toward me, and I recognized a few of them as belonging to the herd which we had brought from our camp. In a few seconds more I saw that we had some wild ones, too. They whirled back when they saw me, only to find a rider wherever they might turn. The decoy cattle were fairly quiet, simply milling around through the thicket, and the wild ones were soon thoroughly mingled with them." Cook and the other cowboys now had little difficulty driving the combined tame and wild Longhorns into a corral where they were held until time to start an overland drive to market.

The work of rounding up Longhorns gradually developed into an organized routine directed by a man who came to be known as the range boss. During a roundup, his authority was as ironclad as that of a ship's captain. At the beginning of a "gather" the range boss would assemble an outfit of about twenty cowhands, a horse wrangler to look after the mounts and, most important of all, a camp cook. Roundups began very early in the spring because every cattleman was eager to be the first to hit the trail before the grass overgrazed along the route to Kansas.

On the first morning of a roundup the men would be up before sunrise to eat their breakfasts hurriedly at the chuckwagon; then in the gray light of dawn they would mount their best ponies and gather around the range boss for orders. As soon as he had outlined the limits of the day's roundup, the boss would send his cowhands riding out in various directions to sweep the range. When each rider reached a specified point, he turned back and herded all the cattle within his area back into the camp center.

■ ■ *Texas Longhorns are herded across a stream during an 1867 cattle drive. Between 1867 and 1887, a total of 5.5 million head of Texas Longhorns were trailed north.*

After a herd was collected, the second operation of a roundup began. This next step was to separate the young stock which were to be branded for return to the range from the mature animals which were to be driven overland to market. "Cutting out" it was fittingly called, and this performance was, and still is, the highest art of the cowboy. Cutting out required a specially trained pony, one that could "turn on a dime," and a rider who had a sharp eye, good muscular reflexes, and who was an artist at handling a lariat. After selecting an animal to be separated from the herd, the rider and his horse would begin a quick-moving game of twisting and turning, of sudden stops and changes of pace.

Roping, the final act of the cutting out process, also required close cooperation between pony and rider. Forming an oval-shaped noose six or seven feet in diameter, the cowboy would spin it over his head with tremendous speed. A second before making the throw, he would draw his arm and shoulder back, then shoot his hand forward, aiming the noose sometimes for the animal's head, sometimes for its feet. As the lariat jerked tight, the rider instantly snubbed it around his saddle horn. At the same moment the pony had to be stopped short. The position of the pony at the moment of throw was important; a sudden jerk of a taut lariat could spill both horse and rider.

As soon as the unbranded animal was roped, it was immediately herded or dragged to the nearest bonfire where branding irons were kept heated to an orange red. In Texas, all branding was done in a corral, a legal requirement devised to prevent hasty and illegal branding by rustlers on the open range. The first brands in Texas were usually the initials of the owners, and if two cattlemen had the same initials, a bar or a circle distinguished one from the other. Law required that brands be publicly registered by counties in Texas; other Western states had state brand books. In the early years when ranches were unfenced and land boundaries poorly marked, friction over unbranded cattle caused many a gunfight. To discourage rustlers who could easily change a "C" to an "O," an "F" to an "E," a "V" to a "W," ranchers designed unusual brands, some of the more famous being the Stirrup, Andiron, Scissors, Frying Pan, and Dinner Bell.

As soon as the work of branding was completed, preparations for the trail drive began in earnest. The owner of the cattle was responsible for food and other supplies, but each cowboy assembled the personal gear he would need on the journey. Every item he wore or carried was designed for utility. Tents were seldom taken along, two blankets being considered sufficient shelter from the elements. If the weather was warm, the cowboys shed their coats, and if they wore vests they rarely buttoned them because of the rangeland belief that to do so would bring on a bad cold. Most wore leather chaps to protect their legs from underbrush and weather. They put high heels on their boots to keep their feet from slipping through the stirrups, and they wore heavy leather gloves because the toughest palms could be burned raw by the lariats they used constantly in their work. They paid good money for wide-brimmed hats because they served as roofs against rain, snow, and sun. They used bandannas for ear coverings, as dust masks, as strainers when drinking muddy water, for drying dishes, as bandages, towels, slings for broken arms, to tie hats on in very windy weather, and for countless other purposes.

Getting the average trail herd of about 3,000 cattle underway was as complicated an operation as starting a small army on a march across country. Each rider needed several spare mounts for the long journey, and this herd of horses accompanying a cow column was known as the remuda—from a Spanish word meaning re-

placement. A trail boss, sixteen to eighteen cowboys, a cook and chuckwagon, and a horse wrangler for the remuda made up the personnel of an average drive.

It was necessary to move slowly at first until the restive Longhorns grew accustomed to daily routines. To keep a herd in order a wise trail boss would search out a huge dominating animal and make it the lead steer. Charles Goodnight had one called Old Blue which he considered so valuable as a leader that after every long drive he brought the animal back to the home ranch. Two or three quiet days on the trail was usually long enough to calm a herd of Longhorns. After that the cattle would fall into place each morning like infantrymen on the march, each one keeping the same relative position in file as the herd moved along.

Cattleman John Clay left a classic description of an early trail herd in motion: "You see a steer's head and horns silhouetted against the skyline, and then another and another, till you realize it is a herd. On each flank is a horseman. Along come the leaders with a swinging gait, quickening as they smell the waters of the muddy river." The pattern of trail driving soon became as routinized as that of roundups—the trail boss a mile or two out in front, horse herd and chuckwagon following, then the point riders directing the lead steers, and strung along the widening flow of the herd the swing and flank riders, until at the rear came the drag riders in clouds of dust, keeping the weaker cattle moving.

Not many trail drivers had time to keep diaries, that of George Duffield being one of the rare survivors. From it a reader can feel the tensions and weariness, the constant threats of weather, the difficult river crossings, and dangers of stampedes.

May 1: Big stampede. Lost 200 head of Cattle.
May 2: Spent the day hunting & found but 25 Head. It has been Raining for three days. These are dark days for me.
May 3: Day spent in hunting Cattle. Found 23. Hard rain and wind. Lots of trouble.

■ ■ *In 1878, Dodge City was the "king of the trail towns." Longhorns and cattlemen made the city what it was, but their day of glory ended during Dodge's long reign.*

May 8: Rain pouring down in torrents. Ran my horse into a ditch & got my Knee badly sprained—15 miles.

May 9: Still dark and gloomy. River up. Everything looks *Blue* to me.

May 14: Swam our cattle & Horses & built Raft & Rafted our provisions & blanket & covers. Lost Most of our Kitchen furniture such as camp Kittles Coffee Pots Cups Plates Canteens &c &c.

May 17: No Breakfast. Pack & off is the order.

May 31: Swimming Cattle is the order. We worked all day in the River & at dusk got the last Beefe over—I am now out of Texas—This day will long be remembered by me—There was one of our party Drowned today.

George Duffield made his drive along the eastern edge of Indian Territory in 1866. Ten years later the drives were still as wearisome and dangerous, but the trails had shifted much farther westward and there had been a swift succession of trail towns. A new railroad, the Sante Fe, pushed sixty-five miles south of Abilene in 1871, and Newton became the main cattle-shipping town. Newton's reign was brief, however; it was replaced by Ellsworth and Wichita. Although the advancing railroad tracks were a boon to cattlemen seeking shorter routes to markets, they also brought settlers west by the thousands. By 1876 the life of the Chisholm Trail was ending and the Western Trail, or Dodge City Trail, had taken its place.

Dodge City was the king of the trail towns, the "cowboy capital," a fabulous town of innumerable legends for a golden decade. The names survive in history: Long Branch Saloon, the Lady Gay, the Dodge Opera House, Delmonico's, Wyatt Earp, Doc Holliday, Boot Hill, Bat Masterson, Clay Allison, Luke Short, and Big Nose Kate. But it was Longhorns and cattlemen that made Dodge City, and it was during Dodge's long reign that the Longhorns came to the end of their day of glory.

One of the men responsible for the change was Charles Goodnight. In the year that Dodge opened as a cow town, 1875, Goodnight found himself financially destitute for the second time in his life. He had made a fortune with Texas cattle, bought a ranch in Colorado, become a banker, and then lost everything in the Panic of 1873. All he had left in 1875 was a small herd of unmarketable Longhorns, and he decided it was time to return to Texas and start all over again.

He chose an unlikely region, the Texas Panhandle, an area long shunned by cattlemen because it was supposed to be a desert. Goodnight, however, recalled the immense herds of buffalo which had roamed there for centuries, and he reasoned that wherever buffalo could thrive so could Longhorns. He found a partner, John Adair, to furnish the capital and drove his Longhorns into the heart of the Panhandle, to the Palo Duro Canyon, where he discovered plenty of water and grass. There he founded the JA Ranch. Soon after starting operations, Goodnight began introducing Herefords and shorthorns, cross-breeding them at first with Longhorns so that his cattle produced more and better beef, yet retained the ability to flourish on the open range and endure long drives to Dodge City.

Other ranchers soon followed his example, and "White Faces" instead of "Longhorns" gradually became the symbol of trail cattle. After a continuing flood of homesteaders, brought west by the proliferating railroads, made it necessary to close the trail to Dodge City, one more overland route—the National Trail to Wyoming and Montana—saw the last treks of the Longhorns.

As the 19th century came to an end, so did open range ranching and trail driving. There was no longer any place for rangy Longhorns. Until the day he died, however, Charles Goodnight kept a small herd of them to remind him of the old days. A few specimens survive today in wildlife refuges and on larger ranches as curiosities, or for occasional use in parades and Western movies. But most of these animals are descendants of crossbreds. The day of the genuine Texas Longhorn—with his body tucked up in the flanks, his high shoulder-top thin enough to split a hail stone, his ribs flat, his back swayed, his ability to outwalk any other breed of cattle—now belongs to history.

■ ■ ■

STUDY QUESTIONS

1. What were the origins of the Texas Longhorn? Why were they so well suited for the long drive?

2. How did the Civil War affect the cattle business?

3. Why did Joseph McCoy choose to drive cattle to Abilene?

4. What was life like on the long drive?

5. Why did the drives end?

BIBLIOGRAPHY

Ray Allen Billington's *The Far Western Frontier* (1963) and *Westward Expansion* (1974) are excellent introductions to the westward movement. Ernest S. Osgood, *The Day of the Cattlemen* (1929) is a classic work on the subject, and Lewis Atherton, *The Cattle Kings* (1961) is a more recent study. Gene M. Gressley, *Bankers and Cattlemen* (1966) deals with Eastern as well as Western interests. Wayne Gard, *The Chisholm Trail* (1954) is an outstanding study of the Long Drive, and J. Frank Dobie *The Longhorns* (1941) tells the story delightfully well. Robert R. Dykstra, *The Cattle Town* (1968) and Joe B. Frantz and J. E. Choate, *The American Cowboy* (1981) remove the myths that surround their subjects.